BEFORE THE
GREGORIAN
REFORM

JOHN HOWE

BEFORE THE GREGORIAN REFORM

THE LATIN CHURCH
AT THE TURN OF THE
FIRST MILLENNIUM

CORNELL UNIVERSITY PRESS

ITHACA AND LONDON

First published 2016 by Cornell University Press

Printed in the United States of America

Library of Congress Cataloging-in-Publication Data

Names: Howe, John, 1947 March 13– author.
Title: Before the Gregorian reform : the Latin Church at the turn of the first millennium / John Howe.
Description: Ithaca : Cornell University Press, 2016. | Includes bibliographical references and index.
Identifiers: LCCN 2015044155 | ISBN 9780801452895 (cloth : alk. paper)
Subjects: LCSH: Church history—10th century. | Church history—11th century. | Church renewal—Catholic Church—History—To 1500. | Europe—Church history—600–1500.
Classification: LCC BX1070 .H69 2016 | DDC 270.3–dc23
LC record available at http://lccn.loc.gov/2015044155

Cloth printing   10   9   8   7   6   5   4   3   2   1

To Ann,

Dignas grates tibi non agere possum.

Quamvis amplae sint, parum sunt.

Semper amaberis.

CONTENTS

ILLUSTRATIONS

Maps

Figures

ACKNOWLEDGMENTS

This book has been almost two decades in the making. In *Church Reform and Social Change: Dominic of Sora and His Patrons* (1997), I presented the career of Dominic of Sora—a hermit monk who wandered through central Italy around the millennium—as a microhistory that revealed a different way to envision the process of Church reform, a perspective that was earlier, more local, more Mediterranean, more rooted in social and political history, more patron-driven than the standard narrative. Yet that conclusion would remain no more than an interesting suggestion unless it could be corroborated by a broader survey of ecclesiastical change. I was rash enough to contemplate undertaking such a project because much of my research deals with its tangential aspects. Hence this book, an ultimate goal pursued in fits and starts, often laid aside. What appears here, after many years, has benefited from more help than can ever be acknowledged.

Thanks are due to Texas Tech University (my employer for more than thirty years), its Department of History, and its library. The High Plains of Texas is not universally recognized as the epicenter of medieval studies, and what I have managed to accomplish owes a great deal to departmental-level accommodations, to college-level support for medieval studies in general and the TTU Medieval and Renaissance Studies Center in particular, and to university help in the form of library services and faculty development leaves. Research directly related to this project has been aided by fellowships and readerships from the Institute for Advanced Study in Princeton (spring 2001), from the Erasmus Institute of the University of Notre Dame (2003–4), and from the Center for Medieval and Renaissance Studies of UCLA and the Getty Research Institute (2013–14). Publication was aided by Texas Tech University's Department of History, Humanities Center, Institute for the Study of Western Civilization, and Office of the Vice President for Research.

There is no way to acknowledge the intellectual debts owed to colleagues and collaborators who have answered queries, discussed ideas, suggested examples, and offered encouragement. Recommenders who supported aspects of this project at various times include Giles Constable, John Contreni, Patrick Geary, Thomas Noble, John McCulloh, and Maureen Miller. Good ideas and help (even from those who found my approach somewhat eccentric) have come from England's splendid cohort of scholars of medieval Italy, including the late H. E. J. Cowdrey, Graham Loud, and Chris Wickham. Special thanks are due to Peter Potter, editor in chief of Cornell University Press, for queries about this project, for encouraging its submission to Cornell University Press, and for all the efforts he has made to bring it to a successful conclusion. Thanks are also due to Cornell's readers and editors.

The members of my family—my wife, Ann Hanson Howe, and children, Joseph, Thomas, and Anna—have shared in the travails of this research. Daughter-in-law Chiara joined this team in mid-project. I am very grateful for their support, their patience when I was away on research trips, and their gracious acceptance of life with a writer who sometimes disappears into his garret. My special thanks to Ann for spending the 2013–14 year with me in the wilds of Los Angeles, facilitating my efforts to wrestle this manuscript into final form.

ABBREVIATIONS

AASS   *Acta Sanctorum*. 68 vols. Antwerp: Société des Bollandistes, 1643–1940.

AHR   *American Historical Review*

ASOSB   *Acta Sanctorum Ordinis S. Benedicti in Saeculorum Classes Distributa*. 9 vols. Venice: Sebastian Colet, 1733–40.

BAV   Biblioteca Apostolica Vaticana (Vatican City)

CCCM   Corpus Christianorum, Continuatio Mediaevalis. 320+ vols. Turnhout: Brepols, 1966–.

CCM   *Cahiers de civilisation médiévale, X^e–XIIe siècle*

CCSL   Corpus Christianorum, Series Latina. 201+ vols. Turnhout: Brepols, 1953–.

CHR   *Catholic Historical Review*

Chron. Casin.   *Chronica Monasterii Casinensis*, ed. Hartmut Hoffmann, *Die Chronik von Montecassino*, MGH *SS* 34. Hannover: Hahn, 1980.

CISAM   Centro italiano di studi sull'alto medioevo (Spoleto)

CNRS   Centre national de la recherche scientifique (Paris)

Corp CM   *Corpus Consuetudinum Monasticarum*, original series, ed. Kassius Hallinger. 12 vols. in 16. Siegburg: F. Schmitt, 1963–1987.

CRAHAM or CRAHM   Centre de recherches archéologiques et historiques anciennes et médiévales or Centre de recherches archéologiques et historiques médiévales (Caen)

CSEL   Corpus Scriptorum Ecclesiasticorum Latinorum. 100+ vols. Vienna: Österreichischen Akademie der Wissenschaften, 1866–.

DOML   Dumbarton Oaks Medieval Library, 39+ vols. Washington, DC: Dumbarton Oaks Research Library, 2010–.

ÉFR   École française de Rome

EHR	*English Historical Review*
Hagiographies	*Hagiographies*. Vols. 1–5, ed. Guy Philippart, vols. 6–, ed. Monique Goullet. Corpus Christianorum Hagiographies. 6+ vols. Turnhout: Brepols, 1994–.
IRHT	Institut de recherche et d'histoire des textes (Paris)
ISIME	Istituto Storico Italiano per il Medioevo (Rome)
JEH	*Journal of Ecclesiastical History*
MGH	Monumenta Germaniae Historica (Munich)
MGH *Epp*	MGH *Epistolae* in quarto. 8 vols. Berlin: Weidmann, 1891–1925.
MGH *Epp Sel*	MGH *Epistolae Selecta in Usum Scholarum Separatim Editae*. 5 vols. Berlin: Weidmann, 1916–52.
MGH *SS*	MGH *Scriptores* in folio. 39+ vols. Hannover: Hahn 1826–.
MGH *SS Rer Germ*	MGH *Scriptores Rerum Germanicarum in Usum Scholarum Separatim Editi*. 78+ vols. Hannover: Hahn, 1871–.
MGH *SS Rer Germ ns*	MGH *Scriptores Rerum Germanicarum Nova Series*. 25+ vols. Hannover: Weidman, 1922–.
Migne, *Pat. Lat.*	*Patrologia Cursus Completus*, Series Latina, ed. Jacques-Paul Migne. 212 vols. Paris: Migne, 1844–65.
NCMH	*The New Cambridge Medieval History*. 7 vols. in 8. New York: Cambridge University Press, 1995–2005.
Papsturkunden 896-1046	*Papsturkunden, 896–1046*, ed. Harald Zimmermann. 3 vols. Österreichische Akademie der Wissenschaften, Denkschriften, Philosophisch-historische Klasse 174, 177, and 198. Vienna: Österreichischen Akademie der Wissenschaften, 1984–89.
PIMS	Pontifical Institute of Mediaeval Studies (Toronto)
RHE	*Revue d'histoire ecclésiastique*
SISMEL	Società internazionale per lo Studio del Medioevo Latino
TRHS	*Transactions of the Royal Historical Society* (Cambridge)
Typologie	Typologie des Sources du Moyen Âge Occidental. 88+ vols. Turnhout: Brepols, 1972–.

INTRODUCTION

A PRE-GREGORIAN REFORM?

In 865, while Vikings were pillaging the monastery of Saint-Benoît-sur-Loire at Fleury, its monks took refuge in Orléans and its vicinity. When they finally straggled back it was no happy homecoming. According to Fleury's chronicler Adrevaldus (d. 878), "after the monastery had been destroyed by a great raging fire, there was nothing good left, no temples suitable for divine worship, no hearths for various uses, no granaries, no provisions, absolutely nothing that was either decorative or useful; bare masonry walls shocked those gazing at them, a spectacle of horror rather than of dignity or glory."[1] The monks crowded into a small dormitory, part of which they walled off as a chapel for their treasured relics of St. Benedict,[2] and they remained there until the Vikings briefly drove them away again in 879.[3] Fleury had lost more than monastic amenities. When the monks "occupied again that holy place," they had "divided minds" and "did not hold the property of the monastery in common, but parceled it out among themselves as they were able or as seemed good to them." Much later a local count, perhaps supported by the French king, called in St. Odo of Cluny (d. 944) to reorganize Fleury, but its monks responded by arming themselves with swords and spears, manning the walls, and holding off the reformers for several days until Odo rode in by himself on a donkey and managed to make peace. Subsequent negotiations remained tense.[4]

---

1. Adrevaldus, *Miracula Benedicti* I xxxv, ed. Eugène de Certain, in *Les Miracles de Saint Benoît* (Paris: Mme Ve Jules Renouard, 1858), 1–83, esp. 76. For context, see Thomas Head, *Hagiography and the Cult of the Saints: The Diocese of Orléans, 800–1200* (Cambridge: Cambridge University Press, 1990), 52–55.

2. On the relics of Benedict at Fleury, see Walter Goffart, "Le Mans, St. Scholastica, and the Literary Tradition of the Translation of Benedict," *Revue bénédictine* 77 (1967): 107–41, esp. 108–31; Head, *Hagiography and the Cult of the Saints*, 135–43.

3. Adrevaldus, *Miracula Benedicti* I xxxv, Certain, 76.

4. John of Salerno, *Vita Odonis Abbatis* III viii–ix, ed. *ASOSB* 7:179–81, trans. Gerard Sitwell, *St. Odo of Cluny: Being the Life of St. Odo of Cluny by John of Salerno and the Life of St. Gerald of Aurillac by St. Odo* (London: Sheed & Ward, 1958), 79–81. John Nightingale, "Oswald, Fleury, and Continental Reform," in

A century later this dysfunctional community had become one of the most distinguished monasteries in Europe. A Fleury customary composed in the early eleventh century claims that this "head of the monasteries of France" had three hundred monks.[5] Its impressive properties[6] were protected by legal privileges that included a charter from Pope Gregory V (996–99) making its abbot "preeminent throughout France [*primus inter abates Galliae*]".[7] From its library some six hundred to eight hundred medieval manuscripts still survive today, most from the tenth, eleventh, and twelfth centuries.[8] A historian writing in the 1040s described the community as a "torrent of the liberal arts and a gymnasium of the school of the Lord," mixed metaphors he explicates in a chapter devoted to its early eleventh-century scholars.[9] Its church was intended to be "an example to all France."[10] Its customs and school influenced monks in England, Spain, northern France, the Low Countries, and Germany.[11]

St. Oswald of Worcester: Life and Influence, ed. Nicholas Brooks and Catherine Cubitt (London: Leicester University Press, 1996), 34–39, cautions that the most negative depictions of the Fleury community were written by its Cluniac competitors.

5. Thierry of Amorbach, *Libellus de Consuetudinibus et Statutis Monasterii Floriacensis* I prol., ed. Anselme Davril and Lin Donnat, *Consuetudinum Saeculi X/XI/XII Monumenta Non-cluniacensia, Corp CM* 7(3) (Siegburg, Ger.: Schmitt, 1984), 7–9, ed. and trans. Davril and Donnat, in *L'abbaye de Fleury en l'an Mil*, IRHT Sources d'histoire médiévale 32 (Paris: CNRS, 2004), 170–73.

6. Elizabeth Dachowski, *First among Abbots: The Career of Abbo of Fleury* (Washington, DC: Catholic University of America Press, 2008), 85–86 and 148.

7. Head, *Hagiography*, 236–40, 255–57; Dachowski, *First among Abbots*, 166–69 and 178–86. The quotation is from Gregory V's letter to Abbot Abbo of Fleury (13 November 996), ed. Harald Zimmermann, *Papsturkunden 896–1046* (Vienna: Österreichischen Akademie der Wissenschaften, 1984–89), 2:655–57.

8. Fleury's library is analyzed by Marco Mostert in *The Political Theology of Abbo of Fleury: A Study of the Ideas about Society and Law of the Tenth-Century Monastic Reform Movement* (Hilversum, Neth.: Verloren, 1987), 32–34; *The Library of Fleury: A Provisional List of Manuscripts* (Hilversum: Verloren, 1989); and "La bibliothèque de Fleury-sur-Loire," in *Religion et culture autour de l'an Mil: Royaume capétien et Lotharingie: Actes du Colloque Hugues Capet 987–1987. La France de l'an Mil, Auxerre, 26 et 27 juin 1987—Metz, 11 et 12 septembre 1987*, ed. Dominique Iogna-Prat and Jean-Charles Picard (Paris: Picard, 1990), 119–23.

9. Andrew of Fleury, *Vita Gauzlini* I ii, ed. Robert-Henri Bautier and Monique Labory, *André de Fleury Vie de Gauzlin, Abbé de Fleury*, Sources d'histoire medieval publiées par l'IRHT 2 (Paris: CNRS, 1969), 32–39. On this chapter, see Dachowski, *First among Abbots*, 220–23.

10. The phrase from the *Vita Gauzlini* I xliv, Bautier and Labory, 80–91, refers specifically to the great tower constructed by Abbot Gauzlinus (1004–30). On the larger context, see Éliane Vergnolle, *Saint-Benoît-sur-Loire et la sculpture du XIᵉ siècle* (Paris: Picard, 1985), 275–76, and "Les débuts de l'art roman dans le royaume franc (ca. 980–ca. 1020)," *CCM* 43 (2000): 183–84.

11. For an overview see Donnat, "Recherches sur l'influence de Fleury au Xᵉ siècle," in *Études ligériennes d'histoire et d'archéologie médiévales: Mémoires et exposés présentés à la Semaine d'études médiévales de Saint-Benoît-sur-Loire du 3 au 10 juillet 1969*, ed. René Louise (Auxerre: Société des fouilles archéologiques et des monuments historiques de l'Yonne, 1975), 165–74; and his "Les coutumes monastiques autour de l'an Mil," in Iogna-Prat and Picard, *Religion et culture autour de l'an Mil*, 17–24. Regional studies of Fleury's influence include Louis Gougaud, "Les relations de l'Abbaye de Fleury-sur-Loire avec le Bretagne armoricaine et les îles britanniques (Xᵉ et XIᵉ siècles)," *Mémoires de la Société d'histoire et d'archéologie de Bretagne* 4 (1923): 2–30; Bautier and Labory, "Fleury et la Catalogne au début du XIᵉ siècle," in *André de Fleury, Vie de*

Fleury's spectacular revival, although aided by its relics of St. Benedict, was by no means unique. The destruction the Latin West experienced turned out to have been creative destruction. Aristocrats and churchmen rebuilt the churches lost to barbarian raids and civil disorders and then built new ones, competing against each other so that church building, like castle building, acquired its own momentum.[12] Patrons strove to improve ecclesiastical furnishings, liturgy, and spirituality. Schools were built to staff the new churches. The result was that by the mid-eleventh century a wealthy, unified, better-organized, better-educated, more spiritually sensitive Latin Church was assuming a leading place in the broader Christian world.

This story has not been adequately told. One obstacle is that Church historians have focused more on the late eleventh- and early twelfth-century Gregorian Reform, offering a narrative that emphasizes the investiture controversy between popes and emperors and culminates in the "papal monarchy" of the High Middle Ages.[13] Although historians recognize earlier reforms, especially the revival often somewhat simplistically associated with the monastery of Cluny, they normally separate the anticipatory movements from the main event. Augustine Fliche, who popularized the term "Gregorian Reform," surveyed its earlier roots in *La Réforme grégorienne* but privileged the story of a movement developing in the Rhineland in the early to mid-eleventh century, brought to Rome during the pontificate of Leo IX (1049–54), and ascendant by the start of the twelfth.[14] Although strong continuities between tenth- and eleventh-century reform movements and the Gregorian Reform might seem to undercut this perspective,[15] Gerd Tellenbach, in a synthesis first expounded

Gauzlin, 169–85; Nightingale, "Oswald, Fleury and Continental Reform," 23–45; and Mostert, "Relations between Fleury and England," in *England and the Continent in the Tenth Century: Studies in Honour of Wilhelm Levison (1876–1947)*, ed. David Rollason, Conrad Leyser, and Hannah Williams (Turnhout, Belg.: Brepols, 2010), 185–208.

12. John Howe, "The Nobility's Reform of the Medieval Church," *AHR* 93 (1988): 317–39.

13. Surveys of the literature can be found in Uta-Renate Blumenthal, *The Investiture Controversy: Church and Monarchy from the Ninth to the Twelfth Century* (Philadelphia: University of Pennsylvania Press, 1988); Maureen C. Miller, "The Crisis in the Investiture Crisis Narrative," *History Compass* 7, no. 6 (2009): 1570–80, doi:10.1111/j.1478-0542.2009.00645.x; and Michel Sot, "La réforme grégorienne: Une introduction," *Revue d'histoire de l'Église de France* 96 (2010): 5–10.

14. Augustin Fliche, *Études sur la polémique religieuse à l'époque de Grégoire VII: Les prégrégoriens* (Paris: Société française d'imprimerie et de librairie, 1916), and, more influentially, in *La réforme grégorienne*, vol. 1, *La formation des idées grégoriennes* (Paris: Université Catholique, 1924), vi, viii, 6, 17, 39–148.

15. See, for example, William Ziezulewicz, "The School of Chartres and Reform Influences before the Pontificate of Leo IX," *CHR* 77 (1991): 383–402; Howe, "*Gaudium et Spes*: Ecclesiastical Reformers at the Start of a 'New Age,'" in *Reforming the Church before Modernity: Patterns, Problems, and Approaches*, ed. Christopher M. Bellitto and Louis I. Hamilton (Burlington, VT: Ashgate, 2005), 21–35; and Greta Austin, *Shaping Church Law around the Year 1000: The "Decretum" of Burchard of Worms* (Burlington, VT: Ashgate, 2009), esp. 60–67, 103–4, 123–26.

in 1936, dismissed earlier "monastic reforms" as otherworldly coenobitic projects quite different from mid eleventh-century papal reforms dedicated to making the world more Christian.[16] His division still holds the field today, albeit with more and more qualifications. For André Vauchez, for example, the Gregorian Reform is a movement "toward a spirituality of action" in which the popes took the lead after the mid-eleventh century; yet he recognizes that nonpapal reformers had anticipated the drive for the Christianization of the world and that the papal reform cannot be treated exclusively in political institutional terms since it reflects a spirituality that struggled against evil, within and outside the Church.[17] Dominique Iogna-Prat, whose studies have greatly illuminated monastic spirituality, still starts a new era with the advent of the papal reform party in the 1040s, even while claiming that "the Gregorian Reform was largely prepared by the monastic movement of the first half of the eleventh century."[18] On the other hand, some English-speaking scholars, following the lead of Karl Leyser, have actually sharpened the distinction between the Gregorian Reform and earlier ecclesiastical movements by championing a "Gregorian Revolution" or a mid-eleventh-century "formation of a persecuting society."[19] True, researchers interested in millenarianism have recently been attempting to shift discussion back toward the year 1000, attributing ecclesiastical growth and development first to a hidden millennial excitement and then to the reaction to its failure, but the resulting debates, while documenting increasing eschatological interest, have not justified a focus on any single year.[20] Now in the twenty-first century

16. Gerd Tellenbach, *The Church in Western Europe from the Tenth to the Early Twelfth Century*, trans. Timothy Reuter (Cambridge: Cambridge University Press, 1993), defended the theoretical structure he had already set up in *Libertas: Kirche und Weltordnung im Zeitalter des Investiturstreites* (Stuttgart: W. Kohlhammer, 1936), trans. R. F. Bennett, *Church, State, and Christian Society at the Time of the Investiture Contest* (Oxford: Blackwell, 1940).

17. André Vauchez, *The Spirituality of the Medieval West: From the Eighth to the Twelfth Century*, trans. Colette Friedlander (Kalamazoo, MI: Cistercian Publications, 1993), 66–68.

18. Dominique Iogna-Prat, *La Maison Dieu: Une histoire monumentale de l'Église au Moyen Âge (v. 800–v. 1200)* (Paris: Éditions du Seuil, 2006), esp. 360.

19. Karl Leyser, *Communications and Power in Medieval Europe: The Gregorian Revolution and Beyond*, ed. Timothy Reuter (London: Hambledon, 1994); Robert I. Moore, *The Formation of a Persecuting Society: Power and Deviance in Western Europe 950–1250* (New York: Blackwell, 1987); Moore, *The First European Revolution, c. 970–1215* (Oxford: Blackwell, 2000).

20. The historiography of the "terrors of the year 1000" is surveyed in Edward Peters, "Mutations, Adjustments, Terrors, Historians, and the Year 1000," in *The Year 1000: Religious and Social Response to the Turning of the First Millennium*, ed. Michael Frassetto (New York: Palgrave Macmillan, 2002), 9–28; and Levi Roach, "Emperor Otto III and the End of Time," *TRHS*, 6th ser., 23 (2013): 75–102, esp. 76–77. For broader millennial context, see Richard Landes, *Heaven on Earth: The Varieties of the Millennial Experience* (Oxford: Oxford University Press, 2011) and the website for the Center for Millennial Studies, http://www.mille.org.

scholars are beginning to recognize that systematic ecclesiastical reform began even earlier.[21]

The tenth- and early eleventh-century Latin Church, or more concisely the millennial Church, needs to be studied so that we can comprehend not only ecclesiastical history but also the broader history of Western civilization. The narrative linking ecclesiastical revival to the Gregorian Reform has become increasingly problematic because it no longer synchronizes with the rest of Western history. In the twentieth century, scholars such as Marc Bloch, Georges Duby, and André Vauchez had assumed that ecclesiastical revival had occurred in tandem with an economic, social, and cultural revival of the West, which they dated to the late eleventh century, part of a "spectacular leap forward in all fields."[22] Yet today's scholars now situate the start of the rise of the West well before the mid-eleventh century, even well before the turn of the millennium. Many now see the mid-tenth century as the launching pad for the High Middle Ages, citing the revival of long-distance trade, the growth of cities, the birth of the village, the rise of technology, the "feudal mutation" or "feudal revolution," and the spread of Frankish culture. Others place the new movement even earlier, back during Charlemagne's era, and see it hitting full stride in the tenth after overcoming some post-Carolingian challenges. But whatever the exact chronology of the start of the great medieval revival, a consensus now exists that it was well under way back in the tenth century.[23]

21. Timothy Reuter, preface and introduction to, NCMH, vol. 3, 900–1024, ed. Reuter (Cambridge: Cambridge University Press, 1999), xv–xvii and 1–24, utilizes the concept of a "long tenth century" to integrate much of the period covered here and treat ecclesiastical topics in a forward-looking fashion. Michel Parisse, who spent his career investigating the Lorraine and Saxony, describes a relatively seamless tenth- and eleventh-century monastic reform, most recently in Religieux et religieuses en Empire du Xᵉ au XIIᵉ siècle (Paris: Picard, 2011), esp. 28–31 and 85–86. A new interest in bishops, expressed by the academic society Episcopus founded in 2004, treats bishops as an element of continuity in tenth-, eleventh-, and twelfth-century Europe. This perspective is exemplified in Miller, The Formation of a Medieval Church: Ecclesiastical Change in Verona, 950–1150 (Ithaca: Cornell University Press, 1993); John Ott and Anna Trumbore Jones, eds., The Bishop Reformed: Studies of Episcopal Power and Culture in the Central Middle Ages (Aldershot, UK: Ashgate, 2007), esp. 4; and Francesca Tinti, Sustaining Belief: The Church of Worcester from c. 870 to c. 1100 (Burlington, VT: Ashgate, 2010), esp. 225.

22. The quotation is from Vauchez, Spirituality of the Medieval West, 75. On this historiographical assumption, see Heinrich Fichtenau, Living in the Tenth Century: Mentalities and Social Orders, ed. and trans. Patrick J. Geary (Chicago: University of Chicago Press, 1991), esp. 435–38; and Thomas F. X. Noble, introduction to European Transformations: The Long Twelfth Century, ed. Noble and John Van Engen (Notre Dame: University of Notre Dame Press, 2012), 1–16, esp. 4.

23. Howe, "Re-Forging the 'Age of Iron': Part 1: The Tenth Century as the End of the Ancient World?," History Compass 8, no. 8 (2010): 866–87, doi:10.1111/j.1478–0542.2010.00707.x, and "Re-Forging the 'Age of Iron': Part 2: The Tenth Century in a New Age?," History Compass 8, no. 9 (2010): 1000–1022, doi:10.1111/j.1478–0542.2010.00708.x.

This present book attempts to reinsert the history of the Church into the story of the rise of West. It presents ecclesiastical reform as a central part of the post-Carolingian, postinvasion revival. The Church embodied and defined a rising Europe. The Gregorian Reform that centralized and developed ecclesiastical structures in the late eleventh and early twelfth centuries still remains the proximate background for what has been called the "Renaissance of the twelfth century" and the "Reformation of the twelfth century."[24] Yet those achievements rested on earlier ones. This book studies the Christendom that the mid-eleventh-century Latin reformers inherited. Its goal is to present the millennial Church in its appropriate context, the resurgence of the Latin West, and to understand its ecclesiastical developments as bases for later reform programs rather than as dead ends. In addition, by going beyond traditional political and institutional perspectives, this book seeks to better align Church history with the current fascination with material culture and social history.[25]

One challenge, however, relates to the reform paradigm itself. Ecclesiastical changes in the central Middle Ages are usually discussed in terms of reform. What exactly does this mean? Is reform a modern analytical construct anachronistically applied by today's scholars to a past context? Or is it a medieval concept animating and shaping the changes it describes? If medieval, does it designate ideological ideals or objective realities? And should discussion of reform be limited to concepts explicitly articulated by medieval people themselves or can it be expanded to include a broader implicit range of reform dynamics revealed by their actions? This last dilemma is very familiar to medieval historians who have discovered that important medieval intellectual structures often tend to "go without saying," evoking little debate or definition until some malcontent or heretic begins to raise difficulties. Modern scholars, undeterred by these and other epistemological problems, still often speak indiscriminately about reform.[26] That they will continue to do so is suggested by the 220 special

---

24. Charles Homer Haskins, *The Renaissance of the Twelfth Century* (Cambridge: Harvard University Press, 1927), supplemented by Robert L. Benson and Giles Constable, eds., *Renaissance and Renewal in the Twelfth Century* (Cambridge: Harvard University Press, 1982), a fifty-year retrospective volume; Constable, *The Reformation of the Twelfth Century* (New York: Cambridge University Press, 1996); R.N. Swanson, *The Twelfth-Century Renaissance* (Manchester, UK: Manchester University Press, 1999).

25. Van Engen, "The Future of Medieval Church History," *Church History* 71 (2002): 492–522, esp. 495–97; Austin, "Bishops and Religious Law, 900–1050," in Ott and Jones, *Bishop Reformed*, 40–57, esp. 41.

26. Julia Barrow, "Ideas and Applications of Reform," in *Early Medieval Christianities, c. 600–c. 1100*, ed. Noble and Smith, The Cambridge History of Christianity 3 (Cambridge: Cambridge University Press, 2008), 345–62.

sessions and round tables that the International Medieval Congress at Leeds in 2015 devoted to its theme of Reform and Renewal.

The most systematic attempt to define and categorize concepts of reform was made by Gerhart B. Ladner, whose *Idea of Reform* recently celebrated its fiftieth anniversary.[27] Appearing on the eve of the Second Vatican Council, this book identified reform as a basic Christian dynamic, one given a unique shape in Latin Christianity by Augustine, whose preoccupations with the creation of man in the image and likeness of God (Gen. 1:26–27; 5:6; and 9:6) and with the salvation offered by Jesus Christ had led him to conclude that human beings could never return to a restored paradisial state, as many Greek fathers had envisioned; rather, because God had become man, it was now impossible to get back to the garden—reform would have to be progress toward a better state (*reformatio ad melius*). In retrospect Adam's sin would turn out to have been a "happy fault [*felix culpa*]." Augustine imagined Christian life moving forward, not backward. The "city of God" would be a pilgrim city, unable to be completely perfected in earthly institutions or even on earth, undergoing a never-ending process of reform as it moves toward its fulfillment of the divine plan. Reform would mean corrections based upon an authoritative past. But Ladner emphasized that reform movements in the medieval Latin Church, in contrast to later Protestant attempts at reformation guided by "Scripture alone [*sola scriptura*]," referenced multiple authorities including the Bible, the fathers and tradition, and even Constantinian, canonical, and Carolingian legislation. Although Ladner's work launched a small school of reform studies,[28] inherent in his explications of reform was a tension between the dispassionate technical analysis of a former MGH scholar and the theological vision of a Jewish convert to Catholicism who had come to believe that "the idea of reform . . . was to remain the self-perpetuating core, the inner life spring of Christian tradition through greater and lesser times."[29] While historians can argue, as did R. W. Collingwood, that the essence of history is the history of thought, Ladner's conception of reform as animating thought may be close enough to the *Logos* to make nontheistic historians hesitate.

---

27. Gerhart B. Ladner, *The Idea of Reform: Its Impact on Christian Thought and Action in the Age of the Fathers* (Cambridge: Harvard University Press, 1959). Note also Ladner, "Terms and Ideas of Renewal," in Benson and Constable, *Renaissance and Renewal*, 1–33.

28. On the influence of *The Idea of Reform*, see Christopher M. Bellitto and David Zachariah Flanagin, eds., *Reassessing Reform: A Historical Investigation into Church Renewal* (Washington, DC: Catholic University of America Press, 2012); and Lester L. Field Jr., *Gerhard Ladner and the Idea of Reform: A Modern Historian's Quest for Ancient and Medieval Truth* (Lewiston, NY: Edwin Mellen, 2015), esp. 353–416.

29. Ladner, *Idea of Reform*, 423.

Here a disclaimer is in order: Ladner was my dissertation director at UCLA, and this book owes much, consciously and unconsciously, to his vision of a European ecclesiastical community haltingly and fitfully attempting to reform itself. I employ reform language, although I tend to use "revival" and "renewal" to describe the recovery of existing institutions, and "restoration" to describe the re-creation of institutions lacking direct continuity with their prototypes. "Reform" here designates attempts at reshaping existing ecclesiastical structures in order to make them better conform to ancient norms, attempts that could never fully succeed in an imperfect world and that tended to reveal in their limited successes the tensions between tradition and innovation that are inherent in any attempt at reformation for the better.

From this perspective, reform offers a dynamic narrative. Even the most conservative medieval reformers were innovative, despite themselves, because in order to establish some usable past as a benchmark, they had to resolve the conflicts in their sources and prioritize ancient norms in the light of their own knowledge and concerns. Other reformers deliberately embraced "a certain measure of revolt."[30] The result is that it is less a question of "reform" than of "reforms," and today's scholars increasingly emphasize diversity and local features.[31] Monastic reform remains a central interest, though now it is a question of many reforms, multiple reformers, and irregular initiatives that often depended upon the fates of particular patrons.[32] The story line is less about organized linear progress than about minimally coordinated advances and retreats. Reformation provides a framework inclusive enough to link together the changes that millennial churchmen made in the material, institutional, and intellectual culture of the medieval Church, changes that would help shape the civilization of the Latin West.

My use of reform terminology to describe the development of the millennial Church may draw fire from scholars who question whether an allegedly chaotic "Age of Iron" could actually manifest reform. Ladner himself wrote that "before the Hildebrandian age, reform had ... been primarily individual or personal, and monastic. There was no full realization that the

30. Van Engen, "The Twelfth Century: Reading, Reason, and Revolt in a World of Custom," in Noble and Van Engen, *European Transformations*, 17–44, esp. 24.

31. Howe, *Church Reform and Social Change in Eleventh-Century Central Italy: Dominic of Sora and His Patrons* (Philadelphia: University of Pennsylvania Press, 1997), esp. 162; William North, Jay Rubenstein, and John D. Cotts, "The Experience of Reform: Three Perspectives," *Haskins Society Journal* 10 (2001): 111–61, esp. 111–12.

32. Joachim Wollasch, "Monasticism: The First Wave of Reform," in *NCMH*, 3:163–85, surveys recent trends.

Church as a whole might be in need of reform."[33] In Christopher Belitto's *Renewing Christianity: A History of Church Reform from Day One to Vatican II*, a book directly inspired by Ladner's work, one reads, after a discussion of the Carolingian Renaissance, "The next important chapter in the history of reform begins about 1050 with a series of reform minded popes."[34] This present book argues, to the contrary, that ecclesiastical structures were significantly reformed back in the tenth and early eleventh centuries. In part this conflict stems from the fact that scholars in Ladner's tradition have usually studied ecclesiastical reforms through written documents. Reform back to the Bible? Back to the norms of the apostolic Church? Back to the canon laws of Late Antiquity and of the Carolingians? Back to ancient monastic rules? Back to customaries documenting monastic best practices? In the relatively unreflective millennial Church, however, actions were often more important than words. A dynamic of reform is manifest in material culture, ecclesiastical structures, liturgy, education, and spirituality, not just in literary discourses on reform. As will be seen below, the gritty character of this reform is evident in the earliest reappearances in the post-Carolingian world of the word *reformare*, where it refers to real estate, not theology, to the literal "re-forming" of ecclesiastical patrimonies disrupted during the invasions and civil wars of the late ninth and early tenth centuries. It was possible to re-form property and buildings, customs and costumes. Reforms in the material and customary realms, although sometimes humble, were the necessary prerequisites for the loftier theoretical developments of the Gregorian Reform. Ladner himself might have been open to this extension of his concept inasmuch as he had defined reform, without regard to media, as the "free, intentional and ever perfectible, multiple, prolonged and ever repeated efforts by man to re-assert and augment values pre-existent in the spiritual-material compound of the world."[35]

Other objections will come from a very different direction, from scholars who have concluded that traditional reform terminology now carries so much baggage that it ought to be dropped. It has been argued that monastic-reform master narratives produced in the mid-twentieth century by scholars such as Ernst Sackur and Kassius Hallinger may cause scholars to overlook the varying situations of individual ecclesiastical institutions. If the major narrative becomes reformed vs. unreformed,

33. Ladner, "*Reformatio*," in *Ecumenical Dialogue at Harvard: The Roman Catholic-Protestant Colloquium*, ed. Samuel H. Miller and G. Ernest Wright (Cambridge, MA: Belknap Press, 1964), 172–90, esp. 172.

34. Bellitto, *Renewing Christianity: A History of Church Reform from Day One to Vatican II* (New York: Paulist Press, 2001), 35 and 47.

35. Ladner, *Idea of Reform*, 35.

then debates tend to center more on abstract models such as monasticism and hierarchy and less on concrete institutional realities involving patrons operating in unique social and political situations. Traditional reform narratives emphasize charismatic leaders, overlooking the successors who often did the heavy lifting required to turn ideals into institutional realities. These and other objections were made recently in Steven Vanderputten's *Monastic Reform as Process: Realities and Representations in Medieval Flanders, 900–1100*, which attempts to test the historiography of monastic reform by examining seven Flemish monasteries. He concludes that reform terminology is a "black hole" into which all sorts of historical reality get sucked.[36] Yet his straw men have been attacked before: current research views institutional reform not as a single flashpoint event but as a halting and sporadic process; scholars do recognize the need to contextualize reforms in terms of different generational cohorts and goals; they know to approach with caution the alleged "crisis of monasticism."[37] Vanderputten's concerns relate more to specific misuses of reform paradigms than to the actual paradigms themselves, whose validity his attacks on individual scholarly malpractices cannot logically falsify.

~

This book is addressed not only to professional medievalists but also to general readers interested in medieval and Church history, and therefore it attempts to explain basic concepts, often, I hope, in fresh ways. The initial chapters are more narrative, the later ones more topical, but all seek to highlight changes in the Church in an age of transition. I use thick description to portray a world in which introspective analysis was rare. This story necessarily discusses ideals because the Church postulated the existence of and oriented itself toward a more perfect world. Skeptics might object that the aspirations of a few literate clerks would not have been representative of all Latin Christians, most of them illiterate, some perhaps still living in the "pagan Middle Ages."[38] But the "greater tradition"—articulated by reforming churchmen, backed by powerful patrons, and embodied in

---

36. Steven Vanderputten, *Monastic Reform as Process: Realities and Representations in Medieval Flanders, 900–1100* (Ithaca: Cornell University Press, 2013), esp. 186–89. Along these same lines, see Christopher A. Jones, "Aelfric and the Limits of 'Benedictine Reform,'" in *A Companion to Aelfric*, ed. Hugh Magennis and Mary Swan (Leiden, Neth.: Brill, 2009), 67–108, esp. 70–72, 82–88.

37. Van Engen, "The Crisis of Monasticism Reconsidered: Benedictine Monasticism in the Years 1050–1150," *Speculum* 81 (1986): 269–304; Constable, *Reformation of the Twelfth Century*, 4; Wollasch, "Monasticism," 163–85.

38. Van Engen, "The Christian Middle Ages as an Historiographical Problem," *AHR* 91 (1986): 519–52, esp. 519–22, 538; Ludo Milis, ed., *The Pagan Middle Ages*, trans. Tanis Guest (Woodbridge, UK: Boydell, 1998).

a host of costly institutions and popular practices—is a legitimate subject of inquiry, perhaps more historically consequential than the medieval world's myriad local folk and minority traditions.

Is it possible to write a unified text about a regional world? The aftermath of the collapse of Carolingian central government has been described as *encellulement*, the division of the Latin world into townships and castellanies like the discrete cells enclosing the enamels on a cloisonné vase. And if this was the Frankish heartland, then what about the surrounding Celts, Scandinavians, Slavs, Hungarians, and other peoples? And what about the Mediterranean world, where Latin, Greek, and Eastern Christians, incestuously connected by their "corrupting sea," sometimes seem to have had more in common among themselves than with their brethren north of the Alps?[39] Yet certain themes help unify this diversity: reforms involved the ideals of Rome and Christendom, Carolingian civilization and its legacy, and an ecclesiastical internationalism promoted by an increasingly interrelated community of literary professionals. Reforms manifested a common tension between practice and theory that was being generated as a world based upon custom and ritual was transforming itself into a world privileging written law and true doctrine.

It is impossible to describe each piece of the elaborate mosaic that constitutes the pre-Gregorian Church. My research over the years has centered on France and Italy, though bordering regions in England and the Lorraine have always been in the background. Examples from other places are drawn more heavily from the secondary literature. It can be objected that such a perspective tends to favor Latin Europe's core over its peripheries. Scholars who specialize in Spain, maritime Italy, the Celtic World, Eastern Europe, or Scandinavia will have no problem identifying other possible approaches, but, given the aim of this book and the types of historical sources that survive, a focus on central Francia is hard to avoid. The Latin Church was a hierarchical organization run by literate clergymen whose status in peripheral areas was based in large part on their ability to promote institutional core values. Yet although I can justify the Frankish heartland's presence on center stage, I try not to let the actors on the frontiers fade into the scenery.

The study of the tenth- and early eleventh-century Church is easier now that the surviving historical evidence has become more accessible. Despite the tenth century's famous obscurity, much can be discovered. Monastic chronicles and histories are not as numerous as today's historians would wish, but idiosyncratic voices, oddly local and universal, are

---

39. The phrase echoes Peregrine Horden and Nicholas Purcell, *The Corrupting Sea: A Study of Mediterranean History* (Oxford: Blackwell, 2000), esp. 32–34, 522–23, 541, and 637–41.

provided by chroniclers such as Rodulfus Glaber, Adémar of Chabannes, Flodoard and Richer of Rheims, Thietmar of Merseburg, and others. Tens of thousands of charters survive, not randomly distributed but in clusters such as those from Catalonia and from the monasteries of Cluny and Monte Cassino. Less traditional sources are now entering the public domain: early collections of canon laws that reveal legal minds at work long before Gratian, compendiums of texts produced by schoolmasters and their pupils, practical liturgical manuals, and hagiographies that are now exploited as sources for cultural history as well as for information about their heroes.[40] Architecture and art offer vital perspectives on a largely oral culture.[41] Although medieval archeology is a relatively new discipline, it has much to teach.

ॐ

It may be helpful to conclude this introduction by signaling some conventions this book adopts. One is to speak of the "millennial Church," While the "millennial Church" is a simpler label than "the tenth- and early eleventh-century Church," it risks evoking eschatological resonances. Nevertheless, its benefits may outweigh its deficits, especially now that "millennial" has become a term chronologically neutral enough to designate one group of this book's potential readers, the "millennials" who are members of the 1980–2000 generational cohort. I also employ the names of contemporary national and geographical entities such as "Germany" or "Italy" or "Poland," which are potentially misleading when applied to their very different medieval analogues, but I use them when they are the best communicative signs available and attach warning flags when they are particularly problematic. Personal names are presented in English whenever there is a widely accepted English form; when there is none, the Latin name is the default option. Exceptions include instances where aesthetic dissonance or long use encourage alternative forms: hence "Rodulfus Glaber" instead of "Bald Ralph" or "Sainte Foy" instead of "St. Faith." Names of places and churches still existing today, or that did exist well into the modern period, are presented in their current vernacular form unless they have a generally accepted English name. If a medieval place has no continuity into the modern era, its name appears in Latin.

---

40. For the sources available, see Reuter, "Introduction: Reading the Tenth Century," in *NCMH*, 3: 1–24; Noble, "The Interests of Historians in the Tenth Century," in Rollason et al., *England and the Continent*, 495–513.

41. Michael Camille, "Art History in the Past and Future of Medieval Studies," in *The Past and Future of Medieval Studies*, ed. Van Engen (Notre Dame: University of Notre Dame Press, 1994), 362–82, esp. 366 and 371.

CHAPTER 1

"WOLVES DEVOURING THE LAMBS OF CHRIST"

Then the wolves of slaughter rushed forward, they cared nothing for the water, the host of vikings, west across the Blackwater, across the shining stream they carried their shields, . . . The roar of battle was lifted up there, ravens circled, the bird of prey eager for carrion; there was bedlam in the land. . . . The onslaught of battle was terrible, warriors fell on either side, young men lay dead.

—*The Battle of Maldon*, lines 96–98, 106–107, 111–112

The epic *Battle of Maldon*, composed in eleventh-century English, relates how Ealdorman Byrhtnoth defied Viking invaders on a beach near Maldon in 991.[1] He was killed, but most of his retainers fought on, presumably until they too were slaughtered (the surviving text lacks a conclusion and perhaps some front matter). This invasion was the first in a series of attacks that ultimately resulted in the 1016 crowning of Cnut as king of England. Although the *Anglo-Saxon Chronicle* and other sources note the battle and mention some participants, the only surviving description is this single poem transmitted in a defective manuscript that was itself destroyed by fire in 1731.[2]

1. Quotation is from Donald Scragg, "*The Battle of Maldon*," in *The Battle of Maldon AD 991*, ed. Scragg (Oxford: Basil Blackwell in Association with the Manchester Center for Anglo-Saxon-Studies, 1991), 1–36, esp. 22–23.

2. For general information on the poem, see Scragg, *The Battle of Maldon*, esp. 15–17, and Scragg, *The Return of the Vikings: The Battle of Maldon, 991* (Stroud, UK: Tempus, 2006).

But what do we really know? Critics claim that *The Battle of Maldon* is "not a historical document except insofar as it illustrates literary history."[3] Even scholars who accept it as historical admit that the poet, lacking embedded reporters, must have invented all the heroic challenges and speeches. Some skeptics question whether Byrhtnoth and his men could even have understood their Danish foes.[4] How would they have informed their compatriots about their final moments? Why were they assembled as a classical Germanic war band, an epic structure otherwise unattested in the unified English monarchy? And what about all the details that historians of today would want to know, such as the numbers of combatants, the subsequent fate of the raiders, and their impact on the Essex countryside?

Yet *The Battle of Maldon* is less problematic in some ways than are many other sources. At least it is relatively contemporary with the battle it describes, unlike some chronicles' descriptions of events occurring centuries earlier. Because the poet used his own English language, he did not need to wrestle with the genre expectations and clichés of an alien Latin. He was probably no churchman, unlike most of the writers of the time, who were clerks with dogmatic views about what their literary communities should hear and very little sympathy for the alien other.

The difficulties that historians face when reading *The Battle of Maldon* are found in varying degrees in virtually all the accounts describing post-Carolingian barbarian devastation. This presents a problem for the present book because up until the middle of the twentieth century the deficiencies of the unreformed pre-Gregorian Church were usually blamed on non-Christian invaders. According to the traditional narrative, Vikings, Muslims, and Magyars smashed the empire of Charlemagne (768–814), whose incompetent successors were unable to defend it. Carolingian cultural achievements survived only as isolated ruins in a cataclysmic landscape. Out of the chaos emerged lawless military elites who preyed upon the remains of the institutional Church until the Gregorian reformers began to counter their abuses. But now this grand narrative is in trouble. If the same severe source criticism that can be applied to *The Battle of Maldon* can be applied to all the surviving historical sources that describe the barbarian invasions, then once the documentary witnesses have been thoroughly deconstructed and dispatched, revisionists

3. Earl R. Anderson, "The Roman Idea of a *Comitatus* and Its Application to *The Battle of Maldon*," *Mediaevalia* 17 (1991): 15–26, esp. 24.

4. Peter H. Sawyer, *Kings and Vikings: Scandinavia and Europe, AD 700–1100* (London: Methuen, 1982), 101.

are free to depict the invaders as minor nuisances whose contributions to crafts and commerce compensated in the long run for whatever temporary inconveniences they might have caused. Therefore, before examining how the Church was reformed in the tenth century, it is necessary to address some preliminary historical questions. What happened during the invasions? How did these events affect Christian morale? What survived to be reformed? What reconstruction was required? Like Byrthnoth and his men on the beach, we too must confront the post-Carolingian "barbarians."

THE CAROLINGIAN EMPIRE

There is a new Carolingian Renaissance, not the ninth-century cultural reawakening that this label usually designates but a contemporary rebirth of interest in the Carolingian world. Charlemagne had always attracted attention, even though his attempt to create a new *imperium Christianum* was long viewed as a quixotic dead end. But after competing nation states nearly destroyed themselves in two world wars, Europeans began to take another look, and now they hail Charlemagne as the creator of the first Common Market, "the father of Europe."[5] Moreover, he has a new economic context thanks to scholarly attempts to test the thesis of Henri Pirenne (d. 1935) that Roman economic and cultural systems had continued on after the end of the Western Roman Empire until Islam disrupted the Mediterranean. Pirenne's claims of cultural continuity have held up better than his economic analyses, and today scholars studying the Latin West tend to see the sixth and seventh centuries as the nadir of urban life and posit a subsequent revival.[6] By the eighth century local power structures and aristocracies were gaining strength in many regions, and the secret of Charlemagne's success appears to have been his ability to harness the new elites.[7] Coin hoards and archeology now reveal a new world far from the closed Carolingian Europe that Pirenne had postulated,

---

5. For Charlemagne as father of Europe, see Janet Nelson, "Charlemagne: 'Father of Europe'?," *Quaestiones Medii Aevi Novae* 7 (2002): 1–20; and Alessandro Barbero, *Charlemagne: Father of a Continent*, trans. Allan Cameron (Berkeley: University of California Press, 2004).

6. For Carolingian cities, see Richard Hodges and Brian Hobley, eds., *The Rebirth of Towns in the West, AD 700–1050* (London: Council for British Archaeology, 1988); Adriaan Verhulst, *The Rise of Cities in Northwest Europe* (Cambridge: Cambridge University Press, 1999); Hodges, *Towns and Trade in the Age of Charlemagne* (London: Duckworth, 2000).

7. Chris Wickham, *Framing the Middle Ages: Europe 400–800* (Oxford: Oxford University Press, 2005), esp. 827–28; Mathew Innes, "Charlemagne's Government," in *Charlemagne: Empire and Society*, ed. Joanna Story (Manchester, UK: Manchester University Press, 2005), 71–89, esp. 74–76 and 86–87.

one "deeply open to new people, new things, new ideas."[8] Instead of the twilight of Antiquity, the age of Charlemagne now seems more like a new dawn.[9]

Insofar as a Frankish warlord could, Charlemagne re-created Christian Rome. He and his successors filled Europe with churches modeled on Constantine's basilicas, especially on St. Peter's.[10] He built a Late Antique imperial palace complex at Aachen, which included a model of Justinian's church of San Vitale at Ravenna (incorporating *spolia* from Rome and Ravenna), a swimming pool evoking a Roman bath, and decorative touches such as an imported "statue of Constantine" and a giant stone pine cone echoing the one found at the Lateran.[11] His residence was hailed as a new Lateran Palace.[12] His faux Roman coins celebrated "Karolus Imperator Augustus,"[13] and his seal was an ancient Roman intaglio bearing the inscription "Renovatio Romani Imperii."[14] His son Louis received an imperial crown from the pope that was allegedly the actual diadem of Constantine.[15] Charlemagne himself, albeit only on the rarest of occasions, could be coerced into forgoing his normal Frankish dress and donning formal Roman garments, and he was ultimately laid to rest shrouded in rich silks.[16] Although his persona as a German warlord at first evoked negative comments,[17] later

8. Michael McCormick, *Origins of the European Economy: Communications and Commerce, A.D. 300–900* (Cambridge: Cambridge University Press, 2001), 791.

9. Howe, "Re-Forging the 'Age of Iron': Part II," 1004–7.

10. Richard Krautheimer, "The Carolingian Revival of Early Christian Architecture," *Art Bulletin* 25 (1942): 1–38.

11. Günter Bandmann, *Early Medieval Architecture as Bearer of Meaning*, trans. Kendall Wallis (New York: Columbia University Press, 2005), 195–201; Janet L. Nelson, "Aachen as a Place of Power," in *Topographies of Power in the Early Middle Ages*, ed. Mayke de Jong and Frans Theuws (Leiden, Neth.: Brill, 2001), 217–42; Charles B. McClendon, *The Origins of Medieval Architecture: Building in Europe, A.D. 600–900* (New Haven: Yale University Press, 2005), 105–27.

12. Bandmann, *Early Medieval Architecture*, 295, note 144.

13. Simon Coupland, "Charlemagne's Coinage: Ideology and Economy," in Story, *Charlemagne*, 211–29.

14. Percy Ernst Schramm, "Drei Nachträge zu den Metallbullen der Karolingischen und Sächsischen Kaiser," *Deutsches Archiv* 24 (1968): 1–15, esp. 7–10 and plate 2; Reinhard Schneider, "Vor- und Frühformen einer *Renovatio Imperii* in christlichen Germanenreichen der Völkerwanderungszeit," *Zeitschrift für antikes Christentum* 4 (2000): 325–37.

15. Wolfgang Wendling, "Die Erhebung Ludwigs des Frommen zum Mitkaiser im Jahre 813 und ihre Bedeutung für Verfassungsgeschichte des Frankenreiches," *Frühmittelalterliche Studien* 19 (1985): 201–38, esp. 226.

16. Einhard, *Vita Karoli* xxiii, ed. Georg Waitz and Oswald Holder-Egger, MGH SS Rer Germ 25 (Hannover: Hahn, 1911), 29, trans. David Ganz, *Two Lives of Charlemagne: Einhard and Notker the Stammerer* (London: Penguin, 2008), 35.

17. Paul Edward Dutton, *The Politics of Dreaming in the Carolingian Empire* (Lincoln: University of Nebraska Press, 1994), esp. 76–80; Roger Collins, "Charlemagne and His Critics, 814–29," in *La royauté et les élites dans l'Europe carolingienne: Début IXᵉ siècle aux environs de 920*, ed. Régine Le Jan (Lille: Université de Charles-de-Gaulle Lille III, 1998), 193–211.

on, looking back from more chaotic ages, people began to acclaim him as "St. Charlemagne."[18]

Louis the Pious, Charlemagne's sole surviving legitimate son, inherited a united empire. Because he had served as sub-king of Aquitaine since 781, he was able to bring to Aachen not only political and military experience but also his own tested ministers. He evicted his sisters, who had become increasingly powerful during the old emperor's final years.[19] He fostered monastic reform.[20] He sponsored efforts to Christianize the Scandinavians.[21] But his idealism made it difficult for him to maintain Charlemagne's careful balance between German warlord and Roman emperor, and ultimately not even his own sons would obey him, disgusted as they were by his innovations and by the machinations of their stepmother. The empire divided. In 841, two of Charlemagne's grandsons took the famous oaths at Strasbourg, where the troops of Charles Bald swore in the *lingua Romana* and the troops of Louis the German in the *Teudisca lingua* (i.e., in their French and German vernaculars).[22] The ultimate result was the Treaty of Verdun in 843, which divided the empire in a way that foreshadowed the future France and Germany and the contested territories lying between them.

This disintegration of the Frankish realm was nothing new. Frankish kings almost always disputed royal inheritances. The smooth transition from Charlemagne to Louis the Pious had occurred only because the old emperor had managed to outlive all but one primary heir. His own succession, his father's, and his grandfather's had been far messier, and during the preceding Merovingian dynasty the realm had frequently disintegrated into Aquitania, Burgundy, Neustria (the "western kingdom" of northern

18. The apotheosis of Charlemagne in memory is analyzed in Robert Morrissey, *Charlemagne and France: A Thousand Years of Mythology*, trans. Catherine Tihanyi (Notre Dame: University of Notre Dame Press, 2003); Matthew Gabriele, *An Empire of Memory: The Legend of Charlemagne, the Franks, and Jerusalem before the First Crusade* (Oxford: Oxford University Press, 2011), esp. 1–9; and in Anne A. Latowsky, *Emperor of the World: Charlemagne and the Construction of Imperial Authority, 800–1229* (Ithaca: Cornell University Press, 2013), esp. 59–98. On his status as saint, see Jürgen Petersohn, "Die päpstliche Kanonisationsdelegation des 11. und 12. Jahrhunderts und die Heiligsprechung Karls des Grossen," in *Proceedings of the Fourth International Congress of Medieval Canon Law, Toronto, 21–25 August 1972*, ed. Stephan Kuttner (Vatican City: BAV, 1976), 163–206.

19. Nelson, "La cour impériale de Charlemagne," in Le Jan, *La Royauté et les élites*, 177–91.

20. Josef Semmler, "Le monachisme occidental du VIIIᵉ au Xᵉ siècle: Formation et réformation," in *Revue bénédictine* 103 (1993): 68–89, esp. 83–86; Egon Boshof, *Ludwig der Fromme* (Darmstadt: Wissenschaftliche Buchgesellschaft, 1996), 123–26.

21. James T. Palmer, "Rimbert's *Vita Anskarii* and Scandinavian Mission in the Ninth Century," *JEH* 55 (2004): 235–56, esp. 235–36 and 248 and 251–52.

22. *Annales Bertiniani* 842, ed. Félix Grat, *Annales de Saint-Bertin* (Paris: Klincksieck, 1964), 41, trans. Nelson, *The Annals of St-Bertin* (Manchester, UK: Manchester University Press, 1991), 52; Nithard, *Historiarum IV Libri* III v, ed. Georg Pertz and Ernest Müller, MGH SS Rer Germ (Hannover: Hahn, 1965), 35–37, trans. Bernhard Walter Scholz, *Carolingian Chronicles: "Royal Frankish Annals" and Nithard's "Histories"* (Ann Arbor: University of Michigan Press, 1970), 161–63.

Francia), and Austrasia (the ancient homeland of the Franks around the lower Rhine). Yet it was always reassembled by great leaders or at least by long-lived ones. Despite the fierceness of the civil wars among Charlemagne's grandsons and great-grandsons, anyone knowledgeable about the acrimonious history of the Franks expected that these divisions would be quickly transcended.

But this time things were different. Just as had happened to the Western Roman Empire centuries earlier, the arrival of foreign invaders tipped the balance. In the second half of the ninth and the first half of the tenth century, the Carolingian world was attacked from all sides by Vikings, Muslims, and Magyars, with a little help from the Slavs. The Franks had brought some of these troubles upon themselves. By conquering Frisians, Saxons, and Avars they had eliminated potential buffers against Scandinavians, Slavs, and Magyars; by trading with Scandinavians they had helped these dangerous neighbors develop their deadly maritime expertise; and by becoming players in Mediterranean affairs they had added the more civilized polities of Umayyad Spain and the Byzantine Empire to their roster of potential enemies. The Franks would reap what they had sown.

THE VIKINGS

The most successful invaders were Scandinavians. Medieval English writers, who could speak precisely about "Danes" and "Northmen," called some of them "Vikings," a word whose disputed etymology is usually linked to a notion of traveling, perhaps out of bays or fiords.[23] On the Continent the raiders were "Danes," "Northmen," "heathen men," "pagans," "pirates," or "enemies of God."[24] All of these terms are unsatisfactory in that the more general names obscure differences among ethnically diverse bands that could unite for mutual advantage and then turn on each other just as readily, while national labels such as "Danes," "Norwegians," and "Swedes"

---

23. For the English terminology, see Alfred P. Smyth, "The Emergence of English Identity, 700–1000," in *Medieval Europeans: Studies in Ethnic Identity and National Perspectives in Medieval Europe*, ed. Smyth (London: Macmillan, 1998), 24–52, esp. 35–39; David N. Dumville, "Vikings in Insular Chronicling," in *The Viking World*, ed. Stefan Brink and Neil Price (London: Routledge, 2008), 350–67; and Robert Ferguson, *The Vikings: A History* (New York: Penguin, 2009), 2–5. Linguistic arguments based on Scandinavian sources are presented in Judith Jesch, *Ships and Men in the Late Viking Age: The Vocabulary of Runic Inscriptions and Skaldic Verse* (Woodbridge, UK: Boydell, 2001), 44–68; and Tette Hofstra, "Changing Views on the Vikings," *TijdSchrift voor Skandinavistiek* 24 (2003): 147–60.

24. For Continental terminology, see Horst Zettel, *Das Bild der Normannen und der Normanneneinfälle in westfränkishen, ostfränkishen und Angelsächsischen Quellen des 8. bis 11. Jahrhunderts* (Munich: Wilhelm Fink, 1977).

evoke kingdoms that had not yet coalesced and obscure the ad hoc mixed composition of many expeditions.[25] Also misleading is the hindsight that allows today's historians to focus on the groups that endured and to disregard the more ephemeral ones, an advantage not shared by the people under attack.[26]

While the Carolingian Franks were creating an empire, their Scandinavian neighbors were busy increasing their trade with France and England and quietly colonizing the Orkneys, Hebrides, and other outer British isles.[27] In 793, in a dramatic debut as maritime raiders, they sacked the sacred island monastery of Lindisfarne and another Northumbrian monastery, probably Jarrow.[28] Then they began to systematically attack all the island monasteries of the Irish Sea.[29] Alcuin (d. 804), the head of Charlemagne's "brain trust," an Englishman who had formerly been the schoolmaster at York, expresses his shock in seven surviving letters: "Never before has such an atrocity appeared in Britain as we have now suffered at the hands of a pagan people. Such a voyage was not thought possible. The church of St. Cuthbert is now spattered with the blood of the priests of God, stripped of all its furnishings, exposed to the plundering of pagans."[30]

25. Nelson, "The Frankish Empire," in *The Oxford Illustrated History of the Vikings*, ed. Sawyer (Oxford: Oxford University Press, 1997), 19–47, esp. 35–36 and 38, discusses Viking divisions. Nils Blomkvist, *The Discovery of the Baltic: The Reception of a Catholic World System into the European North (A.D. 1075–1225)* (Boston: Brill, 2005) argues that myriad quasi-independent Baltic and North Sea communities were not effectively integrated into larger states until the twelfth century.

26. Anne Niessen Jaubert, "Some Aspects of Viking Research in France," *Acta Archaeologica* 71 (2001): 159–69, esp. 159. For a less teleological contemporary perspective, note how the Normans of the Loire are treated in a parallel fashion to those of the Seine (today's Normans) in Flodoard of Rheim's *Annales*, ed. Philippe Lauer, *Les Annales de Flodoard*, Collection de texts pour servir à l'étude et à l'enseignement de l'histoire 39 (Paris: Alphonse Picard et Fils, 1906), trans. Steven Fanning and Bernard Bachrach, *The Annals of Flodoard of Reims, 919–966* (Peterborough, ON: Broadview, 2004).

27. The archaeological evidence for Viking infiltration into the outer islands is discussed in Olwyn Owen, "The Scar Boat Burial—and the Missing Decades of the Early Viking Age in Orkney and Shetland," in *Scandinavia and Europe, 800–1350: Contact, Conflict, and Coexistence*, ed. Jonathan Adams and Katherine Holman (Turnhout, Belg.: Brepols, 2004), 3–33, esp. 25; and in James Graham-Campbell, "Les traces archéologiques des peuplements scandinaves en Occident," in *Les fondations scandinaves en Occident et les débuts du duché de Normandie: Colloque de Cerisy-la-Salle (25–29 septembre 2002)*, ed. Pierre Bauduin (Caen: CRAHAM, 2005), 13–23, esp. 13–16.

28. *Anglo-Saxon Chronicle* 793–94, ed. Susan Irvine, *The Anglo-Saxon Chronicle: A Collaborative Edition*, vol. 7, *MS E* (Cambridge: D.S. Brewer, 2004), 42, trans. Dorothy Whitelock, *The Anglo-Saxon Chronicle: A Revised Translation* (New Brunswick, NJ: Rutgers University Press, 1961), 36.

29. *Annales Ultonienses* 794, 795, 798, 802, 806, ed. and trans. Seán Mac Airt and Gearóid Mac Niocaill, *The Annals of Ulster* (Dublin: Institute for Advanced Studies, 1983), 250–53, 258–59, 262–63.

30. Alcuin, *Epist.* xvi (to Ethelred, King of Northumbria, late 793), ed. Ernst Dümmler, MGH *Epp* IV: Karolini Aevi 2 (Berlin: Weidmann, 1895), 42–49, esp. 42, trans. (as *Epist.* xii) Stephen Allott, *Alcuin of York, c. A.D. 732 to 804—His Life and Letters* (York, UK: William Sessions, 1974), 18–20, esp. 18. The full correspondence is discussed in Donald A. Bullough, "What Has Ingeld to Do with Lindisfarne," *Anglo-Saxon England*

FIGURE 1. Viking longship, replica of the Oseberg ship from the early ninth century. Bergen Maritime Museum, Norway. Photo credit: HIP/Art Resource, NY.

Northmen also hit the Frankish heartland. During Charlemagne's last years, increased tension between Franks and Danes had resulted in a more elaborate *Danevirke*, a system of fortifications that cut Denmark off from the empire. That situation was temporarily defused by the succession disputes following King Godfred's death in 810. Louis the Pious tried to prolong these distractions by subsidizing pretenders to the Danish crown, but this policy kept the Danes far too well informed about Francia

22 (1993): 93–125; and in *Alcuin, Achievement and Reputation: Being Part of the Ford Lectures Delivered in Oxford in Hilary Term 1980* (Leiden, Neth.: Brill, 2004), 410–18.

and its problems. Stronger kings ultimately emerged in Scandinavia, a development that hurt the Franks both by facilitating mass mobilizations within the new northern kingdoms and by causing discontented groups of more independent warriors to decide to seek their fortunes elsewhere. Raids increased. Large Danish forces attacked major ports during the Carolingian civil wars of the 830s; hundreds of ships sailed up the Seine, the Loire, and the Garonne during the succession struggles of the early 840s, looting monasteries and towns all along the way. Fleets ravaged the coasts of Brittany and Aquitaine and even attacked Spain and Italy. At first the raiders sailed directly from their homelands, but soon seasonal campaigns were replaced by overwintering on riverine islands and then by more permanent Irish, English, and Continental bases.[31]

The "great armies" retained their mobility for a long time. When Charles the Bald (840–877) strengthened his defenses in the 870s, using tactics such as fortified bridges (which, alas, tended to concede the watersheds below them to the raiders), Vikings shifted their attention to England, where they won control over the kingdoms of Northumbria and Mercia and threatened Wessex, the last holdout. King Alfred (871–99) stabilized the situation and began a systematic reconquest that would not be completed until 954 when Eric Bloodaxe was driven out of York, ending nearly a century of Viking rule there. Some Vikings avoided Alfred's forces during the 880s and 890s by returning to the Continent to attack the Low Countries, part of the fractured Middle Kingdom of Charlemagne's grandson, Emperor Lothar (840–55), but despite initial successes they failed to establish a permanent beachhead there.[32] In Western Francia, however, the Vikings who settled at the mouth of the Seine were recognized around 911 as the protectors of Rouen by King Charles the Simple (893–923), and by 933 they had taken control over almost all the territory that would become the Duchy of Normandy.[33]

31. Viking books arrive in hordes. General introductions with select bibliographies include Angelo Forte, Richard Oram, and Frederik Pederson, *Viking Empires* (Cambridge: Cambridge University Press, 2005); Martin Arnold, *The Vikings: Wolves of War* (Lanham, MD: Rowman & Littlefield, 2007); I. P. Stephenson, *Viking Warfare* (Stroud: Amberly, 2012); Neil Oliver, *The Vikings* (New York: Pegasus Books, 2013); Philip Parker, *The Northmen's Fury: A History of the Viking World* (London: Jonathan Cape, 2014).

32. Stéphane Lebecq, "Les Vikings en Frise: Chronique d'un échec relatif," in Bauduin, *Les fondations scandinaves en Occident*, 97–112; Egge Knol, "Frisia in Carolingian Times," and W.J.H. Verwers, "Vikings in the Lower Rhine Area?," in *Viking Trade and Settlement in Continental Western Europe*, ed. Iben Skibsted Klaesø (Copenhagen: Museum Tusculanum Press, University of Copenhagen, 2010), 43–60 and 61–80.

33. Bauduin, *Le monde franc et les Vikings, VIII ᵉ–X ᵉ siècle* (Paris: Albin Michel, 2009), 347–51. On problems inherent in the traditional story of the 911 Treaty of Saint-Clair-sur-Epte, see Dumville, "Vikings in the British Isles," in *The Scandinavians from the Vendel Period to the Tenth Century: An Ethnographic Perspective*, ed. Judith Jesch (Woodbridge: Boydell, 2002), 209–250, esp. 214.

Vikings became victims of their own success. When they established themselves permanently in Ireland, Scotland, England, and northern France, they lost mobility. To accommodate themselves to their new neighbors, they accepted local systems of property, government, and religion. Although Scandinavian settlers continued to arrive in Normandy throughout the tenth century, independent Viking raids gradually diminished in frequency and scale, with the last major one in France occurring in 1006.[34] In the eleventh century would-be Vikings went on to related careers: Northmen fought for both sides during the Norman conquest of Greek southern Italy, served in the Byzantine Varangian guard, and participated in final assaults on England.[35]

England became a target once more. Raiders from Ireland in the 980s had begun to menace the kingdom united by Alfred's descendants. Major forces from Denmark arrived from 991 on, undeterred by the heroic efforts of Byrhtnoth and his men at Maldon. King Aethelred (978–1016) attempted to buy safety by paying protection money (*Danegeld*), which only exacerbated his problems. By 1013 Sven Forkbeard had conquered the country.[36] Both he and Aethelred soon died, leaving Swen's son Cnut (1016–35) as the universally recognized king of England.[37] Yet entrepreneurial maritime raiders reaped no benefits from the Danish triumph because now England had an effective navy.[38] When English magnates tired of financing the capricious Scandinavian political adventures of Cnut's heirs, they arranged for the crown to revert to Edward the Confessor (1042–66), Aethelred's son. Although attempts to retake England continued through the end of the century, no other Scandinavian king could replicate Cnut's success.[39]

---

34. On late ninth-century Viking activity, see Nelson, "The Frankish Empire," in Sawyer, *Oxford Illustrated History of the Vikings*, 19–47. Frankish countermeasures are now less derided: see Nelson, *Charles the Bald* (New York: Longman, 1992), and Simon McLean, *Kingship and Politics in the Late Ninth Century: Charles the Fat and the End of the Carolingian Empire* (Cambridge: Cambridge University Press, 2003). On the defeat of the duke of Aquitaine by a large force of Vikings who landed at Saint-Michel-en l'Herm in August of 1006, see Bernard Bachrach, "Toward a Reappraisal of William the Great, Duke of Aquitaine (995–1030)," *Journal of Medieval History* 5 (1979): 11–21, esp. 13–14.

35. Jesch, "Vikings on the European Continent in the Late Viking Age," in Adams and Holman, *Scandinavia and Europe*, 255–68, esp. 266–67.

36. Simon Keynes, "Historical Context of the Battle of Maldon," in Scragg, *Battle of Maldon*, 81–113; Keynes, "The Vikings in England, c. 790–1016," in Sawyer, *Oxford Illustrated History of the Vikings*, 48–82, esp. 73–82; Ian Howard, *Swein Forkbeard's Invasions and the Danish Conquest of England, 991–1017* (Woodbridge, UK: Boydell, 2003).

37. On Cnut scholarship, see Timothy Bolton, *The Empire of Cnut the Great: Conquest and Consolidation of Power in Northern Europe in the Early Eleventh Century* (Leiden, Neth.: Brill, 2009), 1–5.

38. Ryan Lavelle, *Alfred's Wars: Sources and Interpretations of Anglo-Saxon Warfare in the Viking Age* (Woodbridge, UK: Boydell, 2010), 141–76, surveys the earlier naval situation.

39. Kelly DeVries, *The Norwegian Invasion of England in 1066* (Woodbridge, UK: Boydell, 1999); Parker, *Northmen's Fury*, 264, 301–6, 315.

THE MUSLIMS

Muslims also attacked. Although "the monstrous Hagarenes [gens Agarenorum nefanda]" were notorious for their resounding trumpets and fierce battle cries, often they were more urbane, literate, and better armed than their Western opponents.[40] John of Gorze (d. 974), on an embassy from the king of Germany to the court at Cordova during the years 953–56, had ample time to be impressed with the caliph's great wealth and elaborate protocol.[41] A century or more later, the *Roland* poet could imagine splendidly equipped Islamic armies marching from wealthy cities and nations beyond number. Muslims, on the other hand, saw the "Franks" as an unwashed, smelly people, an ill-defined Christian group dwelling between Spain and the Slavs on the far edge of the civilized world whose real center lay in the Near East.[42]

Islamic raids ranged from small campaigns led by freebooters to major expeditions authorized by self-proclaimed caliphs in Cordoba and al-Mahdiyya. Although Islamic states fought among themselves as least as much as they did with their Christian neighbors, they did share common strategic interests. In the post-Roman world, as Michael McCormick has demonstrated by exhaustively tabulating known travelers and coin hoards, the western Mediterranean had long remained a "Roman lake" with local trading areas connected by a major route running from the west to Constantinople. Although Byzantine hegemony was unaffected by half-hearted Carolingian attempts to establish naval bases at Pisa and Genoa, the ninth-century Islamic conquests of Sicily and Crete suddenly threatened to turn the Mediterranean into a "Mare Arabicum."[43] Islamic leaders

40. The citation refers to a tenth-century attack on Brindisi recorded in the *Chronicon Salernitanum* lxxii, ed. Ulla Westerbergh, *Chronicon Salernitanum: A Critical Edition with Studies on Literary and Historical Sources and on Language* (Stockholm: Almquist & Wiksell, 1956), 70. For a comparison of early Frankish and Islamic military technology, see Bernard Bachrach, *Early Carolingian Warfare: Prelude to Empire* (Philadelphia: University of Pennsylvania Press, 2001), 175–77.

41. Francisco Fernández, "Die Gesandschaft des Johannes von Gorze nach Cordoba," in *Otto der Grosse, Magdeburg und Europa*, ed. Matthias Puhle, 2 vols. (Mainz, Ger.: P. von Zabern, 2001), 525–36. On the archeological remains of tenth-century Cordova, see the articles by Antonio Vallejo Triano, Antonio Almagro, and Glaire D. Anderson, in *Revisiting Al-Andalus: Perspectives on the Material Culture of Islamic Iberia and Beyond*, ed. Anderson and Mariam Rosser-Owen (Leiden, Neth.: Brill 2007), 3–26, 27–52, 53–79; and Anderson, *The Islamic Villa in Early Medieval Iberia: Aristocratic Estates and Court Culture in Umayyad Córdoba* (Burlington, VT: Ashgate, 2013), esp. 172–76.

42. André Miquel, *La géographie humaine du monde musulman jusqu'a milieu du 11ᵉ siècle*, 4 vols. (Paris: Mouton, 1967–88), 2:354–59. Nizar F. Hermes, *The [European] Other in Medieval Arabic Literature and Culture: Ninth-Twelfth Century AD* (New York: Palgrave Macmillan, 2012), esp. 39–80 and 173, argues against the stereotype that Islamic views of the West were always negative and uniformed.

43. McCormick, *Origins of the European Economy*, esp. 787 and 795. For effects on Greece, see Florin Curta, *The Edinburgh History of the Greeks, c. 500 to 1050: The Early Middle Ages* (Edinburgh: Edinburgh University Press, 2011), 146–47 and 152–53. On the conquest of Sicily, see Leonard C. Chiarelli, *A History*

understood trade routes and centers of wealth and planned their campaigns accordingly.[44] Muslim pirates proliferated, and the successful ones inspired greater rulers to take an interest in their existing lairs and in new forward bases, just as successful Viking raiders sometimes enticed northern kings into their operations. Some pirate bases were temporary, others more permanent. From them raiders could attack sea routes and hinterlands; in them they could accumulate and exchange booty and hostages.[45] Yet the different Mediterranean theaters featured very different casts of characters.

Soon after the Muslim conquest of Spain in 711, the pattern of future interactions was set. Islamic Spain dominated the southern half of the peninsula, separated from the residual Christian principalities in the north by a shifting no-man's-land peopled by miscellaneous frontiersmen. This balance of power was little affected by Charlemagne's Spanish campaigns, whose only fruits were a precarious Frankish march and the military disaster that inspired the *Song of Roland*. In fact, early medieval Muslim geographers believed that Islamic Spain's most formidable opponents were the Basques and other local Christians, not the Franks.[46] After the Carolingian Empire imploded, the part of the Spanish march not reclaimed by Islam became the County of Barcelona.

Islamic Spain's complex politics limited its ability to exploit ninth- and tenth-century Frankish troubles. Following the triumph of the Abbasid caliphs in Baghdad in 750, a dispossessed Umayyad heir made his way into Spain. The Umayyads ruled out of Cordova by carefully balancing Arab, Berber, Jewish, and Mozarabic constituencies, though at times their actual power did not extend very far beyond the capital.[47] Cordova was frequently at odds with Saragossa, the major city in the north (each larger than any in contemporary Latin Christendom), instability that

---

of Muslim Sicily (Sta Venera, Malta: Midsea Books, 2011), esp. 13–142. The quoted phrase is from Martin Goffriller, "The Castral Territory of the Balearic Islands: The Evolution of Territorial Control in Mallorca during the Middle Ages," in *Château et représentations: Actes du Colloque International de Stirling (Écosse), 30 août–5 septembre 2008*, ed. Peter Ettel, Anne-Marie Flambard Héricher, and Tom E. McNeill (Caen: CRAHM, 2010), 109–13, esp. 110.

44. Ekkehard Eickhoff, *Seekrieg und Seepolitik zwischen Islam und Abendland: Das Mittelmeer unter byzantinischer und arabischer Hegemonie (650–1040)* (Berlin: Walter de Gruyter, 1966), esp. 117–19, 351–56, and 396–97.

45. Travis Bruce, "The Politics of Violence and Trade: Denia and Pisa in the Eleventh Century," *Journal of Medieval History* 32 (2006): 127–42.

46. Miquel, *La géographie humaine du monde musulman*, 2:351–53; Hermes, *The [European] Other*, 55–56 and 63–67.

47. Janina M. Safran, *The Second Umayyad Caliphate: The Articulation of Caliphal Legitimacy in al-Andalus* (Cambridge: Center for Middle Eastern Studies of Harvard University, 2000); Maribel Fierro, *Abd al-Rahman III: The First Cordoban Caliph* (Oxford: One World, 2005).

contributed to independent raids and to unauthorized alliances with northern Christians. Coastal emirs could sponsor their own adventures, such as the conquest of the Balearics in 903.[48] The height of Cordovan rule was reached when a chamberlain seized effective power in 981 and ruled until his death in 1002 as Al-Mansur (the victorious). He mobilized Muslims against Christians, leading, often in person, what Islamic writers claimed were fifty-two separate raids against the major cities and strongpoints of Christian Spain.[49] He targeted churches and monasteries, especially the bell towers that were the Christian equivalent of minarets, and he sent the confiscated bells of Santiago de Compostela to Cordova, where, inverted, they served as braziers in the Great Mosque until after the Christian conquest of Cordova in 1236.[50] However, the pendulum swung the other way after Al-Mansur's death, and Christian kingdoms benefited greatly from Islamic civil wars that featured the sack of Cordova in 1013, the elimination of the last Umayyad claimant in 1031, and the emergence, out of the wreckage, of nearly two dozen *taiffa* kingdoms.

North Africa had also broken free from the political authority of the Abbasid caliphate. In 789 Morocco became independent under the Idrisid dynasty; in 800 much of North Africa passed to the Aghlabids of Tunis. After a Byzantine rebel invited an Egyptian fleet into Sicily in 827, the Aghlabids joined campaigns there that culminated in the fall of Syracuse in 878. The Byzantines never gave up: Taormina held until 902, sporadic revolts broke out long afterwards, and expeditions seeking reconquest continued up into the 1030s.[51] Nevertheless, for nearly two centuries Sicily was an important Islamic province. Its capital, Palermo, larger than any contemporary Latin city and famed throughout Islam for its jurists and poets, was hailed as "a city of more than 300 mosques."[52]

48. Goffriller, "Castral Territory of the Balearic Islands," in Ettel et al., *Château et représentations*, 109–113.

49. Amancio Isla, "Warfare and Other Plagues in the Iberian Peninsula around the Year 1000," in *Europe around the Year 1000*, ed. Przemysław Urbańczyk (Warsaw: Polish Academy of Sciences Institute of Archaeology and Ethnology, 2001), 233–246, esp. 237–39.

50. Janice Mann, "A New Architecture for a New Order: The Building Projects of Sancho el Mayor (1004–1035)," in *The White Mantle of Churches: Architecture, Liturgy, and Art around the Millennium*, ed. Nigel Hiscock (Turnhout, Belg.: Brepols, 2003), 233–48, esp. 233–35. The return of Santiago's bells triumphantly concludes Lucas of Tuy's *Chronicon*, ed. Emma Falque, *Lucas Tudensis Chronicon Mundi*, CCCM 74 (Turnhout, Belg.: Brepols, 1973), 326–27.

51. Graham A. Loud, *The Age of Robert Guiscard: Southern Italy and the Norman Conquest* (Harlow, UK: Pearson Education Limited, 2000), 78–79.

52. Ibn Ḥauḵal, *Image of the Earth* (ca. 972), ed. J.H. Kramers, *Opus Geographicum Auctore Ibn Ḥauḵa (Abū 'L-Kāsim ibn Hauḵal al Naṣ ībī), secundum Textum et Imagines Codicis Constantinopolitani Conservati in Bibliotheca Antiqui Palatii N°. 3346 Cui Titulus Est "Liber Imaginis Terrae,"* Bibliotheca Geographicorum

In the tenth century, Shiite revolution captivated or captured North Africa. An imported leader who traced his descent from Mohammed's daughter Fatima proclaimed himself caliph. He took the title *al-Mahdi* and ruled from 921 on out of a massively fortified capital city near Carthage, named in his honor al-Mahdiyya. Its great gate controlled access by land; its rectangular harbor and shipyards, carved out of rock and protected by two huge towers and a chain, controlled access by sea. From there the Fatimids, bankrolled by West African gold, were able to dispatch fleets and armies in all directions. They took control over hard-to-rule Sicily, ruthlessly shifting populations, even arranging in 962 for the mass circumcision of fifteen thousand young men, who did receive generous gifts in compensation.[53] In 969, after many attempts, the Fatimids finally conquered Egypt. They had missionaries and allies throughout the Near East and central Asia. They had armies of slaves, which they trusted far more than the local forces of the countries they conquered.[54] The Fatimid quest for Shiite supremacy would ultimately be thwarted by Turks entering the Arab world from the north, but for a time the fate of Islam hung in the balance. This epic struggle benefited the Christian West because, when the Fatimid caliph moved to Cairo and got distracted by events farther east, his governors in North Africa and Sicily were able to break away to pursue their own independent dynastic interests.

Islamic pirate bases dotted southern France in the swampy lawless Camargue and elsewhere, but the most famous was at Fraxinetum, today's Garde-Freinet, on the French Riviera about ten miles from Saint-Tropez. Andalusian pirates landed there in 889, established a fort, and expanded outward, crossing the Maritime Alps and even the Alps themselves.[55] They controlled several major passes and dominated the central valley of the Rhone, colonizing as well as raiding. For nearly a century no one could evict them. A major theme of the *Annals* of Flodoard of Rheims (d. after 966) is the harm they inflicted on pilgrims:

Arabicorum 2 (Leiden, Neth.: Brill, 1967), 118–31, esp. 120, trans. Bernard Lewis, *Islam from the Prophet Muhammad to the Capture of Constantinople*, 2 vols. (New York: Walker and Company, 1976), 2:87–101, esp. 89. Another version is translated in William Granara, "Ibn Hawqal in Sicily," *Alif: Journal of Comparative Poetics* 3 (1983): 94–99. For context, see Chiarelli, *History of Muslim Sicily*, 112–15 and 289–335.

53. Chiarelli, *History of Muslim Sicily*, 67–93, 226, and 180.

54. Michael Brett, *The Rise of the Fatimids: The World of the Mediterranean and the Middle East in the Fourth Century of the Hijira, Tenth Century CE* (Leiden, Neth,: Brill, 2001), esp. 142–52.

55. On the ruins and alleged ruins of this Islamic occupation, see Manfred W. Wenner, "The Arab/Muslim Presence in Medieval Central Europe," *International Journal of Middle East Studies* 12 (1980): 59–97; Gabriele Crespi, *The Arabs in Europe* (New York: Rizzoli, 1986), 64–74.

in 921 travelers were "killed by stones in the defiles of the Alps by the Saracens"; in 923 English pilgrims were "slaughtered in the Alps by the Saracens"; in 929 "the Saracens blocked the Alpine paths and turned back many who wished to travel to Rome"; in 936 "the Saracens raided Alamannia and, as they were returning, they killed many who were travelling to Rome."[56] In 972 they went too far when they captured and held for ransom Abbot Maiolus of Cluny (965–994), the most distinguished Latin churchman of his day. The response was a retaliatory alliance of regional notables led by Count William the Good of Arles and seconded by Gibelin Grimaldi of Genoa, whose reward was the hillside village that would become Grimaud, the eponymous home of today's Grimaldi princes of Monaco.[57]

Other bases were located on Sardinia, Corsica, and the Balearics. The embattled Byzantine Empire had left local Sardinian officials to fend for themselves, and they were unable or unwilling to oppose Muslim infiltration. In 849 Sardinia was the rendezvous point for a fleet directed at Rome that was wrecked by a storm outside Ostia. It harbored Muslim forces sporadically until Pisa and Genoa took the fight directly to the island itself in the early eleventh century and then to North Africa.[58] Islamic pirates had attacked Corsica several times during Charlemagne's reign and subsequently expanded their influence there despite the attempts of the marquesses of Tuscany to defend it: some Corsican territory remained under Muslim control until about 930. Malta was Muslim from about 870 until 1091, when Normans from Sicily occupied it, thereby becoming rulers of a substantial Islamic population. The Spanish Muslims who conquered the Balearics in 903 held them until the early thirteenth century.

Directly in the line of fire lay Italy. Muslims had often traded with the nominally Byzantine coastal republics such as Naples and Amalfi, perhaps even serving as their mercenaries. Starting in the 820s or 830s, Islamic forces from Sicily began to annex sections of the mainland. Temporarily they held most of the Basilicata, Calabria, and Apulia, lands that were

56. *Flodoard, Annales* 921, 923, 929, and 936, Lauer, 5, 19, 44–45, 65, Fanning and Bachrach, 5, 10, 19, 28.

57. Maiolus's capture is described in his hagiographical *vitae* and in Rodulfus Glaber, *Historiae* I ix, ed. and trans. John France, *Rodulfus Glaber: The Five Books of the Histories* (Oxford: Clarendon, 1989), 18–23. See Scott G. Bruce, *Cluny and the Muslims of La Garde-Freinet: Hagiography and the Problem of Islam in Medieval Europe* (Ithaca: Cornell University Press, 2015), 10–40.

58. Eickhoff, *Seekrieg und Seepolitik*, 398–400; H.E.J. Cowdrey, "The Mahdia Campaign of 1087," *EHR* 92 (1977): 1–29; Travis Bruce, "Politics of Violence and Trade: Denia," 127–142.

ruled out of Bari from 847 to 871 by an emir who presented himself as the counterpart of the powerful emir of Sicily. A fleet from Palermo sacked the suburbs of Rome in 846, looting the basilica of St. Peter's so thoroughly that "along with the very altar that had been placed above his tomb, they carried off all the ornaments and treasures."[59] That focused everyone's attention and made attitudes toward the Muslims much less tolerant. Pope Leo IV (847–55) surrounded the Constantinian basilica with the Leonine walls whose vestiges survive today in the papal gardens, witnesses of the original Vatican City. An alliance of Byzantine, Frankish, and Lombard forces led by Charlemagne's great-grandson Emperor Louis II (850–875) finally reconquered Bari, and Byzantines and Lombards successfully retook the rest of the mainland cities.[60]

Yet Christian Italy remained in danger. Southern Italy existed under unofficial Islamic hegemony: its cities frequently paid tribute to Muslim Sicily; in Calabria and parts of Campania the Sicilian dinar was the major currency.[61] According to one calculation, 13 percent of the people in Reggio Calabria had Islamic names.[62] It ought not to be surprising that Muslim geographers knew southern Italy better than any other region of Christian Europe.[63] After the loss of Bari, Islamic raiders based themselves in fortified entrepôts from which they attacked and destroyed nearly all of the central and southern Italian monasteries. Their most famous redoubt was a camp at the mouth of the Garigliano, which operated for decades until it was eliminated in 915 by an international Lombard, Byzantine, and papal force assembled by Pope John X (914–28). In 982, the emir of Sicily, campaigning in southern Italy near Crotone, defeated the Holy Roman Emperor Otto II so decisively that he escaped only by swimming from the shore to a Byzantine spy ship, an ordeal from which he never fully recovered.[64] Around the year 1000, Doge Pietro Orseolo led the Venetian forces that broke a Muslim siege of Bari. The Sardinian-based fleet of an Andalusian emir captured Luni in 1014, prompting a counterattack not only from

59. *Annales Bertiniani* 846, Grat, 52, Nelson, 63.

60. Clemens Gantner, "New Visions of Community in Ninth-Century Rome: The Impact of the Saracen Threat on the Papal World View," in *Visions of Community in the Post-Roman World: The West, Byzantium and the Islamic World, 300–1100*, ed. Walter Pohl, Clemens Gantner, and Richard Payne (Burlington, VT: Ashgate, 2012), 403–21.

61. Chiarelli, *History of Muslim Sicily*, 99–100, 115, 250.

62. Loud, *Age of Robert Guiscard*, 52; see also Chiarelli, *History of Muslim Sicily*, 99.

63. Miquel, *La géographie humaine du monde musulman*, 2:366–68.

64. Gunther Wolf, "Kaiser Otto II. (973–983) und die Schlacht von Crotone am 13. Juli 982," in *Kaiserin Theophanu: Prinzessin aus der Fremde—des Westreichs Grosse Kaiserin*, ed. Wolf (Cologne: Böhlau, 1991), 155–61; Dirk Alvermann, "La battaglia di Ottone II contro i Saraceni nel 982," *Archivio storico per la Calabria e la Lucania* 62 (1995): 115–30 (who contests Wolf's identification of the battle site); Eickhoff, *Theophanu und der König: Otto III. und seine Welt* (Stuttgart: Klett-Cotta, 1996), 57–79.

Pisa and Genoa but also from the pope, who proclaimed a minicrusade complete with promises of spiritual rewards.[65]

The Fatimid expansion also affected the Latin presence in Jerusalem that Charlemagne had subsidized.[66] As the dueling caliphs in Cairo and Baghdad faced off, Jerusalem would change hands several times. In 1009 the Fatimid caliph Hakim (996–1021), who had first favored but then attacked local Christians, ordered the destruction of Christian pilgrimage churches, including the Church of the Holy Sepulchre. Byzantine aid later restored many, but the Church of the Holy Sepulchre was not rebuilt until midcentury, and the Martyrion of Constantine that had connected Calvary and Christ's tomb was still in ruins at the time of the First Crusade.[67]

The destruction in Jerusalem completed a tragic trifecta: within a century and a half, Islamic forces had sacked all three of Latin Christendom's major pilgrimage destinations—St. Peter's in Rome, St. James's (Santiago) at Compostela, and the Church of the Holy Sepulchre in Jerusalem. All visitors to these holy sites would have heard about the sacrileges and seen the evidence. Western Christians would not forget. In the early eleventh century Rodulfus Glaber reported a vision of ghostly soldiers journeying onward to their heavenly reward, men who had died in battle against the Saracens.[68] It ought not to be all that surprising that Urban II's call for a crusade in 1095 received an enthusiastic response.

THE MAGYARS

Charlemagne's destruction of the Avars created a power vacuum in east-central Europe that the Magyars soon filled. They were Finno-Ugric speakers from the steppes of Russia, nomads who were still developing their own national identity in the later ninth century, even while they were migrating into the former homeland of the Huns. These "Hungarians" disrupted the surrounding Slavic communities. Invited into Italy as

---

65. Silvia Orvietani Busch, "Luni in the Middle Ages: The Agony and Disappearance of a City," *Journal of Medieval History* 17 (1991): 283–96, esp. 288.

66. On Frankish involvement in Jerusalem, see McCormick, *Charlemagne's Survey of the Holy Land: Wealth, Personnel, and Buildings of a Mediterranean Church between Antiquity and the Middle Ages* (Washington, DC: Dumbarton Oaks, 2011), 76–91.

67. Colin Morris, *The Sepulchre of Christ and the Medieval West: From the Beginning to 1600* (Oxford: Oxford University Press, 2005), 92–93, 134–39, and 189–203; Thomas Pratsch, ed., *Konflikt und Bewältigung: Der Zerstörung der Grabeskirche zu Jerusalem im Jahre 1009* (Berlin: De Gruyter, 2011), esp. 1–66, 139–58.

68. Rodulfus Glaber, *Historiae* II xix, France, 82–85. For commentary on this story, see Dennis M. Kratz, "Monsters and Monstrous Visions: The Art of Rodulfus Glaber's *Historiarum Libri Quinque*," in *Latin Culture in the Eleventh Century: Proceedings of the Third International Conference on Medieval Latin Studies, Cambridge, September 9–12 1998,* ed. Michael W. Herren, C.J. McDonough, and Ross G. Arthur, 2 vols. (Turnhout, Belg.: Brepols, 2002), 1:508–19, esp. 512–13 and 515.

mercenaries, at the Battle of the Brenta in 899 they soundly defeated the army of King Berengar (887–924), who later was their occasional ally. They also targeted Germany, especially during the weak reigns of Louis the Child (899–911) and Conrad of Franconia (911–918). They were forced to change strategy when Henry the Fowler (918–36), the first of the Saxon kings, established his credentials and his dynasty by assembling the forces and fortresses that allowed him to defeat them decisively at Riade in 933—afterwards they campaigned extensively in Germany only when aided by local rebels.

The usual Magyar *razzia* was a swift-moving grab for loot and slaves made by mounted warriors who could ride hundreds of miles and still return home by winter. To go this fast they avoided sieges and sought targets of opportunity. Annals list nearly three dozen such campaigns between 899 and 955, emphasizing their destructiveness. Magyars raided the Balkans, Italy, northern France, Belgium, Burgundy, and even Spain.[69]

APOCALYPTIC DESTRUCTION?

Medieval authors describe alien attacks in apocalyptic terms. Abbo of Saint-Germain-des-Prés (d. c. 923) offers a long catalog of "rapacious wolves . . . devouring the lambs of Christ"; these included Northmen, Muslims, Hungarians, eastern peoples, heretics, and "false Christians who destroy the Church."[70] The Vikings, according to Archbishop Hincmar of Rheims (845–882) writing in the *Annals of Saint-Bertin*, spent the year 873 in Anjou "ravaging various towns, razing fortresses to the ground, burning churches and monasteries, and turning cultivated land into a desert."[71] The *Annals of Saint-Vaast* present the Viking campaigns of the 880s in the Low Countries as systematic genocide: "The Northmen never stopped capturing and killing the Christian people, pulling down their churches, destroying their walls, and burning their cities. In every street were lying the bodies of the clergy, of noble laymen, and of

---

69. Lellia Cracco Ruggini and Mechthild Schulze-Dörrlamm, "Die Ungareinfälle des 10. Jahrhunderts im Spiegel archäologischer Funde," in *Europa im 10. Jahrhundert: Archäologie einer Aufbruchszeit: Internationale Tagung in Vorbereitung der Ausstellung "Otto der Grosse, Magdeburg und Europa,"* ed. Joachim Henning (Mainz am Rhein: Philipp von Zabern, 2002), 109–22, esp. 109; Charles R. Bowlus, *The Battle of Lechfeld and Its Aftermath, August 955: The End of the Age of Migrations in the Latin West* (Aldershot, UK: Ashgate, 2006), 73–95. On the somewhat slim archaeological evidence for their raids, see Aldo A. Settia, "Gli Ungari in Italia e i mutamenti territoriali fra VIII e X secolo," in *Magistra Barbaritas: I Barbari in Italia,* ed. Maria Giovanna Arcamone et al. (Milan: Garzanti, 1984), 185–218, esp. 189–200 and 218; Ruggini and Schulze-Dörrlamm, "Die Ungareinfälle," 110.

70. Abbo, *Sermo de Fundamento et Incremento Christianitatis,* ed. Ute Önnerfors, *Abbo von Saint-Germain-des Prés: 22 Predigten: Kritische Ausgabe und Kommentar* (Frankfurt: Peter Lang, 1985), 133–46, esp. 145–46.

71. *Annales Bertiniani* 873, Grat, 193, Nelson, 183.

others; of women, of young men and of infants. There was sorrow and tribulation to all who were seeing the Christian people being laid waste to the point of extinction."[72] Some twentieth-century Danish scholars attempted to assemble all early Latin texts referring to the Vikings, but the grim collection that resulted consisted almost entirely of accounts of raids, attacks, and devastations.[73] The earliest vernacular sources are equally negative.[74]

The Vikings were not the only invaders to receive bad reviews. According to the *Destructio Farfensis*, a lament on the afflictions suffered by the imperial monastery of Farfa, a day's journey north of Rome, "The multitude of the pagans, that is the nation of the Hagarenes, entered Italy. As much as the military power of the Italians waned, theirs grew, so that . . . there were few cities, beyond Rome and Ravenna, which they did not destroy and subjugate to their hegemony. They completely depopulated those provinces and cities they were taking by force, and everything found there they took for themselves."[75] The *Monte Cassino Chronicle* claims that "not only the monastery [of Monte Cassino, largely abandoned from 883 to 949] but all the plains around it were so deserted because of the assaults of the Saracens that only a rare man—or no man at all—could be found dwelling there who would give due allegiance to the monks."[76] Even the more transient Magyars allegedly left little standing. Flodoard, for example, states that in a 924 raid they "set fire to the rich and populous *urbs* of Pavia, destroying vast resources there. Forty-four churches were set afire and the bishop of that city [John], along with the bishop of Vercelli [Ragamfridus], who had been with him, was killed by the fire and the smoke. From the almost innumerable multitude of inhabitants of Pavia, only 200 are said to have survived. They gave the Magyars eight measures of silver gathered from the ashes in the remains of the city, thus ransoming the life and walls of the empty *civitas*."[77]

Historians formerly accepted such accounts at face value but now are more cautious, warned by the "linguistic turn" in historical scholarship that assumes that written sources express authorial ideological agendas,

72. *Annales Vedastini* 884, ed. Georg Heinrich Pertz, MGH *SS* 2 (Hannover: Hahn, 1829), 196–209, esp. 200.

73. *Diplomatarium Danicum*, sect. 1, vol. 1, *Regester 789–1052*, ed. C.A. Christensen and Herluf Nielsen (Copenhagen: C.A. Reitzels, 1975).

74. Régis Boyer, *Le mythe viking dans les lettres françaises* (Paris: Porte-Glaive, 1986), 19–39.

75. Hugh of Farfa, *Destructio Farfensis*, ed. Ugo Balzani, in *Il Chronicon Farfense di Gregorio di Catino. Procedono la Constructio Farfensis e gli scritti di Ugo di Farfa*, 2 vols., Fonti per la storia d'Italia 33–34 (Rome: Istituto storico italiano, 1902), 1:25–51, esp. 28–29.

76. *Chron. Casin.* II i, ed. Hartmut Hoffmann, *Die Chronik von Montecassino*, MGH *SS* 34 (Hannover: Hahn, 1980), 166.

77. Flodoard, *Annales* 924, Lauer, 22, Fanning and Bachrach, 11.

often by using ancient clichés.[78] Today's historians examine the narratives of destruction more skeptically.[79] They recognize that medieval authors had incentives to overemphasize catastrophes: by using biblical topoi of destruction, they could present Latin Christians as new Israelites; by darkening the bad old days, they could valorize present times; and by blaming foreigners for deleterious changes, they could avoid offending the powerful. Thus, for example, a hagiographer who could attribute the disappearance of a local saint's relics, ancient records, and treasures to the ravages of barbarians might be able to avoid possibly embarrassing questions regarding the malfeasance of local lords clerical and secular. Other factors contributed to a reevaluation. Advances in medieval archaeology reveal positive aspects of the invaders unmentioned in the chronicles, particularly their roles as traders who could develop and expand commercial networks. Enhanced interest in the Carolingian era lends support to a less cataclysmic perspective because it reveals that the late ninth-century cultural landscape was no total wasteland. Indeed, contrarians might observe that some of the worst attacks occurred at the same time as impressive cultural achievements at the courts of Alfred in England, Charles the Bald in France, and the popes in Rome.

As a result, the historical narrative is now being revised, perhaps too drastically. One of the most prominent revisionists, Peter H. Sawyer, concluded that "however destructive the Vikings were, they often made a very positive and significant contribution to the development of western Europe, especially as conquerors and colonists."[80] It has been suggested that invasions actually helped monasteries by encouraging them to develop their less exposed properties.[81] Some also assert that the disappearance of monasteries "owes more to the changing standards of later generations

78. On the complexity of the "linguistic turn," see Judith Surkis, "*AHR* Forum: When Was the Linguistic Turn? A Genealogy," *AHR* 117 (2012): 700–22 (cf. response, ibid., 796–98). For Viking destruction as a topos, see Zettel, *Bild der Normannen*; on its use in hagiographies, see Felice Lifshitz, "The Migration of Neustrian Relics in the Viking Age: The Myth of Voluntary Exodus, the Reality of Coercion and Theft," *Early Medieval Europe* 4 (1995): 175–92, and her related studies cited therein.

79. The pioneers who in the 1960s began to take a more skeptical view of the accounts of Viking destruction were Lucien Musset, *Les invasions. Le second assaut contre l'Europe chrétienne (VIIᵉ–XIᵉ siècle)* (Paris: Presses universitaires de France, 1965; 2nd ed., 1972) and Albert d'Haenens, *Les invasions normandes en Belgique au IXᵉ siècle: Le phénomène et sa répercussion dans l'historiographie médiévale* (Louvain: Bureaux du Recueil, Bibliothèque de l'Université et Publications universitaires de Louvain, 1967). D'Haenens went on to survey all Francia in "Les invasions normandes dans l'empire franc au IXᵉ siècle: Pour une rénovation de la problématique," in *I Normanni e la loro espansione in Europa nell'alto medioevo, 18–24 aprile 1968*, Settimane di studio del CISAM 16 (Spoleto: CISAM, 1969), 233–98.

80. Sawyer, *Kings and Vikings*, 97. See also Sawyer, *Age of the Vikings* (London: Edward Arnold, 1962), 147.

81. Hélène Noizet, "Les chanoines de Saint-Martin de Tours et les Vikings," in Baudin, *Les fondations scandinaves en Occident*, 53–66.

than to Viking depredations."[82] Others have argued that the brutality of the Vikings was "no worse than that of their contemporaries."[83] Some scholars drastically minimize the effects of the raids: for example, it is claimed that in Normandy "every indicator of concrete 'reality' evidences relative continuity and minimal disruption, from Carolingian Neustria to Viking Normandy."[84] It is also said that in Ireland the Vikings "made little or no impact on secular society."[85] Such sanguine evaluations have not gone unchallenged.[86]

Why are scholars divided? Frequently they are not actually looking at the same things. Some geographical areas were hit harder than others. Different elements of society were affected differently. For example, continuities in field patterns, land documents, and village names suggest that peasant farmers often maintained their traditional ways of life despite the invasions. Boundary lines and place names reveal such underlying continuities even in areas where colonization occurred.[87] Many cities, despite damage to their suburban churches, actually gained population when refugees sought greater safety within their walls: this is what archaeology suggests happened at Auxerre, Barcelona, Dublin, Rouen, Winchester, York, and other places.[88] More extended commercial networks certainly

82. Sawyer, *Kings and Vikings*, 96.

83. David M. Wilson, preface to *The Vikings*, ed. James Graham Campbell and Dafydd Kidd (New York: Metropolitan Museum of Art, 1980), 7.

84. Lifshitz, *The Norman Conquest of Pious Neustria: Historiographic Discourse and Saintly Relics, 684–1090* (Toronto: PIMS, 1995), 12.

85. Donnchadh O'Corráin, *Ireland before the Normans* (Dublin: Gill and Macmillan, 1972), 83.

86. For historiographical debates about the impact of the Vikings, see Michel Rouche, "The Vikings versus the Towns of Northern Gaul: Challenge and Response," in *Medieval Archaeology: Papers of the Seventeenth Annual Conference of the Center for Medieval and Early Renaissance Studies*, ed. Charles L. Redman (Binghamton: SUNY Press, 1989), 41–56; Smyth, "The Effect of Scandinavian Raiders on the English and Irish Churches: A Preliminary Reassessment," in *Britain and Ireland 900–1300: Insular Responses to Medieval European Change*, ed. Brendan Smith (Cambridge: Cambridge University Press, 1999), 1–38; Dumville, "Vikings in the British Isles," 209–50, esp. 236–30; and Mary A. Valante, *The Vikings in Ireland: Settlement, Trade, and Urbanization* (Dublin: Four Courts, 2008), 81.

87. Nevertheless note the caveat of Smyth, "Effect of Scandinavian Raiders," in Smith, *Britain and Ireland 900–1300*, 13–14.

88. For Auxerre, see Xavier Barral i Altet, *The Early Middle Ages: From Late Antiquity to A.D. 1000* (Cologne: Taschen, 2002), 174–78 and 181. For Barcelona, see Felipe Fernández-Armesto, *Barcelona: A Thousand Years of the City's Past* (Oxford: Oxford University Press, 1992), 6–20. For Dublin, see Howard Brian Clarke, "The Social Structure and Topography of Dublin from the Viking Period to the End of the Thirteenth Century," in *Europäische Städte im Mittelalter*, ed. Ferdinand Opil and Christoph Sonlechner (Innsbruck: Studien Verlag, 2010), 179–96, esp. 179–98. For Rouen, see Jacques Le Maho, "Les Normands de la Seine à la fin du IXᵉ siècle," in Bauduin, *Les fondations scandinaves en Occident*, 161–79, esp. 168–73. For Winchester, see T. B. James, *The Book of Winchester* (London: English Heritage, 1997), 49. For York, see Richard A. Hall, "York, 700–1050," in Hodges and Hobley, *Rebirth of Towns in the West*, 125–32, esp. 129–30. That fortified cities in general tended to grow in the tenth century is cautiously suggested in Renato Bordone, "La città nel X secolo," in *Il secolo di ferro: Mito e realtà del secolo X, 19–25 aprile 1990*, 2 vols., Settimane di studio del CISAM 38 (Spoleto: CISAM, 1991), 1:517–63.

did create patches of prosperity in places such as York and Palermo, where Vikings and Muslims dominated.

The subject of this book, however, is the Latin Church, and its institutions were hit hardest. Raiders targeted ecclesiastical gold, silver, and jewels because they were relatively poorly protected. Although most church leaders came from families of the warrior aristocracy, they had been trained from childhood to pray, not fight. Secular and regular clergy were professionally unarmed (*inermes*), and killing pagans was officially a bar to their ecclesiastical advancement.[89] Nuns were especially vulnerable because their ability to defend themselves was limited not only by their religious status but also by gender roles.[90] Those church leaders who did successfully fortify their buildings, hire soldiers, and mobilize the forces needed for siege defense did so in spite of rather than because of their clerical status. The apocalyptic tone adopted by ecclesiastical writers is therefore understandable. But was it justified?

Church Buildings Destroyed?

Chronicles and saints' lives claim that the invaders systematically burned churches and monasteries.[91] They were not just making things up. One scholar's attempt to correlate the written claims of Viking destruction with archeological evidence for the destruction of buildings and settlements concludes that "the written sources of the ninth century were generally quite accurate when they reported on the level of destruction at various sites."[92] Destruction of churches is attested by legal sources: a Frisian law proscribing Viking activities itemizes four: burning houses, raping women, killing men, and setting fire to churches.[93]

---

89. *Concilium Meldense* (Meaux/Paris 845/846) xxxvii, ed. Wilfried Hartmann, MGH *Concilia*, vol. 3, *Die Conzilien der karolingischen Teilreich 843–845* (Hannover: Hahn, 1984), 61–133, esp. 102; Nicholas I, *Epist.* cxxxiv (867, to Bishop Wifred of Thérouanne), ed. Migne, *Pat. Lat.* 119:1129.

90. On damaged convents see Jane Tibbetts Schulenburg, *Forgetful of Their Sex: Female Sanctity and Society ca. 500–1100* (Chicago: University of Chicago Press, 1998), 142–55.

91. Delphine Planavergne, "Les Normands avant la Normandie: Les invasions scandinaves en Neustrie au IXe siècle dans l'hagiographie franque," in Bauduin, *Les fondations scandinaves en Occident*, 37–52, esp. 46; Simon Coupland, "Holy Ground? The Plundering and Burning of Churches by Vikings and Franks in the Ninth Century," *Viator* 45 (2014): 73–98, esp. 91–93.

92. Lesley Anne Morden, "How Much Material Damage Did the Northmen Actually Do to Ninth-Century Europe?" (PhD diss., Simon Fraser University, 2007), esp. iv, 175–222, http://summit.sfu.ca/system/files/iritems1/2654/etd2893.pdf.

93. *Das Rüstringer Recht* IV q 20, ed. Wybren Jan Buma and Wilhelm Ebel, Altfriesische Rechtsquellen 1 (Göttingen: Muster-Schmidt, 1963), 54.

Yet the destruction of individual churches was only part of the problem. Early medieval churches burned down fairly often, even without any help from alien arsonists. Although no one has ever attempted to integrate all the surviving records into one giant database, anecdotal evidence suggests that, on average, major churches experienced major fires every couple of centuries. The ecclesiastical corporations that survived were the ones that had the resources needed to rebuild. What was distinctive about the late ninth and early tenth centuries was not that churches burned but that they were not rebuilt, at least not immediately. This perspective reveals the weakness of Peter Sawyer's attempt to minimize the impact of the Vikings by maintaining that "although many houses were destroyed by Viking raiders, losing their libraries and their treasures, many recovered in a remarkable way."[94] The unusual aspect of the late ninth and early tenth centuries was not that some churches and monasteries recovered, which was the default scenario, but that many did not. Their ruins were left untended or inhabited by hermits, irregular clergymen, or other caretakers. By the start of the tenth century such desolations included virtually all the monasteries and convents in England and Normandy;[95] most in southern France; and even the greatest Italian houses such as Farfa, San Vincenzo al Volturno, and Monte Cassino.

To understand why reconstruction was delayed it is necessary to understand how ecclesiastical communities worked. Early medieval cathedrals and megamonasteries depended on resources drawn from their subsidiary churches and estates. By owning properties in diverse ecological niches, they could operate their own vineyards, olive groves, woodlands, sheep farms, horse ranches, fisheries, feedlots, and other specialized enterprises. Historians miss much of the story if they look only at direct attacks on cathedrals and motherhouses, which were the headquarters of much larger corporations, and ignore what happened to the *episcopia* or *abbatia* (the whole body of the estates and rights under a bishop's or abbot's jurisdiction). A diocese or monastery could normally repair major buildings, even though this would require great effort and generous outside help. But if chaos in the countryside made it unproductive to attempt to move goods from subsidiary estates to the center, then a community would eventually reach a tipping point at which it became more efficient

94. Sawyer, *Kings and Vikings*, 97.

95. Sarah Foote, *Veiled Women*, 2 vols. (Aldershot, UK: Ashgate, 2000), 1:71–96 and 2:1–2; Mathieu Arnoux, "Ermites et ermitages en Normandie (XIe–XIIIe siècles)," in *Ermites de France et d'Italie (XIe–XVe siècle)*, ed. Vauchez (Rome: ÉFR, 2003), 115–35, esp. 116; John Blair, *The Church in Anglo-Saxon Society* (Oxford: Oxford University Press, 2005), 127–29, 291–97.

to move the canons, monks, nuns, and other clerical personnel out to the peripheral estates (usually to fortified places near them).[96] Although a flip from the center to the peripheries could be logical economically, Church authorities tried to avoid it if at all possible because there were negative consequences for estate control, ecclesiastical discipline, and spiritual life.

To document this dynamic in detail is another project.[97] Here let a good example suffice, an account of the 897 destruction of the imperial monastery of Farfa, written by an anonymous but nearly contemporary monk:

> The Saracens, who already occupied everything around it, came to the monastery itself, which they tried to attack from every direction but which they were unable to take [presumably thwarted by Farfa's high walls and towers]. The venerable abbot Peter, relying on the help of God and the support of his knights, frequently repelled them from the boundaries of the monastery and had them pursued for considerable distances. But these dangerous men, since they had subjugated and devastated all the neighboring places, always returned to fight him. The abbot together with his monks endured this oppression for seven straight years. He saw that because of the Christian people's evil nature God was handing them over to oblivion and to the power of the pagans. Seeing no reason to delay the matter any further, after he had taken council, he divided the monks and the treasures into three parts. He sent one part to Rome; another to the city of Rieti, and the third part, including himself, took refuge in the county of Fermo.

The result was destruction. Before the monks left Farfa, they dismantled and hid whatever valuables were too heavy to transport. After they departed, the Saracens moved in and took up residence. One night some impoverished Christian thieves from Catino, prowling around the monastery, accidentally set it on fire.[98] The monks endured further misfortunes in their multiple places of exile, and more than a generation would pass before a few were finally able to return to the ruins of the motherhouse. Farfa's story demonstrates how even a successful defense of corporate headquarters was insufficient without control over the countryside.

Because construction projects required access to distant resources, the invaders who disrupted ecclesiastical economies deserve to be blamed not only for the churches they destroyed but also for the (re)building projects they halted. It is impossible to quantify churches never built, but written and archaeological sources are suggestive. In England in the

---

96. Schulenburg, *Forgetful of Their Sex*, 142, discusses the movement of female religious communities from earlier "open sites" into houses within city walls.

97. Howe, "To Kill a Monastery: Images and Realities of Monastic Disruption" (in progress).

98. Hugh of Farfa, *Destructio Farfensis*, Balzani, 31–32.

ninth century, literary references reveal a little ecclesiastical construction during the first massive but sporadic Viking invasions, though no single building actually survives that can be located within that era. In the early eleventh century, however, in the face of large standing armies and huge demands for Danegeld, there is no evidence for any sort of church construction.[99] On the Continent, it is hard to document ecclesiastical building in the areas of greatest warfare, such as Normandy and Brittany. Some late Carolingian projects continued in Germany, and a century of invasions and civil wars seems to have produced similar mixed results in Italy.[100]

Ecclesiastical Personnel Attacked?

Raiders targeted church leaders. Some were legitimate targets, leaders of military forces who met their deaths at or around battlefields. Among these were bishops Diethard and Markward in Saxony in 882; three bishops killed with the duke of Bavaria during the Magyar victory at Pressburg (Bratislava) in 907; three Catalan bishops who died at the siege of Cordoba in 1010; and Bishop Eadnoth of Dorchester and Abbot Wulfsige of Ramsey, who fell at the battle of Ashingdon in 1016.[101] Other high-status ecclesiastical personnel, however, seem to have been killed more arbitrarily. One of these was the aged Abbot Bertharius of Monte Cassino, whom Muslims slaughtered in 883 as he prayed at the altar of San Salvatore (the lower abbey at Monte Cassino, his residence after Muslims had already looted the more famous mountaintop monastery).[102] Others were casualties of botched hostage takings. Examples included Bishop Immo of Noyon, a prisoner slain on the march in 859 by a band that had already dispatched two other bishops; Archbishop Roland of Arles, whose death in captivity in 869 was concealed until his community had paid his ransom, whereupon his body was left on shore, neatly arrayed in his pontifical robes

99. Ernest Arthur Fisher, *An Introduction to Anglo-Saxon Architecture and Sculpture* (London: Faber and Faber, 1957), 52; Helen Gittos, "Sacred Space in Anglo-Saxon England: Liturgy, Architecture, and Place" (PhD diss., University of Oxford, 2001), 152 and 160; Gittos, *Liturgy, Architecture, and Sacred Places in Anglo-Saxon England* (Oxford: Oxford University Press, 2013), 85.

100. McClendon, *Origins of Medieval Architecture*, 173–94.

101. Adam of Bremen, *Gesta Hammaburgensis* I xxxviii, ed. Bernhard Schmeidler, *Adam von Bremen, Hamburgische Kirchengeschichte*, MGH *SS Rer Germ* 2 (Hannover: MGH, 1917), 41, trans. Francis J. Tschan, *History of the Archbishops of Hamburg-Bremen* (New York: Columbia University Press, 1959), 37; Paul H. Freedman, *The Diocese of Vic: Tradition and Regeneration in Medieval Catalonia* (New Brunswick, NJ: Rutgers University Press, 1983), 20; Keynes, "Ely Abbey 672–1109," in *A History of Ely Cathedral*, ed. Peter Meadows and Nigel Ramsey (Woodbridge, UK: Boydell, 2003), 2–58, esp. 231.

102. Alessandro Pratesi, "Bertario" *Dizionario biografico degli italiani*, 82– vols. (Rome: Istituto della Enciclopedia italiana, 1960–), 9:477–80.

and seated on his episcopal throne; and Archbishop Aelfheah of Canterbury (d. 1012), who, unransomed for many months, was eventually killed by bones thrown at him by drunken Vikings, a sadistic food fight with some Scandinavian parallels.[103]

Less elite clergymen and their dependents were not much safer. If they attempted to defend their communities, attackers showed little mercy. In 806, when the island monastery of Iona was attacked for the third time, the Vikings are said to have killed sixty-eight members of the monastic *familia*, a claim circumstantially supported by the subsequent shift of monastic resources to the mainland daughterhouse of Kells and the apparent reduction of Iona's status to that of a hermitage.[104] In 881, the Islamic attackers of San Vincenzo al Volturno allegedly slaughtered nine hundred monks and dependents who had successfully defended it until some traitorous retainers helped the attackers outflank them.[105] Members of wealthy communities could be taken as hostages. The Muslim pirates who attacked Marseilles in 838 "carried off all the nuns, of whom there was a great number living there, as well as all the males, both clergy and laymen, laid waste the town and took away with them en masse the treasures of Christ's churches."[106]

Ransoms were an important part of the pillaging business. Alcuin, in his early description of the attack on Lindisfarne, notes that boys studying there had been carried off by the raiders and he pledges to try to get Charlemagne to help redeem them.[107] According to the *Annals* of Saint-Wandrille, in 841 the monastery ransomed sixty-eight prisoners from Vikings who sailed up the Seine by paying 26 pounds of silver, a big sum considering that on this occasion the money paid out to protect the monastery itself was only 6 pounds.[108] Charlemagne's grandson Abbot Hilduin of Saint-Denis, captured by the Seine Vikings in 858, was freed for 686 pounds of gold and

103. On Bishop Immo see *Annales Bertiniani* 859, Grat, 81, Nelson, 91. On Bishop Roland, see *Annales Bertiniani* 869, Grat, 165–66, Nelson, 163. The sources on Aelfheah's death are analyzed in Ian McDougall, "Serious Entertainments: An Examination of a Peculiar Type of Viking Atrocity," *Anglo-Saxon England* 22 (1993): 201–25.

104. *Annales Ultonienses* 806, Mac Airt and Mac Niocaill, 262–63; Smyth, "Effect of Scandinavian Raiders," 11–12.

105. John the Monk, *Chronicon Vulturnense*, ed. Vincenzo Federici, *Chronicon Vulturnense del Monaco Giovanni*, 3 vols. (Rome: ISIME, 1925–40) 1:359, 362, 368, 370; Hodges, "The Sack of San Vincenzo, 10 October 881," in *Light in the Dark Ages* (Ithaca: Cornell University Press, 1997), 144–53; Hodges, Sarah Leppard, and John Mitchell, "The Sack of San Vincenzo al Volturno, 10 October 881, Reconsidered by Archaeology," *Acta Archaeologica* 82 (2011): 286–301.

106. *Annales Bertiniani* 838, Grat, 24, Nelson, 39.

107. Alcuin, *Epist.* xx (to *Higbald, Bishop of Lindisfarne*, late 793), Dümmler, 56–58, Allott (as *Epist.* xxvi), 36–38.

108. *Fragmentum Chronici Fontanellensis* 841, ed. Georg Heinrich Pertz, MGH *SS* 2 (Hannover: Hahn, 1829), 301–4, esp. 301.

FIGURE 2. Viking hoard, found at Cuerdale, Lancashire, England: more than 8,500 objects, mostly "hacksilver" and coins, none later than ca. 905. British Museum. © Trustees of the British Museum.

3,250 pounds of silver, a ransom that "drained dry . . . many church treasuries in Charles's realm [that is, Charles the Bald, 840–77, Hilduin's second cousin], at the king's command . . . large sums were eagerly contributed also by the king, and by all the bishops, abbots, counts and other powerful men."[109] Abbot Maiolus of Cluny was treated respectfully by the Muslims of La Garde-Freinet until his huge ransom was paid.[110]

Less well-connected people whose families and friends were unable to ransom them could be enslaved, a practice that made foreign invaders more terrifying than criminous local Franks, who did not normally enslave their fellows. Large numbers might be taken. In 951 Northmen from Dublin allegedly rounded up three thousand people from the monasteries of Meath in eastern Ireland (in addition to cattle and horses).[111]

109. *Annales Bertiniani* 858, Grat 77, Nelson, 86.

110. Michael Meckler, "Wolves and Saracens in Odilo's *Life of Mayeul*," in Herren et al., *Latin Culture in the Eleventh Century*, 2:116–28; Scott G. Bruce, *Cluny and the Muslims*, 10–40.

111. *Annales Ultonienses* 951, Mac Airt and Mac Niocaill, 396–97. On the importance of the slave trade in this region, see Valante, *Vikings in Ireland*, 86–90.

A pilgrim passing through Muslim-held Taranto in the 860s claimed to have encountered nine thousand Christian prisoners in the process of being transported into North Africa.[112]

It can be objected that the well-documented cases of church leaders killed or held for ransom amount to only a few dozen.[113] But that number of incidents alone, although certainly not all that occurred, could have caused many threatened bishops, abbots, and abbesses to keep low profiles or to seek their safety in exile. Some archbishops even developed procedures to handle the requests for episcopal transfers *propter infestationem paganorum* that came from bishops whose sees had become too dangerous (or who perhaps in some cases were just seeking a legal way to switch sees).[114]

Ecclesiastical Furniture Looted?

Above all, the invaders wanted to grab valuable movable property—and they did! Today the monastic, cathedral, and royal treasuries of large sections of Europe contain no preinvasion artifacts. Except for an occasional early treasure hoard, almost no Anglo-Saxon metal work remains. Few manuscripts created by Celtic scribes during Ireland's Golden Age survive, and most that do had been shipped off island before the Vikings arrived. Rouen, the capital of ancient Armorica, has no early medieval treasures left.[115] Pavia, burned by the fiery arrows of the Hungarians, left Liudprand of Cremona lamenting the loss of its gold and silver in epic verse.[116]

Why such losses? Real surprise attacks must have been relatively rare. Lightning assaults were possible along coastlines, but it took time for large fleets to thread their way up sinuous rivers and for armies encumbered by hostages and wagonloads of plunder to plod on to their next destinations. Normally the owners of precious things should have had time to move their valuables to safety (assuming safer places existed). Probably it was the owners themselves who actually handed over their treasures, using

112. Bernardus Francus, *Itinerarium* iv, ed. Josef Ackermann, *Das "Itinerarium Bernardi Monachi": Edition-Übersetzung-Kommentar*, MGH Studien und Texte 50 (Hannover: Hahn, 2010), 117 (context 106–8).

113. Nelson, "The Frankish Empire," 26–29 and 37, offers tables of French churchmen killed or held by Vikings; Schulenburg, *Forgetful of Their Sex*, 145 and 459n77, lists some captive abbesses.

114. Pierre Bauduin, "En marge des invasions vikings: Actard de Nantes et les translations d'évêques *propter infestationem paganorum*," *Le Moyen Âge* 117 (2011): 9–20.

115. Jacques Le Maho, "Le trésor de la cathédrale de Rouen de l'époque mérovingienne aux premières années du XIIIᵉ siècle," in *Les trésors de sanctuaires, de l'Antiquité à l'époque romane: Communications présentées au Centre de recherches sur l'Antiquité tardive et le haut Moyen Âge de l'Université de Paris X-Nanterre (1993–1995)*, ed. Jean-Pierre Caillet (Paris: Picard, 1996), 123–35, esp. 123.

116. Liudprand, *Antapodosis* III ii–iii, ed. Paolo Chiesa, *Liudprandi Cremonensis Opera Omnia*, CCCM 156 (Turnhout, Belg.: Brepols, 1998), 1–150, esp. 68–70, trans. Paolo Squatriti, in *The Complete Works of Liudprand of Cremona* (Washington, DC: Catholic University of America Press, 2007), 40–202, esp. 112.

them to ransom hostages and properties and to help finance regional defense.[117] Vikings happily accepted protection money—it was less trouble than fighting—and they carried their own scales to count it out more efficiently.[118]

Archival and Cultural Destruction?

From a historian's viewpoint, some of the worst losses involved irreplaceable books and documents. The irony here is that Latin texts were of no interest to Vikings, Muslims, and Magyars. These raiders did covet the gold, jewels, and ivories incorporated into the covers of splendid liturgical books, but the deluxe volumes were probably stored in strong rooms and sacristies along with the liturgical vessels. The reason that raiders found themselves routinely rifling through all books, documents, and parchment scraps is that these were stored in the same types of chests (*armaria*) as those used to hold textiles, metal work, and other valuables. The only thing that disappointed looters could get from texts was fuel. This is illustrated by archaeological work on San Vincenzo al Volturno, where Muslim attackers caused massive conflagrations by shooting heavily weighted fire arrows but also burned selectively, first ransacking the iron-bound chests, then setting fire to their contents.[119]

Although ideologically motivated book burning has a long history, late ninth- and early tenth-century raiders just seem to have liked to burn things.[120] That churchmen could save their best manuscripts by moving them out of harm's way is evident from the thousands of preinvasion volumes that survive today, despite the fact that only a handful of monasteries entirely avoided looting. What we do not know is how much more was lost. Communities whose *scriptoria* had been active for centuries would have produced far more written material than could ever have been spirited away. A recent survey of European manuscript production, compiled on the basis of gross searches of all surviving catalogs, postulates steady increases in the number of books in the West from the sixth century on, except for dramatic declines in England in the ninth century and France in the tenth, and moderate tenth-century declines all over the rest of Europe

117. Nelson, "The Frankish Empire," 19–47, esp. 36–38; Loud, *Age of Robert Guiscard*, 8–9.

118. *Annales Bertiniani* 866, Grat, 125, Nelson, 130, note that when Charles the Bald bought peace with a band of Northmen he pledged four thousand pounds of silver to be weighed "according to their scales."

119. Hodges, *Light in the Dark Ages*, 144–61.

120. For the history, Judith Herrin, "Book Burning as Purification," in *Transformations of Late Antiquity: Essays for Peter Brown*, ed. Philip Rousseau and Manolis Papoutsakis (Burlington, VT: Ashgate, 2009), 205–22.

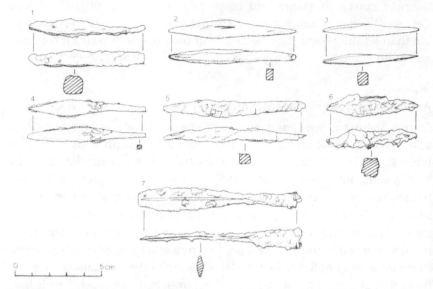

FIGURE 3. Arrow points from Islamic mercenaries at San Vincenzo al Volturno, excavated from the buildings destroyed in 881. Reproduced by permission from Richard Hodges, *Light in the Dark Ages: The Rise and Fall of San Vincenzo al Volturno* (Ithaca: Cornell University Press, 1997), 148.

except for Christian Spain, anomalies best explained by the destructions described in this chapter.[121]

In some areas the invaders nearly destroyed manuscript culture itself. In early medieval England the break caused by the Viking invasions is so striking that historians use it to separate "Early Anglo-Saxon" from "Later Anglo-Saxon."[122] Few preinvasion English books exist, and much of what remains seems to have been preserved on the Continent. Regional manuscript survival correlates inversely with Viking activity. In heavily populated and invaded East Anglia almost no documents survived the Danish

121. Eltjo Buringh, *Medieval Manuscript Production in the Latin West: Exploration with a Global Database* (Leiden, Neth.: Brill, 2011), esp. 255–63, 333–42.

122. Helmut Gneuss, "King Alfred and the History of Anglo-Saxon Libraries," in *Modes of Interpretation in Old English Literature: Essays in Honour of Stanley B. Greenfield*, ed. Phyllis Rugg Brown, Georgia Ronan Crampton, and Fred C. Robinson (Toronto: University of Toronto Press, 1986), 29–49, esp. 36–38; Dumville, *Liturgy and the Ecclesiastical History of Late Anglo-Saxon England: Four Studies* (Woodbridge: Boydell, 1992), 96–98; Dawn M. Hadley, *The Northern Danelaw: Its Social Structure ca. 800–1100* (London: Leicester University Press, 2000), 16. Robert Deshman signaled "a hiatus in large scale artistic production that lasted almost a century," in *"Christus Rex et Magi Reges*: Kingship and Christology in Ottonian and Anglo-Saxon Art," *Frühmittelalterliche Studien* 19 (1976): 367–405, esp. 367, repr. with additional bibliography in *Eye and Mind: Collected Essays in Anglo-Saxon and Early Medieval Art*. ed. Adam S. Cohen (Kalamazoo, MI: Western Michigan University Medieval Institute Publications, 2010), 137–71, esp. 137.

occupation.[123] Aspects of discontinuity in the *scriptoria* of Lindisfarne and York and Canterbury and of continuity in the more Western monastery at Worcester also fit this pattern.[124] Few manuscripts survived in Ireland and Scotland. Scholars today concur in seeing a "near collapse of Latinate culture in England, Scotland, and perhaps Ireland."[125]

Normandy had a similar experience. The great monasteries that had flourished in Merovingian times and had had their ups and downs during the Carolingian triumph lost most of their institutional memory during the late ninth and early tenth centuries. Carolingian Saint-Wandrille, for example, once had so many thousands of books and charters that to store them it needed both a dedicated archive building and a library,[126] but today all that survives from preinvasion Saint-Wandrille are a few manuscripts that left the monastery before the Normans arrived and a small number of working texts that the community carried off into exile.[127] At Jumièges in the mid-tenth century writers had little access to earlier monastic records, and there are no new charters during a documentary gap in the tenth century.[128] No preinvasion manuscripts survive from Saint-Ouen at Rouen.[129] To measure the effects of these destructions, note the difference between the heavily documented historical research found in the early ninth-century *Deeds of the Abbots of Saint-Wandrille* and the fanciful oral sources underlying the early eleventh-century *History of the Normans* by Dudo of Saint-Quentin.[130]

123. Keynes, "Ely Abbey 672–1109," 3–58, esp. 14–16; Tim Pestell, *Landscapes of Monastic Foundations: The Establishment of Religious Houses in East Anglia, c. 650–1200* (Woodbridge, UK: Boydell, 2004), 9, 18, 73, 98–99; Lesley Abrams, "Les fondations scandinaves en Angleterre," in Bauduin, *Les fondations scandinaves en Occident*, 133–44, esp. 133; Helmut Gneuss, "A Handlist of Anglo-Saxon Manuscripts: Origins, Facts, and Problems," in *Anglo Saxon Books and Their Readers: Essays in Celebration of Helmut Gneuss's* Handlist of Anglo-Saxon Manuscripts, ed. Thomas N. Hall and Donald Scragg (Kalamazoo, MI: Western Michigan University Medieval Institute Publications, 2008), 1–19, esp. 11–14.

124. Dumville, *Liturgy*, 98–99; Richard W. Pfaff, *The Liturgy in Medieval England* (Cambridge: Cambridge University Press, 2009), 50–51.

125. Michael Lapidge and Rosalind C. Love, "The Latin Hagiography of England and Wales (600–1550)," in *Hagiographies*, 3:203–25, esp. 216; Dumville, "Vikings in the British Isles," 209–50, esp. 229.

126. *Gesta Sanctorum Patrum Fontanellensis Coenobii* xiii 5, ed. Pascal Pradié, in *Chronique des Abbés de Fontenelle (Saint-Wandrille)*, Les classiques de l'histoire de France au Moyen Age (Paris: Belles Lettres, 1999), 170–71.

127. Leif Errol Pierson, "Evidence for Viking Disruption from Early Norman Histories and Commemorations of Saints" (MA thesis, Texas Tech University, 1999); Howe, "The Hagiography of Saint-Wandrille (Fontenelle) (Province of Haute-Normandie): Sources Hagiographiques de la Gaule 8," in *L'hagiographie du haut moyen âge en Gaule du Nord: Manuscrits, textes et centres de production*, ed. Martin Heinzelmann, Beihefte der Francia 52 (Stuttgart: Jan Thorbecke, 2001), 127–92, esp. 127–28.

128. Mathiu Arnoux, "Disparition ou conservation des sources et abandon de l'acte écrite: Quelques observations de l'actes de Jumièges," *Tabularia "Études"* 1 (2001): 1–10; Jacques Le Maho, "La production éditoriale à Jumièges vers le milieu du Xᵉ siècle," *Tabularia "Études"* 1 (2001): 11–32, esp. 23.

129. Le Maho, "La production éditoriale à Jumièges," 11–32, esp. 130.

130. Pierson, "Evidence for Viking Disruption."

Archival destruction is manifested in various ways. Ecclesiastical institutions sometimes replaced lost documents with universal charters that listed all their property claims. Charles the Bald (840–877), who ruled devastated West Francia, issued many such *pancartes*, some specifically drafted to replace archives destroyed by Northmen.[131] An example of this genre is a charter Carloman II (879–84) issued for Bishop Gauterius of Orléans, dated August 11, 883, a confirmation of an earlier grant from Charles the Bald, issued "because by the lamentable persecution of the Northmen this charter together with many other copies of books and documents of this church had perished in fiery destruction, a fact established by most certain proofs, not only by the testimony of our honest and faithful men but also by the basilica of this mother church, burned by the aforesaid persecutors of the kingdom."[132] The monastery of St. Mary at Verdun ordered a commission of eminent canons and tenants to help re-create the charters and land surveys lost in a great fire in 916–17 and in the Magyar incursion of 926.[133] Or institutions could just cut corners and silently (re)create the lost documentation: one estimate is that the texts of perhaps 50 percent of all known early medieval charters have been forged or altered substantially.[134] For example, the monastery of St. Maximin (Trier), which lost its archives in 882, wound up replacing its missing deeds with confected ones, in part to rebut the claims made by the archbishop of Trier's own late tenth-century collection of forgeries.[135]

Genre studies offer another way to analyze the destruction of high culture. Latin hagiography, for example, virtually ceased to be composed in England between ca. 800 and ca. 950.[136] Ireland offers a similar

---

131. On *pancartes* as a literary form, see Parisse, "Les pancartes: Étude d'un type d'acte diplomatique," in *Pancartes monastiques des XIᵉ et XIIᵉ siècles*, ed. Parisse, Pierre Pégeot, and Benoît-Michel Tock (Turnout: Brepols, 1998), 1–62, esp. 26–35. Note the charters Charles the Bald issued for church of Rouen (863) and for the monasteries of Saint Martin of Tours (854), Fossés (864), Saint-Bavo (864), and Solignac (865), in *Recueil des actes de Charles II le Chauve, roi de France*, ed. Arthur Giry, Maurice Prou, and Georges Tessier, 3 vols. (Paris: Imprimerie nationale, 1943–55), 2:86–89, 1:438–42, 2:99–101, 2:115–17, 2:125–27 (nos. 259, 167, 266, 274, and 283).

132. Christensen and Nielsen, *Diplomatarium Danicum*, sect. 1, vol. 1, 58–86 (doc. 206), available online in the *Cartulaire de Sainte-Croix d'Orléans (814–1300)*, ed. Joseph Thillier, Bibliothèque de l'École nationale des chartes Cartulaires numérisé d'Île-de-France, http://elec.enc.sorbonne.fr/cartulaires/scroix/actepdf36/pdf.

133. Nightingale, *Monasteries and Patrons in the Gorze Reform: Lotharingia ca. 850–1000* (Oxford: Clarendon, 2001), 98.

134. Mostert, "Forgery and Trust," in *Strategies of Writing: Studies on Text and Trust in the Middle Ages: Papers from "Trust and Writing in the Middle Ages" (Utrecht, 28–29 November 2002)*, ed. Petra Schulte, Mostert, and Irene van Renswoude (Turnhout, Belg.: Brepols, 2008), 37–59, esp. 38.

135. Nightingale, *Monasteries and Patrons*, 169.

136. Lapidge and Love, "The Latin Hagiography of England and Wales (600–1550)," in *Hagiographies*, 3: 203–325, esp. 216.

story.[137] Very little comes from Christian Spain in the late tenth and early eleventh century.[138] Almost everywhere, hagiographical production suffered.[139] Parallel disruptions can be found in annals, biography, canon law, written legislation, and poetry.[140]

PSYCHOLOGICAL DAMAGE

Perhaps the worst consequences were psychological. How could the enemies of God be winning? Following the lead of the Hebrew Bible, churchmen were quick to blame the victims. Alcuin had already sounded this theme back in 797 at the very start of the troubles: "I fear the pagans—men who in earlier times did not dare to navigate our sea and devastate the coast of our fatherland—because of our sins [*timeo paganos propter peccata nostra*]."[141] A council held at Meaux in 845 declared that "because there had not been obedience to divine commandments, the lord sent . . . the Northmen, the cruel and most monstrous persecutors of Christianity."[142] Six councils in the Lorraine affirmed that Viking and Magyar raids were divine chastisements.[143] Thietmar of Merseburg (d. 1018), reflecting on the successes of the pagan Hungarians against the Germans, explains "based on my personal knowledge and what I have learned from books" that "with divine consent they were aroused as God's vengeance for our sins and we fled like cowards, terror-stricken because of our injustice. So it happened that we, who rejected the fear of the Lord in prosperous times, rightly endured the lash of the Lord. Having made no attempt to placate the anger of heaven, we were not heard when we cried out to God."[144] In England's

---

137. Lapidge and Richard Sharpe, *A Bibliography of Celtic Latin Literature, 400–1200* (Dublin: Royal Irish Academy, 1985), 101–30.

138. Manuel C. Díaz y Díaz, *Index Scriptorum Latinorum Medii Aevi Hispanorum*, 2 vols. (Salamanca: Universidad de Salamanca, 1958–59). The manuscript evidence is itemized in José Carlos Martín, "Códices hagiográficos latinos de origen hispanico de los siglos IX–XIV," *Analecta bollandiana* 127 (2009): 313–63.

139. For a rough index of hagiographical decline, see the century-by-century lists of saint's vitae in Felix Vernet, "Biographies spirituelles," *Dictionnaire de Spiritualité*, vol. 1 (1937), cols. 1624–1719. There Italy, for example, shows almost no hagiographical production in the tenth century.

140. Georges Duby, *L'An mil* (Paris: Collection "Archives," 1967), 18; Howe, "Re-Forging the 'Age of Iron': Part I," 867–68. For a "real interruption of documentary tradition" involving the papacy, see Tommaso di Carpegna Falconieri, "Osservazioni sulle edizioni dei documenti romani dei secoli IX–XII, con particolare riferimento alla storia ecclesiastica," in *Das Papsttum und das vielgestaltige Italien: Hundert Jahre "Italia Pontificia,"* ed. Klaus Herbers und Jochen Johrendt (Berlin: Walter de Gruyter, 2009), 389–401, esp. 394.

141. Alcuin, *Epist.* cxxx (to the people and kings of Britain, ca. 797), Dümmler, 193.

142. *Canones* (Meaux/Paris 845/846) praef., ed. Hartmann, MGH *Concilia*, 3:82–83; Michael Edward Moore, *A Sacred Kingdom: Bishops and the Rise of Frankish Kingship, 300–850* (Washington, DC: Catholic University of America Press, 2010), 363–65.

143. Nightingale, *Monasteries and Patrons*, 219.

144. Thietmar, *Chronicon* II vii, ed. Robert Holtzmann, *Die Chronik des Bischofs Thietmar von Merseburg*

bleak year of 1014, Wulfstan's "Sermon of the Wolf to the English" itemizes a long list of moral and social failings and concludes that "it is clear and manifest in all of us that we have previously transgressed more than we have amended, and therefore much is assailing this people. . . . There has been devastation and persecution in every district again and again, and the English have been for a long time now completely defeated and too greatly disheartened through God's anger; and the pirates so strong with God's consent that often in battle one puts to flight ten, and sometimes less, sometimes more, all because of our sins."[145] Sampiro, the bishop of Astorga around 1035, claimed that Al-Mansur triumphed because of "Christian sins [*peccata populi Christiani*]."[146] Scholars have sketched the general history of the topos of divine chastisement and have explicated its Carolingian manifestations in detail.[147]

Churchmen harping on this theme may have intended to offer a ray of hope: if sinfulness leads to chastisement, then repentance should inspire mercy. Abbo of Saint-Germain-des-Prés (d. ca. 923) in a sermon "Against Those Who Take the Goods of Others" expresses this in painfully simple terms to a lay audience: "The good tree is the good person who makes good fruit, that is, good works; the bad tree is the bad person making bad fruit, that is, bad works. So if up to now you have been bad trees, from now on be good trees, that is, good men, and produce the fruit of good works, and in that very instant God will be pious and merciful toward you. But how can you please God and get a victory, you who forever have your hands full of perjuries and plunderings?"[148] The problem here is that the

---

und ihre Korveier Überarbeitung, MGH SS *Rer Germ* 9 (Berlin: Weidmann, 1955), 46–47, trans. David A. Warner, *Ottonian Germany: The Chronicon of Thietmar of Merseburg* (Manchester, UK: Manchester University Press, 2001), 96–97.

145. Wulfstan, "The Sermon of the Wolf to the English," ed. Whitelock, *Sermo Lupi ad Anglos* (New York: Appleton-Century Crofts, 1966), 47–67, esp. 53–55, 58–59, trans. Whitelock, *English Historical Documents*, 1:854–59, esp. 856–57. For historiographical debates on the date of this piece, see Renée R. Trilling, "Sovereignty and Social Order: Archbishop Wulfstan and the *Institutes of Polity*," in Ott and Jones, *Bishop Reformed*, 58–91, esp. 58; and Hugh Magennis, *The Cambridge Introduction to Anglo-Saxon Literature* (Cambridge: Cambridge University Press, 2011), 140–43.

146. Felipe Fernández-Armesto, "The Survival of a Notion of *Reconquista* in Late Tenth- and Eleventh-Century León," in *Warriors and Churchmen in the Middle Ages: Essays Presented to Karl Leyser*, ed. Timothy Reuter (London: Hambledon, 1992), 123–43, esp. 137.

147. d'Haenens, "Les invasions normandes dans l'Empire franc au IXᵉ siècle," 286–87; Simon Coupland, "The Rod of God's Wrath or the People of God's Wrath? The Carolingian Theology of the Viking Invasions," *JEH* 42 (1991): 535–54.

148. Abbo of Saint-Germain des Prés, *Sermo adversus Raptores Bonorum Alienorum* ix, ed. Ute Önnerfors, *Abbo von Saint-Germain-des Prés: 22 Predigten: Kritische Ausgabe und Kommentar*, Lateinische Sprache und Literatur des Mittelalters 16 (Frankfurt: Peter Lang, 1985), 94–99, esp. 94–95.

proffered hope could be quickly dashed if Christians heeded the message, repented, did penance, and then got crushed again. During the chaotic last years of King Aethelred's reign, the English bishops exhorted the nation to undertake joint fasts and required every priest in every church to sing the "Mass against the Pagans" every Wednesday.[149] The 1009 "Edict When the Great Army Came to England," whose English version is found in the works of Wulfstan (d. 1023) and is written in his characteristic vocabulary, connects the raising of the Danegeld to fasts, Masses, confessions, and barefoot processions. The liturgical close of the fuller Latin text prays that "Almighty God might be merciful to us and may give us triumph over our enemies and peace, Whom we beg assiduously that here we will experience his mercy and grace and in the future his rest without end, Amen." The Old English version concludes more cogently but perhaps less hopefully: "God help us! Amen."[150] Then the Danes won once more. Such crises of theodicy could have self-perpetuating military consequences because spiritual hope was a major element in the battlefield effectiveness of early medieval armies.[151]

Especially galling was the fact that some Christians helped the invaders. Modern historians and a large slice of the popular media pay more attention to alien barbarians than to the local thugs who benefited from the chaos that they caused. We picture hordes of Vikings in motley but spectacular barbarian armor, perhaps including the anachronistic horned helmets popularized in the operas of Richard Wagner.[152] We assume that tenth-century Muslim pirates shared the implacable anti-Western hostility of today's most extreme jihadis. We can imagine the Magyars as they appear in their nineteenth-century bronze memorial in Budapest, fierce

149. Aelfric, *Epistola de Canonibus* ꝗ 175, in *Councils & Synods with Other Documents Relating to the English Church*, vol. 1, pt. 1, *871–1066*, ed. Whitelock, Martin Brett, and Christopher N. L. Brooke (Oxford: Clarendon, 1981), 191–226, esp. 226.

150. Wulfstan, "Latin Version: Edict When the Great Army Came to England," esp. ꝗ 1–4, in Whitelock et al., *Councils & Synods*, vol. 1, pt. 1, 373–78, esp. 375–77; Wulfstan, Old English Version: ꝗ 1–8, in ibid., 379–82. On the overt and subtle political messages in these decrees, see M. K. Lawson, "Archbishop Wulfstan and the Homiletic Element in the Laws of Aethelred II and Cnut," in *The Reign of Cnut, King of England, Denmark, and Norway*, ed. Alexander R. Rumble (London: Leicester University Press, 1994), 141–64. Wulstan employs the same closing in the similarly demoralizing "Sermon of the Wolf," Whitelock, *Sermo Lupi*, 67, Whitelock, *English Historical Documents*, 859.

151. David Bachrach, *Religion and the Conduct of War, c. 300–1215* (Woodbridge: Boydell, 2003), esp. 8, 42, 62–63, 68–69; Bernard Bachrach, *Early Carolingian Warfare*, 132–69; David Bachrach, *Warfare in Tenth-Century Germany* (Woodbridge: Boydell, 2012), 169–92.

152. Roberta Frank, "The Invention of the Viking Horned Helmet," in *International Scandinavian and Medieval Studies in Memory of Gerd Wolfgang Weber: Ein runder Knäuel, so rollt' es uns leicht aus den Händen*, ed. Michael Dallapiazza, Olaf Hansen, Preben Meulengracht-Sørensen, and Yvonne S. Bonnetain (Trieste: Parnaso, 2000), 199–208.

mustachioed mounted warriors eager to slash, burn, and enslave. The reality was somehow worse. Contemporary ninth- and tenth-century charters and chronicles blame the destruction not only on "pagans" but also on "bad Christians."[153] The problem was not so much the relatively few Frankish Christians who actually joined the marauding bands.[154] Greater harm was probably done by profiteers who provided the food and horses that enabled the raiders to maintain their armies in the field.[155] Then there were the opportunistic Christians who grabbed unguarded lands and governmental powers for themselves after the raiders had driven out monks, canons, and secular officials. Moreover, any clear line between Christians and pagans would have begun to blur as early adapters in Viking and Magyar armies converted to Christianity. Muslims may not have converted as readily, but Al-Mansur was able to force so many Christian "volunteers" to participate in his campaigns that these have been described as a virtual civil war among Christians.[156]

The pagans were even helped by God's anointed kings. At one time or another almost every Frankish ruler from Louis the Pious onward allied with bands of raiders. Sometimes these were aggressive partnerships, as when Emperor Lothar hired Vikings to attack his brothers' lands or when King Berengar of Italy directed Magyars against his foes or when the lords of Naples tacitly supported Muslim attacks on independent monasteries in their region. The more common scenario, however, was that kings who paid non-Christian raiders protection money were forced to ally with them because the neutralized bands needed exit plans. Hapless kings considered these bargains lesser evils but their subjects could be outraged.[157] Prudentius of Troyes (d. 861), the author of a section of the *Annals of Saint-Bertin*, was horrified at Emperor Lothar's Frisian grant to the

---

153. Christensen and Nielsen, *Diplomatarium Danicum*, sect. 1, vol. 1, 35, 42, 44, 59, 61, 79, 80, 18, 85, 87, 92, 99, 104 (2x), 106, and 127–28 (docs. 83, 99, 104, 139, 144, 190, 191, 194, 204, 210, 223, 243, 255, 256, 260, and 324). For further examples, see Anna Jones, "Pitying the Desolation of Such a Place: Rebuilding Religious Houses and Reconstructing Memory in Aquitaine in the Wake of the Viking Incursions," *Viator* 37 (2006): 85–103, esp. 90–92; and Coupland, "Holy Ground?," 73–97.

154. Smyth, "Effect of Scandinavian Raiders," 27.

155. Charles the Bald, *Capitula Pistensia* (864), ed. Alfred Boretius and Victor Krause, MGH *Legum Sectio II: Capitularia Regna Francorum*, 2 vols. (Hannover: Hahn, 1883–1897), 2:310–28, esp. 328 (no. 273). For the context of this assembly, see Nelson, *Charles the Bald*, 207–09.

156. Isla, "Warfare and Other Plagues in the Iberian Peninsula," in Urbańczyk, *Europe around the Year 1000*, 233–46, esp. 237–38; Thomas Deswarte, *De la destruction à la restauration: L'idéologie du royaume d'Oviedo-Léon (VIIIe–XIe siècles)* (Turnhout, Belg.: Brepols, 2003), 295–96.

157. Some alliances are listed in Sawyer, *Kings and Vikings*, 98–100; and in Bauduin, *Le monde franc et les Vikings VIIIe–Xe siècle* (Paris: Albin Michel, 2009), 313–41. For Vikings viewed not as alien outsiders but as actual participants in European politics, see Niels Lund, "Allies of God or Man? The Viking Expansion in a European Perspective," *Viator* 20 (1989): 45–59.

Viking Harald and denounced it as "surely an utterly detestable crime."[158] Liudprand of Cremona (d. ca. 972) frets about hypocritical Christians who seek infidel aid against fellow Christians, undermine Christianity, and provoke God's vengeance, and he blames such men for the arrival of the Muslims and Magyars.[159] Aelfric (d. ca. 1010), in his Old English *Lives of the Saints*, emphasizes steadfast faith and refusal to compromise with paganism, perhaps a veiled attack on his fellow Englishmen who allied with the Danes.[160] Later on people preferred to forget about the bad Christians and to embrace the narrative of "Christians vs. pagans": Rodulfus Glaber (d. ca. 1046) begins the first book of his *Histories* with the Saxon emperors and the invasions of the Muslims, Vikings, and Magyars, and neglects to mention any Christian culpability.[161] But while the invasions were actually in progress, people would have been painfully aware of the collaborators in their midst.

---

158. *Annales Bertiniani* 841, Grat, 39, Nelson, 51.

159. Liudprand, *Antapodosis* I ii–iv, xxxvi, Chiesa, 6–7, 26, Squatriti, 45–47, 66–67. This theme is explicated in Jon N. Sutherland, *Liudprand of Cremona, Bishop, Diplomat, Historian: Studies of the Man and his Age* (Spoleto: CISAM, 1988), 58–63; and Karl Leyser, "Ends and Means in Liutprand of Cremona," *Byzantinische Forschungen* 13 (1988): 119–43, esp. 143.

160. Malcolm R. Godden, "Aelfric's Saints' Lives and the Problem of Miracle," *Leeds Studies in English*, n.s., 16 (1985), 83–100, esp. 97.

161. John France, "War and Christendom in the Thought of Rodulfus Glaber," *Studia Monastica* 30 (1989): 105–19, esp. 109–10, 113.

CHAPTER 2

"ENTER CONFIDENTLY INTO THE WAR OF THE LORD GOD"

> Enter confidently into the war of the Lord God. And when you enter
> into the war of God, everyone call out in a loud voice "Christus vincit,
> Christus regnat, Christus imperat!" At that instant the devil, the prince
> of the pagans, will flee when he has heard the terrifying shout of the
> Christians. And then the pagans will flee after their devil prince. And
> so you who will have God for your king and prince will receive the
> victory.
>
> —Abbo of Saint-Germain, *Sermo adversus Raptores*

Western morale did improve, in tandem with the success of Western arms.[1]
At the end of the eleventh century, descendants of the demoralized Latin
Christians who in the tenth century were being mugged by Vikings, Muslims, and Magyars would fight their way through Greek, Turkish, and Arab
empires to raise the Latin cross over Jerusalem. What changed!? The success of the Crusaders caused the Byzantine princess Anna Comnena (d.
ca. 1153) to conclude that "a Frank on horseback is invincible, and would
even make a hole in the walls of Babylon."[2] But the achievement was more
than military. No Frankish knights would have been in Babylon's vicinity
had there not been resources to train, equip, and supply them. And the
decision to invest great wealth in such an improbable cause presupposed

1. For the introductory quotation, see Abbo, *Sermo adversus Raptores Bonorum Alienorum* ix, ed. Ute
Önnerfors, *Abbo von Saint-Germain-des-Prés: 22 Predigten* (Frankfurt: Peter Lang, 1985), 98–99. On the
chanting of "Christus vincit" before battles, see David Bachrach, *Religion and the Conduct of War*, 34.

2. Anna Comnena, *Alexiad* XIII viii, trans. Elizabeth A.S. Dawes (London: Routledge & Kegan Paul,
1967), 342.

an extraordinary faith that "God wills it!" and a shared commitment to do God's will. A quick survey of the military, political, and ecclesiastical history of the tenth-century Latin West will reveal that the rise of the West and the revival and reform of the Latin Church are actually interrelated aspects of the same story.

INTERNAL FORTIFICATIONS AND THEIR CONSEQUENCES

Recovery required military security, and this was achieved through "encastellation," the development of extensive internal fortifications.[3] Early medieval Western Europe had a heritage of strongholds, including hilltop ringforts left over from the Iron Age, abandoned Roman military camps, and some turreted city walls from Late Antiquity. Although this internal military infrastructure was of little consequence so long as the Carolingian kings could provide peace and security, it suddenly became important when Vikings, Muslims, Magyars, and *mali Christiani* began sacking undefended villas, churches, and monasteries, and even attacking cities. More defenses were needed. The invaders with their island bases, pirate nests, and ad hoc camp defenses unintentionally offered tutorials to the Latin West on how to construct them cheaply.

One expedient was to "harden" manor houses. Fortified villas in Late Antiquity are known from mosaic images, but although villa archaeology has made great strides, the surviving foundations and ground plans do not reveal much about possible window protections, towers, crenulations, and other military features. As the Carolingian Empire disintegrated, lower-story windows and doors were sealed and hardened on some manor houses and other modifications added to make them more defensible.[4]

3. General studies include *L'Incastellamento: Actas de las reuniones de Girona, 26–27 noviembre 1992, y de Roma, 5–7 mayo 1994/L'Incastellamento: Actes des rencontres de Gérone, 26–27 novembre 1992, et de Rome, 5–7 mai 1994*, ed. Miquel Barceló and Pierre Toubert (Rome: ÉFR & Escuela Española de Historia y Arqueología en Roma, 1998); Riccardo Francovich, "Changing Structures of Settlements," in *Italy in the Early Middle Ages, 476–1000*, ed. Cristina La Rocca (Oxford: Oxford University Press, 2002), 144–67, esp. 158–67; Francovich and Hodges, *Villa to Village: The Transformation of the Roman Countryside in Italy, c. 400–1000* (London: Duckworth, 2003), 75–105.

4. Michel de Boüard, "De l'aula au *donjon*: Les fouilles de la motte et de La Chapelle à Doué-la-Fontaine (Xe–XIe siècle)," *Archéologie médiévale* 3–4 (1973–74): 5–110, esp. 37 and 58–79; Ross Samson, "The Residences of *Potentiores* in Gaul and Germania in the Fifth to Mid-Ninth Centuries" (PhD diss., University of Glasgow, 1991), 120–40, 172–73, 183–84. On the fortification of palaces during the ninth and tenth centuries, see Annie Renoux, "*Palatium* et *castrum* en France du Nord (fin IXe–début XIIIe siècle)," in *The Seigneurial Residence in Western Europe, AD c 800–1600*, ed. Gwyn Meirion-Jones, Edward Impey, and Michael Jones (Oxford: Archaeopress, 2002), 15–26.

FIGURE 4. Fortified villa of Junius of Carthage, fifth-century mosaic. Musée du Bardo, Tunis. Photo credit: HIP/Art Resource, NY.

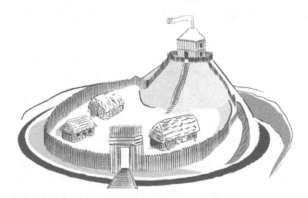

FIGURE 5. Digital rendering of a motte-and-bailey castle.
Illustration by Holt Haley-Walker. Reproduced by permission.

FIGURE 6. Stone tower, Donjon of Loches (the surrounding curtain walls represent a later phase), one of the many castles of Count Fulk Nerra of Anjou (987–1040). Photo credit: Gianni Dagli Orti/The Art Archive at Art Resource, NY.

Transalpine fortifications were usually constructed using earth and timber. Simple ditch and wall enclosures sited on hills, harking back to centuries of pre-Roman fortifications, are called ringworks by English scholars, *castella* in some Continental Latin sources.[5] The more innovative solution, adopted when resources and topography permitted, was the motte-and-bailey castle, a *castrum* in some Continental sources. The motte was a fortified mound that anchored and dominated the bailey, an enclosed fortified courtyard below it, both of which were surrounded by an artificial ditch (whose former fill contributed to the motte). Palisades and a platform or tower on top protected archers and offered them good fields of fire.

5. D.J.C. King and Leslie Alcott, "Ringworks of England and Wales," in *Chateau Gaillard 3. Conference at Battle, Sussex, 19–24 September 1966*, ed. A.J.P. Taylor (London: Phillimore, 1969), 90–127; Bernard Bachrach, "Early Medieval Fortifications in the 'West' of France: A Revised Technical Vocabulary," *Technology and Culture* 16 (1975): 531–69, esp. 562–65; John R. Kenyon, *Medieval Fortifications* (New York: St. Martin's, 1990), 2–7 and 23–28.

More expensive stone towers appear early in some parts of northern Europe, especially in the ambient of Fulk Nerra (987–1040), a count of Anjou who presented himself as a "consul" and seems to have been ideologically attracted to Roman-style fortifications.[6] Yet up until the thirteenth century the majority of northern European castles remained timber-built.[7] The timber palisades surrounding their upper and lower levels made them appear more like the frontier forts of the Wild West than the fantastic stone castles imagined by Disney. Motte-and-bailey castles appeared in northern France in the tenth century and spread widely; rare in pre-Conquest England, after 1066 they would anchor the new Norman elite.[8]

In eastern Francia, a system of defense in depth, originally developed on the Carolingian frontiers, secured local defenses with strategically placed modular earth and wood structures that guarded transportation routes and complicated the lives of mobile raiders. This world is known mostly through its remains: for example, of the more than 250 fortifications from ca. 700–ca. 1000 now known archaeologically in northern Bavaria, only about 30 appear in the surviving written records. These defensive systems expanded as the German kings extended their influence farther east.[9] Private fortifications for individual lords began to develop away from the frontiers.[10]

Towns improved their fortifications. Whereas Henri Pirenne saw Charlemagne ruling an empire of great rural estates, today's scholars identify market centers already developing in Carolingian times, places that, when

---

6. Bernard Bachrach, "Fortifications and Military Tactics: Fulk Nerra's Strongholds circa 1000," *Technology and Culture* 20 (1979): 531–49; Bernard Bachrach, *Fulk Nerra, the Neo-Roman Consul 987–1040: A Political Biography of the Angevin Count* (Berkeley: University of California Press, 1993), 49–50, 95–97, and 255.

7. Robert Higham and Philip Parker, *Timber Castles* (London: B. T. Batsford, 1992), esp. 17 and 30–31.

8. Kenyon, *Medieval Fortifications*, 1–38; C. J. Spurgeon, "Mottes and Castle-Ringworks in Wales," in *Castles in Wales and in the Marches: Essays in Honour of D.J. Cathcart King*, ed. John R. Kenyon and Richard Avent (Cardiff: University of Wales Press, 1987), 23–49; Bernard Bachrach and David Bachrach, "Saxon Military Revolution, 912–973? Myth and Reality," *Early Medieval Europe* 15 (2007): 186–222, esp. 216–19; Kelly DeVries and Robert Douglas Smith, *Medieval Military Technology*, 2nd ed. (Toronto: University of Toronto Press, 2012), 199–233.

9. Bowlus, *Battle of Lechfeld*, 138–62; Hans-Wilhelm Heine, "Der 'Heidenwall' in Oldenburg (Oldb.): Eine Holz-Erde-Burg, Datiert auf 1032/33 bzw. 1042," in *Château et représentations: Actes du Colloque international de Stirling (Écosse), 30 août–5 septembre 2008*, ed. Peter Ettel, A.-M. Flambard-Héricher, and T. E. McNeill (Caen: CRAHAM, 2010), 115–21; David Bachrach, "Exercise of Royal Power in Early Medieval Europe: The Case of Otto the Great," *Early Medieval Europe* 17 (2009): 389–419, esp. 382n–393n; David Bachrach, *Warfare in Tenth-Century Germany* (Woodbridge, UK: Boydell, 2012), xiii, 24–32, 56–57, 71–77, and 220–25.

10. Jean-Michel Rudrauf, "L'apparition des premiers châteaux en Alsace entre le début du Xe et le milieu du XIe siècle," in *Léon IX et son temps*, ed. Georges Bischoff and Benoît-Michel Tock (Turnhout, Belg.: Brepols, 2006), 543–66.

challenged, took steps to better fortify themselves.[11] Some former Roman cities retained potentially useful elements of their old walls,[12] and, as noted earlier in the discussion of barbarian attacks, might actually gain population when refugees sought shelter from disorder in the countryside.

In the Mediterranean world, encastellation was more a question of walled hilltop villages than of fortified lordly residences or military redoubts. Italian settlement patterns were easy to turn to military advantage because farmers preferred elevated sites, above the flood-prone malarial river valleys, where they could practice terraced mixed-crop agriculture and access higher-altitude forests and pastures. In this milieu it was easy to site concentrated settlements on defensible outcroppings, and these could be fortified using Italy's abundant workable limestone or the cut stone left by earlier civilizations. Yet even in Italy strongholds could be made of wood.[13] The fortified villages that the Italians call *castelli* were promoted by great landowners, especially by property-rich ecclesiastical corporations that were attempting to repopulate their lands by granting leases to noble developers and privileges to new settlers. Tighter fortified communities replaced dispersed farmsteads in a land that, formerly the center of a world empire, had now become a frontier.[14]

Hastily built internal fortifications were still vulnerable to determined assaults, but at what cost? Attackers, perhaps burdened by ladders as well as armor, had to cross well-designed killing fields, clamber down and up the sides of ditches and up hills while dodging missile fire from enemies occupying higher ground, and, once they did reach the walls, survive everything that creative defenders could drop on them. A versified account of the defense of Paris in 885–86 describes a tower protected not only by the spears and arrows of its defenders but also by "rocks thudding on painted shields," a "huge wheel thrown down from the top of the tower," and "oil, wax, and pitch, which was all mixed up together and made into a hot liquid on a furnace."[15] The longer raiders were delayed by sieges, the

11. Rouche, "Vikings versus the Towns of Northern Gaul," 41–56; Verhulst, *Rise of Cities in Northwest Europe*, 44–67.

12. Jean Hubert, "Evolution de la topographie et de l'aspect des villes de Gaule du Vᵉ au Xᵉ siècle," in *La città nell'alto Medioevo*, Settimane di Studio del CISAM 6 (Spoleto: CISAM, 1959), 529–58, esp. 533.

13. For a dramatic mid-eleventh-century story about the burning of the castle of Belvedere, see Amatus of Montecassino, *Ystoire de li Normant* II xxxix, ed. Michèle Guéret-Laferté, *Aimé du Mont-Cassin: Ystoire de li Norman: Édition du manuscrit BnF fr. 688* (Paris: Honoré Champion, 2011), 302–3, trans. Prescott N. Dunbar and Graham A. Loud, *Amatus of Montecassino: The History of the Normans* (Woodbridge: Boydell, 2004), 82 (where the division is II xxxx).

14. Howe, *Church Reform*, 10–17.

15. Abbo of Saint-Germain-des-Prés, *Bella Parisiacae Urbis* I, lines 78–171, ed. and trans. Nirmal Dass, *Viking Attacks on Paris: The "Bella Parisiacae Urbis" of Abbo of Saint-Germain-des-Prés*, Dallas Medieval Texts and Translations 7 (Paris: Peeters, 2007), 32–37.

more exposed they were to potential counterattacks from relieving armies. Successful besiegers could hope to capture livestock, enslave survivors, and celebrate the destruction of annoying adversaries, but would those rewards be worth the casualties? As Europe became better fortified, raiding became less profitable.

It has been claimed that "more surplus resources were devoted to the preparation for war, the conduct of war, and war's aftermath than to any other activity during the tenth century."[16] Scholars who doubt that the post-Carolingian invasions had any decisive impact would need to explain such expenditures. One might argue that the Carolingians had already directed great resources toward military expansion and frontier fortifications, but this fails to explain the new shift toward internal fortifications. It has been objected that most castles were built only after the major raids had ceased, but this is exactly what one would expect inasmuch as war leaders in all eras prepare to fight their previous wars. Pierre Toubert once famously attempted to argue that encastellation originated as a new system of seigniorial exploitation unrelated to military considerations, but he ultimately retreated from that position and admitted that the new fortifications originally responded to military necessities.[17] In support of his reconsideration it might be observed that in Greek southern Italy, which still possessed a more centralized Late Roman governmental system, Islamic raids resulted in the same shift toward fortified hilltop villages that occurred just to the north in Latin Italy. If a different political system faced with the same military challenges develops in a similar way, then the similarity probably ought to be explained in military rather than political terms.[18] Yet even if encastellation originated as a response to external military attacks, it soon achieved its own momentum when lords found themselves erecting castles and countercastles across disputed borders. The late ninth- and early tenth-century attacks ultimately led to a restructured Europe, to tighter, more intensely exploited military districts, a change that would have great demographic, social, and political consequences, not least for the rebuilding and reformation of the Latin Church.

The new fortifications were most effective when manned by or at least supervised by military professionals. The old Germanic ideal of a nation

---

16. David Bachrach, *Warfare in Tenth-Century Germany*, 102, 170.

17. Howe, *Church Reform*, 10–12.

18. Jean-Marie Martin and Ghislaine Noyé, "Guerre, fortifications et habitats en Italie méridionale du Vᵉ au Xᵉ siècle," in *Castrum 3: Guerre, fortification et habitat dans le monde méditerranéen au moyen âge*, ed. André Bazzana (Madrid: Casa de Velázquez / ÉFR, 1988), 225–36; Loud, *Age of Robert Guiscard*, 21 and 55–56. In Byzantine provinces outside southern Italy, fortification was normally a large-scale imperial endeavor: see Leonora Neville, *Authority in Byzantine Provincial Society, 950–1100* (New York: Cambridge University Press, 2004), 42–44.

in arms, defended by all its free men, was increasingly obsolete. Regino of
Prüm (d. 915) tells that when a Viking raiding party arrived at the monastery of Prüm on the feast of the Epiphany, a holiday time when the men
from the farms and villages could be easily assembled into one host, the
invaders were quick to recognize that "this crowd of common people
[*ignobile vulgus*] was not so much unarmed as bereft of military training
[*disciplina militare nudatum*], . . . [and they] rushed on them with a shout
and cut them down in such a bloodbath that they seemed to be butchering
dumb animals rather than men [*ut bruta animalia*]."[19] Tenth-century warfare required not an "ignoble crowd" but a more noble one, professional
well-equipped men-at-arms who were trained to fight together. Despite
the famous dictum of Lynn White Jr. that "Antiquity imagined the Centaur;
the early Middle Ages made him the master of Europe," the supremacy of
the heavily armored knight on the tenth- and early eleventh-century battlefield was by no means clear.[20] In any case, such battlefields were relatively rare because prudent commanders preferred to avoid unpredictable
field battles in favor of the more pedestrian work of building, besieging,
and relieving castles, operations in which mounted shock combat had little to contribute. However, the most common use of military force was to
harass the countryside, and here the new castles provided perfect havens
for heavily armored soldiers who could ride out to trample crops, burn
thatched huts, and confiscate livestock until peace and tribute could be
reestablished on a more satisfactory basis.[21]

A NEW EUROPE

Encastellation reshaped the political order, but it was a difficult tool to
wield, especially by Charlemagne's hapless descendants. The later Carolingians, according to Edward Gibbon "no longer exhibited any symptoms
of virtue or power, and the ridiculous epithets of the *bald*, the *stammerer*,

19. Regino of Prüm, *Chronicon* 882, ed. Friedrich Kurze, MGH *SS Rer Germ* 50 (Hannover: Hahn, 1890),
118, trans. Simon MacLean, *History and Politics in Late Carolingian and Ottonian Europe: The "Chronicle" of
Regino of Prüm and Adalbert of Magdeburg* (Manchester, UK: Manchester University Press, 2009), 61–283,
esp. 185.

20. Lynn White Jr., *Medieval Technology and Social Change* (London: Oxford University Press, 1962), 38.
On the subsequent debate, see Alex Roland, "Once More into the Stirrups: Lynn White Jr., *Medieval Tech-
nology and Social Change*," *Technology and Culture* 44 (2003): 574–85, esp. 577–78; Bachrach and Bachrach,
"Saxon Military Revolution," 188–89.

21. Michael Mitterauer, *Why Europe? The Medieval Origins of Its Special Path*, trans. Gerald Chapler
(Chicago: University of Chicago Press, 2010), 115–16, claims that the connection between heavy cavalry and
encastellation and this system's coexistence with other types of fortification were Western developments
unprecedented and unmatched in other civilizations.

the *fat*, and the *simple* distinguished the tame and uniform features of a crowd of kings alike deserving of oblivion."[22] Some of these rulers look less inept when their careers are examined seriously, and some did grasp the importance of new internal fortifications. The *Annales of Saint-Bertin* describe Charles the Bald building forts, ordering towns to fortify, and legislating garrison duties.[23] His fortified bridges proved effective against the "cruelest enemies of God."[24] But even Charles had to order the dismantling of "castles and strong points [*castella et firmitates*]" that were popping up throughout his realm without royal authorization.[25]

Internal political disintegration was what really handicapped the later Carolingians. In 884 Charlemagne's great-grandson Charles the Fat temporarily inherited nominal lordship over almost the whole empire, but things fell apart when he was deposed in parts of his realm in 887 and died in January of 888. Regino of Prüm saw this as a turning point: "After his [Charles the Fat's] death, the kingdoms which had obeyed his authority, just as though a legitimate heir were lacking, dissolved into separate parts and, without waiting for their natural lord, each decided to create a king from its own guts. This was the cause of great wars. . . . None so outshone the others that the rest deigned to submit to his rule."[26] At various times royal status was claimed by rulers in France (West Francia), Brittany, Lotharingia (the Lorraine), Provence, Aquitaine, Burgundy, Upper Burgundy, Italy, and Germany (East Francia). This forced international aristocratic lineages to choose sides, thus putting at risk all the properties they owned outside the realms of the lords they chose.[27]

Who would control the castles? In England, Germany, and Spain, which were still fighting wars against non-Christians, there remained a need for strong kings who could oversee the process of fortification. The border kingdoms were a special case, however, and elsewhere initiative tended to

22. Edward Gibbon, *History of the Decline and Fall of the Roman Empire*, ed. J. B. Bury, 3 vols. (New York: Heritage, 1946), 3:1704.

23. *Annales Bertiniani* (868, 869), Grat, 150, 152, 166, Nelson, 151, 153, 164.

24. Carroll Gillmor, "The Logistics of Fortified Bridge Building on the Seine under Charles the Bald," and Brian Dearden, "Charles the Bald's Fortified Bridge at Pitres (Seine): Recent Archaeological Investigations," *Anglo-Norman Studies: Proceedings of the Battle Conference* 11 (1989): 87–107 and 107–32. The phrase *inimices Dei cruentissimi* is from Charles the Bald, *Carta* cclxxxvii (16 January 866), ed. Arthur Giry, Maurice Prou, and Georges Tessier, *Recueil des actes de Charles II le Chauve, roi de France*, 3 vols. Chartes et diplômes relatifs à l'histoire de France 8 (Paris: Imprimerie nationale, 1943–1955), 2:132–36, esp. 135.

25. Charles the Bald, *Capitula Pistensia* (864), ed. Alfred Boretius and Victor Krause, MGH *Legum Sectio II: Capitularia Regum Francorum*, 2 vols. (Hannover: Hahn, 1883–90), 2:310–28, esp. 328 (no. 273). For the context of this assembly, see Nelson, *Charles the Bald*, 207–9.

26. Regino of Prüm, *Chronicon* 888, Kurze, 129, MacLean, 199.

27. Simon Maclean, *Kingship and Politics in the Late Ninth Century: Charles the Fat and the End of the Carolingian Empire* (New York: Cambridge University Press, 2003), esp. 1–11.

pass to those dukes, marcher lords, and counts who still remained powerful after central authority had collapsed. For example, the counts of Flanders, descended from the Carolingians through the female line, dominated the castles in their territories while reigning out of their own fortified, almost-royal palace at Bruges.[28] Such lords acquired the public lands, judicial powers, and ecclesiastical patronage that had formerly belonged to kings and emperors. In places where invaders and usurpers had smashed even the comital level of administration, power devolved to lesser nobles or independent castellans. The result was *encellulement des hommes*, the fragmentation of Europe into small tight sections like the enamel-filled cells in cloisonné jewelry.[29] The much-debated model of a "feudal revolution" around the year 1000, when disorderly knights everywhere allegedly usurped the powers of the old nobility and made knightly violence the order of the day, now seems at best to describe only certain local situations.[30] Yet the very fact that scholars could have a lively debate over whether or not Europe experienced a feudal revolution demonstrates how great and confusing were the regional differences, not only between eastern and western Francia but also among kingdoms, provinces, and even microregions. To appreciate the fragmented political background of Church reform, it may be helpful to survey quickly, region by region, the major polities that emerged out of the wreckage.

Germany

East Francia was the great success story. Until the reign of Charlemagne, Saxons, Bavarians, and other distant Germans were basically independent, but after they had been definitively conquered, they clung to their newly acquired Carolingian institutions with the tenacious loyalty of recent converts. Although Germany's mostly inland geography made it less vulnerable to maritime raiders, it still faced severe challenges that included internal power struggles, a problematic Slavic frontier, and the arrival of the Magyars. German dukes responded by clinging to the Carolingian dynasty of Louis the German despite the uninspiring reigns of Arnulf the Bastard (d. 899)

28. Karine Ugé, *Creating the Monastic Past in Medieval Flanders* (York: York Medieval Press, 2005), 7–10. On the comital palace, see Renoux, "Palatium et castrum," in Meirion-Jones et al., *Seigneurial Residence in Western Europe*, 17.

29. Robert Fossier, *Enfance de l'Europe: X^e–XIIe siècle. Aspectes économique et sociaux*, 2 vols. (Paris: Presses universitaires de France, 1982), 288 and 346; also Susan Reynolds, *Kingdoms and Communities in Western Europe 900–1300* (Oxford: Clarendon, 1984), iv. For the pivotal role of castles in this change, see André Debord, "The Castellan Revolution and the Peace of God in Aquitaine," in *The Peace of God: Social Violence and Religious Response in France around the Year 1000*, ed. Thomas Head and Richard Landes (Ithaca: Cornell University Press, 1992), 135–64, esp. 148–55.

30. Christian Lauranson-Rosaz, "Le débat sur la 'mutation féodale': État de la question," in Urbańczyk, *Europe around the Year 1000*, 11–40; Howe, "Re-Forging the 'Age of Iron': Part I," 869–71.

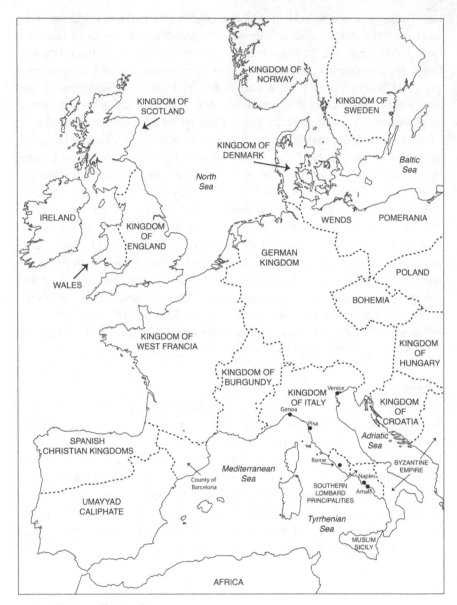

MAP 1. Western Christendom ca. 1000. Map by Holt Haley-Walker Graphic Design & Illustration. Reproduced by permission.

and Louis the Child (d. 911). Devotion to the Carolingians probably also helps explain the coronation of Conrad of Franconia (d. 918), a relative of Louis the Child through the maternal line, a loyal Carolingian supporter who ruled the original Frankish homeland. After he too failed to make headway against rebellious dukes and invading Hungarians, the crown was passed to one of his rivals, Henry the Fowler of Saxony (d. 936), who, as the most powerful duke, was presumably best able to unite the kingdom.[31]

A century of Saxon rule brought imperial greatness. Henry initially allowed the dukes considerable independence, but he took more control over the Lorraine, scored military successes against many eastern tribes, and was able to cease paying tribute to the Magyars after he defeated them at the Battle of Riade in 933. When his son Otto inherited the crown in 936, he was able to stage his coronation at Charlemagne's chapel at Aachen, following the rite with a banquet at which the dukes of the realm served him at table.[32] Otto I was no Arnulf the Bastard, the most recent German imperial claimant.[33] His pretensions are revealed by his dynasty's marriage politics. His first wife, Edith, was the granddaughter of Alfred the Great; his second wife, Adelaide, was the daughter of the king of Burgundy and the widow of the king of Italy, connected by marriage to the Bosonids, a lineage that once threatened to rival the Carolingians. Otto decided that his own son Otto II should wed a Byzantine princess, an ambition he achieved despite Greek recalcitrance so great that the marriage negotiations required three diplomatic missions.[34] Otto's brother Henry groomed his daughter to marry Romanus II, the heir to the eastern imperial throne. An aggressive foreign policy expanded German power in Burgundy, the Lorraine, Eastern Europe, and Italy. The victory over the Magyars at the Battle of the Lechfeld in 955 cemented Otto's position as a pan European figure and positioned him to acquire the imperial crown in 962. Byzantine emperors justifiably felt threatened.[35]

The Saxon rulers relied heavily on the Church, particularly on ecclesiastical vassals who often also held secular political offices. The imperial

31. Hagen Keller and Gerd Althoff, *Die Zeit der späten Karolinger und der Ottonen: Krisen und Konsolidierung, 888–1024*, vol. 3 of *Gebhardt: Handbuch der deutschen Geschichte*, 10th ed. (Stuttgart: Klett-Cotta, 2008), 54–85.

32. Keller, *Ottonische Königsherrschaft: Organisation und Legitimation königlicher Macht* (Darmstadt: Wissenschaftliche Buchgesellschaft, 2002), 91–130; Keller and Althoff, *Zeit der späten Karolinger und der Ottonen*, 148–56; David Bachrach, *Warfare in Tenth-Century Germany*, 14–69.

33. On Arnulf's tribulations, see Carl I. Hammer, "Crowding the King: Rebellion and Political Violence in Late Carolingian Bavaria and Italy," *Studi medievali*, 3rd ser., 48 (2007): 493–541, esp. 493–500.

34. Jonathan Shepard, "Marriages toward the Millennium," in *Byzantium in the Year 1000*, ed. Paul Magdalino (Turnhout, Belg.: Brepols, 2002), 1–33, esp. 4.

35. For overviews, see chapters 9–13 of Reuter, *NCMH*, 3:235–328; and Keller and Althoff, *Die Zeit der späten Karolinger und der Ottonen*, 148–239.

chancery prepared clerks for ecclesiastical leadership so efficiently that by the early eleventh century most German bishops had apprenticed in the royal chapel. Though scholars have questioned whether or not this condominium constitutes an "imperial Church system," it was certainly an imperial Church.[36] Kings expressed their power and position through ecclesiastical ceremony.[37] The most outstanding in this regard was (St.) Henry II (1002–25) who staged myriads of formal crowning ceremonies, regularly attended the great church consecrations of his day (he helped choreograph them), and often took a place at the altar with the clergy even during liturgical services normally off limits to laymen, an indulgence he could justify in that he was not only king but also an honorary canon of many of the great churches of his realm.[38] Some German scholars have presented the Saxon rulers as "kings without a state," governing primarily through the power of symbolism and ceremony, and, although this hyperbole has provoked counterarguments showcasing their bureaucratic accomplishments, no scholars question the tremendous importance of imperial sacral power.[39]

36. The existence of an imperial Church system was questioned in Reuter, "The Imperial Church System of the Ottonian and Salian Rulers: A Reconsideration," *JEH* 33 (1982): 347–74, esp. 352–54. On the subsequent debates, see John Ott and Anna Jones, "Introduction: The Bishop Reformed," and Jones, "Lay Magnates, Religious Houses, and the Role of the Bishop in Aquitaine (877–1050)," in Ott and Jones, *Bishop Reformed*, 1–20, esp. 9, and 21–39, esp. 22. For the current state of the question, see Herwig Wolfram, *Conrad II (990–1039): Emperor of Three Kingdoms*, trans. Denise A Kaiser (University Park: Pennsylvania State University Press, 2006), 251–54; Steffen Patzold, *Episcopus: Wissen über Bischöfe im Frankenreich des späten 8. bis frühen 10. Jahrhunderts* (Ostfildern: Jan Thorbecke, 2008), 521–26; and John Eldevik, *Episcopal Power and Ecclesiastical Reform in the Greater German Empire: Tithes, Leadership, and Community, 950–1150* (Cambridge: Cambridge University Press, 2012), 7–10.

37. Joachim Wollasch, "Kaiser und Könige als Brüder der Mönche: Zum Herrscherbild in liturgischen Handschriften des 9. bis 11. Jahrhunderts," *Deutsches Archiv* 40 (1984): 1–20; Karl Leyser, "Ritual, Zeremonie, und Gestik: Das ottonische Reich," *Frühmittelalterliche Studien* 27 (1993): 1–26; Gerd Althoff, *Spielregeln der Politik im Mittelalter: Kommunikation in Frieden und Fehde* (Darmstadt: Primus, 1997), 21–56; David Warner, "Ritual and Memory in the Ottonian Reich: The Ceremony of *Adventus*," *Speculum* 76 (2001): 255–82; Hagen Keller, "Ritual, Symbolik und Visualisierung in der Kultur des ottonischen Reiches," *Frühmittelalterliche Studien* 35 (2001): 23–59.

38. Hartmut Hoffmann, *Mönchskönig und Rex Idiota: Studien zur Kirchenpolitik Heinrichs II. und Konrads II.*, MGH Studien und Texte 8 (Hannover: Hahn, 1993); Stefan Weinfurter, "Authority and Legitimation of Royal Policy and Action: The Case of Henry II," in *Medieval Concepts of the Past: Ritual, Memory, Historiography*, ed. Althoff, Johannes Fried, and Patrick J. Geary (Washington, DC: German Historical Institute, 2002), 19–37, esp. 30.

39. Althoff, *Die Ottonen: Königsherschaft ohne Staat* (Stuttgart: Kohlhammer, 2000). For conflicting views on Saxon administrative competence, contrast Karl Leyser, "*Theophanu Divina Gratia Imperatrix Augusta*: Western and Eastern Emperorship in the Later Tenth Century," in *The Empress Theophano: Byzantium and the West at the Turn of the First Millennium*," ed. Adelbert Davids (Cambridge: Cambridge University Press, 1995), 1–27, esp. 1–14 and 27, with David Bachrach, "Exercise of Royal Power," 389–419, esp. 389–91 and 419, and "Feeding the Host: The Ottonian Royal Fisc in Military Perspective," *Studies in Medieval and Renaissance History*, 3rd ser., 9 (2012): 1–43.

Italy

Italy was the home of the last effective Carolingian emperor, Louis II (850–75), Charlemagne's great-grandson, the emperor who led the alliances that expelled the Muslims from the mainland Italian cities. Unfortunately for the peace of Italy, he left no direct heir and therefore bequeathed potential claims on the Italian throne to his uncles and cousins, the kings of France, Germany, and Burgundy. From 875 to 962, during the "national period" of the *Regnum Italicum*, dozens of candidates contended for the crown, including some Italian magnates such as the marquesses of Spoleto and Friuli who were handicapped vis-à-vis their northern rivals because they had fewer resources and more local enemies. Central government deteriorated, even though there was still some bureaucratic competence left at the old royal capital of Pavia and some possibility of successful rule, at least temporarily, by installing crowds of relatives in positions of power.[40] The exception to general governmental decline was wealthy southern Italy, where the Eastern Roman Empire, ruled by the Macedonian dynasty (867–1028), was able to expand its territory in the heel and toe of the Italian boot at the expense of the southern Lombard princes.[41] Byzantine momentum in southern Italy would be slowed by Muslim raids and German emperors and then halted in the eleventh century by the arrival of uncontrollable Norman mercenaries "eager for plunder [*ad rapinam avidi*]."[42]

In 962 Otto I, who had been intervening in Italy sporadically since 950, secured his coronation as emperor. From then on the Saxon emperors would spend about a third of their time in Italy but would never find an effective way to govern it. Italian nobles were deferential when imperial armies were present but did as they pleased when they were away. The emperors failed to effectively harness the last remnants of Lombard bureaucracy, and when the archives of Pavia burned in 1022, no attempt was made to restore them. Instead the emperors attempted to project power by establishing control over major Italian bishoprics and monasteries, strong points important to

40. For overviews, see Giuseppi Sergi, "The Kingdom of Italy," in Reuter, *NCMH*, 3:346–71; François Bougard, "Public Power and Authority," and Stefano Gaspari, "The Aristocracy," in La Rocca, *Italy in the Early Middle Ages*, 34–58, 59–84.

41. André Gillou, "Production and Profits in the Byzantine Province of Italy (Tenth to Eleventh Centuries): An Expanding Society," *Dumbarton Oaks Papers* 28 (1974): 89–109; Michael McCormick, "The Imperial Edge: Italo-Byzantine Identity, Movement, and Integration, A.D. 650–950," in *Studies on the Internal Diaspora of the Byzantine Empire*, ed. Hélène Ahrweiler and Angeliki E. Laiou (Washington, DC: Dumbarton Oaks, 1998), 17–52; Loud, *Age of Robert Guiscard*, 18–21 and 50–54.

42. On the arrival of the Normans see Loud, *Age of Robert Guiscard*, 60–91. Phrase from Desiderius, *Dialogi de Miraculis S. Benedicti* I xi, ed. Gerhard Schwartz and Adolf Hofmeister, MGH SS 30(2) (Leipzig: Karl Hiersemann, 1929), 1113–74, esp. 1124.

an itinerant imperial court that required hospitality.[43] The greatest potential power base was the papacy, which the emperors sometimes dominated but never securely controlled. In the late tenth century, they fought bloodily with Roman noble factions in support of their favored papal candidates; in the early eleventh, popes from the family of the counts of Tuscolo artfully strove to accommodate both Roman and German interests; at midcentury, a Roman reform party appeared that became resolutely opposed to imperial control. The Italians had little love for their Roman emperors: a chronicler at San Andrea del Soratte (just north of Rome) complained that the arrival of Germans was always associated with bloodshed, plague, and cattle rustling;[44] from the other side Bishop Thietmar of Merseberg lamented, "Alas there are many conspiracies in the regions of Rome and Lombardy. For all visitors there is scant affection."[45]

Struggles over the Italian crown permitted dynamic changes at lower levels. Effective power devolved to marcher lords, counts, gastalds (managers of former royal properties), bishops, members of lineages that owned castelli—basically to anyone who could control territory and the soldiers it supported.[46] The new nucleated settlements produced agricultural surpluses that could support larger populations. Maritime cities developed international trade by piggybacking onto existing commercial systems. Venice, Bari, Amalfi, and Naples—never effectively conquered by either Lombards or Franks—proclaimed their theoretical Byzantine connections so long as these were profitable. Venice signed a special trade agreement with Constantinople in 992; some doges acquired elite Byzantine marriage connections.[47] Maritime cities also prospered through their less reputable connections to the Islamic world. Amalfi's surprisingly large merchant colony in Egypt may have originated in trading links established while the

43. Mathilde Uhlirz, "Die italienische Kirchenpolitik der Ottonen," *Mitteilungen des Instituts für Österreichische Geschichtesforschung* 48 (1934): 201–321; John W. Bernhardt, *Itinerant Kingship and Royal Monasteries in Early Medieval Germany, c. 936–1075* (Cambridge: Cambridge University Press, 1993), esp. 290–95; Thomas Vogtherr, *Die Reichsabteien der Benediktiner und das Königtum im hohen Mittelalter (900–1125)* (Stuttgart: Jan Thorbecke, 2000), 167–88.

44. Benedict of San Andrea del Soratte, *Chronicon*, ed. Giuseppe Zucchetti, *Il Chronicon di Benedetto Monaco di S. Andrea del Soratte e il Libellus de Imperatoria Potestate in Urbe Roma*, Fonti per la storia d'Italia 55 (Rome: Tipografia del Senato, 1920), esp. 186–87.

45. Thietmar, *Chronicon* VII ii, Holtzmann, 400; Warner, 309.

46. Roland Pauler, *Das Regnum Italiae in ottonischer Zeit: Markgrafen, Grafen und Bischöfe als politische Kräfte* (Tübingen: Max Niemeyer, 1982). For Florence, see Maria Elena Cortese, *Signori, castelli, città: L'aristocrazia del territorio fiorentino tra X e XII secolo* (Florence: Leo S. Olschki, 2007); for the Abruzzo and northeastern Lazio, see Howe, *Church Reform*, 10–18 and 123–48.

47. Claudio Azzara, "Important Figures in Italy in the Year 1000," in Urbańczyk, *Europe around the Year 1000*, 221–32, esp. 228; Antonio Carile, "Venezia e Bisanzio," in *Le relazioni internazionali nell'alto medioevo, Spoleto, 8–12 2010*, Settimane di studio della Fondazione CISAM 58 (Spoleto: CISAM, 2011), 629–90.

Fatimids were still in al-Mahdiyya.[48] The Islamic government in Cordoba, which recognized that Western trade could be profitable, issued treaties of safe-conduct to merchants from Amalfi, Barcelona, Narbonne, and Sardinia.[49] The collapse of the Umayyad caliphate at the start of the eleventh century freed Muslim pirates and local rulers to attack Sardinia, Luni, Calabria, Liguria, and other targets, but these expeditions provoked countercampaigns that culminated in a 1087 proto-Crusade that temporarily captured al-Mahdiyya and definitively gave the Italian city states the upper hand.[50] The leaders here were Pisa and Genoa, more Frankish than Byzantine in their orientation, who had a consistent interest in the islands of the western Mediterranean.[51] As trading and raiding brought gold into Italy, the prosperity of the commercial centers spread to the inland cities able to supply them with resources.[52]

France

West Francia was a mess. With the death of Charles the Fat in 888, the crown went to Odo (888–898), a son of Robert the Strong of Anjou who had distinguished himself against the Vikings. But Odo was soon opposed by a legitimist Carolingian faction, and in subsequent generations the crown would pass back and forth between the Robertians and the Carolingians, a rivalry abetted by the powerful rulers of East Francia who were not eager to see a strong French government near their borders. The relative strength of the competing Frankish monarchs may be indicated by the number of surviving royal charters issued by Louis the Foreigner (936–54) and Lothar (954–82), which amounts to about a fifth of the number issued by Otto I (936–72).[53] The rivalry degenerated to comic opera status when King Lothar, making a last West Frankish attempt at empire, invaded the Lorraine in 976, occupied Aachen, and reversed the eagle on Charlemagne's palace chapel complex, turning it from east to west so that it faced

48. Claude Cahen, "Un texte peu connue relatif au commerce d'Amalfi au Xᵉ siècle," *Archivio storico per le Province Napoletane* 34 (1953–54): 3–8; Patricia Skinner, *Medieval Amalfi and Its Diaspora, 800–1250* (Oxford: Oxford University Press, 2013), esp. 212–33.

49. Travis Bruce, "Politics of Violence and Trade," 127–42, esp. 130–31.

50. Cowdrey, "Mahdia Campaign," 1–29.

51. Steven A. Epstein, *Genoa and the Genoese, 958–1528* (Chapel Hill: University of North Carolina Press, 1996), 15–24.

52. Bryan Ward Perkins "The Towns of Northern Italy: Rebirth or Renewal?," in Hodges and Hobley, *Rebirth of Towns*, 16–27.

53. References cited in Hoffmann, "Der König und seine Bischöfe in Frankreich und in Deutschen Reich 936–1060," in *Bischof Burchard von Worms, 1000–1025*, ed. Wilfried Hartmann (Mainz, Ger.: Gesellschaft für mittelrheinische Kirchengeschichte, 2000), 79–127, esp. 81.

his own land—an irate Otto II chased him back to Paris, burning every-thing along the way.[54]

The battle for the West Frankish crown was settled in 987 by the corona-tion of Hugh Capet, a Robertian heir. Hugh directly controlled only about two and half counties (the Île de France), but he quickly made his son Robert co-king, an expedient that, repeated by his successors for two centuries, elim-inated vacancies on the throne and set the stage for Capetian rule throughout the High Middle Ages.[55] Some of the vassals who elevated Hugh Capet had more land than he did. Major territorial principalities in the north included Flanders, Normandy, Brittany, Anjou, and Blois-Chartres (amalgamated with Champagne after 1021). Long lineages skilled in marriages, acquisitions, and encastellation had assembled Flanders, Anjou, and Champagne. Ethnic ele-ments helped define Celtic Brittany and Viking Normandy, whose "pirates" soon became "Franks." The principalities south of the Loire such as Gascony (an ethnic unit), Aquitaine, Provence, and Catalonia, were less cohesive, less connected to the French crown, and more likely to be involved in Iberian affairs.[56] Although the early Capetian kings are often dismissed as nonenti-ties, they did distinguish themselves by surviving.

England

Tiny Wessex led England's revival, guided by the oldest royal family in Europe, kings the *Anglo-Saxon Chronicle* traces back to Cerdic and Cynric at the end of the fifth century. At first the Viking destruction of the island monasteries at the end of the eighth century had little effect on Wessex. More dangerous was the arrival of the "Great Army" around 865 that dom-inated York, Mercia, and East Anglia. Wessex fought back under Alfred (871–99), Edward the Elder (899–924), and Athelstan (924–39), winning the Danelaw piece by piece until York was finally conquered in 954.[57] The drive north included conquests, conversions, and institutional rebuilding

54. Thietmar, *Chronicon* III viii, Holtzmann, 106–7, Warner, 133. See Theo Riches, "The Carolingian Cap-ture of Aachen in 978 and Its Historiographical Footprint," in *Frankland: The Franks and the World of the Early Middle Ages. Essays in Honour of Dame Jinty Nelson*, ed. Paul Fouracre and Ganz (Manchester, UK: Manchester University Press, 2008), 191–208.

55. Jean Dunbabin, "West Francia: The Kingdom," in Reuter, *NCMH*, 3:372–97; Constance Brittain Bouchard, "The Kingdom of the Franks to 1108," in *NCMH* 4, pt. 2, ed. David Luscombe and Jonathan Riley-Smith (Cambridge: Cambridge University Press, 2004), 120–53; Jim Bradbury, *The Capetians: Kings of France, 987–1328* (New York: Hambledon Continuum, 2007), 67–128.

56. Jan Dhondt, *Études sur la naissance des principautés territoriales en France (IXᵉ–Xᵉ siècle)* (Bruges, Belg.: de Tempel, 1948), is the classic discussion of French territorial principalities. For current debates, see David Bates, "The Northern Principalities," and Michel Zimmermann, "Western Francia: The Southern Prin-cipalities," in Reuter, *NCMH*, 3:398–419 and 420–55.

57. On Wessex's triumph, see Sarah Foote, *Aethelstan: The First King of England* (New Haven: Yale University Press, 2011).

featuring boroughs or *burhs* (fortified settlements), shire reeves (sheriffs representing the king), and a pioneering use of the English vernacular in official documents.[58] The kingdom that resulted was relatively urbanized and prosperous.[59] It so effectively restored Latinate culture by importing texts and personnel from the Continent that scholars today now find it convenient to treat Late Saxon England as a cultural part of the Frankish heartland.[60] Here was one of Europe's strongest governments. Alfred ambitiously saw himself as an island-wide "king of the Anglo-Saxons"; some of his descendants claimed to be *imperator* and even *basileus* (the title used by the Byzantine emperor).[61] They legislated more than their Continental counterparts.[62] Marriage connections linked them to the Continent.[63]

Part of the strength of the English monarchy was a strong partnership with its church. Political discourse was "increasingly sacralized."[64] Its Church became monasticized as kings and queens supported new monasteries and protected them against both canons and lay lords. Dunstan (909–88), a nobleman who became a hermit at Glastonbury, was appointed abbot there by King Edmund (922–46); exiled to Ghent in 956, he returned in 957 to become bishop of London and Worcester, then archbishop of Canterbury (960–88). Together with Aethelwold (bishop of Winchester, 963–84) and Oswald (bishop of Worcester 962–92; archbishop of York, 972–92), Dunstan was the most distinguished of a triumvirate of

---

58. Lavelle, *Alfred's Wars*, 141–76.

59. Richard H. Britnell, *The Commercialization of English Society, 1000–1500*, 2nd ed. (Manchester, UK: Manchester University Press, 1996), esp. 5–22; Peter Sawyer, *The Wealth of Anglo-Saxon England* (Oxford: Oxford University Press, 2013).

60. For England as a "Carolingian state," see James Campbell, "Observations on English Government from the Tenth to the Twelfth Century," *TRHS*, 5th ser., 25 (1975): 39–54; H.R. Loyn, "Church and State in England in the Tenth and Eleventh Centuries," in *Tenth-Century Studies: Essays in Commemoration of the Millennium of the Council of Winchester and Regularis Concordia*, ed. David Parsons (London: Phillimore, 1975), 94–102 and 229–30; and Chris Wickham, *The Inheritance of Rome: Illuminating the Dark Ages, 400–1000* (New York: Penguin, 2009), 453–71. This idea is now so generally accepted that Simon Keynes, "England, 900–1016," in Reuter, *NCMH*, 3:456–84, is placed in the section on "Post-Carolingian Europe" rather than in the section on "Non-Carolingian Europe."

61. Keynes, "Edward, King of the Anglo-Saxons," in *Edward the Elder, 899–924*, ed. N.J. Higham and D.H. Hill (London: Routledge, 2001), 40–66, esp. 44–48; Lynn Jones, "From *Anglorum Basileus* to Norman Saint: The Transformation of Edward the Confessor," *Haskins Society Journal* 12 (2002): 99–120, esp. 108–13; Wickham, *Inheritance of Rome*, 457–58; Foote, *Aethelstan*, 212–16.

62. Nelson, "Rulers and Government," in Reuter, *NCMH*, 3:95–129.

63. Sheila Sharp, "The West Saxon Tradition of Dynastic Marriage with Special Reference to the Family of Edward the Elder," in Higham and Hill, *Edward the Elder*, 79–88; Foote, "Dynastic Strategies: The West Saxon Royal Family in Europe," in Rollason et al., *England and the Continent*, 237–53; Elizabeth M. Tyler, "Crossing Conquests: Polyglot Royal Women and Literary Culture in Eleventh-Century England," in *Conceptualizing Multilingualism in Medieval England, c. 800–c. 1250*, ed. Tyler (Turnhout, Belg.: Brepols, 2011), 171–96, esp. 176–83.

64. Mary Frances Giandrea, *Episcopal Culture in Late Anglo-Saxon England* (Woodbridge: Boydell, 2007), 55.

reformers who founded and restored monasteries, keeping certain ones under their own direct control even while they were serving as the king's favored bishops. David Knowles, who was unable to document any organized English Benedictine house at the start of the tenth century, found more than thirty communities of monks and a half dozen of nuns at its close, the pre-Conquest apogee.[65] In 963, papal approval was obtained to eject the secular canons from Winchester Cathedral and to hand it over to monks, initiating a trend that would ultimately result in nearly half of the dioceses in England having monks as their episcopal electors, a practice unique in Western Christendom.[66]

Spain

With the death of Al-Mansur (970–1002) and the ascent of Sancho el Mayor (1004–35), suddenly the Muslims were in disarray and the Christians united. Christian political unity would end when the dying Sancho divided his realm into fourths, and Spanish Muslims would later temporarily reunite twice more under some oppressive African "allies," the Almoravids and the Almohades, but momentum had shifted. Enriched by booty and tribute, the frontier states of Léon, Navarre, Aragon, and Barcelona soon blossomed.[67] The County of Barcelona in particular was able to create the "richest archives of eleventh-century Europe."[68] As a result, historians can study all sorts of social interactions, including many property disputes that have given rise to debates about whether or not Catalonia experienced its own feudal revolution around the year 1000.[69] On the other extreme, the realm of Léon-Castile was more court-centered, run by

65. David Knowles, *The Monastic Order in England: A History of Its Development from the Times of St. Dunstan to the Fourth Lateran Council, 943–1216* (Cambridge: Cambridge University Press, 1941), 31–36, 48, and 695.

66. Catherine Cubitt, "The Tenth-Century Benedictine Reform in England," *Early Medieval Europe* 6 (1997): 77–94; Mechtild Gretsch, *The Intellectual Foundations of the English Benedictine Reform* (Cambridge: Cambridge University Press, 1999); Blair, *Church in Anglo-Saxon Society*, 350–67; Julia Barrow, "The Chronology of the Benedictine 'Reform,'" in *Edgar, King of the English, 959–975: New Interpretations*, ed. Donald Scragg (Woodbridge: Boydell, 2008), 211–23.

67. General studies include Roger Collins, *Early Medieval Spain: Unity in Diversity, 400–1000* (New York: St. Martin's, 1983); Collins, "The Spanish Kingdoms," in Reuter, *NCMH*, 3:670–91; and Simon Barton, "Spain in the Eleventh Century, in Luscombe and Riley-Smith, *NCMH*, 4, pt. 2, 154–90.

68. Pierre Bonnassie, preface to *Els pergamins de l'Arxiu Comtal de Barcelona de Ramon Borrell a Ramon Berenguer I*, ed. Gaspar Feliu and Josep M. Salzach, 3 vols. Fundació Noguera Diplomataris 18–20 (Barcelona: Fundació Noguera, 1999), 1:9–16, esp. 9.

69. Bonnassie, *La Catalogne du milieu du Xᵉ à la fin du XIᵉ siècle: Croissance et mutations d'une société*, 2 vols. (Toulouse: Université de Toulouse-Le Mirail, 1975–76), portrays feudal disruption in Catalonia. Jeffery A. Bowman, *Shifting Landmarks: Property, Proof, and Dispute in Catalonia around the Year 1000* (Ithaca: Cornell University Press, 2004), esp. 211–25, questions some of Bonnassie's interpretations.

a self-proclaimed "emperor" whose neo-Gothic grand strategy of recon-quest would come to underpin much of the ideology of *reconquista*.[70]

How these little states were related to the rest of the Latin West is a subject of scholarly debate. Some claim that northern Spain in the tenth century was "a whole other world."[71] Yet many documents in the archives of the County of Barcelona were carefully dated with the regnal years of Hugh Capet and Robert the Pious, weak and distant kings but titular leaders of "Gallia" nonetheless. Interaction with the north was certainly increasing. Ecclesiastical reform movements such as the Peace of God appear early.[72] Rodulfus Glaber encountered Spanish monks at Cluny.[73]

Scandinavia

Scandinavia pivoted from predation to exploitation, converting not only to Christianity's books, Latin, and learning but also to its more organized governmental and economic systems. Did the decline of Viking raiding cause these developments or result from them? There is no clear answer. Fortification in depth was diminishing the profitability of attacks on Frank-ish Europe just as the Scandinavians were adopting many aspects of its civilization.

The traditional stories of conversions achieved by saintly missionar-ies and pioneering kings are now treated as insufficient by scholars who stress that prior to Christian "mission" and "institutionalization" there had been "infiltration," which some Christian-themed grave goods document at least for the wealthier people who had long-distance contacts.[74] The earliest Scandinavians to convert formally were members of the Viking diaspora who adopted the religion of their neighbors. In Normandy, despite immigration that lasted into the eleventh century, Scandinavian

70. Felipe Fernández-Armesto, "The Survival of a Notion of *Reconquista* in Late Tenth- and Eleventh-Century León," in Reuter, *Warriors and Churchmen*, 123–43; Deswarte, *De la destruction à la restauration*, esp. 46–65.

71. Achim Arbeiter, "Nordspanien zwischen Atlantik und Pyrenäen um das 10. Jahrhundert: Bau- und Kunstdenkmäler der erstarkenden christlichen Territorien," in Henning, *Europa im 10. Jahrhundert*, 337–50.

72. Bowman, "Councils, Memory, and Mills: The Early Development of the Peace of God in Catalonia," *Early Medieval Europe* 8 (1999): 99–129.

73. Rodulfus Glaber, *Historiae* III iv, France, 114–15. Debates over the extent of Cluniac influence in tenth- and eleventh-century Spain are discussed in Carlos M. Reglero de la Fuente, *Cluny en España: Los prioratos de la provincia y sus redes sociales (1073–ca. 1270)* (Léon: Centro de Estudios e Investigación "San Isidoro," 2008), esp. 59–100.

74. Sawyer, *Kings and Vikings*, 131–43; Stefan Brink, "New Perspectives on the Christianization of Scan-dinavia and the Organization of the Early Church," in Adams and Holman, *Scandinavia and Europe*, 163–75, esp. 164; Alexandra Sanmark, "The Role of Secular Rulers in the Conversion of Sweden," in *The Cross Goes North: Processes of Conversion in Northern Europe, AD 300–1300*, ed. Martin Carver (York: York Medieval Press, 2003), 551–563; Brink, "Christianization and the Emergence of the Early Church in Scandinavia," in Brink and Price, *Viking World*, 621–28.

"alienness" was soon reduced to some unusually tenacious family and community ties and a few new words associated with place names and sailing.[75] Anglo-Scandinavians, despite some Nordic idiosyncrasies, were soon worshipping in churches and getting buried in Christian graveyards.[76] The fortified Viking settlements of Ireland that in the ninth and tenth centuries had dominated its pastoral hinterlands, controlled its international commerce, and profited greatly from merchant fees, the slave trade, rents, and other sources of income had by the eleventh century become Ireland's first effective urban centers, now Christianized and under the control of Irish kings.[77] But diaspora conversions did not immediately result in religious change back home: the *Annals of Saint-Bertin* complain that after Charles the Bald had arranged for the baptism of a band of Vikings, showered them with gifts, and "sent them back to their own people, . . . afterward, like typical Northmen, they lived according to their pagan custom [*ritus*] just as before."[78]

Yet the same dynamics that caused the Vikings residing in greater Francia to regularize their religious beliefs ultimately also triumphed in Scandinavia. Latin kings and emperors systematically tried to convert their northern counterparts. Christian kings eventually emerged in Denmark with Harold Bluetooth ca. 960; in Norway with Olaf Tryggvason in 994; and in Sweden with Olaf Erikson, baptized ca. 1008—kings who freely accepted Christianity and eagerly employed it in state building.[79] New

75. Bates, *Normandy before 1066* (London: Longman, 1982), 15–24; Eleanor Searle, *Predatory Kinship and the Creation of Norman Power, 840–1066* (Berkeley: University of California Press, 1988), esp. 230–49; Elisabeth Ridel, "The Linguistic Heritage of the Scandinavians in Normandy," in Adams and Holman, *Scandinavia and Europe*, 149–59, esp. 151–52; Pierre Bauduin, *Le monde franc et les Vikings VIIIᵉ–Xᵉ siècle* (Paris: Albin Michel, 2009), esp. 343–51.

76. Lesley Abrams, "The Conversion of the Danelaw," in *Vikings and the Danelaw: Selected Papers from the Proceedings of the Thirteenth Viking Congress, Nottingham and York, 21–30 August 1997*, ed. James Graham-Campbell, Richard Hall, Judith Jesch, and David N. Parsons (Oxford: Oxbow Books, 2001), 31–44; Philip Rahtz and Lorna Watts, "Three Ages of Conversion at Kirkdale, North Yorkshire," in Carver, *Cross Goes North*, 289–309; Dawn Hadley, *The Vikings in England: Settlement, Society, and Culture* (Manchester, UK: Manchester University Press, 2006), esp. 192–236 and 262–64.

77. Benjamin Hudson, *Viking Pirates and Christian Princes: Dynasty, Religion, and Empire in the North Atlantic* (Oxford: Oxford University Press, 2005), 79–106; Valante, *Vikings in Ireland*, esp. 14, 47–48, 133–34, 150–51, and 161–64.

78. *Annales Bertiniani* 876, Grat, 206, Nelson, 195.

79. Coviaux, "Baptême et conversion des chefs scandinaves du IXᵉ eu XIᵉ siècle," in Bauduin, *Fondations scandinaves en Occident*, 67–80, charts the major conversions. See also Sverre Bagge, "The Transformation of Europe: The Role of Scandinavia," in *Eurasian Transformations, Tenth to Thirteenth Centuries: Crystallizations, Divergences, Renaissances*, ed. Johann P. Arnason and Björn Wittrock (Leiden, Neth.: Brill, 2004), 131–65, esp. 133–37; Luts E. von Padberg, "Der Abschluss der Missionsphase in Skandinavien durch die Errichtung der Kirchenprovinzen im 12. Jahrhundert," in *Vom Umbruch zur Erneuerung? Das 11. und beginnende 12. Jahrhundert: Positionen der Forschung*, ed. Jörg Jarnut and Matthias Wemhoff (Munich: Wilhelm Fink, 2006), 469–85; Nora Berend, ed., *Christianization and the Rise of Christian Monarchy: Scandinavia, Central Europe and Rus' c. 900–1200* (New York: Cambridge University Press, 2007), 73–213; Anders Winroth,

saints enhanced national identity.[80] There would still be many setbacks, the sparsely populated interior would require centuries to convert, and some of the seminomadic Sami seem to have retained their traditional religions until the modern era. Yet Adam of Bremen, writing in the third quarter of the eleventh century, could still claim with pride, "Behold that exceedingly fierce race of the Danes, of the Norwegians, or of the Swedes . . . that piratical people, by which, we read, whole provinces of the Gauls and of Germany were at one time devastated and which is now content with its bounds, and . . . everywhere admits eagerly, now that the native fury of its folk has been subdued, the preachers of the truth; and, since the altars of demons have been torn down, it builds churches far and wide."[81]

Eastern Europe

While the Vikings were attacking the West, their Swedish relatives were traveling east along the great rivers. These Rus' found no isolated churches ripe for plunder, and after Constantinople blocked their advance they settled down as traders, intermarried with local Slavic peoples, and built cities that included Novgorod and Kiev. Although the Rus' ultimately embraced Greek rather than Latin Christianity, Russia continued to provide a potential bridge between the two. In the Latin West in the eleventh and twelfth centuries Kievan princesses were in special demand thanks to a stricter interpretation of the laws prohibiting marriage among kin, which made it more difficult for the interrelated Frankish royal families to find legal marriage partners closer to home.[82]

The Conversion of Scandinavia: Vikings, Merchants, and Missionaries in the Remaking of Northern Europe (New Haven: Yale University Press, 2014), esp. 4, 112–18. For Norway alone, see Bagge, From Viking Stronghold to Christian Kingdom: State Formation in Norway, c. 900–1350 (Copenhagen: Museum Tusculanum Press, 2010), esp. 21–40.

80. Erich Hoffmann, "Politische Heilige in Skandinavien und die Entwicklung der drei nordischen Reiche und Völker," in Politik und Heiligenverehrung in Hochmittelalter, ed. Jörgen Petersohn (Sigmaringen: Jan Thorbecke, 1994), 277–324; Haki Antonsson, "The Early Cult of Saints in Scandinavia and the Conversion: A Comparative Perspective," and Åslaug Ommundsen, "The Cults of Saints in Norway before 1200," in Saints and Their Lives on the Periphery: Veneration of Saints in Scandinavia and Eastern Europe (c. 1000–1200), ed. Haki Antonsson and Ildar H. Garipzanov (Turnhout, Belg.: Brepols, 2010), 17–37 and 67–93.

81. Adam of Bremen, Gesta IV xliv, Schmeidler, 280, Tschan, 222–23. Adam's claims are nuanced in Anne-Sofie Gräslund, "New Perspectives on an Old Problem: Uppsala and the Christianization of Sweden," and Henrick Janson, "Adam of Bremen and the Conversion of Scandinavia," in Christianizing Peoples and Converting Individuals, ed. Guyda Armstrong and Ian N. Wood (Turnhout, Belg.: Brepols, 2000), 61–82, 83–88; also in Hans-Werner Goetz, "Constructing the Past: Religious Dimensions and Historical Consciousness in Adam of Bremen's Gesta Hamburgensis Ecclesiae Pontificum," in The Making of Christian Myths in the Periphery of Latin Christendom (c. 1000–1300), ed. Lars Boje Mortensen (Copenhagen: Museum Tusculanum Press, 2006), 17–51.

82. In general, see Thomas S. Noonan, "Scandinavians in European Russia," in Sawyer, Oxford Illustrated History of the Vikings, 134–55; Shepard, "The Origins of Rus' (c.900–1015)," and Simon Franklin, "Kievan Rus' (1015–1125)," in The Cambridge History of Russia, vol. 1, From Early Rus' to 1689, ed. Maureen Perrie (Cambridge:

In East Central Europe, Carolingian and German expansion had resulted in a German/Slavic frontier that stretched from the Baltic to the Adriatic.[83] German imperialism catalyzed the creation of counterstates. Defeat at the battle of the Lechfeld in 955 led to Hungarian state formation under the Arpad dynasty. Prince Géza converted toward Christianity in 972, still continuing to offer pagan sacrifices but explaining to shocked missionaries that he was wealthy enough to afford this particular indulgence. His less heterodox son, (St.) Stephen (1000–1038), received a crown from the pope, ruthlessly abolished tribal divisions, and amalgamated the Magyars and Slavs of the realm (privileging the former).[84]

The new Hungarian state bisected the Slavs of Eastern Europe. Those to the south fell under Byzantine domination.[85] Those in East Central Europe developed their institutions in the Frankish style. Bohemia, protected from the Hungarians by its mountains, greatly influenced by Bavaria, and blessed with a major market at Prague, took shape under the Přemyslid dynasty under the early-converting martyred king Vaclav (St. Wenceslas, 921–35). The Piast dukes of Poland, relatives and rivals of Bohemia's rulers, announced the conversion of prince and people in 966. The usual backsliding ensued. Around the year 1000 Emperor Otto III, in keeping with his vision of multiple realms united under his imperial rule, authorized episcopates and crowns for the new states. Military confrontations resumed after his death, and a Polish bid for hegemony over the western Slavs waxed and waned. While Polabians, Pomeranians, and other smaller groups tended to fall through the cracks, Bohemia and Poland ultimately developed national identities, institutions, and even an occasional awareness of common interests.[86]

Cambridge University Press, 2006), 47–72 and 73–97; and Shepard, "Rus'," in Berend, *Christianization and the Rise of Christian Monarchy*, 369–416. On brides from Kiev, see Nicolas de Baumgarten, *Généalogies et mariages occidentaux des Rurikides russes du Xe au XIIIe siècle* (Rome: Pontificium Institutum Orientalium Studiorum, 1927). Cautions about Baumgarten's methodology are expressed in Alexander Kazhdan, "Rus'-Byzantine Princely Marriages in the Eleventh and Twelfth Centuries," *Harvard Ukrainian Studies* 12–13 (1988–89): 414–29, esp. 428–29.

83. Wolfram, "New Peoples around the Year 1000," in Urbańczyk, *Europe around the Year 1000*, 391–408; Giuseppe Fornasari, "La cristianizzazione degli slavi: Problemi e prospettive di ricerca a partire da un recente volume," *Studi medievali*, 3rd ser., 47 (2006): 855–75. For the advent of the Slavs in Eastern Europe, see Florin Curta, *The Making of the Slavs: History and Archaeology in the Lower Danube* (New York: Cambridge University Press, 2001).

84. Marianne Sághy, "The Making of the Christian Kingdom in Hungary," in Urbańczyk, *Europe around the Year 1000*, 451–64; Berend, *At the Gate of Christendom: Jews, Muslims, and "Pagans" in Medieval Hungary, c. 1000–c. 1300* (New York: Cambridge University Press, 2001), 1–33; Berend, József Laszlovszky, and Béla Zsolt Szakács, "The Kingdom of Hungary," in Berend, *Christianization and the Rise of Christian Monarchy: Scandinavia*, 319–68.

85. Paul Stephenson, *Byzantium's Balkan Frontier: A Political Study of the Northern Balkans, 900–1204* (Cambridge: Cambridge University Press, 2000), esp. 117–50; Curta, *Southeastern Europe in the Middle Ages, 500–1250* (Cambridge: Cambridge University Press, 2006), 111–310.

86. Gábor Klaniczay, "The Birth of a New Europe about 1000 CE: Conversion, Transfer of Institutional Models, New Dynamics," in Arnason and Wittrock, *Eurasian Transformations*, 99–129, surveys the

The new Eastern European states, like their Scandinavian counterparts, adeptly adopted Frankish institutions to bolster monarchical power. They created new national identities out of new religious identities that were fostered by the cults of royal and national saints.[87] One distinctive characteristic of the Magyar and Slavic frontier polities was their ability to accommodate an impressive variety of minority peoples including Jews, Armenians, Orthodox Greeks, and pagan Turks. The eastern frontier states alternated between collaborating and fighting with the Rus' and the Greeks.[88]

∼

By the turn of the millennium, Latin Europe was well along on its way to recovery. Mass demographic migrations had largely ceased. In fact, a map of Europe's major ethnic groups around the year 1000 would be broadly accurate today, with the exception of the Turks, who were delayed a bit by Byzantines and Crusaders. Post-Carolingian political units had largely stabilized—even troubled West Francia, whose survival as a kingdom had at times appeared improbable.

There were changes. Brittany had lost its king, emerging from the chaos with a *dux* who was clearly affiliated with France. Kings had failed to establish themselves permanently in Provence, Burgundy, and other northern parts of the fragmented middle kingdom of Emperor Lothar. The old Anglo-Saxon kingdoms that had once constituted an alleged seven-kingdom "heptarchy" were casualties of the Viking invasions and the triumph of Wessex. The last Lombard duchies in Italy lost ground to the resurgent Western and Eastern empires and would ultimately fall to the same Norman mercenaries who would destroy Byzantine Italy. On balance, the Europe that emerged was a recognizable, reasonably stable prototype of today's Europe. It included many well-fortified microregions and some very powerful states, particularly on greater Francia's English,

---

historiography. See also Jerzy Strzelczyk, "Bohemia and Poland: Two Examples of Successful Slavonic State Formation," in Reuter, NCMH, 3:514–35; Petr Sommer, Dušan Třeštik, and Josef Žemlička, "Bohemia and Moravia," and Urbańczyk and Stanisław Rosik, "The Kingdom of Poland, with an Appendix on Polabia and Pomerania between Paganism and Christianity," in Berend, *Christianization and the Rise of Christian Monarchy*, 214–62 and 263–318. Andrzej Pleszczyński, *Birth of a Stereotype: Polish Rulers and Their Country in German Writings c. 1000 A.D.* (Leiden, Neth.: Brill, 2011), links early Polish development and eastern Saxon politics.

87. Aleksander Gieysztor, "Politische Heilige im hochmittelalterlichen Polen und Böhmen," and Gábor Klaniczay, "Königliche und dynastische Heiligkeit in Ungarn," in Petersohn, *Politik und Heiligenverehrung*, 325–41 and 343–61; Klaniczay, *Holy Rulers and Blessed Princesses: Dynastic Cults in Medieval Central Europe*, trans. Éva Pálmai (Cambridge: Cambridge University Press, 2002); Maria Bláhová, "The Function of the Saints in Early Bohemian Historical Writing," and László Veszprémy, "Royal Saints in Hungarian Chronicles, Legends, and Liturgy," in Mortensen, *Making of Christian Myths*, 83–119, 217–45.

88. Berend, "How Many Medieval Europes? The 'Pagans' of Hungary and Regional Diversity in Christendom," in *The Medieval World*, ed. Peter Linehan and Nelson (London: Routledge, 2001), 77–92.

Spanish, and German borders. The kings and ruling elites of this new order were eager to consolidate their power and to fix what had been broken.

REBUILDING THE CHURCH

One of the highest priorities was to rebuild the Church. In a world where ecclesiastical infrastructure and personnel had been severely disrupted and where the process of encastellation was reshaping the demography of countrysides, villages, and towns, what was required was a very literal ecclesiastical re-formation, one proceeding church by church. Elites had many reasons to take action, some of which were mundane. Families of any eminence held miscellaneous rights of patronage and privilege over churches within their jurisdictions, and they would have wanted to get these churches back into satisfactory operation.[89] Unattended ruined buildings and disputed properties were ongoing administrative and legal headaches. Moreover, increasingly concentrated settlement patterns required new churches to anchor and serve new villages. Conversely, the demographic shifts worked to the disadvantage of some older rural and suburban churches, which had suffered badly during the invasions and now needed not only reconstruction but also repurposing as chapels or hermitages subject to more central churches.[90]

Beyond the practicalities, there were more exalted spiritual reasons to take action. Organized prayers were part of the economy of salvation.[91] Their absence caused the sort of anxiety that King Lothar of France expressed in the mid-tenth century in regard to the monastery of St. Bavo in Ghent: "For many years, both because of the attacks of the pagans and the negligence of the inhabitants it has been deserted and turned into a solitude and made almost completely uninhabitable, to such an extent that almost nothing of the divine office is celebrated there."[92] To restore liturgy required habitable institutions and proper inhabitants for them: that is, priests, monks, and nuns living holy lives appropriate to their stations and performing the work of God.

Patrons quickly discovered that dedicated religious personnel were hard to find. Monastic chroniclers are negative about exiled monks, who were usually hard-pressed to maintain their traditional monastic observances

---

89. Susan Wood, *The Proprietary Church in the Medieval West* (New York: Oxford University Press, 2006), esp. 584–658.

90. Miller, *Formation of a Medieval Church*, 32–34, offers examples from the diocese of Verona.

91. Helen Foxhall Forbes, *Heaven and Earth in Anglo-Saxon England: Theology and Society in an Age of Faith* (Farnham, UK: Ashgate, 2013), 219–64.

92. Lothar, Charter issued at Laon on 11 December 954 or 958 (no. 2027 in Johann Friedrich Böhmer, *Regesta Chronologico-Diplomatica Karolorum* [Frankfurt-am-Main: Franz Varrentrapp, 1833], 192), in Christensen and Nielsen, *Diplomatarium Danicum*, sect. 1, 1:127–28 (doc. 324).

and who had often compromised their personal poverty by splitting up whatever corporate assets their communities still possessed. Exiled monks and nuns found it hard to train their replacements. The result was that even so dedicated and resourceful a patron as King Alfred was unable to assemble the personnel he needed to establish an edifying community at his new monastery at Athelney.[93] St. Gerald of Aurillac (d. 909), known in detail thanks to his *vita* written by Abbot Odo of Cluny (d. 942), also found this an impossible task: after the first monastery he had attempted to build collapsed because of a poor foundation, he did manage to succeed architecturally but "he was always turning over in his mind where to find monks of good character who would live in the place according to their rule." He sent some noble youths to a monastery famed for its discipline, but

> when these same youths were ordered to return, they became relaxed with a feminine softness through lack of masters, and neglected the rigor of their rule, and so the plan came to nothing. . . . Consequently, his mind was in a turmoil day and night, and he could not forget his wish to gather a community of monks. He often spoke of it with his household and friends. He was so moved by his desire for this that sometimes he exclaimed, "O, if it might be granted to me by some means to obtain religious monks, how I would give them all I possess."

Gerald never got his wish. As he lay dying, he looked down from his castle at his empty monastery and wept, lamenting that "only the monks are missing; they alone could not be found." Gerald, according to Odo, attended church services frequently and therefore ought to have been unusually knowledgeable about monastic worship, but if even a dedicated and wealthy patron could not find competent monks, then who could?[94]

In today's corporate terms, reform involved both physical plant and human resource issues. Unlike the Carolingian world, where monastic reform meant legalistic attempts at restructuring institutions according to the Benedictine Rule,[95] tenth- and early eleventh-century reforms, under-

---

93. Asser, *Life of King Alfred* xcii–xcviii, ed. William Henry Stevenson, *Asser's Life of King Alfred Together with the* Annals of Saint Neots *Erroneously Ascribed to Asser* (Oxford: Clarendon, 1904), 1–96, esp. 79–85; trans. Alfred P. Smyth, *The Medieval* Life of King Alfred the Great: *A Translation and Commentary on the Text Attributed to Asser* (New York: Palgrave, 2002), 1–54, esp. 45–48.

94. Odo of Cluny, *Vita S. Geraldi* II iv–viii and III i, ed. Anne-Marie Bultot-Verleysen, *Odon de Cluny: Vita sancti Geraldi Auriliacensis. Édition critique, traduction française, introduction et commentaires*, Subsidia Hagiographica 89 (Brussels: Bollandistes, 2009), 202–9 and 246–47, trans. Sitwell, *St. Odo of Cluny*, 89–180, esp. 136–40 and 162. On Gerald and on an alternative version of the vita, see Mathew Kuefler, *The Making and Unmaking of a Saint: Hagiography and Memory in the Cult of Gerald of Aurillac* (Philadelphia: University of Pennsylvania Press, 2014).

95. Josef Semmler, "Das Erbe der karolingischen Klosterreform im 10. Jahrhundert," in *Monastische Reformen im 9. und 10. Jahrhundert*, ed. Raymond Kottje and Helmut Maurer (Sigmaringen: Jan Thorbecke, 1989), 29–77, esp. 31–50.

taken in the wake of widespread destruction and disruption, were forced to start at a much more basic level. Ruined churches had to be rebuilt. Clerks whose ways of life had become irregular needed to be reformed, and new clerks had to be educated correctly. Ecclesiastical reformation in the High Middle Ages began as a very literal rebuilding and re-formation of the Latin Church, associated with encastellation, the rise of new local and regional authorities, and increasing prosperity.

A necessary first step was to re-form ecclesiastical patrimonies. Established institutions ideally controlled the resources they needed in order to operate independently. Churches had lost control over many properties during the chaos of the late ninth and early tenth centuries, and these proved to be very hard to reclaim. Neighbors of abandoned or poorly administered lands exploited them for hunting, pasturage, and forest products; more intensive and permanent encroachments soon followed. The most desirable lands would gravitate to the most powerful lords, those best able to defend their usurpations against all challengers. For example, for many years the dukes of Normandy lived in a major palace complex located within the former convent of Fécamp.[96] Thanks to encastellation, unwanted tenants could be very securely anchored.

In theory ecclesiastical property was protected by spiritual sanctions, but in practice these did not deter *mali Christiani* very effectively. Even the Carolingians, ostensible partners of the Church, had a spotty record of respecting ecclesiastical possessions.[97] A settlement between Louis the Pious and his son Pepin in 837, for example, involved an assembly of bishops that warned Pepin at some length about his own imperiled salvation and urged him to "restore to God's churches the property which had previously been battened on and ruined by his own supporters," but despite Pepin's repentance future ecclesiastical assemblies continued to demand restitutions.[98] The partial *Register* of Pope John VIII (872–82), the only curial collection of papal documents surviving from the late ninth through the early eleventh century, consists mostly of supernatural threats against those who were contemplating seizing Church property and anathemas against those who already had.[99]

The earliest use of the word *reformare* in the post-Carolingian world concerns real estate, not theology. Sources speak of re-forming the patrimonies of churches, that is, of reassembling lands lost to ecclesiastical control

---

96. Renoux, *Fécamp: Du Palais ducal au palais de Dieu: Bilan historique et archéologique des recherches menées sur le site du château des ducs de Normandie, IIe siècle A.C.–XVIIIe siècle P.C.* (Paris: CNRS, 1991).

97. Ian Wood, "Entrusting Western Europe to the Church, 400–750," *TRHS*, 6th ser., 23 (2013): 37–73, esp. 60–62.

98. *Annales Bertiniani* 837, Grat 21, Nelson, 36. For specific background, see Moore, *Sacred Kingdom*, 343–48; for the Carolingian record in general, see Susan Wood, *Proprietary Church*, 215–18, 247–51.

99. John VIII, *Epistolae et Decretae*, ed. Migne, *Pat. Lat.*, 126:651–966.

during the period of the barbarian invasions and Carolingian disintegration.[100] Even the most well-intentioned lords found this process difficult. In the Lorraine, for example, Bishop Adalbero of Metz (929–62) had trouble returning Gorze's property because so much of it was held by members of his own family; and bishop (St.) Gerard of Toul (963–994), as he reveals in a 974 charter, felt definitively compelled to return the possessions of Saint-Mansuy of Toul only after he had been "overcome by the extreme exhaustion of a fever, brought near death, . . . worn down by the violence of the disease."[101] Three generations of Ottos would reign before the territories of St. Maximin at Trier were largely restored.[102] Norman dukes were confronted on multiple occasions by monks carrying the relics of St. Wandregiselus but still took decades to agree to Saint-Wandrille's refoundation and to return some of its property; the campaign to persuade them to agree to restore Jumièges and its lands lasted well into the eleventh century.[103] Many properties never returned. The Italian border monasteries of Charlemagne's day never fully regained their immense holdings: San Vincenzo al Volturno in particular reclaimed only a sliver of its ninth-century wealth, and that very precariously. The English monasteries and convents of the first Saxon Age that had been restructured or dissolved during the Viking invasions never got back much of their former land.[104]

Generous new gifts helped compensate. Donations came from kings, great lords, and bishops, often working in partnership. When scholars combine all the restorations and new donations (which, given the

100. For examples, see Charles the Bald's charters to restore the ruinous church of Saint-Nazaire in Autun (26 July 854) and to reaffirm and reconstitute the possessions of Saint-Èvre (24 November 869), in Giry et al., *Recueil des actes de Charles II*, 1:432–34 (no. 165) and 2:328–35 (no. 330); or a Senlis charter (18 March 868), in Christensen and Nielsen, *Diplomatarium Danicum*, sect. 1, 1:63 (doc. 147). For this usage in *miracula*, see Aimoinus of Fleury, *Miracula Benedicti* II ii, Certain, 90–137, esp. 97; and Andrew of Fleury, *Miracula Benedicti* VI ii, Certain, 173–276, esp. 219. Reform may also refer to the restoration of rights and privileges, as in Ruotger, *Vita Brunonis* x (written in the late 960s), ed. Irene Ott, MGH SS *Rer Germ* n.s. 10 (Cologne: Böhlau, 1958), 10, where Bruno "reformed a monastery with its original privileges and immunities [*privilegis et immunitatibus pristinis reformavit*]." Some additional examples are in Lin Donnat, "L'idée de réforme monastique aux VIIe–XIe siècles," in *Abbon, Un abbé de l'an mil*, ed. Annie Dufour and Gillette Labory (Turnhout, Belg.: Brepols, 2008), 69–79, esp. 73–76.

101. John Nightingale, "Bishop Gerard of Toul (963–94) and Attitudes to Episcopal Office," in Reuter, *Warriors and Churchmen*, 41–62, esp. 52–55; Nightingale, *Monasteries and Patrons*, 71–86; Parisse, *Religieux et religieuses en Empire du Xe au XIIe siècle* (Paris: Picard, 2011), 44–45 and 55–71.

102. Nightingale, *Monasteries and Patrons*, 235–49.

103. On Saint-Wandrille, see Alain Dierkens, *Abbayes et chapitres entre Sambre et Meuse (VIIe–XIe siècles): Contribution à l'histoire religieuse des campagnes du haut Moyen Âge* (Sigmaringen: Jan Thorbecke, 1985), 243–44; Cassandra Potts, *Monastic Revival and Regional Identity in Early Normandy* (Woodbridge: Boydell, 1997), 24–25. See also Lucien Musset, "Jumièges," in *Jumièges: Congrès scientifique du XIII. centenaire, Rouen, 10–12 juin 1954*, 2 vols. (Rouen: Lecerf, 1955), 1:49–55.

104. Robin Flemming, "Monastic Lands and England's Defense in the Viking Ages," *EHR* 395 (1985): 247–65.

fragmentary state of the documentation, are impossible to separate), many conclude that the volume of ecclesiastical donations in the late tenth and early eleventh centuries is unparalleled and that more land was transferred to the Church at that time than ever before or since.[105] An analysis of several thousand charters from the monastery of Cluny places the high point of donations in the late tenth century.[106] A study of 7,500 private acts surviving from Carolingian and post-Carolingian Italy likewise puts the peak in donations in the late tenth century.[107]

By itself reconstitution of ecclesiastical patrimony did not solve the personnel problem. Patrons who tried to recruit their own holy canons, monks, and nuns ran the risk of being disappointed, just as King Alfred and Count Gerald of Aurillac had been. Over the course of the tenth century most found it expedient to outsource this job to ecclesiastical professionals, a process that turned some successful abbots into directors of international monastic federations. "Families" of monasteries had been an ancient tradition, and, although the *Rule of Benedict* may appear to envision isolated unaffiliated monasteries, Benedict himself had once supervised a dozen houses.[108] Because of the usefulness of monastic federations in reform, they became the norm in the millennial Church.[109] Communities could be linked by obedience to the same abbot and by the long-lasting spiritual bonds that could be established when an abbot shared treasured relics and saints' lives among his charges or established confraternities that featured the names of deceased monks of affiliated communities in the same books of prayer (*libri vitae*).[110] Scholars have marveled at the apparent spontaneity of the monastic revival that swept through Europe in the tenth and eleventh century.[111] It becomes easier to understand if

105. David Herlihy, "Church Property on the European Continent, 701–1200," *Speculum* 36 (1961): 81–105, esp. 95–97; Georges Duby, *The Early Growth of the European Economy: Warriors and Peasants from the Seventh to the Twelfth Century* (Ithaca: Cornell University Press, 1974), 165–66; Parisse, *Religieux et religieuses*, 50–52; Eldevik, *Episcopal Power*, 183–85.

106. Barbara Rosenwein, *To Be the Neighbor of Saint Peter: The Social Meaning of Cluny's Property, 909–1049* (Ithaca: Cornell University Press, 1989), 199.

107. Francois Bougard, "Actes privés et transferts patrimoniaux en Italie centro-septentrionale (VIIIᵉ–Xᵉ siècle)," *Mélanges de l'ÉFR—moyen âge*, 111 (1999): 487–987, esp. 539–62.

108. Gregory I, *Dialogi* II iii, ed. Adalbert de Vogüé and Paul Antin, *Grégoire le Grand: Dialogues*, 3 vols., Source chrétiennes 251, 260, and 265 (Paris: Éditions du Cerf 1979), 2:148–49, trans. Odo John Zimmerman, *Saint Gregory the Great: Dialogues*, Fathers of the Church 39 (Washington, DC: Catholic University of America Press, 1959), 66. Benedict's vita in *Dialogi* II is available in multiple English translations, some listed in Robert Godding, *Bibliografia di Gregorio Magno 1890/1989* (Rome: Città Nuova Editrice, 1990), 113–15.

109. Howe, *Church Reform*, 80–86; Constable, *The Abbey of Cluny: A Collection of Essays to Mark the Eleven-Hundredth Anniversary of Its Foundation* (Berlin: LIT, 2010), 86–87; Susan Wood, *Proprietary Church*, 413–33.

110. Parisse, *Religieux et religieuses*, 76–81.

111. Vauchez, *Spirtuality*, 36–37.

MAP 2. Centers of ecclesiastical activity in the millennial church. Map by Holt Haley-Walker Graphic Design & Illustration. Reproduced by permission.

we view it less as a sudden manifestation of monastic general will and more as the logical consequence of the process whereby kings, nobles, and bishops all across Europe secured help with monastic reforms from directors of international monastic *familia*.

The classic example is the monastery of Cluny, the centerpiece of discussions about monastic revival.[112] Count William of Aquitaine (d. 918) inherited an estate complex at Cluny in French Burgundy from his sister Ava[113] and dedicated it in 910 to Saints Peter and Paul in a famous foundation charter, whose provisions for monastic liberty are actually not all that different from similar language found in many charters of family monasteries.[114] The dedication to Peter and Paul would ultimately be parlayed into immense privileges and protections from the See of Peter, but that would take two centuries of litigation.[115] Also helpful was the custom, adopted in the same century in which the Capetian kings had begun to make their sons co-kings, by which the abbots of Cluny designated their own successors: seamless succession systems could reduce the possibility of outside interference and shift allegiances toward institutions rather than persons. The abbots of Cluny had excellent connections with the local nobility, which resulted in many early donations.[116] Because Cluny was distinguished by economic prosperity and impressive liturgical services, its customs were recorded and widely circulated.[117] Lay patrons begged the abbots of Cluny to reform their monasteries, which they did while gradually developing tighter ways to connect reformed monasteries to the motherhouse. Scholars have debated about whether there was an early "order of Cluny," as opposed to personal or temporary allegiances to the abbot, and, if so, when it would have first appeared—estimates range from the tenth century to as late as 1200.[118]

---

112. On Cluny as a monastic "system," see Rosenwein, *Rhinoceros Bound: Cluny in the Tenth Century* (Philadelphia: University of Pennsylvania Press, 1982), 3–29; Constable, "Cluny in the Monastic World of the Tenth Century," in *Secolo di ferro*, 1:391–448, esp. 391–92; and Dominique Iogna-Prat, "Cluny comme 'système ecclesial,'" in *Die Cluniazenser in ihrem politisch-sozialen Umfeld*, ed. Constable, Gert Melville, and Jörg Oberste (Münster: LIT, 1998), 13–92.

113. Constable, *Abbey of Cluny*, 1–4.

114. Scholars place the year of foundation in 909 or 910, based upon their assessments of the charter's inconsistent dating elements: Constable, *Abbey of Cluny*, 13–14, surveys the dispute and presents the case for 910. On parallels to this charter, see Howe, "*Monasteria Semper Libera*: Cluniac-Type Monastic Liberties in Eleventh-Century Central Italian Monasteries," *CHR* 78 (1992): 19–34; and Susan Wood, *Proprietary Church*, 374–75.

115. Susan Wood, *Proprietary Church*, 839–40; Constable, *Abbey of Cluny*, 23–30.

116. Rosenwein, *To Be the Neighbor of Saint Peter*, esp. 45–46.

117. Susan Boynton and Isabelle Cochelin, eds., *From the End of Night to the End of Day: The Medieval Customs of Cluny* (Turnhout, Belg.: Brepols, 2005), esp. 29–83.

118. Rosenwein, *Rhinoceros Bound*, 44–56; Constable, *Abbey of Cluny*, 46, 58, and 88–91; Odon Hurel and Denyse Riche, *Cluny: De l'abbaye à l'ordre clunisien, Xe–XVIIIe siècle* (Paris: Armand Colin, 2010), 20–74.

Monastic reform, however, is no longer a Cluniac story. Upon closer inspection, Cluny's system of monasteries looks more local, ad hoc, and ephemeral.[119] Its houses and liturgies were slow to arrive in England, where monastic restoration was an idiosyncratic royal initiative.[120] In the Aquitaine and other parts of France, while specific details of Cluniac customs had great influence, Fleury's customs embodying older usages may have animated a related and yet somewhat independent reform tradition.[121] In the mid-twentieth century Kassius Hallinger documented German liturgical reforms developing independently from Cluny, a movement he traced to the monastery of Gorze, although other institutions such as St. Maximin at Trier may have been more proximately responsible for disseminating Gorze liturgical practices to greater Germany.[122] Today even local reform studies find it difficult to define clear models and patterns. The study of monastic reform has become more fragmented, more evolutionary than revolutionary, less focused on single houses and heroes, more conscious of the central roles played by lay and ecclesiastical patrons.[123]

While it may be premature to speak of religious orders in the tenth century, individual impresarios of reform certainly did create their own personal temporary monastic federations. Gerard of Brogne (d. 959), a former soldier who had entered monastic life at Saint-Denis in France, returned to Flanders where he established a Benedictine monastery at Brogne (displacing some canons) and soon found himself asked by Count Arnulf the Great (918–65) to help other monasteries move toward a stricter Benedictinism.[124] Aethelwold (d. 984), starting with Abingdon in 954, founded or

---

119. Rosenwein, introduction to *Rhinoceros Bound*, esp. xiii; Bouchard, "Merovingian, Carolingian and Cluniac Monasticism: Reform and Renewal in Burgundy," *JEH* 41 (1990): 365–88.

120. Pfaff, *Liturgy in Medieval England*, 102 and 243–48.

121. Donnat, "Les coutumes monastiques autour de l'an Mil," in Iogna-Prat and Picard, *Religion et culture autour de l'an Mil*, 17–24, esp. 20–23.

122. Kassius Hallinger, *Gorze-Kluny. Studien zu den monastischen Lebensformen und Gegensätzen im Hochmittelalter*, 2 vols. (Rome: "Orbis Catholicus" Herder, 1950–51); Nightingale, *Monasteries and Patrons*, esp. 1–3; T.I.I.J. McCarthy, *Music, Scholasticism, and Reform: Salian Germany, 1025–1125* (Manchester, UK: Manchester University Press, 2009), esp. 11–13.

123. The current historiography is surveyed in *Ecclesia in Medio Nationis: Reflections on the Study of Monasticism in the Central Middle Ages*, ed. Steven Vanderputten and Brigitte Meijns (Louvain, Belg.: Leuven University Press, 2011), esp. 7–45.

124. Gerard's career, reconstructed from late and tendentious sources, is analyzed in Daniel Misonne, "Gérard de Brogne e sa dévotion aux reliques," *Sacris Erudiri* 25 (1982): 1–26; and Dierkens, *Abbayes et chapitres entre Sambre et Meuse*, 197–243. On his comital support, see Walter Mohr, *Studien zur Klosterreform des Grafen Arnulf I. von Flandern: Tradition und Wirklichkeit in der Geschichte der Amandus-Klöster* (Louvain: Leuven University Press, 1992); Ugé, *Creating the Monastic Past in Medieval Flanders*, 4–6 and 31–35; and Vanderputten, *Monastic Reform as Process*, 34. For skepticism about his vita's list of eighteen monasteries reformed, see Vanderputten and Meijns, "Gérard de Brogne en Flandre, État de la question sur les réformes monastiques du Xe siècle," *Revue du Nord* 92 (2010): 271–95.

reformed six to ten abbeys in England, providing much of the dynamism for the tenth-century English monastic reform.[125] Poppo of Stavelot Malmedy reformed twenty houses.[126] Romuald, the emblematic saint of the Italian eremitical revival who founded or was given dozens of monasteries by patrons who included Emperor Otto III, gained fame as "the father of the reasonable hermits who lived according to a rule."[127] William of Volpiano (d. 1031), born into a noble family near Turin, attached himself to Abbot Maiolus of Cluny and was invited in 989 to reform Saint-Bénigne at Dijon; then imperial bishops in the Lorraine asked for his help; in 1000–1001 he was able to found Fruttuaria on his Italian family's own estates; in 1001 Duke Richard II of Normandy (996–1026) invited him to reform the new monastery located at his palace at Fécamp, a base from which William ultimately reformed Jumièges, Saint-Michel, Saint-Ouen at Rouen, and other monasteries (his biography claims forty; modern scholars have managed to document thirty-three).[128] Richard of Saint-Vanne (d. 1046) spent more than forty years promoting disparate reforms in monasteries and houses of canons in northeastern France and the upper Lorraine.[129]

As ecclesiastical rebuilding progressed, reconstructing existing churches became less important than building new ones. New foundations increased in tenth- and eleventh-century France.[130] In Anjou, for example, restorations, not new foundations, were favored by Geoffrey Greymantle (960–87), new foundations by Fulk Nerra (987–1040).[131] Burgundian nobles built relatively few new churches in the tenth century, more family foundations in the

---

125. Michael Lapidge, "Three Latin Poems from Aethelwold's School at Winchester," *Anglo-Saxon England* 1 (1972): 85–137, esp. 92.

126. Dorothee Schäfer, "Studien zu Poppo von Stablo und den Klosterreformen im 11. Jahrhundert" (PhD diss., University of Munich, 1991); Philippe George, "Un réformateur lotharingien de choc: L'abbé Poppon de Stavelot (987–1048)," *Revue Mabillon*, n.s., 10 (1999): 89–111.

127. Jean Leclercq, "Saint Romuald et le monachisme missionaire," *Revue bénédictine* 72 (1962): 307–323; Howe, "The Awesome Hermit: The Symbolic Significance of the Hermit as a Possible Research Perspective," *Numen* 30 (1983): 106–19. The quotation is from Bruno of Querfurt, *Vita Quinque Fratrum* ii, ed. and trans. Marina Miladinov, in *Vitae Sanctorum Aetatis Conversionis Europae Centralis (saec. X–XI)*, ed. Gábor Klaniczay (Budapest: Central European University Press, 2013), 183–313, esp. 204–5.

128. The major source for William of Volpiano is Rodulfus Glaber, *Vita Willelmi*, ed. Neithard Bulst, repr., and trans. France and Paul Reynolds, and appended to *Rodulfus Glaber: The Five Books of the Histories*, ed. France, 254–99. Explications are in Bulst, *Untersuchungen zu den Klosterreformen Wilhelms von Dijon (962–1031)* (Bonn: Ludwig Röhrscheid, 1973); Véronique Gazeau, "Guillaume de Volpiano en Normandie: état des questions," *Tabularia "Études"* 2 (2002): 35–47, http://www.unicaen.fr/mrsh/craham/revue/tabularia/pdf/gazeau.pdf ; and Mariano del Omo, "Guglielmo da Volpiano e l'ambiente spirituale del suo tempo," *Studia monastica* 46 (2004): 349–63.

129. Vanderputten, *Imagining Religious Leadership in the Middle Ages: Richard of Saint-Vanne and the Politics of Reform* (Ithaca: Cornell University Press, 2015), esp. 165–67.

130. Susan Wood, *Proprietary Church*, 372.

131. Bernard Bachrach, *Fulk Nerra*, 88.

eleventh.[132] New churches were required by a new ecclesiastical "grid." In Latin Europe each diocese was divided up into geographical units based upon particular churches, and each Christian was affiliated to one of them, depending upon his or her place of residence. This parish system was an innovation. The ancient Church had emphasized the central importance of dioceses and their cathedral churches but had shown less concern about more local places of worship. The same people often worshipped at small churches built by the great landowners; sought baptisms, burials, and other services at more distant episcopal "baptismal churches" staffed by groups of clergymen; and flocked to cathedral churches on special feasts. Although these possibilities were not eliminated in the High Middle Ages, a tighter administrative structure was developing that depended more on the local church. One cause of the shift was Carolingian tithe legislation because, in order to verify payment, each family needed one official place to tithe.[133] Tithe boundaries were hardening in the tenth century, and questions about who owed tithes to whom were increasingly debated.[134] In the areas bordering the Frankish realm, the same process occurred slightly later. In England new villages became centers for new parishes not only because of the introduction of more formal tithing but also because of the partial breakdown of the earlier collegiate churches, the minsters, which had been damaged by Viking attacks and undermined by a changing landscape of new *burhs* and disintegrating royal estates.[135] Although questions about the shape and meaning of parishes would not be completely settled until the thirteenth century, the period between 950 and 1050, when specific churches came to serve the inhabitants of well-defined blocks of territory, has been hailed as a *mutation de la situation ecclésiastique locale*.[136] Old and new ecclesiastical infrastructure had to be accommodated to the new system.

132. Bouchard, *Sword, Miter, and Cloister: Nobility and the Church in Burgundy, 980–1198* (Ithaca: Cornell University Press, 1987), 102–3.

133. Constable, *Monastic Tithes: From Their Origins to the Twelfth Century* (Cambridge: Cambridge University Press, 1964), 34–39. On the possibility that the changes also reflect non-tithe-related developments in lordship and social structure, see Michel Lauwers, ed., *La Dîme, l'Église et la société féodale* (Turnhout, Belg.: Brepols, 2012), esp. 12–14, 87–90, and 107.

134. Eldevik, *Episcopal Power*, esp. 75–76 and 92–96.

135. Norman J. G. Pounds, *A History of the English Parish: The Culture of Religion from Augustine to Victoria* (Cambridge: Cambridge University Press, 2000), 17–40; Blair, *Church in Anglo-Saxon Society*, 295–323, 345–46, 368–425.

136. Joseph Avril, "La 'paroisse' dans la France de l'an Mil," in *Le roi de France et son Royaume autour de l'an Mil: Actes du Colloque Hugues Capet 987–1987, La France de l'an Mil, Paris–Senlis, 22–25 juin 1987*, ed. Parisse and Barral i Altet (Paris: Picard, 1992), 203–18, esp. 204 and 212; Brigitte Resl, "Material Support I: Parishes," in *Christianity in Western Europe, c. 1100–c. 1500*, ed. Miri Rubin and Walter Simons, Cambridge History of Christianity 4 (Cambridge: Cambridge University Press, 2009), 99–106. On the ultimate shape of

Church building was uniting Latin Christians spiritually at the very same time that encastellation was sharpening their local political divisions. To understand this paradox it is necessary to recognize that rebuilt and new churches tended to be more connected to the greater "catholic" Church: first, because the builders and artisans were often imported; second, because priests, monks, and nuns all had to come from somewhere, and while local personnel almost always dominated, some new clerks were out- siders affiliated with or employed by monastic confederations prosperous enough to have surplus personnel and resources. Schoolmasters and choir- masters were especially likely to be imported, often on the recommendation of well-traveled reformers. A great deal of scholarly energy has been spent attempting to define sharply contrasting "national churches" such as Celtic vs. English, French vs. German, or Latin vs. Greek, but the movement to rebuild and reform tended to erode rather than enhance these divisions.[137]

The Norman Church offers a striking example of the universalizing effects of ecclesiastical rebuilding. This was not true of the Norman bish- ops themselves, who during the tenth century went from perhaps a single resident bishop at Rouen to a full complement in the major dioceses but who, insofar as they can be traced, seem to have been local men, some connected to the ducal family; the deans and archdeacons exhibit sim- ilar local roots.[138] The newly rebuilt monasteries, however, were much more international. Although all the old Norman monasteries had been destroyed by the Vikings, they were refounded with the aid of the Norman dukes: their numbers increased from perhaps one in 950, to five in 990, to thirty-three in 1070.[139] The dukes were eager to recruit qualified person- nel, with the result that in the millennial Church their abbots exhibited

parishes, see Léopold Genicot, *Rural Communities in the Medieval West* (Baltimore: Johns Hopkins Univer- sity Press, 1974), esp. 90–107.

137. John Blair and Richard Sharpe, introduction to *Pastoral Care before the Parish*, ed. Blair and Sharpe (Leicester: Leicester University Press, 1992), 1–10, esp. 2, make this point for the Celtic/English division.

138. Lucien Musset, "Un millénaire oublié: La remise en place de la hiérarchie épiscopale en Normandie autour de 990," in *Papauté, monachisme et théories politiques: Études d'histoire médiévale offertes à Mar- cel Pacaut*, ed. Pierre Guichard, Marie-Thérèse Lorcin, Jean-Michel Poisson, and Michel Rubellin, 2 vols. (Lyon: Centre interuniversitaire d'histoire et d'archéologie médiévales/Presses universitaires de Lyon, 1994), 2:563–73. On lesser officials, see David S. Spear, "Les doyens du chapitre cathédral de Rouen durant la péri- ode ducale," *Annales de Normandie* 33 (1983): 91–119; and Spear, "Les archidiacres de Rouen au cours de la période ducale," *Annales de Normandie* 34 (1984): 15–50.

139. Bates, *Normandy before 1066*, 189 and 218; Musset, "Monachisme d'époque franque et mona- chisme d'époque ducale en Normandie: Le problème de la continuité," in *Aspectes du monachisme en Normandie (IVᵉ–XVIIIᵉ siècles: Actes du Colloque scientifique de l' "Année des abbayes normandes," Caen, 18–20 octobre 1979* (Paris: Vrin, 1982), 55–74; Anne Goulet, "Les invasions normandes entre Loire et Seine (840–930): Le répercussions sur les établissements monastiques," *Positions des thèses soutenues par les élèves de la promotion pour obtenir le diplôme d'archiviste paléographe* (1989): 85–94, esp. 92–93; Potts,

an "astonishing diversity of origins": about 15 percent are known to have been born outside Normandy; at one time or another at least sixteen of the thirty-three monasteries were ruled by a foreign abbot.[140] Outsiders included William of Volpiano (d. 1031), who was charged by Duke Richard II with the reorganization of many Norman monasteries; several Italian monks who arrived in his wake and became abbots themselves, including Abbot John of Fécamp (1028–78); several abbots from Germany; and many more.[141] For broader European history the most important were two extraordinary Italian schoolmasters: Lanfranc of Pavia, later archbishop of Canterbury (1070–89), who crossed the Alps ca. 1030, worked as a teacher, and then became prior of Bec (ca. 1045–63);[142] and Anselm of Aosta, philosopher and later archbishop of Canterbury (1093–1109), who, perhaps attracted by Lanfranc's fame, joined him at Bec in 1059.[143] Ultimately the monastic schools shaped by these foreigners helped train many Norman bishops, abbots, and other officials, and in the wake of the Norman conquests clerks trained in Normandy's cosmopolitan monasteries would become prominent in the episcopates of England, southern Italy, and the Holy Land.

Revival heartened the West. The demoralization caused by the invasions is encapsulated by the depressing *Annals of Xanten*, which report that in 848 "the pagans, as they were accustomed to do, severely injured the Christians"; and in 849 that "paganism [*gentilitas*] from the north as usual severely injured Christianity [*Christianitas*]."[144] God was chastising his people. By the millennium things had changed. Violence had not been ended by the process of internal fortification and the creation of the new kingdoms—quite the contrary—but Europe was more prosperous and confident. Church leaders viewed the change of fortune in religious terms, and they claimed that the proper way to give thanks to God was to rebuild the Church.

Monastic Revival, 19–35; Gazeau, *Normannia monastica: Princes normandes et abbés bénédictins (Xᵉ–XIIᵉ siècle)*, 2 vols. (Caen: CRAHM, 2007), 1:7–17.

140. Gazeau, *Normannia monastica*, 1:193 and 197.

141. Gazeau, ibid., 1:193–229, discusses abbots who came from outside Normandy. Volume 2 of *Normannia monastica* is a monastery-by-monastery prosopographical dictionary of Norman abbots from the tenth to the twelfth century.

142. Margaret Gibson, *Lanfranc of Bec* (Oxford: Clarendon, 1978), 20–28; Gazeau, *Normannia monastica*, 1:194. For an Italian perspective on his career, see *Lanfranco di Pavia e l'Europa del secolo XI nel IX centenario della morte (1089–1989): Atti del convegno internazionale di studi (Pavia, Almo Collegio Borromeo, 21–24 settembre 1989)*, ed. Giulio D'Onofrio (Rome: Herder, 1993).

143. Richard Southern, *Saint Anselm: A Portrait in a Landscape* (Cambridge: Cambridge University Press, 1990), 3–18, explores what is known about Anselm's arrival in Normandy. For a recent overview, see Sally N. Vaughn, *Archbishop Anselm, 1093–1109: Bec Missionary, Canterbury Primate, Patriarch of Another World* (Burlington, VT: Ashgate, 2012).

144. *Annales Xantenses* 848–49, ed. Bernhard von Simson, MGH *SS Rer Germ* 12 (Hannover: Hahn, 1909), 16.

CHAPTER 3

"A WHITE MANTLE OF CHURCHES"

> Just before the third year after the millennium, throughout the whole
> world, but most especially in Italy and Gaul, men began to recon-
> struct churches, although for the most part the existing ones were
> properly built and not in the least unworthy. But it seemed as though
> each Christian community were aiming to surpass all others in the
> splendour of construction. It was as if the whole world were shaking
> itself free, shrugging off the burden of the past, and cladding itself
> everywhere in a white mantle of churches. Almost all the episcopal
> churches and those of monasteries dedicated to various saints, and lit-
> tle village chapels, were rebuilt better than before by the faithful.
>
> —Rodulfus Glaber (d. ca. 1046), *Historiae Libri Quinque*

A WORLD OF NEW CHURCHES?

Rodulfus Glaber, in one of the most memorable images coined by a medieval chronicler, envisions millennial Europe donning a "white mantle
of churches."[1] To portray the dynamism of the action he surrounds the
phrase with transitive verbs. To stress its universality he invokes "the
whole world" and specifies the churches of "each Christian community"
from little village chapels to great cathedrals. Rodulfus's white mantle is
even shinier in Latin than in English: the *vestis* of the new churches is
candida, "shining white," an adjective reserved in the New Testament for

1. Rodulfus Glaber, *Historiae* III iv (cf. III vi), France, 114–17 (cf. 126–27). The iconic status of this meta-
phor is indicated by its presence in titles such as "A White Garment of Churches: Romanesque and Gothic
Art" (video recording), Art of the Western World 2 (New York: PBS, 1989) and Hiscock, *White Mantle of
Churches*.

the garments of angels and of Christ after his resurrection. A *vestis candida* would have been a gloriously white piece of clothing. Was it a baptismal robe?[2] Or perhaps an alb, the full-length white garment donned by priests when they vested for the liturgy? The alb would have been the only white outer garment that the black-robed monk Rodulfus would ever have had any occasion to wear, either as a celebrant of the Mass or as a participant in very special processions. Yet a closer examination of the new churches themselves might lead one to imagine that Rodulfus's white mantle could have been a Roman toga.

The new churches proclaimed *Romanitas* (Romanness) by their construction in stone, Rome's premier building material. In transalpine Europe builders favored gleaming white limestone, in Italy marble. They deliberately sought whiteness.[3] The nineteenth-century romantics, who rediscovered medieval churches only after they had been darkened by the coal smoke of the Industrial Revolution, imagined them as dark, brooding structures. Now, thanks to cleaning with high-pressure water spray, we can recognize in temporarily gleaming Romanesque and Gothic buildings what Rodulfus meant, at least until modern pollution resumes its work of destruction. Stone was not an inevitable choice. In most non-Mediterranean regions the primary building material had been wood.[4] The verb for "to build" in Old English was *timbran*.[5] What was novel about Rodulfus's white mantle of churches was that in some regions stone was triumphing over wood. In others it was eclipsing brick banding and rubble construction. And although the chronological pace varied regionally, stone vaults and towers were starting to replace wooden roofs and steeples.

2. White baptismal gowns are assumed in *The Bobbio Missal: A Gallican Mass-Book (MS Paris Lat. 13246)*, 3 vols., ed. Elias Avery Lowe (London: Henry Bradshaw Society, 1920), 2:75. They became so universal that baptism itself could be designated by the Anglo-Saxon term *Fulwiht*: see Peter Brown, *The Rise of Western Christendom: Triumph and Diversity, A.D. 200–1000*, 2nd ed. (Oxford: Blackwell, 2003), 487.

3. Renoux, *Fécamp*, 454–56, discusses the tricks master builders used to enhance whiteness. Christ's tomb in the Old English "Dream of the Rood" was of "bright stone": see Edward B. Irving, Jr., "Crucifixion Witnessed or Dramatic Interaction in *The Dream of the Rood*," in *Modes of Interpretation in Old English Literature: Essays in Honour of Stanley B. Greenfield*, ed. Phyllis Rugg Brown, Georgia Ronan Crampton, and Fred C. Robinson (Toronto: University of Toronto Press, 1986), 101–12, esp. 109.

4. Although dated in many respects, still unsurpassed in breadth is Josef Strzyygowski, *Early Church Art in Northern Europe with Special Reference to Timber Construction and Decoration* (New York: Harper & Brothers, 1928). See also Günter P. Fehring, "Die Stellung des frühmittelalterlichen Holzkirchenbaues in der Architekturgeschichte," *Jahrbuch des Römisch-Germanischen Zentralmuseums Mainz* 14 (1967): 179–97. The symbolism of the shift from wood to stone is discussed in Bandmann, *Early Medieval Architecture*, 143–46.

5. Fisher, *Introduction to Anglo-Saxon Architecture*, 24; Nicholas Howe, "The Landscape of Anglo-Saxon England: Inherited, Invented, Imagined," in *Inventing Medieval Landscapes: Senses of Place in Western Europe*, ed. John Howe and Michael Wolfe (Gainesville: University Press of Florida, 2002), 91–112, esp. 96.

Stone's triumph was Rome's triumph. The new churches "copied" specific ancient churches, especially Constantine's St. Peter's basilica in Rome, which has been acclaimed "the most important church design ever composed" and the "most imitated model in the Latin West,"[6] and Constantine's Anastasis rotunda above the Holy Sepulchre in Jerusalem.[7] The importance of these prototypes is easy to overlook because medieval architects—unlike their modern counterparts, who tend to equate imitation with reproduction—evoked their sacred models symbolically, which was possible through minimal similarities in name, detail, material, gross form, or function.[8] The spatial arrangement of interrelated churches could mark a city as a "new Rome" or a "new Jerusalem." Also indicative of Roman inspiration is the use of *spolia*, architectural elements taken from old Roman buildings.[9] In regions where Roman ruins were common this might have been nothing more than opportunistic recycling, but in many cases the builders transported their Roman souvenirs over long distances, despite great difficulty and expense. Masons also attempted, with widely varying degrees of success, to re-create versions of Roman columns, capitals, arcades, and other features.

6. Quotations from Kenneth John Conant, *A Brief Commentary on Early Medieval Church Architecture, with Especial Reference to Lost Monuments* (Baltimore: Johns Hopkins University Press, 1942), 6. Concerning this see Richard Gem, "St. Peter's Basilica in Rome c. 1024–1159: A Model for Emulation?," in *Romanesque and the Past: Retrospection in the Art and Architecture of Romanesque Europe*, ed. John McNeill and Richard Plant (Leeds: British Archaeological Association, 2013), 49–66, esp. 59–62. Even (old) Saint Peter's painting programs had great influence in Italy and beyond: see especially William Tronzo, "The Prestige of St. Peter's: Observation on the Function of Monumental Narrative Cycles in Italy," in *Pictorial Narrative in Antiquity and the Middle Ages*, ed. Herbert L. Kessler and Marianna Shreve Simpson (Washington, DC: National Gallery of Art, 1985), 93–114; Tronzo, "I grandi cicli pittorici romani e la loro influenza," in *La Pittura in Italia: L'Altomedioevo* (Milan: Electa, 1994), 355–68; and Herbert L. Kessler, *Old St. Peter's and Church Decoration in Medieval Italy*, CISAM 17 (Spoleto: CISAM, 2002), esp. 45–96.

7. Richard Krautheimer, "Introduction to an Iconography of Medieval Architecture," *Journal of the Warburg and Courtauld Institutes* 5 (1942): 1–33, esp. 3–20 and 31–33; repr. with a postscript in his *Studies in Early Christian, Medieval, and Renaissance Art* (New York: New York University Press, 1969), 115–50, esp. 118–35 and 147–50. Hesitations about Krautheimer's faith in the seminal role played by ancient models are presented in Catherine Carver McCurrach, "*Renovatio* Reconsidered: Richard Krautheimer and the Iconography of Architecture," *Gesta* 50 (2011): 41–69.

8. Krautheimer, "Introduction to an Iconography," 13–17 or 128–31; Bandmann, *Early Medieval Architecture*, 38 and 50; Morris, *Sepulchre of Christ*, 58–67, 120–26, and 153–65. Current theories of architecture as image are surveyed in Carolyn Marino Malone, *Saint-Bénigne de Dijon en l'an Mil, Totius Galliae Basilicis Mirabilior: Interprétation politique, liturgique et théologique* (Turnhout, Belg.: Brepols, 2009), 11–22.

9. On spolia, see Dale Kinney, "The Concept of Spolia," in *A Companion to Medieval Art: Romanesque and Gothic in Northern Europe*, ed. Conrad Rudolph (Oxford: Blackwell, 2006), 233–52. On how intentionally re-use recalls Rome, contrast John McNeill, "*Veteres Statuas Emit Rome*: Romanesque Attitudes to the Past," in *Romanesque and the Past*, ed. McNeill and Plant, 1–24, esp. 16–17, with Michael Greenhalgh, *Marble Past: Monumental Present: Building with Antiquities in the Mediaeval Mediterranean* (Leiden, Neth.: Brill, 2009), esp. 525.

Tenth-century Romanitas was often mediated through Carolingian models, so much so that some art historians have advocated lumping Carolingian and early Romanesque architecture together as a "First Romanesque" style, which would have preceded a more refined and decorated "Second Romanesque."[10] This might tempt an observer to conclude that what appear to be echoes of the glories of ancient Christian Rome are really imitations of the Carolingian Renaissance. Yet Rome's influence is also obvious in non-Carolingian areas such as pre-Viking England, as Nicholas Howe demonstrated in a study strikingly titled "Rome: Capital of Anglo-Saxon England."[11] People participated in a timeless, ideal Roman Empire, and, although intermediate architectural models existed, all Roman echoes, direct and indirect, potentially glorified Rome, its Church, and the unity of Latin Christendom.

OTTONIAN ARCHITECTURE

Rodulfus Glaber located his postmillennial building boom "especially in France and Italy," the regions he knew best. He failed to note that, decades earlier, eastern Francia had begun enshrining its imperial pretensions in grand new cathedrals and monasteries. Similar myopia has afflicted Spanish, French, British, and American scholars who until the mid-twentieth century failed to recognize the role Ottonian architecture played in the transition from Carolingian to Romanesque.[12]

10. Krautheimer, "The Carolingian Revival of Early Christian Architecture," *Art Bulletin* 24 (1942): 1–38; repr. with a postscript in his *Studies*, 203–65. For the ensuing scholarly discussion, see Rosamond McKitterick, *Perceptions of the Past in the Early Middle Ages* (Notre Dame: University of Notre Dame Press, 2006), 106–7, note 31; Judson J. Emerick, "Building *More Romano* in Francia during the Third Quarter of the Eighth Century," in *Rome across Time and Space: Cultural Transmission and the Exchange of Ideas c. 500–1400*, ed. Claudia Bolgia, McKitterick, and John Osborne (Cambridge: Cambridge University Press, 2011), 127–50, esp. 142–47; McCurrach, "*Renovatio* Reconsidered," 41–69. On debates over the meaning of "Romanesque," see Eric Fernie, "Romanesque Architecture," in Rudolph, *Companion to Medieval Art*, 295–313, esp. 301–6, and Fernie, "The Concept of the Romanesque," in *Romanesque and the Past*, ed. McNeill and Plant, 283–89.

11. Nicholas Howe, "Rome: Capital of Anglo-Saxon England," *Journal of Medieval and Early Modern Studies* 34 (2004): 147–72. See also Jane Hawkes, "*Iuxta Morem Romanorum*: Stone and Sculpture in Anglo-Saxon England," in *Anglo-Saxon Styles*, ed. Catherine E. Karkov and George Hardin Brown (Albany: SUNY Press, 2003), 69–99, esp. 87–88.

12. Outside of Germany, "Ottonian architecture" rarely appeared as an analytical category prior to the publication of Louis Grodecki, *L'Architecture ottonienne* (Paris: Armand Colin, 1958). For debates about this periodization, see Richard Plant, "Architectural Developments in the Empire North of the Alps: The Patronage of the Imperial Court," in Hiscock, *White Mantle of Churches*, 29–56, esp. 29–31; and Willibald Sauerländer, "Romanesque Art 2000: A Worn Out Notion?," in *Romanesque Art and Thought in the Twelfth Century: Essays in Honor of Walter Cahn*, ed. Colin Hourihane (University Park: Princeton Index of Christian Art with Penn State University Press, 2008), 40–56, esp. 41–42.

The leaders of this rebuilding were the Saxon kings, the Latin West's most impressive and effective rulers. They attempted to wield power through military force, control of local elites, and personal presence, and to do this successfully they needed spiritual authority. Sacral kingship required elaborate ceremonies.[13] To stage these, the German rulers spent much of their wealth creating grand imperial monasteries and churches that offered an itinerant court not only venues for hospitality but also spectacular theatrical backdrops analogous to those found in Rome, Aachen, and Constantinople. The term "Ottonian architecture" highlights this imperial initiative, though it needs to be construed flexibly because the Saxon dynasty and its architectural projects do not perfectly align: ecclesiastical construction was less dramatic during the earlier years, and some characteristic projects still continued long after the Salian dynasty had taken over.

The Carolingian influence on Ottonian architecture is easy to understand. Carolingian buildings were abundant in the Frankish political heartland between the Meuse and the Moselle, where the greatest concentration of Carolingian family properties had been located, and in the area between the Moselle and the Rhine, which included Aachen, Charlemagne's imperial capital. German kings resided in Carolingian palace complexes at Nijmegen and Frankfurt, and they could visit living examples of late Carolingian architecture at Seligenstadt (built by Einhard, around 832–840), Corvey (its abbey church rebuilt 873–85), and Werden (825–75), with a slightly later "west work" (a massive entrance complex opposite the main altar at the eastern end of the church), buildings so respected that they escaped extensive remodeling during the tenth and eleventh centuries. Alpine monastic centers such as Reichenau and Saint-Gall still preserved Carolingian buildings and libraries. Direct sources of classical inspiration could be found in Italy itself, where, following the imperial coronation of 962, the Ottonian court often resided.

In evoking Rome, the earliest Ottonian churches remained faithful to Carolingian prototypes and incorporated their characteristic innovations such as double-apsed designs;[14] west works;[15] the use of prominent

---

13. Karl Leyser, "Sacral Kingship," in his *Rule and Conflict in an Early Medieval Society: Ottonian Saxony* (Bloomington: Indiana University Press, 1979), 75–107; Michael McCormick, *Eternal Victory: Triumphal Rulership in Late Antiquity, Byzantium, and the Early Medieval West* (New York: Cambridge University Press, 1986), 362–87; Yitzhak Hen, *The Royal Patronage of Liturgy in Frankish Gaul to the Death of Charles the Bald (877)* (London: Boydell for the Henry Bradshaw Society, 2001), esp. 16–19, 81–83, and 120–46.

14. Bandmann, *Early Medieval Architecture*, 219–22; McClendon, *Origins of Medieval Architecture*, 159–60.

15. For debates on the term "west work," see Bandmann, *Early Medieval Architecture*, 201–12; Dagmar von Schönfeld de Reyes, *Westwerkprobleme: Zur Bedeutung des Westwerke in der kunsthistorischen Forschung* (Weimar: Verlag und Datenbank für Geisteswissenschaften, 1999); and McClendon, *Origins of Medieval Architecture*, 188–93.

flanking towers in the west works;[16] and the addition of multiple radiating chapels around choirs to accommodate increasing numbers of ordained canons and monks.[17] From the mid-tenth century onward, Ottonian architecture began to feature more original touches such as smoother integration of transept and nave, alternation of pillar and pier supports in the nave to produce ordered divisions of space, and wall decorations that included recesses, pilasters, and blind arches echoing Italian stonework. Love of symmetry characterizes Ottonian architecture, reflecting the learning of builders who were knowledgeable about Euclidian geometry, Christian number symbolism, and the Roman architectural lore of Vitruvius.[18]

All the Saxon emperors sponsored ecclesiastical building projects, beginning with Otto I (936–973) at Magdeburg, a marketplace that drew visitors from all over Europe. There he constructed a grand palace and a royal monastery that he ultimately converted into the cathedral of St. Maurice, his burial place. Although Otto's cathedral was destroyed by fire in the early thirteenth century, archaeological excavation suggests that it was originally a two-apsed basilica with an atrium in the west. Its somewhat archaic columnar supports were spolia—Late Antique marble, porphyry, and granite columns—transported all the way from the area of Rome to their new home on the Elbe.[19] According to Thietmar

16. Classical Western basilicas lacked church towers. Jean Hubert, *L'Art préroman* (Chartres: Jacques Laget, 1974), 13–15, 22–23, 80–85, presents evidence for their origin as stone and wood towers in northern France and soon in Anglo-Saxon England in the sixth and seventh century, perhaps analogous to the corner towers of fortified villas. Caillet, "Le mythe du renouveau architectural roman," *CCM* 43 (2000): 341–69, esp. 352, argues that basilican churches with towers had developed originally in the Late Antique East, citing archaeological evidence from Cilicia and northeastern Syria as well as an unprovenanced mosaic in the Louvre. On the early medieval diffusion of towers, see Roger Stalley, *Early Medieval Architecture* (Oxford: Oxford University Press, 1999), 121–30.

17. Ambulatories with radiating chapels are not securely documented in the West prior to the late sixth century. See Gillian Mackie, *Early Christian Chapels in the West: Decoration, Function, and Patronage* (Toronto: University of Toronto Press, 2003), 69–80; and McClendon, *Origins of Medieval Architecture*, 204–6. On their proliferation in Carolingian churches, see Cyrille Vogel, "Note et communication: La multiplication des messes solitaires au moyen âge, essai de statistique," *Revue des sciences religieuses* 55 (1981): 206–13, esp. 206–10.

18. Hiscock, *The Wise Master Builder: Platonic Geometry in Plans of Medieval Abbeys and Cathedrals* (Aldershot, UK: Ashgate, 2000), 25–95; and Tessa Morrison, "Architectural Planning in the Early Medieval Era," *Journal of the Australian Early Medieval Association* 5 (2009): 147–63.

19. Cord Meckseper, "Antike Spolien in der ottonischen Architektur," in Poeschke, *Antike Spolien in der Architektur*, 179–204, esp. 179–88; Joachim Ehlers, "Magdeburg—Rom—Aachen—Bamberg: Grablege des Königs und Herrschaftsverständnis in ottonischer Zeit," in *Otto III.— Heinrich II. Eine Wende?*, ed. Bernd Schneidmüller and Stefan Weinfurter (Sigmaringen: Jan Thorbecke, 1997), 47–76, esp. 49–55; and Matthias Puhle and Gabriele Klöster, eds., *Otto der Grosse und das Römische Reich: Kaisertum von der Antike zum Mittelalter, Austellungskatalog: Landesausstellung Sachsen-Anhalt aus Anlass der 1100. Geburtstages Ottos des Grossen* (Regensburg: Schnell & Steiner, 2012), esp. 623–27.

of Merseburg (d. 1018), who had spent much of his life as a Magdeburg clerk, "The emperor had precious marble, gold, and gems brought to Magdeburg. And he ordered that relics of the saints should be enclosed in all the columns."[20] This was certainly a grand statement of Romanitas whether Otto's ostentation was inspired by the basilicas of Christian Rome, his increasing involvement in Italy, his imperial pretensions, or all of the above.

In Saxony Otto pursued similar projects, including a new basilica and diocese at Merseburg and major building campaigns at Gernrode and Quedlinburg. Archbishop Bruno of Cologne, Otto's half-brother and chancellor, had inherited an impressive cathedral church which he seems to have expanded into a five-aisle basilica like St. Peter's or St. John Lateran; Bruno also began to grandly rebuild St. Pantaleon's Abbey, today one of the best preserved of these imperial projects, which became a burial place for him and later for Otto's Byzantine daughter-in-law, the empress Theophanu.[21]

The geographical arrangement of churches might have imperial resonances. Emperor Henry II (1002–25) created a new Rome at Bamberg on properties belonging to him and his wife, Kunegunde. At the Council of Frankfurt in 1007, he announced to the assembled bishops that "because there remains to me no hope of acquiring offspring, I have made Christ my heir. For some time now, I have secretly offered my most valued possessions as a sacrifice to the Unborn Father, namely my own person and whatever I have acquired or am yet to acquire. . . . I have already conceived the desire to establish a bishopric in Bamberg and today I wish to bring this just plan to fruition."[22] After some drama, Henry won their assent. He built a giant cathedral, with double apses and double crypts and a transept in the west, dedicating the main altar to Peter and Paul. The city of Bamberg itself became "equal to the city of Rome [*Arcem Romanam se gestit*

---

20. The foundation of Magdeburg is described in Thietmar's *Chronicon* II iii–xxii, esp. xvii, Holtzmann, 40–65, esp. 58–59, Warner, 91–108, esp. 104.

21. Hans Joachim Kracht, *Geschichte der Benediktinerabtei St. Pantaleon in Köln, 965–1250* (Siegburg, Ger.: Franz Schmitt, 1975), 4–51; Günther Binding, "Ottonische Baukunst in Köln," and Hans Peter Neuheuser, "Der Kölner Dom unter Erzbischof Bruno," in *Kaiserin Theophanu: Begegnung des Ostens und Westens um die Wende des ersten Jahrtausends*, ed. Anton von Euw and Peter Schreiner, 2 vols. (Cologne: Schnütgen-Museum, 1991), 1:281–98, 1:299–310; Anne Behrend-Krebs, *Die ottonischen und romanischen Wandmalereien in St. Gereon, St. Maria im Kapitol und St. Pantaleon in Köln* (Münster: Tebbert KG, 1994), 272–344, esp. 272–73.

22. Thietmar of Merseburg, *Chronicon* VI xxxi, Holtzmann, 310–13, Warner, 258. See Helmut Fussbroich, "Das Grab der Kaiserin Theophanu in Sankt Pantaleon zu Köln," in *Kaiserin Theophanu: Prinzessin aus der Fremde—des Westreichs Grosse Kaiserin*, ed. Gunther Wolf (Cologne: Böhlau, 1991), 295–300.

FIGURE 7. Ottonian architecture, St. Pantaleon façade, Cologne, late tenth century.
Photo credit: Erich Lessing/Art Resource, NY.

habere coaequam]."[23] Among the similarities signaled by Henry's biographers were its exalted new church dedicated to St. Peter, its alleged seven hills, a cross-shaped pattern of five churches built within and around the city that was supposed to evoke Rome's ecclesiastical geography, and, not

23. Gerhard of Seeon, *Dedicatio Libri*, ed. Karl Strecker, MGH *Poetae Latini Medii Aevi* 5 (Leipzig: Karl W. Hiersemann, 1937), 396–98, esp. 397; discussed in Stefan Weinfurter, *Heinrich II (1002–1024): Herrscher am Ende der Zeiten* (Regensburg: Friedrich Pustet, 1999), 250–51 and 323.

least, the city's status as an imperial capital, Henry II's favored residence and chosen burial site.[24]

German prince bishops constructed other great churches. Archbishop Bruno's Cologne was rivaled by Mainz, the city that claimed the right to crown the king. Archbishop Willigis of Mainz (975–1011), perhaps the most influential bishop of his era, built an ambitious new cathedral, one of the largest churches in Christendom. Although it burned to the ground on the day of its consecration in 1009, it was rebuilt and dedicated again in 1036.

The cathedral of Mainz had a three-aisled nave and an unusually long west transept, longer even than the present 380-foot structure that stops short of the bishop's chapel, today unconnected to it, where part of the original end wall can still be seen in the chapel's external wall. In the early tenth century, the former cathedral, which had been dedicated to St. Peter, had already been rebuilt outside the walls, like St. Peter's in Rome, and had been integrated into a stational liturgical cycle like Rome's. Willigis's new cathedral deepened the architectural parallels, echoing St. Peter's in its associated buildings, its atrium, and its bronze doors. He made it possible to stage the royal coronation at Mainz in a way that would echo the imperial coronation rites in Rome.[25]

All the *gesta* and vitae of Ottonian bishops praise their heroes as great builders.[26] Some were even hailed as urban planners.[27] After the reign

---

24. Adalbertus of Bamberg, *Vita S. Heinrici Regis* ix–xiii, ed. Marcus Stumpf, MGH SS *Rer Germ* 69 (Hannover: Hahn, 1999), 223–324, esp. 246–642; Ehlers, "Magdeburg–Rom–Aachen–Bamberg," 47–76, esp. 64–71; Garrison, *Ottonian Imperial Art and Portraiture: The Artistic Patronage of Otto III and Henry II* (Burlingon, VT: Ashgate, 2012), 113–63; Ulrike Siewert, "Die Bedeutung des Kollegiatstiftes St. Stephan in der Bischofsstadt Bamberg von der Bistumsgründung bis zum ausgehenden Mittalalter," in *Bischofsbild und Bischofssitz: Geistige und geistliche Impulse aus regionalen Zentren des Hochmittelalters*, ed. Hanns Peter Neuheuser (Münster: Aschendorff, 2013), 63–88, esp. 63–68.

25. Dethard von Winterfeld, *Die Kaiserdome Speyer, Mainz, Worms und ihr romanisches Umland* (Wurzburg: Zodiac–Echter, 1993), 116–64; Michael Matheus, "Zur Romimitation in der *Aurea Moguntia*," in *Landesgeschichte und Reichsgeschichte: Festschrift für Alois Gerlich zum 70. Geburtstag*, ed. Winfried Dotzauer, Wolfgang Kleiber, Michael Matheus, and Karl-Heinz Spiess (Stuttgart: Franz Steiner, 1995), 35–49; Weinfurter, *Heinrich II*, 47–50.

26. Hatto Kallfelz, ed., *Lebensbeschreibungen einiger Bischöfe des 10.–12. Jahrhunderts* (Darmstadt: Wissenschaftliche Buchgesellschaft, 1973), 8–10; Wolfgang Giese, "Zu Bautätigkeit von Bischöfen und Äbten des 10. bis 12. Jahrhunderts," *Deutsches Archiv* 38 (1982): 388–438; Stephanie Haarländer, Vitae Episcoporum: *Eine Quellengattung zwischen Hagiographie und Historiographie, Untersucht an Lebensbeschreibungen von Bischöfen des Regnum Teutonicum im Zeitalter der Ottonen und Salier* (Stuttgart: Anton Hiersemann, 2000), 200–224. For attestations in illustrated lives, see Cynthia Hahn, *Portrayed on the Heart: Narrative Effect in Pictorial Lives of Saints from the Tenth through the Thirteenth Century* (Berkeley: University of California Press, 2001), 151–52 and 204.

27. Steffen Patzold, "L'épiscopat du haut Moyen Âge du point de vue de la médiévistique allemande," *CCM* 48 (2005): 341–58, esp. 353–54.

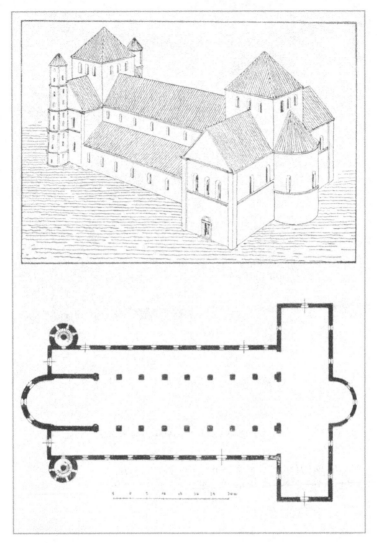

FIGURE 8. Mainz cathedral of Archbishops Willigis and Bardo, early eleventh century. From Rudolf Kautzsch, *Die Romanischen Dome am Rhein* (Leipzig: E. A. Seemann, 1922), 13.

of Henry II, when emperors became less active in church construction, the imperial bishops still carried on, especially in the Rhineland. Later on some Gregorian reformers faulted the German bishops of the late tenth and early eleventh centuries for being far too involved in the political and military affairs of this world and too willing to tolerate lay domination of the Church. But these righteous critics were often preaching from pulpits built by their predecessors.

FIGURE 9. Rome re-created, bronze door framed with Corinthian capitals from the cathedral of Willigis of Mainz. Photo credit: Max Hirmer, Max Hirmer Verlag #784.2978.

OTTONIAN INFLUENCE

In *The Making of the Middle Ages*, Richard W. Southern identified as the major feature of the cultural geography of the West "the distinction between the lands of Germanic and Romance speech," which constituted a "widening . . . gulf between the eastern and western halves of the Latin world."[28] During the tenth and eleventh centuries, however, that gulf was still fairly easy to cross thanks to the way the German and Romance worlds merged in the former Middle Kingdom of Emperor Lothar—that

28. Richard W. Southern, *The Making of the Middle Ages* (New Haven: Yale University Press, 1953), esp. 16–20.

is, the Low Countries (where the Dutch were still Deutsch), the Lorraine, Burgundy, and Italy. The western and southern lands of the Reich were able to transmit Ottonian architecture to a wider world.[29]

Liège was the Ottonian St. Petersburg. Its location on the River Meuse, an important trade artery, allowed counts of Flanders and western tradesmen to participate directly in the life of the empire. From Liège, literate émigrés could launch themselves even farther west. Prior to the investiture controversy, its prince bishops were usually drawn from the imperial court, and the most famous was Bishop Notker (972–1008), a Swabian noble who had served Otto I for many years before he received the diocese of Liège together with its overlapping, although slightly smaller, secular principality.[30] Liège prospered after Notker walled and developed it. His major church was the H-shaped cathedral of Saint-Lambert, built in a two-transept design that would spread throughout the empire. It was intended to rival the greatest churches of Germany and to provide a setting suitable for the emperor himself. On its eastern end Notker constructed associated churches like those surrounding the atrium of Old St. Peter's in Rome.[31] His cathedral anchored a citywide pattern of churches laid out *in modum crucis*, evoking not only Rome but also Jerusalem (as did the several copies of the Church of the Holy Sepulchre that would be built in this diocese during the eleventh and twelfth centuries).[32] A triumphal column surmounted by a cross invoked the grandiose imperial columns of Rome. The Church of St. John the Evangelist was inspired by the palace chapel at Aachen, although it was destined to be the burial place of Notker, not Charlemagne.[33] Liège has been described as a "city of clerks."[34] Perhaps its ecclesiastical activity limited it to some extent, for even though it was able to weather the investiture contest by backing the emperors, it fared poorly in local conflicts after the imperial power had been weakened. Bruges ultimately inherited much of its commerce.

There were similar imperial outposts to the south in the Lorraine; these included Verdun, where Bishop Haymon (988–1024) built an Ottonian cathedral complex, and Cambrai-Arras, whose eleventh-century cathedral was a project of Gerard I (1012–51) and his nephew Lietbert (1051–76),

29. Ingrid Voss, "La Lotharingie, terre de rencontres, X^e–XIe siècles," in Iogna-Prat and Picard, *Religion et culture autour de l'an Mil*, 266–72.

30. For the political and intellectual situation of Notker and Liège, see J.R. Webb, "Hagiography in the Diocese of Liège (950–1130)," in *Hagiographies*, 6:809–904, esp. 809–22.

31. Elizabeth den Hartog, *Romanesque Architecture and Sculpture in the Meuse Valley* (Leeuwarden, Neth.: Eisma, 1992), 46–50.

32. On the argument for Jerusalem symbolism, see ibid., 33–42.

33. On copies of the Palace Chapel, see McClendon, *Origins of Medieval Architecture*, 197–99.

34. Luc-François Genicot, introduction to *Les Églises mosanes du XIe siècle* (Louvain: Publications universitaires de Louvain, 1972), xxxiv–xxxvi, attempts to tabulate the clerical population.

descendants of the dukes of Lower Lotharingia who were ecclesiastical suffragans of the Archbishop of Rheims.[35] The Lorraine hosted some of the most influential monastic reformers, including Gerard of Brogne (d. 959), John of Gorze (d. 974), and William of Volpiano (d. 1031). The decentralized reforms associated with Gorze and with St. Maximin at Trier, which generally deferred to imperial bishops, spread throughout Germany and the Kingdom of Burgundy. Their architectural concomitants have not been systematically studied, although a case has been made for associating the Gorze reforms with the construction of outer crypts on the eastern apse, permitting some simplification of the grand entrance constructions of the west work.[36]

Germany's architectural revival found echoes in distant places, including Normandy. The Normans appropriated the Carolingian past, finding architectural inspiration in surviving buildings such as Saint-Riquier and Corvey. They were also inspired by contemporary Ottonian churches such as St. Pantaleon at Cologne and St. Michael's at Hildesheim, which provided useful structural solutions for configuring west works, ambulatories, chapels, and supporting columns.[37] Thanks in part to the German and Italian abbots the dukes recruited, Normandy developed its own early Romanesque style ahead of many other French regions.

The Anglo-Saxons rebuilt their churches. William of Malmesbury (d. ca. 1143), in an image worthy of Rudolphus Glaber, reports that in mid-tenth-century England monasteries and convents of monks and nuns "were rising up in a wave [*surgebant*]."[38] Anglo-Saxon builders emphasized continuity with the early English Church by constructing their new churches on ancient sites, modifying rather than destroying old buildings. Often they used groups of churches, each usually built to a smaller scale than the

35. On Verdun, see Jean-Pol Evrard, "Verdun, au temps de l'évêque Haymon (988–1024)," in Iogna-Prat and Picard, *Religion et culture autour de l'an Mil*, 273–78, esp. 276–78. On Cambrai-Arras, see T.M. Riches, "Bishop Gerard I of Cambrai-Arras, the Three Orders, and Human Weakness," and Ott, "Bishop Lietbert of Cambrai and the Construction of Episcopal Sanctity in a Border Diocese around the Year 1100," in Ott and Jones, *The Bishop Reformed*, 122–36 and 137–60.

36. Warren Sanderson, "Monastic Reform in Lorraine and the Architecture of the Outer Crypt, 950–1100," *Transactions of the American Philosophical Society*, n.s., 61 (1971): 17–36, and "Monastic Architecture and the Gorze Reforms Reconsidered," in Hiscock, *White Mantle of Churches*, 81–90 (includes bibliography).

37. Maylis Baylé, "L'Architecture romane en Normandie," and Carol Heitz, "Influences carolingiennes et ottoniennes sur l'architecture religieuse normande," in *L'architecture normande au moyen age*, vol. 1, *Regards sur l'art de bâtir. Actes du colloque de Cerisy-la-Salle (28 septembre—2 octobre 1994)*, ed. Baylé (Caen: Presses universitaires de Caen, 1997), 13–35 and 37–48, esp. 16–19, 42–48.

38. William of Malmesbury, *Gesta Pontificum Anglorum* I xviii, ed. and trans. Michael Winterbottom, *William of Malmesbury: "Gesta Pontificum Anglorum": The History of the English Bishops*, vol. 1, *Text and Translation* (Oxford: Clarendon, 2007), 34–35. See also Wulfstan, *Vita Aethelwoldi* xxvii, ed. and trans. Michael Lapidge and Winterbottom, *Wulfstan of Winchester: The Life of St Aethelwold* (Oxford: Clarendon, 1991), 42–43.

major churches of the Continent. They favored traditional cruciform patterns with a central tower and perhaps another tower at the west entrance, external decorative carving, and elaborate ecclesiastical furniture.[39] Yet they did borrow sporadically from Continental traditions: English monastic reformers had close contacts with the monastery of Fleury, as well as with Saint-Bertin in Ghent on the edge of the Gorze reform.[40] The New Minster at Winchester was constructed after Alfred's death to suit the requirements of Grimbald of Saint-Bertin.[41] In the late tenth century Winchester's cathedral boasted a Germanic-style west work, known from liturgical documents.[42] The old cathedral at Canterbury appears to have had a double apse, multiple altar chapels, large stair turrets, and a crypt modeled on that of St. Peter's—all echoing similar imperial constructions.[43] It has been claimed on the basis of such details that there was an "English Ottonian style."[44] Yet the Westminster of King Edward (1042–66) seems to have reflected his Norman connections, and the precise architectural affiliations of major late Saxon churches are unclear because all of them were soon systematically dismantled by the conquering Normans.[45]

39. Richard Gem, "Tenth-Century Architecture in England," in *Il secolo di ferro*, 2:803–36, esp. 829–31; John Blair, "Anglo-Saxon Minsters: A Topographical Review," in Blair and Sharpe, *Pastoral Care before the Parish*, esp. 246–58; Gittos, "Sacred Space in Anglo-Saxon England," 75–116; Gittos, *Liturgy, Architecture*, 85–102. The surviving examples of stone carving in Saxon churches are itemized in Fisher, *Introduction to Anglo-Saxon Architecture*, 63–96.

40. Gem, "Tenth-Century Architecture in England," in *Il secolo di ferro*, 2:803–36, esp. 807–8, 810, 824–25, and 832; Philip Grierson, "The Relations between England and Flanders before the Norman Conquest," in *Essays in Medieval History Selected from the TRHS on the Occasion of Its Centenary*, ed. R. W. Southern (London: Macmillan, 1968), 61–92.

41. Grierson, "Grimbald of St. Bertin's," *EHR* 55 (1940): 529–61, esp. 530–31. Because the New Minster was built to suit Grimbald, one would expect Continental influence, but R. N. Quirk, "Winchester New Minster and Its Tenth-Century Tower," *Journal of the British Archaeological Association*, 3rd ser., 24 (1961): 16–54, indicates how much remains unknown.

42. Quirk, "Winchester Cathedral in the Tenth Century," *Archaeological Journal* 114 (1957): 28–68, esp. 49–53 and 61–64; Martin Biddle, "Archaeology, Architecture, and the Cult of Saints in Anglo-Saxon England," in *The Anglo-Saxon Church: Papers on History, Architecture, and Archaeology in Honour of Dr. H.M. Taylor*, ed. L.A.S. Butler and R.K. Morris (London: Council for British Archaeology, 1986), 1–31, esp. 22–25; Martin Biddle, "*Felix Urbs Winthonia*: Winchester in the Ages of Monastic Reform," in Parsons, *Tenth Century Studies*, 123–40, esp. 138.

43. H.M. Taylor, "The Anglo-Saxon Cathedral at Canterbury," *Archaeological Journal* 126 (1969): 101–30, esp. 116–18; Taylor, "Tenth-Century Church Building in England and on the Continent," in Parsons, *Tenth-Century Studies*, 141–68, esp. 153–58; Kevin Blockley, *Canterbury Cathedral Nave: Archaeology, History, and Architecture* (Canterbury: Canterbury Archaeological Trust, 1997), 100–111.

44. Fisher, *Introduction to Anglo-Saxon Architecture*, 32–34.

45. Warwick Redwell, "New Glimpses of Edward the Confessor's Abbey at Westminster," and Gem, "Craftsmen and Administrators in the Building of the Confessor's Abbey," in *Edward the Confessor: The Man and the Legend*, ed. Richard Mortimer (Woodbridge, UK: Boydell, 2009), 151–57 and 168–72. On the larger problem of what influenced Anglo-Saxon architecture, see Gem, "Tenth-Century Architecture in England," in *Il secolo di ferro*, 2:803–36, esp. 830–32.

PRE-ROMANESQUE ARCHITECTURE IN THE LATIN MEDITERRANEAN

While Ottonian architecture was developing in the north, a different "pre-Romanesque" or "proto-Romanesque" architecture was evolving in the Mediterranean south. This "premier art roman" was identified at the start of the twentieth century by Josep Puig i Cadafalch, a Catalan architect with a dramatic vision of a new architectural style, indebted to the Lombards of Italy, spreading from Catalonia to Dalmatia and ultimately up the Rhone Valley into central France.[46] French scholars, although slightly less enthusiastic about Catalan roots, were happy to situate the development of the Romanesque style in France. They attempted to define regional schools, and they brought a surprisingly large corpus of buildings and building fragments into the debate.[47] Although these scholars were perhaps too quick to accept as the essential features of the Romanesque style whatever elements had advanced further in France than in Germany, they did demonstrate that important structural solutions and decorative effects originated in a Mediterranean world where the Carolingian footprint was less heavy and the architectural traditions of Islamic Spain, Byzantium, and the Roman Empire itself were closer at hand.

Lombard art and architecture, occasionally dismissed as barbaric, sometimes produced work so sophisticated that today scholars debate whether particular architectural productions are Roman or Lombard.[48] Masons developed new techniques for arches and vaults.[49] "Lombard bands" or "Lombard arcades" were a decorative system of vertical stone bands raised out from the walls that joined into a line of small arcades placed just below the eaves. This version of wall decoration, which has late classical antecedents, seems to have taken shape in northern Italy in the tenth century, become common there in the eleventh, and then ultimately helped inspire the blind arcades and decorative arches that proliferate in pre-Romanesque style.

---

46. On the debates surrounding the work of Puig i Cadafalch, see Marcel Durliat, "La Catalogne et le 'premier art roman,'" *Bulletin monumental* 147 (1989): 209–38; Éliane Vergnolle, "Le 'premier art roman' de Josep Puig i Cadafalch à nos jours," in *Le "premier art roman" cent ans après: La construction entre Saône et Pô autour de l'an mil. Études comparatives*, ed. Vergnolle and Sébastien Bully (Besançon: Presses universitaires Franc-Comtoises, 2012), 17–64.

47. Hubert, *L'Art préroman*, exemplifies the traditional French perspective on the rise of the Romanesque. For a rapid inventory of the relevant architectural evidence, see Vergnolle, "Les débuts de l'art roman," 172–83.

48. John Mitchell, "The Use of *Spolia* in Lombard Italy," in Poeschke, *Antike Spolien in der Architektur*, 93–116; McClendon, *Origins of Medieval Architecture*, 48–58.

49. C. Edson Armi, *Design and Construction in Romanesque Architecture: First Romanesque Architecture and the Pointed Arch in Burgundy and Northern Italy* (Cambridge: Cambridge University Press, 2004), esp. 14–15, 25–48.

In Italy regionalism prevailed. Its millennial architectural styles included Late Antique, Byzantine, Lombard, and Carolingian.[50] Perhaps the Italians, less than enthused about German domination, consciously or unconsciously were affirming their own identities by reiterating their traditional regional styles. The result was frequently architectural conservatism. Wooden roofs continued to appear on Italian basilicas long after stone vaulting had triumphed elsewhere. Although Italian baptisteries were usually Late Antique constructions, in the tenth century many were refurbished, suggesting that, unlike in the rest of Europe, independent baptisteries were still used—the fiercely conservative archdiocese of Milan even built new ones.[51] When communes developed, urban baptisteries would become symbols of Christian and civic community.[52] Bell towers were added to existing churches. In Italy these *campanili* were usually free-standing because to actually attach them to the ancient churches might produce differential ground pressures and destructive settling.[53] *Campanili* were often impressive arcaded affairs, ancestors of the famous Leaning Tower of Pisa. They found echoes in distant places, perhaps even in far-off Ireland.[54]

Despite their regional distinctiveness, Italian buildings, especially those with links to the German emperors, could incorporate northern ideas. For example, San Salvatore on Monte Amiata (near Siena), rebuilt by Abbot Winizo (1004–35), while decorated with Lombard bands and other Italian features, included northern-style towers in gray granite as well as an impressive hall crypt.[55] The cathedral of Aosta, reconstructed ca.

---

50. A rare overview can be found in McClendon, "Church Building in Northern Italy around the Year 1000: A Reappraisal," in Hiscock, *White Mantle of Churches*, 221–32.

51. Manuel Kling, "Einige Gliederungsformen am Aussenbau zehn anderer romanischer Baptisterien in Oberitalien," in *Baukunst des Mittelalters in Europa: Hans Erich Kubach zum 75. Geburtstag*, ed. Franz J. Much (Stuttgart: Stuttgarter Gesellschaft für Kunst und Denkmalpflege, 1988), 415–22; McClendon, "Church Building in Northern Italy," 221–32, esp. 223–26.

52. Augustine Thompson, *Cities of God: The Religion of the Italian Commune, 1125–1325* (University Park: Pennsylvania State University Press, 2005), 26–33, 309 14.

53. Ann Priester, "The Italian Campanile: Where Did It Come from?," in *Pratum Romanum: Richard Krautheimer zum 100. Geburtstag*, ed. Renate L. Colella, Meredith J. Gill, Lawrence A. Jenkins, and Petra Lamers (Wiesbaden: Dr. Ludwig Reichert, 1997), 259–75, introduces major theories of its origin, including the suggestion that freestanding minarets in Islamic Spain could have influenced Spanish and Italian Christian parallels.

54. Stalley, "Sex, Symbol, and Myth: Some Observations on the Irish Round Towers," in *From Ireland Coming: Irish Art from the Early Christian to the Late Gothic Period and Its European Context*, ed. Hourihane (Princeton: Princeton University Press, 2001), 27–47, esp. 29–30; Tadhg O'Keeffe, *Ireland's Round Towers* (Stroud, UK: Tempus, 2004), esp. 117–31; Tomás Ó Carragáin, *Churches in Early Medieval Ireland: Architecture, Ritual, and Memory* (New Haven: Yale University Press, 2010), 161–65.

55. Much, "Beobachtungen an der Abteikirche von Abbadia San Salvatore (Siena)," in Much, *Baukunst des Mittelalters in Europa*, 445–78; Much, "L'Abbazia di San Salvatore: Storia e archeologia dell'architettura,"

FIGURE 10. Lombard architecture, chancel and apsidal bell towers of the cathedral at Ivrea, built by Bishop Warmond (ca. 968–1004).
Photo credit: Gianni Dagli Orti/The Art Archive at Art Resource, NY.

1020–40, featured a large T-shaped basilica, reminiscent of old St. Peter's except for twin towers on the arms that were probably based on northern models, perhaps St. Maximin in Trier.[56] Early in the eleventh century apses *en echelon* (staggered in a hieratic order) and square twin towers

in *L'Amiata nel medioevo*, ed. Mario Ascheri and Wilhelm Kurze (Rome: Viella, 1989), 323–60; McClendon, "Church Building in Northern Italy," 221–32, esp. 226–30. On the northern origin of hall crypts, a matter debated by some Italian scholars, see Günter Fehring, *The Archaeology of Medieval Germany: An Introduction*, trans. Ross Samson (London: Routledge, 1991), 81–82.

56. Renato Perinetti, "Le choeur occidental de le cathédrale de Aoste (XIᵉ siècle)," in *Avant-nefs & espaces d'accueil dans l'église entre le IVᵉ et le XIIᵉ siècle*, ed. Christian Sapin (Paris: Comité des travaux historiques et scientifiques, 2002), 372–77, esp. 374 and 377; McClendon, "Church Building in Northern Italy," 221–32, esp. 222–23.

were added to Florence's cathedral, Santa Reparata, an arrangement that suggests foreign influence since all five Italian complexes known to have featured square towers flanking an apse—an arrangement common in the Lorraine and occasionally found in France and Germany—were located in towns or abbeys of special importance to the Reich.[57]

In Christian Spain both the widespread destruction caused by Al-Mansur (d. 1002) and the new prosperity that followed his death led to an architectural revolution.[58] Eleventh-century Spanish ecclesiastical leaders wanted to re-create Visigothic shrines and dioceses, and when they reconstructed churches, they not only preserved their surviving subterranean crypts but also attempted to echo their vaulting in the churches built above, eliminating wooden roofs that were too easily destroyed. Spanish builders abandoned the Islamic-looking horseshoe arch in favor of round arches and began to use the creative carved capitals that would become a hallmark of Romanesque architecture, including not only vegetative variations on Corinthian forms but also historiated capitals with figural carving.[59] Walls featured new types of blind arcading, and builders were quick to utilize Italian, Islamic, and Byzantine models.[60] A prime example is Saint-Vincent de Cardona in Catalonia, a completely vaulted domed church rebuilt in the 1030s, perhaps proximately inspired by Italian models but ultimately resembling the Bodrum Camii church in Constantinople, with barrel vaults throughout the main parts of the church and Lombard-style blind niches around the interior of the apse and choir.[61] The Catalan counts had properties and dynastic

57. Franklin K. Toker, "Early Medieval Florence: Between History and Archaeology," in *Medieval Archaeology: Papers of the Seventeenth Annual Conference of the Center for Medieval and Early Renaissance Studies*, ed. Charles L. Redman (Binghamton: SUNY Press, 1989), 261–83, esp. 281–82. For fuller explication of Toker's analysis, see *The Florence Duomo Project: On Holy Ground: Liturgy, Architecture, and Urbanism in the Cathedral and the Streets of Medieval Florence*, Florence Duomo Project 1 (Turnhout, Belg.: Brepols, 2009), esp. 11, 41; *Archaeological Campaigns below the Florence Duomo and Baptistery, 1895–1980*, Florence Duomo Project 2 (Turnhout, Belg.: Brepols, 2013); and two additional volumes still in progress.

58. On the tenth-century Spanish Christian architecture that was largely destroyed by Al-Mansur, see Achim Arbeiter, "Nordspanien zwischen Atlantik und Pyrenäen," in Henning, *Europa im 10. Jahrhundert*, 337–50.

59. Janice Mann, "A New Architecture for a New Order: The Building Projects of Sancho el Mayor (1004–1035)," in Hiscock, *White Mantle of Churches*, 233–48. For the spread of Corinthian capitals in France, see Vergnolle, "Fortunes et infortunes du chapiteau corinthien dans le monde roman," *Revue de l'art* 90 (1990): 21–34, esp. 12, who describes these capitals as "a major theme of Romanesque architectural decoration." Durliat, "La sculpture du XIᵉ en Occident," *Bulletin monumental* 192 (1994): 129–213, esp. 142–64, offers a lengthy series of photographic examples.

60. Jerrilynn D. Dodds, *Architecture and Ideology in Early Medieval Spain* (University Park: Pennsylvania State University Press, 1990), 83–94.

61. Charles M. Radding and William W. Clark, *Medieval Architecture, Medieval Learning: Builders and Masters in the Age of Romanesque and Gothic* (New Haven: Yale University Press, 1992), 12–16; Eric C. Fernie, "Saint-Vincent de Cardona et la dimension méditerranéenne du premier art roman," *CCM* 43 (2000): 243–56.

connections in southern France that facilitated the spread of their architecture to the north and enriched it with the classical traditions of Provence.

THE EMERGENCE OF THE ROMANESQUE IN CENTRAL FRANCE

If Rodulfus Glaber had been thinking of a specific church when he envisioned his white mantle of churches, it would probably have been Saint-Bénigne in Dijon, where he began his *Five Books of History*. His mentor, William of Volpiano, had begun to rebuild this church soon after the year 1000, supported by the bishop of Langres.[62] Rodulfus says William rebuilt it according "to such a wonderful plan that it would be difficult to find another as beautiful" and indeed had "planned to build a church more wondrous than those of all Gaul and incomparable in its situation."[63] A Saint-Bénigne chronicler says William imported masters of the different arts (from his native Italy?) and that "both by bringing together these masters and by giving orders to the workers, . . . constructed a temple worthy of the divine cult," a building that included "columns of marble and stone from all over," 371 according the chronicler's count.[64] The most striking feature was a rotunda at the end of the nave, replacing the standard choir, which was lit by an *oculus*, a circular "eye" open to the sky, echoing the *oculus* of the Pantheon in Rome. Although there were local precedents, the rotunda and extended inner crypt built by William exhibited Italian features and a variety of Lombard details, and it was surely more than coincidence that he chose to dedicate his church to Mary, the patroness of the Pantheon, on May 13, the anniversary feast of the Pantheon's own Christian dedication.[65] The superstructure seems to have been intended from the first to support masonry vaulting. William, who at various times ruled over dozens of monasteries, had influence far beyond this house, especially at Saint Germain de Près and in Normandy.[66] Not only did he bring Italian features north,

---

62. Malone, *Saint-Bénigne de Dijon*, 29–72, presents the historical and archaeological sources.

63. Rodulfus Glaber, *Historiae* III v, and *Vita Willelmi* viii, France and Reynolds, 120–21 and 276–77.

64. *Chronicon S. Benigni*, ed. Louis Emile Bougaud and Joseph Garnier, in *Chronique de l'Abbaye de Saint-Bénigne de Dijon suivie de la Chronique de Saint-Pierre de Bèze* (Dijon: Darantière, 1875), 1–195, esp. 138–42; partially ed. in Andrew Martindale, "The Romanesque Church of Saint-Bénigne at Dijon and MS 591 in the Bibliothèque municipale," *Journal of the British Archaeological Association* 25 (1962): 21–54, esp. 47–50.

65. Martindale, "The Romanesque Church of Saint-Bénigne at Dijon," 36–37; Wilhelm Schlink, "La rotonde de Guillaume," in *Guillaume de Volpiano et l'architecture des rotondes: Actes du colloque de Dijon, Musée Archéologique, 23–25 septembre 1993*, ed. Monique Jannet and Sapin (Dijon: Éditions de l'Université de Dijon, 1996), 35–43; Barral i Altet, *Early Middle Ages*, 174–78; Malone, *Saint-Bénigne*, 49–73 and 93–113.

66. On William's Saint-Germain-des-Près, see Baylé, "La place des sculptures de Saint-Germain-des-Prés dans le cheminement des formes au XIᵉ siècle," in *De la création à la restauration: Travaux d'histoire de l'art offerts à Marcel Durliat pour son 75ᵉanniversaire* (Toulouse: Atelier d'histoire de l'art méridional, 1992),

but he also brought northern features south, founding Fruttuaria in 1003 on familial property near his native Volpiano (diocese of Ivrea, in the Piedmont) as a monastery to be run by his brothers—what survives today is a monumental northern-style square bell tower.[67]

Despite the spiritual and political significance of the monastery of Cluny, its role in the development of Romanesque architecture is less clear than might be expected. Its best-known church, Cluny III, built from 1088 to 1130, was a five-aisled, six-towered basilica, the largest church in Christendom until surpassed by the modern St. Peter's, a church intended to be a "new Rome" in accordance with its dedication to St. Peter and its papal privileges.[68] It epitomized the fully developed Romanesque style and remained impressive until the early nineteenth century, when contractors converted most of it into paving stone.[69] Yet Cluny III does not seem to have been extraordinarily influential, except perhaps on a few later Burgundian houses, because new Cistercian architectural ideals and the development of Gothic soon challenged its architectural hegemony.[70] More important to the millennial Church was the preceding church, Cluny II, probably built 948–81, which was destroyed to make room for its more famous successor.[71] Speculations about its shape are based on liturgical details found in Cluniac customaries and on comparisons to apparently related churches such as Payerne and Romanmôtier.[72]

205–13; Danielle Johnson, "The Architecture and Sculpture of the Eleventh-Century Church of St Germain-de-Près," in Hiscock, *White Mantle of Churches*, 189–94. On his influence in Normandy, see Heitz, "Influences carolingiennes et ottoniennes," 37–48, esp. 44.

67. Luisella Pejrani-Baricco, "L'église abbatiale de Fruttuaria à la lumière des dernières fouilles archéologique," in Jannet and Sapin, *Guillaume de Volpiano*, 75–108.

68. Ann Baud, "Cluny: La *Maior Ecclesia*—1088 (?)–1130," in *Vom Umbruch zur Erneuerung? Das 11. und beginnende 12. Jahrhundert: Positionen der Forschung*, ed. Jörg Jarnut and Matthias Wemhoff (Munich: Wilhelm Fink, 2006), 219–30; Constable, *Abbey of Cluny*, 30–40.

69. On the fate of Cluny, see Janet T. Marquardt, *From Martyr to Monument: The Abbey of Cluny as Cultural Patrimony* (Newcastle: Cambridge Scholars Publishing, 2007); and Didier Méhu, ed., *Cluny après Cluny: Constructions, reconstructions et commemorations, 1790–2010: Actes du colloque de Cluny, 13–15 mai 2010* (Rennes: Presses universitaires de Rennes, 2013).

70. Iogna-Prat and Sapin, "Notes critiques: Les études clunisiennes dans tous leur états, Rencontre de Cluny, 21–23 septembre 1993," *Revue Mabillon*, n.s., 5 (1994): 233–58, esp. 237–39.

71. Conant, *Cluny: Les Églises et la maison du chef d'ordre* (Cambridge: Mediaeval Academy of America, 1968), 54–59. Criticisms of this reconstruction are summarized in Sapin, "Cluny II et l'interprétation archéologique de son plan," in Iogna-Prat and Picard, *Religion et culture autour de l'an Mil*, 85–89. For a popular explication, see Edwin Mullins, *In Search of Cluny* (Oxford: Signal Books, 2006), 23–35.

72. Conant, *Cluny*, 55, offers a list of related churches; two are analyzed in more detail in Hans Rudolf Sennhauser, *Romainmôtier und Payerne: Studien zur Cluniazenerarchitektur des 11. Jahrhunderts in der Westschweiz* (Basel, Switz.: Alkuin-Verlag, 1970). On the question of Cluniac sculpture, see Sapin, "Architecture et décor des débuts du XIe siècle en Bourgogne: Nouvelles recherches archéologiques et perspectives," *Les Cahiers de Saint-Michel de Cuxa* 32 (2001): 51–63, esp. 52–53.

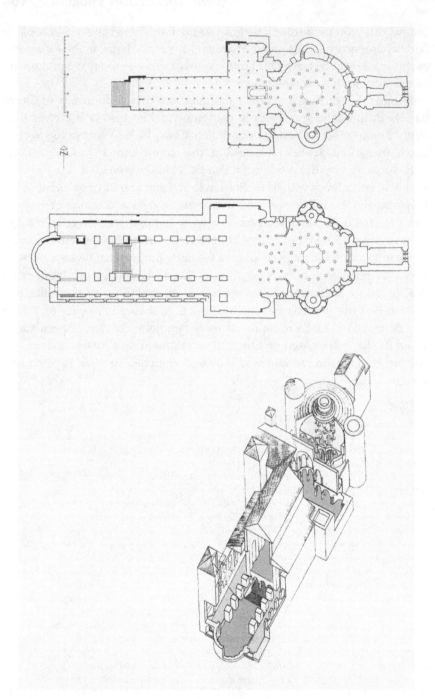

FIGURE 11. Pre-Romanesque architecture in France, St. Bénigne, Dijon, as rebuilt by William of Volpiano (d. 1031). Plan and reconstruction reproduced by permission from Carolyn Malone.

FIGURE 12. Cluniac influence, the Abbey of Romanmôtier, Switzerland. Photo credit: ©Roland Zumbühl 9.10.06, courtesy of Picswiss.

Cluny II presumably included triple apses *en echelon* and a hall around the choir to facilitate access to the chapels (a deambulatory). A two-story chapel structure in the west work, an *avant-nef* or *galilaea*, common in Burgundian buildings, has been linked to Cluniac liturgical practice.[73] Scholars are increasingly skeptical of the claim that Cluny played a major early role in the development of early Romanesque decorative sculpture.[74] Though there are many questions about the details, Burgundy was

73. Conant, *Cluny*, 59; Kristina Krüger, "Architecture and Liturgical Practice: The Cluniac *Galilaea*," in Hiscock, *White Mantle of Churches*, 138–59, esp. 146 and 149–52.

74. Neil Stratford, *Studies in Burgundian Romanesque Sculpture*, 2 vols. (London: Pindar, 1998), 1:1–21, esp. 6.

undeniably one of the greatest centers of monastic reform, and Cluny's prestige certainly helped to disseminate its architectural plans, technical ideas, and even craftsmen.

The monastery of Fleury may have played a significant role in sculptural development. After most of its monastic complex was destroyed in a great fire in 1026, Abbot Gauzlinus (1004–30) utilized squared blocks of good stone shipped down the Loire from the Nivernais to rebuild his western tower, suggesting a growing professionalism among stoneworkers, and he imported marbles from "Romania" to decorate the choir.[75] The plan of Gauzlinus featured an open porch on the ground floor, with a variety of piers furnished with engaged shafts linked to the arches above in a way that unified the structure, a solution that, with improvements, soon spread widely.[76] Perhaps because of its close contacts with Catalonia, Fleury had historiated capitals and friezes and other sculptural decoration by the mid-eleventh century.[77] It appears to have influenced a wide range of construction not only because it was a popular pilgrimage center but also because its schools produced an intellectual "curia of senators," learned ecclesiastics who traveled widely, occupied influential positions far from home, and brought with them knowledge of the new architecture.[78]

LESSER CONSTRUCTION

It is harder to investigate Rodulfus Glaber's further claim that "little village chapels were rebuilt better than before by the faithful." Most of these were probably built out of wood and other transient materials, and they would have been rebuilt or remodeled as the population exploded. Churches on rural estates frequently remain undocumented until they show up as donations to dioceses or monasteries. The holes in the evidence are huge: in Scotland, for example, no church can be solidly dated to the tenth and eleventh centuries;[79] in England the early church buildings surviving

75. Andrew of Fleury, *Vita Gauzlini* I xliv, Bautier and Labory, 80–81.

76. Stalley, *Early Medieval Architecture*, 192–93.

77. Bautier and Labory, *André de Fleury: Vie de Gauzlin*, 169–85, itemize and reproduce the literary evidence for Catalan contact. Vergnolle, *Saint-Benoît sur Loire et la sculpture*, traces the development of sculptured capitals and reliefs through many churches of the Loire valley, also in articles reprinted as *L'Art monumental de la France romane: Le XIe siècle* (London: Pindar, 2000), and he offers a list of the surviving eleventh-century Loire churches in "Le première sculpture Romane de la France moyenne (1010–1050)" ([Varzi, Italy]: Guardamagna Editori, 1996). See also Baylé, "La place des sculptures de Saint-German-des-Prés au XIe siècle," 205–13; and Uwe Geese, "Romanesque Sculpture," in *Romanesque: Architecture, Sculpture, Painting*, ed. Rolf Toman (Cologne: Könemann, 1997), 256–323, esp. 256–84.

78. Andrew of Fleury, *Vita Gauzlini* I ii, Bautier and Labory, 32–33, uses the senatorial metaphor.

79. Barbara E. Crawford, "Alba: The Kingdom of Scotland in the Year 1000," in Urbańczyk, *Europe around the Year 1000*, 271–87, esp. 282.

today are almost all from the surge of church building that followed the Conquest.[80] Yet extrapolation of the Suffolk section of the 1086 Domesday Survey (a rare region where the survey conscientiously listed churches) suggests that there were then well over five thousand rural churches in England and that in some regions by 1066 virtually all the churches had been established that would provide pastoral care up through the mid-nineteenth century.

New small churches were required as the parish system and villages coalesced. "Settlement mobility" (communities periodically shifting their locations) had characterized Transalpine Europe from the Neolithic through the early medieval centuries, but it largely ended in the millennial era.[81] Some parish communities coalesced around existing private, monastic, and episcopal churches, but those centered on new villages and castelli often would have required new construction. In the archdeaconry of Xanten (in the Rhineland near Cologne), for example, eight churches are mentioned prior to 900, twelve prior to 1100.[82] In recently converted Scandinavia, there appeared wooden churches of increasing sophistication, many with structurally compromising wooden apses attempting to imitate the apses of stone churches; thousands of stone churches would soon follow.[83] The wave of construction included new churches within cities, which had tended to survive the barbarian attacks relatively well and were adding new, smaller churches to supplement their rebuilt cathedrals, a process well documented, for example, in Cologne and in Worcester and other late Anglo-Saxon cities.[84] In the diocese of Verona, which is known in detail thanks to its well-preserved and well-analyzed records, it is possible to plot the total number of ecclesiastical institutions in half-century intervals, a number that tripled from 84 in 900 to 254 in 1150. Most of this expansion involved new rural churches, many of which were "baptismal churches" that toward the end of this period were almost all securely under episcopal control. After 1000, 90 percent of the new churches were diocesan churches devoted to the care of souls. Small and great churches

80. Richard K. Morris, "The Church in the Countryside: Two Lines of Inquiry," in *Medieval Villages: A Review of Current Work*, ed. Della Hook, Archaeology Monographs 5 (Oxford: Oxford University Committee for Archaeology, 1985), 47–60, esp. 49–53; Pounds, *History of the English Parish*, 32 and 114; Blair, *Church in Anglo-Saxon Society*, 368–504.

81. Helena Hamerow, *Early Medieval Settlements: The Archaeology of Rural Communities in North-West Europe, 400–900* (Oxford: Oxford University Press, 2002), 104–6.

82. Genicot, *Rural Communities*, 91.

83. Roar Hauglid, "Features of the Origin and Development of the Stave Churches in Norway," *Acta Archaeologia* 49 (1979): 37–60.

84. Marcus Trier, "Köln im frühen Mittelalter: Zur Stadt des 5. bis 10. Jahrhunderts aufgrund archäologischer Quellen," in Henning, *Europa im 10. Jahrhundert*, 301–10, esp. 308; Tinti, *Sustaining Belief*, 269–77.

were also reconstructed, although this is less easy to determine from documents, and the story is complicated by massive rebuilding necessitated by a major earthquake in 1117. But the villages around Verona, well before and well after the millennial year, do seem to have been donning their own new mantle, in this case one embroidered not only with grand white limestone buildings but also with a multitude of relatively humble tufa and brick ones.[85]

～

The image of postmillennial Europe donning a white mantle of churches may be slightly misleading if it is interpreted to mean that an unprecedented architectural Renaissance followed the year 1000.[86] The actual building boom had begun much earlier in Germany, the Lorraine, and elsewhere. But Rodulfus never claims that a destroyed and neglected ecclesiastical infrastructure was suddenly re-created—on the contrary, what he sees as novel is that churches were being rebuilt even though "for the most part the existing ones were properly built and not in the least unworthy." Though he errs in extolling the churches of France and Italy above those of other lands, he is describing what he knew.

Rodulfus claims that "each Christian community" attempted to surpass the others in building churches. Perhaps inspired by this hint, some scholars have focused on "the people."[87] Yet the popular character of this architectural renaissance can easily be overemphasized: Rodulfus and other chroniclers credit kings, dukes, counts, archbishops, bishops, and other great patrons; later writers will more frequently mention viscounts, knights, and other lesser members of the ruling elite.[88] An increasing "democratization" of ecclesiastical patronage would eventually allow others to share in these good works: in 1066, out of the fervor of their faith, the people of Monte Cassino's estates (the Terra Sancti Benedicti) helped haul columns imported from Rome up to the top of Monte Cassino for the building of the new basilican church.[89] It would not be long until the famous "miracle of the carts," related by Abbot Suger (d. 1151), when all the faithful helped haul stones for the new church of Saint-Denis.

---

85. Miller, *Formation of a Medieval Church*, esp. 22–40, 63, and 185–87.

86. For an implicit debate on the degree of innovation, contrast Caillet, "Le mythe du renouveau architectural roman," *CCM* 43 (2000): 341–69, with Vergnolle, "Les débuts de l'art roman," 161–94.

87. Puig i Cadafalch considered his subject *art populaire*, a position described—and criticized—in Durliat, "La Catalogne et le 'premier art roman,'" 209–38, esp. 211–14. For a recent identification of popular enthusiasms as the "socio-religious foundations of the campaign of church building," see Landes, "The White Mantle of Churches: Millennial Dynamics and the Written and Architectural Record," in Hiscock, *White Mantle of Churches*, 249–64, esp. 253.

88. Howe, "Nobility's Reform," 325–28.

89. *Chron. Casin.* III xxvi, Hoffmann, 394.

The heroes of the age were great builders, some of whom won praise for actually getting their hands dirty. Abbot Aethelwold (d. 984), an acclaimed builder at Winchester, was hit by a falling post and knocked into a pit "while the man of God was laboring on the structure."[90] Fulk Nerra, Count of Anjou, cleared and leveled land for his new church of Saint Nicholas at Angers.[91] The penitent duke of the Upper Lorraine Godfrey the Bearded (d. 1068) helped with his own hands the common laborers who were rebuilding the main church at Verdun in 1046 (work necessary because the duke had accidentally destroyed the former church while besieging the city).[92] Building was virtuous. And it was also Roman, so much so that contemporaries identified two great builders of the age, abbots Odilo of Cluny and Gauzlinus of Fleury, as new Caesars, hailing them with variations of Augustus's boast, relayed by Suetonius, that he had found Rome brick and left it marble.[93] Patrons rebuilt, reformed, and dramatically expanded the ecclesiastical infrastructure of the Latin West. Far from revealing a "mutation" coincident with the Gregorian Reform or even with the alleged millennial "Feudal Revolution," tenth- and early eleventh-century architectural reconstruction began earlier, after the post-Carolingian chaos, and expressed in stone a more confident and universal Roman identity.

90. Wulfstan, *Vita Aethelwoldi* xv, Lapidge and Winterbottom, 28–29.

91. Bernard Bachrach, "Neo-Roman vs. Feudal: The Heuristic Value of a Construct for the Reign of Fulk Nerra, Count of the Angevins (987–1040)," *Cithara* 30 (1990): 3–30, esp. 7, analyzes the texts concerning the count's labors.

92. Lampert of Hersfeld, *Annales* (1046), ed. Oswald Holder-Egger, MGH SS Rer Germ 38 (Hannover: Hahn, 1894), 60.

93. Jotsaldus of Saint-Claude, *Vita Odilonis* I xiii, ed. Johannes Staub, MGH SS Rei Germ 68 (Hannover: Hahn, 1999), 171; Andrew of Fleury, *Vita Gauzlini* xliv, Bautier and Labory, 134–35. Imperial analogies for Cluniac builders continue in Gilo, *Vita S. Hugonis* II i, ed. Cowdrey, *Two Studies in Cluniac History, 1049–1126* (Rome: Libreria Ateneo Salesiano, 1978), 41–109, esp. 91.

CHAPTER 4

"TO ROUSE DEVOTION IN A CARNAL PEOPLE"

[King Robert the Pious of France, who ruled independently from
996–1031] this servant of the Lord [*servus Dei*] became the greatest
guardian of the body and blood of the Lord and of the sacred vessels.
. . . He delighted in following the service—although placed on earth,
he was already in heaven. He rejoiced in the holy relics of saints which
he himself had had well ornamented with gold and silver, in the white
albs, in priestly vestments, in precious crosses, in chalices made with
fine gold, in censers excellently bringing forth incense, in silver vases
for the washing of the hands of priests.

—Helgaudus of Fleury (d. ca. 1050), *Vita Roberti*

GOLD AND GOD

When King Robert the Pious (d. 1031) rebuilt the monastery of Sainte-Marie
near the royal residence at Poissy, "he rendered it so honorable with ornaments and clergy, with gold and silver, that there the praising of God
never had an end."[1] Viewed critically, such delight in gold and silver seems
to value the material more the spiritual, creatures more than the Creator.
Is it idolatrous? Conscientious churchmen fretted about the merits and
demerits of ecclesiastical luxury. In the medieval Latin West, however, a
consensus gradually emerged that rich and splendid art had a role to play

---

1. Epigraph from Helgaudus of Fleury, *Vita Regis Roberti* vii, ed. Robert-Henri Bautier and Gillette Labory,
Vie de Robert le Pieux, Epitoma Vitae Regis Rotberti Pii [par] Helgaud de Fleury, Sources d'histoire médiéval
publiées par l'IRHT 1 (Paris: CNRS, 1965), 66–69. Subsequent citation ibid., 70–71.

in helping lead simple souls to God.[2] In the twelfth century some church-men would express this quite bluntly. According to William of Malmes-bury (d. ca. 1143), "Certainly, the more grandly constructed a church is, the more likely it is to entice the dullest minds to prayer and to bend the most stubborn to supplication."[3] Even Bernard of Clairvaux (d. 1153), famous as a critic of monastic art, still admitted that, unlike monks who were rela-tively isolated in their monasteries, "bishops have a duty toward both wise and foolish. They have to make use of material ornamentation to rouse devotion in a carnal people, incapable of spiritual things."[4]

Opulent worship was an ancient tradition. The Greeks and Romans had built grand temples to the Olympian gods, endowing them with shares of the spoils of their victories.[5] Later Roman emperors made huge dona-tions to Christian churches. Constantine offered to St. John Lateran alone, 4,390 *solidi* for lamps, 180 pounds of gold for liturgical vessels, and more than 1,700 pounds of silver.[6] Justinian provided unspecified amounts of gold and 40,000 pounds of silver for Hagia Sophia.[7] This imperial largesse would be imitated by post-Roman rulers, German kings who, according to the surviving fragments of their epics, had had their own traditions of bedecking shrines with precious offerings, and who, soon after conver-sion, encouraged by churchmen who had theological qualms about grave goods and were increasingly committed to burials in consecrated ground near churches, began to bestow their gold and silver treasures on churches themselves, no longer burying them in their tombs or in cenotaphs like the one at Sutton Hoo.

2. On patristic opinions about the value of art for simple souls, see Thomas F.X. Noble, *Images, Iconoclasm, and the Carolingians* (Philadelphia: University of Pennsylvania Press, 2009), 10 45, esp. 20–21, 35, and 42–43.

3. William of Malmesbury, *De Antiquitate Glastonie Ecclesie* xix, ed. and trans. John Scott, *The Early History of Glastonbury* (Woodbridge, UK: Boydell, 1981), 66–69.

4. Bernard of Clairvaux, *Apologia ad Guillemum Abbatem* xxviii, ed. Jean Leclercq, Charles H. Talbot, and Henri Rochais, in *Sancti Bernardi Opera*, 8 vols. (Rome: Editiones Cistercienses, 1957–77), 3:61–108, esp. 104–5. For a translation of the passages on art, as well as bibliography and extended comments, see Conrad Rudolph, *The "Things of Greater Importance": Bernard of Clairvaux's Apologia and the Medieval Attitude toward Art* (Philadelphia: University of Pennsylvania Press, 1990), esp. 10–12, 278–85, and 330–36.

5. François Baratte, "L'argent et la foi: Réflexions sur les trésors de temple," in *Les trésors de sanctuaires, de l'Antiquité à l'époque romane: Communications présentées au Centre de recherches sur l'Antiquité tardive et le haut Moyen Âge de l'Université de Paris X-Nanterre (1993–1995)*, ed. Jean-Pierre Caillet (Paris: Picard, 1996), 19–34 (devoted mostly to the better-documented Greek temples).

6. *Liber Pontificalis* xxxiiii, ed. Louis Duchesne, *Le Liber Pontificalis: Texte, introduction, et commentaire*, 2nd ed., 3 vols. (Paris: E. de Boccard, 1955–1957), 172–74, trans. Raymond Davis, *The Book of Pontiffs* (Liber Pontificalis): *The Ancient Biographies of the First Ninety Roman Bishops to AD 715* (Liverpool: Liverpool University Press, 1989), 16–18, explicated in Charles Pietri, *Roma Christiana: Recherches sur l'Église de Rome, son organisation, sa politique, son idéologie de Miltiade à Sixte III (311–440)* (**Rome:** ÉFR, 1976), 4–90, esp. 79.

7. Procopius, *On the Buildings* I i, ed. and trans. H.B. Dewing, *Procopius*, 7 vols., Loeb Classical Library (London: W. Heinemann, 1940), 7:28–29.

Charlemagne, according to Einhard, not only bestowed "an abundance of sacred vessels made of gold and silver and . . . a great number of clerical vestments" on his own palace chapel at Aachen but also poured into the treasury of his favorite church, St. Peter's in Rome, "a vast wealth of gold, silver, and precious stones . . . [and] great and countless gifts to the pope."[8] Some kings donated their own crown jewels and regalia, donations proudly reported by hagiographers and chroniclers.[9] Ecclesiastical treasuries kept written inventories.[10] Nor did they forget to memorialize lost items, as exemplified by an *indicium* from Waltham, Prince Harold's favorite church, that nostalgically laments gifts from Harold that had been "taken away by William [the Conqueror] out of envy":

> seven shrines of which three were gold and four silver-gilt, full of relics and precious jewels; four codices, ornamented with gold, silver, and jewels; four large gold and silver censers; six candlesticks of which two were gold and the remainder silver; three large cruets of Byzantine workmanship, silver and gilt; four crosses made from gold, silver, and jewels; one cross that was cast from fifty gold marks; five very precious priestly vestments ornamented with gold and jewels; five chasubles ornamented with gold and jewels, in one of which were twelve gold marks; two copes ornamented with gold and jewels; five chalices, two gold and the remainder silver; four altars with relics, one of which was gold and the remainder silver gilt; one silver drinking horn for wine, valued at a hundred shillings; ten reliquaries, one of which was made from two marks of gold and jewels, the remainder from gold and silver; two horse cloths and ladies' saddles worked with a great deal of gold;

8. Einhard, *Vita Karoli* II xxvi–xxvii, Waitz and Holder-Egger, 30–32, Ganz, 37, explicated in Neil Christie, "Charlemagne and the Renewal of Rome," in Story, *Charlemagne*, 167–82; and McCormick, *Charlemagne's Survey of the Holy Land*, 186.

9. The *Liber Tramitis* 13.4, 31.3, 54.2, 72, 150.3, ed. Peter Dinter, *Liber Tramitis Aevi Odilonis Abbatis, Corp CM* 10 (Siegburg, Ger.: Franz Schmid, 1980), 23, 42, 68, 108, 151, specifies that Henry II's orb, scepter, crown, and cross of gold were shown at Cluny on Christmas, the Purification, Palm Sunday, the Ascension, and the Assumption. See also Edmond Ortigues and Dominique Iogna-Prat, "Raoul Glaber et l'historiographie clunisienne," *Studi medievali*, 3rd ser., 26 (1985): 537–72, esp. 558–62. The first donation of crown jewels recorded in England was by Cnut to Canterbury in 1023: see Jan Gerchow, "Prayers for King Cnut: The Liturgical Commemoration of a Conqueror," in *England in the Eleventh Century: Proceedings of the 1990 Harlaxton Symposium*, ed. Carola Hicks (Stamford, UK: Paul Watkins, 1992), 210–38, esp. 228. Other notable English donations are itemized in Richard Gameson, *The Role of Art in the Late Anglo-Saxon Church* (Oxford: Clarendon, 1995), 250.

10. Treasure lists from greater Germany are edited in Bernhard Bischoff, *Mittelalterliche Schatzverzeichnisse*, vol. 1, *Von der Zeit Karls des Grossen bis zur Mitte des 13. Jahrhunderts*, Veröffentlichungen des Zentralinstituts für Kunstgeschichte 4 (Munich: Prestel-Verlag, 1967). For France, see Émile Lesne, *Histoire de la propriété ecclésiastique en France*, 6 vols. in 8, Mémoires et travaux publiés par des professeurs des facultés catholiques de Lille 6, 19, 30, 34, 44, 46, 50, and 53 (Lille: R. Giard, 1910–1943), esp. vol. 3, *L'inventaire de la propriété: Eglises et trésors des églises, du commencement du VIIIe siècle à la fin du XIe siècle*. For Italy, see François Bougard, "Trésors et *mobilia* italiens du haut Moyen Âge," in Caillet, *Les trésors de sanctuaires*, 161–97. Caillet, "Le trésor, de l'Antiquité à l'époque romane: Bases de la recherche actuelle et éléments de problématique," in ibid., 5–18, esp. 6–12, contains an excellent overview of the relevant scholarly literature.

and two valuable bells . . . and many other things which it would take too long to mention.[11]

Great lords who gave generously were adopting and usurping the pre-rogatives of their kings. Nobles on the rise such as Count Fulk Nerra of Anjou were proud to provide their ecclesiastical foundations with "books, holy vestments, vessels for the altar, incense holders, candelabra, crosses, and phylacteries."[12] Norman dukes were famously generous.[13] Bishops had additional models to inspire them since the popes were known as great benefactors.[14] Glorious ecclesiastical furniture was produced by great prelates such as Archbishop Egbert of Trier (977–93) and Bishop Bernward of Hildesheim (993–1022).[15]

Although Christianity was committed to a kingdom of God not of this world, ecclesiastical ostentation had an inherent logic. Post-Roman civilization measured status by wealth.[16] This disadvantaged a Church whose most prized possessions had little material value—the Eucharist in its outward form was tiny bits of bread and wine, relics of the saints were just fragments of bone and rags, sacred books were scraps of animal skin stained with ink. How could "a carnal people incapable of spiritual things" ever comprehend the links between this detritus and the world of eternal glory? Through dazzling packaging! The true value of apparently humble elements would be revealed by associating them with the richest possible materials. Grand altars, liturgical vessels, reli-quaries, book covers, art works, and regalia of all sorts could showcase

11. *Vita Haroldi Regis* iii, ed. Walter de Gray Birch, *The Romance and Life of Harold, King of England* (London: Elliot Stock, 1885), 24–25, trans. Michael Swanton, *Three Lives of the Last Englishmen* (New York: Garland, 1984), 1–40, esp. 8. For more laments about lost treasures, see D.M. Wilson, "Tenth-Century Metalwork," in Parsons, *Tenth-Century Studies*, 200–207; and Charles R. Dodwell, "Anglo-Saxon Art and the Norman Conquest," in his *Anglo-Saxon Art: A New Perspective* (Ithaca: Cornell University Press, 1982), 216–234.

12. Bernard Bachrach, *Fulk Nerra*, 109.

13. On Norman donations, see Lucien Musset, "Le mécénat des princes normands au XIe siècle," in *Artistes, artisans et production artistique au moyen âge: Colloque international, Centre national de la recherche scientifique Université de Rennes II—Haute Bretagne, 2–6 mai 1983*, ed. Xavier Barral i Altet, 3 vols. (Paris: Picard, 1986–1990), 2:121–34.

14. Franz Alto Bauer, "The Liturgical Arrangement of Early Medieval Roman Church Buildings: Architec-tural Changes at Santa Maria Maggiore and Santa Maria in Trastevere," *Mededeelingen van het Nederlandsch Historisch Instituut te Rome* 59 (2000): 101–28, esp. 120; Rosamond McKitterick, "Roman Texts and Roman History in the Early Middle Ages," in Bolgia et al., *Rome across Time and Space*, 19–34, esp. 24–26 concerning descriptions of papal largesse in the *Liber Pontificalis*.

15. Thomas Head, "Art and Artifice in Ottonian Trier," *Gesta* 36 (1997): 65–82; Michael Brandt and Arne Eggebrecht, eds., *Bernward von Hildesheim und das Zeitalter der Ottonen: Katalog der Ausstellung Hildesheim 1993*, 2 vols. (Hildesheim: Bernward Verlag, 1993).

16. Jean-Pierre Devroey, Laurent Feller, and Régine le Jan, eds., *Les élites et la richesse au haut Moyen Âge* (Turnhout, Belg.: Brepols, 2010), esp. 5 and 511; Jamie Keiner, "About the Bishop: The Episcopal Entourage and the Economy of Government in Post-Roman Gaul," *Speculum* 86 (2011): 321–60, esp. 321–28.

the liturgy, honor the saints, witness essential truths, and celebrate the devotion (and identity) of ecclesiastical patrons. All this splendor might even inspire believers to contemplate the glories of heaven itself, the new Jerusalem of pure gold, a spectacular place with pearly gates, jasper walls, and foundations set with every precious stone (Rev. 21).[17]

ALTARS AND RELIQUARIES

Altars were both tables for celebrating the Eucharist and containers for the relics of saints. In the ancient world, it was forbidden to disturb the dead and bring their bodies into the sacred confines of the ancient cities, a taboo that separated the relics of the martyrs from the urban churches. If early Christians wanted to assemble with their martyrs, they had to meet in suburban cemeteries. In the Later Roman Empire the new Christian authorities worked to resolve this problem by encouraging the moving (translating) of the bodies of the saints into cities and by requiring that all altars contain bones, artifacts, or other relics.[18]

Early medieval altars were boxlike affairs, normally of simple stone, although wooden altars were known in England and elsewhere in northern Europe until the increased emphasis on stone displaced them.[19] To celebrate the Eucharist, the top surface had to be large and flat. Elaborate relief work, even if confined to the outer edges, threatened the stability of liturgical vessels, especially since the altar table was usually covered by an altar cloth during services.[20] Some altar tables did acquire memorial inscriptions, such as the altar in the church of Saints Peter and Paul in Reichenau-Niederzell, discovered in 1976 during the relocation of the main altar, which features 341 names engraved or inscribed in ink between the ninth and the eleventh century.[21] Nevertheless, the front and the sides facing the congregation were better locations for inscriptions, carvings, or metal frontals.

Architecture attempted to showcase altars. Side altars were framed by the chapels that surrounded them, the main altar by the general lines of

17. Vauchez, *Spirituality*, 46.

18. Peter Brown, *The Cult of the Saints: Its Rise and Function in Latin Christianity*, 2nd ed. (Chicago: University of Chicago Press, 2015), esp. 1–49; G. C. J. Snoeck, *Medieval Piety from Relics to the Eucharist; A Process of Mutual Interaction* (Leiden, Neth.: Brill, 1995), 175–86; John Crook, *The Architectural Setting of the Cult of Saints in the Early Christian West, c. 300–1200* (Oxford: Clarendon, 2000), 12–13 and 65–68; McClendon, *Origins of Medieval Architecture*, 23–34.

19. Charles Cox and Michael Harvey, *English Church Furniture* (New York: E. P. Dutton, 1907), 1–2.

20. Durliat, "La sculpture du XIe en Occident," esp. 138–39.

21. Dieter Geuenich, Renate Neumüllers-Klauser, and Karl Schmid, eds., *Die Altarplatte von Reichenau-Niederzell*, MGH *Libri Memoriales et Necrologia*, n.s. 1: Supplementum (Hannover: Hahn, 1983).

the church as well as by the choir (apse). Altars were placed on elevated platforms requiring stairs and were often surrounded by impressive liturgical paraphernalia such as candlesticks and crosses. In larger churches, a baldachin over the main altar could add dignity and help focus the attention of the congregation. The main altar could become even more prominent if it was shifted toward the eastern wall and acquired the protection of a rood screen, an innovation already attested at Fleury in the eleventh century.[22]

Side altars proliferated from the Carolingian period forward. More were required by ever-larger communities of cathedral canons and monks, many of whom now were priests.[23] Multiple altars evoked Rome, where martyrs had been translated during Carolingian times from insecure tombs outside the city walls into new side altars in urban churches.[24] Altars could be located symbolically: larger churches in Saxon England sometimes arranged them in a cruciform pattern; throughout northern Europe, the towering gate-like entrance structures of the west work often included an altar to St. Michael, the heavenly defender.[25] At a time when the eastern end of the church was the domain of choirs of clerks, new altars in the western end permitted smaller, more private services in areas accessible to lay folk.[26]

Architectural historians are sometimes able to reconstruct the plans of destroyed churches by using lists of altar dedications, as, for example, at

22. Allan Doig, *Liturgy and Architecture from the Early Church to the Middle Ages* (Aldershot, UK: Ashgate, 2008), 123.

23. Otto Nussbaum, *Kloster, Priestermönch und Privatmesse: Ihr Verhältnis im Westen von den Anfänge bis zum hohen Mittelalter* (Bonn: Peter Hanstein, 1961), esp. 132–33, claims that from the ninth to the tenth century the portion of monks who were ordained priests increased from about one-third to more than one-half; he offers parallel data for the steadily increasing number of altars (185–203). See also Leclercq, "Le sacerdoce des moines," *Irénikon* 36 (1963): 5–40, esp. 11–15; and "Deux conséquences de l'eschatologie grégorienne: La multiplication des messes privées et les moines-prêtes," in *Grégoire le Grand: Chantilly, Centre culturel Les Fontaines, 15–19 septembre 1982*, ed. Jacques Fontaine, Robert Gillet, and Stan Pellistrandi, Colloques internationaux du CNRS (Paris: CNRS, 1986), 267–76, esp. 271–74.

24. Bauer, "Liturgical Arrangement," 114–17; McClendon, *Origins of Medieval Architecture*, 33, 142–43, and 176.

25. On altars symbolically arranged, see Helen Gittos, "Architecture and Liturgy in England c. 1000: Problems and Possibilities," in Hiscock, *White Mantle of Churches*, 91–106, esp. 95–96. Some entrance altars dedicated to Michael are listed in Carol Heitz, "Le modèle du Saint-Sépulcre," in Jannet and Sapin, *Guillaume de Volpiano*, 229–36, esp. 235; and in Maylis Baylé, "L'architecture liée au culte de l'Archange," in *Culte et pèlerinages à saint Michel en Occident: Trois monts dédiés à l'Archange*, ed. Pierre Bouet, Giorgio Otranto, and André Vauchez (Rome: ÉFR, 2003), 448–65, esp. 448–49 and 457–64.

26. Caillet, "Reliques et architecture religieuse aux époques carolingienne et romane," in *Les reliques: Objets, cultes, symboles; Actes du colloque international de l'Université du Littoral-Côte d'Opale (Boulogne-sur-Mer) 4–6 septembre 1997*, ed. Edina Bozóky and Anne-Marie Helvétius (Turnhout, Belg.: Brepols, 1999), 169–97; Gittos, "Sacred Space in Anglo-Saxon England," 174–75; Gittos, *Liturgy, Architecture*, 179–81, 257–74.

Saint-Riquier, Saint-Bénigne in Dijon, and St. Maximin at Trier.[27] Medieval clerks may have compiled these lists by recording actual inscriptions displayed on the altars themselves. Rodulfus Glaber tells how, when he was temporarily exiled at the monastery of Seignelay (near Auxerre), he attempted to earn his keep by renewing "the inscriptions on the altars . . . written by scholarly men long before, but through the passage of time, like most things, they were no longer legible. . . . Within the great church there were twenty-two altars, on all of which, with red ochre, I duly restored the inscriptions in hexameters, along with the epitaphs of the saints."[28] To pray at each individual altar was a pious practice. It was said of Bishop Wulfstan of Worcester (d. 1095) that "seven times a day would he prostrate himself before all the eighteen altars in the Old Church," although sometimes in the midst of this devotion he would fall asleep and "lie on the ground with his head on the steps before the altar."[29]

The multiplication of altars had been facilitated by a multiplication of relics.[30] Adémar of Chabannes (989–1034) hails a relic revival.[31] Rodulfus Glaber claims a relic resurrection:

> When the whole world was, as we have said, clothed in a white mantle of new churches, a little later, in the eighth year after the millennium of the

27. For Saint-Riquier see Hariulf, *Chronicon Centulense* II viii, ed. Ferdinand Lot, *Hariulf: Chronique de l'Abbaye de Saint-Riquier (Vᵉ siècle–1104)* (Paris: Alphonse Picard et Fils, 1894), 58–61; for Saint-Bénigne, see *Chronicon S. Benigni*, Bougaud and Garnier, 141–46, Martindale, 47–50 (see also appendix 52–54), a list discussed in Malone, *Saint-Bénigne de Dijon*, 147–70; for St. Maximin at Trier, see Heinrich V. Sauerland, "Bau und Grundriss der Trierer Maximinkirche vor 950 Jahren," *Pastor Bonus* 1 (1889): 310–20.

28. Rodulfus Glaber, *Historiae* V viii, France, 226–27. Fragments of the inscriptions Rodulfus describes still remain but reveal more about the initial Carolingian work than about his: see Maurice Prou, "Inscriptions carolingiennes des crypts de Saint-Germain d'Auxerre," *Gazette archéologique: Recueil de monuments pour servir à la connaissance & à l'histoire de l'art dans l'antiquité et le moyen-âge* 14 (1888): 299–303. On the ancient tradition of such verses, see Jean Michaud, "Culte des reliques et épigraphie: L'exemple des dédicaces et des consécrations d'autels," in Bozóky and Helvétius, *Reliques*, 199–212.

29. William of Malmesbury, *Vita Wulfstani* I iii, ed. Michael Winterbottom and Rodney M. Thomson, *William of Malmesbury, Saints' Lives: Lives of SS. Wulfstan, Dunstan, Patrick, Benignus and Indract* (Oxford: Clarendon, 2002), 26–27.

30. Bernhard Töpfer, "Reliquienkult und Pilgerbewegung zur Zeit der Klosterreform im Burgundisch-Aquitanischen Gebiet," in *Vom Mittelalter zur Neuzeit: Zum 65. Geburtstag von Heinrich Sproemberg*, ed. Hellmut Kretzschmar (Berlin: Rütten & Loening, 1956), 420–39, esp. 421 and 429–30; Angelus Albert Häussling, *Mönchskonvent und Eucharistiefeier: Eine Studie über die Messe in der abendländischen Klosterliturgie des frühen Mittelalters und zur Geschichte der Messhäufigkeit*, Liturgiewissenschaftliche (Münster: Aschendorff, 1973), 218–25. For an "efflorescence," and a " bouillement du culte des saints," see Guy Lobrichon, "Le culte des saints, les rire des hérétiques, le triomphe des savants," in Bozóky and Helvétius, *Reliques*, 95–108, esp. 96–97. For a relic "frénésie," see Barral i Altet, "Les moines, les évêques et l'art," in Iogna-Prat and Picard, *Religion et culture autour de l'an Mil*, 71–83, esp. 74–76. For an English revival, see Pestell, *Landscapes of Monastic Foundations*, 89–91.

31. Adémar, *Chronicon* III lvi, ed. Pascale Bourgain, *Ademari Cabannensis Chronicon*, CCCM 129 (Turnhout, Belg.: Brepols, 1999), 175–77.

Saviour's Incarnation, the relics of many saints were revealed by various signs where they had long lain hidden. It was as though they had been waiting for a brilliant resurrection and were now by God's permission revealed to the gaze of the faithful; certainly they brought much comfort to men's minds.[32]

Where would churchmen put the new relics? Within the altar there was a dedicated recess (the *sepulchrum*) into which they could place little box- or purse-shaped reliquaries made of precious metals and gems. In the millennial Church, however, much larger reliquaries suddenly came into fashion, some so large that when they have a flat surface on top, art historians find themselves debating whether to describe them as large reliquaries or small portable altars.[33] Note the scene in the Bayeux tapestry in which Prince Harold swears his allegiance to Duke William: Harold is flanked by two huge reliquaries, one of which clearly rests on an altar, while the other—which either has processional handles or else is borne on a litter—rests on an altar or covered table.

The story of a giant reliquary built for St. Sabinianus was recorded by its maker, the monk Odorannus (984/985–1046), who was a chronicler as well as a craftsman at Saint-Pierre-le-Vif (Sens). His masterpiece, he explains, required nearly twenty years to complete because of his own temporary exile, the disruptions of war, and its royal patron's vacillations. It finally debuted in a grand translation ceremony in 1028 when King Robert and one of his sons carried in the reliquary on their own shoulders and revealed it to the crowd. It was a box several feet long, covered with silver plaques worked into elaborate relief and topped with a peaked roof that recalled a traditional tomb monument. Such megareliquaries were an innovation in Odorannus's time, but he could have known at least two prototypes at Fleury, the original motherhouse of many of Saint-Pierre's monks. Unfortunately, Odorannus's great reliquary incorporated so much silver that it was quickly dispatched to the mint when the French Revolution broke out.[34]

32. Rodulfus Glaber, *Historiae* III vi, France, 126–27.

33. Barbara Drake Boehm, "Body-Part Reliquaries: The State of Research," *Gesta* 36 (1997): 8–19, esp. 15; Peter Lasko, "Roger of Helmarshausen, Author and Craftsman: Life, Sources of Style, and Iconography," in *Objects, Images, and the Word; Art in the Service of the Liturgy*, ed. Colum Hourihane (Princeton: Index of Christian Art, 2003), 180–201, esp. 185–86. Éric Palazzo, *L'espace rituel et le sacré: La liturgie de l'autel portative dans l'Antiquité et au Moyen Âge* (Turnhout, Belg.: Brepols, 2008), esp. 156–80, finesses the problem by creating an independent category for "altar reliquaries."

34. Odorannus of Sens, *Liber Opusculorum* ii, ed. Bautier and Monique Gilles, *Odorannus de Sens: Opera Omnia*, Sources d'histoire médiévale publiées par l'IRHT 4 (Paris: CNRS, 1972), 100–111 (commentary by Bautier and Gilles, 16–25). Odorannus's reliquary is also mentioned in Helgaudus of Fleury, *Vita Regis Roberti* xv, Bautier and Labory, 88–89.

FIGURE 13. Giant reliquaries, scene 23 of the Bayeux Tapestry, depicting Harold of England in 1064, stretching between two reliquaries as he swears to support Duke William. City of Bayeux Musée de la Tapisserie de Bayeux. Photo credit: Gianni Dagli Orti/ The Art Archive at Art Resource, NY.

Perhaps reliquaries helped bring three-dimensional sculpture back into the artistic repertoire of the West.[35] One new type was a *majestas* reliquary, a "majesty," a jeweled bust or full-bodied image of a saint with eyes that could gaze at or through a devotee; also emotionally powerful, though first documented in the later eleventh century, were reliquaries shaped like forearms and hands.[36] Some scholars have contested the received opinion that majestas reliquaries were originally a Mediterranean phenomenon, but the preponderance of early evidence does come from south of the Loire, from cult centers along the pilgrimage routes toward Santiago de Compostella.[37]

35. Jean-Claude Schmitt, *Le corps des images: Essais sur la culture visuelle au moyen âge* (Paris: Gallimard, 2002), 28–29 and 77–79.

36. Barbara Drake Boehm, "Medieval Head Reliquaries of the Massif Central," 2 vols. in 1 (PhD diss., Institute of Fine Arts, New York University, 1990), esp. 1:47, which lists the earliest examples. On body part reliquaries, see Cynthia Hahn, "The Voices of the Saints: Speaking Reliquaries," *Gesta* 36 (1997): 20–31; Bruno Reudenbach, "Visualizing Holy Bodies: Observations on Body Part Reliquaries," in Hourihane, *Romanesque Art and Thought*, 95–106.

37. That early Christian sculptured cult images appeared away from "the ancient soil of the former Roman Empire" and drew on a Germanic heritage of images was claimed by Hans Belting, *Likeness and Presence:*

The earliest surviving majestas reliquary is the statue of St. Faith, better known as Sainte Foy, the titular patroness of Sainte-Foi at Conques. This figure, about three feet in height, is intended to represent an enthroned crowned virgin martyr of the early fourth century, but it was constructed by incorporating part of a Late Antique imperial bust made of gold plates into the (disproportionate) head of a seated figure grandly clothed in gold and jewels.[38] The core of the statue is probably from the mid-tenth century, but much of its splendor may have been acquired around the year 1000, when it was "completely reformed [de integra reformata]."[39] The crowds mentioned in the saint's Latin texts may have been assembled by jongleurs singing some of the earliest surviving romance verse, the Provençal Song of Sainte-Foy, which may be associated with the transfer of her relics to a new sanctuary under the reign of Abbot Odolric (d. 1065).[40]

Bernard of Chartres, writing around 1015, admits that at first he had believed that majestas reliquaries were a superstitious form of devotion, arguing that

> the saints ought to be commemorated by displaying for our sight only truthful writing in a book or insubstantial images depicted on painted walls. For we allow the statues of saints for no reason other than very old, incorrect practice and the ineradicable and innate custom of simple people. This incorrect practice had such influence in the places I just mentioned earlier [centered on France's Massif central] that, if I had said anything openly then against Saint Gerald's image [at Aurillac], I would probably have been punished as if I had committed a great crime.

Ultimately, however, the wonder-working abilities of the image of Sainte Foy caused Bernard to change his mind and to conclude, after a miracle of vengeance, that

> after that no room was left for argument as to whether the shaped image of Sainte Foy ought to be held worthy of veneration, because it was manifestly

A History of the Image before the Era of Art, trans. Edmund Jephcott (Chicago: University of Chicago Press, 1994), 297. But this is not supported by the early evidence outlined in Boehm, "Medieval Head Reliquaries, 1:49–51 and 113–16, and cataloged there, 1:180–550. See also Amy G. Remensnyder, "Un problème de cultures ou de culture? La statue-reliquaire et les joca de sainte Foy de Conques dans le Liber Miraculorum de Bernard d'Angers," CCM 33 (1990): 351–79, esp. 353 and 368.

38. Jean Taralon, "La majesté d'or de Saint Foi de Conques," Bulletin monumental 155 (1997): 11–77, esp. 51; Jean Wirth, L'Image médiévale: Naissance et développements (VIᵉ–XVᵉ siècle) (Paris: Méridiens Klincksieck, 1989), 171–94. On the significance of the throne, see André Grabar, "Le trône des Martyrs," Cahiers archéologiques 6 (1952): 31–42.

39. Debates on the dating, partially resolved during the 1954–55 restoration, are summarized in Pamela Sheingorn, preface to The Book of Sainte Foy, trans. Sheingorn (Philadelphia: University of Pennsylvania Press, 1995), 16; and Taralon, "La majesté d'or," 16–17.

40. Sheingorn, preface to Book of Sainte Foy, 18 and 26.

FIGURE 14. Reliquary of Sainte Foy, tenth century, Abbaye de Sainte-Foi, Conques. Photo credit: Gianni Dagli Orti/The Art Archive at Art Resource, NY.

FIGURE 15. Reliquary of Sainte-Foy, Abbaye de Sainte-Foi, Conques. Detail of head incorporating Late Antique gold mask. Photo credit: Gianni Dagli Orti/The Art Archive at Art Resource, NY.

clear that he who criticized the statue was punished as if he had shown disrespect for the holy martyr herself . . .

The image represents the pious memory of the holy virgin before which, quite properly and with abundant remorse, the faithful implore her intercession for their sins. Or the statue is to be understood most intelligently in this way; it is a repository of holy relics, fashioned into a specific form only because the artist wished it. . . . Because of her merits, divine goodness performs such great feats that I have neither known nor heard that their like was done through any other saint, at least not in these times. Sainte Foy's image ought not to be destroyed or criticized, for it seems that no one lapses into pagan errors because of it, nor does it seem that the powers of the saints are lessened by it, nor indeed does it seem that any aspect of religion suffers because of it.[41]

SHRINES

The word "shrine" derives from the Latin *scrinium*, a container for scrolls and other important papers, later a reliquary, later still its associated structures and architectural context or even by extension a whole pilgrimage church.[42] Here "shrine" refers to a reliquary's immediate architectural frame. Because the new large reliquaries of the tenth and eleventh centuries did not fit within altars, they required new architectural settings. Of course it was possible to store them in ecclesiastical treasuries and bring them out only on special occasions, but when unseen how could they "rouse devotion in a carnal people"? Moreover, some donors wanted their largesse publicly displayed; Count Fulk Nerra, for example, after some caskets of relics had been found at Saint-Aubin of Angers, awarded Saint-Aubin "decorations worthy of an entire monastery" but specified that his gifts and the saints' relics had to be ensconced where visitors to the shrine could see them and learn the proper way to honor the saints.[43] How might this be done? A large reliquary placed on top of an altar could interfere with the celebration of the Mass: Odo of Cluny (d. 942) tells how St. Waldburgis miraculously warned her sick devotees that they would not be cured because her relics had been placed on the Lord's altar, where only the dignity of the divine mystery should be celebrated.[44] A large reliquary might be enshrined in a niche above the altar or on a monument adjacent to it in order to free up the altar table while still displaying the reliquary to good advantage. If an altar was located against a wall, then reliquaries might be displayed in a retable above it, a solution increasingly popular in later centuries.[45]

Although churchmen promoted relic cults, they also had to work to control them because the crowds attracted by dramatic shrines could disrupt liturgical services. In the Merovingian world, tomb shrines were often located behind the high altar, either with a monument over the tomb or with the sarcophagus itself forming part of an elevated monument, which could be situated to be viewed from a little window

---

41. Bernard of Chartres, *Miracula Fidis* I xiii, ed. Auguste Bouillet, *Liber Miraculorum Sancte Fidis* (Paris: Alphonse Picard et Fils, 1897), 47–49, trans. Sheingorn, *Book of Sainte Foy*, 78–79.

42. Crook, *Architectural Setting of the Cult of Saints*, 242–43.

43. Saint-Aubin, *Carta* cccxcvii, ed. Bertrand de Broussillon, *Cartulaire de l'abbaye de Saint-Aubin d'Angers*, 3 vols. (Angers: Germain et Grassin, 1903), 2:5. See Bernard Bachrach, *Fulk Nerra*, 157 and 236–37.

44. Odo of Cluny, *Collationum Libri Tres* II xxviii, ed. Migne, *Pat. Lat.* 133:573.

45. Snoeck, *Medieval Piety*, 202–26, lists some alternatives for enshrining relics.

behind the altar, in back of the choir, opening onto an exterior court-yard where devotees could stand.[46] The Carolingians, who looked to Rome for inspiration, preferred to use a subchurch like the ring crypt built for Old St. Peter's around 600.[47] Such crypts had surprising consequences. By channeling pilgrims through tight entrances into enclosed underground spaces, they created a much more personal spiritual experience, offering intimate private contact between devotee and saint.[48] Elaborate frescoes could increase the awesomeness.[49] Crypts created feelings of liminality, of testing, of descent into an underworld. For example, Sainte Foy was alleged to become so unhappy "at anyone who thoughtlessly dared to enter her sanctuary while in a defiled condition" that, as a local suppliant related, "if at any time after sexual intercourse, even if it was legitimate, he passed beyond the first set of iron grills without having washed himself, he would never complete that day unpunished."[50] Contained space also reinforced hierarchy because the treasurers and sacristans—the masters of gates, locks, descents, and hidden treasures—were able to reveal or conceal the sacred mysteries of their churches.

In the millennial Church, architectural accommodations for larger and showier reliquaries continued to evolve. Ring crypts imitating St. Peter's had proliferated from Carolingian times onward. Ottonian architects expanded these into hall crypts, sometimes nearly as large as the upper churches, and began to use them for purposes other than relic cults. But around the millennium some churchmen in France decided that crypts were not grand enough to properly display the relics of their greatest patrons.[51] After many experiments, Fleury took the

---

46. Hahn, "Seeing and Believing: The Construction of Sanctity in Early-Medieval Saints' Shrines," *Speculum* 72 (1997): 1079–1106, esp. 1092–98; Werner Jacobsen, "Saints' Tombs in Frankish Church Architecture," *Speculum* 72 (1997): 1107–43, esp. 1114–34.

47. On St. Peter's annular crypt and its influence, see McClendon, *Origins of Medieval Architecture*, 25–34.

48. Crook, *Architectural Setting of the Cult of Saints*, 80–160; Crook, "The Enshrinement of Local Saints in Francia and England," in *Local Saints and Local Churches in the Early Medieval West*, ed. Alan Thacker and Richard Sharpe (Oxford: Oxford University Press, 2002), 189–224, esp. 210–24.

49. Most extant medieval fresco work survives in crypts. For examples, see Hahn, "Seeing and Believing," 1101–4, and plates 15–20 (from Saint-Germain, Auxerre). Yet the remains of some Late Antique churches suggest that elaborate painting and bright colors were once widespread; see Elizabeth S. Bolman, "The Red Monastery Conservation Project, 2004 Campaign: New Contributions to the Corpus of Late Antique Art," in *Interactions: Artistic Interchange between the Eastern and Western Worlds in the Medieval Period*, ed. Hourihane (University Park: Penn State University Press, 2007), 261–81. On fresco work in the early medieval Latin West, see Noble, *Images, Iconoclasm*, 338–40.

50. Bernard of Chartres, *Miracula Fidis* I xxvii, Bouillet, 71, Sheingorn, 97.

51. Jacobsen, "Saints' Tombs," esp. 1141; Crook, *Architectural Setting of the Cult of Saints*, 160.

casket containing the body of St. Benedict out of the crypt and translated it into a shrine in the rebuilt upper church where carved capitals
presented scenes from Benedict's life.[52] In 1049, in a famous elevation
directed by Pope Leo IX, Rheims brought St. Remigius up to its highest
altar.[53] Pilgrimage churches came to prefer the accessibility offered by
the apse-and-ambulatory solution, which allowed pilgrimage traffic to
circulate at ground level while routing it around the sides of the church
to altars and shrines in side chapels.[54] Crypts became less fashionable.
Under the Anglo-Normans, for example, east-end crypts were built only
sporadically, apparently more for reasons involving ground level than
for the cult of the saints.[55] In Germany's more traditional imperial architecture, however, the relic crypt lived on.[56]

It has been claimed that the cult of relics produced the Romanesque
building style. Allegedly relics made it necessary to widen the narrow
aisles and crypts of pre-Romanesque buildings in order to accommodate pilgrims; then the resulting churches had to continue to adapt in
order to handle increasing crowds.[57] This scenario oversimplifies a little.
A saint's cult could dominate a pilgrimage church, but most saints stayed
modestly in the background except during their feast days, processions,
and fairs. The importance of relics varied regionally and chronologically:
in England, for example, Anglo-Saxon churchmen cultivated saints and
pilgrims, while the Normans who supplanted them found it odd that "a
saint or saints should be visibly the chief inhabitants of a church."[58] Yet the
multiplication of altars and reliquaries in crypts, side chapels, and shrines
undoubtedly did help shape ecclesiastical architecture.

52. The sources are not precise: compare Aimoinus, *Miracula Benedicti* II vi and II xviii, Certain, 106 and
121–23; Andrew, *Miracula Benedicti* V viii and VII v, Certain, 208 and 155; and *Additamenta ad Miracula Benedicti* VII xvi, Certain, 275. Reconstructions are attempted in Vergnolle, *Saint-Benoît-sur-Loire et la sculpture*,
13–15 and 249–53; and Caillet, "Reliques et architecture religieuse," esp. 180 and 193.

53. *Itinerarium Leonis IX an.1049 in Galliam*, ASOSB 6, pt. 1 (1701), 711–27.

54. Beat Brink, "Les églises de pèlerinage et le concept de prétention," in *Art, Cérémonial et Liturgie au
Moyen Âge: Actes du colloque de 3e Cycle Romand de Lettres, Lausanne-Fribourg, 24–25 mars, 14–15 avril,
12–13 mai 2000*, ed. Nicolas Bock, Peter Kurmann, Serena Romano, and Jean-Michel Spieser (Rome: Viella,
2002), 125–39, esp. 125–26, reviews the scholarly bibliography on "deambulatories." See also Barral i Altet,
"Les moines, les évêques et l'art," in Iogna-Prat and Picard, *Religion et culture autour de l'an Mil*, 71–80, esp. 73.

55. Crook, *Architectural Setting of the Cult of Saints*, 185, 188, 244.

56. Jacobsen, "Saints' Tombs," 1107–43, esp. 1142.

57. Töpfer, "Reliquienkult und Pilgerbewegung," 432.

58. Christopher Brooke, "Princes and Kings as Patrons of Monasteries: Normandy and England," in *Il
Monachesimo et le riforma ecclesiastica (1049–1122): Atti della quarta Settimana internazionale di studio
Mendola, 23–29 agosto 1968* (Milan: Vita e pensiero, 1971), 125–52, esp. 132; Jay Rubenstein, "Liturgy against
History: The Competing Visions of Lanfranc and Eadmer of Canterbury," *Speculum* 74 (1999): 279–309,
esp. 295.

CROSSES AND CRUCIFIXES

By the close of the High Middle Ages, a great crucifix hung above the main altar of every Latin-rite church. This had not always been the case. Although the cross was a universal Christian symbol, the crucifix, a cross with a depicted or attached representation of the suffering body of Christ, was rare in the early medieval Latin West, even absent among the Celts, whose freestanding, monumental "high crosses" rose throughout Ireland and Northumbria in the eighth century and continued to be produced in Ireland through the tenth.[59] The ninth century, however, saw "a surge in the imagery of the crucifixion."[60] By the year 1000 the body of the crucified Christ was becoming a standard feature on processional and monumental altar crosses, and life-sized wood or bronze crucifixes had begun to appear.[61] The earliest and perhaps most famous—made for Archbishop Gero of Cologne (969–76), a onetime ambassador to Constantinople—is distinguished not only for its monumentality but also for its impressive presentation of a dead Christ with head bowed and eyes closed, an image probably inspired by Greek prototypes.[62]

Crosses and crucifixes suspended above altars were increasingly common. At Reichenau, in the crypt of the church of Saint George of Oberzell,

59. Étienne Delaruelle, "Le crucifix dans la piété populaire et dans l'art, du VIe au XIe siècle," in *Études ligériennes d'histoire et d'archéologie médiévales: Mémoires et exposés présentés à la Semaine d'études médiévales de Saint-Benoit-sur-Loire du 3 au 10 juillet 1969*, ed. René Louise (Auxerre: Société des fouilles archéologiques et des monuments historiques de l'Yonne, 1975), 133–44; Schmitt, "Rituels de l'image e récits de vision," in *Testo e immagine nell'alto medioevo: 15–20 aprile 1993*, 2 vols., Settimane di Studio del CISAM 41 (Spoleto: CISAM, 1994), 1:419–62, esp. 420–31; Michael Herity, "Buildings and Layout of Early Irish Monasteries," in *Studies in the Layout, Buildings, and Art in Stone of Early Irish Monasteries* (London: Pindar, 1995), 19–56, esp. 28 and 43–49; Richard Viladesau, *The Beauty of the Cross: The Passion of Christ in Theology and the Arts, from the Catacombs to the Eve of the Renaissance* (Oxford: Oxford University Press, 2006), 48–55 and 62–69.

60. Celia Chazelle, *The Crucified God in the Carolingian Era: Theology and Art of Christ's Passion* (Cambridge: Cambridge University Press, 2001), 135 and 239 (quoted); Lawrence Nees, *Early Medieval Art* (Oxford: Oxford University Press, 2002), 195. Noble, *Images, Iconoclasm*, 276–77, 293–94, 336–37, and 351, analyzes Carolingian attitudes toward adoration of the cross.

61. Barbara C. Raw, *Anglo-Saxon Crucifixion Iconography and the Art of the Monastic Revival* (Cambridge: Cambridge University Press, 1990), esp. 40–54; Delaruelle, "Crucifix dans la piété populaire," 133–44, esp. 139, where tenth- and eleventh-century life-sized examples are presented as "absolutely novel"; Nees, *Early Medieval Art*, 227–28.

62. Thietmar of Merseburg, *Chronicon* III ii, Holtzmann, 98–101; Warner, 128, describes the crack in Gero's cross still visible today in Cologne's surviving monumental crucifix. See Reiner Haussherr, *Der Tote Christus am Kreuz zur Ikonographie des Gerokreuzes: Inaugural-Dissertation zur Erlangung der Doktorwürde der Philosophischen Fakultät der Rheinischen Friedrich-Wilhelms-Universität zu Bonn* (Bonn: Rheinische Friedrich-Wilhelms-Universität, 1962), 14–16. For its priority and influence on later German monumental crucifixes, see Hausherr, ibid., 16–30; Paul Thoby, *Le crucifix des origines au Concile de Trente: Étude iconographique, Supplèment* (Nantes: Bellanger, 1963), 14–16 (plates 402–8); and Paulus Hinz, "*Traditio* und *Novatio* in der Geschichte der Kreuzigungsbilder und Kruzifixe bis zum Ausgang des Mittelalters," in *Traditio—Krisis—Renovatio aus theologischer Sicht: Festschrift Winfried Zeller zum 65. Geburtstag*, ed. Bernd Jaspert and Rudolf Mohr (Marburg: N.G. Elwert, 1976), 599–608, esp. 605.

FIGURE 16. Monumental crucifix of Archbishop Gero of Cologne (969–76). Cologne Cathedral. Photo credit: Foto Marburg/Art Resource, NY.

FIGURE 17. Crucifix of Archbishop Gero, head and upper torso. Cologne Cathedral. Photo credit: Foto Marburg/Art Resource, NY.

two altars had tenth-century frescoes above them that depicted crosses.[63] Tenth-century written sources from Anglo-Saxon England frequently mention crucifixes and crosses, although none still in situ predate the late tenth.[64] Monumental crosses were proliferating. For example, an inventory taken at Ely in 1073, reflecting pre-Conquest wealth, notes "nineteen large crosses" (at least one of which was life size), and "eight small"; an inventory from 1093 also mentions twenty-seven crosses, presumably the same ones, and specifies that "all the crosses. . .[were] ornamented with gold and silver."[65] Yet monumental crucifixes above main altars were not instantly universal, and some English parish churches

63. Matthias Exner, "Die Wandmalereien der Krypta von St. Georg in Oberzell auf der Reichenau," *Zeitschrift für Kunstgeschichte* 58 (1995): 153–80, esp. 154–57.

64. Gittos, "Sacred Space in Anglo-Saxon England," 183–90, and *Architecture, Liturgy*, 207–10.

65. *Liber Eliensis* II cxiv and cxxxix, ed. E. O. Blake (London: Royal Historical Society, 1962), 196 and 223, trans. Janet Fairweather, *Liber Eliensis: A History of the Isle of Ely from the Seventh Century to the Twelfth Century* (Woodbridge, UK: Boydell, 2005), 234 and 268. Note also Keynes, "Ely Abbey 672–1109," in Meadows and Ramsey, *History of Ely Cathedral*, 2–58, esp. 40.

from as late as the end of the twelfth century still retain traces of different painted programs on their chancel arches.[66]

The new norm may have been another example of *imitatio Romae*. A monumental painted crucifix above the altar of Saints Simon and Jude in the center of the left nave wall of Old St. Peter's has been interpreted as a seventh-century Byzantine-inspired innovation.[67] Recent work places the monumental crucifix tradition in central Italy much earlier than previously believed, with some famous crosses fronted by Christ in majesty now dated back in their original forms to Carolingian times. A tenth- or eleventh-century origin is now claimed for the locally characteristic large painted wooden crucifixes (most familiar to non-Italians through the crucifix of San Damiano, whose role in the conversion of Francis of Assisi is described in Thomas of Celano's second *Vita Francisci*).[68]

Processional crosses and crucifixes are often depicted resting on altar tables or standing nearby. Humble wooden ones have disappeared, and those that survive are the more spectacular crosses made of precious metals, sometimes jeweled, a style popularized in Late Antiquity, when it seems to have originated with large cross-shaped reliquaries containing fragments of the "true cross" that were prominently displayed in Jerusalem, Rome, and Constantinople.[69] Opulent jeweled crosses often were actual reliquaries, cross-shaped *staurothecae* containing bits of the wood of the cross or other holy material.[70] In the Latin West during the tenth,

---

66. Gittos, "Sacred Space in Anglo-Saxon England," 188–89.

67. William Tronzo, "The Prestige of St. Peter's: Observations on the Function of Monumental Narrative Cycles in Italy," in *Pictorial Narrative in Antiquity and the Middle Ages*, ed. Herbert L. Kessler and Marianna Shreve Simpson (Washington, DC: National Gallery of Art, 1985), 93–114. For Roman echoes see Nees, *Early Medieval Art*, 147–49; for Greek antecedents, see Curta, *Edinburgh History of the Greeks*, 26.

68. For new ninth-century dates for the Volto Santo of Lucca and for the wooden crucifix of Sansepolcro, see Gabriella Rosetti, ed., *Santa Croce e Santo Volto: Contributi allo studio dell'origine e della fortuna del culto del Salvatore (secoli IX–XV)* (Pisa: Gruppo Interuniversitario per la Storia dell'Europe Mediterranea, 2002), esp. 4 and 87–88; Michele Bacci, "Il *Volto Santo*'s Legendary and Physical Image," in *Envisioning Christ on the Cross: Ireland and the Early Medieval West*, ed. Juliet Mullins, Jenifer Ní Ghrádaigh, and Richard Hawtree (Dublin: Four Courts Press, 2013), 214–33, esp. 222. On the panel crucifixes, see Belting, *Likeness and Presence*, 299 and 308; Katharina Schüppel, "Medieval Painted Crosses in Italy: Perspectives of Research," in Mullins et al., *Envisioning Christ on the Cross*, 248–61.

69. Hinz, "*Traditio* und *Novatio*," in Jaspert and Mohr, *Traditio—Krisis*, 599–608, esp. 602; Sible de Blaauw, "Jerusalem in Rome and the Cult of the Cross," in Colella et al., *Pratum Romanum*, 55–73, esp. 66–67; Holger A. Klein, *Byzanz, der Westen und das "wahre" Kreuz: Die Geschichte einer Reliquie und ihrer künstlerischen Fassung in Byzanz und im Abendland* (Wiesbaden: Reichert, 2004), 32–47, 69–78, 93–103; Ian Wood, "Constantinian Crosses in Northumbria," in *The Place of the Cross in Anglo-Saxon England*, ed. Catherine E. Karkov, Sarah Larratt Keefer, and Karen Louise Jolly (Woodbridge: Boydell, 2006), 1–13. For the use of jeweled crosses as decorative elements in Late Antiquity, see Galit Noga-Banai, *The Trophies of the Martyrs: An Art Historical Study of Early Christian Silver Reliquaries* (Oxford: Oxford University Press, 2008), esp. 123–30.

70. Whether or not a particular jeweled cross or crucifix was intended to be a reliquary is not always clear: see Anatole Frolow, *Les Reliquaires de la Vrai Croix* (Paris: Institut français d'études byzantines, 1965), 9–10.

eleventh, and twelfth centuries, relics of the true cross are mentioned more and more frequently,[71] and they appear in some of the most popular miracle stories.[72] Jeweled altar crosses (*cruces gemmatae*) became so common that there are special blessings for "decorated crosses," which a Canterbury service book defines as those "decorated with silver or gold or gems."[73] The late tenth-century English "Dream of the Rood" opens with a vision of such a cross.[74]

Some precious crosses were exotic. Mieszko II of Poland (king, 1025–32, duke, 1032–34), included in the furnishings of his lavish new cathedral at Gniezo a cross fabricated from three times his weight in gold, which required a dozen clergymen to carry.[75] The *Miracles* of Sainte Foy tell how Count Raymon II of Rouergue gave Sainte-Foi a saddle "estimated to be worth at least a hundred pounds" that he had won in battle from a Spanish Muslim: it was "taken apart into separate pieces and made into a great silver cross without breaking or damaging the Saracen engraving."[76] A striking example of this sort of recycling is the Lothar Cross, a golden cross about sixteen by twelve inches, a spectacular example of Ottonian metal work probably made shortly before the year 1000, that is treasured today in the Museum of Charlemagne's palace chapel at Aachen. Although it bears the name of Emperor Lothar (840–855), whose seal it incorporates into its base, an even more striking attachment is the first-century sardonyx cameo portrait of Augustus that occupies the center. What do these reuses signify? Do the imperial mementoes glorify Christ simply because of their intrinsic value? Or did images of the emperors evoke Romanness?

---

71. Frolow, *La Relique de la Vrai Croix; Recherches sur le développement d'un culte* (Paris: Institut français d'études byzantines, 1961), iii, graphs the incidence of cross relics, whose individual data points are discussed in an appendix, 153–61; Iogna-Prat, "Le croix, le moine et l'empereur: Dévotion à la croix et théologie politique à Cluny autour de l'an mil," in *Études clunisiennes*, ed. Iogna-Pratt (Paris: Picard, 2002), 74–92, esp 75–76; Klein, *Byzanz, der Westen und das "wahre" Kreuz*," esp. 287–88, places the major jump in cross relics in the West later, in the twelfth century.

72. Guy Philippart and Michel Trigalet, "L'hagiographie latine du XI° siècle dans la longue durée: Données statistiques sur la production littéraire et sur l'édition médiévale," in Herren et al., *Latin Culture in the Eleventh Century*, 2:281–301, esp. 292.

73. Richard W. Pfaff, "The Anglo-Saxon Bishop and His Book," *Bulletin of the John Rylands University Library of Manchester* 81 (1999): 3–24, esp. 13.

74. "The Dream of the Rood," ed. John C. Pope, in *Eight Old English Poems*, 3rd ed. by R.D. Fulk (New York: Norton, 2001), 9–14, trans. Robert Boenig, in *Anglo-Saxon Spirituality: Selected Writings* (New York: Paulist Press, 2000), 259–66. On the possibility that the original version of the poem was much earlier than the surviving text, see Éamonn Ó Carragáin, "Sources or Analogues? Using Liturgical Evidence to Date the *Dream of the Rood*," in *Cross and Cruciform in the Anglo-Saxon World: Studies to Honor the Memory of Timothy Reuter*, ed. Keefer, Jolly, and Karkov (Morgantown: West Virginia University Press, 2010), 135–65.

75. Cosmas of Prague, *Chronica Boemorum* II v (1038), ed. Bertold Bretholz, MGH *SS Rer Germ*, n.s., 2 (Berlin: Weidmann, 1923), 96.

76. Bernard of Chartres, *Miracula Fidis* I xii, Bouillet, 42, Sheingorn, 73.

FIGURE 18. Lothar Cross, jeweled side (ca. 1000), Cathedral Treasury, Aachen. Photo credit: Pitt Siebigs/© Domkapitel Aachen.

FIGURE 19. Lothar Cross, engraved side (ca. 1000), Cathedral Treasury, Aachen. Photo credit: Pitt Siebigs/© Domkapitel Aachen.

Or does an imperial symbol in Christ's place implicitly make the emperor an *alter Christus*? The more standard etched crucifixion on the other side may be more religiously inspiring, but it would have been far less visible in processions.[77]

STATUES

The reappearance of three-dimensional religious statues in the tenth-century Latin West is somewhat surprising. Images had been under attack. The Greek Church had been wracked by struggles over iconoclasm (image breaking) from 726 to 787 and again from 814 to 843. In the Latin West the debate over images was framed differently, thanks in large part to

77. Peter Lasko, *Ars Sacra, 800–1200*, 2nd ed. (New Haven: Yale University Press, 1994), 101; Garrison, *Ottonian Imperial Art*, 44–45, 60–78. On similar reuse of gems, see Klein, *Byzanz, der Westen und das "wahre" Kreuz*, 165–66; and Dale Kinney, "Ancient Gems in the Middle Ages: Riches and Ready-Mades," in *Reuse Value: Spolia and Appropriation in Art and Architecture from Constantine to Sherrie Levine*, ed. Richard Brilliant and Kinney (Burlington, VT: Ashgate, 2011), 97–120.

the teaching of Pope Gregory I (590–604), who had famously identified ecclesiastical images as the Bible of the illiterate, approving their use for decoration, for memorials, and for teaching, although not necessarily for veneration or for arousing religious emotion.[78] Thus the Western Church was less concerned about whether images should be allowed than about their proper use. During Charlemagne's reign, members of his circle tried to restrict the use of images and to stake out a middle position between Greek iconoclasm and Greek iconophilia.[79] Ultimately, however, an expansive view of the value of images triumphed. Walafrid Strabo (d. 849), for example, champions their ability to evoke emotions, observing that "sometimes we see that the simple and unlettered folk, who can scarcely be led to give credence to events presented in words, are so moved by a painting of the Lord's passion or other marvelous events that they show by their tears that the outward images have been imprinted upon their heart as if painted with a brush stroke."[80] It would probably have been hopeless to attempt to insist on the primacy of the word over images in a world where people read Old Testament stories not according to the letter but as symbols of what was to come; thus, for example, the Eucharist is foreshadowed in the offering of Melchisedec (cf. Gen. 14:17–20 and Heb. 5:6 and 7:1–28) and Christ's crucifixion in Moses's brazen serpent (cf. Num. 21: 9 and John 3:14).[81] In a world featuring visually oriented exegesis, there was no way to limit images to only conveying the words of the Bible. Biblical texts could be translated

78. Gregory I, *Epist. ad Serenum*, in *Registrum* IX x, ed. Dag Norberg, 2 vols., CCSL 140–140A (Turnhout, Belg.: Brepols, 1982), 2:873–76 (esp. 874). On the earlier underlying traditions, see Wirth, *L'Image médiévale*, 79–107; and Noble, *Images, Iconoclasm*, esp. 10–45. On the fate of Gregory's dictum, and its limitations, see Lawrence G. Duggan, "Was Art Really the 'Book of the Illiterate'?," *Word & Image* 5 (1989): 227–51. For more recent bibliography, see Herbert L. Kessler, "Pictures as Scripture in Fifth-Century Churches," in his *Old St. Peter's and Church Decoration in Medieval Italy* (Spoleto: CISAM, 2002), 15–43, esp. 21; and also his "Diction in the 'Bibles of the Illiterate,'" in ibid., 125–39, esp. 126.

79. Gerhart B. Ladner, "Die Bilderstreit und die Kunst-Lehren der byzantinischen und abendländischen-Theologie," *Zeitschrift für Kirchengeschichte* 50 (1931): 1–23; repr. in his *Images and Ideas in the Middle Ages: Selected Studies in History and Art*, 2 vols. (Rome: Edizioni di storia e letteratura, 1983), 1:13–33, with corrigenda, 2:1011–1020; Wirth, *L'Image médiévale*, 139–62; Ann Freeman, "Scripture and Images in the *Libri Carolini*," in *Testo e imagine nell'altomedioevo: 15–21 aprile 1993*, 2 vols., Settimane di studio del CISAM 41 (Spoleto: CISAM, 1994), 1:163–95; Chazelle, *Crucified God in the Carolingian Era*, 39–52; David Appleby, "Instruction and Inspiration through Images in the Carolingian Period," in *Word, Image, Number: Communication in the Middle Ages*, ed. John J. Contreni and Santa Casciani (Turnhout, Belg.: Brepols for SISMEL Edizioni del Galluzzo, 2002), 85–111, esp. 89–90; Noble, *Images, Iconoclasm*, 158–206.

80. Walafrid Strabo, *Libellus de Exordiis* viii, ed. Alice L. Harting-Correa, *Walahfrid Strabo's Libellus de Exordiis et Incrementis Quarundam in Observationibus Ecclesiasticis Rerum: A Translation and Liturgical Commentary* (Leiden, Neth.: Brill, 1996), 72–81, esp. 80–81.

81. On the potential of scriptural synthesis to destabilize the primacy of the text, see Kessler, "*Facies Bibliothecae Revelata*: Carolingian Art as Spiritual Seeing," in *Testo e imagine nell'altomedioevo*, 2:533–94, esp. 582–83.

FIGURE 20. Statue of the Virgin and Child commissioned by Bishop Stephen II of Clermont at the end of the tenth century. Drawing found in Patrimonial Library of Clermont-Community, MS 145, fol. 130v. Image courtesy of the Bibliothèque patrimoine, Clermont-Ferrand, France.

into "narrative imagery" in frescoes, in carved capitals, and in stained glass, but symbolic images could also be "revelations" in their own right.[82]

82. Schmitt, "Rituels de l'image," 1:419–62, esp. 447. For debates on the return of sculpture to the West, see the literature cited in Belting, *Likeness and Presence*, 297. The earliest surviving pieces are from the tenth century, but on possible Carolingian prototypes see Ilene H. Forsyth, *The Throne of Wisdom: Wood Sculptures of the Madonna in Romanesque France* (Princeton: Princeton University Press, 1972), 68–82. For a statue

In the millennial Church all sorts of statues suddenly began to appear. Enthroned images of the Virgin and infant Jesus had prototypes in icons, illuminated manuscripts, and Roman frescoes.[83] Now they began to appear as freestanding statues. A gilded reliquary statue of Mary and Jesus, about three feet in height, commissioned during the reign of Bishop Stephen II (ca. 945–984/990), was treasured at Clermont until it was sent to the mint in 1792—its general appearance is known from a medieval rendering.[84]

Essen cathedral still boasts a gilded Madonna, somewhat less than life size, from around 980.[85] The dying Abbot Gauzlinus of Fleury (d. 1030) is said to have gone to pray before a carved wooden statue of Our Lady in the crypt of Notre Dame at Châtillon-sur-Loire (a Fleury possession), which had been sculpted by Prior John the Saracen during the time of Abbo (d. 1004).[86] A life-sized Madonna and Child enthroned above the altar at Ely had been crafted by Abbot Aeflsige himself (996/99–1012/1016) "to an exceptionally high standard from gold and silver and jewels, beyond price" (another casualty of William the Conqueror's 1071 sack of Ely).[87] A now doubly headless gilded Madonna and Child, which may once have contained relics, survives from the Hildesheim of Bernward (d. 1022).[88] Recognizably in the Romanesque tradition is the wooden Virgin and Child of Bishop Imad of Paderborn (1051–76).[89] Such statues became so common that Archbishop Stigand of Canterbury (1052–70) included in his pontifical a "Blessing for an Image of Holy Mary Which Would Have Been Made Out of Gold and Other Beautiful Materials."[90]

---

commissioned by Gregory III and displayed on a pillar, as tenth-century northern statues seem to have been, see Noble, *Images, Iconoclasm*, 125–26.

83. Forsyth, *Throne of Wisdom*, 8–30, 92, and 156–203 ("Register of Principal Examples").

84. Ibid., 31–32, 67, 91, and 95–99; Schmitt, "Rituels de image," 1:419–62, esp. 441–47; Monique Goullet and Iogna-Prat, "La Vierge en Majesté de Clermont-Ferrand," in *Marie: Le culte de la Vierge dans la société medievale*, ed. Iogna-Prat, Palazzo, and Daniel Russo (Paris: Beauchesne, 1996), 383–405. The dates given here for the reign of Stephen II are those of Jean-Pierre Chambon and Christian Lauranson-Rosaz, "Un nouveau document à attribuer à Étienne II, évêque de Clermont (*ca 950–ca 960*)," *Annales du Midi* 114 (2002): 351–63.

85. Lasko, *Ars Sacra*, 102–5; William J. Diebold, *Word and Image: An Introduction to Early Medieval Art* (Boulder, CO: Westview, 2000), 104–6; Birgitta Falk, "Die Schatzkunst," in *Der Essener Domschatz*, ed. Falk (Essen: Klartext, 2009), 45, 62–63.

86. Andrew of Fleury, *Vita Gauzlini* II lxxiv, Bautier and Labory, 146–47. This statue is also mentioned in Andrew, *Miracula Benedicti* V ix, Certain, 207.

87. *Liber Eliensis* II lx and cxi, Blake, 132 and 195, Fairweather, 158–59 and 231.

88. Brandt and Egebrecht, *Bernward von Hildesheim*, 2:500–3 (catalog item no. VII. 32).

89. Lasko, *Ars Sacra*, 138.

90. Cambridge Corpus Christi College MS 44, pp. 137–40, cited from Jean-Marie Sansterre, "*Omnes qui coram hac imagine genua flexerint* . . . La veneration d'images de saints et de la Vierge d'après les texts écrits en Angleterre du milieu du XIe aux premières décennies du XIIIe siècle," *CCM* 49 (2006): 257–94, esp. 280.

In the millennial Church freestanding statues of the Savior are attested more rarely. One vested in gold and silver was at Fleury prior to the end of the tenth century.[91] Another was the pivot of an anti-simony story from around 1040, a statue into whose right hand Emperor Henry III inserted a pastoral staff of office so that a scrupulous abbot-elect could accept it without taking it from "any mortal man."[92] Abbot Gerbert of Saint-Wandrille (d. 1089) deplored the way images of the Savior in Normandy were poorly maintained.[93]

Large statues of the saints were rarer still. A few appear in Saxon England, which had its own distinctive tradition of sculpture,[94] probably reflecting both northern Germanic carving traditions and England's love of imitating Rome.[95] At Ely, Abbot Bryhtnoth (970–996/99) commissioned, in addition to a life-sized gold and silver crucifixion group and a life-sized enthroned Madonna, four gem-studded gold and silver statues of the royal ladies Aethelthryth, Seaxburh, Eormenhild, and Wihtburg whose shrines at the east end of the rebuilt church offered an unparalleled display of statues of local or national saints in Anglo-Saxon England.[96] Cnut's benefactions were said to have included a "great statue" for Winchester Cathedral as well as two large gold and silver images of Mary and John for New Minster in Winchester.[97] St. Swithun was well memorialized: Bishop Ealdred of Worcester (1046–62), while returning

91. Rodulfus Tortarius, *Miracula Benedicti* VIII xxviii, Certain, 277–356, esp. 325.

92. Rodulfus Glaber, *Historiae* V viii, France, 226–27.

93. François Dolbeau, "Passion et résurrection du Christ, selon Gerbert, abbé de Saint-Wandrille," in Herrin et al., *Latin Culture in the Eleventh Century*, 1:223–49, esp. 228, 233, and 243–44.

94. Rosemary Cramp, "The Furnishing and Sculptural Decoration of Anglo-Saxon Churches," in *The Anglo-Saxon Church: Papers on History, Architecture, and Archaeology in Honour of Dr. H.M. Taylor*, ed. L.A.S. Butler and R.K. Morris (London: Council for British Archaeology, 1986), 101–4; Durliat, "La sculpture du XIᵉ en Occident," 129–213; Diebold, *Word and Image*, 104–5.

95. On Saxon *imitatio Romae*, see Nicholas Howe, "Rome: Capital of Anglo-Saxon England," 147–72; Hawkes, "*Iuxta Morem Romanorum*: Stone," in Karkov and Brown, *Anglo-Saxon Styles*, 69–99, esp. 87–88. On pagan northern precedents, see Christopher D. Morris, "From Birsay to Brattahlíð: Recent Perspectives on Norse Christianity in Orkney, Shetland, and the North Atlantic Region," in Adams and Holman, *Scandinavia and Europe*, 177–95, esp. 187.

96. *Liber Eliensis* II vi and cxi, Blake, 79 and 195, Fairweather, 102–3 and 231. See C.R. Dodwell, *Anglo-Saxon Art: A New Perspective* (Manchester, UK: Manchester University Press, 1982), 211–15; Keynes, "Ely Abbey 672–1109," 2–58, esp. 25–26 and 41–42.

97. A *magnum imaginem* is noted in the *Annales de Wintonia*, ed. Henry Richards Luard, *Annales Monastici*, 5 vols. Rerum Britannicarum Medii Aevi Scriptores 36, pts. 1–5 (London: Longman, 1864–69), 2:16; on the somewhat later tradition concerning the figures accompanying Cnut's giant cross, see Henry Wharton, *Anglia Sacra*, 2 vols. (London: Richard Chiswell, 1691), 1:249. For bibliography and context, see T.A. Heslop, "The Production of *Deluxe* Manuscripts and the Patronage of King Cnut and Queen Emma," *Anglo-Saxon England* 19 (1990): 151–95, esp. 156–58 and 186–87.

from the Continent in 1054, provided silver to erect a statue of him at Winchester, which around 1100 was "still today to be seen by onlookers"; a second statue, the focus of many miracle stories, was given by the monks of Old Minster to Bishop Aelfwold of Sherborne (1045–62).[98] Virtually all late Anglo-Saxon metal work has been lost, including Ely's royal ladies, who were stripped of their valuables by William the Conqueror, but soon the Anglo-Norman Church had its own statues.[99]

Statues of saints also began to appear on the Continent. At Saint-Martial in Limoges, at the end of the tenth century, a monk allegedly made a "golden image of St. Martial with his right hand blessing the people and his left hand holding the gospel."[100] At Cluny, judging from the edition of its customs made for Farfa in the 1030s, there was a reliquary image of St. Peter so large that it required four or more bearers to move it in procession.[101] Dominic of Sora (in Lazio in central Italy) had a wooden cult statue situated above his tomb, placed there well before the end of the eleventh century.[102] Yet this must have been a slow process. "Images" of the saints are absent in the earliest rituals of "humiliation of the saints," a ceremony wherein the devotees of a saint whose rights had been offended attempt to goad their saint into action by stripping his or her altar of reliquaries, cross, and Gospel book, laying those sacred things on sackcloth on the floor and saying various prayers. If a saint had a cult statue, then it too ought to have been debased, but in the major study of the ritual the earliest mention of saints' images (*imagines*) comes from Le Mans in 1090.[103]

---

98. *Miracula Sancti Swithuni* xliii and xliv, ed. and trans. Michael Lapidge, in *The Cult of St. Swithun*, ed. Lapidge (Oxford: Clarendon, 2003), 678–81. See also Robert Deshman, "Saint Swithun in Early Medieval Art," in ibid., 179–90, repr. with additional bibliography in *Eye and Mind*, 91–103. The text of a blessing for a statue of St. Swithun, perhaps connected to Ealdred's statue, survived on the Continent: see Lapidge, *Cult of St. Swithin.*, 137–38.

99. For early statues of Saints Ithmar, Ives, Oswin, and Swithun see Sansterre, "*Omnes qui coram hac imagine genua flexerint,*" 264–66.

100. Adémar, *Commemoratio Abbatum Lemovicensium*, ed. Migne, *Pat. Lat.* 141:82. Adémar is notoriously untrustworthy about the cult of St. Martial, but at least his testimony proves that he was able to imagine such a statue prior to his death in 1034.

101. *Liber Tramitis* vi (54.2) and xxxi (189), Dinter, 68 and 260. For references to discussions, see Constable, *Abbey of Cluny*, 27–28.

102. Sansterre, "Un saint récent et son icône dans la Latium méridional au XIe siècle: A propos d'un miracle de Dominique de Sora," *Byzantinoslavica* 56 (1995): 447–52; Howe, *Church Reform*, 152–53. The material of this statue is inferred from a local tradition claiming that Napoleonic troops used it for firewood.

103. Patrick J. Geary, "Humiliation of Saints," in *Saints and Their Cults: Studies in Religious Sociology, Folklore, and History*, ed. Stephen Wilson (Cambridge: Cambridge University Press, 1983), 123–40. On the incident in question, see Orderic Vitalis, *Historia Aecclesiastica* VIII xi, ed. Marjorie Chibnall, *The Ecclesiastical History of Orderic Vitalis*, 6 vols. (New York: Oxford University Press, 1969–80), 4:194.

The revival of religious statuary occurred despite the earlier Carolingian reservations attested in the *Libri Carolini* and resulting commentaries. Perhaps statues gained legitimacy through majestas reliquaries, three-dimensional images that were acceptable because devotees were paying homage to the relics within rather than to the image itself. Statues were no distant step, and it is noteworthy that many of the earliest were gilded so that they looked like metal reliquaries. The matter is not entirely clear, however, since the most vibrant and best-attested sculptural revival occurred in Saxon England, far from the area where majestas reliquaries were most common. The reappearance of statues might also have been aided by a revival of tomb sculptures related to the general revival of things Roman: Fulk Nerra, consul of Anjou (d. 1040), had his tomb decorated with a recumbent statue (a *gisant*).[104] Tomb commemoration and the cult of the saints were so linked that when Rodulfus Glaber was describing how he renewed the labels on the altars in the crypt at Saint-Germain (Auxerre), he added that "I even so honoured the tombs of some of the religious."[105] And, of course, cult statues became easier to commission once pre-Romanesque sculptors had increased their skills by transitioning from re-creating vegetative capitals to carving elaborate narrative ones incorporated into more extensive programs of architectural relief.

ECCLESIASTICAL PARAPHERNALIA

The new churches with their shrines and crosses and statues needed ministers to celebrate the liturgies. And those ministers required appropriate vestments, books, and equipment to celebrate services properly. Their accessories had to harmonize with the surrounding ecclesiastical opulence. All sorts of ecclesiastical paraphernalia were crafted to help bring simple souls to God.

Vestments

The quotation that opens this chapter praises King Robert the Pious of France for his delight not only in liturgical gold and silver but also in "white albs and priestly vestments." Liturgical garments could be treasures. In the post-Carolingian world, perhaps even earlier in localities such as England, elite liturgical vestments were becoming much more ornate, with the most deluxe made of silk featuring bands of golden embroidery. There were also increasingly elaborate staffs (crosiers), rings, and miters. Although

---

104. Bernard Bachrach, *Fulk Nerra*, 244–46.
105. Rodulfus Glaber, *Historiae* V iii, France, 220–21.

Carolingian officials had occasionally criticized extravagant ecclesiastical dress, these criticisms became rarer from the tenth through twelfth centuries. Fancy clerical regalia expressed the hierarchy of ministers symbolically in that the most exalted would wear the most exalted vestments; it signaled the greatest feasts and occasions through the use of the most spectacular items. The study of clerical dress, long relegated to liturgists and antiquarians, has recently entered the academic mainstream, not only because of new interest in material culture but also because of the advent of women's studies (up through the twelfth century embroidery and silk work were usually women's work).[106]

Less precious clerical garb marked the boundaries of "clerical culture."[107] White robes were prized for elaborate liturgical ceremonies, and some cathedral canons seem to have worn white.[108] Although Benedict had envisioned monks wearing the standard garments of the poor, by the end of the sixth century their clothing had begun to differ from standard lay dress, and from Carolingian times on, monastic customaries describe increasingly distinctive costumes, some rather elegant.[109]

Books

Christianity was a religion of the book, and that book could be deluxe. The most prestigious volumes had authority, dignity, and impressive illuminations.[110] Some were protected by jeweled covers, perhaps even

106. Anna Muthesius, *Byzantine Silk Weaving, AD 400 to AD 1200* (Vienna: Fassbaender, 1997), esp. 119–26; Maureen Miller, *Clothing the Clergy: Virtue and Power in Medieval Europe, c. 800–1200* (Ithaca: Cornell University Press, 2014), esp. 96–140, 156n, 238–42.

107. For a general survey of clerical costume, see Louis Trichet, *Le costume du clergé: Ses origins et son évolution en France d'après les règlements de l'Église* (Paris: Cerf, 1986).

108. Rodulfus Glaber, *Historiae* III xiv, France, 118–19; Julia Barrow, *The Clergy in the Medieval World: Secular Clerics, Their Families and Careers in North-Western Europe, c. 800–c. 1200* (Cambridge: Cambridge University Press, 2015), 127.

109. Contrast Benedict, *Regula* lv, ed. and trans. Bruce L. Venarde, *The Rule of Saint Benedict*, DOML 6 (Cambridge: Harvard University Press, 2011), 178–81, with Gregory, *Moralia in Job "Epist. ad Leandrum"* i, ed. Marcus Adriaen, 3 vols., CCSL 143, 143A, 143B (Turnhout, Belg.: Brepols, 1979–85), 1:1. See Désirée Koslin, "The Robe of Simplicity: Initiation, Robing, and Veiling of Nuns in the Middle Ages," in *Robes and Honor: The Medieval World of Investiture*, ed. Stewart Gordon (New York: Palgrave Macmillan, 2001), 255–74.

110. McKitterick, "The Church," and Wollasch, "Monasticism," in *NCMH* 3:145–46, 156–59, and 165–66, cite some outstanding examples of liturgical book production. A census of manuscripts from England is presented in Helmut Gneuss, "Liturgical Books in Anglo-Saxon England and Their Old English Terminology," in *Learning and Literature in Anglo-Saxon England: Studies Presented to Peter Clemoes on the Occasion of His Sixty-Fifth Birthday*, ed. Lapidge and Gneuss (Cambridge: Cambridge University Press, 1981), 91–141; elucidated in David N. Dumville, "Liturgical Books from Late Anglo-Saxon England: A Review of Some Historical Problems," in *Liturgy and the Ecclesiastical History*, 96–152. Deluxe German ecclesiastical codices are described in Hartmut Hoffmann, *Buchkunst und Königtum im ottonischen und frühsalischen Reich*, 2 vols. (Stuttgart: Anton Hiersemann, 1986).

by built-in relics.[111] Precious books were included in lists of treasures, as in Charlemagne's last will and testament, where he lumps together the Palace Chapel's "vessels, books, or other adornments."[112] They evoked Rome.[113] They honored God and awed the faithful. They had even helped to convert Europe: Boniface, when missionizing pagan Germans, wrote back to England to ask for a New Testament written in gold (he supplied the gold) in order "to impress honor and reverence for the Sacred Scriptures visibly upon the carnally minded to whom I preach."[114] The princes of Bohemia wore military belts featuring cast-metal images of books in order to advertise their new Christian allegiance.[115] Celtic clergy kept their ornate books in elaborate locked jeweled carrying cases, book shrines that were displayed in grand processions and even carried into battle—these are best attested at the height of Celtic monasticism in the eighth century, but some continued in use and were refurbished during the tenth and eleventh.[116] When ecclesiastical reformers wanted to express their dedication, they commissioned elaborate books.[117]

How service books were organized and used is a subject for the chapter on liturgy that follows, but here it should be noted that they could be ostentatious material objects. Sacramentaries displayed on the altar in grand public services might be outstandingly decorated. So also the lectionaries containing epistle and Gospel readings that deacons carried in procession.[118] Bishops might still wrestle with elaborate scrolls, all the more impressive just because they were archaic.[119] "Lectern Bibles," giant

111. Frolow, *Reliquaires de la Vrai Croix*, 71–73 and 292–93, notes examples, including Brussels BR MS Lat. 11970, an eleventh-century evangeliary/epistolary that incorporates into its binding a fragment of the true cross, a book on which the counts of Namur would swear oaths. Ibid., 292–93.

112. Charlemagne's testament, transmitted in Einhard, *Vita Karoli Magni* xxxiii, Waitz and Holder-Egger, 40, Ganz, 43; and in Hariulf, *Chronicon Centulense* II x, Lot, 67–70.

113. Donald A. Bullough, "Roman Books and Carolingian *Renovatio*," in *Renaissance and Renewal in Christian History*, ed. Derek Baker, Studies in Church History 14 (Oxford: Ecclesiastical History Society, 1977), 23–50.

114. Boniface, *Epistola* xxxv, ed. Michael Tangl, MGH *Epp Sel* 1, 2nd ed. (Berlin: Weidmann, 1955), 60, trans. C. H. Talbot, *The Anglo-Saxon Missionaries in Germany*, rev. ed. (London: Sheed and Ward, 1985), 91.

115. Dušan Třestik, "Bohemia's Iron Year," in Urbańczyk, *Europe around the Year 1000*, 427–50, esp. 434.

116. Diebold, *Word and Image*, 28–31. A metal shrine (a *cumhdach*), probably created around 1090 for a partial psalter associated with St. Columba (d. 597), is described in Herity and Aidan Breen, *The Cathach of Colum Cille: An Introduction* (with interactive CD-ROM) (Dublin: Royal Irish Academy, 2002), 8–11.

117. Carl Nordenfalk, *Early Medieval Book Illumination* (New York: Skira Rizzoli, 1988), 96–97, 112.

118. Heslop, "Production of *Deluxe* Manuscripts," 151–52, suggests that Gospel books were the most frequently illustrated liturgical books just because they were the ones least subject to obsolescence.

119. The most famous scrolls are the *Exultet* rolls of southern Italy, which could be draped impressively over lecterns. Concerning the thirty examples that still survive, see Guglielmo Cavallo, Exultet: *Rotuli liturgici del medioevo meridionale* (Roma: Libreria dello stato, 1994); Thomas Forrest Kelly, *The Exultet in Southern Italy* (New York: Oxford University Press, 1996); Palazzo, *L'Évêque et son image: L'illustration du pontifical*

physical symbols of the unity of scripture, were so valued by reformed monasteries that these volumes, which became fashionable at the end of the tenth century, were carried back and forth between choir and refectory despite weighing fifty pounds or more: their practical use is shown not only by glosses and annotations but also by the omission of the Psalms and the Gospels (accessed more easily in other books).[120]

Books naturally recalled the heavenly "Book of Life" (*Liber Vitae*), the roster of the saved (cf. Exod. 32:32; Dan. 12:1; Luke 10:20; Phil. 4:3; Rev. 3:5; 13:8; 17:8; 20:12; 20:15).[121] *Liber vitae* is also the technical term for a liturgical book containing names of a church's personnel, friends, and donors, often a sacramentary placed upon the altar that could be referenced during Mass.[122] Note, for example, the *Golden Gospels of Echternach*, probably produced around 1030–40 but bound in gold and ivory covers made from ornaments given to Echternach decades before by Theophanu and Otto III. On the second folio, it displays Christ in Majesty, a beardless Christ in a golden mandorla, surrounded by roundels containing the symbols of the four evangelists and representations of four prophets; Christ raises his right hand in blessing while holding in his left hand an open book wherein is read "Rejoice that your names are written in the book of life."[123] Emperors and other patrons must have felt thoroughly protected when their names were inscribed into such a volume.

A pilgrimage church often possessed a special book dedicated to its patron saint, a hagiographical *libellus*, a "little book," containing the dossier of a saint,

au moyen âge (Turnhout, Belg.: Brepols, 1999), 39; and John Lowdon, "Illuminated Books," in Hourihane, *Objects, Images, and the Word*, 17–53, esp. 22–29. On the several late medieval pontifical rolls that survive from England, see Pfaff, "Anglo-Saxon Bishop and His Book," 3.

120. Diane J. Reilly, *The Art of Reform in Eleventh-Century Flanders: Gerard of Cambrai, Richard of Saint-Vanne and the Saint-Vaast Bible* (Leiden, Neth.: Brill, 2006), 1, 46, 66, 73, 83–90; Reilly, "Lectern Bibles and Liturgical Reform in the Central Middle Ages," and Lila Yawn, "The Italian Giant Bibles," in *The Practice of the Bible in the Middle Ages: Production, Reception, and Performance in Western Christianity*, ed. Susan Boynton and Diane J. Reilly (New York: Columbia University Press, 2011), 105–25 and 126–56.

121. On the heavenly "Book of Life," see Leo Koep, *Das himmlische Buch in Antike und Christentum: Eine religionsgeschichtliche Untersuchung zur altchristlichen Bildersprache* (Bonn: Peter Hanstein, 1952), 31–100 and 117–27; and Claudia Rapp, "Safe-Conducts to Heaven: Holy Men, Mediation and the Role of Writing," in Rousseau and Papoutsakis, *Transformations of Late Antiquity*, 187–203, esp. 195–98.

122. On liturgical memorial books, see Koep, *Das himmlische Buch*, 100–116; and Nicolas Huyghebaert, *Les documents nécrologiques*, Typologie 4 (Turnhout, Belg.: Brepols, 1972), esp. 13–16. Huyghebaert's conclusion that the liber vitae was a particularly Carolingian phenomenon, replaced after the tenth century by necrologies (lists of dead patrons), requires some qualification in the light of eleventh-century examples from Winchester, Thorney, Farfa, and elsewhere.

123. Nürnburg, Germanisches Nationalmuseum MS 156142 (K.G. 1138, *Codex Aureus Epternacensis*), cover and fol. 2v. For commentary, reproductions, and dates, see Peter Metz, *The Golden Gospels of Echternach (Codex Aureus Epternacensis)* (London: Thames and Hudson, 1957); Gunther Wolf, "Zur Datierung des Buchdeckels des *Codex Aureus Epternacensis*," in Wolf, *Kaiserin Theophanu*, 240–45.

FIGURE 21. *Liber vitae*, the Echternach *Golden Gospels*, front cover. German National Museum. Image courtesy of Germanisches Nationalmuseum, Nürnberg.

ideally including a short life, a long life, a verse life, a book of miracles, a sermon, hymns, and liturgical readings for the saint's feast day.[124] Some also

124. Nonillustrated hagiographical libelli have not been systematically studied. Some are discussed in François Dolbeau, "Notes sur l'organisation interne des légendiers latins," in *Hagiographie, cultures et sociétés, IVᵉ–XIIᵉ siècles: Actes du Colloque organisé à Nanterre et à Paris (2–5 mai 1979)* (Paris: Études augustiniennes, 1981), 11–31, esp. 12 and 24; Philippart, *Les Légendiers latins et autres manuscripts hagiographiques*, Typologie 24–25 (Turnhout, Belg.: Brepols, 1994), 99–101; Lapidge, "Editing Hagiography," in *La critica del testo mediolatino: Atti del Convegno (Firenze 6–8 dicembre 1990)*, ed. Claudio Leonardi (Spoleto: CISAM, 1994), 239–57, esp. 243–44; and Dumville, "Liturgical Books from Late Anglo-Saxon England," in *Liturgy and the Ecclesiastical History*, 96–152, esp. 108–11 and 139–41.

FIGURE 22. *Liber vitae*, the Echternach *Golden Gospels*, Majestas Domini image, German National Museum MS 156142, fol. 2v. Image courtesy of Germanisches Nationalmuseum, Nürnberg.

contained impressive cycles of illustrations.[125] Since the days of Augustine (d. 430) churches had recorded miracles worked by their saints, but around the millennium more churches than ever were memorializing these records in impressive display volumes that pilgrims could admire.[126]

125. On illustrated hagiographical libelli, see Leslie Ross, *Text, Image, Message: Saints in Medieval Manuscript Illustrations* (Westport, CT; Greenwood, 1994), 39–63; Barbara Fay Abou-el-Haj, *The Medieval Cult of Saints: Formations and Transformations* (Binghamton: SUNY Press, 1994), esp. 137–55 (an inventory of examples); and Hahn, *Portrayed on the Heart*, 18–26.

126. On the increasing frequency of miracle books, see Töpfer, "Reliquienkult und Pilgerbewegung," 420–39, esp. 434. An example of one being shown to pilgrims is in Bernard of Chartres, *Miracula Fidis* II vii, Bouillet, 112; Sheingorn, 130.

FIGURE 23. King Edgar offers Christ the charter of New Minster, Winchester (966). © The British Library Board, Cotton Collection MS Vespasian A. VIII, fol. 2v.

Even charters might be showpieces. King Edgar's "Privilege for New Minster Winchester" is a document from 966, written partially in rhymed prose, lettered and framed in gold, preceded by a full-page picture showing Edgar, flanked by the Virgin and St. Peter, holding up the charter toward Christ, who is seated in glory and surrounded by angels. This document, drafted by Bishop Aethelwold, as he himself attests, specifies how often and for what reasons it is to be read to the brethren.[127] The monastery at Abingdon is also

127. King Edgar, *Privilegium*, survives as London, BL, Cotton Vespasian MS A.viii, most recently, ed. Sean Miller, in *Charters of the New Minster, Winchester*, Anglo-Saxon Charters 9 (Oxford: Oxford University

said to have had "privileges of perpetual liberty, written on God's and the king's authority. . . . kept there to this day, sealed with gold leaves."[128]

Liturgical Equipment

Gold and silver were commonly used in liturgical vessels, not only because they were symbolically impressive but also because they were easy to cleanse to a state of ritual purity. The monastic craftsman "Theophilus" (probably Roger of Helmarshausen), writing at the start of the twelfth century, discusses precious liturgical paraphernalia including smaller chalices, larger chalices, patens, *fistulae* (liturgical "straws"), strainers, cruets, censers (with their chains or cables), church organs of different kinds, large cast bells, small bells, and even smaller bells.[129] He could have added candle-holders, vessels and pitchers for the priest's washing of hands (an aqua-manile and associated vessels), basins for holy water, flasks for liturgical oils, dippers for baptism, and many other things. Since Late Antiquity some liturgical vessels had been made out of precious metals, and, in perhaps one more homage to Rome, Carolingian legislation required them, a norm that spread to England during the reforms of the late tenth century.[130] Carolingian precedents also helped determine the forms.[131] Unique seasonal props are sometimes mentioned in local monastic customaries: the *Regularis Concordia*, for example, describes the Holy Week rite for the blessing of the new fire, a rite that seems to have been borrowed from Fleury: "The brethren proceed to the church doors bearing with them a staff on which is a candlestick shaped like a serpent [the Fleury version specifies a dragon]; fire is struck from a flint and is blessed by the abbot; then the candle which is in the mouth of the serpent is blessed from that fire."[132]

Press for the British Academy, 2001), 95–111; and ed. and trans. Alexander Rumble, in *Property and Piety in Early Medieval Winchester: Documents Relating to the Topography of the Anglo-Saxon and Norman City and Its Minsters* (Oxford: Clarendon, 2002), 65–97. Artistic analysis in Gameson, *Role of Art*, esp. 6–9, 130–31, 200–202, and 265; and Nees, *Early Medieval Art*, 191–92.

128. Wulstan, *Vita Aethelwoldi* xxi, Lapidge and Winterbottom, 36–37.

129. Theophilus, *De Diversis Artibus* III, ed. and trans. Charles Reginald Dodwell, *Theophilus: The Various Arts* (London: Thomas Nelson, 1961), 61–171, treats the art of the metalworker. See Peter Lasko, "Roger of Helmarshausen, Author and Craftsman: Life, Sources of Style, and Iconography," in Hourihane, *Objects, Images, and the Word*, 180–201.

130. Carol Neuman de Vegvar, "A Feast to the Lord: Drinking Horns, the Church, and the Liturgy," in Hourihane, *Objects, Images, and the Word*, 231–56, esp. 231–32. On allowed materials, see Walafrid Strabo, *Libellus de Exordiis* xxv, Harting-Correa, 150–51.

131. Victor H. Elbern, *Der Eucharistische Kelch im frühen Mittelalter* (Berlin: Deutscher Verein für Kunstwissenschaft, 1964), 34–57, esp. 38.

132. Thomas Symons, "*Regularis Concordia*: History and Derivation," in Parsons, *Tenth-Century Studies*, 37–59, esp. 51–52.

Bells resounded throughout the new churches. For example, in the monastic liturgy codified in England around 970, four sets were required just to begin evening prayers. First the great bells in the bell towers announced the office. A small bell (*tintinnabulum*) rang continuously as the children entered the church; a second bell (*secundum signum*) announced the joint recitation of selected psalms; the nocturns did not actually start until, those psalms having ended, "the remaining bells were rung [*pulsates reliquis signis*]."[133] Over time the bells were increasingly likely to be accompanied by and perhaps partially replaced by pipe organs (reintroduced into the West by Byzantium in the Carolingian era): around the year 1000 "a spate of organs" allegedly appeared.[134]

THE WEALTH OF THE CHURCH

Although the "dead hand of the Church" is proverbially famous for sequestering money and land in perpetuity, ecclesiastical property was really quite fungible. Churchmen could liquidate assets not only, as has been seen, to pay ransom and protection money but also to cover other emergencies. St. Lawrence (d. 258), the martyred deacon of Rome who had handed over his church's assets to the poor rather than to its persecutors, boasted that "the wealth of the Church is the patrimony of the poor," a dictum subsequently echoed by a host of church fathers.[135] Around 900 Leofric of St. Alban's sold off classical gems in the face of famine; a few decades later Aethelwold at Winchester took similar actions.[136] The *Chronicle of Dijon*, after describing how the tomb of Benignus had formerly been "completely covered with gold and silver and displayed the story of the Lord's birth and passion in wonderful relief work," laments that it and a "golden chest wonderfully decorated with gems, as well as three tablets

---

133. *Regularis Concordia Anglicae Nationis* xviii, ed. Thomas Symons, Sigrid Spath, Maria Wegener, and Kassius Hallinger, *Consuetudininum Saeculi X/XI/XII Monumenta Non-cluniacensia, Corp CM* 7 (3) (Siegburg, Ger.: Schmitt, 1984), 61–147, esp. 82, trans. Symons, *Regularis Concordia: The Monastic Agreement of the Monks and Nuns of the English Nation* (London: Thomas Nelson, 1953), 13 (chapter xvii in the translation). Description and bibliography in Pfaff, *Liturgy in Medieval England*, 78–81. On bells in general, see John H. Arnold and Caroline Goodson, "Resounding Community: The History and Meaning of Medieval Church Bells," *Viator* 43 (2012): 99–130.

134. Henry Mayr-Harting, "Artists and Patrons," in *NCMH* 3:212–30, at 212–13. The evidence for the presence of organs in churches around the millennium is evoked in a contentious debate about whether the Winchester organ that Wulfstan of Winchester described in 992–994 as a four hundred-pipe machine played by two brethren "of concordant spirit" was real or imagined: see James W. McKinnon, "The Tenth Century Organ at Winchester," *Organ Yearbook* 5 (1974): 4–19; Christopher Page, "The Earliest English Keyboard," *Early Music* 7 (1979): 308–14, on 309; and Kees Velekoop, "Die Orgel von Winchester: Wirklichkeit oder Symbol?," *Basler Jahrbuch für historische Musikpraxis* 8 (1984): 183–96.

135. Rudolph, *"Things of Greater Importance,"* 80–103.

136. Gervase Rosser, "The Cure of Souls in English Towns before 1000," in Blair and Sharpe, *Pastoral Care before the Parish*, 267–84, esp. 281; Wulfstan, *Vita Aethelwoldi* xxix, Lapidge and Winterbottom, 44–47.

and two silver thuribles and crosses, each one ornamented in gold and silver" were "sold by Abbot William [of Volpiano] in time of famine for the benefit of the poor."[137] During the famine of 1031–33, Abbot Odilo of Cluny sold off his most spectacular treasure—Henry II's donated imperial crown.[138] Bishops and abbots were certainly not eager to liquidate ancient artwork in order to meet the demands of short-term crises, but sometimes they did.

The treasures of the Church could be traded. In a society that depended upon personal relationships, bishops and abbots, like kings and nobles, were great gift givers. Leo IX (1049–54), whenever he participated in a major church dedication, left a liturgical vestment behind: some churches treasured his souvenir chasubles, tunics, and capes for centuries.[139] Wealthy bishops could undertake even more direct largesse.[140] For example, an entry in a Sankt Gall manuscript indicates that in 929 Bishop Coenweald of Worcester (929–57)—who may have been in Germany in connection with the arrangements for the marriage of Princess Edith of Wessex to the future Otto I—distributed gifts of silver in the name of King Athelstan among cloisters "throughout Germany [*per totam Germaniam*]."[141] His fellow English bishops and abbots were also famous for their aristocratic generosity, giving away crosses, liturgical vessels, and books produced by their own workshops, sometimes even by their own hands.[142] Episcopal gifts might coax other gifts, as when Bishop Thierry II of Orléans (1008/1013–1021) gave a grand chalice to the church of Saint-Croix, prompting Robert the Pious, "with a humble heart, touched by the love of God," to join him and commission a matching paten; Robert also made later gifts to the church, presenting them to subsequent bishops of Orléans.[143] Holy gifts could help unite sacral kings: when Emperor Henry II met Robert the Pious on the Meuse in 1023, he turned down "vast presents," taking from Robert only a "gospel-book set with gold and precious stones, and a similar reliquary containing the tooth of St. Vincent, deacon and martyr; his wife

137. *Chronicon S. Benigni*, Bougaud and Garnier, 145–46, Andrew Martindale, 24–25 and 50.

138. Jotsaldus, *Vita Odilonis* I ix, ed. Oswald Holder-Egger, MGH *SS* 15:813.

139. Charles Munier, *Le Pape Léon IX et la réforme de l'Église, 1002–1054* (Strasbourg: Éditions du Signe, 2002), 190.

140. Palazzo, *L'Évêque et son image*, 56–71.

141. The account, written on a supplementary leaf of St. Gall, Stiftsbibliothek MS 915, p. 5, is edited in Whitelock et al., *Councils & Synods*, 40–43. See also Karl Leyser, "Die Ottonen und Wessex," *Frühmittelalterliche Studien* 17 (1983): 73–97, esp. 87.

142. Mary Francis Smith, Robin Fleming, and Patricia Halpin, "Court and Piety in Anglo-Saxon England," *CHR* 87 (2001): 569–602.

143. Helgaudus of Fleury, *Vita Regis Roberti* xv, Bautier and Labory, 86–87.

would only take a pair of golden vessels."[144] In court societies, such as Byzantium, emperors reinforced their ascendancy by giving gold, silver, silk, and other wealth, establishing themselves as the source of special luxury goods. In a similar way the Latin Church expressed and maintained its exalted position by possessing and distributing items linked to the worship of God. The treasuries of monasteries and churches both witnessed and established their places within society.

144. Rodulfus Glaber, *Historiae* III viii, France, 108–11. Much of this account, including the gift of the relic of St. Vincent of Saragossa, is corroborated in Gerard of Cambrai, *Gesta Pontificum Cameracensium* xxxvii, ed. Ludwig Konrad Bethmann, MGH *SS* 7 (Hannover: Hahn, 1846), 393–489, esp. 480.

CHAPTER 5

"FOLLOWING IN THE FOOTSTEPS OF THE SAINTS"

Monks and nuns vied with one another in following in the footsteps of the saints; for they were united in one faith, though not in one manner of monastic usage. Exceedingly delighted with such great zeal the aforesaid king [Edgar of England (959–975)], after deep and careful study of the matter, commanded a Synodal Council to be held at Winchester [ca. 970], To this assembly . . . moved by the grace of Christ, he urged all to be of one mind as regards monastic usage, to follow the holy and approved fathers and so, with their minds anchored firmly on the ordinances of the Rule, to avoid all dissension, lest differing ways of observing the customs of one Rule and one country should bring their holy conversation into disrepute.

—Aethelwold of Winchester, *Regularis Concordia*

LITURGY

The liturgy, communal public worship in all its forms, animated the ecclesiastical revival.[1] In the new churches, architecture, art, treasures, and worshippers were all intended to praise God as a liturgical ensemble. This is not always obvious to today's tourists, who encounter medieval churches as public monuments and see liturgical artifacts in museums. It is further obscured by the failure of the liturgy to consistently dictate architectural forms. Ornate Roman columns, semicolumns, entablatures, and other decorative features lack distinct liturgical purposes; evocations of St. Peter's in

---

1. Epigraph: *Regularis Concordia* iv, ed. Symons et al., 70–71, trans. Symons, 2–3.

Rome, the Church of the Holy Sepulchre in Jerusalem, and other famous prototypes were ideological statements at least as much as practical expedients; ancient liturgical paraphernalia and vestments could be more conservative than functional. Nevertheless, all this weight of tradition was intended to enhance the gravitas and dignity of liturgical celebrations.[2]

The West employed the Romano-Frankish liturgy that was created when Charlemagne's churchmen attempted to conform Frankish liturgy more closely to Roman usage. Around the year 1000 there were still pockets of earlier Western liturgical traditions—Celtic in Ireland, Visigothic in Spain, Ambrosian around Milan, archaic Roman practices in central Italy, Lombard and Greek liturgies further south—but their influence was waning in a Latin world that looked increasingly to Rome.[3] Liturgical history has usually been left to the liturgists, but even they have often ignored the millennial Church, dismissing it as a sort of liturgical dark age lacking any surviving theoretical treatises.[4] This negative perspective fails to recognize that, despite a lack of written theory, the pre-Gregorian liturgy made great progress in practice. Liturgical experiments led to a plethora of books and tools that preserved, standardized, and spread ritual procedures, prompting some liturgical scholars to begin to reinterpret the age as "a phase of profound change and renewal."[5]

THE MASS

The principal medieval act of worship was the Mass (Holy Communion, the Eucharist, the Lord's Supper)—that is, the preparation, consecration, and consumption of the bread and wine that was believed to become Christ himself upon the repetition of Christ's words "This is my body. . . . This is my blood." In the Mass a liturgy of readings and processions varying according to the seasons (the Proper of the Mass, now usually designated the Liturgy of the Word) was followed by the fixed prayers centered

2. On failure to recognize the centrality of the liturgy, see Beth Williamson, "Altarpieces, Liturgy, and Devotion," *Speculum* 79 (2004): 342–406, esp. 341–42; Doig, *Liturgy and Architecture*, xvii.

3. General surveys include John Harper, *The Forms and Orders of Western Liturgy from the Tenth to the Eighteenth Century: A Historical Introduction and Guide for Students and Musicians* (Oxford: Clarendon, 1991); and Marcel Metzger, *History of the Liturgy: The Major Stages*, trans. Madeleine Beaumont (Collegeville, MN: Liturgical Press, 1997). For a document-oriented bibliography, see Cyrille Vogel, *Medieval Liturgy: An Introduction to the Sources*, trans. William G. Storey and Niels Krogh Rassmussen (Washington, DC: Pastoral Press, 1986). On English liturgy, see Pfaff, *Liturgy in Medieval England*, 8–12.

4. John F. Romano, *Liturgy and Society in Early Medieval Rome* (Burlington, VT: Ashgate, 2014), 207, laments the neglect of liturgical history.

5. Roger E. Reynolds, "Liturgical Scholarship at the Time of the Investiture Controversy: Past Research and Future Opportunities," *Harvard Theological Review* 71 (1978): 109–24; Éric Palazzo, "La liturgie de l'Occident médiéval autour de l'An mil: État de la question," *CCM* 43 (2000): 371–94, esp. 393.

on the consecration itself (the Ordinary of the Mass, then frequently called the canon, now the Eucharistic prayer). The Latin ceremony, based upon ancient precedents, reached its mature form in Rome between the fifth and seventh centuries.[6] During the Carolingian Empire, churchmen made great efforts to ensure that the Mass was celebrated properly.

Latin priests sang most of the Mass prayers, both fixed and variable (their Greek and Oriental counterparts sang everything). Although priests knew the fixed prayers by heart, they were advised to keep a written text at hand.[7] They read the variable prayers out of a book called a sacramentary, but a formal service might involve many more books. Extracts from the Epistles and the Gospels could be read, often by a deacon, from separate epistolaries and gospel lectionaries (also known as evangeliaries or evangelistaries). Sung prayers assigned to a choir might be accessed from a book called a gradual by the *precentor* (sometimes called the cantor) who was stationed on the altar steps (*gradus*). The tropes and sequences added to the prayers of the Mass could be collected into tropers. The new white mantle of churches would have required an avalanche of new liturgical books.[8]

Also proliferating, although rarely preserved today, were liturgical libelli, sometimes no more than a single unbound quire, which could contain many or all of the texts needed to celebrate special Masses or to hold services in places that lacked liturgical books. These pamphlets often contained the rites for blessings and anointings performed outside of a church. They wore out easily and were quickly discarded except on the rare occasions when a conscientious librarian decided to bind a bundle of them together. Yet they could be important vehicles for liturgical innovation and creativity.[9]

Multiple service books worked well when priests were assisted by deacons, precentors, and choirs but not when a single priest was handling

6. Harper, *Forms and Orders of Western Liturgy*, 109–26, describes the ritual of the Mass. Still basic is Josef A. Jungmann, *The Mass of the Roman Rite: Its Origins and Development*, 2 vols., trans. Francis A. Brunner (1951–55, repr., Westminster, MD: Christian Classics, 1986).

7. Wulfstan, *Canons of Edgar* (1005–1008) q 32, ed. Whitelock et al., *Councils & Synods*, 313–38, esp. 324–25, trans. Andrew Rabin, *The Political Writings of Archbishop Wulfstan of York* (Manchester, UK: Manchester University Press, 2015), 85–100, esp. 92: "It is right that a priest never celebrate mass . . . but the canon is to be before his eyes. He may consult it if he wishes, so as not to make a mistake." Editions and manuscripts surveyed in Pfaff, *Liturgy in Medieval England*, 66–67.

8. Andrew Hughes, *Medieval Manuscripts for Mass and Office: A Guide to Their Organization and Terminology* (Toronto: University of Toronto Press, 1982), esp. 81–99; Metzger, *Les Sacramentaires*, Typologie 70 (Turnhout, Belg.: Brepols, 1994); Palazzo, *A History of Liturgical Books from the Beginning to the Thirteenth Century* (Collegeville, MN: Liturgical Press, 1998), 19–63; Gunilla Iversen, *Laus Angelica: Poetry in the Medieval Mass*, ed. Jane Flynn, trans. William Flynn (Turnhout, Belg.: Brepols, 2010), 5–19.

9. Palazzo, "Le role des *Libelli* dans la pratique liturgique du haut moyen âge: Histoire et typologie," *Revue Mabillon*, n.s., 1 (62) (1990): 9–36; Palazzo, *History of Liturgical Books*, 63–105.

all the parts of the Mass by himself, as increasingly happened in the side chapels of large churches and in the new parish churches. The extent of the problem becomes clear if one compares two lists of the books that a priest needed, both compiled by the English scholar Aelfric of Eynsham (d. ca. 1010): the first list, written in Latin, requires a Mass book, a book of epistles, a hymnbook, a reading book, a psalter, a manual, a *computus* (for calculating dates of Church feasts), an evangeliary, a passional, and "songbooks," but even the bookish Aelfric must have recognized that this was burdensome, since his parallel list written in Old English omits the evangeliary, passional, and songbooks.[10] Even the abbreviated list might still have challenged those Saxon priests denounced by contemporaries as incompetent, uneducated, and unable to read Latin well.[11]

The first systematic response to the problem of too many books was an impressive initiative in the wrong direction. Between 970 and 1020 the monks of the monastery of Fulda produced a "supersacramentary." They united local celebrations and variations into one grand book that contained an extravagant number of prayers.[12] Some copies were profusely illustrated, most famously the Warmund Sacramentary, composed for the imperial bishop Warmund of Ivrea (ca. 980–1011).[13] But an unwieldy sacramentary encompassing all the liturgical variations of the Mass was not the solution needed.

What did succeed was the missal, a handier Mass book containing the fixed and variable prayers for a liturgical year as well as rubrics that specified the accompanying actions. Missals had to truncate or abbreviate some texts in order to present the whole annual liturgical cycle, often reducing litanies and psalms to a couple of lines.[14] They are the end result of a long development. Some Carolingian sacramentaries had already moved toward such a format by adding glosses for the first lines of the gradual (sung) prayers. Some libelli had included all the prayers and liturgical

10. Contrast Aelfric, *First Old English Letter to Wulfstan* q 157–60, in Whitelock et al., *Councils & Synods*, 1, pt. 1, 255–302, esp. 290–92, with Aelfric, *Epistola de Canonibus* q 52–55, in ibid., 191–226, esp. 206–7. On his book lists, see Joyce Hill, "Monastic Reform and the Secular Church: Aelfric's Pastoral Letters in Context," in Hicks, *England in the Eleventh Century*, 103–17, esp. 110–11; and Pfaff, *Liturgy in Medieval England*, 47 and 66–68.

11. Clerical education is discussed in chapter 8 below, in the section "Secular Priests."

12. Palazzo, *Les sacramentaires de Fulda: Étude sur l'iconographie et la liturgie à l'époque ottonienne* (Münster: Aschendorff, 1994); Palazzo, *History of Liturgical Books*, 56.

13. For bibliography on Warmund's grand liturgical books, including references to facsimile editions, see Mirelle Ferrari, "Libri e testi del Mille," and Simona Gavinelli, "Alle origini della Biblioteca Capitolare," in *Storia della Chiesa di Ivrea dalle origini al XV secolo*, ed. Giorgio Cracco (Rome: Viella, 1998), 511–33 and 535–65, esp. 535–44.

14. Palazzo, *History of Liturgical Books*, 107–10.

instructions needed for particular services. The result was the appearance of recognizable missals in various regions around the year 1000. There is no shortage of praise for Charlemagne's scholars who developed Carolingian minuscule and its accompanying punctuation, thereby making liturgical books easier to read. Yet praise should also be given to their successors who facilitated liturgical celebrations by condensing multiple liturgical books into a single manageable volume. Other liturgical books also became more practical: in the eleventh and twelfth centuries epistolaries and evangeliaries yielded to combined lectionaries.[15] Bishops, beginning in Carolingian times and generally by around the year 1000, consolidated the texts and directions for their many duties into "pontificals," a development whose high points included the imperially sponsored Romano-German Pontifical in Germany and all sorts of Anglo-Saxon pontificals.[16] Standardization and consolidation had a price: the new books may have "restrained in a way the prevailing liturgical creativity and ingenuity which characterized Frankish Gaul throughout the early Middle Ages."[17] Nevertheless, the result was a more coherent and universal Latin liturgy.

The Mass lent its solemnity to many other rituals. Masses accompanied sacramental rites such as clerical ordinations, public vows of marriage, ceremonies of public penance, and even baptism.[18] They were also associated with coronations of kings, prayers for victory in battle, funerals, and excommunications. Donations of property or children, when made at Mass, were serious commitments that what had been given would not be taken back.[19] Liturgical dramas could be part of the entrance rites.[20] Exorcisms could occur.[21] For judicial ordeals an oath of innocence was taken by

15. Hughes, *Medieval Manuscripts for Mass and Office*, 124–59; Aimé-Georges Martimort, *Les lectures liturgiques et leurs livres*, Typologie 64 (Turnhout, Belg.: Brepols, 1992); Palazzo, *History of Liturgical Books*, 83–105, esp. 99.

16. Pfaff, "Anglo-Saxon Bishop and His Book," 3–24; Sarah Hamilton, "The Early Pontificals: The Anglo-Saxon Evidence Reconsidered from a Continental Perspective," in Rollason et al., *England and the Continent*, 411–428.

17. Hen, *Royal Patronage of Liturgy in Frankish Gaul*, 147.

18. Pierre-Marie Gy, "Sacraments and Liturgy in Latin Christianity," in *Christian Spirituality: Origins to the Twelfth Century*, ed. Bernard McGinn and John Meyendorff (New York: Crossroad, 1985), 365–81.

19. Howe, *Church Reform*, 60; Mayke De Jong, *In Samuel's Image: Child Oblation in the Early Medieval West* (Leiden, Neth.: Brill, 1996), 171–85 and 195.

20. Timothy James McGee, "The Liturgical Origin and Early History of the *Quem Quaeritis* Dialogue" (PhD diss., University of Pittsburgh, 1974); Bernard J. Quint, "The *Quem Quaeritis*: Its Context as Liturgical Drama" (PhD diss., Arizona State University, 1976), esp. 150–98; Michal Kobialka, *This Is My Body: Representational Practices in the Early Middle Ages* (Ann Arbor: University of Michigan Press, 1999), 18–24 and 35; Iversen, *Laus Angelica*, esp. 49–62.

21. For examples, see Piroska Nagy, *Le Don des larmes au moyen âge: Un instrument spirituel en quête d'institution (V^e–XIIIe siècle)* (Paris: Albin Michel, 2000), 229–31; Florence Chave-Mahir, *L'exorcisme des possédés dans l'Église d'Occident (X^e–XIVe siècle)* (Turnhout, Belg.: Brepols, 2011), esp. 110–11, 117, 144, 148–49.

the accused party just before communion, and then after the service the water, iron, or other medium was blessed.[22] The "clamor" and the "humiliation of saints," were conducted in and around the Mass, with the saints challenged in the presence of Christ, "before your altar and before your all holy body and blood."[23] The tenth century is said to have seen the advent of a new "dramatic liturgy,"[24] but the anchor of that liturgy was the Mass.

Masses were becoming private as well as public celebrations. Gregory the Great makes some of the earliest allusions to private daily Masses, but he presents them as the exceptional practices of some pious secular priests.[25] Irish and English sources mention them more frequently, even for monks; Carolingian *ordines* recognize a *missa solitaria* celebrated by only one priest and an assistant, or even by one priest alone.[26] Yet private Masses remained somewhat anomalous. Fulbert of Chartres (d. 1028) advised a priest not to celebrate Mass "without at least two or three of the faithful present," although he was so unsure about his canonical grounds here that he promised his interlocutor that "if in reading new works or re-reading old ones I should find anything more definite about this, out of charity I shall write and let you know. But if you yourself should come across something first, please show the same charity."[27] The opposite conclusion was reached by the Italian reformer Peter Damian (d. 1072/1073), who justified the solitary Masses of hermit priests by arguing that at these services the whole Church was cosmically present.[28] Monk priests tried to

22. Robert Bartlett, *Trial by Fire and Water: The Medieval Judicial Ordeal* (Oxford: Clarendon, 1986), 41, 54, 95, and 120; Snoeck, *Medieval Piety*, 149–58. On the place of the Mass in this rite, see the *Ordines Judicii Dei*, ed. Karl Zeumer, in *Formulae Merowingi et Karoli Aevi*, MGH *Legum, Sectio* 5: *Formulae* (Hannover: Hahn, 1882), 599–722, esp. 638, 641, 843, 647, 648; and Derek A. Rivard, *Blessing the World: Ritual and Lay Piety in Medieval Religion* (Washington, DC: Catholic University of America Press, 2009), 253–64.

23. Geary, "Humiliation of Saints," in Wilson, *Saints and Their Cults*, 123–40; Snoeck, *Medieval Piety*, 159–73 and 365–67, esp. 168 (a list of liturgical references).

24. M. Bradford Bedingfield, *The Dramatic Liturgy of Anglo-Saxon England* (Woodbridge, UK: Boydell, 2002).

25. Gregory, *Dialogi* IV lvii, lviii, lx, de Vogüé and Antin, 3:184–203, esp. 3:186–87, 194–95, and 202–3, Zimmerman, 266–73. For a claim that Gregory's eschatology helped to promote private Masses, see Cyrille Vogel, "Deux conséquences de l'eschatologie grégorienne: La multiplication des messes privées et les moines-prêtes," in *Grégoire le Grand: Chantilly, Centre culturel Les Fontaines, 15–19 septembre 1982*, ed. Jacques Fontaine, Robert Gillet, and Stan Pellistrandi (Paris: CNRS, 1986), 267–76, esp. 270–71.

26. Nussbaum, *Kloster, Priestermönch und Privatmesse*, 138–50; Angelus Albert Häussling, "Ursprünge der Privatmesse," *Stimmen der Zeit* 176 (1965): 21–28; Häusling, *Mönchskonvent und Eucharistiefeier*, 243–51 and 265–68.

27. Fulbert of Chartres, *Epist.* xx (mid-1008 or later), ed. and trans. Frederick Behrends, *The Letters and Poems of Fulbert of Chartres* (Oxford: Clarendon, 1976), 26–27.

28. Peter Damian, *Epist.* xxviii, ed. Kurt Reindel, *Die Briefe des Petrus Damiani*, 4 vols., MGH *Briefe der deutschen Kaiserzeit* 4, pts. 1–4 (Munich: MGH, 1983–93), 1:248–78, esp. 256–57, trans. Owen J. Blum, *The Letters of Peter Damian*, 6 vols. (the last two with Irven M. Resnick), The Fathers of the Church Mediaeval

celebrate their private Masses so that they would not disturb the liturgy of the hours, but the logistics could be challenging. According to Rodulfus Glaber, an eyewitness to the situation at Cluny, "The number of brethren in that house was so great that it was the custom to celebrate Mass without interruption from day-break to dinner time. These masses are so reverently, piously, and worthily performed that you would have thought them the work of angels rather than men."[29]

If the devotional needs of congregations did not determine how many Masses a priest could celebrate, then what did? Monk priests said their own private Masses in addition to the community Mass. Although according to the formal language of the monastic customaries their extra altar service was voluntary, in practice they found themselves obligated by community pledges to celebrate large numbers of votive Masses[30] and by the expectation that they would offer thirty memorial Masses for each deceased fellow monk.[31] How many Masses could a priest say each day? Carolingian scholars were uncertain.[32] Doubts are suggested by a query from Archbishop Wulfstan of York to Aelfric of Eynsham, whose reply cited his beloved master Aethelwold's preference for only one celebration per day.[33] Wulfstan, however, apparently found that practice too limiting for his own generation, since the *Canons of Edgar*, which he helped write, offer more latitude: "And it is right that a priest not celebrate Mass more than three times in one day at most."[34] Piety may explain this proliferation, since if Masses could help save

---

Continuation 1–3 and 5–7 (Washington, DC: Catholic University of America Press, 1989–2005), 1:255–89, esp. 1:262–64. See Alessandro Azzimonti, "Pietro Damiani e la legittimità della liturgia dei solitari," *Aevum* 85 (2011): 341–52. On his revised death date, see John Howe, "Did St. Peter Damian Die in 1073? A New Perspective on His Final Days," *Analecta Bollandiana* 128 (2010): 67–86.

29. Rodulfus Glaber, *Historiae* V xiii, France, 236–37.

30. Nussbaum, *Kloster, Priestermönch und Privatmesse*, 159–62 and 206–7.

31. On the ancient and Carolingian background of Masses for the dead, see Constable, "The Commemoration of the Dead in the Early Middle Ages," in *Early Medieval Rome and the Christian West: Essays in Honour of Donald A. Bullough*, ed. Julia M.H. Smith (Leiden, Neth.: Brill, 2000), 169–95. The custom of offering thirty days of Masses for a deceased monastic brother appears in Gregory I, *Dialogi* IV lvii, de Vogüé and Antin, 3:188–94, Zimmerman, 266–72. It became widespread: the *Regularis Concordia*, for example, requested that for thirty days after the death of a monk, each of the priests of the monastery celebrate thirty Masses for the repose of his soul. See Symons, "*Regularis Concordia*: History and Derivation," in Parsons, *Tenth Century Studies*, 56–57, who also notes a Continental parallel at Verdun. Peter Damian assumes a thirty-day Mass obligation for the deceased in his *Epist.* xviii and l, Reindel, 1:248–78, esp. 1:275, and 2:77–131, esp. 2:98–99, Blum, 1:159–70, esp. 166 and 2:289–334, esp. 304. On the parallel Cluniac custom, see Iogna-Prat, "Le croix, le moine et l'empereur," 74–92, esp. 76–77.

32. Divergent practices are cited ca. 840 in Walafrid Strabo, *Libellus de Exordiis* xxii, Harting-Correa, 122–25.

33. Aelfric, *Epist. ad Uulstanum* xiii, in Whitelock et al., *Councils & Synods*, 242–55, esp. 251–52 (discussed 243–44).

34. Wulfstan, *Canons of Edgar* (1005–1008) q 37, Whitelock et al., *Councils & Synods*, 326, Rabin, *Political Writings*, 93. Three Masses is also the limit in the *Northumbrian Priests' Law* (ca. 1008–1023)' q 18, Whitelock et al., *Councils & Synods*, 449–68, esp. 456, Rabin, *Political Writings*, 197–206, esp. 20.

souls, then it would be charitable to offer as many as possible.[35] Or, as some commentators hinted, priests motivated by greed might multiply Masses to gain money or fame.[36] Whatever the motives, the end result was an increase so great that the tenth and eleventh centuries have been dubbed "the blossoming time of the private Mass [*die Blütezeit der Privatmesse*]."[37]

The proliferation and prestige of priests' private Masses subtly marginalized nonordained monks and nuns. One way to involve them more in Eucharistic piety was to encourage daily communion for all religious, a movement that arose in the late Carolingian world in parallel with the proliferation of monk priests.[38] In England around 970 the *Regularis Concordia* became the first customary to insist that all religious should take communion daily.[39] A century later, Gregory VII would be promoting this practice to pious laywomen.[40]

LITURGY OF THE HOURS: CANONICAL AND MONASTIC

Christian scriptures urge unceasing prayer (Matt. 7:7–12; Luke 11:5–13, 18:1–8, and 21:36; Eph. 6:18, Col. 4:2, 1 Thess. 5:16–18), an ideal that could be realized in part by offering regular prayers at fixed hours following the biblical injunction to pray seven times per day (Psalms 118:164). The singing of psalms went back to Judaism, but in the liturgy of the hours these were supplemented by all sorts of other prayers, chants, and readings, many unique to particular regions or even to particular communities. The liturgy of the hours blossomed when the fourth-century liberation of the Church made possible elaborate public prayers. In theory the bishop or abbot or abbess led the prayers, but in practice designated specialists

35. Rodulfus Glaber, Jotsaldus, and Peter Damian all relate versions of a hermit's vision validating the efficacy of Cluniac Masses in extricating souls from Purgatory. On these stories and their afterlife, see Iogna-Prat, "Les morts dans la compatibilité céleste des Clunisiens aux XIᵉ et XIIᵉ siècles," in his *Études clunisiennes*, 125–50, esp. 125–26.

36. Aelfric, *Epistola ad Uulstanum* xiii, in Whitelock et al., *Councils & Synods*, esp. 251–52.

37. Nussbaum, *Kloster, Priestermönch und Privatmesse*, 274.

38. Around 840, Walafrid Strabo, *Libellus de Exordiis* xxi, Harting-Correa, 114–23, urged daily communion for professional religious but noted that this custom contrasted with the practice of "earlier generations."

39. *Regularis Concordia* xxix, ed. Symons et al., 89, trans. Symons, 18–19, explicated in Symons, "*Regularis Concordia*: History and Derivation," in Parsons, *Tenth Century Studies*, 37–59, esp. 44–45. Aelfric of Eynsham, *Epistola* viii, ed. and trans. Christopher Jones, *Aelfric's Letter to the Monks of Eynsham* (Cambridge: Cambridge University Press, 1998), 112–13 and 157, wavers a little on this practice. For a comparison with the Gorze tradition, see Hallinger, *Gorze-Kluny*, 2:975–76.

40. Gregory VII, *Epist. ad Mathildem* (16 February 1074), *Register* I xlvii, ed. Erich Caspar, 2 vols., MGH *Epp Sel* 2 (Berlin: Weidmann, 1920–23), 71–73, trans. H. E. J. Cowdrey, as *The Register of Gregory VII, 1073–1085: An English Translation* (Oxford: Oxford University Press, 2002), 51–53. On women's special association with frequent reception of the Eucharist, see Caroline Walker Bynum, *Holy Feast and Holy Fast: The Religious Significance of Food to Medieval Women* (Berkeley: University of California Press, 1987), 80–91.

usually presided. Though variations and combinations were possible, the fixed hours became fairly standard (see table 1).

The Latin liturgy of the hours coalesced from the fifth through the eighth centuries, heavily influenced by Eastern practices and by the Mass, with which it shared hymns, prayers, and liturgical cycles. Western monks adopted the common prayers of urban Christian communities but then developed them independently, thus bifurcating the liturgical tradition. Carolingian officials, despite their love of liturgical standardization, had to be content here with requiring cathedral canons to follow the liturgy of the hours as outlined in the *Rule of Chrodegang of Metz* (d. 766) and monks to follow the *Rule of Benedict*.[41] Around the millennium, the evidence for the secular liturgy of the hours is sketchy,[42] but possible problems are suggested by the amount of time and effort that the Gregorian reformers devoted to regularizing and upgrading the canonical clergy and their liturgies. The monastic liturgy, on the other hand, was in the midst of a well-documented phase of expansion in which monks and nuns were lengthening liturgical prayers at the expense of Benedict's parallel emphasis on manual labor. This liturgical inflation is more evident in the eleventh century than in the tenth. The monastery of Cluny, whose ritualism is usually blamed here, had for a long time remained faithful to Carolingian Benedictine liturgical reforms, but then, under abbots Odilo (994–1049) and Hugh (1049–1109), the number of recited psalms increased by about a third.[43]

Monks described their liturgies in their customaries.[44] In the tenth and eleventh centuries they produced the vast majority of the texts that fill the sixteen quarto volumes of the *Corpus Consuetudinum Monasticarum*.[45] The customaries in themselves document a desire for reform because in a well-functioning monastery the monks would not have needed to write

41. For general surveys, see Josef A. Jungmann, *Pastoral Liturgy* (London: Challoner, 1962), 105–22; Robert F. Taft, *The Liturgy of the Hours in East and West: The Origins of the Divine Office and Its Meaning for Today* (Collegeville, MN: Liturgical Press, 1986), 3–213; Harper, *Forms and Orders of Western Liturgy*, 73–108; Palazzo, *History of Liturgical Books*, 113–67.

42. Pfaff, *Liturgy in Medieval England*, 98; Jesse D. Billett, "The Divine Office and the Secular Clergy in Later Anglo-Saxon England," in Rollason et al., *England and the Continent*, 429–71, esp. 429–31.

43. Constable, *Abbey of Cluny*, 1, 48–49, and 78; Iogna-Prat, "Coutumes et statuts clunisiens comme sources historiques (ca. 990–ca. 1200)," *Revue Mabillon*, n.s., 3 (1992): 23–48, esp. 35.

44. Donnat, "Les coutumes monastiques autour de l'an Mil," in Iogna-Prat and Picard, *Religion et culture autour de l'an Mil*, 17–24, esp. 17n; Joachim Wollasch, "Reformmönchtum und Schriftlichkeit," *Frühmittelalterliche Studien* 26 (1992): 274–86, quoted 278. See also Aimé-Georges Martimort, *Les "ordines," les ordinaires et les cérémoniaux*, Typologie 56 (Turnhout, Belg.: Brepols, 1991); Palazzo, *History of Liturgical Books*, 213–32.

45. *Corp CM*, 16 vols., ed. Kassius Hallinger (Siegburg, Ger.: Franz Schmitt, 1963–87), discussed in Donnat, "Les coutumiers monastiques: Une nouvelle enterprise et un territoire nouveau," *Revue Mabillon*, n.s., 3 (1992): 5–21.

Table 1. Liturgy of the hours

Hour	Time celebrated	Clock time (at equinox)
Matins	Eighth hour of the night	2:00 a.m.
Lauds	Daybreak	About 5:30 a.m.
Prime	First hour of the day	6:00 a.m.
Terce	Third hour of the day	9:00 a.m.
Sext	Sixth hour of the day	12:00 noon
None	Ninth hour of the day	3:00 p.m.
Vespers	Before dark	About 5:30 p.m.
Compline	Before retiring	

Sources: Chart adapted from Lila Collamore, "Prelude: Charting the Divine Office," in *The Divine Office in the Latin Middle Ages: Methodology and Source Studies, Regional Developments, Hagiography, Written in Honor of Professor Ruth Steiner*, ed. Margot E. Fassler and Rebecca A. Baltzer (Oxford: Oxford University Press, 2000), 3–11, esp. 3. The prayers covered at each of these hours in the Rule of Benedict are charted in Sally Elizabeth Roper, *Medieval English Benedictine Liturgy: Studies in the Formation, Structure, and Content of the Monastic Votive Office, c. 950–1540* (New York: Garland, 1993), table 1.1 on 181–86; and in Susan Boynton, "The Bible and the Liturgy," in *The Practice of the Bible in the Middle Ages: Production, Reception, and Performance in Western Christianity*, ed. Boynton and Diane J. Reilly (New York: Columbia University Press, 2011), 10–33, esp. 14–17.

down their local customs, which the *seniores* already knew and modeled. If, however, a monastery was seeking to reform by adopting the best practices of another house, then, unless it could import a critical mass of monks trained in the new system, it needed a written memorandum. We know the early usages of the monastery of Cluny, for example, less from its own documents than from descriptions of Cluniac customs made for other communities. Fleury's customary was specifically intended to document "imitable customs [*imitabiles consuetudines*]," allegedly practices that were "according to the model of the early Church."[46]

In the tenth and eleventh centuries, pious lay folk could participate in the monastic liturgy of the hours.[47] Monastic churches were usually large enough to accommodate the people of the neighborhood and had bells to summon them. Customaries such as the *Regularis Concordia* assume the presence of a popular community, especially on great feasts such as Holy Saturday, the vigil prior to Easter. Anecdotes mentioning such attendees

46. Thierry from Amorbach (fl. early 11th cent.), *Libelli de Consuetudinibus*, prol., ed. Davril and Donnat, 8, ed. and trans. Davril and Donnat, 172–73. The reform orientation of Fleury's *imitabiles consuetudines* was signaled in Wollasch, "Reformmönchtum und Schriftlichkeit," 278–79.

47. Jean Hubert, "La place faite aux laïcs dans les églises monastiques et dans les cathédrales aux XIe et XIIe siècles," in *I laici nella societas christiana dei secoli XI e XII, Atti della terza Settimana internazionale di studi 3, 21–27 agosta 1965* (Milan: Vita e pensiero, 1968), 470–87, esp. 474; Rosser, "Cure of Souls in English Towns," in Blair and Sharpe, *Pastoral Care before the Parish*, 270.

include a tale by Rodulfus Glaber about a man who mistook funeral bells for service bells: "Nearby there lived a fellow who was deeply religious though he was only a layman. He did not know of the brother's death and thought the bells were ringing for matins; so he set out, as he often did, to go to church."[48]

Architecture showcased this liturgy. Although clerics traditionally stood around the main altar in the east end of the church, the new churches offered more possibilities. A description in the customs of Fleury in the early eleventh century compares the church to a castle, a fortified Jerusalem guarded by members of the choir and defended by the arms of prayer, with the most senior monks placed at the balustrade of the sanctuary, guarding the entrance to the camp, and other arrangements of choirs and seats serving as additional battle stations.[49] Galleries, surviving earliest at Gernrode around 960 and featured in a number of German churches over the following decades, had Byzantine parallels but were probably intended to provide potential theatrical space for choirs.[50] It has been suggested that in some of the imperial German convents, new lateral galleries might have held choirs of nuns while the abbess would have been enthroned in the west work; the later provision of galleries over the arms of the transept might have brought canonesses and nuns nearer to the priest conducting services in the sanctuary.[51] Archaeological traces of diagrams for basic music instruction support the claims of late writers that the west work at Corvey was a place where a "chorus angelicus" of young children sang.[52] Western galleries also offered potential space for pipe organs. The gradual shift toward tunnel vaulting, evident first in the Mediterranean and then progressing north, probably produced acoustical changes that ecclesiastical musicians would have had to take into account.

The liturgy of the hours incorporated processions that took advantage of the symbolic values of different sites within the grand new churches. For example, the *galilea*, constructed as part of the west work, a sort of entrance hall to the nave with a second-floor chapel above, became

48. Rodulfus Glaber, *Historiae* II xx, France, 86–87. Other miracle stories involving laymen present at the monastic offices are found in Bernard of Chartres, *Miracula Fidis* I xxii and II xii, Bouillet, 59–60 and 120–22, Sheingorn, 88, 137–39.

49. Thierry of Amorbach, *Libelli de consuetudinibus* II xxiv, ed. Davril and Donnat, 34–35, ed. and trans. Davril and Donnat, 210–13.

50. Hiltje F. H. Zomer, "The So-Called Women's Gallery in the Medieval Church: An Import from Byzantium?," in Davids, *Empress Theophano*, 290–306; Plant, "Architectural Developments in the Empire," in Hiscock, *White Mantle of Churches*, 29–56, esp. 39.

51. Taylor, "Tenth-Century Church Building," in Parsons, *Tenth-Century Studies*, 141–68, esp. 142.

52. McClendon, *Origins of Medieval Architecture*, 192–93.

popular in French Burgundy, where Cluniac monks used it for burial rituals and prayers for the dead so that, as they marched through that porch on their way to choir, moving from the realm of death to the wide space where they would recite the office, they were reversing the route along which one day their own bodies would be carried, making each liturgical office a "new Easter."[53] Out of the liturgy came the *prosae*, the writing of separate syllables for each note; then followed all sorts of tropes, sequences, and notation systems; then out of the dialogued tropes came plays, the *ludi*, which contributed to the development of liturgical dramas. These could utilize the whole church. Tower porches, important in the Loire and the Île de France, helped to stage the trope of *Quem Quaeritis?* (Whom Do You Seek?), in which symbolically vested monks took the parts of the angel and of the women at the tomb of Christ, exchanging dialogue antiphons until the final *Te Deum Laudamus* when all the bells rang out.[54]

Illustrations of this event, which situate the women and the angel in an elaborate tower, simultaneously evoke both Constantine's circular church over the Holy Sepulchre and the church towers that clerics used in reenacting the *Quem Quaeritis*: see particularly the images of the visit to the Holy Sepulchre in a famous eleventh-century Winchester psalter leaf, reproduced here, and in the *Benedictional of Aethelwold*.[55] Because the women at the tomb were known through an ancient iconographic tradition, here architecture, art, and liturgy all converge.[56]

53. Extensive discussion of this architectural feature can be found in the section "La Bourgogne et le galilée clunisienne," in Sapin, *Avant-nefs*, 397–437; and in Kristina Krüger, "Architecture and Liturgical Practice: The Cluniac *Galilea*," in Hiscock, *White Mantle of Churches*, 138–159; and Krüger, "Monastic Customs and Liturgy in the Light of the Architectural Evidence: A Case Study on Processions (Eleventh-Twelfth Centuries)," in *From Dead of Night to End of Day: The Medieval Customs of Cluny*, ed. Susan Boynton and Isabelle Cochelin (Turnhout, Belg.: Brepols, 2005), 191–220. According to Frederick S. Paxton, *The Death Ritual at Cluny in the Central Middle Ages* (Turnhout, Belg.: Brepols, 2013), 30–33, the funerary use and symbolism of the *galilea* chapel became less important in Cluny III. On the symbolism see Gilo, *Vita Hugonis* II i, Cowdrey, 91.

54. A detailed early account from ca. 970 is found in the *Regularis Concordia* lxxviii–lxxix, ed. Symons et al., 123–27, trans. Symons, 49–50. This rite is explicated in G. W. G. Wickham, "The Romanesque Style in Medieval Drama," in Parsons, *Tenth Century Studies*, 115–22, esp. 119; and in Kobialka, *This Is My Body*, 18–24 and 77–79. On the use of the west work as a stage backdrop, see Éliane Vergnolle, "Un carnet de modèles de l'an Mil originaire de Saint-Benoît-sur-Loire (Paris, B.N. lat. 8318 + Rome, Vat. Reg. Lat. 596)," *Arte medievale* 2 (1984): 23–56, esp. 40–41.

55. The Psalter leaf, found in British Library, Cotton MS Tiberius C.VI, fol. 13v, is discussed in Carol Heitz, "The Iconography of Architectural Form," in *The Anglo-Saxon Church: Papers on History, Architecture, and Archaeology in Honour of Dr. H. M. Taylor*, ed. L. A. S. Butler and R. K. Morris (London: Council for British Archaeology, 1986), 90–100, esp. 95–96. The image in the *Benedictional of Aethelwold*, British Library Add MS 49598, fol. 51v, is discussed in Kobialka, *This Is My Body*, 89–92. On the Aethelwold Psalter, which is datable to 971–84, see Pfaff, *Liturgy in Medieval England*, 81–83.

56. See Heitz, "*Sepulcrum Domini*: Le sépulcre visité par les saintes femmes (IX⁰–XI⁰ siècle)," in *Haut moyen-âge: Culture, éducation et société: Études offertes à Pierre Riché*, ed. Michel Sot (La Garenne-Colombes: Editions européennes Erasme, 1990), 389–400; Bedingfield, *Dramatic Liturgy of Anglo-Saxon England*, 156–70.

FIGURE 24. Women visit the tomb of Christ, imagined in a way that evokes both the Church of the Holy Sepulchre in Jerusalem and the new ecclesiastical architecture used in the *Quem Quaeritis* liturgy. © The British Library Board, Cotton Collection MS Tiberius C. VI, fol. 13v.

The new three-dimensional art could also be integrated into the dramatic liturgy when the Magi at the end of their quest would witness the unveiling of a beloved statue of Mary and the infant Jesus or when the great crucifix would be taken down after the Good Friday service and laid on wrappings in a tomb.[57] Here teaching by word and deed had developed to the point where "the monks were the book."[58] The ceremony of the Easter

---

57. Forsyth, *Throne of Wisdom*, 49 and 52–59.

58. Cochelin, "When the Monks Were the Book: The Bible and Monasticism (6th to 11th Centuries)," in Boynton and Reilly, *Practice of the Bible*, 61–83.

sepulchre would develop in later centuries to include elaborate rites, impressive monuments, and lots of lay participation and fund-raising.[59]

The divine office has been hailed as the "perfect expression and synthesis" of monastic learning and prayer.[60] New feasts required new offices, and old offices were constantly revised. Thousands of monastic hymns were written, in dozens of musical forms each of which had its own laws and history. The language and music became increasingly sophisticated. The tenth century saw the spread of rhymed prose, two-syllable rhyming at full stops,[61] and of *cursus*, the use of specific prose rhythms at full stops.[62] Liturgical music was increasingly standardized as a result of new systems of recording music, the use of the organ in both the liturgy and music teaching, and early experiments with polyphony.[63] Pessimistic observers may regard all these bells and whistles as proof that liturgical Latin had become so poorly understood that a sonorous liturgical ambience was now more important than clearly sung, easily understandable prayer. This theory sounds plausible, but it fails to explain why prose rhythm also appears in Old English sermons and hagiography, in which linguistic obscurity should not have been such an issue.[64] In both cases the goal may simply have been a more elevated style.

The tenth-century liturgy of the hours also required many books.[65] This was a problem because the fourth chapter of the Rule of Chrodegang and the fiftieth chapter of the Rule of Benedict urge clerks to recite the hours in private when they are not able to celebrate them in common. New developments made this easier. Books of hours began to be produced for private

---

59. Pamela Sheingorn, *The Easter Sepulchre in England* (Kalamazoo, MI: Western Michigan University Medieval Institute, 1987), esp. 6–32.

60. Jean Leclercq, *The Love of Learning and the Desire for God: A Study of Monastic Culture*, trans. Catharine Misrahi (New York: Fordham University Press, 1961), esp. 287–308.

61. Karl Polheim, *Die lateinische Reimprosa* (Berlin: Weidmann, 1925); Jean-Yves Tilliette, "La poésie métrique latines: Ateliers et genres," in Iogna-Prat and Picard, *Religion et culture autour de l'an Mil*, 103–9, esp. 107; Gunilla Björkvall and Andreas Haug, "Performing Latin Verse: Text and Music in Early Medieval Versified Offices," in *Divine Office in the Latin Middle Ages: Methodology and Source Studies, Regional Developments, Hagiography, Written in Honor of Professor Ruth Steiner*, ed. Margot E. Fassler and Rebecca A. Balzer (Oxford: Oxford University Press), 278–99.

62. Tore Janson, *Prose Rhythm in Medieval Latin from the 9th to the 13th Century* (Stockholm: Almqvist & Wiksell, 1975), esp. 35–64 and 104. Janson's gross generalizations still stand, even though his pioneering application of statistical methodology to the measurement of cursus has been criticized and refined. On Wulfstan's use of cursus, for example, see Michael Lapidge and Michael Winterbottom, eds., introduction to *Wulfstan of Winchester: Vita Aethelwoldi* (Oxford: Clarendon, 1991), cx–cxi.

63. Giovanni Varelli, "Two Newly Discovered Tenth-Century Organa," *Early Music History* 32 (2013): 277–315, esp. 315.

64. Peter Clemoes, "Late Old English Literature," in Parsons, *Tenth Century Studies*, 102–14, esp. 114; Haruko Momma, "Rhythm and Alliteration: Styles of Aelfric's Prose up to the *Lives of the Saints*," in Karkov and Brown, *Anglo-Saxon Styles*, 253–69, esp. 255.

65. Hughes, *Medieval Manuscripts for Mass and Office*, 160–244.

offices and even for the standard offices themselves. The eleventh century experimented with special books for each hour of prayer—*nocturnalis liber, diurnale, matutinale* or *liber matutinalis*—but these proved to be liturgical dead ends.[66] Consolidation triumphed: autonomous hymnals are mentioned with increasing frequency in monastic customaries of the tenth and eleventh centuries; liturgical homilaries are incorporated into office lectionaries; hagiographical readings appear in passionals and legendaries.[67] The ultimate result of these various experiments was the breviary, which appears widely in the eleventh century, although one can find fragmentary antecedents from the ninth and tenth. Just as the missal had abstracted readings from many different sorts of Mass books so that it presented in one place everything a priest would need to conduct a service, so also the breviary sought to combine readings from all the different books required to celebrate the offices. To keep the breviary from being too unwieldy, many of the pieces were shortened so that psalms and litanies were often reduced to a few sentences, or even a few words.[68]

INTO THE WORLD

Processions of pagan priests had confirmed ancient cities as symbolic temples and celebrated the numinous springs, caves, groves, and mountains that surrounded them. Claiming this sacred landscape for Christ would not be easy. Even in Rome itself, Constantine's grand new basilicas were built out in the suburbs, insufficient to Christianize either the civic center still dominated by pagan temples or the countryside beyond. To claim the public square, Christianity needed to step out into the world. It did. Early medieval Rome has been described as a city united by liturgy.[69] Processions, pilgrimages, and blessings flourished and developed.[70] Processions would be a particularly lively part of the millennial Church's attempts to Christianize the world.

Many took place within church precincts. In theory the Mass itself included at least three processions: a formal entry (the *introit*), an offertory

---

66. Palazzo, *History of Liturgical Books*, 131–32.

67. Ibid., 143, 156, 157.

68. Pierre Salmon, *The Breviary through the Centuries*, trans. Sister David Mary (Collegeville, MN: Liturgical Press, 1962), esp. 11–12; Taft, *Liturgy of the Hours in East and West*, 297–306, esp. 299–300; Pierre-Marie Gy, "Les premiers bréviaires de Saint-Gall (deuxième quart du XIᵉ s.)," in *Liturgie, Gestalt und Vollzug*, ed. Walter Dürig (Munich: M. Hueber, 1963), 104–113; Palazzo, *History of Liturgical Books*, 169–72.

69. Romano, *Liturgy and Society*, esp. 109–39.

70. On Christian processions and recent scholarly interest in them, see Kathleen Ashley, "Introduction: The Moving Subjects of Professional Performance," and C. Clifford Flanigan, "The Moving Subject: Medieval Liturgical Processions in Semiotic and Cultural Perspective," in *Moving Subjects: Processional Performance in the Middle Ages and the Renaissance*, ed. Ashley and Wim Hüsken (Amsterdam: Rodopi, 2001), 7–34 and 35–51; Palazzo, *L'espace rituel et le sacré*, esp. 24–41; Rivard, *Blessing the World*, 217–67.

during which gifts were brought to the altar, and a communion service in which worshippers came forward to receive the sacrament. Processions inside a church implicitly presuppose that some areas are holier than others. There is the sanctuary itself, the space around the high altar; there are side altars, often elevated on steps and located in architecturally demarcated chapels. In monastic or collegiate churches the eastern end with its high altar is associated with the clergy and the opposing west end with the lay folk. For example, the mid-tenth-century Ottonian monastery of St. Maximin at Trier has a nave of nearly ninety yards divided by a central altar that separates the eastern half, with its three parallel apses, reserved for the monastic community, from the western half with its "mighty tower" reserved for the laity.[71] Processions could display, affirm, and explain such features. For example, William of Volpiano's extravagant Saint-Bénigne at Dijon has left three surviving customaries that describe in detail a variety of liturgical processions utilizing the new spaces and the many altars.[72] The main doorway of a church—usually integrated into an impressive west work, tower, or decorative porch—was a portal between the sacred and the profane and thus the natural place for liminal rituals such as the announcement of betrothals, the reintegration of public penitents, and, of course, the entrances and exits of processions.[73]

Late Antique churches had formal *atria* beyond their entrances, courtyards whose porticos provided open yet restricted space. Thanks to the penchant for copying Old St. Peter's, *atria* do appear occasionally in prestigious Carolingian and millennial churches, as, for example at Cluny II, but most sacred entrances were not so monumentally framed. Small country churches were lucky if their churchyards were fenced and gated well enough to keep out the pigs. Nevertheless, a penumbra of sacredness surrounded all a church's properties because they too were theoretically protected by the celestial patron(s) At Fleury, for example, during a famine so great that a wolf carried off a women's baby, the wolf allegedly dropped the infant as soon as it entered the lands of St. Benedict;[74] near Conques men who wished to usurp Sainte Foy's territory were struck blind as soon as they rode across the property line.[75] The precincts of churches had their own sacred geographies that processions could trace.

---

71. Bandmann, *Early Medieval Architecture*, 42; Warren Sanderson, "Considerations on the Ottonian Monastic Church of Saint Maximin at Trier," in Much, *Baukunst des Mittelalters*, 173–98, esp. 173.

72. Malone, *Saint-Bénigne de Dijon*, 171–225.

73. On the roles of the entrance complex, see Alain Dierkens, "Avant-corps, galilées, massifs occidentaux: Quelques remarques méthodologiques en guise de conclusions," in Sapin, *Avant-nefs*, 495–97.

74. Adrevaldus, *Miracula Benedicti* I xxxix, Certain, 82–83.

75. Bernard of Chartres, *Miracula Fidis* III xiv, Bouillet, 140, Scheingorn, 162–63.

Certain rites, however, naturally brought the liturgy into the world. One was the burial service. After a funeral Mass and various rites, clergy and laypeople would escort the body to a tomb in consecrated ground. This might involve nothing more than a simple procession from the church to an adjacent cemetery, usually accompanied by ringing bells. Yet some good-byes were more elaborate. This might be expected in the case of Otto III (d. 1002), who died in Italy in January and whose body, carried across the Alps despite the winter, traversed Germany in a dramatic Lenten procession, challenged along the way by would-be claimants to the crown. It stopped at Augsburg, where Otto's entrails were interred; sojourned during Holy Week at Cologne, where his procession visited the major churches and merged into the rites of the reconciliation of penitents; and culminated with a novel Easter burial at Aachen.[76] A lesser state occasion was the funeral of Bishop Burchard of Worms (d. 1025), where "his knights were present at his exequies, venerable and illustrious men, and after bearing the body around to all the monasteries, they brought it to his principal seat [that is, to his actual throne in the cathedral]," where on the next day it was buried in the western side of the choir.[77] Perhaps more surprising is a mutilated fragment from a Winchester sacramentary, written ca. 1000, which describes the route of a procession, beginning and ending at Winchester's cathedral, the "Old Minster," in which the body of a dead monk of St. Swithun's was taken to a string of local churches, with stops at each one for special intercessory prayers, effectively transforming all of Winchester into ritual space.[78]

External processions were also required to consecrate the new buildings of the white garment of churches.[79] Ecclesiastical dedications were so important that they constitute about a tenth of the ordines and nearly a quarter of the word count in the *Romano-German Pontifical*. They had to be impressive because they established sacred space. Only bishops could dedicate churches, often in association with visiting bishops (perhaps even the pope himself after the mid-eleventh century) and accompanied by sec-

76. Theitmar, *Chronicon* IV l–liii, Holtzmann, 189–95, Warner, 187–90. Context in Nicholas Gussone, "Religion in a Crisis of Interregnum: The Role of Religion in Bridging the Gap between Otto III and Henry II," in *Monotheistic Kingship: The Medieval Variants*, ed. Aziz Al-Azmeh and Janos M. Bak (Budapest: Central European University Press, 2004), 119–35.

77. Ebbo of Worms (?), *Vita Burchardi Episcopi* xxv, ed. Georg Waitz, MGH *SS* 4 (Hannover: Hann, 1844), 829–46, esp. 846.

78. Worcester, Worcester Chapter Library, MS F.173, fol. 21r, ed. Cuthbertson H. Turner, in "The Churches at Winchester in the Early Eleventh Century," *Journal of Theological Studies* 17 (1916): 65–68.

79. For studies, see Iogna-Prat, *La Maison Dieu*, esp. 172–76, 259–95; Louis I. Hamilton, *A Sacred City: Consecrating Churches and Reforming Society in Eleventh-Century Italy* (Manchester, UK: Manchester University Press, 2010), esp. 13–55.

ular officials ranging from local notables to kings and emperors. Processions were required to bring the bishop and the relics to the new church and to circumambulate its boundaries. Then followed an elaborate entry ritual, accompanied by a litany, in which the bishop was required to knock on the church door three times with his staff before he was finally admitted, as illustrated here in an early eleventh-century English pontifical.[80]

The interior of the church, depending upon the details of the rite, was "baptized" and/or "confirmed," procedures requiring much holy water, many crosses applied in holy oil, and even an X of obscure origins spanning the church, drawn by the bishop with his staff, using the Latin alphabet for one diagonal and the Greek for the other.[81] The climax of the interior ceremony was the deposition of relics into the altar, but there might also be separate dedications and blessings for side altars, furnishings, and the churchyard. These elaborate ceremonies were all expressions of reform: a ruined church would be reconsecrated to its original holy purpose; the rocks, timbers, spolia, and relics of a newly built church would be repurposed into a structure intended to praise their ultimate creator; the new church would help convert the surrounding wilderness or urban chaos into a Christian landscape. Peter Damian, in a sermon on church dedications, analogizes the inscription of divine law on the human heart with the "inscription of the law" into a church building where the Bible would be proclaimed.[82]

Elaborate processions were associated with feasts of local patron saints and with Palm Sunday. One way to involve many churches in these rites was a system of "stational liturgy," technically "a service of worship at a designated church, shrine, or public place in or near a city or town, on a designated feast, fast, or commemoration, which is presided over by the bishop or his representative and intended as the local church's main liturgical celebration of the day."[83] The elaborate stational and processional liturgies of Jerusalem, Rome, and Constantinople were famous. Perhaps originally these were attempts to link together communities where social differences, schisms, or heretical movements had previously threatened

80. Rouen Bibliothèque Municipale MS A.27 (cat. 368) (*Pontificale Lanaletense*), fol. 2v.

81. *Pontificale Romano-Germanicum* xxxiii–lv, ed. Cyrille Vogel and Reinhard Elze, *Le Pontifical romano-germanique du dixième siècle*, 3 vols. (Vatican City: BAV, 1963–1972), 1:82–194, offers a multitude of dedications, blessings, and symbolic explanations thereof, rites generally involving processions into and within the new church, often specified as *cum clero et populo*.

82. Peter Damian, *Sermo* lxxii, ed. Giovanni Lucchesi, *Petrus Damiani Sermones*, CCCM 57 (Turnhout, Belg.: Brepols, 1983), 421–30, esp. 422. See Jennifer A. Harris, "Peter Damian and the Architecture of Self," in *Das Eigene und das Ganze: Zum Individuellen im mittelalterlichen Religiosentum*, ed. Gert Melville and Markus Schürer (Münster: LIT, 2002), 131–57, esp. 140–43.

83. John F. Baldovin, *The Urban Character of Christian Worship: The Origins, Development, and Meaning of Stational Liturgy* (Rome: Pontificium Institutum Studiorum Orientalium, 1987), 37; Iogna-Prat, *La Maison Dieu*, 183–88.

FIGURE 25. A bishop consecrates a church, as illustrated in the "Lanalet Pontifical" of the early eleventh century. Rouen Bibliothèque Municipale MS A.27 (cat. 368), fol. 2v. Image from Collections de la Bibliothèque municipale de Rouen.

unity. In theory bishops could arrive at the designated church unheralded or with only a modest escort, but in practice the episcopal comings and goings naturally inspired formal processions.[84] Stational processions are documented earliest in the East at Antioch, Constantinople, and Jerusalem.

84. Maureen C. Miller, "The Florentine Bishop's Ritual Entry and the Origins of the Medieval Episcopal *Adventus*," *RHE* 98 (2003): 5–28, esp. 10–15; followed by Miller, "Urban Space, Sacred Topography, and Ritual Meanings in Florence: The Route of the Bishop's Entry, ca. 1200–1600," in Ott and Jones, *Bishop Reformed* (Aldershot, UK: Ashgate, 2007), 237–49.

Although Rome's stational liturgy was very early, its assembly places for the associated popular processions are not documented until the end of the seventh century and the start of the eighth.[85] Its ecclesiastical processions were probably influenced by those in Constantinople, judging from their relatively late emergence, the introduction of the Kyrie, the use of Greek technical terms such as *letania* (litany) and *antiphonia* (antiphon), and the use of similar processional crosses featuring triple candles.[86] The Roman stational liturgy ultimately found echoes in places such as Angers, Augsburg, Autun, Chartres, Cologne, Limoges, Mainz, Metz, Paris, Pavia, Strasbourg, Tours, Trier, and Verona.[87] Studies on individual ecclesiastical buildings and processions may miss the point that "it was precisely the city as a whole which was to be the locus of the Church."[88]

Outdoor ceremonies were often impressive. A papal procession, as described in an *Ordo Letaniae Maioris*, starts with the poor from the poor house, who carry the painted wooden cross and cry "Kyrie eleison" as they exit the church; after them come seven cross bearers, carrying the seven stational crosses each with three lighted candles; then come the bishops or priests and the subdeacons; the pope himself follows with deacons, preceded by two silver crosses carried by subdeacons and by censers borne by the officers of the church; after him marches the *schola cantorum* singing.[89] Processional order might have symbolic significance. For example, an abbot of Saint-Riquier commanded his monks to travel in the Easter procession in ranks seven by seven in order to demonstrate the sevenfold grace of the Holy Spirit.[90] Yet this was also *imitatio Romae* inasmuch

---

85. Baldovin, *Urban Character of Christian Worship*, 122. According to Jacob A. Latham, "From Literal to Spiritual Soldiers of Christ: Disputed Episcopal Elections and the Advent of Christian Processions in Late Antique Rome," *Church History* 81 (2012): 298–327, ecclesiastical processions in Rome were initially discouraged by its secular aristocracy. Especially important in Rome's development of popular processions were the Syrian Pope Sergius (687–701), who established the first known regularly scheduled processions for the feasts of the Virgin, and the Siculo-Greek Pope Stephen II (752–57), who vastly expanded their number. Ad hoc popular processions had occurred at earlier dates, including the famous response to the plague of 590 organized by Gregory I. For processions involving Rome's icons, see Belting, *Likeness and Presence*, esp. 68–73.

86. Belting, *Likeness and Presence*, 166, 237.

87. Baldovin, *Urban Character of Christian Worship*, 248–49, lists references to nearly two dozen stational liturgies. For an explication of the one at Metz, see Martin A. Claussen, *The Reform of the Frankish Church: Chrodegang of Metz and the* Regula Canonicorum *in the Eighth Century* (New York: Cambridge University Press, 2004), 276–89.

88. Baldovin, *Urban Character of Christian Worship*, 35.

89. *Ordo XXI*, ed. Michel Andrieu, *Les Ordines Romani du haut moyen age*, 5 vols. (Louvain: Spicilegium Sacrum Lovaniense, 1931–1961), 3:237–49, esp. 248.

90. Angilbertus (d. 814), *Institutio* vii, ed. Ferdinand Lot, in *Hariulf: Chronique de l'Abbaye de Saint-Riquier (Vᵉ siècle–1104)* (Paris: Alphonse Picard et Fils, 1894), 296–306, esp. 300.

as the Easter ritual in Rome, according to the ordines, used seven ranks of acolytes.[91]

Monks had grand processions. Monastic complexes often contained multiple churches: San Vincenzo al Volturno had eight, Farfa, six.[92] Evidence for processions linking them together can be found in their architecture: lengthy and elaborate galleries might be constructed to protect processants, most famously at the huge Carolingian Abbey of Saint-Riquier, where arcades spanned the whole monastic settlement.[93]

Processions at their best were models of good order: an early twelfth-century Crusade *chanson*, when attempting to describe a precise military maneuver, says, "All arrived at the mêlée in disorder, but the knights are good / and create a wheeling mass (?) in the midst of the Turks / Such as monks adopt when they are in solemn procession."[94] Cluny's processions were famous.[95] In the detailed Cluniac customary that constitutes the monastery of Farfa's *Liber Tramitis*, the sections discussing the great liturgical seasons and feasts usually start with chapters *De Processione* that read as if they were recipes: they list how many participants of each rank should be in the initial procession, how they should be dressed, and what equipment each should take (how many Gospel books, crosses, censers, candelabra, etc.); next the customary specifies the order of the procession, its prayers, and its destinations.[96] Robert of Arbrissel (d. 1117), when asked whether he would prefer to die at Rome or Jerusalem or Cluny, chose instead his own foundation of Fontevraud but remarked wistfully that Cluny was "where gorgeous processions take place."[97]

In England processions are specified in the earliest of the customaries, the *Regularis Concordia* of around 970, and in almost all that follow.[98] Because English churchmen had tended to rebuild by adding new churches next to

---

91. Baldovin, *Urban Character of Christian Worship*, 132–33.

92. Howe, *Church Reform*, 3–4; Schulenburg, *Forgetful of Their Sex*, 83–84.

93. Taylor "Tenth-Century Church Building," 141–68, esp. 146–52; McClendon, *Origins of Medieval Architecture*, 150–58; Doig, *Liturgy and Architecture*, 126–30. Recent archaeological work at Saint-Riquier has not directly illuminated the exterior processional galleries but has highlighted the way that the whole Carolingian complex was designed for a sort of "stational liturgy": see Honoré Bernard, "Saint-Riquier, fouilles et découvertes récentes," in Sapin, *Avant-nefs*, 88–107, esp. 106.

94. The *Canso d'Antioca: An Occitan Epic Chronicle of the First Crusade*, ed. Carol Sweetenham and Linda M. Patterson (Aldershot, UK: Ashgate, 2003), 234–35.

95. Michel Huglo, "The Cluniac Processional of Solesmes: Bibliothèque de l'Abbaye, Réserve 28," in Fassler and Balzer, *Divine Office in the Latin Middle Ages*, 205–33, esp. 207–8.

96. *Liber Tramitis*, Dinter, esp. 239–43. On the Palm Sunday procession described there, see Forsyth, *Throne of Wisdom*, 41–42.

97. Andrea, *Vita Roberti* q 32, ed. and trans. Jacques Dalarun, *The Two Lives of Robert of Arbrissel, Founder of Fontevraud: Legends, Writings, and Testimonies* (Turnhout, Belg.: Brepols, 2006), 189–300, esp. 250–51.

98. Gittos, "Sacred Space in Anglo-Saxon England," 117–43, and *Architecture, Liturgy*, 103–45, provides the best overview of the evidence.

FIGURE 26. Galleries at Saint-Riquier, built to facilitate ecclesiastical processions. Centula/ St. Riquier, depicted from a 1673 engraving reproducing a lost medieval image reflecting the form of the Carolingian monastery. Reproduced with permission from the Bibliothèque nationale de France, Département des estampes et photographie.

venerable older ones, they had clusters of churches that processions could link. Some additional English processional activity was a legacy from the days when services in the countryside had been administered by communities of clergymen in minsters": although independent parish churches had gradually replaced what was left of that extended system of pastoral care, in some places representatives of former daughter churches continued to bring offerings to former mother churches on their feast days.[99] England's processional season ran from Candlemas to Rogationtide, from early spring

99. P. H. Hase, "The Mother Churches of Hampshire," in *Minsters and Parish Churches: The Local Church in Transition, 950–1050*, ed. John Blair (Oxford: Oxford University Committee for Archaeology, 1988), 45–66, esp. 58, 60, 65–66; Gittos, "Sacred Space in Anglo-Saxon England," 135–38, and *Architecture, Liturgy*, 138–39.

to early summer, but there were additional recurring processions as well as ad hoc ones organized for funerals, translations of saints, royal arrivals, and other events. For the most solemn, the monks were encouraged to put even the choir boys into albs and, if the resources of the house and the weather permitted, to issue each a candle.[100] Early medieval Irish monastic or ere-mitical sites featured processions whose stations were marked by standing stones and inscribed crosses.[101] Irish tribes seem to have often marched with their relics, although few early sources and reliquaries exist because of the depredations of Vikings and later invaders.[102]

The new portable giant reliquaries brought saints out of their churches and into the world. These relatively light, wood-framed, metal-clad con-structions were probably designed specifically for processions (some wear patterns support this theory).[103] Relics in processions appealed especially to the popular imagination. Note the contrasting emphases of the Latin and Old English versions of the 1009 "Edict when the Great Army Came to England" (an ecclesiastical response to the Danish invasion). After requir-ing preparatory prayers and fasting, the version in Latin asks that "each priest with his people go out on procession with bare feet for three days"; the parallel version in English—presumably addressed to a less clerical audience—says that "all are to go out with the relics and to call on Christ eagerly from their inmost hearts.[104] Hagiographical literature suggests that mobile reliquaries, especially the majestas ones, were increasingly pressed into service to protect a monastery's possessions. For example, processions to patrol Sainte Foy's boundaries at Conques, according to Bernard of Chartres writing around 1015, had become almost routine:

> For it is a deeply rooted practice and firmly established custom that, if any land given to Sainte Foy is unjustly appropriated by a usurper for any rea-son, the reliquary of the holy virgin is carried out to that land as a witness in regaining the right to her property. The monks announce that there will be a solemn procession of the clergy and laity, who move forward with great

---

100. *Regularis Concordi* LIII, ed. Symons et al., 101; trans. Symons, 30–31.

101. Michael Herity, "The Antiquity of *an Turas* (the Pilgrimage Round) in Ireland," in *Lateinische Kultur im VIII. Jahrhundert: Traube-Gedenkschrift*, ed. Albert Lehner and Walter Berschin (St. Ottilien: EOS, 1989), 95–143; Herity, "Early Christian Decorative Slabs in Donegal: *An Turas* and the Tomb of the Founder Saint," in *Donegal: History and Society*, ed. William Nolan, Liam Ronayne, and Malread Dunleavy (Dublin: Geog-raphy Publications, 1995), 25–50.

102. Picard, "Le culte des reliques en Irlande (VIIᵉ–IXᵉ siècle)," in Bozóky and Helvetius, *Reliques*, 39–55, esp. 53–55.

103. Snoeck, *Medieval Piety*, 251–68; Forsyth, *Throne of Wisdom*, 8–9 and 38–39.

104. Wulfstan, Latin Version: "Edict When the Great Army Came to England," esp. q 2.2, in Whitelock et al., *Councils & Synods*, 373–78, esp. 376; Wulfstan, Old English version q 2.1, ibid., 379–82, esp. 380. Some background on these penitential processions is provided in Clare A. Lees, *Tradition and Belief: Religious Writ-ing in Late Anglo-Saxon England* (Minneapolis: University of Minnesota Press, 1999), 1–3.

formality carrying candles and lamps. A processional cross goes in front of the holy relics, embellished all around with enamels and gold and studded with a variety of gems flashing like stars. The novices serve by carrying a gospel book, holy water, clashing cymbals, and even trumpets made of ivory that were donated by noble pilgrims to adorn the monastery. It is certainly incredible to report what miracles were worked in processions of this kind.[105]

From the mid-eleventh century on, processions helped raise money for building campaigns and other good works.[106] Relics and reliquaries could be paraded out for oath swearing, for penitential processions, and for judicial ordeals.[107] The Roman liturgy since the seventh century had included elaborate processions in honor of Mary that showcased beloved icons; around the year 1000 Cluniac usage encouraged similar celebrations in monasteries throughout Europe centered on images of Christ and Mary.[108]

The greatest processional activity involving relics was associated with Peace of God and Truce of God movements. These were essentially converging processions. Rodulfus Glaber famously describes enthusiastic "great councils of the whole people, to which were borne the bodies of many saints and innumerable caskets of holy relics. . . . Such enthusiasm was generated that the bishops raised their croziers to the heavens, and all cried out with one voice to God, their hands extended: 'Peace! Peace! Peace!'"[109] Bernard of Chartres offers more detail about the reliquaries brought to such a meeting of saints:

> The most reverent Arnald, bishop of Rodez [post 1004, attested 1025–31), had convened a synod that was limited to the parishes of his diocese. To this synod, the bodies of the saints were conveyed in reliquary boxes or in golden images by various communities of monks or canons. The ranks of saints were arranged in tents and pavilions in the meadow of Saint Felix, which is about a mile from Rodez. The golden majesties of St. Marius, confessor and bishop, and Saint Amans, also a confessor and bishop, and the golden reliquary box of Saint Saturninus, and the golden image of holy Mary, mother of God, and the golden majesty of Sainte-Foy especially adorned that place. In addition to these there were relics of many saints, but I can't give the exact number here.[110]

---

105. Bernard of Chartres, *Miracula Fidis* II iv, Bouillet, 100, Sheingorn, 120–21. These are explicated in Kathleen Ashley and Sheingorn, "*Sainte Foy* on the Loose, or the Possibilities of Procession," in Ashley and Hüsken, *Moving Subjects*, 53–67.

106. Pierre Héliot and Marie-Laure Chastang, "Quêtes et voyages de reliques au profit des églises françaises du moyen âge," *RHE* 59 (1964): 789–822, esp. 799–800, and *RHE* 60 (1965): 5–32; Reinhold Kaiser, "Quêtes itinérantes avec reliques pour financer la construction des églises (XIᵉ–XIIᵉ s.)," *Moyen âge* 101 (1995): 205–25.

107. David Rollason, *Saints and Relics in Anglo-Saxon England* (Oxford: Basil Blackwell, 1989), 190–95.

108. Rachel Fulton, *From Judgment to Passion: Devotion to Christ and the Virgin Mary, 800–1200* (New York: Columbia University Press, 2002), 269–73.

109. Rodulfus Glaber, *Historiae* IV xiv–xvi, France, 194–97.

110. Bernard of Chartres, *Miracula Fidis* I xxviii, Bouillet, 71–72, Sheingorn, 98.

Yet medieval churchmen may have extended their liturgical world a little too well. Although organized processions and outdoor assemblies illustrate and affirm the hierarchies they display, mobilizations can acquire their own momentum. In Western European documents around the year 1000, medieval historians have discovered an unprecedented "emergence of the crowd" and have speculated about possible economic, social, and religious explanations.[111] Yet a more basic question than what motivated the new crowds is how people had learned to participate in them. Peasants living in dispersed homesteads or small villages do not normally congregate in large numbers. Ecclesiastical gatherings taught them how to negotiate mass assemblies. They marched, sang, venerated the relics, and observed the liturgies and the preachers. And from the eleventh century forward, for better and for worse, crowds in the Western world would keep marching on, from peace assemblies to pilgrimages to Crusades to outdoor revivals led by apostolic or heretical preachers, and ultimately to peasant revolts.

111. Debates on the emergence of the crowd are surveyed in Howe, "*Gaudium et Spes*," 27–28; Leidulf Melve, *Inventing the Public Sphere: The Public Debate during the Investiture Contest* (c. 1030–1122), 2 vols. (Leiden, Neth.: Brill, 2007), 1:57–68; and Louis Hamilton, *Sacred City*, 10 and 56–88.

CHAPTER 6

"WHEN MY SOUL LONGS FOR THE DIVINE VISION"

There are many types of contemplation which the soul devoted to you, O Christ, can profit from and enjoy. But my spirit rejoices in none of them so much as in that wherein, putting aside all else, she raises up the simple contemplation of a pure heart to your Godhead alone. What peace, what rest, what delight does the spirit concentrated on you then enjoy! Behold, O Lord, when my soul longs for the divine vision, and, reaching out to capture you, meditates and sings of your glory, the burden of the flesh is less heavy, the tumult of thoughts ceases, the weight of our mortality and the well-rehearsed pattern of our anxieties fade. All things are silent. All is tranquil. The heart is on fire. The spirit rejoices. Remembrance flourishes. The intellect shines. And the whole soul burns with desire for the vision of your beauty, seeing itself taken over by the love of invisible things.

—John of Fécamp, *Confessio Theologica* (written ca. 1017–18)

SPIRITUALITY IN THE TENTH AND ELEVENTH CENTURIES?

The contemplative spirituality of Abbot John of Fécamp, so unexpected at the start of the eleventh century, raises multiple problems.[1] Can we even speak of spirituality in this period? *Spiritualitas* was used by medieval theologians in a general way to indicate spiritual quality independent from matter,

1. John of Fécamp, *Confessio Theologica Recapitulatio*, ed. Jean Leclercq and Jean-Paul Bonnes, in *Un maître de la vie spirituelle au XIᵉ siècle: Jean de Fécamp* (Paris: Vrin, 1946), 109–83, esp. 182.

but only in the nineteenth century did the term "spirituality" acquire its current sense as "the religious dimension of the inner life."[2] Spirituality, according to the mission statement of the series "World Spirituality," is located within the individual, in "the deepest center of the person," where "the person is open to the transcendent dimension" and he or she "experiences ultimate reality"; spirituality pertains to the "discovery of this core," to "prayer, spiritual direction, the various maps of the spiritual journey, and the methods of advancement in the spiritual ascent."[3] These abstractions may be helpful to today's students of comparative religion, but they would have perplexed millennial Latin Christians for whom spiritual ascent was a specifically Christian project guided by the Church. In fact, all human beings, despite occasional attempts at objectivity, necessarily approach the divine in culturally mediated ways, not in quests inspired by religiously neutral terms. This study therefore examines how millennial Latin Christians attempted to approach their God through a specifically Christian theological perspective.

Another stumbling block is the identification of spirituality with individual quest. Were millennial Christians autonomous individuals in the same way as today's citizens of the Atlantic world? Sir Richard Southern's *Making of the Middle Ages* situates the transition "from epic to romance" in the late eleventh and early twelfth centuries; in fact, Southern sometimes came close to seeing the movement toward increased individual self-consciousness that he so beautifully illuminates in his studies on Anselm of Canterbury (d. 1109) as an "Anselmian revolution."[4] Colin Morris's *The Discovery of the Individual, 1050–1200* extrapolates this line of thought to claim that the twelfth century invented "the individual."[5] Critics such as Caroline Bynum point out that the twelfth-century self-consciousness Morris describes differs from the absolute individualism treasured by many people today because it defines a person not in terms of freedom from social bonds but as a product of and a member of sometimes tragically conflicting social communities.[6] Further complicating matters is the

---

2. Vauchez, *Spirituality*, 7.

3. McGinn and Meyendorff, preface to *Christian Spirituality: Origins to the Twelfth Century*, xiii.

4. Southern, *Making of the Middle Ages*, 99–112.

5. Colin Morris, *The Discovery of the Individual, 1050–1200* (New York: Harper & Row, 1972), esp. 158–60.

6. Caroline Bynum, "Did the Twelfth Century Discover the Individual?," in *Jesus as Mother: Studies in the Spirituality of the High Middle Ages* (Berkeley: University of California Press, 1982), 82–109. On the progress of this debate, see Susan R. Kramer and Bynum, "Revisiting the Twelfth-Century Individual: The Inner Self and the Christian Community," in Melville and Schürer, *Das Eigene und das Ganze*, 75–85; Ineke van't Spijker, *Fictions of the Inner Life: Religious Literature and the Formation of the Self in the Eleventh and Twelfth Centuries* (Turnhout, Belg.: Brepols, 2004), esp. 1–15; Steven Lukes, *Individualism* (Colchester, UK: European Consortium for Political Research, 2006), 11–12; and Suzanne Verderber, *The Medieval Fold: Power, Repression, and the Emergence of the Individual* (New York: Palgrave Macmillan, 2013), esp. 5–24.

way that historians of the Renaissance and Enlightenment blithely locate the rise of the modern individual within their own favorite centuries.[7] Were members of the millennial Church self-aware individuals? No universal answer is possible. What can be asserted is that it is possible to find isolated expressions of individual spiritual longing such as the passage quoted at the opening of this chapter from John of Fécamp's *Confessio*.

A third obstacle is the rarity of documented introspection in the late tenth and early eleventh centuries. Members of the millennial Church were far better at doing things than at describing them. Students of spirituality in this period have found "no important compendium of spiritual teaching," "few works of spiritual advice," "no outstanding mystical authors," and in England "no directly monastic spiritual writings at all."[8] Yet if a lack of contemporary theoretical treatises were sufficient to demonstrate the nonexistence of significant spirituality, then parallel *argumenta ex silentio* also ought to demonstrate the absence of architecture, craftsmanship, and liturgical science—conclusions easily falsified by surviving artifacts and cultural ephemera. The problem with spirituality is that events occurring in a person's deepest center do not necessarily leave behind direct material evidence. Nevertheless, hints of changes in religious practice, vocabulary, and interests suggest that many aspects of high medieval spirituality may have roots in the tenth-century ecclesiastical revival.

A final conceptual problem is the diversity of the methods of advancement in the spiritual ascent employed by tenth- and eleventh-century Christians. This diversity is inherent in Christianity itself, whose scriptures enthusiastically incorporate the ancient Greek emphasis on teaching through "word and deed" (e.g., Luke 24:19; Acts 7:22; 2 Cor. 10:13; Rom. 15:18; Col. 3:17; 2 Thess. 2:17).[9] That theme animates patristic sources, particularly Augustine's *On Christian Doctrine*, whose fourth book stresses that a preacher's life must exemplify the doctrine he preaches;[10] Gregory

7. Lewis Hinchman, "Autonomy, Individuality, and Self-Determination," in *What Is Enlightenment? Eighteenth-Century Answers and Twentieth-Century Questions*, ed. James Schmidt (Berkeley: University of California Press, 1996), 488–516; John Martin, "Inventing Sincerity, Refashioning Prudence: The Discovery of the Individual in Renaissance Europe," *AHR* 102 (1997): 1309–42.

8. The quotations are from Jungmann, *Pastoral Liturgy*, 1; Bynum, *Docere Verbo et Exemplo: An Aspect of Twelfth-Century Spirituality* (Missoula, MT: Scholars Press, 1978), 119; McGinn, *The Growth of Mysticism*, vol. 2 of his *The Presence of God: A History of Western Mysticism*, 5 vols. (New York: Crossroad, 1994–), 119; and Knowles, *Monastic Order in England*, 48. Note also Leclercq, "From St. Gregory to St. Bernard: From the Sixth to the Twelfth Century," in *The Spirituality of the Middle Ages*, ed. Leclercq, François Vandenbroucke, and Louis Boyer, trans. Benedictines of Holme Eden Abbey (New York: Seabury, 1968), 1–220, esp. 115.

9. H. Wayne Merritt, *In Word and Deed: Moral Integrity in Paul* (New York: Peter Lang, 1993), esp. 9–109 for the Greek background and 5–6 for a list of Christian citations.

10. Augustine, *De Doctrina Christiana* IV, ed. William M. Green, CSEL 80 (Vienna: Hoelder-Pichler-Tempsky, 1963), 118–69, trans. John J. Gavigan, *Writings of Saint Augustine* IV, Fathers of the Church 2 (New

I's *Pastoral Care*, whose second book is devoted to the "Life of the Pastor" so that his flock "following the teaching and conduct of its shepherd, may proceed the better through example rather than words";[11] and the Benedictine Rule, which enjoins the abbot to "lead his disciples with twofold teaching, that is, he should show all good and holy things in deeds more than words."[12] Millennial Christians assumed that the way to advance in the spiritual life was to follow worthy models. The teacher in the early eleventh-century Latin dialogues of Aelfric Bata could not have been clearer: "I've shown you now . . . what kind of men are good and perfect Christians and what sort are bad and imperfect . . . . Those whom you see to be good, just, pious, and merciful, imitate as you are able while you are young. And as for those whom you recognize as bad, do not follow their bad works."[13] Christians around the millennium sought to reach God through scriptural and sacramental prayer, through holy images, through imitation of holy persons, and through contemplation of creation. What unites these varied spiritual routes is their incarnational character. Seekers attempt to reach the spiritual through the material, advancing from the concrete to the transcendent.

EUCHARISTIC SPIRITUALITY

About 840, in a treatise that has been described as "the first history of the liturgy," Walafrid Strabo explained the Mass as a form of spiritual ascent: "The readings from the Gospel should call to mind the foundation of . . . salvation and faith. . . . Indeed, what is lower in value is placed first, so that the listener's mind might progress from lesser to greater understanding, and gradually ascend from the lowest level to the highest." At the start of the canon "the people's affections are inspired toward the liturgy of thanksgiving, and then permission to join the prayer of human devotion with the praises of the heavenly hosts is urgently requested [that is, with the Sanctus, the angelic prayer of "Holy, Holy, Holy," as in Isaiah 6:3]." "The canon is called the 'action' because in it the Lord's sacraments

York: CIMA Publishing, 1947), 168–235. For commentary, see Mark Levering, *The Theology of Augustine: An Introductory Guide to His Most Important Works* (Grand Rapids: Baker Academic, 2013), 15–17.

11. Gregory I, *Regula Pastoralis* II, esp. iii, ed. E. W. Westhoff, *S. Gregoriae Pape I Cognomento Magni De Pastorale Cura Liber* (Münster in Westphalia: Aschendorff, 1860), 28–71, esp. 31, trans. Henry Davis, *St. Gregory the Great Pastoral Care*, Ancient Christian Writers 11 (Westminster, MD: Newman, 1955), 45–88, esp. 48. Gregory's influence on this topos is discussed in Leclercq, "Le magistère du prédicateur au XIIIᵉ siècle," *Archives d'histoire doctrinale et littéraire du moyen âge* 15 (1946): 105–47, esp. 106–7.

12. Benedict, *Regula* ii, Venarde, 20–27, esp. 23.

13. Aelfric Bata, *Colloquia* xxix, ed. Scott Gwara, trans. David W. Porter, *Anglo-Saxon Conversations: The Colloquies of Aelfric Bata* (Woodbridge, UK: Boydell, 1997), 170–77, esp. 174–75.

are prepared. . . . The Lord's prayer follows, suitably framed with other prayers . . . correctly placed at the conclusion of the sacred canon; purified by this, those who are going to communicate may worthily receive for true salvation what has been solemnly prepared."[14]

The Mass celebrated the unity of the Church in Christ, not only of the priest and people in attendance but also of all the faithful on earth and all the angels and saints in heaven. The Gloria, the Sanctus, and a host of tropes and sequences link the worshippers to the angels praising God.[15] That angels are spectators participating in the worship is presumed in miracle stories relayed by ancient and medieval writers.[16] Thus, according to the creed of the 1025 Synod of Arras, the Mass is "that holy and admirable commerce through which heavenly things are joined to earthly ones."[17] Even its smallest details might have celestial analogues. A monastic follower of Romuald (d. ca. 1027) was granted a vision of two of his deceased colleagues, one of whom was wearing splendid vestments and celebrating a solemn Mass using a book with golden letters, while the other, who had been a less conscientious follower of Romuald's spiritual advice, was cut off from the celebration and had no "beautifully illuminated book"—the community prayed until that monk too got his book.[18] The unity of the Church in the Mass is portrayed symbolically in the Bamberg Apocalypse, a Reichenau manuscript from the early eleventh century, in which the Apocalyptic lamb, wearing Christ's halo, appears on a Eucharistic altar, and the facing page shows the Church (*Ecclesia*) offering the blood of Christ at the cosmic end of the journey of Christian life.

Yet although the Mass was the ultimate community devotion, the proliferation of private Masses in the millennial Church potentially turned it into a private prayer. Some hagiographers in the tenth and early eleventh centuries saw it as an opportunity for the celebrant to commune individually with God. Once when Romuald was saying Mass, as he came to the canon, he was rapt into ecstasy for such a long period of time that all who were present marveled—and in this illumination he gained a new

---

14. Walafrid Strabo, *Libellus de Exordiis* xxi, Harting-Correa, 126–49, esp. 134–35, 140–41, 144–45.

15. Garcia M. Colombas, *Paradis et vie angélique: Le sens eschatologique de la vocation chrétienne*, trans. Suitbert Caron (Paris: Cerf, 1961), 217–27, esp. 217–22; Iversen, *Laus Angelica*, esp. 29–30, 85–86, 136–41, 159, 221, and 256.

16. Peter Browe, *Die Eucharistischen Wunder des Mittelalters* (Breslau: Müller & Seiffert, 1938), 5–12.

17. Gerard of Cambrai, *Acta Synodi Atrebatensis* ii, ed. Steven Vanderputten and Diane J. Reilly, *Gerardi Cameracensis, Acta Synodi Atrebatensis, Vita Autberti, Vita Gaugerici, Varia Scripta ex Officina Gerardi Exstantia*, CCCM 270 (Turnhout, Begl.: Brepols, 2014), 1–75, esp. 27.

18. Peter Damian, *Vita Romualdi* lvii, ed. Giovanni Tabacco, *Peter Damian: Vita Beati Romualdi*, Fonti per la storia d'Italia 94 (Rome: ISME, 1957), 99–100, trans. Henrietta Leyser, in *Medieval Hagiography: An Anthology*, ed. Thomas Head (New York: Garland, 2000), 295–316, esp. 311–12.

FIGURE 27. A liturgical procession through the sacraments and a procession in heaven. Bamberg Staatsbibliothek Kaiser Heinrichs-II Bibliothek ms. Bibl 22, fols. 4v and 5r. Photo credit: Gerald Raab, Bamberg Staatsbibliothek.

understanding of the Psalms and many of the prophets.[19] The gift of tears was associated with Masses celebrated by Romuald, John of Fécamp, and Leo IX.[20]

The Eucharist was more and more central to the millennial Church. This claim contradicts the traditional presentation of pre-Gregorian religion as a mélange of folk practices, relics, and ritual in which the Mass was becoming an opaque drama shrouded in mysterious language and increasingly distant from the faithful.[21] A closer look reveals a new emphasis on the Mass beginning when Carolingian scholars stressed the unique role of

19. Damian, *Vita Romualdi* l, Tabacco, 92–93, Leyser, 310, discussed in Nagy, *Le Don des larmes*, 182–84.

20. Peter Damian, *Vita Romualdi* xxxi, Tabacco, 67–68; John of Fécamp, *Confessio Theologica* III xxviii, Lerclercq and Bonnes, 109–83, esp. 174; and John of Fécamp, *Summe Sacerdos et Vere Pontifex* v, ed. André Wilmart, "L'*Oratio Sancti Ambrosii* du Missel Romain," *Revue bénédictine* 39 (1927): 317–39, esp. 332–33; *Vita Leonis* I xv, ed. Hans-Georg Krause, *Die Touler Vita Leos IX.*, MGH SS Rer Germ 70 (Hannover: Hahn, 2007), 144–45, trans. I. S. Robinson, *The Papal Reform of the Eleventh Century: Lives of Pope Leo IX and Pope Gregory VII* (Manchester, UK: Manchester University Press, 2004), 121. On the connection of this charism to the Eucharist in the mid-eleventh century, see Nagy, "Larmes et eucharistie: Formes du sacrifice en Occident au Moyen Âge central," in *Pratiques de l'eucharistie dans les Églises d'Orient et d'Occident (Antiquité et Moyen Âge)*, ed. Nicole Bériou, Béatrice Caseau, and Dominique Rigaux, 2 vols. (Paris: Institut d'Études Augustiniennes, 2009), 2:1073–1109, esp. 1090–95.

21. For example, Jungmann, *Pastoral Liturgy*, 62–63; Brian Stock, *The Implications of Literacy: Written Language and Models of Interpretation in the Eleventh and Twelfth Centuries* (Princeton: Princeton University Press, 1983), 267; McGinn, *Growth of Mysticism*, 23.

the Eucharist within the Church.[22] By the mid-tenth century most monks were also priests who celebrated the Mass in addition to their monastic office.[23] As small parish communities led by single priests acquired market share at the expense of the larger, old-style baptismal churches and minsters that had the personnel and resources needed to celebrate the full liturgy of the hours, the Mass was increasingly the only liturgical service available.

Histories of Eucharistic theology tend to omit the millennial Church entirely and to jump directly from the mid-ninth-century debates among Carolingian scholars to the mid-eleventh-century debates over the teachings of Berengar of Tours (d. 1088). Yet something very significant must have occurred between those two points. Whereas the Carolingian Eucharistic discussions had been divided and unfocused, the mid-eleventh-century arguments began with such a strong consensus about the transformation of the Eucharistic offerings into the actual body and blood of Christ that not even the learned and clever Berengar was able make any headway against it.[24] This triumph of Eucharistic realism is probably related to an increasing emphasis on the Mass, perhaps to the liturgical piety of Cluny.[25] It certainly must reflect the teaching of the monastic schools, since Berengar's fiercest opponents were monks of Moyenmoutier, Cluny, Mont-Saint-Michel, Bec, Fécamp, and Monte Cassino.[26] Moreover, in the generation before Berengar, Eucharistic realism had been championed by

22. Marta Cristiani, "La controversia eucaristica nella cultura del secolo IX," *Studi medievali*, 3rd ser., 9 (1968): 167–233; Leclercq, "From St. Gregory to St. Bernard," 89–90; Chazelle, *Crucified God in the Carolingian Era*, 209–38, esp. 237; Alex J. Novikoff, "Anselm, Dialogue, and the Rise of Scholastic Disputation," *Speculum* 86 (2011): 387–418, esp. 391, notes 18–19.

23. On the clericalization of monks, see Häussling, *Mönchskonvent und Eucharistiefeier*, 150–61 and 172–73.

24. Summaries of this Eucharistic debate are in Margaret Gibson, *Lanfranc of Bec* (Oxford: Clarendon, 1978), 63–81; Kobialka, *This Is My Body*, 69–72, 102–3, 112, and 118; and Clare Monagle, *Orthodoxy and Controversy in Twelfth-Century Religious Discourse: Peter Lombard's* Sentences *and the Development of Theology* (Turnhout, Belg.: Brepols, 2013), 8–16. Scholars who have recognized its tenth- and early-eleventh-century antecedents include Fulton, *From Judgment to Passion*, 53–54, who discovered a possible shift by examining the circulation of Eucharistic treatises, and Charles M. Radding and Francis Newton, *Theology, Rhetoric, and Politics in the Eucharistic Controversy: Alberic of Monte Cassino against Berengar of Tours* (New York: Columbia University Press, 2003), 5, who recognize that the intellectual ground must have shifted prior to Berengar but duck the problem by claiming that "the evidence is too scattered for us to trace the process [behind it]."

25. Snoeck, *Medieval Piety*, 174.

26. Jotsaldus (d. post 1051), the biographer of Odilo of Cluny, wrote a treatise that has been lost: see Patrick Henriet, *La parole et la prière au Moyen Âge: Le Verbe efficace dans l'hagiographie monastique des XIIᵉ siècles* (Brussels: De Boeck & Larcier, 2000), 90. Anastasius at Mont Saint-Michel wrote a treatise, *De Corpore et Sanguine Domini*, on which see Mathieu Arnoux, "Un Vénitien au Mont-Saint-Michel: Anastase, moine, ermite et confesseur (d. vers 1085)," *Médiévales* 28 (1995): 55–78, esp. 76–78. For the claims that Lanfranc's work on the Eucharist was basically achieved at Bec, and for the argument that some of John of Fécamp's work had Berengar in mind, see H. E. J. Cowdrey, *Lanfranc: Scholar, Monk, and Bishop* (Oxford: Oxford University Press, 2003), 59 and 60. Alberic of Monte Cassino (d. between 1094 and 1098–99), wrote the treatise edited in Radding and Newton, *Theology*, who inventory contemporary Eucharistic writers (5–7).

distinguished teachers such as Heriger of Lobbes (d. 1007),[27] Fulbert of Chartres (d. 1028),[28] and John of Fécamp (d. 1078, writing ca. 1017–18),[29] as well as by Bishop Gerard I of Cambrai-Arras (1012–51), whose *De Corpore et Sanguine Domini* is found in the *Acta* of the 1025 Synod of Arras.[30]

Miraculous visions of the physical body and blood of Jesus in the Eucharist illustrate the new climate. Scholars usually associate their proliferation with the Berengarian debates.[31] Yet these miracle stories had begun to multiply earlier, back at the start of the eleventh century when they were being retailed by chroniclers such as Helgaudus of Fleury, Rodulfus Glaber, and Andrew of Fleury.[32] They could be interpreted as responses to Eucharistic doubts expressed by heretics at Orléans, Périgord, and elsewhere shortly after the year 1000, but that supposition itself presupposes a new emphasis on Eucharistic realism sufficient to inspire an unprecedented counterreaction.[33]

The more concrete understanding of Christ's presence within the Eucharist may have been reinforced by the increasing prominence of relics.[34] Relics privilege physical presence. If the authenticity of a particular relic

27. Heriger of Lobbes (misattributed here to Gerbert), *Libellus de Corpore et Sanguine Domini*, ed. Migne, *Pat. Lat.* 139:179–88. See Charles R. Shrader, "The Surviving Manuscripts of the Eucharistic Treatises of Heriger of Lobbes," in *Canon Law, Religion, and Politics*: Liber Amicorum *Robert Somerville*, ed. Uta-Renate Blumenthal, Anders Winroth, and Peter Landau (Washington, DC: Catholic University of America Press, 2012), 147–62.

28. Fulbert, *Sermo (Fragmentum)* viii, ed. Migne, *Pat. Lat.* 141: 334–36. See Josef Geiselmann, *Die Eucharistielehre der Vorscholastik* (Paderborn: Ferdinand Schöningh, 1926), 286–89; and Frederick Behrends, ed., introduction to *The Letters and Poems of Fulbert of Chartres* (Oxford: Clarendon, 1976), xxiin19.

29. John of Fécamp, *Confessio Theologica* III xxviii, Leclercq and Bonnes, 109–83, esp. 173–75.

30. Gerard I, *Acta Synodi Atrebatensis* ii, ed. Vanderputten and Reilly, 26–34, which raises questions discussed in Erik Mingroot, "*Acta Synodi Atrebatensis* (1025): Problèmes de critique de provenance," *Studia Gratiana* 20 (1967): 201–9; in Guy Lobrichon, "Arras, 1025, ou le vrai procès d'une fausse accusation," in *Inventer l'hérésie? Discours polémiques et pouvoirs avant l'inquisition*, ed. Monique Zerner (Nice: Centre d'études médiévales, 1998), 67–85, esp. 79–80 and 82–84, where the basic authenticity of the *Acta* is defended; and in Fulton, *From Judgment to Passion*, 83–87 and 494–95 (note 90). On Gerard, see T. M. Riches, "Bishop Gerard I of Cambrai-Arras, the Three Orders, and Human Weakness," in Ott and Jones, *Bishop Reformed*, 122–36.

31. See Browe, *Eucharistischen Wunder*, 116; and Snoeck, *Medieval Piety*, 48 and 385.

32. Helgaudus of Fleury, *Vita Regis Roberti* v, Bautier and Labory, 68–69; Rodulfus Glaber, *Historiae* V xi–xiii, France, 230–37; Andrew of Fleury, *Miracula Benedicti* VI xiii, Certain, 237–40. On earlier hesitations about such miracles, see Chazelle, *Crucified God in the Carolingian Era*, 219. Browe, *Eucharistischen Wunder*, 93–171, esp. 139–46, attempts a typology of Eucharistic miracles, and his examples suggest that their popularity started to increase at the end of the tenth century.

33. Michael Frassetto, "The Heresy at Orléans in 1022 in the Writings of Contemporary Churchmen," *Nottingham Medieval Studies* 49 (2005): 1–17, esp. 15–16. On the 1025 Arras synod, see note 30 above; on Heribert's rather generic letter describing heretics disavowing the Mass and the Eucharist, see Guy Lobrichon, "The Chiaroscuro of Heresy: Early Eleventh-Century Aquitaine as Seen from Auxerre," in Head and Landes, *Peace of God*, 80–103 (translating the letter itself, 85–86). Helgaudus of Fleury, *Vita Regis Roberti* v, Bautier and Labory, 68–69, mutters darkly about "perverse dogma [opposed to the proper understanding of the Eucharist] . . . now growing in the world."

34. Snoeck, *Medieval Piety*, 1–4, presents the scant bibliography on the parallels between Eucharistic and relic piety. See also Guy Lobrichon, "Le culte des saints, les rire des hérétiques, le triomphe des savants," in Bozóky and Helvétius, *Reliques*, 95–108, esp. 107.

is disputed, the basic question becomes, who has the body? For example, in regard to the competing claims of Monte Cassino and Fleury-sur-Loire over which monastery possessed the body of St. Benedict, the Fleury side retailed the story of an apparition of Benedict to a Monte Cassino monk to whom Benedict explained that, while he was indeed present *spiritualiter* at his beloved monastery of Monte Cassino, his physical remains were at Fleury.[35] Real relics were more than just spiritual presence.[36] If the bread and the wine of the Eucharist become the body and blood of Christ, they become the ultimate relic, an understanding that required Christ's real presence and not simply something spiritual.

SPIRITUALITY OF THE LITURGY OF THE HOURS

The liturgy of the hours provided a special way for canons, monks, and nuns to approach the heavenly realm. They saw it as the earthly counterpart of the perpetual prayer of the angels, who were assumed to be in attendance.[37] The monks' voices were "angelic."[38] They sang in choirs, like the choirs of angels. Their tonsures were symbolic haloes (*coronae*, literally, crowns). In their words and actions they witnessed the heavenly order.[39] The prayers of the hours were timed according to the rising and setting sun, implicitly anticipating and then celebrating the light of the world, Christ, in both his death and his resurrection.

How did choreographed liturgical teamwork relate to individual religious quest? First of all, it transported monks and nuns into the celestial world. According to Benedict, "We believe the divine presence is everywhere and 'the eyes of the Lord observe the good and the wicked in every place' [Prov. 15:3]. Let us believe this most of all, without a trace of doubt, when we are present at the divine office."[40] His Rule asks monks to recite

---

35. Andrew of Fleury, *Miracula Benedicti* VII xv, Certain, 274.

36. On the centrality of physical relics, see Patrick J. Geary, "The Saint and the Shrine: The Pilgrim's Goal in the Middle Ages," in *Wallfaht Kennt keine Grenzen*, ed. Lenz Kris-Rettenbeck and Gerda Möhler (Munich: Schnell & Steiner, 1984), 265–74; revised in Geary, *Living with the Dead in the Middle Ages* (Ithaca: Cornell University Press, 1994), 163–76.

37. Benedict, *Regula* xix, Venarde, 91. See Leclercq, *Love of Learning*, 251; Colombas, *Paradis et vie angélique*, 203–17.

38. Particular monastic saints are praised for their angelic voices, such as Ysarnus (d. 1047), in his *vita* i, ed. Cécile Caby, Jean-François Cottier, Rosa Maria Dessi, Michel Lauwers, Jean-Pierre Weiss, and Monique Zerner, *Vie d'Isarn, Abbé de Saint-Victor de Marseille (XIᵉ siècle)* (Paris: Les Belles Lettres, 2010), 6–7. On Irish conceptions of the unity of human and celestial singing, see Peter Jeffery, "Eastern and Western Elements in the Irish Monastic Prayer of the Hours," in Fassler and Balzer, *Divine Office in the Latin Middle Ages*, 99–143, esp. 121.

39. Isabelle Cochelin, "When the Monks Were the Book," in Boynton and Reilly, *Practice of the Bible*, 61–83.

40. Benedict, *Regula* xix, ed. Venarde, 90–91.

the psalms of the office so that "our spirits and our voices are in harmony," an enigmatic saying probably best understood if "voice" (*vox*) is read as "our vocal prayer."[41] This liturgy was inherently meditative. According to Jean Leclercq, himself a monk of Clervaux, medieval monks did not privilege interior religion over public worship because their liturgy, the apex of their monastic culture, was their ultimate expression of "the love of learning and the desire for God," and the hours they sang were "the eternal praise that the monks, in unison with the Angels, began offering God in the abbey choir, and which will be perpetuated in Heaven."[42]

The liturgy of the hours united the clerical *familia*. Monks and nuns prayed for their community and their patrons. They honored the dead as well as the living. Early medieval Irish hermits had already envisioned the office and penitential practices associated with it as ways to help suffering souls.[43] The *Regularis Concordia* adds an office of the dead, featuring new prayers several times a day that varied according to the seasons.[44] The monks of Cluny popularized not only necrologies but also All Soul's Day, and their prayers were considered extraordinarily efficacious at freeing souls from Purgatory.[45] The first Tuscolan pope, Benedict VIII (1012–24), after his death was alleged to have appeared in a vision to his brother Pope John XIX (1024–1032), begging him to obtain the salvific prayers of Odilo of Cluny. A later apparition revealed that the psalms, prayers, alms, and Masses offered by Odilo and the rest of the Cluniac monks had managed to carry even the controversial Benedict to the celestial realm.[46] The liturgical office linked the living, the dead, and the angels.[47]

Grand as these liturgies were, and however much they promoted the liturgically oriented meditations of monks and nuns and canons, this

---

41. Ibid. On this phrase and its antecedents, see Giles Constable, "The Concern for Sincerity and Understanding in Liturgical Prayer, Especially in the Twelfth Century," in *Classica et Mediaevalia: Studies in Honor of Joseph Szövérffy*, ed. Irene Vaslef and Helmut Buschhausen (Washington, DC: Classical Folia, 1986), 17–30, esp. 18–20.

42. Leclercq, *Love of Learning*, 251 (cf. 245); Leclercq, "From St. Gregory to St. Bernard," 119–22.

43. Jeffery, "Eastern and Western Elements in the Irish Monastic Prayer," 99–143, esp. 104–05.

44. *Regularis Concordia* xxi and xxvi, ed. Symons et al., 84 and 87, trans. Symons, 15 and 20 (see also 23).

45. Leclercq, "Documents sur le mort des moines," *Revue Mabillon* 45 (1955): 165–80; 46 (1956): 65–81. Pre-Cluniac precedents for general commemorations of the departed are noted in H. R. Philippeau, "Contribution à l'étude du culte collectif des trépassés," *Zeitschrift für schweizerische Kirchengeschichte* (*RHE Suisse*) 51 (1957): 45–57.

46. The story of the salvation of Benedict VIII is told in Peter Damian, *Vita Odilonis*, ed. Migne, *Pat. Lat.* 144: 925–44, esp. 937A–938B. For context see Jacques Le Goff, *The Birth of Purgatory*, trans. Arthur Goldhammer (Chicago: University of Chicago Press, 1984), 201 (although note the cautions in Forbes, *Heaven and Earth in Anglo-Saxon England*, 203–6).

47. Megan McLaughlin, *Consorting with Saints: Prayers for the Dead in Early Medieval France* (Ithaca: Cornell University Press, 1994), 153–65 and 228–29, emphasizes that contemporary donation documents do not single out Masses for the dead but instead cite all the works and prayers of religious communities, including the liturgy of the hours.

elaborate community prayer was beginning to be challenged by increasing individualism. The Masses of monk priests were a potential distraction. And as the quest for the solitude of the desert swept through tenth- and early eleventh-century Italy, individual hermits requested dispensations from parts of the divine office because "it behooves us to weep rather than to sing."[48]

PRIVATE PRAYER

Private prayer overlapped with public prayer, which is no surprise given that private prayer is known only through monastic authors whose liturgical prayers it extended and deepened.[49] It usually consisted of scriptural readings, an orientation reinforced through each year's cycle of variable readings in the Mass and in the liturgy of the hours.[50] A common form of private devotion was to pray supplementary daily offices such as those in remembrance of the dead and in honor of Mary.[51] Because silent reading of any kind was rare prior to the twelfth century, private prayer, like public prayer, meant reading aloud.[52] But this was the slow, devotional, meditative reading that the Rule of Benedict calls the *lectio divina*.[53] What was new at the start of the eleventh century was that John of Fécamp, soon to be followed by Lanfranc and Anselm, began to use technical terms such as *meditatio* to analyze this devotional reading more precisely.[54]

How scripturally based meditation might work in practice is indicated by a summary of Romuald's teaching on prayer, made by Bruno of Querfurt (d. 1009):

> Be seated in your cell as though in paradise; cast to the rear of your memory everything distracting, becoming alert and focused on your thoughts as a good fisherman is on the fish. One pathway [to this state] is through reciting the Psalms; do not neglect this. If you cannot manage to get through them all [at one sitting] as you used to do with the fervor of a novice, take pains to chant the psalms in your spirit, now [starting] from this place, now from that, and to inter-

48. Leclercq, "From St. Gregory to St. Bernard," 115.

49. Constable, *Abbey of Cluny*, 74–76.

50. Jungmann, *Pastoral Liturgy*, 165–70; Boynton, "The Bible and the Liturgy," in Boynton and Reilly, *Practice of the Bible*, 10–33.

51. Sally Elizabeth Roper, *Medieval English Benedictine Liturgy: Studies in the Form, Structure, and Content of the Monastic Votive Office, c. 950–1540* (New York: Garland, 1993), 57–68.

52. Paul Saenger, *Space between Words: The Origins of Silent Reading* (Stanford: Stanford University Press, 1997), esp. 202–4 and 235, links the spread and triumph of silent reading to the clearer word separation and punctuation that became widespread north of the Alps in the eleventh century, in Italy in the twelfth.

53. Benedict, *Regula* xlviii, Venarde, 160–63. See "Lectio Divina," *Dictionnaire de Spiritualité*, 26 vols. (Paris: Beauchesne, 1932–95), 9:470–510; McGinn, *Growth of Mysticism*, 132–38.

54. Saenger, *Space between Words*, 203–4 and 396–98.

pret them in your mind [*intellegere mente*], and when you begin to wander in your reading, don't stop what you are doing, but make haste to correct [*emendare*] by interpreting; place yourself [*pone te*] above all in the presence of God with fear and trembling, like one who stands in the gaze of the emperor; pull yourself in completely and crouch down like a baby chick, content with God's gift, for, unless its mother provides, it neither knows nor gets what it should eat.[55]

The earliest surviving little books of prayers made for individual use (*libelli precum*) are from the Carolingian era.[56] Some were minipsalters.[57] They include the first surviving medieval royal prayer book, a grand illustrated prayer book connecting the king's private piety to exalted rulership, which internal evidence suggests was commissioned sometime between 846 and 869 for Charles the Bald (840–77).[58] Similar royal piety flourished in the tenth century, when a parallel book was produced for Otto III (the style suggests the workshops of Archbishop Willigis of Mainz), a small easily portable codex written in gold ink on purple parchment that owes much to Carolingian prototypes but also incorporates prayers that have been claimed to reflect the emperor's personal piety. It begins with the seven penitential psalms and various litanies and includes five illustrations, most notably the king bowing (in full *proskynesis*) to an opposing image of Christ in Majesty.[59] Early personal prayer books were usually less

55. Bruno of Querfurt, *Vita Quinque Fratrum* xxxii, Miladinov, 310–11. The English translation, including its bracketed notes, is quoted here from Mary Carruthers, *The Craft of Thought: Meditation, Rhetoric, and the Making of Images, 400–1200* (New York: Cambridge University Press, 1998), who explicates the mnemonic devices, 112–15.

56. Henri Barré, *Prières anciennes de l'Occident à la Mère du Saveur: Des origins à saint Anselme* (Paris: Lethielleux, 1963), 4–5 and 59–99; B.J. Jaye, *Artes Orandi*, Typologie 61 (Turnhout, Belg.: Brepols, 1992); Boynton, "Libelli Precum In the Central Middle Ages," in *A History of Prayer: The First to the Fifteenth Century*, ed. Roy Hammerling (Leiden, Neth.: Brill, 2008), 255–318, esp. 255–71.

57. Pierre Salmon, "Psautiers abrégés du Moyen Âge," in his *Analecta Liturgica: Extraits des manuscrits liturgiques de la Bibliothèque Vaticane: Contribution à l'histoire de la prière chrétienne* (Vatican City: BAV, 1974), 67–119; Jean-François Cottier, Anima mea: *Prières privées et textes de dévotion du Moyen Age latin: Autour des Prières ou Méditations attribuées à saint Anselme de Cantorbéry XIe–XIIe siècles* (Turnhout, Belg.: Brepols, 2001), xlvii–liii. For a description written in 841/842, explaining how a layperson might use such a prayer book, see Dhuoda, *Liber Manualis* XI, ed. and trans. Marcelle Thiébaux, *Dhuoda, Handbook for Her Warrior Son: Liber Manualis* (Cambridge: Cambridge University Press, 1998), 232–37.

58. Robert Deshman, "The Exalted Servant: The Ruler Theology of the Prayerbook of Charles the Bald," *Viator* 11 (1980) 385–417, esp. 385–86, 389, and 412–14, repr. with additional bibliography in *Eye and Mind*, 192–219, esp. 192–93, 195, and 213–15; Michael Moore, "The King's New Clothes: Royal and Episcopal Regalia in the Frankish Empire," in Gordon, *Robes and Honor*, 95–135, esp. 113. A counterpart prayer book, probably composed for Louis the German, is signaled in Noble, *Images, Iconoclasm*, 429, note 108.

59. *Das Gebetbuch Ottos III.: Handschrift Clm 30111 der Bayerischen Staatsbibliothek München* (Lucerne: Faksimile Verlag Luzern, 2008). Commentary in Sarah Hamilton, "'Most Illustrious King of Kings': Evidence for Ottonian Kingship in the Otto III Prayerbook (Munich, Bayerische Staatsbibliothek, Clm 30111)," *Journal of Medieval History* 27 (2001): 257–88; and Hermann Hauke and Elisabeth Klemm, *Das Gebetbuch Ottos III: Kommentar zur Faksimile-Edition der Handschrift Clm 30111 der Bayerischen Staatsbibliothek München* (Lucerne: Faksimile Verlag Luzern, 2008).

sumptuously illustrated than later medieval books of hours.[60] These humble collections of individual prayers were generally overlooked by historians up until the middle of the twentieth century, when some Benedictine scholars first began to systematically identify and describe them.[61]

Scholars see a turning point in prayer around the year 1000. According to Patrick Henriet, "In the years following the millennium in Italy, a few decades later in the rest of the West, indications of an interiorization of prayer and of the development of an individual *conscientia* multiply."[62] Piroska Nagy finds in the pre-1018 work of John of Fécamp an "emotional intensity, which, permeating the literature of piety, constitutes a novelty of the eleventh century, and takes up again a style that had disappeared in the West since Augustine, permitting the description of sentiments and, more generally, of movements of interiority."[63] Although the *libelli precum* remained permeated with biblical spirituality, they begin to include more original prayers, at first often as appendixes to standard psalters. These prayers are generally anonymous or (mis)attributed to ancient Church fathers; some may have Celtic antecedents.[64] The great spiritual masters of the eleventh century—John of Fécamp, Peter Damian, and Anselm of Canterbury—chose to present their meditations in letters, treatises, hymns, and prayer collections. John of Fécamp's *Confessio Theologica*, quoted at the head of this chapter, uses the term *confessio* in the same way Augustine did, to designate the confessions of faith of an individual opening his soul to God.[65]

GOD THROUGH IMAGES

Millennial Christians frequently prayed in front of statues and images. Chapter 4 describes changes in the art of this era: movement from cross to crucifix and from triumphant Christ to suffering Christ; the appearance of grand reliquaries, some figural; more frequent three-dimensional cult statues of the Virgin and the saints. Chapter 5 examines how these works of art were used in the liturgy. Here the issue is how they functioned in individual spirituality.

---

60. Jeffrey F. Hamburger, "Before the Book of Hours: The Development of the Illustrated Prayer Book in Germany," in his *The Visual and the Visionary: Art and Female Spirituality in Late Medieval Germany* (New York: Zone Books, 1998), 149–95 and 510–22, esp. 149–52 and 510–12.

61. Surveys of research on medieval prayer books, emphasizing the contributions of Wilmart and Pierre Salmon, can be found in Barré, *Prières anciennes*, 1–3; Salmon, "Livrets de prières de l'époque carolingienne," *Revue bénédictine* 86 (1976): 218–34; and Fulton, *From Judgment to Passion*, 509–15 and 534–35. Salmon inventories Vatican material in "*Libelli Precum* du VIIIe au XIIe siècle," in his *Analecta Liturgica*, 121–94.

62. Henriet, *La parole et la prière*, 14.

63. Nagy, *Don des larmes*, 190–95, esp. 191.

64. Barré, *Prières anciennes*, 8, 52–57, and 63–70.

65. For Augustine's influence on John of Fécamp, see McGinn, *Growth of Mysticism*, 134–38; and Philippe de Vial, introduction to *Jean de Fécamp: La Confession Théologique* (Paris: Cerf, 1992), 66–69.

Basically they offered *praesentia* or *présentification*: that is, like relics and image reliquaries, images themselves in some mysterious manner made present what they represented.[66] It has been suggested that *présentification* was the major impetus for high medieval and late medieval religious art.[67]

Devotional Use of Crosses and Crucifixes

The adoration of the cross, which had originated in Jerusalem, had been part of the Good Friday liturgy in Rome since Late Antiquity.[68] Even Carolingian intellectuals skeptical about other religious imagery accepted the devotional use of the cross,[69] though a few heretics did have their doubts.[70] Bernard of Chartres, writing around 1015, does not hesitate to affirm that "the holy and universal Church accepts this image [the "crucifix of our Lord"], in either carved or modeled form, because it arouses our affective piety in the commemoration of Our Lord's passion."[71]

Devotion to Christ on the cross was enthusiastically promoted in the tenth and eleventh centuries. It is a theme in liturgical prayers from early eleventh-century Nonantola and eleventh-century Farfa.[72] Priests focused on the significance of the Eucharist by contemplating processional crosses

66. Jean-Claude Schmitt, "Les reliques et les images," in Bozóky and Helvétius, *Reliques*, 145–67, esp. 157; Erik Thunø, *Image and Relic: Mediating the Sacred in Early Medieval Rome* (Rome: "L'Erma" di Bretschneider, 2002); Nees, *Early Medieval Art*, 137–51.

67. Wirth, *Image médiévale*, 267–81.

68. Gerhard Römer, "Die Liturgie des Karfreitags," *Zeitschrift für katholische Theologie* 77 (1955): 39–93, esp. 70–86, discusses the first description of the ritual from ca. 700. However, Sible de Blaauw, "Jerusalem in Rome and the Cult of the Cross," in Colella et al., *Pratum Romanum*, 55–73, esp. 71–72, claims that Good Friday adoration in Rome must have begun much earlier, basing her argument largely on the fact that the stational church for this feast was Santa Croce in Gerusalemme, a minor church that lacked its own cross relic after the fifth century. For a survey of the literature, see Chazelle, "The Cross, the Image, and the Passion in Carolingian Thought and Art," 2 vols. (PhD diss., Yale University, 1985), 1:65–68. On the broader question of early devotion to the cross, see Viladesau, *Beauty of the Cross*, 9–47.

69. Noble, *Images, Iconoclasm*, 194, 214, 276–77, 298–301, 309–13, 320–21, 336–37, and 348–51. For the most famous example of this approbation, see Einhard, *Quaestio de Adoranda Cruce*, ed. Karl Hampe, in MGH *Epp*, Sectio 5: *Epp Karolini Aevi*, vol. 3 (Berlin: Weidmann, 1899), 146–49, esp. 149, trans. Paul Edward Dutton, *Charlemagne's Courtier: The Complete Einhard* (Peterborough, ON: Broadview, 1998), 171–74, esp. 174.

70. Noble, *Images, Iconoclasm*, 291, 293–94, 298–301, and 309–13, examines the source problems involved in reconstructing the mid-ninth-century career of Claudius of Turin, who appears to have opposed devotion to the cross. Schmitt, "L' Occident, Nicée II et les images du VIIIe au XIIIe siècle," in *Nicée II, 787–1987*, ed. François Boespflug and Nicholas Lossky (Paris: Cerf, 1987), 271–301, esp. 288–90 and 296, examines the rejection of the cross and crucifix by heretics around the millennium. Some are described in Gerard I, *Acta Synodi Atrebatensis* xiii–xiv, ed. Vanderputten and Reilly, 63–70; Lobrichon, "Chiaroscuro of Heresy," 80–103; Rodulfus Glaber, *Historiae* xi, France, 88–91. On the possibility of a link between heretical iconoclasm and millennial excitation, see Fulton, *From Judgment to Passion*, 78–87.

71. Bernard of Chartres, *Miracula Fidis* I xiii, Bouillet, 46–47; Sheingorn, 77.

72. Wilmart, "Prières médiévales pour l'adoration de la croix," *Ephemerides Liturgicae* 46 (1932): 22–65, esp. 22.

and crucifixes placed on or near the altar, a practice Archbishop Lanfranc assumes in his letter written in 1073 to Gilbert Crispin, in which he explains that he is sending Gilbert a cross containing relics "to look at as you celebrate Mass."[73] The use of the crucifix to aid a priest's recollection is literally canonized in new sacramentaries and missals that turn the T that begins the first offertory prayer of the Canon of the Mass, the *Te igitur*, into a full-page cross on which the crucified Christ hangs. Although there is an early surviving example in the Gellone sacramentary from 750–80, this image remained rare until the end of the tenth century, when it proliferated in sacramentaries and missals to such an extent that by the close of the eleventh it had become nearly universal.[74]

This use of the crucifix during the sacrifice of the Mass to raise feelings of empathy for the suffering Christ probably explains why the traditional image of Christ triumphant in front of the cross was gradually replaced by crucifixes evoking Christ's suffering and death.[75] The congregation could share in this devotion if monumental crucifixes were displayed above the main altars—hence their sudden prominence in millennial churches. Art and liturgical spirituality appear to have developed in parallel.

Devotional reflection on the crucifix became part of private meditation, especially in the Mediterranean world. Romuald's father, Duke Sergius of Ravenna (d. ca. 990?), during his monastic retirement just prior to his death, "had the custom of standing before a certain image of the Savior, and there to afflict himself with great sorrow of heart, praying privately with abundant tears."[76] John Gualbert (d. 1073), in the 1030s was converted to monastic life when, while he was praying in the church of San Miniato, the figure of Christ on a crucifix inclined its head toward him.[77] Peter Damian says that he "often beheld, by an immediate percep-

---

73. Lanfranc, *Epist.* xx, ed. and trans. Helen Clover and Margaret Gibson, *The Letters of Lanfranc, Archbishop of Canterbury* (New York: Cambridge University Press, 1979), 100–103.

74. Rudolf Suntrup, "*Te Igitur*-Initialen und Kanonbilder in mittelalterlichen Sakramentarhandschriften," in *Text und Bild: Aspekte des Zusammenwirkens zweier Künste in Mittelalter und früher Neuzeit*, ed. Christel Meier und Uwe Ruberg (Wiesbaden: Dr. Ludwig Reichert, 1980), 278–382, esp. 281, with illustrations 367–75; Chazelle, *Crucified God in the Carolingian Era*, 86–91; Nees, *Early Medieval Art*, 169–70.

75. Constable, "The Imitation of the Divinity of Christ," in *Three Studies in Medieval Religious and Social Thought* (Cambridge: Cambridge University Press, 1998), 143–248, esp. 164–65, emphasizes the slowness of the transition, lasting into the thirteenth century, in which the dead figure of the suffering Christ replaced the image of Christ in majesty. On the need to also be aware of potential Trinitarian aspects related to this and other imagery, see Rachel Fulton Brown, "Three in One: Making God in Twelfth-Century Liturgy, Theology, and Devotion," in Noble and Van Engen, *European Transformations*, 468–98, esp. 470–72.

76. Peter Damian, *Vita Romualdi*, xiv, Tabacco, 36. The passage is discussed in Nagy, *Don des larmes*, 181–82.

77. Atto of Pistoia, *Vita Altera S. Johannis Gualberti* 1.1–3, ed. *AASS* Jul III 1723, 348–49. Atto actually wrote a century later, but elsewhere he closely follows the contemporary life by Andrew of Strumi, which at this point is missing a section of its original narrative.

FIGURE 28. Crucifix incorporated into the T of the *Te igitur*, opening prayer of the canon of the Mass. Sacramentary illustration from The J. Paul Getty Museum MS Ludwig VI, fol. 2v. Digital image courtesy of the Getty Museum's Open Content Program.

tion of my mind, Christ hanging from the cross fastened with nails, and I thirstily received his dripping blood in my mouth. But if I were to attempt to tell you of the heights of contemplation that were vouchsafed to me, both of our Redeemer's most sacred humanity and of the indescribable glory of heaven, the day would be at an end before I finished." Whether Peter Damian is describing an actual crucifix or a purely visionary image derived from that piety, this is the earliest known account of a vision of a bleeding crucifix, a topos that would be common in the twelfth century.[78]

78. Peter Damian, *Epistola* lxxii, Reindel, 2:326–56, esp. 343, trans. Blum, 3:129–30. Peter Dinzelbacher, "Das Blut Christi in der Religiosität des Mittelalters," in *900 Jahre Heilig-Blut-Verehrung in Weingarten,*

Icons

Tenth- and eleventh-century Italy had a special devotion to icons, two-dimensional holy images devoutly honored as channels of grace. As in Eastern Christianity, true icons made saints present.[79] From the late sixth century on, the churches of Rome had their own ancient wonder-working icons—some from Jerusalem, some from Byzantium, some created by local Greeks—whose legends and traditions continued to flourish despite Eastern iconoclasm and Carolingian hesitation.[80] Venice also had its icons, although these would become much more numerous and prominent after she had increased her power in the Greek East.[81] Ravenna had special images.[82] In Italy, ecclesiastical inventories often list *iconae, yconae,* or *conae,* not only in Greek churches but also in Latin ones in Apulia, the Duchy of Naples, and even in central and northern Italy.[83] This image culture may help explain why Claudius of Turin (originally from Spain or southern France) was so shocked when he found in his new diocese of Milan "all the basilicas filled against the order of truth with foul images" to which "everyone paid cult [*colebant*]" that he embarked upon his notorious career as an iconoclast.[84] Fragmentary evidence suggests that some Italian churches, prior to the purges of the Counter-Reformation, had chancel screens modified to hold icons, functioning much like the iconostasis in an Orthodox

1094–1994, 3 vols. (Sigmaringen: Jan Thorbecke, 1994), 1:415–34, esp. 425, claims this as the earliest such vision focusing on the drinking of the precious blood; on this theme see Caroline Walker Bynum, "The Blood of Christ in the Later Middle Ages," *Church History* 71 (2002): 685–714. Peter Damian also wrote several prayers on the adoration of the cross, on which see Ugo Facchini, *San Pier Damiani: L'Eucologia e le preghiere. Contributo alla storia dell'eucologia medievale: Studio critico e liturgico-teologico* (Rome: Centro Liturgica Vincenziano—Edizioni Liturgiche, 2000), 543–51; Fulton, *From Judgment to Passion,* 501, note 170.

79. David N. Bell, *Orthodoxy: Evolving Tradition,* Cistercian Studies Series 228 (Collegeville, MN: Liturgical Press, 2008), 51.

80. Per Jonas Nordhagen, "Constantinople on the Tiber: The Byzantines in Rome and the Iconography of Their Images," in Smith, *Early Medieval Rome,* 113–34; Jean-Marie Sansterre, "Entre 'Koinè méditerranéenne,' influences byzantines et particularités locales: Le culte des images et ses limites à Rome dans le haut moyen âge," in *Europa medievale e mondo bizantino: Contatti effettivi e possibilità di studi comparati (Tavola rotonda del XVIII Congresso del CISH—Montréal, 29 agosto 1995),* ed. Girolamo Arnaldi and Guglielmo Cavallo (Rome: ISIME, 1997), 109–24; Sansterre, "Entre deux mondes? La vénération des images à Rome et en Italie d'après les textes des VIe–IXe siècles," in *Roma fra Oriente e Occidente, 19–24 aprile 2001,* 2 vols., Settimane di studio del CISAM 49 (Spoleto: CISAM, 2002). 2:993–1052, esp. 993–1027.

81. Belting, *Likeness and Presence,* 195–207 and 332–39.

82. Sansterre, "Le vénération des images à Ravenne dans le haut moyen age: Notes sur une forme de dévotion peu connue," *Revue Mabillon,* n.s., 7 (1996): 5–21.

83. Jean-Marie Martin, "Quelques remarques sur le culte des images en Italie méridionale pendant le haut moyen âge," in *Cristianità ed Europa: Miscellanea di studi in onore di Luigi Prosdocimi,* ed. Cesare Alzati, 2 vols. in 3 (Rome: Herder, 1994–2000), 1:223–36; François Bougard, "Trésors et *mobilia,*" in Caillet, *Les trésors de sanctuaires,* 161–97, esp. 182.

84. Noble, *Images, Iconoclasm,* 188–91.

church.[85] Yet the medieval Latin West never developed a specific theology of icons or a body of theory for their use in personal spirituality, perhaps because it had never faced systematic and widespread iconoclasm on the level of the East.[86]

During the reigns of the Saxon emperors, who spent much of their time in Italy, the veneration of icons began to move north. Henry II's visit to Italy for his coronation in 1014 might be connected to the *icona* contained in his and Kunigunde's 1017 list of donations to her foundation of Sankt-Marien of Kaufungen.[87] At Reichenau, in a poetic commemoration written around 995, Abbot Witigowo (d. 997) is celebrated for building projects that include a stone staircase to the chapel, where "a painted image of the Mother of God, bearing on her lap Christ, the pledge of love, remains on the wall. The brothers, going up the stairs, bending forward, touch it in prayer and bathe it with holy kisses." Witigowo had to have anticipated this veneration when he commissioned an image for such an accessible place. The same poem continues by noting two images of Mark and of Januarius (like Mary, special patrons of Reichenau) that Witigowo had ordered painted so that "these defenders may protect us on all sides from the hostile snares of the enemy," and although these images are not described as receiving the same devotion as the image of Mary, they too apparently made Reichenau's heavenly patrons more present.[88]

Statues

The three-dimensional religious images that appeared in the West from the tenth century on also had parts to play in spiritual ascent. As has been seen, Bernard of Chartres, writing around 1015, ultimately had come to accept Sainte Foy's reliquary as art that "enhances people's recollection and makes the saint more present." In this sense the statue functions as a device crafted to get the attention of devotees. But there is more to the story. Although in the *Miracles* Sainte Foy usually appears to devotees as the young girl of her legend, she sometimes also manifests herself as the imperious figure

---

85. Belting, *Likeness and Presence*, 232–249, esp. 238.

86. Schmitt, "L'historien et les images," in *Der Blick auf die Bilder: Kunstgeschichte und Geschichte im Gespräch*, ed. Otto Gerhard Oexle (Göttingen: Wallstein, 1997), 7–51, esp. 46.

87. Bischoff, *Mittelalterliche Schatzverzeichnisse*, 1:125–26 (no. 123).

88. Purchart, *Gesta Witigowonis*, lines 344–54, ed. Walter Berschin and Johannes Staub, *Die Taten des Abtes Witigowo von der Reichenau (985–997): Eine zeitgenössische Biographie von Purchart von der Reichenau* (Sigmaringen: Jan Thorbecke, 1992), 50–51. These lines are explicated in Sansterre, "Vénération et utilisation apotropaïque de l'image à Reichenau vers la fin du Xᵉ siècle: Un témoignage des *Gesta* de l'abbé Witigowo," *Revue belge de philologie et d'histoire* 73 (1995): 281–85.

of the reliquary.[89] Image and saint have merged, a conflation that is not too unusual. Monks could recognize Benedict in visions because he looked like his artistic image.[90] Around the year 1000, at the death of Adso, the provost of San Benedetto in Marsica, a monk saw the archangel Michael hurrying to claim the provost's soul, looking "as he was accustomed to be painted."[91] One way to explain the correspondences between artistic images and celestial beings is to assume that the artist was divinely inspired, as presumably would have been the case with the majestas of the Virgin found at Clermont from the mid-tenth century on, which was said to have been modeled on the appearance of the mother and child in a dream.[92] In the years around the millennium the Greek East knew many "true images" miraculously "made without hands [acheiropoieta]" or painted by Saint Luke; such images were initially rare in the West but became more common later, partly by importing Eastern images and partly by identifying the miraculous origins of long-cherished Western paintings and statues.

Officially, as Bishop Gerard I of Cambrai-Arras (1012–51) explained to the heretics at the Synod of Arras in 1025, "images of the saints are in the holy Church not to be adored by men but that through them we may be interiorly excited to contemplate the operation of divine grace and to take something out of the acts of those saints for use in our own manner of life."[93] According to this definition, images exist simply to inspire viewers to prayer and virtue. Yet anecdotes suggest that they also somehow mysteriously managed to make heavenly patrons more powerfully present.[94]

HOLY MEN AND WOMEN, DEAD AND ALIVE

If mere art can make the celestial more tangible, then what can actual holy people reveal? Because spiritual leaders are supposed to teach by word

89. Bernard of Chartres, *Miracula S. Fidis* I i, xiii, xvii, xix ; II v, vii, Bouillet, 11, 47–48, 54, 56, 107, 113, Sheingorn, 47, 78–79, 83, 85, 126–27, 131.

90. Benedict is recognized by a persecutor in Adrevaldus of Fleury, *Miracula Benedicti* I xviii, Certain, 15–89 esp. 42–46. Bruno, the future Leo IX, was able to recognize him immediately "by his face and habit [*ex qualitate vultus et habitus*]": see *Vita Leonis* I v, Krause, 102–3, Robinson, 105. On this dynamic, see Schmitt, "Rituels de l'image," in *Testo e immagine*, esp. 1:447–57.

91. *Chron. Casin.* II xxxiv, Hoffmann, 233. Peter the Deacon, retouching the original text of the *Chronicle* by Leo Marsicanus, added to "as he was accustomed to be painted" the words "by artists." Ibid. This same story also appears in Desiderius, *Dialogi* II vi, Schwartz and Hofmeister, 1130.

92. Schmitt, "Rituels de image," 1:419–59, esp. 441–47. See figure 20 above. On links between dreams and visions and Byzantine true images, see Henry MacGuire, *The Icons of Their Bodies: Saints and Their Images in Byzantium* (Princeton: Princeton University Press, 1996), 5–47.

93. Gerard I, *Acta Synodi Atrebatensis* xiv, ed. Vanderputten and Reilly, 66. The teaching on images is discussed in Fulton, *From Judgment to Passion*, 83–87.

94. On this complex relationship see Paroma Chatterjee, *The Living Icon in Byzantium and Italy: The Vita Image, Eleventh to Thirteenth Century* (Cambridge: Cambridge University Press, 2014), esp. 8–12.

and deed, the saints ought to be models. Yet few Christians thought they could imitate the extraordinary sanctity and works of power of the saints, and, in any case, the human dimensions of many saints had been lost to memory. Saints were usually more important as intercessors, powerful figures in the heavenly court to whom people could appeal. Although churchmen encouraged their flocks to pray for help along the lines of the litany formula "Ora pro nobis" (Pray for us), they did not always succeed, and in miracle stories popular saints often appear to be operating as independent agents. What was novel in the millennial Church was the reappearance of new saints, recent saints, who were able to serve as living models.

Many saints of the early medieval Latin West were generic. Their relics were often jumbled together in altars and reliquaries. The readings for the feasts of martyrs, saints, and Mary seem to place "less emphasis on their lives as models for spirituality than on their relationship to the paschal mystery, their entry (*natale*) into the afterlife, their tomb as a scene of local cult, as well as their intercession and efficacious presence in the Church."[95] When peace movements or other local assemblies brought together large numbers of reliquaries, even those saints who were well known became abstract witnesses. Yet somehow anonymous crowds of saints led devotees back to the broader mystery of Christ's incarnation. The power of the saints rests ultimately on the triumph of Jesus Christ, which martyrs and confessors, *membra Christi*, shared by having imitated him in heroic virtue and wonders.[96] A positive perspective on this saintly anonymity was expressed by Aelfric:

> An earthly king hath many servants
> and diverse stewards; he cannot be an honoured king
> unless he have the state which befitteth him,
> and as it were serving-men, to offer him their obedience.
> So likewise it is with Almighty God who created all things;
> It befitteth Him that He should have holy servants
> who might fulfill His will, and of these there are many
> even amongst mankind whom He chose out of this world,
> so that no scribe, though he know much,
> may write their names, because no man knoweth them.
> They are innumerable, as befitteth God.[97]

95. Pierre-Marie Gy, "Sacraments and Liturgy in Latin Christianity," in McGinn and Meyendorff, *Christian Spirituality*, 365–81, esp. 373.

96. Constable, "Imitation of the Divinity of Christ," in *Three Studies*, 143–248, esp. 145–50; Snoeck, *Medieval Piety*, 198–201.

97. Aelfric, *Prefatory Letter to Aethelwerd*, ed. Wilcox, *Aelfric's Prefaces*, 120–21, trans. Walter W. Skeat, *Aelfric's* Lives of the Saints *Being a Set of Sermons on Saints' Days formerly Observed by the English Church*, 2 vols. (London: Early English Text Society, 1881 and 1885), 1:4–7, esp. 6–7.

Around the millennium Mary seemed to become more present, especially in England. Although the chain of evidence is complex, a Winchester tradition, found in a twelfth-century collection of materials pertaining to Aethelwold (d. 984), associates him with special private devotions, including one to the Virgin Mary. An anonymous office of the Virgin, exhibiting many of Aethelwold's stylistic features, combines traditional antiphons with new prayers (some featuring the Grecisms characteristic of Winchester). It emphasizes chastity, mercy, and Mary's role as an intercessor. If this office is Aethelwold's, it places tenth-century England at the start of the tradition of the *Hours of the Blessed Virgin*, which soon became a favored private devotion.[98]

In the early eleventh century Marian piety also flourished on the Continent, where it found expression in the sermons of Fulbert of Chartres and Peter Damian.[99] The new popularity is evidenced in Henri Barré's inventory of prayers to Mary written prior to Anselm, four-fifths of which cluster in the early eleventh century.[100] Medieval Christians were beginning to learn the Ave Maria (Hail Mary) to go along with their Pater noster (Our Father) and Credo (Apostles' Creed).[101] Marian piety would become a hallmark of the spirituality of the Gregorian Reform.[102]

Even more concrete, however, were the new saints of the late tenth and early eleventh century. Carolingian churchmen had acclaimed few of their colleagues as holy: instead, motivated by love of Rome and tradition, they had preferred to import relics of ancient Roman martyrs and to rewrite the

98. Fulton, *From Judgment to Passion*, esp. 60–64. Roper, *Medieval English Benedictine Liturgy*, 47–50 and 71–74, offers references supporting her claim that the "tenth century marked the beginnings of English interest in Marianism; an interest which had almost reached cult proportions by the Norman Conquest." Lapidge and Winterbottom, introduction to *Wulfstan of Winchester: Life of St Aethelwold*, lxviii–lxxvii, discuss and edit this private office.

99. On Fulbert's Mariology, see his *Sermones*, ed. Migne, *Pat. Lat.* 141:317–40. For context see Barré, *Prières anciennes*, 150–53; Fulton, *From Judgment to Passion*, 219–21; and Fassler, *The Virgin of Chartres: Making History through Liturgy and the Arts* (New Haven: Yale University Press, 2010), 79–89, 112–16. On Peter Damian's Mariology, see Facchini, *San Pier Damiani: L'Eucologia*, 535–42 and 609; contextualized in Jennifer A. Harris, "Peter Damian and the Architecture of Self," in Melville and Schürer, *Das Eigene und das Ganze*, 148–50.

100. Barré, *Prières anciennes*, 311–12, in which only the first fifteen of the seventy-five prayers he lists fall outside the section on "L'essor marial du XIe siècle."

101. Ibid., 1–21.

102. Cowdrey, "The Spirituality of Gregory VII," in *The Mystical Tradition and the Carthusians*, ed. James L. Hogg (Salzburg: Institut für Anglistik und Amerikanistik, 1998), 1–22; Fulton, *From Judgment to Passion*, 224–35. Marian miracles associated with Gregory VII became part of later Marian collections as described in Horst Fuhrmann, "Zu den Marienwundern in der *Vita Gregorii VII Papae* des Paul von Bernried," in Ecclesia et Regnum: *Beiträge zur Geschichte von Kirche, Recht und Staat im Mittelalter: Festschrift für Franz-Josef Schmale zu seinem 65. Geburtstag*, ed. Dieter Berg and Hans-Werner Goetz (Bochum: Winkler, 1989), 111–19.

FIGURE 29. Anonymous saint appearing in the margins of a Gospel book *incipit* page. © The British Library Board, BL Royal 1 D. IX ("Cnut Gospels") fol. 111.

stories of long-dead local apostles.[103] In the millennial Church, hagiographers began to make up for lost time: they reversed the decline in saints' lives associated with invasions and warfare, and they honored not only traditional saints, whose rewritten lives continued to constitute the overwhelming bulk of hagiographical production, but also new contemporary heroes.[104]

---

103. Pierre Riché, "Les carolingiens en quête de sainteté," *in Les fonctions des saints dans le monde occidental (IIIᵉ–XIIIᵉ siècle): Actes du Colloque organisé par l' ÉFR avec le concours de l'Université de Rome "La Sapienza,"* Rome, 27–29 octobre 1988 (Rome: ÉFR, 1991), 217–24.

104. Ludwig Zoepf, *Das Heiligen-Leben im 10. Jahrhundert* (Leipzig: B. G. Teubner, 1908), 240–45; Guy Philippart and Michel Trigalet, "L'hagiographie latine du XIᵉ siècle," in Herren et al., *Latin Culture in the Eleventh Century*, 2:281–301, esp. 287–89.

The new saints were diverse. Kings admired those who were members of their own families.[105] Sainted kings came from the heart of Francia and from its peripheries, especially from the newly Christianized areas to the north and east that often honored royal martyrs who died defending their new faith and their political factions.[106] Canonized members of royal families included thirteen royal women from the house of Wessex, six Ottonians from the empire, two Arpads from Hungary, a couple of Premislyds from Bohemia, and other potential dynastic saints whose popular acclaim never received official recognition.[107]

Elite saints are to be expected in a hierarchical society, but they were more common in the tenth and eleventh centuries than in the Carolingian era. Bishops were canonized, especially the powerful German prince bishops whose hagiographical vitae and/or political gesta lauded both their sanctity and their administrative skills.[108] Successful monastic founders and reformers were remembered and honored by their new ecclesiastical communities.[109] Gerard of Brogne, John of Gorze, William of Volpiano, and others whose reforming work was mentioned above became saints. Elite saints could have popular cults: Maiolus of Cluny (d. 994), for example, attracted crowds of pilgrims to his tomb at Souvigny.[110] However, new categories of saints also appeared, including a plethora of low-born Italian

---

105. Robert Folz, *Les saints rois du moyen âge en occident, VIᵉ–XIIIᵉ siècles* (Brussels: Bollandistes, 1984). For debates on sacral kingship, see Janet L. Nelson, "Royal Saints and Early Medieval Kingship," *Studies in Church History* 10 (1973): 39–44; Gábor Klaniczay, "The Birth of a New Europe about 1000 CE: Conversion, Transfer of Institutional Models, New Dynamics," in Arnason and Wittrock, *Eurasian Transformations*, 99–129, esp. 120–23.

106. František Graus, "La sanctification du souverain dans l'Europe centrale des Xᵉ et XIᵉ siècles," in *Hagiographie, cultures, et sociétés, IVᵉ–XIIᵉ siècles: Actes du Colloque organisé à Nanterre et à Paris (2–5 mai 1979)* (Paris: Études augustiniennes, 1981), 559–72; Klaniczay, "From Sacral Kingship to Self-Representation: Hungarian and European Royal Saints in the 11th–13th Centuries," in *Continuity and Change: Political Institutions and Literary Monuments in the Middle Ages: A Symposium*, ed. Elisabeth Vestergaard (Odense, Den.: Odense University Press, 1986), 61–86. Sainted kings are discussed in more detail in chapter 8 below.

107. Patrick Corbet, *Les saints ottoniens: Sainteté dynastique, sainteté royale et sainteté feminine autour de l'an Mil* (Sigmaringen: Jan Thorbecke, 1986); Rollason, *Saints and Relics*, 137–44; Klaniczay, *Holy Rulers and Blessed Princesses*, 108–13, 123–50.

108. Oskar Köhler, *Das Bild des geistlichen Fürsten in den Viten des 10., 11. und 12. Jahrhunderts* (Berlin: Verlag für Staatswissenschaft und Geschichte, 1935); Hatto Kallfelz, *Lebenbeschreibungen einiger Bischöfe des 10.–12. Jahrhunderts* (Darmstadt: Wissenschaftliche Buchgesellschaft, 1973); Stephanie Coué, "Acht Bischofsviten aus der Salierzeit," in *Gesellschaftlicher und ideengeschichtlicher Wandel im Reich der Salier*, vol. 3 of *Die Salier und das Reich*, ed. Stefan Weinfurter (Sigmaringen: Jan Thorbecke, 1992), 347–413.

109. Roman Michalowski, "Il culto dei santi fondatori nei monasteri tedeschi dei secoli XI e XII—Proposte di ricerca," in *Culto dei santi, istituzioni e classi sociali in età preindustriale*, ed. Sofia Boesch Gajano and Lucia Sebastiani (L'Aquila, It.: L. U. Japadre, 1984), 105–40.

110. Constable, "Souvigny and Cluny," in *Abbey of Cluny*, 213–34, esp. 219–22.

hermits,[111] and even some exotic eastern holy men who haphazardly wandered west.[112]

From the mid-tenth century on, both old and new saints were increasingly commemorated by "professional" hagiographers. Some of these were educated clerks, exiled by choice or bad fortune, who paid for hospitality by writing or rewriting liturgical texts. Some were the schoolmen discussed in the next chapter. Although professionalization encouraged standardization, the cult of the saints in the millennial Church continued to vary geographically. Millennial Italy was filled with contemporary hermit saints, whereas the north had relatively few.[113] Belgium produced much hagiography but few new saints.[114] Spain had little hagiography and almost no new saints.[115] Celtic traditions were largely oral.

Did this increase of contemporary saints affect spirituality? Hagiographers use the same traditional models to describe them.[116] For example, saints routinely imitate the wonders of Christ and the apostles, even in such details as the healing gesture, the imposition of hands (to which the sign of the cross may be equated), and power transferred to objects that the saint has touched (contact is important with living saints, as with relics).[117] The most cited models are generic rather than individual: lives portray saints living angelically, speaking out prophetically, imitating Christ,

111. Pierre Toubert, *Les Structures du Latium médiéval: Le Latium méridional et la Sabine du IXe siècle à la fin du XIIe siècle*, 2 vols. (Rome: ÉFR, 1973), 43–47; John Howe, "St. Benedict the Hermit as a Model for Italian Sanctity: Some Hagiographical Witnesses," *American Benedictine Review* 55 (2004): 42–54.

112. Howe, "Greek Influence on the Eleventh-Century Western Revival of Hermitism," 2 vols. (PhD diss., UCLA, 1979), 1:36 and 2:365; Howe, "Western Monks and the East, 850–1050," in *Cambridge History of Medieval Western Monasticism*, ed. Alison Beach and Isabelle Cochelin (New York: Cambridge University Press, forthcoming). On these new saints, see chapter 9 below.

113. Judging on the basis of hagiographical production, northern hermits were rare in this period. See Howe, "Greek Influence,"1:18–33 and 2:365. Yet that does not rule out the possibility that they had existed but failed to gain the recognition accorded to their Italian colleagues—see Fichtenau, *Living in the Tenth Century*, 246–52.

114. Almost no lives of contemporary saints are listed in Paul-Irénée Fransen and H. Maraite, "Oeuvres hagiographiques, X{e}–XIe siècle" and "Oeuvres hagiographiques, XIe siècle," in *Index Scriptorum Operumque Latino-Belgicorum Medii Aevi. Deuxième partie: XIe siècle*, ed. Paul Tombeur and Léopold Genicot (Brussels: Académie Royale de Belgique Comité national du Dictionnaire du latin médiéval, 1976). Belgian hagiographers were more concerned with ancient heroes, as described in Léon Van der Essen, *Étude critique et littéraire sur les vitae des saints mérovingiens de l'ancienne Belgique* (Paris: Albert Fontemoing, 1907); and Webb, "Hagiography in the Diocese of Liège," esp. 812–25.

115. Díaz y Díaz, *Index Scriptorum Latinorum Medii Aevi Hispanorum*, is arranged century by century with *Vita, Passio*, etc. included in the final index.

116. Leclercq, "From Saint Gregory to Saint Bernard," in Leclercq et al., *Spirituality of the Middle Ages*, 103.

117. Pierre-André Sigal, *L'Homme et le miracle dans la France médiévale (XIe–XIIe siècle)* (Paris: Cerf, 1985), 17–78, esp. 32–35.

leading the apostolic life, and pursuing holy careers resembling those of universal saints such as Martin of Tours or Benedict of Nursia.[118] Pictures of saints in frescoes, manuscripts, and sculpture symbolically reinforce such universal models.[119]

Nevertheless, the living holy people who were in the vanguard of the late tenth- and early eleventh-century ecclesiastical revival would not have been remembered unless they had somehow been influential. In fact, they were part of a larger spectrum of charismatic figures found at this time in the West: perhaps because social, ecclesiastical, and political institutions were still in the process of reconstruction, the gaps and conflicts in law and custom required leaders able to transcend them through power of personality. Chroniclers, like hagiographers, emphasize personal qualities: kings must be wellborn, wise, generous, mild toward good men and severe toward evildoers; nobles must be brave, strong, and militarily skilled, while also being affable and pleasant, wise in council, and lavish in generosity.[120] Potential saints had to meet and exceed similar standards for holiness, and in doing so their actual historical deeds could offer potential examples for imitation. By being contemporary they somehow gained *praesentia*—otherwise hagiographers would not so often specify eyewitness testimony.

Latin Christians even attempted to identify living saints, a dubious pursuit inasmuch as theologians believed that salvation could be assured only through a good death. Nevertheless, Romuald had to sneak out of the area around the monastery of Cuxà because neighbors were plotting to kill him in order to acquire his relics.[121] A less violent spiritual path did lie open to those who were able to follow a (potential) saint. William of Volpiano impressed his many disciples so much that they made him their unofficial heavenly intercessor even when he was still alive: according to Rodulfus Glaber, when William's men were traveling and things were not going well, "they were wont to say: 'Lord, in the faith of Father William,

118. On hagiographical images in texts, see Leclercq, *La Vie parfaite: Points de vue sur l'essence de l'état religieux* (Paris: Brepols, 1948); Jean-Yves Tilliette, "Les modèles de sainteté du IXᵉ au XIᵉ siècle, d'après le témoignage des récits hagiographiques en vers métriques," in *Santi e demoni nell'alto medioevo occidentale (secoli V–XI), 7–13 aprile 1988*, 2 vols., Settimane di Studio del CISAM 36 (Spoleto: CISAM, 1989), 1:381–409. On the angelic life in particular, see Scott Bruce, *Silence and Sign Language in Medieval Monasticism: The Cluniac Tradition c. 900–1200* (Cambridge: Cambridge University Press, 2007), 1–28. For an explication of how such images could operate in a particular cult, that of Dominic of Sora (d. 1032), see Howe, *Church Reform*, 66–71. On the influence of Benedict, see Howe, "St. Benedict the Hermit," 42–54.

119. Hahn, *Portrayed on the Heart*, esp. 33–34.

120. Fichtenau, *Living in the Tenth Century*, 138–41, 166–70, 197.

121. Peter Damian, *Vita Romualdi*, xiii, Tabacco, 35 (where notes indicate related stories told about the desert fathers), Leyser, 301.

do to us as thou knowest'. . . . None who said this ever wanted for any-thing."[122] When Benedict of Benevento (d. 1003) found Romuald, "Benedict was glad that he had found a master at last, believing that nothing was right or sacred except what Romuald said, and he mortified his will imperiously and eagerly followed the admonishments of his harsh mentor"; according to another disciple, John Gradenigo, Romuald was "living . . . in great humility albeit on splendid heights, and he has taught us which is the right way."[123] Of course, spiritual masters had to be chosen with great care. Some of the new heretical groups also followed charismatic leaders: the Arras heretics, for example, were devoted to the "law and discipline which we received from our master" (an otherwise unknown "Gundolph" from Italy).[124]

Leaders could extend their charisma by presenting their followers as examples. Bruno of Querfurt (d. 1009) describes how "Master Romuald praised Benedict, affirming that he was "like a rock [*quasi saxum*] in fasting and vigils; and because of the innocent obedience and chaste behavior, in which he walked with joy, as God is witness, Romuald deservedly recommended him in extraordinary terms [*eum . . . mirabiliter predicavit*] to me [Bruno] and to all others."[125] Peter Damian, who devoted a considerable part of his literary career to praising his disciples, instructed the priors of his hermitages, "Whenever you are citing an example of someone who is performing heroically, withhold his name if he belongs to the community; but if he is someone outside our hermitage, you may say who it is. It is more effective to use recent examples rather than older ones."[126]

Living people vividly modeled asceticism. *Askēsis* is a Greek term that originally referred to programs of physical exercises undertaken to train for athletic contests; then ancient philosophers used it to designate the spiritual training required by the philosophic life; Greek Christians who believed that the monastic life was the true "philosophic life" turned *askēsis* into Christian asceticism.[127] These exercises sought to help a seeker of

122. Rodulfus Glaber, *Vita Domni Willelmi* xii, Bulst, France and Reynolds, 286–87.

123. Bruno of Querfurt, *Vita Quinque Fratrum* ii, Miladinov, 204–7.

124. Gerard I, *Acta Synodi* i, ed. Vanderputten and Reilly, 17–18. For a sociological analysis of the charismatic leadership of these early heretical groups, see Lutz Kaebler, *Schools of Asceticism: Ideology and Organization in Medieval Religious Communities* (University Park: Pennsylvania State University Press, 1998), 120–23.

125. Bruno of Querfurt, *Vita Quinque Fratrum* ii, Miladinov, 206–7.

126. Peter Damian, *Epistola* l, Reindel, 2:77–131, esp. 126, Blum, 2:289–334, esp. 329.

127. Michel Olphe-Galliard, "L'ascèse païenne," *Dictionnaire de spiritualité*, 17 vols. (Paris: Gabriel Beauchesne et ses fils, 1932–95), 1:940–960; Vincent L. Wimbush, introduction to *Ascetic Behavior in Greco-Roman Antiquity: A Sourcebook* (Minneapolis: Fortress Press, 1990), 1–11. Wimbush and Richard Valantasis, introduction to *Asceticism*, ed. Wimbush and Valantasis (New York: Oxford University Press, 1995), xix–xxxiii, esp.

divine wisdom avoid worldly distractions: poverty was an antidote to the snares of wealth, chastity to the cares of family life, obedience to the corrupting effects of pride and power. Also important were arduous physical practices such as fasts, vigils, and repeated genuflections.

Asceticism could serve as penance, a way to atone for or at least to demonstrate sorrow for faults. This promoted self-criticism. Italian hermits at the millennium quoted a dictum, perhaps echoing contemporary Greek spirituality, that "nor is it a small approach to blessedness, when a man has come to know his own wretchedness."[128] Eleventh-century Western Europe saw the flowering of the cult of Mary Magdalene, who allegedly had spent her last decades living as a preeminent model of tearful repentance in the wilds of southern France.[129] Spiritual writers in the Greek East, however, following Origen (d. 253/254), envisioned asceticism not as penance for its own sake but as a potential first step in a larger program of mystical ascent. In a common scheme, asceticism served to neutralize the passions: those who achieved "apathy" might then fight against demons; the spiritual warrior who triumphed over evil spirits might hope to apprehend celestial images and ideas or perhaps even to touch the indescribable realm beyond them.[130] In the early medieval Latin West, such step-by-step mystical itineraries had been rare, but in early eleventh-century Italy that situation was beginning to change. Peter Damian discussed several models.[131] This era saw the reemergence of the word "ecstasy," a loanword from Greek mysticism indicating that the spirit literally "stood outside" itself as it sought union with the divine.[132] The

xix–xxv, survey some of the bibliography. On the origins of Christian asceticism, see Samuel Rubenson, "Christian Asceticism and the Emergence of the Monastic Tradition," and McGinn, "Asceticism and Mysticism in Late Antiquity and in the Early Middle Ages," in Wimbush and Valantasis, *Asceticism*, 49–75 and 58–74.

128. Bruno of Querfurt, *Vita Quinque Fratrum* vii, Miladinov, 232–33.

129. Nagy, *Don des larmes*, 256–67, offers an overview of the Magdalene's place in penitential spirituality. On this devotion, see Victor Saxer, *Le culte de Marie Madeleine en Occident: Des origines à la fin du moyen âge*, 2 vols. (Auxerre: Société des Fouilles Archéologiques et des Monuments Historiques de l'Yonne, 1959); and in Élisabeth Pinto-Mathieu, *Marie-Madeleine dans la littérature du Moyen Âge* (Paris: Beauchesne, 1997), 89–109.

130. Tomáš Špidlík, *The Spirituality of the Christian East: A Systematic Handbook*, trans. Anthony P. Gythiel (Kalamazoo, MI: Cistercian Publications, 1986), 68–71, 177–82, 233–38, and 327–49; McGinn, The *Foundations of Mysticism*, vol. 1 of *The Presence of God: A History of Western Mysticism*, 5 vols. (London: Crossroads, 1992), 148–57 and 218–27; Hilarion Alfeyev, *St. Symeon the New Theologian and Orthodox Tradition* (Oxford: Oxford University Press, 2000), esp. 228 and 249–55.

131. McGinn, *Growth of Mysticism*, 144–46. These schemes include a four-stage ascent corresponding to four stages in the life of St. Alexius, in Peter Damian, *Sermo* xxviii, Lucchesi, 162–70; also a Leah and Rachael allegory in *Epist*. cliii, Reindel, 4:13–67, esp. 29–32, Blum, 6:33–36. Peter is clear that asceticisms are antidotes to money, sex, food, and other things that impede the soul from rising in contemplation: see, for example, *Epistola* xcvi, Reindel, 3:46–64, esp. 47–49, Blum, 4:51–67, esp. 52–54.

132. Charles Baumgartner, "Extase," *Dictionnaire de Spiritualité*, 26 vols. (Paris: Beauchesne, 1932–95), 4:2045–189, esp. 2110–11; Alfeyev, *St. Symeon*, 241–49.

word *exstasis* had appeared in Christian Latin in Late Antiquity but never caught on: it is found only twice in the Vulgate, and even though Augustine used it in biblical commentaries to describe states of prophetic inspiration, it is almost completely absent in authors such as Gregory the Great.[133] Starting in the late tenth century, however, "ecstasy" begins to reappear in the Latin West.[134] Examples associated with recent holy people include the various ecstatic experiences that Peter Damian describes in his life of Romuald (d. 1027), visions and healings received by the young Leo IX while in ecstasy, an ecstatic visionary at Monte Gargano who announced a Christian victory over the Spanish Muslims in 1041, and the ecstatic experience that Berthold of Reichenau attributes to Hermannus Contractus (d. 1054).[135] Likewise, the quest for the "gift of tears" in prayer, considered as a sign of perfection as well as divine grace, allegedly attained its maximum importance around the year 1000 among Italian hermits.[136]

Although the lives of holy people hint at changes in prayer and piety around the year 1000, it was still a time of transition. In Italian hermitism and in John of Fécamp (himself a native of Ravenna) one finds a new emotionalism and interiority. Private prayers were becoming more individual and explicit. But only in later generations—in the monastic tradition of Anselm, William of Saint-Thierry, and Bernard—is there a consistent, self-conscious effort to systematize this spirituality and to align the eremitical love of literal solitude more closely with the quest for interior solitude.[137]

GOD IN NATURE

Nature is God's art. Walafrid Strabo unambiguously made this point around 840 while he was defending sacred images against the charge that they could lead to idolatry: "Of course, if anyone thinks the art of painting or sculpture should be censured because things made by artists and sculptors might, by

---

133. McGinn, *Growth of Mysticism*, 448n224.

134. For *exstasis* around the millennium, see Howe, "Greek Influence," 1:142–49 and 2:440–42.

135. Peter Damian, *Vita Romualdi* xiv and l, Tabacco, 36–37 and 93; *Vita Leonis* I v and xvii, Krause, 102–2 and 152–53, Robinson, 105 and 125; Andrew of Fleury, *Miracula Benedicti* IV xi, Certain, 190; Berthold, *Annales* (1054), ed. Georg Pertz, MHG *SS* 5 (Hannover: Hahn, 1844), 264–326, esp. 268.

136. Nagy, *Don des larmes*, esp. 38, 166, 174–76. Anselm had a very short "prayer for the grace of tears" (*Oratio* xvi *ad Christum*), ed. Migne, *Pat. Lat.* 158: 892–94.

137. Henriet, *La parole et la prière*, 97–141; Leclercq, "Pierre le Vénérable et l'érémitisme clunisien," in *Petrus Venerabilis, 1156–1956: Studies and Texts Commemorating the Eighth Centenary of His Death*, ed. Constable and James Kritzeck (Rome: Herder, 1956), 99–120; Leclercq, "'Eremus' et 'eremita': Pour l'histoire du vocabulaire de la vie solitaire," *Collectanea Ordinis Cisterciensium Reformatorum* 25 (1963): 8–30; Fulton, *From Judgment to Passion*, 198–99; Constable, "Spiritual Emptiness and Ascetic Exile in the Middle Ages," in *On the Shoulders of Giants: A Festschrift in Honour of Glenn Olsen*, ed. David Appleby and Teresa Olsen Pierre (Toronto: PIMS, 2015), 135–58.

their grace and elegance, entice the foolish to worship them, logically he could also object to the works of God—why has God created the heavenly bodies of such splendour or the plants and vegetables of such loveliness and fragrance that these, like other created things, have been adored and worshipped in the liturgy by the deluded?"[138] Although Christianity has often been criticized for its alienation from nature, at least as compared with the embrace of nature in the cults of the Olympian deities, there has always been a profound Christian natural theology.[139] This would ultimately blossom in the twelfth century's preoccupation with nature as revelation.[140]

In the late tenth and early eleventh centuries, hermits and their patrons valued nature as a venue for meditation.[141] Romuald of Ravenna, prior to his monastic conversion, discovered a "pleasant place [*locus amoenus*]," and was inspired to soliloquize about "O how well hermits would be able to dwell in the recesses of these woods, how nicely they could meditate here away from all the disturbances of secular strife."[142] Otto III proposed to send missionaries to establish a monastery on the edge of Christendom in the "beautiful forests" and "golden solitudes" of his realm; he was proud to possess "many beautiful solitudes" in which it would be "possible to lead the solitary life."[143] The *locus amoenus* where one can find leisure and rest is a classical rhetorical topos.[144] Yet any doubt that it could be connected to an objective reality can be dispelled by touring eleventh-century hermitage sites such as John Gualbert's Vallombrosa, Peter Damian's Fonte Avellana, or Dominic of Sora's many retreats—hermitages with these spectacular vistas must have been chosen for aesthetic as well practical reasons.[145] The claim that appreciation of landscape is a renaissance innovation does not stand.[146]

---

138. Walafrid Strabo, *Libellus de Exordiis* xxii, Harting-Correa, 72–81, esp. 74–77.

139. For debates on medieval natural theology, see Howe and Michael Wolfe, introduction to *Inventing Medieval Landscapes: Senses of Place in Western Europe*, ed. Howe and Wolfe (Gainesville: University Press of Florida, 2002), 1–10, esp. 10.

140. Constable, *Reformation of the Twelfth Century*, 140–41; Henriet, *La parole et la prière*, 117–19.

141. McGinn, *Growth of Mysticism*, 128–30.

142. Peter Damian, *Vita Romualdi* i, Tabacco, 14.

143. Bruno of Querfurt, *Vita Quinque Fratrum* ii and ix, Miladinov, 210–11, 238–39.

144. The topos of the *locus amoenus* received its classic description in Ernst Robert Curtius, *European Literature and the Latin Middle Ages*, trans. Willard R. Trask, Bollingen Series 36 (1953, repr., Princeton: Princeton University Press, 1990), 183–202.

145. Visual or verbal descriptions are in *Vallombrosa: Santo e meraviglioso luogo*, ed. Roberto Paolo Ciardi (Florence: Banca Toscana, 1999), 5–28; Luigi Michelini Tocci, *Eremi e cenobi del Catria* (Pesaro: Cassa di Risparmio di Pesaro, 1972); and Stefania Mezzazappa, "L'impronta di Domenico nei luoghi emblematici della sua presenza," in *La tradizione storica di San Domenico di Sora: Iconografia, fonti, luoghi. Atti dei Convegni del millenario*, ed. Luigi Gulia (Sora: Edizioni Casamari, 2012), 167–211, esp. 193–210. See Nees, *Early Medieval Art*, 132, for the claim that early medieval monastic sites in general are "uncommonly beautiful."

146. For other instances of medieval privileging of natural vistas, see Oliver H. Creighton, *Designs upon the Land: Elite Landscapes of the Middle Ages* (Woodbridge: Boydell & Brewer, 2009).

This respect for nature extended on rare occasions to Franciscan-like concern for its creatures. The hermit Guthlac (d. 714), in the Old English *Guthlac A*, which is usually assumed to reflect the spirituality of England's mid-tenth-century Benedictine reform, is blessed by the birds because "daily from his own hand he gave them food appropriate to their kind."[147] Thietmar tells how Otto I's widow Mathilda, dwelling at Quedlinburg, arranged to feed both paupers and birds; he also relates how an old noble bishop, Ansfrid of Utrecht (995–1010), after losing his eyesight, became a monk on a mountain, where he fed and washed poor folk and in winter hung bundles of food in trees to feed the birds.[148]

Love of nature did not prevent attempts to improve it. The countryside was Christianized with chapels, wayside crosses, and pilgrimage shrines.[149] The solar year became the liturgical cycle, its solstices and equinoxes tracked by great Christian festivals (Christmas, Annunciation, St. John's Day, St. Martin's Day). Saints' days dictated fasts and feasts, when to plant, when to hold markets, and even when to pay taxes (church offerings were due on specific feasts). The logical consequence was a proliferation of shrines and dedications that led to the maximal Christianization of nature, toward what Edward Muir has labeled "the ubiquity of the sacred."[150]

By the mid-eleventh century the sacred geography of Western Christendom was essentially in place. Like the west works of its churches, whose entrances were guarded by their Michael chapels, its frontiers were protected by the Archangel himself, whose banner had led the German armies to victory against the Hungarians and whose sanctuaries included Monte Gargano in southern Italy, Mont Saint-Michel in Normandy, Michael Mount in Cornwall, and São Miguel do Castello in Portugal.[151] Like a properly defended lordship, Western Christendom had some major strongholds on its frontiers—the three great pilgrimage centers of Jerusalem, Rome, and Santiago de Compostella. Within the European sanctuary, each

147. Guthlac's Old English "*Vita A*" ¶ 9–10, ed. Paul Gonser, *Das angelsächische Prosa-Leben des hl. Guthlac*. Anglistische Forschungen 27 (Heildelberg: Karl Winter, 1909), 97–200, esp. 140–43, trans. Michael Swanton, *Anglo-Saxon Prose* (London: Dent, 1975), 39–62, esp. 51–52.

148. Thietmar of Merseburg, *Chronicon* I xxi and IV xxxvi, Holtzmann, 26–27 and 173, Warner, 82 and 177.

149. Howe, "The Conversion of the Physical World: The Creation of a Christian Landscape," in *Varieties of Religious Conversion in the Middle Ages*, ed. James K. Muldoon (Gainesville: University Press of Florida, 1997), 63–78; and Howe, "Creating Symbolic Landscapes: Medieval Development of Sacred Space," in Howe and Wolfe, *Inventing Medieval Landscapes*, 208–23.

150. Edward Muir, "The Virgin on the Street Corner: The Place of the Sacred in Italian Cities," in *Religion and Culture in the Renaissance and Reformation*, ed. Steven Ozment (Kirksville, MO: Sixteenth Century Journal, 1989), 25–40, esp. 252.

151. *Culte et pèlerinages à Saint Michel*, Bouet et al.

community had its own celestial protectors and patrons, defense in depth that was the spiritual counterpart to the castles of the secular warlords.

How could a geographically rooted Latin Christendom coexist with what was allegedly an increasing emphasis on contempt for the world (*contemptus mundi*)? In Robert Bultot's polemical studies on this theme, John of Fécamp, Peter Damian, Anselm, and others are presented as men who despise the world and its humane secular values. Yet even while advocates of *contemptus mundi* explicitly reject the material world, they seem to protest too much and to be self-consciously spurning something profoundly attractive. As Bultot himself admits, the leaders of the new spirituality consistently affirmed that all God's creations are good and that "all spirit and each creature praise the Creator (cf. Psalm 150: 6)."[152] They disparaged nature and the delights of the world not because they were bad but because they were transitory. This attitude toward all material things is exemplified by one of Jean of Fécamp's poems, which declares that, as in the third chapter of Ecclesiastes, the transient glories of the world are just not enough:

> Woe to man, woe to man, woe to you unhappy man!
> Why do you love the goods of this world which are going to perish?
> Vanity of vanities, all is vanity,
> Everything existing under the sun is vain.
> All the glory of the world is like the flower and the grass.
> The world will pass away with all its desires.[153]

One way to recognize the limits of the world is to look at it from God's perspective. God's ability to be both inside and yet outside and beyond the universe was an intellectual problem that in Late Antiquity preoccupied Augustine and in the eleventh century continued to fascinate John of Fécamp, who incorporated chapters on divine transcendence into his meditative *Confessio Theologica*.[154] In a phenomenon sometimes labeled "dilation," visionaries share this perspective by stretching the mind's interior vision in God so that the seer stands outside and above himself or herself—indeed, above the world itself, which then appears very small (cf. Wisd. of Sol. 11:22). The classic early medieval image of the world transcended is the vision of Benedict, who while praying in a tower saw

---

152. Robert Bultot, Christianisme et les valeurs humaines: *La Doctrine du mépris du monde*, vol. 4, pt. 1, *Pierre Damian*, and vol. 4, pt. 2, *Jean de Fécamp, Herman Contract, Roger de Caen, Anselme de Canterbury* (Louvain: Éditions Nauwelaerts, 1963–64), esp. vol. 4, pt. 1, 13–14, 67–68; vol. 4, pt. 2: 41–42. Quotation from John of Fécamp, *Confessio Theologica* I viii and III xxvi, Leclercq and Bonnes, 109–83, esp. 114 and 171.

153. John of Fécamp, *De Vanitate Mundi*, ed. Wilmart, "Jean de Fécamp, La complainte sur les fins dernières," *Revue d'ascétique et de mystique* 9 (1928): 385–98, esp. 392.

154. John of Fécamp, *Confessio Theologica* I ii–iii and v–vi, Leclercq and Bonnes, 109–83, esp. 110–13 (cf. Augustine, *Confessions*, I ii and iv),

a celestial light poured out from above, which "brought before his eyes the whole world, as though gathered in one ray of the sun."[155] Spiritual seekers around the millennium understood this perspective. Dominic of Sora, while living as a hermit at Monte Argatone above the Lago di Scanno around the year 1000, felt himself lifted above the clouds so that he beheld the whole earth.[156] The young Bishop Bruno of Toul (the future Pope Leo IX, 1049–54), crushed by his inability to protect his diocese from violence, in troubled sleep saw "someone with an angelic face who offered to him a sphere brighter than the sun, which contained within it the mechanism of the whole universe."[157] Related to this perspective are accounts of cosmic journeys, visions of hell and of heaven that reveal the pettiness of the day-to-day human landscape as focus widens to a cosmic perspective.[158] Peter Damian imagines how a sinful soul at death "looks down at the base and loathsome darkness of the world and then marvels at the eternal brilliance above."[159] Although the dilation experience has its own long literary and spiritual life, its eleventh-century manifestations in the Latin Church reveal seekers attempting to transcend the limits of their present world.

155. On this story see Pierre Courcelle, "La vision cosmique de Saint Benoît," *Revue des études augustiniennes* 13 (1967): 93–117, esp. 114–17; Basil Steidel, "Die kosmische Vision des Gottesmannes Benedikt: Beitrag zu Gregor d. gr., Dialog II, Kap. 35," *Erbe und Auftrag* 47 (1971): 187–92, 298–315, and 404–14; and Françoise Monfrin, "Voir le monde dans la lumière de Dieu: A propos de Grégoire le Grand, *Dialogues*, II, 35," in *Les fonctions des saints dans le monde occidental (IIIᵉ–XIIIᵉ siècle): Actes du colloque organisé par l'ÉFR avec le concours de l'Université de Rome "La Sapienza," Rome, 27–29 octobre, 1988* (Rome: ÉFR, 1991), 37–41.

156. Howe, *Church Reform*, 47 and 63.

157. *Vita Leonis* I xvi, Krause, 146–49, Robinson, 122–24.

158. For example, Guthlac's Old English *"Vita A"* q 5, Gonser, 127–35, Swanton, 47–49.

159. Peter Damian, *Epist.* lxvi, Reindel 2:265, Blum 3:56.

CHAPTER 7

"LEARNING IS PART OF HOLINESS"

Without doubt learning is part of holiness, and most of all it drives
away carelessness, expels every avarice, diminishes love of worldly
things, turns the mind toward love of God, and brings it about that we
shun the desires of the present life. In truth, with work learning shall
bring forth all these aforementioned things.

—Anonymous Old English Homily (late tenth century?)

LEARNING AS GRACE

Learning was essential to ecclesiastical reform.[1] The new churches and
monasteries required trained personnel, and in order to produce the necessary religious professionals old schools had to be revived and new ones
established. This movement was inspired by Carolingian precedents but
implemented on a vastly enlarged scale using increasingly refined peda-
gogy and curricula. Its story has not been effectively told.[2] Historians of
education usually jump from Carolingian schools to late eleventh-century
ones, and until recently they have not paid much attention to the actual
formative practices of medieval Christian education.[3] Perhaps one reason

1. *Homily* vii, ed. Donald Scragg, *The Vercelli Homilies and Related Texts*, Early English Text Society, o.s.,
300 (Oxford: Oxford University Press, 1992), 134:1–6, trans. Clare Lees, *Tradition and Belief: Religious Writing
in Late Anglo-Saxon England* (Minneapolis: University of Minnesota Press, 1999), 114.

2. Post-Carolingian education has not been overstudied. Contrast the claim of C. Stephen Jaeger, *The
Envy of Angels: Cathedral Schools and Social Ideals in Medieval Europe, 950–1200* (Philadelphia: University
of Pennsylvania Press, 1994), 1–4, that historians of the post-Carolingian age have neglected cathedral schools
in favor of monastic ones, with the laments over the relative neglect of monastic schools in Sally N. Vaughn
and Jay Rubenstein, introduction to *Teaching and Learning in Northern Europe*, ed. Vaughn and Rubenstein
(Turnhout, Belg.: Brepols, 2006), 1–16, esp. 1–7. The scholarship is summarized in Barrow, *Clergy*, 170–275.

3. See John Van Engen, introduction to *Educating People of Faith: Exploring the History of Jewish and
Christian Communities*, ed. Van Engen (Grand Rapids, MI: Eerdmans, 2004), 1–26, esp. 14–17.

is that systematic historical research on medieval schools was first undertaken by nineteenth- and early twentieth-century English, German, and American scholars who had received classical educations and were far more interested in the fates of pagan authors than in other school studies, which they tended to dismiss as superstitious, dogmatic, and Catholic. They investigated how pagan learning was transmitted and recovered, and they described how new texts and techniques imported from Islam and Byzantium ultimately inspired new types of scholastic learning. These are important story lines, but they deal with impinging factors, not with the core tradition.

It is impossible to understand the central tradition without recognizing that early medieval educators considerd learning a gift from God. Wisdom comes from the Holy Spirit, and thus, according to Pope Gregory the Great, "Unless the Spirit is present in the heart of the hearer, the discourse of the teacher is useless. Nobody should attribute to the one who teaches what he learns from his teaching, since, unless He might be within Who teaches, the speech of the teacher outside operates in a vacuum."[4] According to Rabanus Maurus, "What the Holy Spirit speaks in the Church. / Through grammar the Psalmist brings this to the people / Duly confirming their grasp of the law of God. / So, brethren, we should strive always / With eyes and ears intent, to learn the Word of God."[5] The preface to the Old English *Grammar* of Aelfric (d. ca. 1010), the first Latin grammar written in a vernacular language, explains that the study of grammar leads to wisdom and provides the key to interpreting scripture.[6]

Education guided the ignorant back toward the Savior who was Truth (cf. John 14:6). It was a type of reform involving not only abstract ideas but also practical realities, not just truth and salvation in a world to come but the establishment of right order in the here and now. Scripture had a moral sense from which biblical commentators deduced rules for conduct. Christian teaching, especially when presented by pastors to their less learned flocks, was most often about how to behave. Teachers discriminated sharply between truth and falsehood, good and evil, and if there were any doubts about which was which, they could seek solutions in

---

4. Gregory I, *Homilia xxx*, ed. Raymond Étaix, Georges Blanc, and Bruno Judic, *Grégoire le Grand: Homélies sur l'Évangile*, 2 vols., Sources chrétiennes 485 and 522 (Paris: Cerf, 2005–8), 2:221–49, esp. 228–31.

5. Rabanus Maurus, *De Clericorum Institutione ad Heistulphum Archiepiscopum* prol., ed. Migne, *Pat. Lat.* 107: 203–4, trans. Marcia L. Colish, *A Study in the Medieval Theory of Knowledge* (Lincoln: University of Nebraska Press, 1968), 64.

6. Aelfric, *Grammatica*, preface, ed. Julius Zupitza, *Aelfrics Grammatik und Glossar*, 3rd ed. (pref. from Helmut Gneuss) (Hildesheim: Weidmann, 2001), 2–3; more preface versions in Jonathan Wilcox, ed., *Aelfric's Prefaces*, Durham Medieval Texts 9 (Durham: Durham Medieval Texts, 1994), 36–37, 114–16, 151–53.

ancient books written by Christian fathers and inspired pagans. Respect for books ran high.

THE NEW SCHOOLS

Schools proliferated.[7] The new academic world is illustrated in Peter Damian's story about a Burgundian named Walter who "sought an education throughout Western Europe, moving from one kingdom to another, and travelling to the cities, burghs, and regions not only of Germany and France, but even to those of the Saracens in Spain. After he had scoured the world for its learning, so to speak, he gave up his wandering, settled down, and quietly began to teach boys." This story—actually a cautionary tale about the futility of seeking learning for its own sake, which concludes with Walter's sudden death and dying lament ("Oh, what a loss!")—presupposes that by the mid-eleventh century, as Peter Damian's audience would recognize, an interrelated system of schools and learning had developed throughout the Latin West.[8]

Carolingian educational decrees had fostered schools, but these institutions had all been disrupted to greater or lesser extents: basic educational continuity is evident only in a few cathedral schools such as Laon, Rheims, and Metz, and a few southern German monasteries such as Reichenau.[9] One serendipitous consolation was that the dispersal of teachers and books may actually have helped spread Carolingian learning. Notker the Stammerer (d. 884) mentions a monk, a refugee from the destroyed monastery of Jumièges, who arrived at Saint-Gall in Switzerland with a new system for recording music.[10] Archbishop Fulk of Rheims (882–900), trying to revive his important school, which had declined during the Viking threats that dominated the last years of Archbishop Hincmar (845–82), imported two academic stars, Hucbald of Saint-Amand (d. 930) and Remigius of Auxerre (d. c. 908), who after Fulk's assassination departed quickly for Paris.[11] The predecessors of Peter Damian's wandering Master Walter were not always on the road voluntarily.

7. Pierre Riché, "Essor des écoles occidentales: Milieux Xᵉ–milieu XIᵉ siècle," in his *Écoles et enseignement dans le Haut Moyen Age: Fin du V e siècle–milieu du XI e siècle*, rev. ed. (Paris: Picard, 1989), 119–67.

8. Peter Damian, *Epist.* cxvii, Reindel, 3:316–29, esp. 322, Blum, 4:318–31, esp. 325.

9. Joachim Ehlers, "Dom- und Klosterschülen in Deutschland und Frankreich im 10. und 11. Jahrhundert," in *Schule und Schüler im Mittelalter: Beiträge zur europäischen Bildungsgeschichte des 9. bis 15. Jahrhunderts*, ed. Martin Kintzinger, Sönke Lorenz, and Michael Walter (Cologne: Böhlau, 1996), 29–52, esp. 34–38.

10. Notker Balbulus, *Liber Hymnorum*, preface, ed. Wolfram von den Steinen, *Notkeri Poetae Balbuli Liber Ymnorum* (Bern, Switz.: Francke, 1960), 6–9, trans. Richard Crocker, *The Early Medieval Sequence* (Berkeley: University of California Press, 1977), 1. On the historicity and significance of this much-discussed story, see Michel Huglo, "La diffusion des tropes en France avant l'an Mil," in Iogna-Prat and Picard, *Religion et culture autour de l'an Mil*, 99–102, esp. 99.

11. Michael E. Moore, "Prologue: Teaching and Learning History in the School of Rheims, c. 800–950," in Vaughn and Rubenstein, *Teaching and Leaning*, 19–49, esp. 34–41.

As soon as conditions improved, schools flourished. They were the trimmings on the new white mantle of churches. Ecclesiastical authorities embraced the pursuit of learning as a religious quest that could improve their clergy, their prestige, and perhaps even their incomes.[12] Monastic and cathedral schools now began to develop in different directions because, while many monks and nuns were concerned about forming recruits for the religious life, the cathedral schools, benefiting from their locations in growing cities, increasingly trained not only secular priests but also administrators and courtiers.[13] The educational revival had regional variations. When West Francia was still struggling with raiders and civil wars, the educational center of gravity shifted east. In the last two generations of the tenth century more than a dozen major cathedral schools arose in Germany, well financed and stocked with the best Carolingian school texts.[14] The stereotype that these were uncreative copies of Carolingian schools[15] has been challenged in recent years by C. Stephen Jaeger's vision of a vibrant system of schools, dedicated to training students for courtly life, that cultivated a civic humanism inspired by Ciceronian stoicism and expressed in poetry.[16] Bishops in the Lorraine, who were closely involved in monastic reform, led a world in which cathedral and monastic schools did not bifurcate so radically.[17] At the end of the tenth century, the schools in West Francia began to catch up under the

12. Cowdrey, *Lanfranc*, 19–20, cites evidence suggesting that around 1060 the abbot of Bec, when approving Lanfranc's proposal for a new school, added the stipulation that the gifts it generated should go into the abbey's building fund.

13. Contrast the difference between Thierry Kouamé, who describes Carolingian academic legislation that applied equally to all schools in "La réception de la législation scolaire carolingienne dans les collections canoniques jusqu'au *Décrit* de Gratien (IXe–XIIe siècle)," in *Universitas Scolarium: Mélanges offerts à Jacques Verger par ses anciens étudiants*, ed. Cédric Giraud and Martin Morard (Geneva: Droz, 2011), 3–46, esp. 5–13, and Robert Norman Swanson, *The Twelfth-Century Renaissance* (Manchester, UK: Manchester University Press, 1999), 12–21, who emphasizes the distinctions between tenth- and eleventh-century monastic and cathedral schools.

14. Josef Fleckenstein, "Königshof und Bischofsschule unter Otto dem Grossen," *Archiv für Kulturgeschichte* 38 (1956): 38–62; Rosamond McKitterick, "Continuity and Innovation in Tenth Century Ottonian Culture," in *Intellectual Life in the Middle Ages: Essays Presented to Margaret Gibson*, ed. Lesley Smith and Benedicta Ward (London: Hambledon, 1992), 15–24, esp. 24; Ehlers, "Dom- und Klosterschulen," in Kintzinger et al., *Schule und Schüler*, 29–59; Johannes Staub, "Domschulen am Mittelrhein um und nach 1000," in Hartmann, *Bischof Burchard*, 279–309.

15. Jean-Yves Tilliette, "La poésie métrique latines: Ateliers et genres," in Iogna-Prat and Picard, *Religion et culture*, 103–9, esp. 105–6.

16. Jaeger, *Envy of Angels*, esp. 3, 30, 36, 48. For more references, see Jaeger, "Philosophy, ca. 950–ca. 1050," *Viator* 40 (2009): 17–40, esp. 17–19; and Jaeger, "John of Salisbury, a Philosopher of the Long Eleventh Century," in Noble and Van Engen, *European Transformations*, 499–520, esp. 510–13.

17. Egon Boshof, "Kloster und Bischof in Lotharingien," in Kottje and Maurer, *Monastische Reformen im 9. und 10. Jahrhundert*, 197–245; Pierre Riché, "Éducation et culture autour de l'an Mil: La place de la Lotharingie," in Iogna-Prat, *Religion et culture*, 279–83, esp. 279.

leadership of famous schoolmasters such as Gerbert of Rheims (later Pope Sylvester II, d. 1003), Abbo of Fleury (d. 1004), and Fulbert of Chartres (d. 1028). Now German students started to appear in France.[18] Catalan cathedral schools emerged.[19] Italy, although local and conservative in its traditions, benefited from its international connections to advance rhetoric, law, and medicine, and its scholars migrated north to teach in transalpine schools, most notably in Normandy, which would receive John of Fécamp, Lanfranc, and Anselm.[20]

The new schools spread beyond Charlemagne's old borders. England imported texts and teachers from the Continent, and by the end of the tenth century, according to Michael Lapidge, could boast of "various schools . . . housing Latin scholars on a par with most any of their continental colleagues, producing manuscripts as lavishly decorated as the products of any continental scriptoria."[21] Until well into the twelfth century, England's monastic schools remained livelier than its cathedral schools, and many of its ecclesiastical leaders were actually trained on the Continent, some in monastic schools such as Bec and Jumièges, which produced ecclesiastical administrators as proficiently as any German cathedral school.[22] Newly converted Slavic kingdoms created their own cathedral schools, acquiring scholars and books from Italy, Germany, and France.[23] Whereas Charlemagne's Francia had had to import scholars in order to create its Carolingian Renaissance, by the end of the tenth century Francia was "a net exporter

18. Bernhard Bischoff, "Biblioteche, scuole e letteratura nelle città dell'alto medio evo," and "Literarisches und künstlerisches Leben in St. Emmeram (Regensburg) während des frühren und hohen Mitelaters," in *Mittelalterliche Studien: Ausgewählte Aufsätze zur Schriftkunde und Literaturgeschichte*, 3 vols. (Stuttgart: Anton Hiersemann, 1966–81), 1:122–33, esp. 130; 2:77–115, esp. 82–84; Ehlers, "Deutsche Scholaren in Frankreich während des 12. Jahrhunderts," in *Schulen und Studium im sozialen Wandel des hohen und späten Mittelalters*, ed. Johannes Fried (Sigmaringen: Jan Thorbecke, 1986), 97–120.

19. Ludwig Vones, "Bischofssitze als geistige Zentren eines katalanischen Kulturräumes im 10. Jahrhundert: Barcelona, Vic und Girona," in Neuheuser, *Bischofsbild und Bischofssitz*, 173–203.

20. Cowdrey, "Anselm of Besate and Some North-Italian Scholars of the Eleventh Century," *JEH* 23 (1972): 115–24; Charles M. Radding and Antonio Ciaralli, *The* Corpus Iuris Civilis *in the Middle Ages: Manuscripts and Transmission from the Sixth Century to the Juristic Revival* (Leiden, Neth.: Brill, 2006), esp. 67–84.

21. Michael Lapidge, "Schools, Learning and Literature in Tenth-Century England," in *Il secolo di ferro*, 2:951–1005, esp. 952–53. For a comparison of English schools with their Continental counterparts, see Martin Irvine, *The Making of Textual Culture:* Grammatica and Literary Theory, 350–1100 (Cambridge: Cambridge University Press, 1994), 342–44, 355–64, and 405–66.

22. Julia Barrow, "Recruitment of Cathedral Canons in England and Germany, 1100–1225," *Viator* 20 (1989): 117–38, esp. 130–31. For a list of Bec's distinguished alumni, see Vaughn, "Anselm of Bec: The Pattern of His Teaching," in Vaughn and Rubenstein, *Teaching and Learning*, 99–127, esp. 99.

23. Előd Nemerkényi, *Latin Classics in Medieval Hungary: Eleventh Century* (Budapest: Central European University Press, 2004), esp. 13–30 and 157–80; Nemerkényi, "Fulbert et l'implantation des écoles en Hongrie," in *Fulbert de Chartres, précurseur de l'Europe médiévale?*, ed. Michel Rouche (Paris: Presses de l'Université Paris-Sorbonne, 2008), 43–54; Frank C. Hirschman, "Bischofssitze als Bildungszentren im hohen Mittelalter," in Neuheuser, *Bischofsbild und Bischofssitz*, 1–27, esp. 5.

of culture," dispatching books, scholars, and schools to places well beyond the Carolingian heartland.[24]

Historians focus on well-documented and well-connected schools, but these were the centers of far less visible educational networks. Any church able to secure a recognized schoolmaster and pupils technically possessed a school, and if its graduates became teachers, they could boost the number of schools exponentially. Notker at Liège apparently had a half dozen schools under his cathedral school, which itself included separate divisions for internal and external students.[25] Maureen C. Miller, analyzing developments in the well-documented diocese of Verona, describes how an initial system for the education of its priests, in which the canons living around the cathedral taught young students, was replaced in the tenth century by three new *scole* closely associated with the bishop, which in turn were supplemented in the early eleventh century by many more *scole*, often associated with new churches.[26] These wider ripples were the proximate sources of the more literate world of the High Middle Ages.

CURRICULA

"The early medieval classroom," it has been claimed, "is a subject of which we know very little."[27] This may be true inasmuch as educational programs had profound regional differences and teachers were probably as idiosyncratic as they are today. Nevertheless, considerable evidence about tenth- and eleventh-century classrooms does survive, including monastic customaries, library catalogs, miscellanies (volumes of diverse excerpts whose use as school texts is suggested by arrangement and annotation), introductions to authors and their importance (*accessus ad auctores*), glossed texts, and letters to and from charismatic teachers. While gross generalizations apply to no single school, it is possible to sketch the outlines of the educational system that shaped leaders of the millennial Church, and through them the Latin West.

24. Phrase quoted from John Contreni, "The Tenth Century: The Perspective from the Schools," in *Haut moyen-âge: Culture, education et société. Études offertes à Pierre Riché*, ed. Claude Lepelley, Michel Sot, and Riché (Paris: Editions européennes Erasme, 1990), 379–87, esp. 383.

25. Anselm, *Gesta Episcoporum Tungrensium, Traiectensium et Leodiensium* xxviiii–xxx, ed. Georg Heinrich Pertz, MGH SS 7 (Hannover: Hahn, 1846), 205–6.

26. Miller, *Formation of a Medieval Church*, 42–53.

27. Mariken Teeuwen, "Glossing in Close Cooperation: Examples from Ninth-Century Martianus Capella Manuscripts," in *Practice in Learning: The Transfer of Encyclopaedic Knowledge in the Early Middle Ages*, ed. Rolf H. Bremmer Jr., and Kees Dekker (Paris: Peeters, 2010), 85–99, esp. 93.

Preschool

Religious education began before formal schooling. Following immemorial patterns, families were expected to catechize their infant children, a project involving not just parents but also siblings, aunts, uncles, grandparents, and other extended family members, especially those who were members of the clergy.[28] Very young children learned to celebrate the great feasts of the Church year. They were taught basic Latin prayers known even to people without formal schooling. The sign of the cross (Signum Crucis), for example, was such an omnipresent talisman that medieval people believed panicked Jews could resort to it in a pinch.[29] Fathers and godfathers were enjoined to teach their sons the Our Father (Pater Noster) and the Creed (Credo or Symbolum).[30] The Pater Noster, the Gloria, and the Credo were so well known that they were imbricated into the folk incantations known as "elf charms."[31] Illiterate lay brothers unable to handle simple Latin sentences were still assumed to be able to supply from memory a Pater Noster.[32] Formal invocations of Mary were becoming more common, antecedents of the Hail Mary (Ave Maria), whose combination of Gabriel's and Elizabeth's greetings to Mary (Luke 1:28 and 1:42) became a popular fixed prayer during the twelfth century.

Early religious instruction could help parents judge the aptitude of a child for the religious life. Abbo of Fleury's clerical relatives recognized his

28. Genicot, *Rural Communities in the Medieval West*, 95; Amy Livingstone, *Out of Love for My Kin: Aristocratic Family Life in the Lands of the Loire, 1000–1200* (Ithaca: Cornell University Press, 2010), 34–41.

29. David F. Johnson, "The *Crux Usualis* as Apotropaic Weapon in Anglo-Saxon England," in Karkov et al., *Place of the Cross in Anglo-Saxon England*, 80–95; Ursula Lenker, "Signifying Christ in Anglo-Saxon England: The Old English Terms for the Sign of the Cross," in Keefer et al., *Cross and Cruciform*, 233–75, esp. 235–43. An *exemplum* in which a Jew resorts to the sign of the cross is found in Gregory I, *Dialogi* III vii, de Vogüé and Antin, 2: 280–85, Zimmerman, 120–23, and echoed, among other places, in Jacques de Vitry, *Exempla*, ed. Thomas Frederick Crane, *The Exempla or Illustrative Stories from the* Sermones Vulgares *of Jacques de Vitry* (New York: Lenox Hill, 1971), 59.

30. Rather of Verona, *Epist.* xxv (to the clergy of Verona in 996), ed. Fritz Weigle, *Die Briefe des Bischofs Rather von Verona*, MGH Briefe der deutschen Kaiserzeit 1 (Weimar: Hermann Böhlau, 1949), 124–37, esp. 134, trans. Peter L. D. Reid, *The Complete Works of Rather of Verona* (Binghamton, NY: Center for Medieval and Early Renaissance Studies, 1991), 452–55, esp. 450; Wulfstan, *Canons of Edgar* (1005–1008) q 17 and 22, in Whitelock et al., *Councils & Synods*, 321 and 322, Rabin, *Political Writings*, 90–91. See Forbes, *Heaven and Earth in Anglo-Saxon England*, 1–2, 41–43, and 84–85.

31. On teaching the Lord's Prayer and the Creed, see John Van Engen, "Faith as a Concept of Order in Medieval Christendom," in *Belief in History: Innovative Approaches to European and American Religion*, ed. Thomas Kselman (Notre Dame: University of Notre Dame Press, 1991), 19–67, esp. 36–39. On their use as part of charms, see Karen Louise Jolly, *Popular Religion in Late Anglo-Saxon England: Elf-Charms in Context* (Chapel Hill: University of North Carolina Press, 1996), including 7–8, 93, 117–19, 130, 141, 146, 148, 152, 158, 160–61, 164; and Hugh Magennis, *The Cambridge Introduction to Anglo-Saxon Literature* (Cambridge: Cambridge University Press, 2011), 148–49.

32. Guigo I, *Consuetudines* lxix, ed. by "a Carthusian," *Guigues I*er*: Coutumes de Chartreuse*, Sources chrétiennes 313 (Paris: Cerf, 1984), 276–77.

talents and urged his parents to make him an oblate.[33] The parents of the seven-year-old William of Volpiano (d. 1031) took him to the monastery of San Michele in Lucedio "because of his admirable disposition."[34] Andrew of Fleury (d. mid-eleventh century) had already learned some psalms as a little boy still in his father's house, prior to his entrance into Fleury.[35] Although children could enter monastic or convent or cathedral schools at various ages, depending in part upon what "home school" opportunities they had available, around five to seven years seems to have been most common. Some were oblates, children offered by their parents as apprentices to the religious life.[36] Others were temporary students, who might be either integrated into monastic and cathedral schools or else separately educated in parallel "external" schools.

Joining the Choir

Schoolchildren entered a world of music.[37] Nonliterate cultures organize information musically; literate civilizations abandon this music very slowly, especially where it is foundational to liturgy and ritual. The ancient Sophists, the first recorded Western schoolmasters, still referred to the *choros* of their students. Greeks and Romans chanted their religious formulas. Hebrew chant traditions were inherited by Christians, who developed them extensively. The result was that medieval religious communities had vast repertoires of liturgical music, some of which was sung only once a year. Although performance cues could be provided by neumes and melodic patterns by chant modes, melodies were rarely written down. This abundant music was mastered more easily by children than by adults, which is presumably why the monastery of Fleury required

---

33. Pierre Riché, *Abbon de Fleury: Un moine savant et combatif (vers 950–1004)* (Turnhout, Belg.: Brepols, 2004), 16–17.

34. Rodulfus Glaber, *Vita Willelmi* ii, Bulst, France and Reynolds, 258–59.

35. Andrew of Fleury, *Miracula Benedicti* VII ix, Certain, 257.

36. Patricia A. Quinn, *Better Than the Sons of Kings: Boys and Monks in the Early Middle Ages* (New York: Peter Lang, 1989); Maria Lahaye-Geusen, *Das Opfer der Kinder: Ein Beitrag zur Liturgie- und Sozialgeschichte des Mönchtums im hohen Mittelalter* (Altenberge: Oros, 1991); De Jong, *In Samuel's Image.*

37. The role of music in medieval education has only recently become a major scholarly interest: see Susan Boynton, "Training for the Liturgy as a Form of Monastic Education," in *Medieval Monastic Education*, ed. George Ferzoco and Carolyn Muessig (London: Leicester University Press, 2000), 7–20; Boynton and Isabelle Cochelin, "The Sociomusical Role of Child Oblates at the Abbey of Cluny in the Eleventh Century," in *Musical Childhoods and the Cultures of Youth*, ed. Boynton and Roe-Min Kok (Middletown, CT: Wesleyan University Press, 2006), 3–24; Boynton, "Boy Singers in Medieval Monasteries and Cathedrals," and Anne Bagnall Yardley, "The Musical Education of Young Girls in Medieval English Nunneries," in *Young Choristers, 650–1700*, ed. Boynton and Eric Rice (Woodbridge, UK: Boydell, 2008), 37–48 and 49–67. For the broader context of ecclesiastical musical culture, see Christopher Page, *The Christian West and Its Singers: The First Thousand Years* (New Haven: Yale University Press, 2010).

the head of the choir, the *precentor*, to have been an oblate raised there as a child, not someone who had entered as an adult.[38]

Children's choirs were significant parts of their communities. Some monastic customaries specify the liturgical duties of the oblates, describing when they should enter the church and their special parts and responses.[39] The boys' choirs in the German cathedral schools, once they were provided with an organized system of scholarships, became the major source for recruiting cathedral canons.[40] Palace schools also had their choirs, such as the one at Pavia, where Liudprand of Cremona (d. ca. 972), as a choirboy in the court of King Hugh of Italy (924–48), through the beauty of his voice won the favor of the king, "who was passionately fond of singing."[41] In the necrology of Chartres, Bishop Fulbert is depicted in his new cathedral attended by his community, most proximately by what appear to be the boys of his choir.

Choirs enhanced the grandeur of the new churches. Note how Guido d'Arezzo (d. post 1033) links the rebuilding of Arezzo's cathedral to his own plan for reforming its music and learning:

> Just as you [Bishop Theodaldus of Arezzo (1023–36)] created by an exceedingly marvelous plan the church of St. Donatus, the bishop and martyr [completed in 1032], over which you preside by the will of God and as his lawful vicar, so likewise by a most honorable and appropriate distinction you would make the ministers of that church cynosures for all churchmen throughout almost the entire world. In very truth it is sufficiently marvelous and desirable that even boys of your church should surpass in the practice of music the fully trained veterans of all other places; and the height of your honor and merit will be greatly increased because, though subsequent to the early fathers, such great and distinguished renown for learning has come to this church through you.[42]

When choir-trained children encountered poetry, its fixed rhythms elided naturally into music. That they sang their Horace and Virgil is evident from the scansions, glosses, and neumes that fill ninth- to eleventh-century

---

38. Thierry of Amorbach, *Consuetudines Floriacenses* I vii, ed. Davril and Donnat, in *Corp CM* 7(3), 14, ed. and trans. Davril and Donnat, in *L'abbaye de Fleury*, 180–81.

39. Boynton, "The Liturgical Role of Children in Monastic Customaries from the Central Middle Ages," *Studia Liturgica* 28 (1998): 194–209, esp. 200–204; Boynton and Cochelin, "Sociomusical Role of Child Oblates," 13–17.

40. Barrow, "Recruitment of Cathedral Canons," 120–29.

41. Liudprand, *Antapodosis* IV i, Chiesa, 97, Squatriti, 141. What little is known about Liudprand's childhood and education is explicated in Jon N. Sutherland, *Liudprand of Cremona, Bishop, Diplomat, Historian: Studies of the Man and His Age* (Spoleto: CISAM, 1988), 1–43.

42. Guido of Arezzo, *Micrologus*, introd., ed. Joseph Smits van Waesberghe, *Guidonis Aretini Micrologus*, Corpus Scriptorum de Musica 4 (Nijmegen: American Institute of Musicology, 1955), 82–83, trans. Warren Babb, *Hucbald, Guido, and John on Music: Three Medieval Treatises* (New Haven: Yale University Press, 1978), 57–58.

FIGURE 30. Choirboys with Bishop Fulbert of Chartres (d. 1028) in his new cathedral. Part of a memorial image by "Andrew of Micy" commemorating the recently deceased Fulbert, found in Chartres MS Nouvelle Acquisition 4, fol. 34r. Photo credit: Henri de Feraudy. Image courtesy of Chartres L'Apostrophe-Médiathèque.

manuscripts.[43] More surprisingly, they also sang the Greek terminology of music theory,[44] the calendrical calculations of the computus,[45] and even Hucbald of Saint-Amand's didactically convoluted poem in praise of baldness.[46] Classrooms were musical places, no great surprise in a world where teachers were religious professionals who spent much of their lives chanting the liturgy and where many of their students expected to follow in their footsteps.

43. Solange Corbin, "Notations musicales dans les classiques latines," *Revue des études latines* 32 (1954): 97–99; Corbin, "Comment on chantait les classiques latins au Moyen Âge," in *Mélanges d'histoire et d'esthétique musicales offerts à Paul-Marie Masson, professeur honoraire en Sorbonne, par ses collègues, ses élèves et ses amis*, 2 vols. (Paris: Richard-Masse-Éditeur, 1955), 1:107–13; Andreas Haug, "Ways of Singing Hexameter in Tenth-Century Europe," in *City, Chant, and the Topography of Early Music*, ed. Michael Scott Cuthbert, Sean Gallagher, and Christoph Wolff (Cambridge: Harvard University Press, 2013), 207–28.

44. Michael Bernhard, "Didaktische Verse zur Musiktheorie des Mittelalters," in *Cantus Planus: Papers Read at the Third Meeting of the International Musicological Society Study Group, Tihany, Hungary, 19–24 September 1988*, ed. László Dobszay (Budapest: Hungarian Academy of Sciences Institute for Musicology, 1990), 227–44.

45. Wolfgang Irtenkauf, "Der *Computus Ecclesiasticus* in der Einstimmigkeit des Mittelalters," *Archiv für Musikwissenschaft* 14 (1957): 1–15.

46. Yves Chartier, *L'Oeuvre musicale d'Hucbald de Saint-Amand: Les compositions et le traité de musique* (Saint-Laurent: Bellarmin, 1995), 11–12.

Mastering Latinate Culture

Latin was universal, not local; the language of elite law, history, and high-class poetry; the gateway to ecclesiastical reform, liturgy, and scripture. Children arrived in school already knowing a few simple Latin prayers, but they would become fluent by learning the Psalter. The first educational priority of religious communities was to enable their young students to participate in the daily office by chanting the psalms, which they could memorize by imitating the singing of a teacher.[47] Little students became Latinate by applying the rules and vocabulary found in short grammatical treatises, glossaries, glossed texts, and educational dialogues to material that they had already learned by heart. Early medieval illustrated psalters, which sometimes include children in their pictures, may have been intended to help children relate to the written text.[48]

Younger students had little contact with pagan authors, but their study of the Psalter was supplemented by the introduction to secular poetic literature provided by the *Distichs* of Cato and the fables of Avienus. The Cato in question was an unknown second-century AD writer who moralized in the style of Cato the Censor, presenting both simple precepts ("Be neat," "Yield to your senior," "Read books," "Remember what you read") and epigrams ("Don't worry much about death's certain approach / He who despises life does not fear to die"). These commonplaces on good conduct and fickle fortune had a school reputation comparable to Virgil's, not because of their aesthetic qualities but because they were salutary and easy to read. Avienus, a fourth- or fifth-century pagan writer, transmits forty-two short fables, most of which can be traced back through various intermediaries to Aesop. From at least Carolingian times forward, the *Distichs* of Cato and the fables of Avienus were primers from which students could learn Latin, aided by simple Latin grammars, just as they learned it from their psalms and hymns.[49]

---

47. Boynton, "Training for the Liturgy," in Ferzoco and Muessig, *Medieval Monastic Education*, 7–20, esp. 11 and 14; John Flemming, "Muses of the Monastery," *Speculum* 78 (2003): 1071–1106, esp. 1091. On the ancient antecedents of this tradition, see Robert Louis Wilken, "Christian Formation in the Early Church," in Van Engen, *Educating People of Faith*, 48–62, esp. 53–55.

48. Quinn, *Better Than the Sons of Kings*, 75–97, 225–57.

49. Cato and Avienus can be found together in J. Wight Duff and Arnold M. Duff, *Minor Latin Poets*, Loeb Classical Library (Cambridge: Harvard University Press, 1934), 585–639 and 669–749. On whether the text of "Cato" known from Carolingian times forward is the original or an improved version, see Marcus Boas, *Alcuin und Cato* (Leiden, Neth.: Brill, 1937). Avienus is discussed in Alan Cameron, "Macrobius, Avienus, and Avianus," *Classical Quarterly*, n.s., 17 (1967): 385–89. On the use of these texts in education, see Günter Glauche, *Schullektüre im Mittelalter: Entstehung und Wandlungen des Lektürekanons bis 1200 nach den Quellen dargestellt* (Munich: Arbeo-Gesellschaft, 1970), 26–29, 98–99; and M. D. Reeve, "Avianus," in *Texts and Transmission: A Survey of the Latin Classics*, ed. Leighton Durham Reynolds (Oxford: Clarendon, 1983), 29–32.

The most enduring legacy of ancient pagan education was the study of the *Aeneid*, Virgil's national epic of Rome. Virgil never completely left the classroom because Augustine and Jerome respected him, ancient grammarians often cited him, and churchmen had managed to find ways to interpret Virgil's proclamations of future salvation as proto-Christian prophesy (though these actually anticipate the triumphs of his patron, Augustus). Early manuscript fragments suggest that Virgil continued to be read in some post-Roman schools, especially in Italy and Ireland.[50] As the Carolingians attempted to revive Roman letters, he became universally taught once again but still not universally trusted: Jerome's image of Virgil's poetry as a beautiful vase filled with snakes was not forgotten,[51] and the need for caution was highlighted by the career of Vilgardus of Ravenna, a too-dedicated late tenth-century grammarian who allegedly became convinced that Virgil's gods were real.[52] Perhaps as important as Virgil were Christian poets of Late Antiquity such as Iuvencus (fl. second quarter of fourth cent.), Prosper of Aquitaine (d. c. 455), Prudentius (d. post 505), Avitus of Vienne (d. 523), Sedulius (fl. second quarter of fifth cent.), Arator (fl. mid-sixth cent.), and Venantius Fortunatus (d. ca. 603), whose now neglected verses still abound in tenth- and eleventh-century collections of school texts.[53] Even when additional pagan authors gradually began to appear in fancier curricula, miscellanies suggest that the Late Antique Christian poets did not yield their places quickly.[54]

Learning Latin was related to other skills, including writing in a good hand or hands (some clerks were skilled in multiple scripts). Scripts were often carefully modeled on earlier exemplars, especially Carolingian ones, which is not surprising in a world striving to reform back to what was believed to be traditionally Roman. Letter recognition had to precede reading, and active learning involved practicing letters on wax tablets. The *Colloquia* of Aelfric Bata, eleventh-century classroom dialogues written from a student perspective, include the technical Latin scribal vocabulary for knives, razors, styluses, tablets, awls, etc., and praise writing not only as a useful skill but also as a potentially profitable one inasmuch as good

---

50. Riché, *Education and Culture in the Barbarian West from the Sixth through the Eighth Century*, trans. Contreni (Columbia: University of South Carolina Press, 1976), 198–200; Louis Holtz, "La redécouverte de Virgile aux VIIIᵉ et IXᵉ siècles d'après les manuscrits conservés," in *Lectures médiévales de Virgile: Actes du colloque organisé par l'École française de Rome (Rome, 25–28 octobre 1982)* (Rome: ÉFR, 1985), 9–30.

51. Nalgodus, *Vita S. Odonis Abbatis* viii, ed. *ASOSB*, 7:187.

52. Rodulfus Glaber, *Historiae* II xii, France, 92–93. For context, see Jeffrey Burton Russell, *Dissent and Reform in the Early Middle Ages* (Berkeley: University of California Press, 1965), 110–11.

53. On the prominence of these poets in the earliest surviving collections of school texts, see Glauche, *Schullektüre im Mittelalter*, 364–70.

54. Ibid., 75–100.

scribes could get work on commission.[55] That such motives did not sufficiently inspire all students is suggested by a sketch of a grammar class, from perhaps 1100, in which the classmates with their tablets range from the diligent tonsured young clerk copying away in the center to the two unhappy shirtless boys on the wings who bear the marks of the teacher's discipline.

Another associated skill was poetic composition. Although monastic schools favored hymns and hagiographic verses, cathedral schools, especially those in the Lorraine and Germany, emphasized occasional poetry. Tenth-century West Frankish schools, slower to cultivate this art, have left fewer high-quality poems than survive from the preceding and succeeding periods.[56] This poetry gap probably reflects different audiences. Jaeger argues that East Frankish cathedral schools, which were more concerned with training people for life at court, made the composition of poetry "the major subject . . . from the mid-tenth to the end of the eleventh century . . . the enterprise in which the others culminate."[57] Friendship could be expressed through poetry.[58] When Froumund (d. 1006/12), the schoolmaster of Tegernsee, wanted to scold a lazy student, he began by exhorting him to write more poetry.[59] When Peter Damian wanted to warn against the pursuit of worldly wisdom, he mocked a curial official who could "write verses like Virgil."[60]

The Seven Liberal Arts

According to the standard narrative of intellectual history, the seven liberal arts formed the core curriculum of medieval schools. They first appear as an ensemble in the early fifth century in Martianus Capella's *Marriage of Philology and Mercury*, an elaborate didactic allegory written in poetry and prose, in which the wedding of Mercury ("the god of spring") with the maiden Philology ("learning"), is attended by seven bridesmaids stationed

55. Aelfric Bata, *Colloquia* xiv, xv, and xxiv, Gwara, Porter, 111–17, 133–37; context in Loredana Lazzari, "I *colloquia* nelle scuole monastiche anglosassoni tra la fine del X e la prima metà dell'XI secolo," *Studi medievali*, 3rd ser., 44 (2003): 147–77; Vergnolle, "Un carnet de modèles," 23–56, esp. 31–36 and 51; Lahaye-Geusen, *Opfer der Kinder*, 240–44.

56. Tilliette, "La poésie métrique latine," 103–9. To gain a rough overview of poetic output and trends, glance through MGH *Poetarum Latinorum Medii Aevi*, 6 vols. in multiple parts (Munich: MGH, 1881–).

57. Jaeger, *Ennobling Love: In Search of a Lost Sensibility* (Philadelphia: University of Pennsylvania Press, 1999), esp. 52–53; "Pessimism in the Twelfth-Century 'Renaissance,'" *Speculum* 78 (2003): 1151–83, esp. 1172–73; Jaeger, "The Stature of the Learned Poet in the Eleventh Century," in *Norm und Krise von Kommunication: Inszenierungen literarischer und socialer Interaktion im Mittelalter*, ed. Alois Hahn, Gert Melville, and Werner Röcke (Berlin: LIT, 2006), 417–38, esp. 419.

58. Brian Patrick McGuire, *Friendship and Community: The Monastic Experience, 350–1250* (Ithaca: Cornell University Press, 1988), 141, 150, 174–79, 185.

59. Froumund, *Epist.* lxiv, ed. Karl Strecker, *Codex Epistolarum Tegernseensium*, MGH *Epp Sel* 3 (Munich: MGH, 1978), 72–73.

60. Peter Damian, *Epist.* cxvii, Reindel, 3:316–29, esp. 324, Blum, 4:318–31, esp. 326–27.

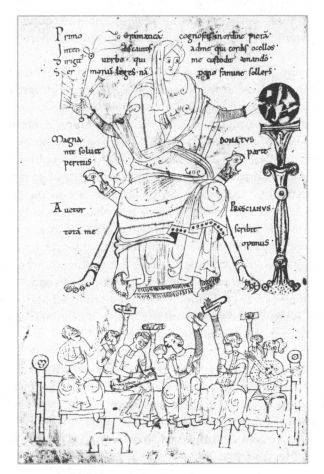

FIGURE 31. Mixed group of students in a grammar class, ranging from a studious clerk in the center to enthusiastic responders waving their writing tablets to shirtless boys on the wings bearing the marks of the master's whip. From an illustration found in a copy of Martianus Capella's *De Nuptiis Philologiae et Mercurii* produced in France ca. 1100. Biblioteca Medicea Laurenziana, Florence. BML MS San Marco 190, fol. 15v. By concession of the MiBACT. Prohibited from further reproduction by any means.

on celestial spheres—Grammar, Logic, Rhetoric, Geometry, Arithmetic, Astronomy, and Music. Each art requires a whole book to detail her attributes (Architecture and Medicine are also present but earthbound and therefore blessedly mute).[61] Later schoolmasters would distinguish

61. Martianus Capella, *De Nuptiis*, ed. James Willis, *Martianus Capella* (Leipzig: Teubner, 1983), following justifications previously published in Willis, *De Martiano Capella Emendando* (Leiden, Neth.: Brill, 1971), trans. William Harris Stahl and Richard Johnson, *Martianus Capella and the Seven Liberal Arts*, 2 vols. (New York: Columbia University Press, 1971), vol. 2.

between the three verbal arts (the *trivium*) and the four mathematical ones (the *quadrivium*). These arts allegedly became the basis of medieval education.

A more complicated picture is emerging. Ancient Roman schools had originally envisioned the *artes* as an educational program in which grammar, taught in grammar schools, was followed by rhetoric, taught in advanced schools, a program that imperial legislation continued to document long after Martianus Capella.[62] When secular schools declined in the post-Roman West, arts instruction was left to conservative churchmen who had few educational resources and great distrust of pagan traditions. Church councils cast aspersions on pagan letters and on bishops who taught them.[63] Over time, perhaps more so in Italy than in France, Christian education was transformed into biblically based training for Church leaders, more circumscribed, more practical, more performance-oriented, and largely restricted to Christian letters.[64] Carolingian scholars revived the arts, seeking to improve the literacy of clerks and to connect their new Frankish empire to imperial Rome.[65] They rediscovered Martianus Capella's allegory, which had dropped out of sight, and scholars began to gloss it extensively from the mid-ninth century onward.[66]

The tenth century became the century of Martianus Capella, but although the model of the seven liberal arts helped to shape the choice of texts to study, a specific canon had not yet crystallized. Disciplinary boundaries were messy. All seven arts were taught by a single master, not by individual subject specialists; the distinctions were further blurred by school texts covering all the arts, such as the *De Nuptis* of Martianus Capella and the *Consolatio Philosophiae* of Boethius. Some arts received

62. Gratian, *Codex Theodosianus* 13.3.11, ed. Clyde Pharr, *The Theodosian Code and Novels and the Sirmondian Constitutions* (Princeton: Princeton University Press, 1952), 389; Justinian, *Novellae* App., VII, 22, ed. Rudolf Schöll, *Corpus Juris Civilis*, 3 vols. (Zurich: Weidmann, 1970–72), 3:802.

63. Paul F. Gehl, "Latin Orthopraxes," in *Latin Grammar and Rhetoric: From Classical Theory to Medieval Practice*, ed. Carol Dana Lanham (London: Continuum, 2002), esp. 7–11.

64. Riché, *Education and Culture*, esp. 79–99; Ralph W. Mathisen, "Bishops, Barbarians, and the 'Dark Ages': The Fate of Late Roman Educational Institutions in Late Antique Gaul," in *Medieval Education*, ed. Ronald B. Begley and Joseph W. Koterski (New York: Fordham University Press, 2005), 3–19; Robert Markus, "Between Marrou and Brown: Transformations of Late Antique Christianity," in Rousseau and Papoutsakis, *Transformations of Late Antiquity*, 1–13, esp. 10–12.

65. Johanes Fried, "Karl der Grosse, die *Artes liberales* und die karolingische Renaissance," and Louis Holtz, "Alkuin et la renaissance des arts libéraux," in *Karl der Grosse und sein Nachwirken: 1200 Jahre Kultur und Wissenschaft in Europa*, ed. Paul Butzer, Max Kerner, and Walter Oberschelp (Turnhout, Belg.: Brepols, 1997), 25–43, 45–60.

66. Stahl, *Martianus Capella*, 1:60–66; Michael Winterbottom, "Martianus Capella," in Reynolds, *Texts and Transmission*, 245–46; Mariken Teeuwen, "Martianus Capella's *De Nuptiis*: A Pagan 'Storehouse' First Discovered by the Irish?," in *Foundations of Learning: The Transfer of Encyclopaedic Knowledge in the Early Middle Ages*, ed. Rolf H. Bremmer Jr. and Kees Dekker (Paris: Peeters, 2007), 51–62.

more attention than others, particularly grammar, which remained the most important. Arts education around the millennium was still a developing program.

Its heart was the trivium, which included the traditional mainstays of grammar and rhetoric, as well as logic, which was becoming increasingly popular. Grammar was basic literary study, the fundamental art, the source of all other lines of intellectual inquiry, the center of early medieval education.[67] The Carolingian Renaissance reinforced its importance by using ancient texts to establish empire-wide standards of correct usage.[68] Whereas we might envision grammar as a bookish discipline, tenth- and eleventh-century teachers were very concerned about vocalization. They worried about how to speak Latin properly in a world still dominated by oral communication, one in which poetry was expected to scan in spite of all the confusions introduced by different regional accents and in which ecclesiastical leaders could be evaluated according to their ability to read, recite, and sing. More theoretical study of grammar built on the Carolingian glossed tradition of Priscian, although the more practically focused schools of northern Italy promoted linguistic studies through word lists and the abridgement of Priscian by Papias of Pavia (ca. 1050).[69] Rhetoric was also beginning to develop an independent commentary tradition based on Ciceronian works whose copies proliferated in the tenth and eleventh centuries, but systematic guides to eloquent letter writing (the *ars dictaminis*) still lay in the future.[70] The new popularity of logic may have been related to rhetoric because logic could be used to propound

67. Irvine, *Making of Textual Culture*, esp. 1–8 and 327–31; Lanham, *Latin Grammar and Rhetoric*.

68. Joyce Hill, "Aelfric's Grammatical Triad," in *Form and Content of Instruction in Anglo-Saxon England in the Light of Contemporary Manuscript Evidence: Papers Presented at the International Conference, Udine, 6–8 April 2006*, ed. Patrizia Lendinara, Loredana Lazzari, and Maria Amalia D'Aronco (Turnhout, Belg.: Brepols, 2007), 285–308, esp. 300–301.

69. For surveys on the use of Priscian in late ninth- and tenth-century schools, see David W. Porter, *Excerptiones de Prisciano: The Source for Aelfric's Latin-Old English Grammar* (Woodbridge, UK: Boydell, 2002), 9–33; Rita Copeland and Inneke Sluiter, "Glosses on Priscian by Remigius and His Followers (Ninth and Tenth Centuries)," in *Medieval Grammar and Rhetoric: Language Arts and Literary Theory, AD 300–1475*, ed. Copeland and Sluiter (Oxford: Clarendon, 2009), 299–310; *Priscien: Transmission et refoundation de la grammaire de l'Antiquité aux Modernes*, ed. Marc Baratin, Bernard Colombat, and Louis Holtz (Turnhout, Belg.: Brepols, 2009), 427–86; Gibson, *Lanfranc of Bec*, 11–15.

70. Thomas Haye, "Mündliche und schriftliche Rede: Ein Beitrag zur rhetorischen Kompetenz des Abbo von Fleury," *Frühmittelalterliche Studien* 35 (2001): 273–92, esp. 289–92; Ronald Witt, "Rhetoric and Reform during the Eleventh and Twelfth Centuries," in *Textual Cultures of Medieval Italy*, ed. William Robins (Toronto: University of Toronto Press, 2005), 53–79; John O. Ward, "The Medieval and Early Renaissance Study of Cicero's *De Inventione* and the *Rhetorica ad Herennium*: Commentaries and Contexts," and Ruth Taylor-Briggs, "Reading between the Lines: The Textual History and Manuscript Transmission of Cicero's Rhetorical Works," in *The Rhetoric of Cicero in Its Medieval and Early Renaissance Commentary Tradition*, ed. Virginia Cox and John O. Ward (Leiden, Neth.: Brill, 2006), 3–75, esp. 20–23, and 77–108, esp. 77–78 and 97.

convincing and conclusive arguments.[71] Boethius came into his own in the tenth century and was glossed and commented upon in new ways, emphasizing logic and language, with Abbo of Fleury stressing his more Aristotelian features and Gerbert his more Platonic ones.[72] Gerbert's scholastic program at Rheims, which heavily emphasized logic, is known in unusual detail,[73] and his improvements to the arts appear to have been adopted by later masters such as his pupil Fulbert of Chartres and Anselm when he taught arts at Bec.[74]

The quadrivium, although overshadowed by the trivium, was increasingly lively.[75] Charlemagne's court scholars had made real advances in arithmetic and astronomy, but they were more concerned with calculating the dates of Church feasts (the computus) than with the quadrivium per se.[76] In the tenth and eleventh centuries, the mathematical arts were more practical than theoretical. Students of arithmetic could master number systems that included Roman numerals and shortcuts for using them, hand calculations to 9,999, abacus calculations, and perhaps even the newly arrived Hindu-Arabic numerals.[77] Considerable geometry was known,

---

71. Wilfried Hartmann, "Rhetorik und Dialektik in der Streitschriftenliteratur des 11./12. Jahhunderts," in *Dialektik und Rhetorik im früheren and hohe Mittelalter*, ed. Fried (Munich: R. Oldenbourg, 1997), 73–95, esp. 73–79.

72. John Marenbon, *Early Medieval Philosophy (480–1150)*, 2nd ed. (London: Routledge, 1988), 47–49, 77–81; Marenbon, "Carolingian Thought," in *Carolingian Culture: Emulation and Innovation*, ed. McKitterick (Cambridge: Cambridge University Press, 1994), 171–92, esp. 174–76.

73. Richer, *Historiae* III xlvi–xlvii, ed. and trans. Justin Lake, *Richer of Saint-Rémi: Histories*, 2 vols., DOML 10 (Cambridge: Harvard University Press, 2011), 2:68–75. For context see Jason K. Glenn, "Master and Community in Tenth-Century Rheims," in Vaughn and Rubenstein, *Teaching and Learning*, 51–68, esp. 63–66.

74. Claude Genin, *Fulbert de Chartres: Une grande figure de l'Occident chrétien au temps de l'an Mil* (Paris: Société archéologique d'Eure-et-Loir, 2003), 29–38; Ian Logan, *Reading Anselm's Prosologion: The History of Anselm's Argument and Its Significance Today* (Burlington, VT: Ashgate, 2009), 11–12; McCarthy, *Music, Scholasticism*, 109–20.

75. Guy Beaujouan, "L'enseignement du 'Quadrivium,'" in *La Scuola nell'Occidente Latino dell'alto medioevo, 15–21 aprile 1971*, 2 vols. Settimane di studio del CISAM 19 (Spoleto: CISAM, 1972), 2:639–67; Gillian R. Evans, "The Influence of Quadrivium Studies in the Eleventh- and Twelfth-Century Schools," *Journal of Medieval History* 1 (1975): 151–64, esp. 152–54.

76. Paul Butzer and Dietrich Lohrmann, eds., *Science in Western and Eastern Civilization in Carolingian Times* (Basel, Switz.: Birkhäuser, 1993); Brigitte Englisch, *Die Artes Liberales im frühen Mittelalter (5.–9. Jh.): Das Quadrivium und der Komputus als Indikatoren für Kontinuität und Erneuerung der exakten Wissenschaften zwischen Antike und Mittelalter* (Stuttgart: Franz Steiner, 1994); Paul L. Butzer and Karl W. Butzer, "Mathematics at Charlemagne's Court and Its Transmission," in *Court Culture in the Early Middle Ages: The Proceedings of the First Alcuin Conference*, ed. Catherine Cubitt (Turnhout, Belg.: Brepols, 2003), 77–89. For an introduction to and editions of computistic material, see Arno Borst, ed., *Schriften zur Komputistik im Frankenreich von 721 bis 818*, 3 vols., MGH Quellen zur Geistesgeschichte des Mittelalters 21 (Hannover: Hahn, 2006).

77. Alison Peden, "Unity, Order, and Ottonian Kingship in the Thought of Abbo of Fleury," in *Belief and Culture in the Middle Ages: Studies Presented to Henry Mayr-Harting*, ed. Richard Gameson and Henrietta Leyser (Oxford: Oxford University Press, 2001), 158–68; J. Lennart Berggren, "Medieval Arithmetic: Arabic Texts and European Motivations," in Contreni and Casciani, *Word, Image, and Number*, 351–65. On the

and several new treatises appeared in the tenth century even though early medieval knowledge of Euclid still remained fragmentary.[78] Astronomical diagrams and spatial understanding developed, laying the conceptual groundwork for the fruitful encounter between Arabic and Latin astronomy that would soon follow.[79] Music relied on some practical techniques and on the difficult Greek theories transmitted in Boethius's *De Musica*.[80] But what most distinguished the quadrivium in the tenth and eleventh centuries was the advent of new tools. The monochord, traditionally used to explain musical ratios, could now be supplemented by the organ. The celestial globe moved within a generation from Fatimid Egypt to Spain to Gerbert's France.[81] The astrolabe, celestial globe, and planetarium all helped to conceptualize astronomy in a way that increased chronological precision and promoted abstract and symbolic thought.[82] Now the cosmos appears as a *machina mundi*, and God, the creator who "ordered all things in measure, and number, and weight" (Wisd. of Sol. 11:21), is the *Deus geometra* who uses a compass and scales at Winchester in a Gospel book around from around 1025 and in the Tiberius Psalter from around 1050. God as *Deus geometra* also appears in some later eleventh-century Bibles and will become a standard figure in illustrated Bibles.[83] For medieval scholars, numbers measured unity and diversity and, ultimately, cosmic order.

---

earliest Arabic numerals in the West, see Paul Kunitsch, "The Transmission of Hindu-Arabic Numerals Reconsidered," in *The Enterprise of Science in Islam: New Perspectives*, ed. Jan P. Hogendijk and Abdelhamid I. Sabra (Cambridge: MIT Press, 2003), 3–21, esp. 11 and 15.

78. Marie-Thérèse Zenner, "Imagining a Building: Latin Euclid and Practical Geometry," in Contreni and Casciani, *Word, Image, and Number*, 219–46, esp. 126–27; Wesley M. Stevens, "Euclidean Geometry in the Early Middle Ages: A Preliminary Reassessment," in *Villard's Legacy: Studies in Medieval Technology, Science, and Art in Memory of Jean Gimpel*, ed. Zenner (Burlington, VT: Ashgate, 2004), 229–64.

79. Bruce Eastwood, "Plinian Astronomical Diagrams in the Early Middle Ages," in *Mathematics and Its Applications to Science and Natural Philosophy in the Middle Ages: Essays in Honor of Marshall Clagett*, ed. Edward Grant and John E. Murdoch (New York: Cambridge University Press, 1987), 141–72; Stephen C. McCluskey, *Astronomies and Cultures in Early Medieval Europe* (Cambridge: Cambridge University Press, 1998), 157–87.

80. McCarthy, *Music, Scholasticism*, 16–33, 214–15, 220–23.

81. Arianna Borrelli, *Aspects of the Astrolabe*: Architectonica Ratio *in Tenth- and Eleventh-Century Europe* (Stuttgart: Franz Steiner, 2008), 181 and 192–95.

82. Borst, *Astrolab und Klosterreform an der Jahrtausendwende* (Heidelberg: Carl Winter, 1989), esp. 21–30, 53–84; McCluskey, *Astronomies and Cultures*, 171–80; David A. King, "The Neglected Astrolabe: A Supplement to the Standard Literature on the Favourite Astronomical Instrument of the Middle Ages," in his *In Synchrony with the Heavens: Studies in Astronomical Timekeeping and Instrumentation in Medieval Islamic Civilization*, 2 vols. (Leiden, Neth.: Brill, 2004–5), 2:339–402, esp. 379–82; Borrelli, *Aspects of the Astrolabe*, 26, 104–7, and 159–60.

83. John Block Friedman, "The Architect's Compass in Creation Miniatures of the Later Middle Ages," *Traditio* 30 (1974): 419–29, esp. 423 and fig. I-III. On this shift to more abstract thought, see Radding and Clark, *Medieval Architecture*, esp. 12 and 18–19.

Although the seven liberal arts were accepted as a way to organize knowledge, few schools taught them all in any depth. To fill in the gaps, the great scholars of the age had to travel. Odo of Cluny, who had studied in the monastery of Saint-Martin at Tours, went to Paris to study dialectic and music under Remigius of Auxerre.[84] Despite the extraordinary educational resources available at Fleury, Abbo still had to go to Paris and Rheims, and he had to hire a private tutor in music, causing him to grumble throughout his life about avaricious scholars who taught for pay.[85] Gerbert left the monastery of St. Gerald at Aurillac to study the quadrivium in Catalan Spain and then went to Rheims to study dialectic.[86]

Beyond the Seven Liberal Arts

The seven liberal arts do not include all the subjects that medieval schools taught, either within the arts curriculum or parallel or subsequent to it. It was an intellectual paradigm awkwardly superimposed over the ancient system of education that had proceeded from grammar schools to rhetorical schools, had then been modified by the Church for its own purposes, and had then been revised by late and post-Carolingian educators who were dedicated to a revival of things Roman and captivated by Martianus Capella. Earlier structures did not disappear. In the schools of the millennial Church, in addition to the seven liberal arts, students might also learn, among other things, history, vernacular languages, Greek, law, medicine, and, most important in the eyes of churchmen, the Bible. To view the school curriculum through the lens of the seven liberal arts risks overlooking or minimizing whatever did not fit neatly into that framework.

History, although not one of the seven liberal arts, permeated education. The biblical books presented theology as a historical narrative.[87] World chronicles explicated salvation history, often beginning with the six days of Creation, the making of Adam in God's image, and the fall of

---

84. John of Salerno, *Vita Odonis* I xix, ed. *ASOSB*, 7:154, trans. Sitwell, *St. Odo of Cluny*, 21–23.

85. Abbo, *Explanatio in Calculo Victorii* I ii, ed. Peden, *Abbo of Fleury and Ramsey: Commentary on the Calculus of Victorius of Aquitaine*, Auctores Britannici Medii Aevi 15 (Oxford: Oxford University for the British Academy, 2003), 64; Aimoinus, *Vita Abbonis* I iii, ed. and trans. Robert-Henri Bautier and Monique Labory, in *L'abbaye de Fleury en l'an Mil*, *IRHT sources d'histoire médiévale 32* (Paris: CNRS, 2004), 9–137, esp. 48–49. See Riché, *Abbon de Fleury*, 25–28; Elizabeth Dachowski, *First among Abbots: The Career of Abbo of Fleury* (Washington, DC: Catholic University of America Press, 2008), 45–47.

86. Riché, "Gerbert de Aurillac en Catalogne," in *Catalunya i França meridional a l'entorn de l'any mil, Barcelona, 2–5 juliol 1987*, ed. Xavier Barral i Altet, Iogna-Prat, Anscari Manual Mundó, Josep M. Salrach, and Michel Zimmermann (Barcelona: Generalitat de Catalunya, 1991), 374–77.

87. Jennifer A. Harris, "The Bible and the Meaning of History in the Middle Ages," in Boynton and Riley, *Practice of the Bible*, 84–104.

FIGURE 32. God the Creator, using scales and compass, illustration from the Tiberius Psalter (Winchester ca. 1050). © The British Library Board, BL Cotton Tiberius C. VI, fol. 7v.

humanity from grace.[88] In cataloging books, librarians moved in chronological order from Bibles and biblical aids to patristic commentaries.[89] Canon law collections were usually chronological rather than topical. As part of the Carolingian classical revival, its scholars produced freestanding private and public histories, local histories of ecclesiastical and secular

88. McKitterick, *Perceptions of the Past*, 7–14.

89. On "The Organization of Written Knowledge," see McKitterick, *The Carolingians and the Written Word* (Cambridge: Cambridge University Press, 1989), 165–210, esp. 180 and 196–98.

institutions, and political polemic.[90] Building on these traditions, the tenth century became "an age of great historians."[91] Classical histories were taught as part of grammar, and, insofar as they organized events and presented them dramatically, as part of rhetoric.[92] The new Western emperors and their minions actively encouraged the study of the history of the Roman Empire.[93]

Latinate culture cultivated its conquerors. Medieval vernacular languages are known today because Latin-trained scholars wrote them down, sometimes Latinizing their grammars in the process.[94] Vernacular study varied geographically, and in areas where popular romance speech was still close to Latin, written vernacular texts are rare.[95] Germany's revived schools, on the other hand, aided by earlier Carolingian work, had German vocabulary lists, vernacularly glossed Latin texts, and even translations of Latin school texts produced by Notker Labeo (d. 1022), all attempting to facilitate knowledge of Latin rather than replace it.[96] Yet German scholars also valued their vernacular for its own sake and wrote down and preserved functional Germanic texts and oral materials.[97] Some fretted that

90. Matthew Innes and McKitterick, "The Writing of History," in McKitterick, *Carolingian Culture*, 193–220.

91. Phrase from Reuter, "Introduction: Reading the Tenth-Century," in *NCMH* 3: 3.

92. Riché, "Les lettrés du Xe siècle et l'histoire de Rome," in *Le nombre du temps: Mélanges Paul Zumthor* (Paris: Champion Slakine, 1988), 247–54; McKitterick, "The Reading of History at Saint-Amand in the Ninth and Tenth Centuries," in *Reading and the Book in the Middle Ages*, ed. Susan J. Ridyard (Sewanee, TN: University of the South Medieval Colloquium, 2001), 39–46; Michel Sot, "Pratique et usages de l'histoire chez Abbon de Fleury," in *Abbon, un abbé de l'an Mil*, ed. Annie Dufour and Gilette Labory (Turnhout, Belg.: Brepols, 2008), 205–23; Michael E. Moore, "Prologue: Teaching and Learning History in the School of Rheims, c. 800–950," in Vaughen and Rubenstein, *Teaching and Learning in Northern Europe*, 19–49, esp. 20–23.

93. Paolo Chiesa, "Storia romana e libri di storia romana fra IX e XI secolo," in *Roma antica nel Medioevo: Mito, rappresentazioni, sopravvivenze nella 'Respublica Christiana' dei secoli IX–XIII. Atti della quattordicesima Settimana internazionale di studio Mendola, 24–28 agosto 1998* (Milan: Vita e Pensiero, 2001), 231–258, esp. 257–85. For Emperor Henry II's gift of Roman histories to Bamberg in 1007, see Wolfgang Huschner, *Transalpine Kommunication im Mittelalter: Diplomatische, kulturelle und politische Wechselwirkungen zwischen Italien und dem nordalpinen Reich (9.–11. Jahrhundert)*, 3 vols. (Hannover: Hahn, 2003), 2:471–76, and Marek Thue Kretschmer, *Rewriting Roman History in the Middle Ages: The Historia Romana and the Manuscript Bamberg, Hist. 3* (Leiden, Neth.: Brill, 2007), esp. 1–2 and 55–64.

94. Bischoff, "The Study of Foreign Languages in the Middle Ages," in his *Mittelalterliche Studien*, 2:227–45, esp. 231.

95. Tilliette, "Le Xe siècle dans l'histoire de la literature," in Iogna-Prat and Picard, *Religion et culture*, 93–98; McKitterick, "Latin and Romance: An Historian's Perspective," in *Latin and the Romance Languages in the Early Middle Ages*, ed. Roger Wright (London: Routledge, 1991), 130–45.

96. John Knight Bostock, *A Handbook on Old High German Literature*, 2nd ed. (Oxford: Clarendon, 1976), 90–107; Dennis Howard Green, *Medieval Listening and Reading: The Primary Reception of German Literature 800–1300* (Cambridge: Cambridge University Press, 1994), 47–54; Cyril Edwards, "German Vernacular Literature: A Survey," in McKitterick, *Carolingian Culture*, 141–70.

97. Karl Leyser, "The German Aristocracy from the Ninth to the Early Twelfth Century: A Historical and Cultural Sketch," *Past & Present* 41 (1968): 25–53, esp. 30; Green, *Medieval Listening and Reading*, 95–112.

this study could be carried too far: Meinhard, the master of Bamberg's school, bewailed the way his Bishop Gunther (1057–65)—lacking gravitas and *disciplina* ("Oh mores!")—had put aside Augustine and Gregory for Attila and Dietrich.[98] In England, King Alfred enthusiastically promoted the use of written English because he believed it a necessary expedient in a realm that had nearly lost Latinate culture. Latin was the most esteemed language, and English could serve as a bridge to its mastery as glossaries and other tools demonstrate, but English was also cultivated in order to teach basic literacy, facilitate pastoral duties, accommodate educated laymen, and present a wide variety of humble or practical secular subjects.[99] A team of monks at Canterbury in the 960s produced an Old English version of the Gospels for the secular clergy to use for homiletics, a text carefully copied and still surviving in eight manuscripts.[100] Vernacular saints' lives were common.[101] Tenth-century English became a national language offering a common identity to its speakers.[102]

Scientia divina, which would come to be called theology, had a proud place in millennial schools that scholars today often overlook. Early medieval schools had been pastoral and biblical, emphases always necessary for clerical formation even if they did not fit seamlessly into the structure of the seven liberal arts. Perhaps the arts curriculum could serve as a prologue? It is noteworthy that the interests of Fulbert, Peter Damian, and Lanfranc shifted over time from the liberal arts to sacred scripture.[103] Gozechinus (d. post 1074), who taught at Liège and Mainz, names four

---

98. Meinhard, *Epist.* lxxiiii, ed. Carl Erdmann and Norbert Fickermann, *Briefsammlungen der Zeit Heinrichs IV.*, MGH Briefe der deutschen Kaiserzeit 5 (Weimar: Hermann Böhlaus, 1950), 120–21.

99. Stephanie Hollis, "Anglo-Saxon Secular Learning and the Vernacular: An Overview," in *Secular Learning in Anglo-Saxon England: Exploring the Vernacular*, ed. László Sándor Chardonnens and Bryan Carella (Amsterdam: Rodopi, 2012), 1–43.

100. R. M. Liuzza, ed., *The Old English Version of the Gospels*, 2 vols., Early English Text Society 304 and 314 (Oxford: Oxford University Press, 1994 and 2000).

101. Paul E. Szarmach, ed., *Holy Men and Holy Women: Old English Prose Saints' Lives and Their Contexts* (Albany: SUNY Press, 1996). Sharon M. Rowley, *The Old English Version of Bede's "Historia Ecclesiastica"* (Woodbridge: D. S. Brewer, 2011), 156–94, describes glosses reflecting the use of Bede for hagiographical and pastoral purposes.

102. Helmut Gneuss, "The Emergence of Standard Old English and Aethelwold's School at Winchester," *Anglo-Saxon Studies* 1 (1972): 68–83; Peter Clemoes, "Late Old English Literature," in Parsons, *Tenth-Century Studies*, 102–14, esp. 105; Mechtild Gretsch, "Literacy and the Uses of the Vernacular," and Lendinara, "The World of Anglo-Saxon Learning," in *The Cambridge Companion to Old English Literature*, ed. Malcolm Godden and Michael Lapidge, 2nd ed. (Cambridge: Cambridge University Press, 2013), 273–94, 295–312.

103. Documented transitions from the arts to theology include Fulbert, discussed in Genin, *Fulbert*, 40–46; Peter Damian, as noted in John Howe, "Peter Damian and Monte Cassino," *Revue bénédictine* 107 (1997): 330–51, esp. 350–51; and Lanfranc, as treated in Gibson, *Lanfranc of Bec*, 51, and Cowdrey, *Lanfranc*, 20 and 46.

professors from among the "many and famous" masters who had joined him in moving from the arts to scriptural studies.[104] This trajectory, which receives intellectual support from Augustine's *De Doctrina Christiana*, would ultimately be institutionalized as the formal hegemony of theology in northern universities. But one result of an infusion of arts faculty members into theology was a more abstract logical theology, moving away from the traditional ruminations of biblical commentary. Lanfranc would still gloss scripture, but Anselm would not.[105]

Many more subjects were taught than can be addressed here. Knowledge of Greek was an academic ideal rarely attained but sporadically sought.[106] Law, valued as an independent discipline, advanced in tandem with the reform of monasteries, particularly in the Lorraine, and, as with liturgical studies, scholars sought to consolidate books and eliminate extraneous elements in order to turn unwieldy masses of texts into topically oriented collections.[107] Medicine had a relatively strong school tradition in southern Italy, especially at Salerno, soon to be enhanced by medical translations made by Constantine the African (d. ca. 1087); it also attracted scholars in northern Europe, as exemplified by the journey that Richer of Rheims (fl. late tenth cent.) made to Chartres in order to study the *Aphorisms of Hippocrates*, an ill-fated odyssey involving wrong turns, a broken bridge, a lost page boy, and a dead horse.[108]

Millennial schools also offered leadership training by supplementing the standard educational programs of some select students with "internships." Early customaries note students posted to the abbot's table.[109] Fleury

104. Gozechinus, *Epist. ad Walcherum* xxxiii, ed. R. B. C. Huygens, *Apologiae Duae*, CCM 62:35 (Turnhout, Belg.: Brepols, 1985); Irven M. Resnick, "Attitudes towards Philosophy and Dialectic during the Gregorian Reform," *Journal of Religious History* 16 (1990): 115–25, esp. 121–22, 125.

105. Ian Logan, *Reading Anselm's 'Prosologion,'* 19.

106. Bischoff, "Das griechische Element in der abendländischen Bildung des Mittelalters," in *Mittelalterliche Studien*, 2:46–75; Walter Berschin, *Griechisch-Lateinisches Mittelalter: Von Hieronymus zu Nikolaus von Kues* (Bern, Switz.: Francke, 1980); Michael W. Herren, ed., *The Sacred Nectar of the Greeks: The Study of Greek in the West in the Early Middle Ages* (London: King's College Medieval Studies, 1988).

107. Greta Austin, *Shaping Church Law around the Year 1000: The* Decretum *of Burchard of Worms* (Burlington, VT: Ashgate, 2009), esp. 3–4, 53–74; Alice Rio, *Legal Practice and the Written Word in the Early Middle Ages: Frankish Formulae c. 500–1000* (Cambridge: Cambridge University Press, 2009), 192–97. Roman law developed in Italy in this period through a legal apprenticeship system noted in Radding, *The Origins of Medieval Jurisprudence: Pavia and Bologna, 850–1150* (New Haven: Yale University Press, 1988), 179–80.

108. On Salernitan medicine, see Monica H. Green, ed., *The Trotula: A Medieval Compendium of Women's Medicine* (Philadelphia: University of Pennsylvania Press, 2001), 43–14; Francis Newton, "Constantine the African and Monte Casino: New Elements and the Text of the *Isagoge*," in *Constantine the African and 'Alī ibn al-'Abbās al-Maǧūsī: The "Pantegni" and Related Texts*, ed. Charles Burnett and Danielle Jacquart (Leiden, Neth.: Brill, 1994), 16–47. On Richer's misadventures, see his *Historia* IV l, Lake, 2:304–11; on the Chartres context, see Genin, *Fulbert*, 38–40.

109. De Jong, *In Samuel's Image*, 147–50, 152–53.

customaries specify that a twelve-year old boy from the school was to be assigned to the service of the abbot.[110] The colloquies of Aelfric Bata, written around the millennium, assume that students were stationed as doormen and messengers outside the abbot's quarters.[111] Cluny, according to its customaries, had select groups of six and twelve *pueri*, with special masters and perhaps special liturgical functions, possibly a similar attempt to identify and train potential leaders.[112] These students, just like the pages who assisted secular lords, would have gained breaks from regular routines, opportunities to interact with distinguished visitors, and unique perspectives on what great lords actually do. Perhaps some of the tenth and eleventh century's long-ruling abbots and bishops were able to successfully assume their offices at young ages just because they had been identified early as future leaders and prepared by competition and special training within the schools.

EDUCATION AS CLERICAL REFORM

Education was a type of reform. Human beings, who had become flawed through original sin and ignorance, were to be led out toward Truth (literally "led out" in that education etymologically is *ex duco*). To acquire knowledge is a way to approach God, at least in a semi-Platonic intellectual world where arts and ideas really exist within the Divine Mind. This dynamic makes teachers channels of learning just as saints are channels of sanctity. The professor is more than a messenger—he personifies knowledge and makes it present. To the dismay of historians of education, medieval students have more to say more about the glories of their teachers than about what they actually taught. A charismatic teacher might be "our Socrates" or a "second Cicero."[113] Abbo was a "bright and shining light," one of many teachers acclaimed with light metaphors.[114] Fulbert's students were proud to have studied with him.[115] Lanfranc, as praised by

110. Thierry of Amorbach, *Libellus de consuetudinibus* I iii, ed. Davril and Donnat, 10, ed. and trans. Davril and Donnat, 174–75.

111. Aelfric Bata, *Colloquy* xi, Gwara, Porter, 108–9 (cf. also 7 and 11).

112. Constable, "*Seniores* and *Pueri* at Cluny," in *Histoire et société: Mélanges offerts à Georges Duby*, ed. Médiévistes de l'Université de Provence, 4 vols. (Aix-en-Provence: Université de Provence Service des publications, 1992), 3:17–24, esp. 23–24.

113. Jaeger, "Cathedral Schools and Humanist Learning 950–1150" in *Deutsche Vierteljahrsschrift für Literaturwissenschaft und Geistesgeschichte* 61 (1987): 569–616, esp. 586–88; Jaeger, *Envy of Angels*, esp. 2–4; Édouard Jeauneau, "Fulbert, notre vénérable Socrate," in Rouche, *Fulbert de Chartres*, 19–32, esp. 22.

114. Amoinus, *Vita Abbonis* I vi, Bautier and Labory, 58–59; Cora E. Lutz, *Schoolmasters of the Tenth Century* (Hamden, CT: Archon Books, 1977), 150.

115. Behrends, introduction to *Letters and Poems of Fulbert*, xxviii (see also xxxvi, which lists students and their recollections, esp. Adelman ca. 1050); McGuire, *Friendship and Community*, 163–73; Genin, *Fulbert*, 54–62; Rouche, *Fulbert de Chartres*, 9–10, 63–75, 104–9.

Orderic Vitalis, would have won "the applause of Herodian in grammar, Aristotle in dialectic, Cicero in rhetoric, Augustine, Jerome, and the other commentators on the Old and New Testaments in scriptural studies."[116] These paragons of the arts could lead their students toward the divine light. In 1050 the heretic Berengar, a pupil of Fulbert, justified his work by specifically equating dialectic with reform: "People who have the greatest hearts seek logic in all things, because to seek for it is to seek for reason, and since man is made to the image and likeness of God according to reason, he who does not seek it loses this high honor and is not able to be "renewed [*renovari*] from day to day according to the image of God."[117]

Yet, as in educational systems in all ages, mundane considerations could interfere with the disinterested pursuit of enlightenment. Good schoolmasters were identified not only as embodiments of wisdom but also as those professors whose students got jobs. Wulfstan's *Vita Aethelwoldi*, written around the year 1000, explains that because Aethelwold of Winchester (d. 984) was an outstanding teacher of "the rules of grammar and metric, . . . many of his students became priests, abbots, and notable bishops, some even archbishops, in England."[118] Students of Notker of Liège became important bishops and teachers, triumphs his biographer trumpets despite his fear that ambition for the courts of bishops and kings could distract students from the spiritual life.[119] The chronicle of Dijon itemizes the successful students of William of Volpiano.[120]

Good students were able to get jobs because educational accomplishments were valued. In 996, when Abbo of Fleury first encountered Gregory V (996–99), the pope greeted him enthusiastically because "I have learned you are a very ardent guardian of the Church and of the truth . . . wise in the human and the sacred sciences."[121] This papal respect for learning would steadily increase over succeeding generations. In 1081 Gregory VII rebuked King Alfonso VI of Castile and Léon because he had wanted

116. Orderic Vitalis, *Historia Aecclesiastica* IV ccxi, Chibnall, 2:250–51. See Priscilla D. Watkins, "Lanfranc at Caen: Teaching by Example," in Vaughn and Rubenstein, *Teaching and Learning in Northern Europe*, 71–97, esp. 73–78 and 96.

117. Berengar, *Rescriptum contra Lanfrannum* I, ed. R. B. C. Huygens, CCCM 84 (Turnhout, Belg.: Brepols, 1988), 85; CCCM 84A (Turnhout, Belg.: Brepols, 1988), fol. 36r (facs.).

118. Wulfstan, *Vita Aethelwoldi* xxxi (cf. xxxviii), Lapidge and Winterbottom, 48–49 (cf. 56–57), explicated xcii–xcix. On the actual achievements of Aethelwold's pupils, see Michael Lapidge, "Aethelwold as Scholar and Teacher," in *Bishop Aethelwold: His Career and Influence*, ed. Barbara Yorke (Woodbridge: Boydell, 1998), 89–117, esp. 101–17; Loredana Lazzari, "The Scholarly Achievements of Aethelwold and His Circle," in Lendinara et al., *Form and Content of Instruction*, 309–47.

119. Anselm, *Gesta Episcoporum Leodiensium* xxviii–xxix, ed. Rudolf Koepke, MGH SS 7 (Hannover: Hahn, 1846), 189–234, esp. 205–06.

120. *Chronicon Sancti Benigni*, Bougaud and Garnier, 149–50, 162.

121. Aimoinus, *Vita Abbonis* I xi, Bautier and Labory, 92–93.

to appoint an archbishop of Toledo who "although he seems sufficiently discreet and well-born, yet, as is known to us and as your letter does not deny, he is deficient in the foundation of instruction, which is the knowledge of letters. How necessary this skill is not only for bishops but, in truth, also for priests, you yourself well know, since without it no one can either teach others or defend himself."[122]

Learning opened a path on which men of undistinguished birth might advance to become schoolmasters and perhaps even to enter the ecclesiastical elite: Abbo of Fleury and Gerbert of Rheims, the greatest scholars of the late tenth century, came from free but nonaristocratic families.[123] Fulbert of Chartres was proud to owe his episcopate to neither nobility nor wealth.[124] Similar origins would later characterize the early leaders of the Roman Reform party such as Peter Damian and Hildebrand (Gregory VII).[125]

All in all, Western schoolmen were proud of what they had achieved, perhaps too proud. They began to envision a *translatio studii* in which the seat of knowledge was shifting to the Latin West. A late tenth-century piece by a "Gautbertus," apparently a monk of Saint-Martial of Limoges, presents a genealogy of teachers culminating in the masters of his day.[126] Abbot Gerhard of Sève, in a poem in praise of Bamberg written to Emperor Henry II around 1012, boasts that Bamberg is superb in the arts, both trivium and quadrivium, "never inferior to the Stoics, greater than Athens."[127] Gozechinus of Mainz, once schoolmaster and chancellor at Liège, speaks of his former city as "that very flower of three-fold Gaul, that second Athens, [which] flourishes nobly in the study of the liberal arts and . . . as to the study of literature you would expect nothing more from the Academy of Plato."[128]

---

122. Gregory VII, *Episola* IX ii, Caspar, 569–72, esp. 571, Cowdrey, 39–401, esp. 400.

123. Abbo's ancestry is explicated in Riché, *Abbon de Fleury*, 16, and Dachowski, *First among Abbots*, 24–32; Gerbert's in Edmonde-René Labande, "La formation de Gerbert à St-Géraud d'Aurillac," in *Gerberto scienza, storia e mito: Atti del 'Gerbert Symposium' (Bobbio 25–27 luglio 1983)* (Piacenza: A. S. B. Bobbio, 1985), 21–34, esp. 23–25.

124. Behrends, introduction to *Letters and Poems of Fulbert*, xvii.

125. Lester K. Little, "The Personal Development of Peter Damian" In *Order and Innovation in the Middle Ages: Essays in Honor of Joseph R. Strayer*, ed. William C. Jordan, Bruce McNab, and Teofilo F. Ruiz (Princeton: Princeton University Press, 1976), 317–41 and 523–38, esp. 322–25; Hildbrand is described as a "vir de plebe" by Abbot Walo of St-Arnulf of Metz, *Epist.* i, ed. Bernd Schütte, *Die Briefe des Abtes Walo von St. Arnulf von Metz*, MGH Studien und Texte 10 (Hannover: Hahn, 1995), 51–52, though on the difficulties involved in precisely identifying his original home and family, see Cowdrey, *Pope Gregory VII, 1073–1085* (Oxford: Clarendon, 1998), 27–30; and Uta-Renate Blumenthal, *Gregor VII.: Papst zwischen Canossa und Kirchenreform* (Darmstadt: Wissenschaftliche Buchgesellschaft, 2001), 16–20.

126. Léopold Delisle, "Notice sur les manuscrits originaux d'Adémar de Chabannes," *Notices et extraits* 35 (1896): 241–358, esp. 311–12. See Contreni, "The Tenth Century," 384.

127. Gerhart of Sève, *Epist. Bamburgensis* v, ed. Philippus Jaffé, in *Monumenta Bambergensia* (Berlin: Weidmann, 1869), 482–83, esp. 483.

128. Gozechinus, *Epist. ad Walcherum* vi, Huygens, 15.

CHAPTER 8

"THE BODY IS NOT A SINGLE PART"

> As a body is one though it has many parts, and all the parts of the
> body, though many, are one body, so also Christ. For in one Spirit we
> were all baptized into one body, whether Jews or Greeks, slaves or free
> persons, and we were all given to drink of one Spirit. Now the body is
> not a single part, but many. . . . God has so constructed the body . . . so
> that there may be no division in the body, but that the parts may have
> the same concern for one another. If [one] part suffers, all the parts
> suffer with it; if one part is honored, all the parts share its joy.
>
> —Paul, 1 Corinthians 12:12–14 and 24–26

The millennial Latin Church's corporate structure cannot be described
by any neat institutional flowchart. This admission may surprise Roman
Catholics familiar with a clearly defined administrative hierarchy that
descends from the pope and his curia, through archbishops and bishops, to parish priests. It may also surprise readers familiar with the
"feudal pyramid," the traditional textbook diagram of the feudal system
in which the king is enthroned proudly at the apex, above his greatest
lords, who each in turn preside over subpyramids of vassals, each with
his own knights. But hierarchical models were never so neat in practice,
and they assume work by legal theorists that was still far from complete
back in the tenth and eleventh centuries. Millennial Christians themselves had many different ways to envision lines of authority in society
and Church: the great medievalist Georges Duby identified at around
the year 1000 the earliest recorded attestations of the "three orders
of society"—that is, "those who pray, those who fight, and those who
work," but one could just as easily point to other divinely sanctioned

hierarchies such as "laymen, secular clergy, and monks" or "virgins, widows, and married folk."[1]

Lacking any neat model for tenth- and eleventh-century ecclesiastical organization, this chapter takes its lead from *The Institutes of Polity, Civil and Ecclesiastical* by Archbishop Wulfstan of York, written around the millennium in English rather than in elite Latin. He starts with the heavenly king and the earthly king and then proceeds to discuss bishops, lay magnates and patrons ("earls and generals and such judges of the world"), Mass priests, abbots and abbesses, monks and nuns, and finally lay folk (including a special section on widows).[2] Wulfstan moves from those who have the most power over the Church down to those who have the least—that is, from kings to simple members of the laity. On the other side of Europe there simultaneously appeared a similar ordering of Christian authorities, the *Admonitions* of King Stephen of Hungary written for his son Emeric around 1013–15.[3] These expositions seem muddled when compared with neat diagrams of ecclesiastical and secular hierarchies. Yet they were written for elite lay folk, men and women who would recognize that lordship over the Church was exercised by many officials and patrons, clerical and lay, each of whom assumed that his or her authority came ultimately from God.[4]

The messiness of these models is in itself significant. Christianity has been described by German sociologists and social historians as "a group-friendly religion [*eine gruppenfreundliche Religion*]."[5] This was certainly true of tenth- and eleventh-century Latin Christianity, which featured many interlocking and often potentially conflicting structures,

1. Georges Duby, *The Three Orders: Feudal Society Imagined*, trans. Arthur Goldhammer (Chicago: University of Chicago Press, 1980), 13–20; Constable, "The Orders of Society," in his *Three Studies*, 249–360; Otto Gerhard Oexle, "Perceiving Social Reality in the Early and High Middle Ages: A Contribution to a History of Social Knowledge," in *Ordering Medieval Society: Perspectives on Intellectual and Practical Models of Shaping Social Relations*, ed. Bernhard Jussen, trans. Pamela Selwyn (Philadelphia: University of Pennsylvania Press, 2001), 92–143.

2. Wulfstan of York, *Institutes of Polity*, ed. Karl Jost, *Die "Institutes of Polity, Civil and Ecclesiastical": Ein Werk Erzbischof Wulfstans von York* (Bern, Switz.: Francke, 1959), trans. Rabin, *Political Writings*, 101–24. On this work, see Trilling, "Sovereignty and Social Order," in Ott and Jones, *The Bishop Reformed*, esp. 73

3. Stephen I, *Monita ad Filium* iii, ed. Migne, *Pat. Lat.* 151:1233–54. See Előd Nemerkényi, "The Admonitions of King Saint Stephen of Hungary," in his *Latin Classics in Medieval Hungary*, 31–71, esp. 50–51, and "The Religious Ruler in the *Admonitions* of King Saint Stephen of Hungary," in Al-Azmeh and Bak, *Monotheistic Kingship*, 231–47.

4. Björn Weiler, "The *Rex Renitens* and the Medieval Idea of Kingship, ca. 900–ca. 1250," *Viator* 31 (2000): 1–42, esp. 23–35, juxtaposes royal and ecclesiastical conceptions of God-given authority.

5. Oexle, "Soziale Gruppen in der Ständegesellschaft: Lebensformen des Mittelalters und ihre historischen Wirkungen," in *Die Repräsentation der Gruppen: Texte-Bilder-Objekte*, ed. Oexle and Andrea von Hülsen-Esch (Göttingen: Vandenhoeck & Ruprecht, 1998), 9–44, esp. 36–39.

replete with multiple vertical and horizontal connections. The Church was broadly united in its faith and in its reforming ideals, but individual churches and their communities were rooted in local power structures and manifested the *encellulement* of society. For better or worse, these were communities that could not easily be swayed en masse by the whims of individual emperors, kings, popes, bishops, nobles, or crowds.

THE ECCLESIASTICAL ELITES

Christian Kings

Around a dozen kings were reigning in Western Europe at the start of the eleventh century, not counting some peripheral Celtic chieftains with monarchical pretentions. These kings were major international figures governing in a world in which at one point the German king held the Italian crown and the Danish king the English one, a world where marriage connections could extend to Kiev and Constantinople. Although royal power rested ultimately upon military force and gift-cemented alliances, in day-to-day affairs a king ruled through power in personality. He and his court itinerated throughout his kingdom, and he had extensive direct contact with its elites. He could grant or withhold favor by word and by deed (through gesture, symbolic action, or liturgy), carefully displaying his esteem or his disapproval and shaping his favors or rebukes according to the situation and the rank of the recipient.[6]

Queens helped. Because the king had to preserve his reputation as a firm war leader and stern fountain of justice, the way lay open for the queen to step forward as a patroness and benefactor. Queens were often more international and literate than their husbands inasmuch as in marriages they were the ones who moved from court to court. They were multilingual, and their Latinity and education were important. Queens were becoming more prominent in art. Little wonder then that special coronation rites for queens began to appear just when the Carolingian Empire was disintegrating into a plethora of new states. Although various scholars have credited the emergence of pan-European courtly culture to the high aristocracy, prince bishops, and exotic ambassadors, royal women may have an equally valid claim.[7]

---

6. Gerd Althoff, "(Royal) Favor: A Central Concept in Early Medieval Hierarchical Relations," in Jussen, *Ordering Medieval Society*, 243–69; Philippe Buc, "Political Rituals and Political Imagination in the Medieval West from the Fourth Century to the Eleventh," in Linehan and Nelson, *The Medieval World*, 189–213.

7. Theresa Earenfight, *Queenship in Medieval Europe* (New York: Palgrave MacMillan, 2012) offers an overview and bibliography. On particular points, see Julie Ann Smith, "The Earliest Queen-Making

Kings were holy, at least in their official capacities. Because semidivine kings ruled long before there were Christians, there have been extensive debates over how much medieval kingship owes to pagan royal sacrality.[8] Yet Christian scripture and early tradition left no doubt that kings held their power from God and must be obeyed.[9] Once post-Roman barbarian kings converted, they were able to define their authority in ecclesiastical terms.[10] From Carolingian times forward, kings were "anointed by God."[11] This sacredness could be enhanced by great relic collections, especially those accumulated by the house of Wessex and the Ottonians.[12] It could also be bolstered by the canonization of royal saints. Around 1020 the public piety of kings reached an all-time high when St. Henry II (1002–24) ruled the Western Empire, alongside St. Stephan of Hungary (997–1038) and St. Olaf of Norway (1015–30), all while St. Edward the Confessor (1042–66) was in exile awaiting his English throne and Robert the Pious (996–1021) was being heralded as saintly by his enthusiastic publicist (alas, two irregular marriages complicated his dossier).[13]

How did this royal sacredness affect the Church? When kings claimed power from God to protect their subjects and their churches, they placed themselves so high above parochial concerns that they could credibly arbitrate among the peoples and factions of their realms. Yet this left all their great vassals, ecclesiastical as well as secular, on an undifferentiated plane somewhere far below. Kings were expected to defend the Church militarily, but they could also defend it through ecclesiastical reform.[14]

Rites," *Church History* 66 (1997): 18–35; Elizabeth M. Tyler, "Crossing Conquests: Polyglot Royal Women and Literary Culture in Eleventh-Century England," in *Conceptualizing Multilingualism in Medieval England, c. 800–c. 1250*, ed. Elizabeth M. Tyler (Turnhout, Belg.: Brepols, 2011), 171–96, esp. 172; Catherine E. Karkov, *The Art of Anglo-Saxon England* (Woodbridge: Boydell, 2011), 231–34, 266–71.

8. On the continuity of pagan sacred kingship, contrast William A. Chaney, *The Cult of Kingship in Anglo-Saxon England: The Transition from Paganism to Christianity* (Berkeley: University of California Press, 1970), with Susan J. Ridyard, *The Royal Saints of Anglo-Saxon England: A Study of West Saxon and East Anglian Cults* (New York: Cambridge University Press, 1988), 234–35. For a fairly balanced synthesis, see Francis Oakley, *Kingship: The Politics of Enchantment* (Oxford: Blackwell, 2006), and his *Empty Bottles of Gentilism: Kingship and the Divine in Late Antiquity (to 1050)* (New Haven: Yale University Press, 2010), esp. 18–39, 144–51.

9. Henry A. Meyers and Herwig Wolfram, *Medieval Kingship* (Chicago: Nelson Hall, 1982), 154–25, 137–47, 164–70; Oakley, *Empty Bottles*, esp. 40–142.

10. John Michael Wallace-Hadrill, *Early Germanic Kingship in England and on the Continent* (Oxford: Clarendon, 1971), 47–71.

11. Franz-Reiner Erkens, "Religiöse Herschaftslegitimierung im Mittelalter," *Zeitschrift der Savigny-Stiftung für Rechtsgeschichte: Kanonistische Abteilung* 89 (2003): 1–55; Oakley, *Empty Bottles*, esp. 157–65.

12. Leyser, "Die Ottonen und Wessex," 73.

13. For a list of sainted kings, see Folz, *Les saints rois*, esp. 76–115 and 184–99. On Robert's pretensions to sanctity, see Laurent Theis, "Robert le Pieux était-il pieux?," in Rouche, *Fulbert de Chartres*, 129–35.

14. Moore, *Sacred Kingdom*, esp. 218–33, 279.

FIGURE 33. Sacral ruler: bishops support the arms and orb of Emperor Henry II (compare Aaron and Hur supporting the arms of Moses in Exodus 17:11–12). Bamberg Staatsbibliothek Kaiser Heinrichs-II Bibliothek MS. Bibl. 53, fol. 20. Photo credit: Gerald Raab, Bamberg Staatsbibliothek.

They could admonish and correct, just like their bishops.[15] Indeed, the original meaning of the word *episcopus* was overseer, and the practical similarities that existed between royal and episcopal monitoring led Constantine to "exercise . . . a bishop's supervision over all his subjects" and Charlemagne to be hailed as a "bishop of bishops."[16] Whether kings or their churchmen were the more important "correctors" depended upon

15. Sumi Shimahara, "L'éxégèse biblique et les élites: Qui sont les recteurs de l'Église à l'époque carolingienne?," in *La culture du haut Moyen Âge: Une question d'élites*, ed. François Bougard, Régine Le Jan, and Rosamond McKitterick (Turnhout, Belg.: Brepols, 2009), 201–17.

16. Eusebius, *De Vita Constantini* IV xxiv, ed. Bruno Bleckmann, *Eusebius von Caesarea De Vita Constantini: Über das Leben Konstantins* (Turnhout, Belg.: Brepols, 2007), 434–35, trans. Averil Cameron and Stuart. G. Hall, *Eusebius' Life of Constantine* (Oxford: Clarendon, 1998), 161; Notger, *Gesta* I xxv, Haefele, 33, Ganz, 75.

the relative political and charismatic power of the individuals involved. Early medieval kings mixed secular and sacred government in a way that people today would find shockingly irregular, as a letter written in 1019 or 1020 from King Cnut to the people of England illustrates:

> Now I charge my archbishops and all my subordinate bishops to be conscientious concerning the rights of the Church, each in the region assigned to him; and I also command my ealdormen to support the bishops in advancing the rights of the Church and my royal authority and the welfare of the whole people.
>
> If anyone—either cleric or lay, Danish or English—is so bold as to act in opposition to my royal authority or in opposition to secular law, and he refuses to repent and refrain in keeping with the teaching of my bishops, then I ask, and indeed command, Earl Thurkill to bring the offender to justice, if he can. If he cannot, then I desire him to wipe him from the earth or drive him from the land with our combined strength, whether he is of higher or lower status.[17]

Bishops

Pre-Gregorian bishops have begun to receive positive scholarly attention.[18] Michael Edward Moore argues that "the building of the [Carolingian] Empire and the sense of religious mission which inspired it can, to a significant extent, be attributed to the royal adoption of an episcopal platform."[19] When Robert Bartlett wanted to exemplify the expansion of Latin Christendom, his initial chapter was devoted to the spread of bishoprics.[20] Timothy Reuter discovered a "Europe of bishops" in the tenth and eleventh centuries.[21] Bishops are now recognized not only as spiritual and political leaders but also as sophisticated courtiers who helped shape Western governance and governors.

17. Letter from King Cnut to the People of England (1019–1020) ¶ 8–10 (Old English), in Whitelock et al., *Councils & Synods*, 435–41, esp. 437–38, trans. Rabin, *Political Writings*, 192–96, esp. 194.

18. For scholarship on bishops who were in office from 800 to 950, see Patzold, *Episcopus*, 17–30; for scholarship on bishops in office from 900 to 1200, see Patzold, "L'épiscopat du haut Moyen Âge du point de la vue de la médiévistique allemande," *CCM* 48 (2005): 341–58. Note also Michel Parisse, "The Bishop: Prince and Prelate," in *The Bishop: Power and Piety at the First Millennium*, ed. Sean Gilsdorf (Münster: LIT, 2004), 1–22; Ott and Jones, introduction to Ott and Jones, *The Bishop Reformed*, 1–20; Anna Jones, *"Noble Lord, Good Shepherd": Episcopal Power and Piety in Aquitaine, 877–1050* (Leiden, Neth.: Brill, 2009), 7–11.

19. Moore, *Sacred Kingdom*, 1 and 371–72.

20. Robert Bartlett, *The Making of Europe: Conquest, Colonization, and Cultural Change, 950–1350* (London: Allan Lane, 1993), 5–23.

21. Timothy Reuter, "Ein Europa der Bischöfe: Das Zeitalter Burchards von Worms," in Hartmann, *Bischof Burchard*, 1–28, trans. as "A Nation of Bishops: The Age of Wulfstan of York and Burchard of Worms," in *Patterns of Episcopal Power: Bishops in Tenth and Eleventh Century Western Europe*, ed. Ludger Körntgen and Dominik Wassenhoven (Berlin: Walter de Gruyter, 2011), 17–38.

The bishops of the millennial Church traced their authority back through their predecessors to Jesus Christ, and they were able to do this with increasing directness thanks to a flurry of ahistorical apostolic foundation legends describing the first transalpine bishops as followers of Christ dispatched from Rome by Peter himself.[22] Bishops governed dioceses, which were imagined communities centering on the cathedral where the bishop had his official seat (his *cathedra*), and were often based upon former Roman administrative districts encompassing a city and its countryside (*civitas* and *pagus*).[23] Bishops enjoyed great independence, as is evident from the local achievements their vitae showcase.[24] Yet they were also members of a larger order, and in the later Roman Empire their offices were arranged in a Roman-style administrative hierarchy, leading up from bishops to archbishops to metropolitans to patriarchs. The Eastern Roman Empire generally maintained this system, but in the post-Roman Latin West the metropolitan jurisdictions gradually fell into desuetude because it would be simpler to appeal directly to Rome if oversight were ever to be sought.[25] Bishops and archbishops developed strong horizontal links among themselves when they met at church dedications, at courts, and at local councils where they attempted to decide things *in communis*. Their collegial identity was enhanced when the Carolingians promoted consistent archepiscopal organization.[26]

Wulfstan presents bishops as spiritual leaders who "must learn and rightly teach. . . . And they must preach and sincerely exemplify the spiritual commission to a Christian people. And they must not knowingly permit any injustice but readily promote all that is just . . . [and] always be sure to zealously proclaim the law of God and to forbid injustice. For the shepherd will be judged weak for the flock, who will not defend the flock that he must protect—even by calling [out] if he can do nothing else—if any corrupter of the people begins to pillage there."[27] Bishops

---

22. Michel Sot, "La Rome antique dans l'hagiographie épiscopale en Gaule," in *Roma antica nel Medioevo*, 163–68, esp. 173–86.

23. Michel Lauwers, "*Territorium non Facere Diocesim* . . . Conflits, limites et représentation territoriale du diocèse (V^e–XIIIe siècle)," in *L'espace du diocèse: Genèse d'un territoire dans l'Occident médiéval (V^e–XIIIe siècle)*, ed. Florian Mazel (Rennes: Presses universitaires de Rennes, 2008), 23–65.

24. Haarländer, *Vitae Episcoporum*, 415; Patzold, *Episcopus*, 467–508; Theo Riches, "The Changing Political Horizons of *Gesta Episcoporum* from the Ninth to Eleventh Centuries," in Körntgen and Wassenhoven, *Patterns of Episcopal Power*, 51–62, esp. 62.

25. Thomas F. X. Noble, "The Christian Church as an Institution," in *Early Medieval Christianities, c. 600–c.1100*, ed. Noble and Julia Smith, Cambridge History of Christianity 3 (Cambridge: Cambridge University Press, 2008), 249–74.

26. Ott and Jones, introduction to *The Bishop Reformed*, and Greta Austin, "Bishops and Religious Law," in Ott and Jones, *Bishop Reformed*, 1–20, esp. 1, and 40–57, esp. 40; Moore, *Sacred Kingdom*, 279.

27. Wulfstan, *Institutes of Polity* vi, Jost, 62–63, Rabin, *Political Writings*, 108–9. See Trilling, "Sovereignty and Social Order," 58–91, esp. 73.

led the diocesan liturgy, at least at Easter when they were expected to preside. Their responsibilities included the ordination and subsequent supervision of the priests of their dioceses, a principle established and elaborated in Late Antiquity.[28] While baptism was normally delegated to baptismal churches or to local clergy, bishops did continue to anoint their flocks through the sacrament of confirmation, which required regular itinerations throughout their dioceses that are noted only by chance as when, for example, a clerk in Aethelwold's retinue lost the flask of chrism on the road.[29] One hopes that Aethelwold and his colleagues avoided the procedure, noted by a horrified twelfth-century author, in which a bishop on horseback swept through villages with his retinue and, never actually dismounting, sprinkled chrism on the frightened children his retainers had been able to round up.[30] Bishops administered major public penances, formally reconciling penitents who had been temporarily banned from the Church because of grievous public sin, often in a Lenten rite that culminated in a reconciliation service on the Thursday before Easter.[31] Bishops founded many monasteries and convents.[32] They oversaw these and all the other religious communities within their diocese, except those that had somehow managed to secure guarantees of "exemption" from episcopal authority.[33] As administrators, bishops were necessarily interested in Church law, using it, writing it, and accessing it through compendia of canon laws that paralleled the liturgical compendia that constituted their pontificals.[34]

Bishops were also political leaders. When they assisted in the conversions of post-Roman barbarian kings, they became de facto royal councilors. They were natural mediators between kings and aristocrats and

28. Robert Godding, *Prêtres en Gaule mérovingienne* (Brussels: Bollandistes, 2001), 104–6 and 267–93.

29. Wulfstan, *Vita Aethelwoldi* xxvi, Lapidge and Winterbottom, 42–43. On these iterations, see Tinti, *Sustaining Belief*, 243–45.

30. Adam of Eynsham, *Magna Vita S. Hugonis* III xiii, ed. Decima L. Douie and David Hugh Farmer, *The Life of St. Hugh of Lincoln*, 2 vols. (Oxford: Clarendon, 1985), 1:127–28.

31. Marcus Bull, *Knightly Piety and the Lay Response to the First Crusade: The Limousin and Gascony, c. 970–c. 1130* (Oxford: Clarendon, 1993), 173–76; Sarah Hamilton, *The Practice of Penance, 950–1050* (Woodbridge: Boydell for the Royal Historical Society, 2001), esp. 3–7 and 108–21.

32. For bishops as monastic founders prior to 1050, see Reuter, "A Europe of Bishops?," 37; Haarländer, *Vitae Episcoporum*, 187–99; Jones, "Noble Lord, Good Shepherd," 105–217.

33. On the episcopal supervision of monks envisioned in Carolingian legislation, see Patzold, *Episcopus*, 118–23, 130. Exemptions are treated in Barbara H. Rosenwein, *Negotiating Space: Power, Restraint, and Privileges of Immunity in Early Medieval Europe* (Ithaca: Cornell University Press, 1999), esp. 4–5, 35–36, 171–83.

34. Renato Bordone, "Vescovi giudici e critici della giustizia: Attone di Vercelli," and Wilfried Hartmann, "Probleme des geistlichen Gerichts im 10. und 11. Jahrhundert: Bischöfe und Synoden als Richter im ostfränkisch-deutschen Reich," in *La Giustizia nell'alto medioevo (secoli IX–XI), 11–17 aprile 1996*, 2 vols. Settimane di studio 44 (Spoleto: CISAM, 1997), 1:457–490 and 2:631–72; Austin, "Bishops and Religious Law," 40–57, esp. 40–46.

between competing aristocratic factions.[35] As pastors they were obligated to defend their flocks, especially the poor.[36] Although Carolingian government had been based on a particularly close partnership with bishops, its disintegration was not an unmitigated disaster for the more powerful ones, who benefited just as the more powerful noblemen did. During chaotic times episcopal cities often grew, just because they were more secure than rural areas, and those bishops who could defend them gained new political concessions and privileges.[37] Prince bishops were awarded secular offices that enabled them to officially rule their territories as both bishop and count, and, according to one enumeration, more than seventy bishoprics ultimately received comital rights, most within Germany, many in Italy, and about a half dozen in France.[38]

Even if a bishop was not formally a secular lord, he still had secular duties. He might owe his office directly to the king or to a local lord, depending on the history of the diocese and the supineness of the clergy and people who were the official electors, and when he was ordained he would have been invested by the king with the symbols of his office. His estates were likely to include properties that had been encumbered with military and administrative obligations acquired prior to their donation to the Church. Kings therefore expected bishops to provide whatever hospitality, court service, and military levies had become customary.[39] The single muster roll surviving from the Ottonian era (which may or may not represent normal mobilization procedures since it was a request for emergency reinforcements issued after the disastrous battle with the Muslims at Crotone in 982) shows Emperor Otto II drawing most of his troops from ecclesiastical vassals.[40] Bishops also supervised considerable legal

---

35. Gilsdorf, "Bishops in the Middle: Mediatory Politics and the Episcopacy," in Gilsdorf, *The Bishop*, 51–74; Monika Suchan, "Monition and Advice as Elements of Politics," in Körntgen and Wassenhoven, *Patterns of Episcopal Power*, 39–50; Laurent Jégou, *L'évêque, juge de paix: L'autorité épiscopale et le règlement des conflits entre Loire et Elbe (VIIIe–XIe siècle)* (Turnhout, Belg.: Brepols, 2011), esp. 89–95, 311–41.

36. Moore, *Sacred Kingdom*, 283–85, 293–94.

37. Eldevik, *Episcopal Power*, 5–10, 97–101.

38. Olivier Guyotjeannin, Episcopus et comes: *Affirmation et déclin de la seigneurie épiscopale au nord du Royaume de France (Beauvais-Noyon, X^e–début XIIIe siècle)* (Geneva: Droz, 1987), 3–66, esp. 56–62; Hagen Keller, *Adelsherrschaft und städtische Gesellschaft in Oberitalien, 9.–12. Jahhundert* (Tübingen: Max Niemeyer, 1979), 251–54, 262–69, and 333–42.

39. Friedrich Prinz, *Klerus und Krieg im früheren Mittelalter: Untersuchungen zur Rolle der Kirche beim Aufbau der Königsherrschaft* (Stuttgart: Hiersemann, 1971); Leopold Auer, "Der Kriegsdienst des Klerus unter den sächsischen Kaisern," *Mitteilungen des Instituts für Österreichische Geschichtsforschung* 79 (1971): 316–407 and 80 (1972): 48–70; Franz-Reiner Erkens, ed., *Die früh- und hochmittelalterliche Bischofserhebung im europäischen Vergleich* (Cologne: Böhlau, 1998); Mary Frances Giandrea, "The *Servitium Regis*," in her *Episcopal Culture in Late Anglo-Saxon England*, 35–69; Hartmut Hoffmann, "König und seine Bischöfe," in Hartmann, *Bischof Burchard*, 79–127.

40. *Indiculus Loricatum*, ed. Ludwig Weiland, MGH *Constitutiones et Acta Publica Imperatorum et Regum, 911–1197* (Hannover: Hahn, 1893), 632–33. For context, see Bernhardt, *Itinerant Kingship*, 34–35.

business, administering not only canon law but also whatever secular laws applied to their properties.[41] Kings had good reason to view them approvingly, as does King Stephen of Hungary in the admonitions he wrote for his son: "The order of prelates adorns the royal throne. . . . They shall be, dearest son, your elders, and you shall cherish them as the apple of your eye. If they favor you, you need not fear any enemy . . . because God set them up as guardians over his people, as overseers of souls, and partakers in as well as administrators of the entire ecclesiastical dignity and of all divine sacraments. Without them no kings are made."[42]

Many bishops were rich, even before their elections, and they were expected to contribute some of their personal wealth to their dioceses.[43] High-born bishops could live in aristocratic style.[44] The triumph of the "ornate style" of episcopal liturgical dress has been assigned to the tenth and eleventh centuries.[45] In miracle stories the staff, the stole, and the ring all shine, and mentions of bishops' staffs, rare before the tenth century, become more common.[46] From the tenth century on, episcopal acclamations began to borrow from the *Laudes* given to kings and emperors.[47] The bishop's residence—at least in Italy, where it has been studied—adapted to

41. Hartmann, "L'évêque comme juge: La pratique du tribunal épiscopal en France du Xe au XIIe siècle," in *Hiérarchies et services au Moyen Âge: Séminaire sociétés, idéologies et croyances au Moyen Âge*, ed. Claude Carozzi and Hugutte Taviani-Carozzi (Aix-en-Provence: Publications de l'Université de Provence, 2001), 71–92, esp. 92.

42. Stephen, *Monita ad Filium* iii, ed. Migne, *Pat. Lat.* 151:1233–54, esp. 1238–39. Context in Nemerkényi, "Religious Ruler," 231–47, esp. 235–36.

43. Giandrea, *Episcopal Culture*, 147–50; Ian Wood, "Entrusting Western Europe to the Church," 43–44. Expectations for property donations by bishops could even be written into law: see *Concilium Agathense* (Council of Agde 506), can. xxxiii, ed. Charles Munier, *Concilia Galliae, a. 314–a. 506*, CCSL 148 (Turnhout, Belg.: Brepols, 1963), 189–228, esp. 207, and Edmund's *First Code* (between 941 and 946) q 5, in Whitelock et al., *Councils & Synods*, 60–63, esp. 63. Thietmar's *Chronicon* VI lx, Holtzmann, 322–23, Warner, 264–65, describes in detail how, prior to his episcopal consecration, he was queried about whether he would aid his church with some part of his inheritance.

44. Carlrichard Brühl, "Die Sozialstruktur des deutschen Episkopats," and Gabriella Rossetti, "Origine sociale e formazione del vescovi del '*Regnum Italiae*' nei secoli XI e XII," in *Le istituzioni ecclesiastiche della "Societas Christiana" dei secoli XI–XII: Diocesi, pievi e parrocchie: Atti della Settima internazionale di studio, Milano, 1–7 settembre 1974* (Milan: Vita e Pensiero, 1977), 42–56 and 57–58; Odilo Engles, "Bischofsherrschaft und Adel in Südfrankreich und Katalonien während des Hochmittelalters," in Erkens, *Die früh- und hochmittelalterliche Bischofserhebung*, 259–85, esp. 276–78; Patzold, "L'épiscopat du haut Moyen Âge," 345–52. On episcopal self-presentation, see Heinrich Fichtenau, "Worldly Clerics," in *Living in the Tenth Century*, 217–41.

45. Miller, *Clothing the Clergy*, esp. 96–136.

46. Megan McLaughlin, "The Bishop as Bridegroom: Marital Imagery and Clerical Celibacy in the Eleventh and Early Twelfth Centuries," in *Medieval Purity and Piety: Essays on Medieval Clerical Celibacy and Religious Reform*, ed. Michael Frassetto (New York: Garland, 1998), 209–37, esp. 211–12 and 217–19; Philippe Depreux, "*Investitura per Anulum et Baculum*: Ring und Stab als Zeichen der Investitur bis zum Investiturstreit," in Jarnut and Wemhoff, *Vom Umbruch zur Erneuerung?*, 169–95, esp. 172–73; Patzold, *Episcopus*, 498–99.

47. Ernst H. Kantorowicz, Laudes Regiae: *A Study in Liturgical Acclamations and Mediaeval Ruler Worship* (Berkeley: University of California Press, 1958), 112–25.

chaos and to increased governmental duties first by becoming a fortified lordly house, often with a tower or two; then in 1020, as bishops began to expand their quarters further, the documents begin to speak of the episcopal "palace."[48] A less lordly image was provided by a few monk bishops who insisted on wearing their monastic habits despite their princely responsibilities: although they were relatively rare in the millennial church, their ranks would increase during the Gregorian Reform.[49] Overall, the bishops of the millennial Latin Church were involved in the world to an unusual degree. When Bishop Liudprand of Cremona went east, he was shocked to discover Greek bishops who uncomplainingly paid great sums to their emperor even though their households were so modest that they answered doors themselves.[50] On the other side, Greek bishops viewed their politically powerful Latin counterparts as bloody warlords.[51]

In the background loomed the bishop of Rome, the pope. Bishops in the central Middle Ages have been described as operating "between kings and popes."[52] They welcomed papal authority when they found it advantageous. But if they did not like papal decisions, they could react as Rodulfus Glaber claims they did in regard to a papal intervention against the archbishop of Tours:

> All [the bishops of Gaul] were equally hostile because it was shameful that he who ruled the Apostolic See was breaking the original apostolic intention and the tenor of the canons, especially when it is an old and well-founded rule that no bishop may presume to exercise authority in the diocese of another unless he is asked, or at least permitted, to do so by its own bishop. . . . Although the pontiff of the Roman church, because of the dignity of the Apostolic See, is honoured more than any other bishop, he is not permitted to transgress the canon law in any way. For each bishop of the orthodox church is bridegroom of his own see and equally embodies the Saviour, and so none should interfere insolently in the diocese of another bishopric.[53]

48. Maureen C. Miller, *The Bishop's Palace: Architecture and Authority in Medieval Italy* (Ithaca: Cornell University Press, 2000), 15, 54–56, 61–71, 78–80, 263–74.

49. Haarländer, *Vitae Episcoporum*, 166–71; Bernard Guillemain, "Les moines sur les sièges épiscopaux du sud-ouest de la France aux XIe et XIIe siècles," in *Études de civilisation médiévale IXe au XIIe siècles: Mélanges offerts a Edmonde-René Labande* (Poitiers: C.É.S.C.M., 1974), 377–84; Giandrea, *Episcopal Culture*, 42–47; Catherine Cubitt, "Bishops and Succession Crises in Tenth- and Eleventh-Century England," in Körntgen and Wassenhoven, *Patterns of Episcopal Power*, 11–26, esp. 121–23.

50. Liudprand, *Legatio* lxiii, Chiesa, 185–218, esp. 216, Squatriti, 238–82, esp. 279–80.

51. Tia M. Kolbaba, *The Byzantine Lists: Errors of the Latins* (Urbana: University of Illinois Press, 2000), 48–51.

52. Meyers and Wolfram, *Medieval Kingship*, 163–78.

53. Rodulfus Glaber, *Historiae* II vi and vii, France, 62–65. The proximate circumstances of this particular clash are described in Bernard Bachrach, "Pope Sergius IV and the Foundation of the Monastery at Beaulieu-les-Loches," *Revue bénédictine* 95 (1985): 240–65; the broader context in Horst Fuhrmann, "Widerstände gegen den päpstlichen Primat im Abendland," in *Il primato del vescovo di Roma nel primo millennio:*

Popes

The most prestigious ecclesiastical official in the West and (sometimes) beyond was the bishop of Rome, the pope. The Church of Rome, an early and wealthy Christian community, could boast of Peter and Paul and thousands of other martyrs. Although its bishop claimed Peter as his Church's founder and applied Peter's headship over all the apostles to himself, his preeminence must have owed much to his church's location in the traditional imperial capital inasmuch as the patriarch of Constantinople, despite inferior apostolic credentials, was able to parlay his leadership of the church of "New Rome" into nearly equivalent prestige. The disputed final canons of the Council of Constantinople of 381 acknowledged the theoretical preeminence of the bishop of Rome, but then and later other bishops were not convinced that this status entitled him to intervene in their affairs.[54]

The papacy survived better than the Western Empire. The early medieval bishop of Rome was the city's largest landholder and by default its de facto administrator even when he was still willing to acknowledge the theoretical authority of the Byzantine exarch in Ravenna.[55] In an eighth-century "Roman Revolution," popes shifted their political allegiance from an unhelpful Byzantine emperor to the Carolingian Franks, an alliance consummated by the pope's coronation of Charlemagne as emperor in the year 800.[56] Initially Charlemagne was the senior partner, but his less powerful successors soon found themselves begging for papal support. Some later ninth-century popes were prominent figures throughout the universal Church, aided by Carolingian missionary outreach and by the prestige gained in the resolution of the Eastern Empire's iconoclastic struggles.[57]

Ricerche e testimonianze: Atti del symposium storico-teologico, Roma, 9–13 ottobre 1989, ed. Michele Maccarrone (Vatican City: Libreria Editrice Vaticana, 1991), 707–36, esp. 722–32.

54. For a standard narrative, see Roland Minnerath, "La position de l'Église de Rome aux trois premiers siècles," and Charles Pietri, "La conversion de Rome et la primauté du Pape (IV–VIe S.)," in Maccarrone, *Il primato del vescovo di Roma*, 139–71 and 219–43; for a minimalist view of the Petrine tradition, see George E. Demacopoulos, *The Invention of Peter: Apostolic Discourse and Papal Authority in Late Antiquity* (Philadelphia: University of Pennsylvania Press, 2013), esp. 2. On Rome of the martyrs, see Alan Thacker, "Rome of the Martyrs: Saints, Cults and Relics, Fourth to Seventh Centuries," in *Roma Felix: Formation and Reflections of Medieval Rome*, ed. Éamonn Ó Carragáin and Carol Neuman de Vegvar (Burlington, VT: Ashgate, 2007), 13–50; and Theofried Baumeister, "Konstantin der Grosse und die Märtyrer," in *Martyrium, Hagiographie und Heiligenverehrung im chistlichen Altertum*, ed. Baumeister, *Römische Quartalschrift* Supplementband 61 (Rome: Herder, 2009), 113–37, esp. 123–31.

55. Georg Scheibelreiter," Church Structure and Organization," in *NCMH 1, c. 500–c. 700*, ed. Paul Fouracre (Cambridge: Cambridge University Press, 2005), 675–709, esp. 677–80 ("The Papacy").

56. Noble, *The Republic of St. Peter: The Birth of the Papal State, 680–825* (Philadelphia: University of Pennsylvania Press, 1984).

57. Noble, "The Papacy in the Eighth and Ninth Centuries," in *NCMH 2: c. 700–c. 900*, ed. McKitterick (Cambridge: Cambridge University Press, 1995), 563–86; John Osborne, "Rome and Constantinople in the Ninth Century," in Bolgia et al., *Rome across Time*, 222–37.

These successes proved ephemeral because Rome and the papacy needed effective Carolingian rulers to maintain internal order and external defense. The suspicious death of Pope John VIII in 882 was followed by a disastrous late ninth-century struggle among Roman aristocratic factions during which nearly two dozen popes and antipopes reigned in brief pontificates that were expedited by depositions, imprisonments, and murders.[58] There were intervals of stability. The much-maligned Theophylact family that dominated Rome in the early tenth century had a positive local reputation for monastic patronage; later the bloody stalemate between the aristocratic faction led by the Crescenzi and the newly arrived Ottonian emperors would be resolved by the nepotistic barons of Tuscolo, who installed their sons and nephews as popes from 1012–46 and arbitrated between emperors and aristocratic factions with Machiavellian skill.[59] Yet no one can deny that the popes of the millennial Church were greatly distracted by local fights.

The papacy nevertheless remained significant. The bishop of Rome ruled the greatest city in the Latin West, which, although only a shadow of its antique glory, still boasted more than a hundred notable churches scattered amid its ancient classical monuments.[60] Rome was visited regularly by pious kings; by great bishops seeking their *pallia*; and by crowds of Latin, Greek, and even Armenian religious seekers so great that to accommodate them the English, Franks, Lombards, and Greeks maintained their own Roman *scolae*.[61] Popes presided over grand ceremonies, and in the eleventh century they began to don their own imperial purple robes.[62]

58. J. N. D. Kelly and Michael Walsh, *The Oxford Dictionary of Popes*, 2nd ed. (Oxford: Oxford University Press, 2010), 110–26, attempt a pope-by-pope survey based on the very sketchy and partisan sources from this era.

59. Bernard Hamilton, "The House of Theophylact and the Promotion of the Religious Life among Women in Tenth Century Rome," *Studia Monastica* 12 (1970): 195–217; Klaus Jürgen Herrmann, *Das Tuskulanerpapsttum (1012–1046)* (Stuttgart: Anton Hiersemann, 1973), esp. 8–12, 23–24, 35–37, 166–78; Wickham, "'The Romans according to Their Malign Custom': Rome in Italy in the Late Ninth and Tenth Centuries," in Smith, *Early Medieval Rome*, 151–67; Wickham, *Medieval Rome: Stability and Crisis of a City, 900–1150* (New York: Oxford University Press, 2015), 181–258.

60. David Whitehouse, "Rome and Naples: Survival and Revival in Central and Southern Italy," and Paolo Delogu, "The Rebirth of Rome in the 8th and 9th Centuries," in Hodges and Hobley, *Rebirth of Towns in the West*, 28–31 and 32–42; Noble, "Topography, Celebration, and Power: The Making of a Papal Rome in the Eighth and Ninth Centuries," in De Jong and Theuws, *Topographies of Power*, 45–91.

61. Wilfrid J. Moore, *The Saxon Pilgrims to Rome and the* Schola Saxonum (Fribourg: Society of St. Paul, 1937), esp. 109–18; Veronica Ortenberg, "Archbishop Sigeric's Journey to Rome in 990," *Anglo-Saxon England* 19 (1990): 197–246; Étienne Hubert, "Les residences des étrangers à Rome," in *Roma fra Oriente e Occidente, 19–24 aprile 2001*, 1:175–207. Eastern pilgrims are discussed in more detail in chapter 9 below.

62. Agostino Paravicini-Bagliani, *The Pope's Body*, trans. David S. Peterson (Chicago: University of Chicago Press, 1994), 85–86; Miller, *Clothing the Clergy*, 192–94.

Despite disasters and scandals, popes were developing their office and their court (the *curia*). Petitioners clamored for legal privileges and favors. The documents they received looked imperial in their forms, internal structures, and even minor details. The first surviving pontifical diploma written on parchment (replacing venerable but impractical papyrus scrolls) appeared soon after 967 and was written in the new minuscule cursive called "chancellery hand," which was replacing the curial writing of the traditional Roman notaries. The old seven *judices de clero* were eclipsed by specific officials, first the *bibliothecarius* (literally the librarian) and then the chancellor. Although papal procedure remained notarial and idiosyncratic, the Tuscolan popes were making bureaucratic progress even before the mid-century advent of Henry III's "imperial" popes Clement II, Damasus II, and Leo IX.[63]

A new papal assertiveness was symbolized by new papal names. The first popes to change their names upon election were tenth-century Romans, born in Rome, who wanted new names to cloak the awkward realities of their rise to power. The son of the Theophylact Prince Alberic (932–54), Octavian, who had already been installed as the temporal ruler of Rome, upon his election to the papacy changed his too-imperial name to John XII (955–64), presumably in order to present himself in a more traditional fashion. The usurper Franco, a perpetual candidate of the Crescenzian faction (antipope in 974 and 984–85), apparently hoped to improve his status by styling himself Boniface VII. Peter of Pavia, an imperial appointee, preferred to reign as John XIV (983–84), perhaps because he lacked the hubris to become Peter II. With these precedents in front of them, imperial papal candidates began to assume new names, but if their goal had been simply to replace exotic foreign names with more typically Roman ones, then they would not have favored Late Antique names that no popes had borne for centuries. When Bruno became Gregory V (996–99) and Gerbert became Sylvester II (999–1003), their names recalled predecessors associated with the remaking of Rome. The next name changers were local men. Bishop Peter of Albano, the last Crescenzian pope, became Sergius IV (1009–1012), again avoiding Peter II. The

---

63. Reinhard Elze "Das *Sacrum Palatium Lateranense* im 10. und 11. Jahrhundert," *Studi gregoriani* 4 (1952): 27–54; Herrmann, *Tuskulanerpapsttum*, 23–24; Hans-Henning Kortüm, *Zur päpstlichen Urkundensprache im Frühen Mittelalter: Die päpstlichen Privilegien, 896–1046* (Sigmaringen: Jan Thorbecke, 1995), 385–87, 396–423; Blumenthal, "Papacy, 1024–1122," 17–20; Cristina Carbonelli Vendittelli, "I supporti scrittorii della documentazione: L'uso del papiro," in *L'héritage byzantine en Italia (VIIIᵉ–XIIᵉ siècle)*, vol. 1, *La fabrique documentaire*, ed. Jean-Marie Martin, Annick Peters-Custot, and Vivien Prigent (Rome: ÉFR, 2011), 33–48, esp. 37 and 45.

Tuscolan popes all dropped their Greekish family names: Theophylact became Benedict VIII (1012–44), his brother Romanus became John XIX (1024–32), and a nephew Theophylact became Benedict XIX (1032–44, 1045, 1047–48). The new papal names after the Tuscolaners are clearly programmatic. Potential popes must have studied their ecclesiastical history thoroughly since it would have been hard to find a more impressive list of early popes than those who had first borne the names chosen by Sylvester III (1045), Gregory VI (1045–46), Clement II (1046–49), Damasus II (1048), and Leo IX (1049–54). The new papal names proclaimed clearly that Rome was not just one more imperial bishopric.[64]

Great Secular Lords and Patrons

Also wielding power over the Church were great lay lords, the elite of "those who fight," the arms bearers who possessed extensive lands and castles. Scholars are not sure how to label this secular elite. It might appear to be a high nobility, but that designation can be challenged if nobility is defined technically as a privileged legal status conveyed by blood. The Latin West would ultimately possess such a nobility, a broad caste, defined by feudal laws, that included everyone from the simplest knights to the greatest lords. In the tenth and eleventh centuries, however, while there were people obviously advantaged by birth—such as relatives of emperors and kings, members of long illustrious lineages, and hereditary holders of former Carolingian offices—their class had not yet been legally defined. Moreover, their status was not shared by lesser armigerous folk such as simple household knights or mercenaries employed by churchmen to meet their military obligations. What can be said is that in the millennial Church there were great lords whose family connections, alliances, and properties marked them as socially elite. These lords often chose to express their status through ecclesiastical patronage.[65]

Theologically it is not obvious why great lay lords and ladies should have been great ecclesiastical powers. They were not anointed like kings. They lacked the holy orders of deacons, priests, and bishops. They took no monastic vows to separate themselves from and above the world (except perhaps on their deathbeds as a form of supernatural life insurance). They did take matrimonial vows, but these would require more

64. Kelly and Walsh, *Oxford Dictionary of Popes*, 127–48.

65. Duggan, ed., *Nobles and Nobility in Medieval Europe: Concepts, Origins, and Transformations* (Rochester, NY: Boydell & Brewer, 2000), esp. 1–24, 43–84; Constance Brittain Bouchard, *"Those of My Blood": Constructing Noble Families in Medieval Francia* (Philadelphia: University of Pennsylvania Press, 2001), 13–38; David Crouch, *The Birth of Nobility: Constructing Aristocracy in England and France, 900–1300* (Harlow, UK: Longman, 2005), esp. 2–4, 232–48.

pastoral and legal refinement before they would be recognized as an unmitigated good. Moreover, the life of the arms bearers was spiritually hazardous: membership in a military elite stained them with violence; familial continuity required sexual activity; courtly life presupposed elaborate material trappings. It would be hard to find people more anchored to the world.

Yet, in contrast to the earlier historiography on the Gregorian Reform, these secular elites are now seen less as the enemies of the Church than as its great supporters.[66] In the aftermath of the invasions they rebuilt ruined churches and built new ones. They commissioned the great abbots who reformed and founded monasteries. They worked with ecclesiastical authorities to promote the Peace of God and the Truce of God. They gave not only estates to the Church but even their own children, who were offered to serve as future bishops, canons, monks, and nuns. Not least among these elite patrons were well-educated and important laywomen.[67] Women were the recipients of much of the surviving tenth- and eleventh-century pious literature directed toward laypeople, including the explication of the Antichrist by Adso of Montier-en-Der,[68] an explanation of contemplation and other topics by John of Fécamp,[69] spiritual exhortations from Gregory VII,[70] the prayer collection of Anselm of Lucca,[71] and the two prayer collections of Anselm of Canterbury.[72] Lords and ladies could develop their interior spirituality in their own private chapels: "Whoever has an *oratorium* in his house is able to pray there," notes the

66. Contrast Émile Amann and Auguste Dumas, *L'Église au pouvoir des laïques (888–1057)*, vol. 7 of *Histoire de l'Église depuis les origines jusqu'à nos jours*, ed. Augustin Fliche and Victor Martin (1940, repr., Paris: Bloud & Gay, 1948), with John Howe, "Nobility's Reform," 317–39; Bouchard, *"Strong of Body, Brave and Noble": Chivalry and Society in Medieval France* (Ithaca: Cornell University Press, 1998), 145–71; and Wollasch, "Monasticism," in *NCMH* 3:163–83, esp. 163–65.

67. Johanna Maria van Winter, "The Education of the Daughters of the Nobility in the Ottonian Empire," and Petty Bange, "The Image of Women in the Nobility in the German Chronicles of the Tenth and Eleventh Centuries," in Davids, *Empress Theophano*, 86–98 and 150–68, esp. 162–65.

68. Adso, *De Ortu et Tempore Antichristi* prol. (*Epistola ad Gerbergam*), ed. Daniel Verhelst, *CCCM* 45:20–137, esp. 20–21.

69. John of Fécamp, *Meditatio* (perhaps sent to Empress Agnes between 1063 and 1064): for this version of the text, see André Wilmart, "Formes successive ou paralleles des 'Meditations de saint Augustin,'" *Revue d'ascétique et de mystique* 17 (1936): 335–57, contextualized in Philippe de Vial, introduction to *Jean de Fécamp: La Confession Théologique* (Paris: Cerf, 1992), 16–17; and Rachel Fulton, *From Judgment to Passion*, 155–70 and esp. 522–23.

70. Kathleen G. Cushing, "*Pueri, Iuvenes,* and *Viri*: Age and Utility in the Gregorian Reform," *CHR* 94 (2008): 435–49, esp. 436–37.

71. Wilmart, "Cinq textes de prière composés par Anselme de Lucques pour la comtesse Mathilde," *Revue d'ascétique et de mystique* 19 (1938): 23–72.

72. Fulton, *From Judgement to Passion*, 146–50, with additional reflections on his correspondence with women, 240–43; Vaughn, *St. Anselm and the Handmaidens of God: A Study of Anselm's Correspondence with Women* (Turnhout, Belg.: Brepols, 2002), esp. 2–4, 18–19.

Romano-German Pontifical, which associates private chapels with private prayer and requires explicit episcopal permission to hold public ceremonies in them.[73]

Great lords "owned" many churches. They oversaw private churches that their families had constructed with their own resources on their own estates (theoretically each church's property had been donated to its patron saint). They also could become guardians and "advocates" of preexisting episcopal and monastic churches, especially after 888, when major churches that the Carolingians had formerly protected suddenly found themselves in need of new allies and patrons. What ecclesiastical powers did lords wield? In their private foundations they could usually select the priest or abbot or abbess (though the bishop had the right to approve any priest); in public churches for which nobles had become advocates their power had to be reconciled with earlier traditions of election, but patrons normally had great influence. They received prayers, distinguished places at services, and perhaps burial rights. They might also gain some material profits.[74]

What were the earthly perquisites of patronage? The tithe revenues of churches could be substantial, but in theory they were divided into quarters allocated to the priest, the bishop, the poor, and the fabric of the church—a patron might hope to pocket that last share, but ambitious building projects could quickly consume it. Patrons probably did get some share. Charters in the tenth and early eleventh century mention tithes that had been donated, alienated, and returned, thus indicating that they had become linked to the properties that paid them and probably somehow enriched the owners. Laws recognized owners' rights to retain for their private churches a share of the tithes that would otherwise have been passed on to the titular mother church.[75] Perhaps the ancillary profits were significant: revenue could be generated from building programs, markets, tolls, poor relief, and other church-related economic activities. Indirect benefits might include literate clerks to grace retinues and write charters, schooling for children, and perhaps even medical expertise. There could be legal advantages: churchmen who could write histories and charters were able to help their patrons construct a useful past that could document their

73. *Pontificale Romano-Germanicum* xxxvii, Vogel and Elze, 1:123.

74. Giuseppe Sergi, *L'aristocrazia della preghiera: Politica e scelte religiose nel medioevo italiano* (Rome: Donzelli, 1994), 3–29; Susan Wood, *Proprietary Church*, esp. 339–418; Jones, "Noble Lord, Good Shepherd," 84–86.

75. Michel Lauwers, "Pour une histoire de la dîme et du Dominium ecclésial," in Lauwers, *La Dîme, l'Église*, 11–64, esp. 32–33, and other studies in this volume, esp. 97–99, 230, and 282; Wood, *Proprietary Church*, 486–595.

estates, alliances, and inheritance arrangements in the face of rival claims. No small benefit would have been the "voluntary" loans that hard-pressed patrons might receive from their churches during times of crisis.[76]

Of course, the ostensible reasons for ecclesiastical patronage were spiritual. The opening lines of charters often state that the donors have chosen to sacrifice some transitory goods now in the hope of securing eternal salvation in the future.[77] Most tenth- and eleventh-century documents do not actually request specific prayers for specific beneficiaries, but prayers were certainly expected. They established alliances between the clerks who prayed and the groups and individuals who supported them.[78] Prayers might seek benefits in this life, such as military success.[79] The Romano-German pontifical includes a Mass to be offered "for the intentions of the founder [*in agenda conditoris aecclesiae*]."[80] More commonly the emphasis is on the afterlife, promoted by the Cluniac emphasis on prayers for the dead.[81] Spiritual alliances could be enhanced by special remembrances, such as an annual founder's feast, perhaps subsidized by a donated fish pond that would ensure a festive table.[82] Wealthy people were able to hedge their bets by supporting both reformers and old entrenched establishments. In late Anglo-Saxon England, for example, of the ten wills written between 970 and 1070 that include bequests to monasteries—that is, to the new reformed communities promoted by Dunstan and his circle—eight also remember secular communities.[83]

Lords who were pillars of the Church can be hard to picture. Although elite laymen and laywomen were often literate,[84] it was a mark of their social status that they themselves rarely wrote: they had clerks to read

---

76. Eldevik, *Episcopal Power*, 267; Wood, *Proprietary Church*, esp. 729–829.

77. H. E. J. Cowdrey, "Unions and Confraternity with Cluny," *JEH* 16 (1965): 152–62; Bull, *Knightly Piety*, 157–66; Constable, *Abbey of Cluny*, 6–8.

78. Rosenwein, *Rhinoceros Bound*, esp. 107–10; Rosenwein, *To Be the Neighbor of St. Peter*, esp. 202; Henriet, *La parole et la prière*, 40–45, 81–83, and 145.

79. Katherine Allen Smith, *War and the Making of Medieval Monastic Culture* (Woodbridge: Boydell, 2011), 28–38.

80. *Pontificale Romano-Germanicum* clxvii, Vogel and Elze, 2:321–22.

81. Franz Schmid and Joachim Wollasch, eds., *Memoria: Der geschichtliche Zeugniswert des liturgischen Gedenkens im Mittelalter* (Munich: Wilhelm Fink, 1984), esp. 200–14, 215–32; Tellenbach, *Church in Western Europe*, 101–9; Vauchez, *Spirituality*, 56; Constable, "The Commemoration of the Dead in the Early Middle Ages," in Smith, *Early Medieval Rome*, 169–95.

82. McLaughlin, *Consorting with Saints: Prayer for the Dead in Early Medieval* France (Ithaca: Cornell University Press, 1994), 151–57.

83. John Blair, "Introduction: From Minster to Parish Church," in Blair, *Minsters and Parish Churches*, 1–19, esp. 6; Blair, *Church in Anglo-Saxon Society*, 407–9.

84. David Bachrach, *Warfare in Tenth-Century Germany*, 10 and 102–34; Michael T. Clanchy, *From Memory to Written Record: England 1066–1307*, 3rd ed. (Oxford: Wiley-Blackwell, 2013), esp. 23–35, 233–54.

FIGURE 34. Secular lord at the altar with his entourage, his hand gesture mirroring the deacon's. Benedictional of Engilmar of Parenzo (Regensburg, c. 1030–40). Los Angeles, The J. Paul Getty Museum MS Ludwig VI, fol. 16r. Digital image courtesy of the Getty Museum's Open Content Program.

and write for them and priests to expound their scriptures. A clerical filter separates them from us, and they are lost to us if we believe that they were simple sheep, incapable of independent agency. Yet the surviving documents are so remarkably consistent that it is hard to believe that laypeople disagreed with them and yet continued to donate their lands and children to the Church. Scholars have begun to claim to be able to "hear the authentic voice of a wide swathe of the Carolingian elite" in regard to values and sanctity and have found echoes of it in the tenth century.[85]

85. Noble, "Secular Sanctity: Forging an Ethos for the Carolingian Nobility," and Scott Ashley, "The Lay Intellectual in Anglo-Saxon England: Ealdorman Aethelweard and the Politics of History," in *Lay Intellectuals in the Carolingian World*, ed. Patrick Wormald and Nelson (Cambridge: Cambridge University Press, 2007), 8–36, esp. 26, and 218–45, esp. 232–39. See also Julia Smith, "Religion and Lay Society," in *NCMH* 2, ed. McKitterick, 654–78.

What can be heard is largely a spirituality of action, which is just what one might expect in a world where sermons exhort monks to seek God and laymen to behave better. Among the ways cited for laymen to enter more closely into the community of Christ are donating property to churches, going on pilgrimages, participating in ecclesiastical initiatives such as the movements for the Peace of God and Truce of God, and fighting against the Church's enemies. The arms bearers' spirituality is illustrated in a com-memoration of "Blessed Count Ansfrid" of Brabant (d. 1010), made by Alp-ert of Metz around 1021–23:

> As count in Brabant, Ansfrid was characterized by such high standards that he could not be turned from the correct path either by money or by gifts. His views generally were considered first in both councils and assemblies. Everyone carefully reviewed whatever he said. Ansfrid himself issued legal judgments that no one, in justice, could oppose. His manner of life was so tempered by moderation and discretion that it was said of our count that though he excelled "he did nothing in excess." . . .
>
> He was received frequently by the king, and was held more dearly than others. Ansfrid united even faithless men with his words, and governed the state with peace. . . .
>
> When Bishop Baldwin of Utrecht died, and a messenger arrived in camp, the king took Ansfrid by the hand and offered the bishopric to him. . . . Ans-frid, realizing that he could not resist the king, asked that he be given a chance to discuss the matter with his own men. When Ansfrid had spoken to them about this, and they had agreed, he promised that he would do what the king had ordered. Ansfrid then took up the sword with which he was girded, and placed it on the altar of St. Mary saying: "Up until this time I have obtained earthly honors with this sword. I have driven out the enemies of Christ's poor, and of widows. Now I commend it to my Lady Saint Mary by whose strength I shall gain honor and the salvation of my soul.[86]

Great Abbots and Abbesses

Wulfstan's description of the orders of the Church segues directly from mag-nates to Mass priests, but he would have conformed better to his general trajectory of proceeding from the greatest to the least had he placed his short section on abbots and abbesses here, right after the secular elite. His deci-sion to discuss them later, in the same place as their communities, receives some support from the Benedictine Rule, which condemns "all exaltation" as "a sign of pride" and forbids distinctions between noble and nonnoble, slave

---

86. Alpertus of Metz, *De Diversitate Temporum*, I xi–xii, ed. Hans van Rij, *Alpertus Mettensis: De Diversi-tate Temporum et Fragmentum de Deoderico Primo Episcopo Mettensi* (Amsterdam: Verlorum, 1980), 22–27, trans. David Bachrach, *Warfare and Politics in Medieval Germany ca. 1000: On the Variety of Our Times by Alpert of Metz* (Toronto: PIMS, 2012), 21–24.

and free.[87] Yet Wulfstan seems to recognize that abbots and abbesses were actually part of the elite when he exhorts them to reside in their houses, oversee their flocks, set good examples, preach rightly, and "never ... be concerned too greatly nor all too frequently with wordly cares or idle vanity."[88] In reality they lived above rather than within their religious communities: their commands were to be obeyed "immediately, as if the order were from heaven"; they appointed all monastic officials; they were unilaterally able to suspend the rules for children, the sick, the weak, the old, basically for anyone; they dined at high tables where guests could be received and monastic fasts dispensed.[89] The abbot was not to be addressed as "Brother," but, "because he acts in Christ's place, he should always be addressed as 'Lord' and 'Abbot.'"[90] True, the abbot was enjoined to "strive to be more loved than feared" and some reformers did try to reduce the gap between the leader and the community.[91] Yet that distance could never completely disappear because abbots and abbesses were the ones with supreme authority.

They were also powers to be reckoned with in the greater world. Monasteries and convents could acquire enormous landholdings, and, despite some despoliation by the ascending Carolingians, they had become well integrated into the Frankish political system. Important abbots and abbesses were courtiers on the scale of bishops and magnates. They too might owe hospitality, court duties, and military contingents.[92] Many were aristocrats by birth and, though this was officially deplored, by comportment.[93] Like bishops, they had their own thrones.[94] Some even secured limited papal approval to wear episcopal-style vestments within their own communities; these included some great abbesses who at home could don a miter and wield a crosier.[95]

---

87. Benedict, *Regula* ii, vii, lix, Venarde, 22–23, 44–45, 192–93.

88. *Institutes of Polity* xiii (or xi), Jost, 122–23, Rabin, *Political Writings*, 118–19.

89. Benedict, *Regula* v, xvii, xxxvi–xxxvii, xxxix, xlviii, lii, lvi, lxv, Venarde, 38–39, 106–9, 130–33, 138–39, 162–63, 172–75, 182–83, 210–13. Of course the rule's grant of nearly absolute authority to the abbot was no guarantee that in reality he could always wield it: see Patzold, *Konflikte im Kloster: Studien zu Auseinandersetzungen in monastischen Gemeinschaften des ottonisch-salischen Reichs* (Husum: Matthiesen Verlag, 2000).

90. Benedict, *Regula* lxiii, Venarde, 204–5.

91. Benedict, *Regula* lxiv, Venarde, 208–9; Josef Semmler, "Die Beschlüsse des Aachener Konzils im Jahre 816," *Zeitschrift für Kirchengeschichte* 74 (1963): 15–82, esp. 40–49.

92. Hans-Peter Wehlt, *Reichsabtei und König dargestellt am Beispiel der Abtei Lorsch mit Ausblicken auf Hersfeld, Stablo und Fulda* (Göttingen: Vandenhoeck & Ruprecht, 1970), 74–123; Thomas Vogtherr, *Die Reichsabteien der Benediktiner und das Königtum im hohen Mittelalter* (Stuttgart: Jan Thorbecke, 2000), 153–269.

93. Katherine Smith, *War and the Making of Medieval Monastic Culture*, 42–57.

94. Hans-Werner Goetz, "Das Bild des Abtes in alamannischen Klosterchroniken des hohen Mittelalters," in Berg and Goetz, *Ecclesia et Regnum*, 139–53.

95. Pierre Salmon, *Étude sur les insignes du pontife dans le rite romain: Histoire et liturgie* (Rome: Officium Libri Catholici, 1955), 49–63.

Abbesses were fewer than abbots and often presided over more vulnerable establishments, some of which vanished or were reestablished as male houses during the chaos of the late ninth and early tenth centuries. From the mid-tenth century on, however, and perhaps slightly earlier in Germany, many new women's houses appeared.[96] These were often aristocratic private convents, some of whose charters specified that the abbess must be a member of the founding family.[97] Those supported by kings (perhaps actually by queens) could be grand places, such as the Italian royal nunnery of San Salvatore at Brescia, the seven great Wessex-centered royal convents, and German imperial houses of canonesses such as those at Gandersheim, Essen, and Quedlinburg.[98] Great abbesses could be very powerful, not least when they offered top-level schools for aristocratic children or hosted itinerant royal courts.

A religious community that governed significant territories within a diocese might encounter jurisdictional problems with its bishop. The abbot of Cluny, for example, was far more famous and wealthy than his theoretical superior, the bishop of Mâcon, and even though Cluny at its foundation had been placed under the symbolic protection of St. Peter, throughout the tenth and eleventh centuries its abbots were often petitioning Rome to secure or enhance Cluniac freedoms.[99] Fleury waged a similar battle when in 1007 the bishop of Orléans ordered its submission, prompting a full-scale fight in which many bishops opposed Abbot Gauzlinus, three popes fought to vindicate St. Peter's right to grant exemptions from episcopal authority, and Fleury finally won but only because

96. Mary Skinner, "Benedictine Life for Women in Central France, 850–1100: A Feminist Revival," in *Medieval Religious Women*, vol. 1, *Distant Echoes*, ed. John A. Nichols and Lillian Thomas Shank (Kalamazoo, MI: Cistercian Publications, 1984), 87–113; Parisse, *Religieux et religieuses*, 126–50, 171–72. However, Foote, *Veiled Women*, esp. 2:1–2, locates the proliferation of English convents in the post-Conquest period.

97. Parisse, *Les nonnes au Moyen Âge* (Le Puy: Christine Bonneton, 1983), 116–20, 131, and his *Religieux et religieuses*, 127–31, 153–55. For a genealogy of Ottonian abbesses of royal monasteries, see Van Winter, "Education of the Daughters," 86–98, esp. 87–90.

98. Susan F. Wemple, "S. Salvatore/S. Giuliae: A Case Study in the Endowment and Patronage of a Major Female Monastery in Northern Italy," in *Women of the Medieval World: Essays in Honor of John H. Mundy*, ed. Julius Kirshner and Wemple (Oxford: Blackwell, 1985), 85–102; Barbara Yorke, *Nunneries and Their West-Saxon Royal Houses* (New York: Continuum, 2003), 72–79, 80–92; Katrinette Bodarwé, *Sanctimoniales Litteratae: Schriftlichkeit und Bildung in den ottonischen Frauenkommunitäten Gandersheim, Essen und Quedlinburg* (Münster: Aschendorff, 2004), esp. 15–74; Giancarlo Andenna, "San Salvatore di Brescia e la scelta religiosa delle donne aristocratiche tra età langobarda ed età franca (VIII–IX secolo)," in *Female Vita Religiosa between Late Antiquity and the High Middle Ages: Structures, Developments, and Spatial Contexts*, ed. Gert Melville and Anne Müller (Berlin: LIT, 2011), 209–33. On queens as the special patrons of nunneries, see Simon MacLean, "Monastic Reform and Royal Ideology in the Late Tenth Century: Aelfthryth and Edgar in Continental Perspective," in Rollason et al., *England and the Continent*, 255–74, esp. 260–62.

99. Cowdrey, *The Cluniacs and the Gregorian Reform* (Oxford: Clarendon, 1970), 1–63; Constable, "Cluny and Rome," in Constable, *Abbey of Cluny*, 19–41.

FIGURE 35. Ecclesiastical elites, a bishop and an abbot await heavenly judgment. *Liber Vitae of* New Minster (Hyde), Winchester (ca. 1031). ©The British Library Board: BL MS Stow 944, fol. 6v.

Gauzlinus became the bishop of Orléans.[100] Struggles for monastic exemption from episcopal control were far from universal.[101] Nevertheless, when tenth- and eleventh-century abbots did appeal to Rome against their bishops, the result was to expand papal power at the expense of the local diocesans, not only in the particular cases at issue but also in the broader court of public opinion when monks such as Abbo of Fleury became motivated to write justifications for papal outreach.[102]

100. *Vita Gauzlini* I xviii–xxi, Bautier and Labory, 50–63 and 154–57 (two related letters of Fulbert of Chartres, which equal Fulbert, *Epist.* vii and viii, Behrends, 16–22).

101. Tellenbach, *Church in Western Europe*, 114–18; Jones, "Noble Lord, Good Shepherd," 142–43.

102. Louis-Marie Gantier, *L'abrégé du* Liber Pontificalis *d'Abbon de Fleury (vers 950–1004): Une histoire des papes, en l'an mil* (Brussels: Nauwelaerts, 2004), esp. 194. See Mostert, *Political Theology of Abbo of*

FIGURE 36. A noble canoness with her brother, Abbess Matilda of Essen, in aristocratic dress, and her brother Duke Otto, depicted in an enamel plaque affixed to a cross they donated to Essen between 971 and 982. Essen Cathedral Treasury.
Image courtesy of Wikipedia Commons.

Such quarrels helped prepare the way for the more activist papacy of the Gregorian Reform.

HINGE PEOPLE

There was a gap between the ecclesiastical elites described above and "those who work," the peasant farmers with varying degrees of legal

---

Fleury, 127–33; Pierre Riché, *Abbon de Fleury: Un moine savant et combatif (vers 950–1004)* (Turnhout, Belg.: Brepols, 2004), 171–73; Dachowski, *First among Abbots,* 110–24 and 151–72.

freedom who constituted the overwhelming majority of the population. Hinge persons were needed to join the literate culture of the elites to the little traditions of the villagers. Among those who connected the ecclesiastical leadership to the people were the secular priests who staffed the new parish churches; those professional religious—including canons, canonesses, monks, and nuns—whose lives had points of tangency, direct or indirect, with the care of souls; and pious laymen and laywomen who traveled in clerical circles and involved themselves in liturgy and learning.

Secular Priests

The parish priest brought the Church to the people. He represented his bishop, who was becoming more distant as episcopal obligations increased. The parish priest oversaw the local church, the village's most impressive structure, perhaps its only stone building. He conducted the Sunday services. He baptized the children, except in a few regions (notably in Italy) where baptisteries or baptismal churches still functioned. He blessed marriages and anointed the dying. He administered penance, although the most notorious cases were reserved for the bishop.[103] His cosmic importance was summarized by Peter Damian:

> No mortal man, as I see it, performs greater deeds in relation to God's sacraments than these very men who are secular priests. It is true, of course, that patriarchs and metropolitans and all bishops . . . perform other functions that pertain especially to their privileged status. But neither a bishop, nor chrism, nor anything else in the Church's sacraments is greater than the Body and Blood of the Savior. Priests, therefore, participate in the episcopal dignity in those things which within the Church are of the highest and most sublime value. . . . These very men, who in some matters are inferior, are in things of higher value found to be equal.[104]

Despite this theoretical dignity, parish priests labored in obscurity. Early medieval secular priests were rarely honored as saints. In the village the priest was the person with the widest connections, unless there happened to be an estate manager in residence or a castle nearby, but the village was a very, very small place. Parish communities were minuscule by

---

103. Michel Aubrun, "Le clergé rural dans le royaume franc du IVe au XIIe siècle," in *Le clergé rural dans l'Europe medieval et modern: Actes des XIIIe Journées internationales d'Histoire de l'Abbaye de Flaran, 6–8 septembre 1991*, ed. Pierre Bonnassie (Toulouse: Presses universitaires de Mirail, 1995), 15–27; Alan Thacker, "Priests and Pastoral Care in Early Anglo-Saxon England," in *The Study of Medieval Manuscripts of England: Festschrift in Honor of Richard W. Pfaff*, ed. George Hardin Brown and Linda Ehrsam Voigts (Tempe: Arizona Center for Medieval and Renaissance Studies, 2010), 187–208, esp. 187–190; Tinti, *Sustaining Belief*, 280–314; Charles Mériaux, *Vitae presbyterorum: Remarques sur quelques Vies de prêtres ruraux du haut Moyen Âge*, in *Normes et hagiographie dans l'Occident (IVe–XVIe siécle): Actes du colloque international de Lyon 4–6 octobre 2010*, ed. Marie-Cécile Isaïa and Thomas Granier, Hagiologia 9 (Turnhout, Belg.: Brepols, 2014), 363–78.

104. Peter Damian, *Epist.* xlvii, Reindel, 2:43–51, esp. 47, Blum, 2:252–62, esp. 256.

today's standards, perhaps one hundred to three hundred people, although sizes varied greatly by region, locality, and the peculiarities of the local geography.[105] Parish priests took no vows of poverty,[106] but no rich man would have gained his overlord's or his society's approval to serve as a simple priest. The distance from the elite Church is suggested by the recurring debate over whether, and if so under what circumstances and preconditions, a bishop could ordain a candidate who was not legally free.[107] Most priests were probably local men who were not greatly distinguished from their village neighbors.

Yet reformers considered it abusive if priests lived "in the manner of laymen [*more laicorum*]," and they advocated a higher standard of life for them, more congruent with the emphasis on the real presence of Christ within the Eucharist.[108] Canon law required that a priest be at least thirty years old, but this provision was not consistently followed.[109] Ideally he would be distinguished by being unarmed, clean shaven, and tonsured.[110] He was expected to wear some sort of ecclesiastical garment, at least when in church.[111] He was not allowed to perform as a minstrel in taverns, presumably to avoid cognitive dissonance when he sang his Masses.[112] Sexual purity established a degree of separation, at least in theory. Merovingian and Carolingian conciliar legislation emphasized clerical continence; popes continually reaffirmed it.[113] Nevertheless, in many regions clerical

---

105. Genicot, *Rural Communities*, 10–11, 94.

106. Godding, *Prêtres en Gaule mérovingienne*, 349–52.

107. Ibid., 85–90; Patzold, *Episcopus*, 122; Barrow, *Clergy*, 337.

108. Rosser, "Cure of Souls in English Towns," in Blair and Sharpe, *Pastoral Care before the Parish*, esp. 280. Quotation from Desiderius, *Dialogi* III prol., ed. Schwartz and Hofmeister, MGH *SS*, 30(2): 1141.

109. Godding, *Prêtres en Gaule mérovingienne*, 32–49; Patzold, *Episcopus*, 121. However, see Thietmar, *Chronicon* VII 11, Holtzmann, 398–99, Warner 308, who despairs that "because we have not maintained this, we are wretched sinners."

110. On armed priests, see Rather, *Epist.* xxv (to the clergy of Verona in 996), Weigle, 131, Reid, 448. While Wulfstan, *Canons of Edgar* ¶ 46, in Whitelock et al., *Councils & Synods*, 329, Rabin, *Political Writings*, 95, claims that " it is right that no mass-priest come within the church doors while armed," Aelfric, *Epistola de Canonibus* ¶ 80, Whitelock et al., *Councils & Synods*, 191–226, esp. 212, wants the priest never to bear arms. On bearded priests, see Constable, "Beards in History," in *Apologiae Duae: Gozechini Epistola ad Walcherum; Burchardi, ut Videtur, Abbatis Bellevallis Apologiae de Barbis*, ed. R. B. C. Huyghens, CCCM 62 (Turnhout, Belg.: Brepols, 1985), 74–150; Wulfstan, *Canons of Edgar* (1005–1008), ¶ 47, Whitelock et al., *Councils & Synods*, 313–88, esp. 330, Rabin, *Political Writings*, 95. On the tonsure, see Louis Trichet, *La tonsure: Vie et mort d'une pratique ecclésiastique* (Paris: Cerf, 1990); Godding, *Prêtres en Gaule mérovingienne*, 23–27.

111. Rather, *Epistola* (to the clergy of Verona in 996) xxv, Weigle, 133, Reid, 449; Wulfstan, *Canons of Edgar*" ¶ 47, Whitelock et al., *Councils & Synods*, 313–88, esp. 330, Rabin, *Political Writings*, 95.

112. Wulfstan, *Canons of Edgar* ¶ 59, Whitelock et al., *Councils & Synods*, 313–38, esp. 333, Rabin, *Political Writings*, 97; "The Northumbrian Priests' Law" ¶ 41, Whitelock et al., *Councils & Synods*, 460, Rabin, *Political Writings*, 202.

113. Gabriella Rossetti, "Il matrimonio del clero nella società altomedievale," in *Il matrimonio nella società altomedievale, 22–28 aprile 1976*, 2 vols. Settimane di studio del CISAM 24(1–2) (Spoleto: CISAM,

families appear, attested by documents whose information may under-state their numbers, given that official disapproval ought to have discour-aged their public display.[114] This disjunction between theory and practice bothered people, leading to campaigns against clerical marriage that were under way in millennial popular and legal circles long before the Grego-rian Reform.[115]

Could better education have improved the priesthood? Peter Damian complains that "there are priests who are now so deficient in education that not only do they not understand what they read, but can hardly stammer syllable by syllable through the parts of a clause. And so, what does he ask for the people in his prayers if, like a foreigner, he does not understand what he is saying?"[116] One way to attempt to avoid such prob-lems, a procedure sporadically followed from Late Antiquity, was to give a formal examination to prospective priests.[117] Yet what results could a bishop expect in a world where candidates had unsystematically prepared themselves by serving as acolytes, by assisting priests who were often their uncles or even fathers, and at best by studying for some unspecified period in cathedral or monastic schools? Rather of Liège (d. 974), who was notoriously strict, warned that he would not ordain any candidates "unless they have lived for a time in our city [Verona] or in some monas-tery or at the house of some wise man, and are educated in letters a little so that they seem suitable for the ecclesiastical dignity." He wanted them to be able to recite the canon of the Mass from memory, to pronounce

---

1977), 1:473–567, esp. 473–542; Godding, *Prêtres en Gaule mérovingienne*, 111–54; Mayke De Jong, "*Imitatio Morum*: The Cloister and Clerical Purity in the Carolingian World," in Frassetto, *Medieval Purity and Piety*, 49–80. For late Carolingian concerns, see the Council of Trosly (909) *Capitula viiii*, ed. Wilfried Hartmann, Isolde Schröder, and Gerhard Schmitz, MGH *Concilia* V (Hannover: Hahn, 2012), 497–562, esp. 535–41. Papal policy is described in Georg Denzler, *Das Papsttum und der Amtszölibat*, 2 vols. (Stuttgart: Anton Hiersemann, 1973–76), 1:25–50.

114. Anne Llewellyn Barstow, *Married Priests and the Reforming Papacy: The Eleventh-Century Debate* (New York: Edwin Mellen, 1982), 31–45 and 105–55. Regional and local examples include Toubert, *Struc-tures du Latium médiéval*, 1:779–84 (re Lazio); Rossetti, "Matrimonio del clero," in *Il matrimonio nella so-cietà altomedievale*, 1:542–50 (re Lucca); Miller, *Formation of a Medieval Church*, 96–97 (re Verona); Éric Thoreau-Girault, "L'Usage napolitain du célibat ecclésiastique (XIe-XIIe siècle)," in Puer Apuliae: *Mélanges offerts à Jean-Marie Martin*, ed. Errico Cuozzo, Vincent Déroche, Annick Peters-Custot, and Vivien Prigent, 2 vols. (Paris: Association des amis du Centre d'histoire et civilisation de Byzance, 2008), 653–60 (re Naples); Barrow, *Clergy*, 139–47 and 345 (re England).

115. Johannes Laudage, *Priesterbild und Reformpapsttum im 11. Jahrhundert* (Cologne: Böhlau, 1984), 52–122; Amy G. Remensnyder, "Pollution, Purity, and Peace: An Aspect of Social Reform between the Late Tenth Century and 1076," in Head and Landes, *Peace of God*, 280–307, esp. 28–94; Phyllis G. Jestice, "Why Celibacy? Odo of Cluny and the Development of a New Sexual Morality," in Frassetto, *Medieval Purity and Piety*, 81–115; Kathleen G. Cushing, *Reform and the Papacy in the Eleventh Century: Spirituality and Social Change* (Manchester, UK: Manchester University Press, 2005), 98–99.

116. Peter Damian, *Epist.* 47, Reindel, 2:43–51, esp. 44, Blum, 2:252–62, esp. 252–53.

117. Godding, *Prêtres en Gaule mérovingienne*, 94–95.

the Psalms correctly, to conduct various rituals, to explain the Our Father, and to recite from memory the Apostles' Creed, the Nicene Creed, and the Athanasian Creed.[118] An early eleventh-century English text, "On the Examination of Candidates for Ordination," requires a would-be priest to spend a month with his bishop (at his own expense) during which time he should demonstrate his ability to explain the true faith, priestly ministry, baptism, and the symbolism of the Mass. In addition he should demonstrate some knowledge of the canons and the computus—"If he then knows too little of these things, he is first to learn, and afterwards receive orders."[119] A more positive approach than the examination system is the collections of homilies and saints' lives assembled by Aelfric (d. ca. 1010), in both Latin and English, written to teach and inform the preachers of his day and their lay audiences.[120] Perhaps reformers were more motivated to deplore clerical ignorance than to praise competent priests. Handbook and reference materials suggest that, at least in the Carolingian era, there were priests who could handle Church law with some facility, and Bishop Burchard of Worms (d. 1025) tried to assemble his *Decretum* of authoritative and harmonious canons so that priests without legal training would be able to use it.[121]

Monks and Nuns, Canons and Canonesses

Monks and nuns, canons and canonesses all seem improbable hinge persons inasmuch as their lives were defined by withdrawal from the world. In fact, when the early twelfth-century anonymous author of the *Libellus de Diversis Ordinibus* was attempting to make sense of monastic diversity, he chose as his central organizing principle the quest for solitude, beginning his analysis with hermits, the holy men who in theory most sought isolation, and ending with the canons, whose ecclesiastical responsibilities most enmeshed them in the world.[122] Yet, whether followers of the religious life were unlettered hermits, choir monks and nuns, canons

---

118. Rather, *Epist.* xxv (to the clergy of Verona in 996), Weigle, 125, Reid, 450.

119. Wulfstan, *On the Examination of Candidates for Ordination* (Bodl. MS Junius 121), fols. 34–35v, in Whitelock et al., *Councils & Synods*, 1, pt. 2, 422–27.

120. Lees, *Tradition and Belief*, esp. 106–32.

121. Patzold, "Bildung und Wissen einer lokalen Elite des Frühmittelalters: Das Beispiel der Landpfarrer im Frankenreich des 9. Jahrhunderts," in Bougard et al., *La culture du haut Moyen Âge*, 377–91; Yitzhak Hen, "Knowledge of Canon Law among Rural Priests: The Evidence of Two Carolingian Manuscripts from around 800," *Journal of Theological Studies*, n.s., 50–51 (1999): 117–34; Austin, "Jurisprudence in the Service of Pastoral Care: The *Decretum* of Burchard of Worms," *Speculum* 79 (2004): 929–59, esp. 937; Austin, *Shaping Church Law*, 81–82.

122. Constable and Bernard Smith, eds., *Libellus de Diversis Ordinibus et Professionibus Qui Sunt in Aecclesia* (Oxford: Clarendon, 1972).

in cathedral chapters dominated by the local gentry, or even wealthy German secular canonesses living in aristocratic communities, their vocations all had some social dimensions. All had to wrestle with the Gospel story of Martha and Mary, who were universally understood as figures of the active and contemplative lives, and to position themselves in regard to those polarities.[123] None could entirely escape the world because family ties would not disappear, lay patrons were needed, and Christianity inherently involved obligations of charity to those in need. Moreover, the insulated community that was the Benedictine ideal proved to be porous in practice: lay tenants lived on monastic estates, laypeople could access at least parts of monastic churches, and, for a variety of reasons, lay visitors were often residing inside monastic compounds.[124]

Spiritual kinship connected choir monks and nuns to a wider world. Prayers for the dead, particularly for departed monastic supporters, proliferated in the ninth century with the reforms of Benedict of Aniane and developed in the tenth century in the reformed tradition of Cluny and other houses. Ceremonies connected with great feasts, donations, oblations, and burials united monks, nuns, and canons with their supporters. Religious professionals were themselves a sacrificial offering, and the families who had offered them as sacrifices presumably participated in their merits.[125]

Professional religious and laypeople were also linked by ecclesiastical material culture. The rich liturgical furnishings and devotional items with which the millennial Church attempted to lead simple souls to God were often produced by monks, nuns, and members of episcopal households. Wulfstan in his *Institutes of Polity* recommends that the bishop himself be involved, and he urges "that those in his service practice crafts, so that indeed no one too idle remain there."[126] Manual labor was such an integral part of the vocation of monks and nuns that not only does the Benedictine Rule require that the monastery be laid out to accommodate "various crafts [*diversas artes*]," but it also unselfconsciously uses craft language when describing all of monasticism's good customs as "the

123. Constable, "The Interpretation of Martha and Mary," in *Three Studies*, 1–141.

124. Rosser, "Cure of Souls in English Towns," 270–74; Constable, "Cluny in the Monastic World of the Tenth Century," in Constable, *Abbey of Cluny*, 67–71.

125. Iogna-Prat, *Agni Immaculati: Recherches sur les sources hagiographiques relatives à Saint Maieul de Cluny (954–994)* (Paris: Cerf, 1988), 319–39; Schmid, "Mönchtum und Verbrüderung," in Kottje and Maurer, *Monastische Reformen*, 117–146; Iogna-Prat, *Order & Exclusion: Cluny and Christendom Face Heresy, Judaism, and Islam (1000–1150)*, trans. Graham Robert Edwards (Ithaca: Cornell University Press, 2002), 219–52; Constable, "Commemoration and Confraternity at Cluny during the Abbacy of Peter the Venerable," in Constable et al., *Die Cluniazenser*, 253–78.

126. Wulfstan, *Institutes of Polity* vii, Jost, 74–77, Rabin, *Political Writings*, 111.

tools of the spiritual craft [*instrumenta artis spiritalis*]" and specifying that "the workshops [*officina*] where we should industriously carry out all this [*omnia diligenter operemur*] are the cloisters of the monastery."[127] Some ritualization and marginalization of manual labor would have resulted from the increases in the time spent on prayer in late Carolingian and Cluniac monasticism, but monks and nuns still managed to keep their hands busy. Nuns produced altar linens, vestments, and manuscripts.[128] Monks handled scribal work, and all its subsidiary technologies. Monastic metal work, already noted in chapter 4 above, may have involved fairly elaborate workshops. Those at Cluny probably produced many of the reliquaries mentioned in the Cluniac customaries, and they were able to convert Henry II's donated gold into chalices in 1014, to process other donations of precious metals in 1016 and before and after 1033, and to fabricate the baldachin for the master altar in 1041.[129] Monte Cassino had skilled metal workers.[130] Monks could even handle architecture: an abbot of Saint-Calais was called in by Fleury after its 1026 fire to direct the rebuilding of the south porch; a monk expert in fresco work was summoned to help with the restoration of the church of Saint-Julien of Tours.[131] On a more prosaic level other brothers apparently worked as general laborers on some of the new monastic buildings.[132] Because monks were *both* literati and manual laborers, their technological creativity could benefit from theory and practice.

The most direct hinge role, however, was pastoral work, which was hazardous for monks to undertake because it placed them in direct competition with their bishop's secular clergy. Although most monks were now ordained priests, monasteries were not supposed to be involved in the *cura animarum*, and even for the many rural churches that they acquired through foundation or donation they were still expected to hire secular priests to officiate. Yet the evidence is clear that monks did do "parish work" on an irregular basis, especially in frontier regions such as the

---

127. Benedict, *Regula* iv, xlviii, lxvi, Venarde, 34–37, 160–63, 214–15.

128. Gameson, *Role of Art in the Late Anglo-Saxon Church*, 252–53: Fiona Griffiths, "'Like the Sister of Aaron': Medieval Religious Women as Makers and Donors of Liturgical Textiles," in Melville and Müller, *Female* Vita Religiosa, 343–74, esp. 348–54. Miller, *Clothing the Clergy*, 141–76, describes the role played by women in general, particularly aristocratic women with resources, in producing clerical regalia, but the specific contributions of nuns remain less well documented.

129. Conant, *Cluny: Les Églises et la maison du chef d'ordre* (Cambridge: Mediaeval Academy of America, 1968), 61.

130. *Chron. Casin.* II lv, Hoffmann, 270.

131. Andrew of Fleury, *Vita Gauzlini* II lxii and lxv, Bautier and Labory, 118–119 and 134–35.

132. Rosemary Cramp, "Anglo-Saxon Sculpture of the Reform Period," in Parsons, *Tenth-Century Studies*, 184–99, esp. 184; Howe, *Church Reform*, 83–84.

mountains of Italy, where invasions and encastellation had scrambled ecclesiastical geography; the mixed Greek and Latin areas of southern Italy; the English countryside, where the previous minster system of pastoral care was disintegrating; and areas in eastern and northern Europe where monasteries could serve as self-sufficient bases for mission work.[133] During the excitement of the Gregorian Reform, monks from Vallombrosa and Hirsau stepped out publicly and became prominent preachers of reform, but for this they were much criticized.[134]

Tenth- and eleventh-century writers often contrasted the contemplative life of monks with the active life of canons.[135] Canons were secular clergymen, often priests affiliated with cathedral or collegiate churches, who in addition to their duties involving the liturgy of the hours might be expected to teach and preach. They followed the Rule of Augustine for common life centered on a church, which had been rewritten in the Frankish world by Chrodegang of Metz (d. 766) and modified again by the Council of Aachen in 816: canons were supposed to live in community but, unlike monks, they could enjoy private property, linen, meat, and a far more generous personal wine allowance.[136] In theory the canons were supervised by their bishops, but in practice colleges of canons could become quite independent, especially if their bishops were outsiders or often absent.[137] Judging from the efforts made by mid-eleventh-century churchmen to reform canonical life, many canons must have been absentee, residing in private homes outside the common cloister, or otherwise inconsistent about their duties.[138] In the early eleventh century, however,

---

133. Toubert, *Structures du Latium médiéval*, 2:900–913: Toubert, "Monachisme et encadrement religieux des campagnes en Italiae aux Xe–XIIe siècles," in *Istituzioni ecclesiastiche*, 416–43, esp. 462–31; Valerie Ramseyer, *The Transformation of a Religious Landscape: Medieval Southern Italy, 850–1150* (Ithaca: Cornell University Press, 2006), 69–71; Rosser, "Cure of Souls in English Towns," 267–84, esp. 270–73; Phyllis G. Jestice, *Wayward Monks and the Religious Revolution of the Eleventh Century* (Leiden, Neth,: Brill, 1997), 44–89.

134. Jestice, *Wayward Monks*, 227–65.

135. Constable, "Interpretation of Martha and Mary," in his *Three Studies*, esp. 35–41 and 78–79.

136. On the texts, see George Lawless, *Augustine of Hippo and His Monastic Rule* (Oxford: Clarendon, 1987); Jerome Bertram, *The Chrodegang Rules: The Rules for the Common Life of the Secular Clergy from the Eighth and Ninth Centuries: Critical Texts with Translations and Commentary* (Burlington, VT: Ashgate, 2005), esp. 84–93. On their applications, see Claussen, *Reform of the Frankish Church*, esp. 206–21; *Frühformen von Stiftskirchen in Europa: Funktion und Wandel religiöser Gemeinschaften vom 6. bis zum Ende des 11. Jahrhunderts. Festgabe für Dieter Mertens zum 65. Geburstag*, ed. Sönke Lorenz and Thomas Zotz (Leinfelden-Echterdingen: DRW-Verlag, 2005), esp. 1–18.

137. Miller, *Bishop's Palace*, 80–85; Jones, "Noble Lord, Good Shepherd," 38–50.

138. Giovanni Miccoli, "Pier Damiani e la vita comune del clero," in *La vita comune del clero nei secoli XI e XII: Atti della Settimana di studio: Mendola, settembre 1959*, 2 vols. (Milan: Vita e Pensiero, 1962), 1:186–219; Tellenbach, *Church in Western Europe*, 120–21; Dieter Hägermann, *Das Papsttum am Vorabend*

stricter communities of reformed canons became leaders in the quest for the "apostolic life."[139]

Canonesses were anomalous. Their communities apparently originated among the pious women, especially widows, who always played an important part in church communities. Some organized under the Rule of Augustine. The Council of Aachen in 816 wrote a rule for canonesses, but their customs were so fluid that observers were sometimes confused about whether particular communities of women were living together *regulariter* (under the Benedictine Rule) or *canonice* (observing some sort of rule for canonesses). In the High Middle Ages, many merged into new religious orders, but some aristocratic secular canonesses, particularly in German lands, chose to live guided instead by their own customs, which might allow private property or even freedom to leave the community.[140]

Professional religious influenced the Church through the examples of their lives. They witnessed an order beyond grubby day-to-day existence, modeling an alternative ideal that proved attractive in a rapidly changing, often morally disquieting world. Ecclesiastical reformers found the monastic ideal especially inspirational. They wanted all priests to live like monks, in celibacy and liturgical good order. They wanted canons to abandon their private property and live in well-ordered quasi-monastic communities. They encouraged elite lay men and women to participate in monastic spirituality insofar as their stations in life permitted.[141] Then suddenly, with the election of Leo IX in 1049, papal authority would be marshaled behind this monastic ideal, and soon actual monks—Gregory VII (1073–85), Victor III (1086–87), and Urban II (1088–1099)—would lead the Church, for better or worse, into the investiture controversy.

---

des Investiturstreits: Stephan IX. (1057–1048), Benedict X. (1958), und Nicholas I. (1058–61) (Stuttgart: Anton Hiersemann, 2008), 69–73.

139. Étienne Delaruelle, "La vie commune des clercs et la spiritualité populaire au XIᵉ siècle," and Maccarrone, "I Papi del secolo XII e la vita comune e regolare del clero," in *Vita comune del clero*, 142–85 and 359–411; Gert Melville, *Die Welt der mittelalterlichen Klöster: Geschichte und Lebensformen* (Munich: Beck, 2012), 114–22.

140. Parisse, "Les chanoinesses dans l'Empire germanique (IXᵉ–XIᵉ siècles)," *Francia* 6 (1979): 107–26; Irene Crusius, *Studien zum Kanonissenstift* (Göttingen: Vendenhoeck & Ruprecht, 2001), esp. 9–38; Thomas Schlip, "Die Wirkung der Aachener *Institutio Sanctimonialium* des Jahres 816," in Lorenz and Zotz, *Frühformen von Stiftskirchen*, 163–84.

141. Rosenwein, *Rhinoceros Bound*, 72–83; Iogna-Prat, "La place idéale du laïc à Cluny: D'une morale statutaire à un éthique absolue?," in his *Études clunisiennes*, 93–124, esp. 107–9 and 123; Andrew Romig, "The Common Bond of Aristocratic Masculinity: Monks, Secular Men, and St. Gerald of Aurillac," in *Negotiating Clerical Identities: Priests, Monks, and Masculinities in the Middle Ages*, ed. Jennifer D. Thibodeaux (New York: Palgrave MacMillan, 2010), 39–56.

CROWDS OF CHRISTIANS

The vast majority of Christians were less distinguished folk who held no formal or informal ecclesiastical offices. Because they were baptized, and because to varying extents they celebrated the feasts of the Church, participated in its services, observed its laws, and paid their tithes (freely or not), they knew they were Christians. Scholars today are less certain, raising questions about the violent profusion of sins and sinners, the vitality of ancient folk practices, and the lack of any precise metrics to prove how effectively the average medieval peasant was "churched."[142] These questions are legitimate, but consistency demands that if they are to be asked about the millennial Church, they should be asked about the Church in all European centuries, in which case perhaps no era may merit the label "Christian."

Lay Christianity, as noted above in the discussion of great lords and magnates, was a lived exercise, more concerned with life as a member of the body of Christ on earth than with a contemplative quest for closer union with God in heaven. In the trifunctional model that divided society into those who pray, those who fight, and those who work, only the first group was partially defined by its otherworldly connections, whereas the next two were known for their roles in the here and now. Laypeople were not expected to participate fully in clerical culture. Their Christianity was measured by visible deeds, and it remained anchored in practice even when its interior dimensions deepened.[143] It has been suggested that the faith of many Christians was actually "implicit faith": they had faith in the teachings of their Church, whatever the precise details might be, and trusted its bishops and teachers to understand the true faith and get it right, just as they trusted monks and nuns to pray properly on their behalf.[144]

The gap between clerical and lay culture was probably never fully transcended, not even by those priests and religious who worked regularly with the common people. The linguistic divide alone was challenging. Latin was a cultivated, precise, learned language, often written in analytical prose; vernaculars were more oral and poetic, conveying meaning through repetitive and vivid clichés, formulas, and stories. Even though churchmen knew the local speech, at times they and their flocks must literally have been thinking in different languages. Perhaps a symptom of

142. For debates about whether the Middle Ages were "Christian," see Van Engen, "Christian Middle Ages," 519–52, esp. 519–22, 538; and Milis, introduction to *Pagan Middle Ages*, 5–11.

143. Delaruelle, "La pietà popolare nel secolo XI," in his *La piété populaire au Moyen Âge* (Torino: Bottega d'Erasmo, 1980), 3–26, esp. 13.

144. Van Engen, "Faith as a Concept of Order," in Kselman, *Belief in History*, 41–47.

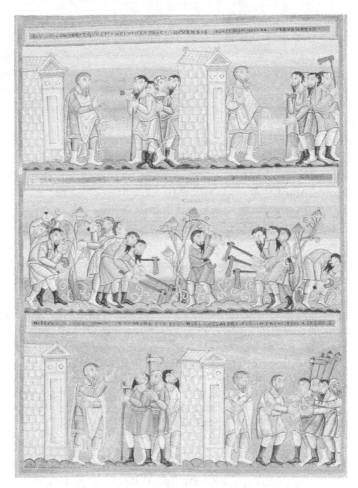

FIGURE 37. "Those who work," the laborers in the vineyard as illustrated in Echternach's *"Golden Gospels."* German National Museum MS 156142, fol. 76. Image courtesy of Germanisches Nationalmuseum, Nürnberg.

this cultural disjunction is the stipulation at Fleury that the monk who ran the guest house for the poor had to be a *conversus*—that is, a former layman who had entered monastic life as an adult and was more familiar with the world—whereas there was no such stipulation for the monk who ran the guest house for elite visitors. Apparently the gap between clerical and popular culture was significantly greater than that between clerical and elite lay culture.[145]

145. Thierry of Amorbach, *Libellus* I xiii–xiv, Davril and Donnat, *Corp CM* 7(3), 24–26, Davril and Donnat, *L'abbaye de Fleury*, 194–97.

In lived religion, gifting was extremely important. It confirmed familial and social connections on earth and presumably also in heaven. Churches needed gift relationships because they were grounded in the material world. It has already been noted that great lords could donate properties and enter into confraternity with religious institutions and could demonstrate their piety by founding churches.[146] Less well recognized is how far down through society this dynamic extended. Some churches were constructed cooperatively by people who were not great lords, such as villagers in Brittany, England, and Spanish and Italian hill towns.[147] And even those who lacked the resources of burgesses could still bring gifts to the altar during the liturgy and thus experience the Mass as a sort of "heavenly commerce" linking heaven and earth in a gift exchange.[148] Special participants in the Mass were the pious women who had made or donated the vestments and altar fittings.[149] Community responsibilities to a church are itemized at the end of a rite for dedicating a church found in the Romano-German Pontifical:

> Once these things [all the elaborate processions and blessings] have been done in proper order, when the bishop will have returned again to the door of the church, and silence has been established, let him have a word with the people [ad plebem] concerning the honor of the church, and the peace that should be accorded to all those coming and going from it, and about the tithes or offerings due to the church, and about the anniversary of the dedication of this church. And both to the clerks and to the people he will proclaim in whose honor the church has been constructed and dedicated and the names of the saints resting therein.[150]

One way to maintain these commitments was to establish a confraternity, a voluntary association dedicated to economic and spiritual goals. These begin to appear in the tenth and eleventh centuries organized around churches, though well-documented organizations with formal statutes are later.[151] Guilds in Anglo-Saxon England, often featuring feasts

---

146. Iogna-Prat, La Maison Dieu, 493–574.

147. Howe, Church Reform, 102–3, 108–11; Bonnassie, "Le clergé paroissal aux IXᵉ–Xᵉ siècles dans les Pyrénées orientales et centrales," in his Le clergé, 153–66, 269–83, reprinted with some comments and a "Bibliographie complémentaire," in Les Sociétés de l'an Mil: Un monde entre deux ages (Brussels: De Boeck & Larcier, 2001), 269–83; Wendy Davies, Small Worlds: The Village Community in Early Medieval Brittany (Cambridge: Cambridge University Press, 1988), 81–83; Remensnyder, Transformation, 9–10, 62–68, and 72–85; Blair, Church in Anglo-Saxon Society, 397–410; Wood, Proprietary Church, esp. 645–58.

148. David Ganz, "Giving to God in the Mass: The Experience of the Offertory," in The Language of Gift in the Early Middle Ages, ed. Davies and Fouracre (Cambridge: Cambridge University Press, 2010), 18–32.

149. Griffiths, "'Like the Sister of Aaron,'" 343–74, esp. 354–65.

150. Pontificale Romano-Germanicum XL cxxviii, ed. Vogel and Elze, Le Pontifical romano-germanique, 1:169.

151. Delaruelle, "La vie commune des clercs et la spiritualité populaire," 142–185, esp. 164–66; Tellenbach, Church in Western Europe, 129–31.

and considerable drinking, began to take charge of maintaining both the fabric of particular churches and local peace in general.[152] Monasteries had their own brotherhoods of supporters, most famously Cluny, where confraternity development seems to have peaked in the early eleventh century.[153] Lay church organizations could parallel and bleed into related organizational efforts such as those involving saint cults, pilgrimages, and the Peace and Truce of God.

Charity was a religious duty. Although it has been disparagingly claimed that in the early Middle Ages charity was "more symbolic than real" and only a concern of "small elites," and basically a "clerical monopoly," there were laypeople involved with poor relief, hospitals, and ransoming societies (lay initiatives that in the High Middle Ages, when they were successful, might be incorporated into or institutionalized as religious orders).[154] Tithes, technically one quarter of them, were supposed to go to the poor, and in theory property donated to the Church funded the poor, the needy, widows, and orphans.[155] As in our own day, people who provided resources to professional charities assumed that they too were participating. Charity was preached by the Church and acted upon by the faithful in various ways. Much direct lay charity, such as alms to beggars or grants of hospitality, would have been spontaneous and undocumented.

In the tenth and eleventh centuries some of the most dramatic manifestations of lay piety were new mass pilgrimages.[156] Crowds of pilgrims literally followed the path of Christ by visiting the sites of his life in the Holy Land and by traveling the way of the cross. They sought out Rome with its many martyrs, including the apostles Peter and Paul; Santiago de Compostella, which boasted of the body of the apostle James; the shrine of the Archangel Michael on Monte Gargano in southern Italy; and many other prestigious destinations. New local pilgrimages resulted from the massive increase in the popularity of saint cults. Pilgrims could don special dress.[157] Because they were travelers by definition, they were the ideal audience to see and admire all the new churches, shrines, and

152. Rosser, "The Anglo-Saxon Guilds," in Blair, *Minsters and Parish Churches*, 31–34.

153. Constable, "Commemoration and Confraternity," in Constable et al., *Die Cluniazenser*, 253–78, esp. 253–54.

154. James William Brodman, *Charity & Religion in Medieval Europe* (Washington, DC: Catholic University of America Press, 2009), esp. 13–14, 41–44; Frederico Botana, *The Works of Mercy in Italian Medieval Art (c. 1050–c. 1400)* (Turnhout, Belg.: Brepols, 2011), esp. 1–5, 9–10.

155. Peter Damian, *Epist.* lxxiv, Reindel, 3:369–75, esp. 370–71, Blum 3:152.

156. Charles Freeman, *Holy Bones, Holy Dust: How Relics Shaped the History of Medieval Europe* (New Haven: Yale University Press, 2011), 97–107.

157. *Chron. Casin.* II xxxvii, Hoffmann, 236, describes the Normans who were going to Jerusalem in 999 as *in habitu peregrino*. On pilgrim insignia, see Constable, "The Cross of the Crusaders," in *Crusading and Crusaders in the Twelfth Century*, ed. Constable (Burlington, VT: Ashgate, 2008), 45–91, esp. 56–61.

ecclesiastical furniture and to personally integrate them into a total religious experience. They brought home their experiences, along with their
stories and badges. Lay folk had churches to build, saints to visit, feasts to
celebrate, and pilgrimages to travel that might take them far beyond the
confines of Latin Christendom.

CHAPTER 9

"ONE SHEPHERD PRESIDES OVER ALL GENERALLY"

Since the Lord suffered in Jerusalem, not the Roman but the Jerusalem church instead ought to be in charge over all the churches. But since according to the authority of the canons the Roman church should hold the first place, the Alexandrian the second, the Antiochene the third, Constantinopolitan fourth, and Jerusalemite the fifth, it follows that the Lord, the Savior, does not preside over any single chair [i.e. any *cathedra*, any episcopal seat] by a special right, but rather the one shepherd presides over all generally. It is clear therefore that the order of the churches is disposed according to the privilege of Peter, not according to the incomparable excellence of the Redeemer.

—Peter Damian, *Letter to Abbot Desiderius of Monte Cassino* (1069)

THE CHRISTIAN WORLD

The Christian world was bigger than the Roman Church.[1] It included the Latin Church itself, with its diminishing Celtic, Visigothic, local Italian, and Greek liturgical traditions. In the non-Islamic eastern Mediterranean, most of the churches were affiliated with the "Universal Patriarch" of Constantinople, whose influence extended not only over his Greek liturgical community but also over Slavic, Russ, Bulgarian, and even some

1. Peter Damian, *Epist.* clix, Reindel, 4:90–99, esp. 99, Blum, 7:94–102, esp. 101–2.

Armenian churches. Beyond "New Rome" lived Oriental Christians out of step with the Councils of Ephesus (431), Chalcedon (451), or Constantinople III (681), including members of ancient Nestorian, Coptic, Ethiopic, Armenian, Syrian, Georgian, and Maronite churches.[2] To this disconcerting diversity there was no practical alternative. Christians believed in one catholic Church (i.e., one universal Church) and yet simultaneously were absolutely convinced that various Christian communities down the road would benefit greatly from a little correction.[3]

Peter Brown offered a way to conceptualize this situation when he described Late Antique "micro-Christendoms" built around a "constellation of centers" scattered throughout the known world from Ireland to central Asia.[4] However, in the ninth century this model becomes less useful as Latin and Greek imperial cores begin to strive for political, cultural, and religious hegemony and to polarize the Christian worlds.[5] In the tenth, as the East Frankish rulers were advancing Romano-Frankish Christianity to the north and east, the Macedonian dynasty was promoting its own ecclesiastical brand, solidifying Byzantine orthodoxy in Greece, which Slavs and Bulgars had turned into a frontier zone, subduing the Bulgarians, and expanding imperial frontiers all the way to Hungary.[6] Greek emperors doubled their holdings in southern Italy and captured Cyprus (958),

2. On eastern Christianities, see David Bundy, "Early Asian and East African Christianities," in *The Cambridge History of Christianity*, vol. 2, *Constantine to c. 600*, ed. Augustine Casiday and Frederick W. Norris (Cambridge: Cambridge University Press, 2007), 118–48; on their medieval challenges, see Michael Gervers and Ramzi Jibran Bikhazi, eds., *Indigenous Christian Communities in Islamic Lands: Eighth to Eighteenth Centuries* (Toronto: PIMS, 1990); and Niall Finneran, "Beyond Byzantium: The Non-Chalcedonian Churches," in *A Companion to Byzantium*, ed. Liz James (Oxford: Wiley-Blackwell, 2010), 199–223. Ashgate sponsors The Worlds of Eastern Christianity, 300–1500, ed. Robert Hoyland and Arietta Papaconstantinou, a series which collects and translates studies on individual traditions, and includes volumes for the churches of the Ethiopians (Alessandro Bausi, 2012), Georgians (Stephan H. Rapp Jr. and Paul Crego, 2012), and Armenians (Tim Greenwood, 2014).

3. Grudging toleration is discussed in Tia M. Kolbaba, "The Orthodoxy of the Latins in the Twelfth Century," in *Byzantine Orthodoxies: Papers from the Thirty-Sixth Spring Symposium of Byzantine Studies, University of Durham, 23–25 March 2002*, ed. Andrew Louth and Casiday (Burlington, VT: Ashgate, 2006), 199–214.

4. Brown, *Rise of Western Christendom*, esp. 13–16 and 41.

5. Vittorio Peri, "'Universalità' culturale cristiana dei due sacri imperi romani," in Arnaldi and Cavallo, *Europa medievale e mondo bizantino*, 124–62. For the formation of the Carolingian Empire as a cause for "the end of the ancient world system," see Ernst Pitz, *Die griechisch-römische Ökumene und die drei Kulturen des Mittelalters: Geschichte des mediterranen Weltteils zwischen Atlantik und Indischem Ozean, 270–812* (Berlin: Akademie Verlag, 2001), 445–96; for Greek expansion as a catalyst for conflict, see Kolbaba, "Byzantine Perceptions of Latin Religious 'Errors,'" in *Doctrine and Debate in the East Christian World, 300–1500*, ed. Averil Cameron and Robert Hoyland (Burlington, VT: Ashgate, 2011), 293–319, esp. 297–99.

6. Stephenson, *Byzantium's Balkan Frontier*, 18–98; Catherine Holmes, *Basil II and the Governance of Empire (976–1025)* (Oxford: Oxford University Press, 2005), 394–428. On Greece in particular, see Florin Curta, "The Beginning of Prosperity (c. 900 to c. 1050)" and "Early Medieval Greece and the Middle Byzantine Economy," in his *Edinburgh History of the Greeks*, 166–208 and 209–29, esp. 223.

Crete (961), Antioch (969), and even much of Armenia, strategically focusing their efforts on traditionally Christian territories.[7] Military success reinforced the ancient belief in the emperor's divine mission: in theory he ruled universally, like God whom he represented, and Constantinople within its sacred walls was "God-protected," an "ark of the covenant."[8]

The rising Christian civilizations collided. Byzantine influence in Scandinavia, through direct connections via pilgrims and mercenaries as well as through artistic and cultural exchange, peaked in the tenth and early eleventh century but then waned.[9] New Latin missionary archbishoprics in Eastern Europe impinged upon Byzantine interests.[10] The dukes and kings of Poland, linked to the eastern Saxon nobility by friendships and enmities, maintained spies in Rome, supported Western missionaries in Eastern Europe, and participated in coups in Kiev.[11] Scholars debate the historicity of the entertaining story of how Duke Vladimir of Kiev auditioned delegations of missionaries in order to decide which religion to join, but it does highlight the ecclesiastical rivalries.[12] The competition

7. Jonathan Shepard, "Emperors and Expansionism: From Rome to Middle Byzantium," and Catherine Holmes, "Byzantium's Eastern Frontier in the Tenth and Eleventh Centuries," in *Medieval Frontiers: Concepts and Practices*, ed. David Abulafia and Nora Berend (Aldershot, UK: Ashgate, 2002), 55–82, esp. 64–76, and 83–104; Gilbert Dagron, *Emperor and Priest: The Imperial Office in Byzantium*, trans. Jean Birrell (Cambridge: Cambridge University Press, 2003), 192–219.

8. Quotations from Peter N. Bell, ed., *Three Political Voices from the Age of Justinian: Agapetus*, Advice to the Emperor; Dialogue on Political Science; *Paul the Silentiary*, Description of Hagia Sophia (Liverpool: Liverpool University Press, 2009), 29–31. On imperial ideology, see Georg Ostrogorsky, *History of the Byzantine State*, trans. Joan Hussey (New Brunswick, NJ: Rutgers University Press, 1957), 192–95; Cesare Alzati, "Gerusalemme, Roma, Bizanzio: Traslazioni di un ideale," in *Roma antica nel Medioevo*, 189–207.

9. Michael Müller-Wille, ed., *Rom und Byzanz im Norden: Mission und Glaubenswechsel im Ostseeraum wahrend des 8.–14. Jahrhunderts* (Mainz, Ger.: Akademie der Wissenschaften und der Literatur, 1997), esp. 291–311 and 405–22; Ildar Garipzanov, "Wandering Clerics and Mixed Rituals in the Early Christian North, c. 1000–c. 1150," *JEH* 63 (2012):1–17.

10. Charles R. Bowlus, "*Mitteleuropa*: The Making of Europe between Byzantium and the Latin West, ca. 800–1025," in *Paradigms and Methods in Early Medieval Studies*, ed. Celia Chazelle and Felice Lifshitz (New York: Palgrave Macmillan, 2007), 185–202; Wolfgang Huschner, "Benevent, Magdeburg, Salerno: Das Papsttum und die neuen Erzbistümer in ottonischer Zeit," in *Das Papsttum und das vielgestaltige Italien: Hundert Jahre Italia Pontificia*, ed. Klaus Herbers und Jochen Johrendt (Berlin: Walter de Gruyter, 2009), 87–108.

11. Gunther Wolf, "Spätkarolingische und ottonische Beziehungen zum Kiever Reich der Rus," in Wolf, *Kaiserin Theophanu*, 146–54; Shepard, "Otto III, Boleslaw Chrobry and the 'Happening' at Gniezno, A.D. 1000: Some Possible Implications of Professor Poppe's Thesis concerning the Offspring of Anna Porphyrogenita," in *Byzantium and East Central Europe*, ed. Günter Prinzing, Maciej Salamon, and Paul Stephenson (Cracow: Historia Iagellonica, 2001), 27–48; Shepard, "Conversion and Regimes Compared: The Rus' and the Poles, ca. 1000," in *East Central and Eastern Europe in the Early Middle Ages*, ed. Curta (Ann Arbor: University of Michigan Press, 2005), 254–82; Pleszczyński, *Birth of a Stereotype: Polish Rulers*, 152–58, 170, 228, 257–63, 318.

12. *The Russian Primary Chronicle: Laurentian Text* (983–988), trans. Samuel Hazzard Cross and Olgerd P. Sherbowitz-Wetzor (Cambridge: Mediaeval Academy of America, 1953), 96–116. On the dating of this work and its literary strategies, see Aleksandr Viktorovich Rukavishnikov, "*Tales of Bygone Years*: The *Russian*

was especially deadly in southern Italy, which both empires claimed.[13] The traditional 1054 date for the schism between Greek and Latin churches increasingly looks misleading,[14] and it would be possible to argue that a more important year was 1059, when the pope allied with the Normans at the Synod of Melfi, leaving them free to destroy Byzantine Italy, a campaign completed by the capture of Bari in 1071 and the subsequent attack on the Eastern Empire in the Balkans.[15] For centuries the Latins and the Greeks had been divided by real theological differences (at minimum by which theologians their churchmen actually read), but as political clashes intensified those differences became more and more difficult to finesse.

This polarization further disadvantaged the eastern Christian communities already stunted by Islam. For example, the Armenians, an ancient people whose homeland lay in a difficult neighborhood, had experienced a resurgence under the Bagratid dynasty (885–1044), which took advantage of the political disintegration of the Abbasid caliphate to facilitate Armenian emigration to Cilicia, Syria, and Mesopotamia. Armenian refugees and mercenaries entered Byzantine frontier zones such as the Balkans and Italy; some elite Armenian families became important in Constantinople.[16] While a minority of Armenians accepted Chalcedonian Orthodoxy, most did not, leaving them divided and distracted by Byzantine efforts to integrate them into the Orthodox theological and liturgical world.[17]

Primary Chronicle as a Family Chronicle," *Early Medieval History* 12 (2003): 53–74; and Sean Griffin, "Byzantine Liturgy and the *Primary Chronicle*" (PhD diss., UCLA, 2014), 143–47.

13. Henry Mayr-Harting, "Liutprand of Cremona's Account of His Legation to Constantinople (968) and Ottonian Imperial Strategy," *EHR* 116 (2001): 539–56, esp. 543–54; Vera von Falkenhausen, "Between Two Empires: Byzantine Italy in the Reign of Basil II," in Magdalino, *Byzantium in the Year 1000*, 135–59.

14. Evangelos Chrysos, "1054: Schism?," in *Christianità d'Occidente e Christianità d'Oriente (secoli V–XI), 24–30 aprile 2003*, 2 vols., Settimane di studio della fondazione CISAM 51 (Spoleto: CISAM, 2004), 1:547–71; Kolbaba, "The Legacy of Humbert and Cerularius: The Tradition of the 'Schism of 1054' in Byzantine Texts and Manuscripts of the Twelfth and Thirteenth Centuries," in *Porphyrogenita: Essays on the History and Literature of Byzantium and the Latin East in Honour of Julian Chrysostomides*, ed. Charalambos Dendrinos, Jonathan Harris, Eirene Harvalia-Crook, and Judith Herrin (Burlington, VT: Ashgate, 2003), 47–61; J. R. Ryder, "Changing Perspectives on 1054" and Kolbaba, "1054 Revisited: Response to Ryder," *Byzantine and Modern Greek Studies* 35 (2011): 20–37 and 38–44.

15. Axel Bayer, *Spaltung der Christenheit: Das sogenannte Morgenländische Schisma von 1054* (Cologne: Böhlau, 2002), 117–24 and 206.

16. Gérard Dédéyan, "Les Armeniens en Occident, fin Xᵉ–début XIᵉ siècle," in *Occident et Orient au Xᵉ siècle: Actes du XIᵉ Congrès de la Société des historiens médiévistes de l'enseignement superior public (Dijon, 2–4 juin 1978)* (Dijon: Société des belles lettres, 1979), 123–139, esp. 123–24; Nina G. Garsoïan, "The Problem of Armenian Integration into the Byzantine Empire," in *Studies on the Internal Diaspora of the Byzantine Empire*, ed. Hélène Ahrweiler and Angeliki E. Laiou (Washington, DC: Dumbarton Oaks, 1998), 53–124.

17. On the origins of the Armenian Church and its monasticism, see Garsoïan, "Janus: The Formation of the Armenian Church from the IVth to the VIIth Century," in *The Formation of a Millennial Tradition: 1700 Years of Armenian Christian Witness (301–2001)*, ed. Robert F. Taft (Rome: Pontificio Istituto Orientale,

Antioch offers another example of a missed opportunity, a city whose ancient patriarchate governed Georgian, Armenian, and Syrian churches and that after its recapture by the Byzantine Empire in 969 might again have become a cosmopolitan religious center. Instead it simply acquired a superstructure of Constantinopolitan Hellenism without successfully developing its own unique Christian identity.[18] Later the Crusaders would arrive, bringing new sets of problems to the Christians of the East.

ECCLESIASTICAL INTERSECTIONS

Despite the political tensions, East and West did meet, often. Every German king and emperor between 936 and 1204 had official diplomatic contacts with Constantinople.[19] Trade linked the peoples of Europe.[20] Pilgrimage traffic greatly increased in the tenth and eleventh centuries, aided by the rise of the Italian maritime republics, the decline of Islamic naval power, and the opening of the overland route to the East.[21] The extent of Latin ecclesiastical contact with this greater world can be appreciated by surveying three prominent meeting places: Monte Cassino, Rome, and Jerusalem.

Monte Cassino owed its international character in part to its proximity to Greek southern Italy. Byzantine hermit saints made regular pilgrimages

---

2004), 79–95, and Garsoïan, "Introduction to the Problem of Early Armenian Monasticism," *Revue des études arméniennes* 30 (2005–07): 177–236, esp. 228–36 (bibliography).

18. Jean-Claude Cheynet, "The Duchy of Antioch during the Second Period of Byzantine Rule," in *East and West in the Medieval Eastern Mediterranean*, vol. 1, *Antioch from the Byzantine Reconquest to the End of the Crusader Principality*, ed. Krijnie N. Ciggaar and David Michael Metcalf (Louvain, Belg.: Peeters, 2006), 1–16, esp. 8–12; Alexander Saminsky, "Illuminated Manuscripts from Antioch," in Hourihane, *Interactions: Artistic Interchange*, 188–208.

19. Shepard, "Courts in East and West," in Linehan and Nelson, *Medieval World*, 14–36; Ciggaar, *Western Travellers to Constantinople: The West and Byzantium, 962–1204: Cultural and Political Relations* (Leiden, Neth.: Brill, 1996), 203; Michael McCormick, "La lettre diplomatique byzantine du premier millénaire vue de l'Occident et l'énigme du papyrus de Paris," in *Byzance et le monde extérieur: Contacts, relations, échanges: Actes de trois séances du XXᵉ Congrès international des Études byzantines, Paris, 19–25 août 2001*, ed. Michel Balard, Élisabeth Malamut, and Jean-Michel Spieser (Paris: Sorbonne, 2005), 83–95.

20. Ciggaar, *Western Travellers to Constantinople*, esp. 21–44; Ewald Kislinger, "Reisen und Verkehrswege zwischen Byzanz und dem Abendland vom neunten bis in die Mitte des elften Jahrhunderts," in *Byzanz und das Abendland im 10. und 11. Jahrhundert*, ed. Evangelos Konstantinou (Vienna: Böhlau, 1997), 231–57; *Voyages et voyageurs à Byzance et en Occident du VIᵉ au XIᵉ siècles: Actes du Colloque international organisé par la Section d'histoire de l'Université libre de Bruxelles en collaboration avec le Départment des sciences historiques de l'Université de Liège (5–7 mai 1994)*, ed. Alain Dierkens and Jean-Marie Sansterre (Geneva: Droz, 2000); Laiou, "Economic and Noneconomic Exchange," and John Day, "The Levant Trade in the Middle Ages," in *The Economic History of Byzantium from the Seventh through the Fifteenth Century*, ed. Laiou, 3 vols. (Washington, DC: Dumbarton Oaks, 2002), 2:681–770, esp. 713–28, and 2:807–14, esp. 807–8.

21. Ciggaar, *Western Travellers to Constantinople*, 21–44; Aryeh Graboïs, *Le pèlerin occidental en Terre sainte au Moyen Âge* (Paris: De Boeck & Larcier, 1998), 30–38; Freeman, *Holy Bones, Holy Dust*, 97–107.

to Rome, sometimes emigrating permanently in order to avoid Muslim raids.[22] Nilus of Rossano (d. 1004), the most famous of these, after forty years of monastic life moved north to Monte Cassino, where, after a grand reception, he spent nearly fifteen years (ca. 980–ca. 994) directing sixty Greek monks at its daughter house of Valleluce. He then went even farther north, first to Gaeta and then to the neighborhood of Rome, where he died in 1004 while establishing the monastery of Grottaferrata for the barons of Tuscolo (the future Tuscolaner popes).[23] Greek monasticism was so respected at Monte Cassino that after Nilus departed, several of its monks headed east. The future Abbot John II of Monte Cassino (996–97) lived six years on Mount Sinai and Mount Athos; the future Abbot Theobald (1023–1035/37) spent time as a hermit at Jerusalem; the monk Liutius (d. post 1038), upon his return from Jerusalem in the late tenth century shocked his brethren with his ascetic lifestyle.[24] A less impressive witness of Greek monasticism was Abbot Basil (1034/1036–38), a "worldly" Calabrian abbot whom the *Monte Cassino Chronicle* disparages as "not so much an abbot as a representative of the prince [that is, of Prince Pandulf IV of Capua (d.1049–50)]."[25] During the reign of Abbot Theobald (1022–35), Monte Cassino had begun to assemble an impressive library that included some Greek fathers and perhaps even some Greek illuminated manuscripts.[26] When Abbot Desiderius embarked upon an almost complete

22. Gennaro Luongo, "Itinerari dei santi italo-greci," in *Pellegrinaggi e itinerari dei santi nel Mezzogiorno medievale*, ed. Giovanni Vitolo (Naples: Liguori, 1999), 39–56; Mario Re, "Italo-Greek Hagiography," in *The Ashgate Research Companion to Byzantine Hagiography*, ed. Stephanos Efthymiadis, 2 vols. (Burlington, VT: Ashgate, 2011–14), 1: 227–58; John Howe, "Western Monks and the East, 850–1050," forthcoming in Beach and Cochelin, *Cambridge History of Medieval Western Monasticism*.

23. Olivier Rousseau, "La visite de Nil de Rossano au Mont-Cassin," in *La Chiesa greca in Italia dall'VIII al XVI secolo. Atti del Convegno storico intereccelsiale (Bari, 30 apr.–4 magg. 1969)*, 3 vols. (Padua: Antenore, 1972–73), 3:1111–37; Herbert Bloch, *Monte Cassino in the Middle Ages*, 3 vols. (Cambridge: Harvard University Press, 1986), 1:10–12, 721–23.

24. *Chron. Casin.* II xii, xx–xxi, xxx, xlii, li, Hoffmann, 190, 203–5, 245–47, 261, 221–23. On the dates of these abbots, see Hoffmann, "Die Älteren Abtslisten von Montecassino," *Quellen und Forschungen aus italienischen Archiven und Bibliotheken* 47 (1967): 224–354, esp. 300–313. For context see Patricia M. McNulty and Bernard Hamilton, "*Orientale Lumen* et *Magistra Latinitatis*: Greek Influences on Western Monasticism (900–1100)," in *Le Millénaire du Mont Athos, 963–1963: Études et mélanges*, 2 vols. (Chevetogne: Éditions du Chevetogne, 1963), 1:181–216, esp. 184–86, 212.

25. *Chron. Casin.* II lvi, lxi–lxii, Hoffmann, 276, 285–88.

26. On the rebuilding of the library, see Bloch, "Monte Casino's Teachers and Library in the High Middle Ages," in *La Scuola nell'Occidente Latino dell'alto medioevo, 15–21 aprile 1971*, 2 vols. Settimane di studio del CISAM 19 (Spoleto: CISAM, 1972), 2:563–613 (note discussion 612–13); Bloch, *Monte Cassino*, 1:383–85; Newton, *The Scriptorium and Library at Monte Cassino, 1058–1105* (Cambridge: Cambridge University Press, 1999), 253–54. On Greek works acquired, see McNulty and Bernard Hamilton, "*Orientale Lumen*," 1:213–14; Newton, *Scriptorium and Library*, 273–74. Many but not all of the Greek fathers were represented by older Latin translations: see Roger E. Reynolds, "The Influence of Eastern Patristic Fathers on the Canonical Collections of South Italy in the Eleventh and Early Twelfth Centuries," in Blumenthal et al., *Canon Law, Religion,*

rebuilding of the monastery, he ordered brass doors, candlesticks, and an iconostasis from Constantinople; he also imported actual Greek craftsmen to help with frescoes, mosaics, and pavements.[27] Greek influence has been identified in some of Monte Casino's subordinate churches.[28]

Rome still retained its links to the Greek East. This international city had hosted so many refugees fleeing from Muslims and iconoclasts that all but two of the thirteen popes who reigned from 678 to 751 were native Greek speakers.[29] At the start of the ninth century at least nine Greek or partially Greek-rite monasteries still remained in Rome.[30] Greek pilgrims continued to flock there until the end of the eleventh century.[31] The Eastern emperors never forgot "Old Rome," and their interest in it was piqued when their Ottonian rivals began to extend their influence into central and southern Italy.[32] Greek agents actively courted the Lombard princes, the abbots of Monte Casino and Farfa, and grecophile aristocrats in Rome; they promoted the coup in which the papacy was seized in 997–98 by the Calabrian John Philagathos (antipope John XVI).[33] Refugees continued to arrive, most notably some Greek monks sponsored by Metropolitan Sergios of Damascus who received from Benedict VII (972–74) the monastery

---

and Politics, 75–106, esp. 87. For speculations about Greek illuminated manuscripts, see Hans Belting, "Byzantine Art among Greeks and Latins in Southern Italy," Dumbarton Oaks Papers 28 (1974):1–29, esp. 17–19.

27. Bloch, "Montecassino, Byzantium, and the West in the Earlier Middle Ages," Dumbarton Oaks Papers 3 (1946): 163–224, esp. 193–206; H. E. J. Cowdrey, The Age of Abbot Desiderius: Montecassino, the Papacy, and the Normans in the Eleventh and Early Twelfth Centuries (Oxford: Clarendon, 1983), 12–19; Bloch, Monte Cassino, 1:1–112, esp. 41, 45, 51–52, 65–67.

28. Ottavio Morisani, Gli affreschi di S. Angelo in Formis (Naples: Di Mauro Editore, 1962), 15–27; Nicola Cilento, "Sant'Angelo in Formis nel suo significato storico (1072–1087)," Studi medievali, 3rd ser., 4 (1963): 799–812; C. R. Dodwell, Painting in Europe, 800–1200 (Baltimore: Penguin, 1971), 118–38, esp. 131–32.

29. Andrew J. Ekonomou, Byzantine Rome and the Greek Popes: Eastern Influences on Rome and the Papacy from Gregory the Great to Zacharias, A.D. 590–752 (Lanham, MD: Lexington Books, 2007); Clemens Gantner, "The Label 'Greeks' in the Papal Diplomatic Repertoire in the Eighth Century," in Strategies of Identification: Ethnicity and Religion in Early Medieval Europe, ed. Walter Pohl and Gerda Heydemann (Turnhout, Belg.: Brepols, 2013), 303–49, esp. 341.

30. Sansterre, Les moins grecs et orientaux à Rome aux époques byzantine et carolingienne (milieu du VIe s.–fin du IXe siècles), 2 vols. (Brussels: Académie royale de Belgique, 1983); Sansterre, "Le monachisme byzantin à Rome," in Bisanzio, Roma e l'Italia nell'altomedioevo, 3–9 aprile 1986, 2 vols., Settimane di studio del CISAM 34 (Spoleto: CISAM, 1988), 2:701–50; Filippo Burgarella, "Presenze Greche a Roma: Aspetti culturali e religiosi," in Roma fra Oriente e Occidente, 19–24 aprile 2001, 2:943–92; John Osborne, "Rome and Constantinople in the Ninth," in Bolgia et al., Rome across Time, 227–36.

31. Enrico Morini, "The Orient and Rome: Pilgrimages and Pious Visits between the Ninth and the Eleventh Century," Harvard Ukrainian Studies 12–13 (1988–89): 849–69.

32. Shepard, "Emperors and Expansionism," in Abulafia and Berend, Medieval Frontiers, 55–82, esp. 61–69.

33. Johannes Irmscher, "Otto III. und Byzanz," in Konstantinou, Byzanz und das Abendland, 207–29, esp. 224–26; Bayer, Spaltung der Christenheit, 29–36. A Greek agent on the scene boasted about Byzantine involvement in the Philagathos affair: see Jean Darrouzès, Épistoliers byzantins du Xe siècle (Paris: Institut français d'études byzantines, 1960), 165–76.

of Boniface and Alexius, creating a joint Latin-Greek community that attracted the favor of Emperor Otto III and influential holy men from East and West.[34] The Tuscolan popes, whose family names and family chapel were Greek, scandalized some Westerners by their willingness to negotiate with Constantinople.[35] When the Normans roiled southern Italy, Leo IX sought to unite with the Greeks against their common enemy.[36] The papal court was well aware of the wider Christian world.

Jerusalem, another international city, had had a significant Frankish presence back in Charlemagne's time, and circumstantial evidence suggests that some form of his Jerusalem guesthouse may have become the Amalfitani guesthouse of St. John the Almoner.[37] Eleventh-century chroniclers were impressed by the numbers of Western pilgrims, some traveling in unprecedented crowds. Rodulfus Glaber claims that around the millennium "an innumerable multitude of people" traveled to Jerusalem; others describe new mass pilgrimages culminating with the alleged seven or even twelve thousand pilgrims who in 1064–65 traveled together with the archbishop of Mainz and the bishop of Bamberg.[38] Among the Jerusalem visitors were important nobles such as Count Fulk Nerra of Anjou, who made the journey four times.[39] It was claimed that Emperor Otto III had intended to retire to become a monk in Jerusalem.[40] Some Western monks actually did.[41] Along the same routes eastern Christians moved west. Most

---

34. Bernard Hamilton, "The Monastery of S. Alessio and the Religious and Intellectual Renaissance in Tenth-Century Rome," *Studies in Medieval and Renaissance History* 2 (1965): 263–310, and Hamilton, "The Monastic Revival in Tenth Century Rome," *Studia monastica* 4 (1962): 35–68; Sansterre, "Otton III et les saints ascètes de son temps," *Rivista di storia della Chiesa in Italia* 43 (1989): 377–412, esp. 380–86; and Sansterre, "Le monastère des Saints-Boniface-et-Alexis sur l'Aventin et l'expansion du christianisme dans le cadre de la *Renovatio Imperii Romanorum* d'Otton III," *Revue bénédictine* 100 (1990): 493–506.

35. Rodulfus Glaber, *Historiae* IV i, France, 172–77. See Karl Leyser, "Ritual, Ceremony, and Gesture: Ottonian Germany," in his *Communications and Power in Medieval Europe*, ed. Timothy Reuter, 2 vols. (Rio Grande, OH: Hambledon, 1994) 1:189–213, esp. 227–28; Bayer, *Spaltung der Christenheit*, 46–53.

36. Bayer, *Spaltung der Christenheit*, 52–96. Leo's attempts at working with Constantinople are discussed in this book's epilogue.

37. McCormick, *Charlemagne's Survey of the Holy Land*, esp. 57–58, 76, 90–91.

38. Rodulfus Glaber, *Historiae* IV xviii–xxi, France, 198–205; Adémar, *Chronicon* III lxv, Bourgain, 184–85; Orderic Vitalis, *Historia Aeclesiastica* III lxv, Chibnall, 2:69; Fritz Lošek, "*Et Bellum Inire Sunt Coacti*: The Great Pilgrimage of 1065," in Herren et al., *Latin Culture in the Eleventh Century*, 2:61–72, esp. 63.

39. Bernard Bachrach, "The Pilgrimages of Fulk Nerra, Count of the Angevins, 987–1040)," in *Religion, Culture, and Society in the Middle Ages: Studies in Honor of Richard E. Sullivan*, ed. Thomas F. X. Noble and John Contreni (Kalamazoo, MI: Western Michigan University Press, 1987), 205–17.

40. Bruno of Querfurt, *Vita Quinque Fratrum* iii, Miladinov, 218–19.

41. *Vita et Miracula S. Bononii* x, ed. Gerhard Schwartz and Adolf Hofmeister, MGH SS 30(2) (Leipzig: Hiersemann, 1934), 1023–33, esp. 1028–29, claims Bononius of Lucca took up residence on Mount Sinai and had a reputation "through all the region of Jerusalem"; see Teemu Immonen, "A Saint as a Mediator between a Bishop and His Flock: The Cult of St. Bononius in the Diocese of Vercelli under Bishop Arderic

FIGURE 38. Greek monastic cap of St. Symeon of Syracuse, preserved at Trier. Trierer Domschatz. Nikolaus Irsch, *Der Dom zu Trier* (Düsseldorf: L. Schwan, 1931), 323 (fig. 210).

FIGURE 39. Residence of the canons of St. Symeon at Trier, built ca. 1040. Symeonstift, Trier. Photo credit: Anne Hanson Howe.

famous of these was Symeon of Syracuse (or of Trier), a Sicilian raised in Constantinople, who had worked as a guide in the Holy Land for seven years and become fluent in five languages. He retired to become a hermit on the banks of the Jordan, a monk at Bethlehem, and a hermit on

---

(1026/7–1044)," *Viator* 39 (2008): 65–91. On monks from Monte Cassino in Jerusalem, see *Chron. Casin.* II xii, xxii, xxx, xxxiii, lii, lxxii, Hoffmann, 190, 206, 221, 229–30, 262, 313.

Mount Sinai. Sent west with a companion to collect a donation promised by Count Richard of Normandy, Symeon met Archbishop Poppo of Trier, whom he accompanied on a pilgrimage to Jerusalem. On their return Symeon became a sort of stylite, living in the eastern tower of Trier's old Roman "Black Gate," and after his death in 1035, Poppo quickly secured his papal canonization.[42] Symeon was only one of many eastern pilgrims, including a half dozen Armenians, who became honored as saints in the Latin West.[43]

INCORPORATING EXOTICISMS

Contact does not guarantee positive interaction, especially in a strained relationship. Even while Westerners were eagerly acquiring Byzantine jewelry, textiles, and relics, they continued to disparage the "effete Greeks" (a pejorative orientalism that had begun with the ancient Romans). They did respect Greek as a language of the Bible, the Church fathers, and the ecumenical councils. Tenth- and eleventh-century Greeks, on the other hand, show very few traces of Latin envy. Given this prickly relationship, it would be easy to envision the Roman Church as developing independently—easy but inaccurate.

The millennial Roman Church was no church's acolyte, but on its own terms it blithely adopted whatever architectural, artistic, literary, liturgical, institutional, and ascetical elements it happened to find attractive. The Latin Church embraced international flair just because it believed that it wore the mantle of St. Peter, an identity reinforced rather than threatened by universal resonances. Latin Christians borrowed to bedeck their traditions, not to replace them. As has been seen, Western leaders attempting to rebuild Europe were systematically incorporating Roman elements into their material, legal, and spiritual culture. The Roman Church concurred and participated, but its horizons extended even farther. Constantinople was more impressive than any city in the West; Jerusalem, where the drama of the Incarnation had played out, was the ultimate pilgrimage destination; beyond Jerusalem lay other Christian communities that boasted their own holy sites, martyrs, and fascinating customs. Although historians formerly thought in

42. Robert Lee Wolff, "How the News Was Brought from Byzantium to Angoulême; or, The Pursuit of a Hare in an Ox Cart," *Byzantine and Modern Greek Studies* 4 (1978): 139–89, esp. 181–89; Michele C. Ferrari, "From Pilgrims' Guide to Living Relic: Symeon of Trier and His Biographer Eberwin," in Herren et al., *Latin Culture in the Eleventh Century* 1:324–44; Alfred Haverkampf, "Der heilige Simeon (gest. 1035): Grieche im fatimidischen Orient und im lateinischen Okzident, Geschichte und Geschichten," *Historische Zeitschrift* 290 (2010): 1–51.

43. Gérard Dédéyan, "Les Arméniens en Occident, fin Xᵉ au débout XIᵉ siècle," in *Occident et Orient au Xᵉ siècle* (Paris: Les Belles lettres, 1979), 123–39; Howe, "Western Monks and the East."

terms of centers and peripheries, in the age of the Internet it is possible to imagine a world in which specific centers are less important. Roads no longer go simply from A to B—they go everywhere. A strength of the millennial Latin Church was its ability to acquire souvenirs along the way.

Literary Connections

It has been claimed that Latin and Greek Christians had such different intellectual and theological presuppositions that they could never have understood each other.[44] At first glance, such pessimism seems supported by the early medieval history of translations of Greek works into Latin, which were relatively rare and yet became even rarer in the tenth and eleventh centuries.[45] In defense of the millennial Church it might be argued that its scholars had only limited access to Greek texts and linguistic skills, but they not only failed to transcend those limitations but even failed to maintain the level of interest and expertise attained by late ninth-century translators such as Anastasius Bibliothecarius and John Eriugena.[46] Perhaps Greek studies were one more casualty of early tenth-century chaos. Among the few literary connections were a late tenth-century translation of the life of St. Margaret featuring a dedication page with a corrupted Greek inscription produced in the grecophile world of the Ottonian court, along with some Greek interlinear psalters and an interlinear epistolary.[47] The late tenth-century Greek and Latin community at Boniface and Alexius in Rome translated an Alexius legend.[48] Several Greek homilies on the dormition

44. André Gillou, "Il monachesimo greco in Italia meridionale e in Sicilia nel Medioevo," in *L'Eremitismo in Occidente nei secoli XI e XII: Atti della seconda Settimana internazionale di studio, Mendola, 30 agosto–6 settembre 1962* (Milan: Società vita e pensiero, 1963), 355–81, esp. 380–81.

45. Sansterre, "Témoignages des textes latins du Haut Moyen Âge sur le monachisme oriental et des textes byzantins sur le monachisme occidental," *Revue Bénédictine* 103 (1993): 12–30, esp. 20–21; Sansterre, "Les moines d'Occident et le monachisme d'Orient du VIe au XIe siècle: Entre textes anciens et réalités contemporaines," in *Christianità d'Occidente e Christianità d'Oriente*, 1:289–335, esp. 295–305. According to Sansterre, the most recent Eastern saints whose lives had been translated into Latin were John the Almoner (d. 617/618) and Alexander of Persia (d. 628).

46. Walter Berschin, *Greek Letters and the Latin Middles Age: From Jerome to Nicholas of Cusa*, rev. ed., trans. Jerold C. Frakes (Washington, DC: Catholic University Press, 1988), 126–200; Pascal Boulhol, *Grec langaige n'est pas doulz au françois: Étude et enseignement du grec dans la France ancienne (IVe siécle–1530)* (Aix-en-Provence: Presses Universitaires de Provence, 2014), 57–72.

47. Hannover Provinzialbibliothek Hs 189, fol. 11v–32 v, ed. Cynthia Hahn, *Passio Kiliani, Ps Theotimus/ Passio Margaretae, Orationes . . .* (Graz: Akademische Druck, 1988); Berschin, *Greek Letters*, 192–98; Willem J. Aerts, "The Knowledge of Greek in Western Europe at the Time of Theophano and the Greek Grammar Fragment in MS Vindob. 114," in *Byzantium and the Low Countries in the Tenth Century: Aspects of Art and History in the Ottonian Era*, ed. V.D. van Aalst and Ciggaar (Hernen: A.A. Brediusstichting, 1985), 78–103; McKitterick, "Ottonian Intellectual Culture," in Davids, *Empress Theophano*, 175, 181–83, 193.

48. Louk J. Engels, "The West European Alexius Legend: With an Appendix Presenting the Medieval Latin Text Corpus in Its Context (*Alexiana Latina Medii Aevi*, I)," in *The Invention of Saintliness*, ed. Anneke B. Mulder-Bakker (London: Routledge, 2002), 93–144.

of Mary were translated in Reichenau around 1000 and gradually disseminated to the West.[49] Greek millenarian speculations arrived somehow, in particular the concept of the Roman "last emperor."[50] The life of Barlaam and Ioasaph, a Christianized story of the Buddha, was Latinized in the early eleventh century, perhaps more than once.[51] The exceptional bright spot for tenth-century translations was Campania, where dozens of Greek lives of martyrs and desert fathers were translated in Naples and Amalfi.[52] Yet these remained peripheral to international Frankish culture until eleventh-century Monte Cassino provided a bridge.

Perhaps the major literary contribution that the millennial Latin Church received from its Greek counterpart was heightened enthusiasm for the literature of the desert fathers. Ascetical writings from the paleomonastic world were central to Italo-Greek spirituality: Nilus, for example, from his youth loved to read sacred scripture and the lives of Anthony, Sabas, Hilarion, and other saints.[53] Although Benedict's rule had recommended reading about the desert fathers, and paleomonastic texts were always treasured in the West, they could still puzzle Latin Christians. Aelfric, in a Latin preface to his lives of the saints, the third book of his homilies, admits that he has avoided this literature: "I hold my peace as to the book called *Vitae Patrum*, herein are contained many subtle points which ought

49. Fulton, *From Judgment to Passion*, 217.

50. Paul J. Alexander, "The Diffusion of Byzantine Apocalypses in the Medieval West and the Beginnings of Joachism," in *Prophecy and Millenarianism: Essays in Honour of Marjorie Reeves*, ed. Ann Williams (Harlow, UK: Longman, 1980), 53–106, esp. 67; Lowell Clucas, "Eschatological Theory in Byzantine Hesychasm: A Parallel to Joachim da Fiore?," *Byzantinische Zeitschrift* 70 (1977): 324–46. On the Greek tradition of the last emperor, see András Kraft, "The Last Roman Emperor *Topos* in the Byzantine Apocalyptic Tradition," *Byzantion* 82 (2012): 213–57.

51. Alexander P. Kazhdan, "Where, When and by Whom Was the Greek Barlaam and Ioasaph Not Written," in *Zu Alexander d. Gr.: Festschrift G. Wirth zum 60. Geburtstag am 9.12.86*, ed. Wolfgang Will, 2 vols. (Amsterdam: Adolf M. Hakkert, 1988), 2:1187–1209. On the Latin version, see Paulus Peeters, "La première traduction latine de *Barlaam et Joasaph* et son original grec," in *Analecta Bollandiana* 49 (1931): 276–312.

52. Paolo Chiesa, "Le traduzioni dal greco: L'evoluzione della scuola napoletana nel X secolo," *Mittellateinisches Jahrbuch* 24–25 (1989–90): 67–86; Berschin, "I traduttori d'Amalfi nell'XI secolo," in *Cristianità ed Europa: Miscellanea di studi in onore di Luigi Prosdocimi*, ed. Alzati, 2 vols. (Rome: Herder, 1994–2000), 1:237–44; Edoardo d'Angelo, "Agiografia latina del Mezzogiorno continentale d'Italia (750–1000)," in *Hagiographies*, 4:41–134, esp. 68–84.

53. Βίος Νείλου ꟼ2, ed. Germano Giovanelli, Βίος και πολιτεία τοῦ ὁσίου πατρὸς ημων Νείλου νέου (Grottaferrata: Badia di Grottaferrata, 1972), 48, trans. (Italian) with notes in Giovanelli, *S. Nilo di Rossano, fondatore di Grottaferrata* (Grottaferrata: Badia di Grottaferrata, 1966), 15; Enrica Follieri, "Echi della *Vita di Antonio* nella *Vita di Nilo da Rossano*," in *L'ellenismo italiota dal VII al XII secolo*: Alla memoria di Nikos Panagiotakis (Athens: National Hellenic Research Foundation, Institute for Byzantine Research, 2001), 19–26, esp. 20. For lists of citations from the lives of the desert fathers in Italo-Greek hagiography, see Fernando Cezzi, "Per una lettura ecclesiologica delle 'Vite' italo-greche," *Nicolaus* 3 (1975): 295–317, esp. 313–16. For some surviving codices, see Follieri, "Attività scrittoria calabrese nei secoli X–XI," in *Calabria bizantina: Tradizione di pietà e tradizione scrittoria nella Calabria greca medievale* (Reggio Calabria: Casa del libro, 1983), 103–42, esp. 108–9, 116, and 125.

not to be laid open to the laity, nor indeed are we ourselves quite able to fathom them."[54] The Latin hermits of Italy, on the other hand, privileged this literature, following the example of their Italo-Greek neighbors.[55] The East certainly gave the millennial Italian Church the lives of Alexius and of Barlaam and Ioasaph, both of which would become wildly popular in northern vernacular translations.[56] If Greek monks did help promote a new interest in severely ascetical monastic literature, then for this reason alone they would deserve some credit for the efflorescence of hermitism in the West in the tenth and eleventh centuries.

Liturgy

In a polarizing Christian world where liturgical language marked religious identity, liturgy seems an improbable point of contact. Yet sometimes Christians could find common ground on a level below the learned words and precise gestures of priests. Pilgrims understood the general import of sacramental celebrations, hymns, prayers, vigils, prostrations, incense, and candles. Processions created a recognizable sacred landscape of piety and power. The same sacred sites could be symbolically accessible not only to different communities of Christians but even to Muslims and Jews.[57]

For liturgical convergence on a popular level, one can look at the Kyrie. The Greek liturgical invocation Kyrie eleison (Lord have mercy) is first attested in Eastern litanies of the fourth century. It entered the Roman liturgy around the sixth, when it became an independent prayer characterized by ninefold repetitions.[58] It spread with the Roman rite throughout the West, along the way acquiring elaborate musical settings with intricate added tropes.[59] "Kyrieleison" even became a battle

---

54. Aelfric, *English Homilies III*, Latin pref., ed. and trans. Wilcox, *Aelfric's Prefaces*, 45–51, 119–20, 131–32.

55. For claim that Romualdian hermitism was based upon the *Vitae Patrum*, see Bruno of Querfurt, *Vita Quinque Fratrum* ii and xii, Miladinov, 204–5 and 254–55. In support, note the many footnotes citing paleo-monastic literary parallels provided throughout Tabacco's edition of Peter Damian's *Vita Romualdi*.

56. On the diffusion of the Alexius legend, see Engels, "West European Alexius Legend," esp. 100–110; on the diffusion of Barlaam and Ioasaph, see John C. Hirsh, introduction to *Barlam and Iosaphat: A Middle English Life of Buddha Edited from MS Peterhouse 257* (London: Oxford University Press, 1986), xiii–xx; Peter Schreiner, "Der Austausch von literarischen Motiven und Ideen zwischen Ost und West im Mittelmeerraum," in Arnaldi and Cavallo, *Europa medievale e mondo bizantino*, 73–80, esp. 75–76, 80.

57. Josef Meri, *The Cult of Saints among Muslims and Jews in Medieval Syria* (Oxford: Oxford University Press, 2002), esp. 5–6.

58. Camillus Callewaert, "Les étapes de l'histoire du Kyrie: S. Gélase, S. Benoît, S. Grégoire," *RHE* 38 (1942): 20–45; Jungmann, *Mass of the Roman Rite*, 1:333–46; Jungmann, *Pastoral Liturgy*, 180–91; Irénée Hausherr, *Noms du Christ et voies d'oraison* (Rome: Pontificium Institutum Orientalium Studiorum, 1960), 217–20.

59. David A. Bjork, "The Early Frankish Kyrie Text: A Reappraisal," *Viator* 12 (1981): 9–35; Richard L. Crocker, "Kyrie Eleison," Grove Music Online, http://www.oxfordmusiconline.com/subscriber/article/grove/music/15736; Iversen, *Laus Angelica*, 63–91.

cry.[60] In the East the repetitions multiplied further, increasing to a three hundred-fold Kyrie with genuflections, which appeared in Rome in the days of Emperor Otto III.[61] Some devotees used the Kyrie as a sort of Jesus prayer to promote unceasing remembrance of God.[62] This prayer offered a potential link between the Latin and Greek churches. In 1022, when Emperor Henry II was besieging the Greek city of Troia in southern Italy, its citizens ordered their children to march out from the city, accompanied by a hermit in monastic dress bearing a cross, to plead for mercy at the emperor's tent by chanting, "Kyrie eleison."[63] The Greek-speaking Nicholas the Hermit (d. 1094) would be popularly acclaimed as a saint in the Latin Church after he arrived in Apulia carrying his cross and shouting, "Kyrie eleison."[64]

Architecture

Pre-Romanesque architecture, especially in its Mediterranean versions, synthesizes Late Antique, Near Eastern, and Greek elements.[65] While it is possible to contrast this style with Charlemagne's "Roman revival" basilican churches that looked back to Constantine's St. Peter's in Rome, Charlemagne himself complicated this contrast by his decision to model his imperial chapel on the church of San Vitale at Ravenna, thus promoting a Western tradition of Greek-style octagonal churches. Nevertheless, continued direct Eastern influence is suggested by the way that Western domes on pendentives clustered around the Mediterranean in the tenth, eleventh, and twelfth centuries. Well-traveled Western builders and their patrons had seen the architecture of Constantinople, Jerusalem, and Greek southern Italy. Eastern elements could be purchased, such as bronze doors that were fabricated in the East and shipped west.[66] Greek craftsmen could be imported, as they were for the cathedral chapel built "per Grecos operarios" for Bishop

---

60. McCormick, *Eternal Victory: Triumphal Rulership in Late Antiquity, Byzantium and the Early Medieval West* (Cambridge: Cambridge University Press, 1966), 354; Dennis H. Green, "The *Ludwigslied* and the Battle of Saucourt," in Jesch, *Scandinavians*, 281–302, esp. 291–92.

61. Jungmann, *Pastoral Liturgy*, 189–91.

62. Alfeyev, *St. Symeon the New Theologian*, 82.

63. Rodulfus Glaber, *Historiae* III iv, France, 102–3.

64. Paul Oldfield, "St. Nicholas the Pilgrim and the City of Trani between Greeks and Normans (c. 1090–c. 1140," *Anglo-Norman Studies* 30 (2007): 168–81; Efthymiadès, "D'Orient en Occident mais étranger aux deux mondes: Messages et renseignements tirés de la *Vie de saint Nicholas le Pèlerin* (BHL 6223)," in Cuozzo et al., *Puer Apuliae: Mélanges offerts à Jean-Marie Martin*, 207–23.

65. See chapter 3.

66. Guglielmo Matthiae, *Le porte bronzee bizantine in Italia* (Rome: Officina Edizioni Roma, 1971), esp. 47–51 (Skinner, *Medieval Amalfi*, 218, signals some problems with this reference); Ursula Mende, *Die Bronzetüren des Mittelalters, 800–1200* (Munich: Hirmer, 1983), 41–44.

Meinwerk of Paderborn (1009–36); for Fleury, where Gauzlinus of Fleury (1004–30) got workers and marbles from "Romania" (i.e., the Byzantine Empire); and for Monte Cassino, where Greeks were recruited to create the mosaics and variegated pavements of the new basilica constructed for Abbot Desiderius (1058–87).[67] Although Byzantine civilization had its own style, its architectural elements and decorative iconography remained important influences on the West up until the triumph of Gothic solutions.[68]

Because there are no surviving treatises on construction composed in pre-Romanesque Europe, architectural influence has to be inferred from structural similarities. Often this is inconclusive because most elements had antecedents in ancient Rome or developed out of the same Roman prototypes, thus allowing parallels to be explained in terms of common origin, direct borrowing, or both. The Franks initially had to borrow because Roman architectural traditions were less continually employed in the post-Roman Latin West than in the Greek East, but by the end of the Carolingian Age the West had already learned much of what the East had to offer. Nevertheless, ecclesiastical architecture in the millennial Church remained connected to a wider world. High galleries, part of the old and new Hagia Sophia, first made their appearance in Ottonian architecture and then spread elsewhere in the West.[69] A late tenth-century Byzantine ivory reliquary has been somewhat speculatively cited as the inspiration for the design and dedications of the 1030–40 Santa Reparata cathedral in Florence.[70] Normans returned to Normandy with Greek loot from their conquests in southern Italy.[71] Perhaps Eastern influence even affected literal orientation: it has been noted that the east–west orientation of ancient churches was more consistently maintained in the Byzantine world than in the West until twelfth-century Western builders began to follow the ancient Eastern practice more faithfully.[72]

67. *Vita Meinwerci* clv, 82, ed. Franz Tenckhoff, MGH *SS Rer Germ* 59 (Hannover: Hahn, 1921), 82; Andrew, *Vita Gauzlini* xliv, lxvii, Bautier and Labory, 80–81, 136–37; *Chron. Casin.* III xxvii, Hoffmann, 396.

68. Wirth, *L'Image médiévale*, 195.

69 Baldovin, *Urban Character of Christian Worship*, 176; Jacqueline Lafontaine-Dosogne, "Aspectes de l'architecture monastique à Byzance du VIIIe au Xe siècle: Topographie et disposition liturgique," *Revue bénédictine* 103 (1993): 186–208, esp. 198–99; Zomer, "The So-Called Women's Gallery," in Davids, *Empress Theophano*, 290–306.

70. Franklin Toker, "A Gap in the Liturgical History of Florence Cathedral, and a Byzantine Casket Rich Enough to Fill It," in *Arte d'Occidente, temi e metodi: Studi in onore di Angiola Maria Romanini*, ed. Alessandro Tomei, Anna Segagni Malacart, Antonio Cadei, and Marina Righetti Tosti-Croce, 3 vols. (Rome: Edizioni Sintesi Informazione, 1999), 2:767–79.

71. Marjorie Chibnall, *The Normans* (Oxford: Blackwell, 2000), 33.

72. Erica Cruikshank Dodd, "Jerusalem: *Fons et Origo*: Sources in *Outremer* for the Development of Medieval Western Art," in Hourihane, *Interactions: Artistic Interchange*, 11–27, esp. 12–13.

Portable Material Culture

Ecclesiastical material culture, as has already been seen, could be an instrument of reform, a way to reorient simple people toward God. Material symbols, however, refuse to stay within cultural boundaries. Westerners were delighted with Eastern metalwork, silks, and marbles.[73] They acquired jewelry, carvings, images, and textiles from all around the Mediterranean and even from across Eurasia. They probably shared the enthusiasm for the exotic expressed by Roger of Helmarshausen in his early twelfth-century "Theophilus *On Diverse Arts*" (note his choice of a Greek-sounding pseudonym):

> If you will diligently examine it [this manual], you will find in it whatever kinds and blends of various colours Greece possesses: whatever Russia knows of workmanship in enamels or variety of niello: whatever Arabia adorns with repoussé or cast work, or engravings in relief: whatever gold embellishments Italy applies to various vessels or to the carving of gems and ivories: whatever France esteems in her precious variety of windows: whatever skillful Germany praises in subtle work in gold, silver, copper, iron, wood, and stone.[74]

There was ample access to Byzantine coins, jewelry, and reliquaries. When Theophanu (d. 991), the Byzantine bride of Otto II, arrived in the West in 972, she must have brought a suitably impressive dowry, but academic attempts to associate her with particular surviving treasures have foundered because there are so many tenth-century Greek luxury items still floating around.[75] One identifiable treasure, which spawned a long tradition of artistic imitation, is Moses's "brazen serpent," brought back to Milan and set up on a porphyry column in Sant-Ambrogio by Bishop Arnulf (998–1018), the leader of the 1002 embassy sent to Constantinople to fetch a bride for Otto III.[76] Cnut's Queen Emma donated a "Greek shrine" filled with relics to the New Minster at Winchester.[77] Among the most prestigious Byzantine diplomatic gifts were ceremonial crowns, whose elements often included easily

73. Ciggaar, "Une description de Constantinople dans le *Tarragonensis 55*," *Revue des études byzantines* 53 (1995): 117–40, esp. 119–20.

74. Theophilus, *De Diversis Artibus* prol., Dodwell, 13. See Lasko, "Roger of Helmarshausen," in Hourihane, *Objects, Images, and the Word*, 180–201.

75. Hiltrud Westermann-Angerhausen, "Spuren der Theophano in der ottonischen Schatzkunst?," in Wolf, *Kaiserin Theophanu*, 263–78; McKitterick, "Ottonian Intellectual Culture," 169–93, esp. 169–71. On Byzantine materials circulating in the Ottonian world, see Arne Effenberger, "Byzantinische Kunstwerke im Besitz deutscher Kaiser, Bischöfe und Klöster im Zeitalter der Ottonen," in *Bernward von Hildesheim und das Zeitalter der Ottonen: Katalog der Ausstellung Hildesheim 1993*, ed. Michael Brandt and Arne Eggebrecht, 2 vols. (Hildesheim: Bernward Verlag, 1993), 1:145–59.

76. John Lowdon, "Illuminated Books and the Liturgy: Some Observations," in Hourihane, *Objects, Images, and the Word*, 17–53, esp. 38.

77. Lynn Jones, "Emma's Greek *Scrine*," in *Early Medieval Studies in Memory of Patrick Wormald*, ed. Stephen Baxter, Catherine E. Karkov, Janet L. Nelson, and David Pelteret (Burlington, VT: Ashgate, 2009), 499–507.

recyclable gold and enamel plaques.[78] Byzantine influence on metalwork was particularly striking along the Rhine, where Roger worked, and in Italy.[79]

The majority of surviving Byzantine ivories date from the tenth and eleventh centuries.[80] Although modern connoisseurs admire the sculpted natural material, microscopic examination indicates that most were once brightly overpainted.[81] Because the size and curvature of elephant tusks limit the potential dimensions of ivory plaques, they are small, easily portable, and potentially suitable for personal use. Evidence of wear suggests that some religious-themed examples may once have been handheld prayer aids, while holes drilled for hinges reveal that others were joined to make diptychs or triptychs that could be used in private devotions. Byzantine craftsmen loved to use ivory plaques to decorate boxes or thrones, but their Western colleagues preferred to employ them in book covers or portable altars, differences that led to frequent reuse and to opportunities for recycling and disseminating artistic motifs.[82]

Deluxe textiles could transmit patterns and images. In the millennial West many of the finest fabrics were imported, including all the silks.[83] Although Eastern emperors tried to control the silk trade, at least at the high end, and many of the surviving pieces may have originally been involved in carefully calculated "silk diplomacy," what remains today is a sample of what ended up in churches. It is claimed that "several thousand Byzantine silks have survived the ravages of time and exist in Western ecclesiastical treasuries, while hundreds more are documented in inventories between the eighth and the twelfth centuries."[84] Churchmen used silks not only for vestments

78. Shepard, "Crowns from the *Basileus*, Crowns from Heaven," in *Byzantium, New Peoples, New Powers: The Byzantino-Slav Contact Zone from the Ninth to the Fifteenth Century*, ed. Miliana Kaimakamova, Maciej Salamon, and Małgorzata Smorąg Różycka (Cracow: Towarzystwo Wydawnicze "Historia Iagellonica," 2007), 127–48, esp. 140–47.

79. Wilhelm Messerer, "Zur byzantinischen Frage in der ottonischen Kunst," *Byzantinische Zeitschrift* 52 (1959): 32–60; Lafontaine-Dosogne, "Émail ou orfèvrerie à Byzance au Xᵉ au XIᵉ siècle, et leur relation avec la Germanie," in von Euw and Schreiner, *Kunst im Zeitalter der Kaiserin Theophanu*, 61–78; Lasko, "Roger of Helmarshausen," esp. 183, 188, 193.

80. Anthony Cutler, *The Hand of the Master: Craftsmanship, Ivory, and Society in Byzantium (9th–11th Centuries)* (Princeton: Princeton University Press, 1994), esp. 199.

81. Carolyn L. Connor, *The Color of Ivory: Polychromy on Byzantine Ivories* (Princeton: Princeton University Press, 1998), 4–6, 14–15.

82. Barbara Zeitler, "The Migrating Image: Uses and Abuses of Byzantine Icons in Western Europe," in *Icon and Word: The Power of Images in Byzantium. Studies Presented to Robin Cormack*, ed. Antony Eastmond and Liz James (Aldershot, UK: Ashgate, 2003), 185–204; Catherine Jolivet-Lévy, "A New Ivory Diptych and Two Related Pieces," in Hourihane, *Interactions: Artistic Interchange*, 107–19.

83. Muthesius, *Byzantine Silk Weaving*, esp. 145–46; Muthesius, "Essential Processes, Looms, and Technical Aspects of the Production of Silk Textiles," in Laiou, *Economic History of Byzantium*, 1:141–68.

84. Muthesius, "The Role of Byzantine Silks in the Ottonian Empire," in Konstantinou, *Byzanz und das Abendland*, 301–17, esp. 310–16; Antonnopouolos and Dendrinos, "Eastern Roman Empire at the Turn," in Urbańczyk, *Europe around the Year 1000*, 167–203, esp. 190.

but also to wrap relics, to enshroud the bodies of bishops and kings, to hang in churches, and to drape over altars, shrines, and tombs.[85] Despite silk's fragility, some pieces are still spectacular. The late tenth-century Byzantine silk chasuble worn by Archbishop Willigis of Mainz (975–1111) is still treasured in the Mainz Cathedral Museum.[86] The Bamberg cathedral's "Starmantle" of Emperor Henry II, bedecked with both the astronomical and the Christian heavens, includes a border inscription claiming that it was given by Duke Melos (Ishmael) of Bari (the Greek capital of Italy), who presumably added his own exotic aesthetic and imperial ideology to a project actually executed by south German seamstresses.[87] Argyros (d. post 1058), the Byzantine *dux* of Italy, when he was received into monastic brotherhood at Farfa, donated a very precious gold-embroidered robe of Byzantine silk.[88] A commemorative silk tapestry celebrating a 1019 triumph of Basil II ultimately became the shroud of the pilgrim Bishop Gunther of Bamberg (d. 1065).[89] Churchmen happily converted impressive Byzantine and even Islamic and central Asian textiles into liturgical items, which when prominently displayed could potentially influence Romanesque decorative motifs.[90]

Books could be purchased or gifted and were easily portable. Byzantine art has been claimed to furnish "*the* basic idiom for figural illustration," and Western illuminated manuscripts produced in the tenth and eleventh centuries certainly exhibit many parallels.[91] Yet the resemblances do not conclusively prove contemporary contact because traits and techniques originating in a common Greco-Roman heritage reentered the Western

85. Xinru Liu, *Silk and Religion: An Exploration of Material Life and the Thought of People, AD 600–1200* (New Delhi: Oxford University Press, 1999), 113–129, esp. 113.

86. See Wilhelm Jung, ed., *1000 Jahre Mainzer Dom (975–1975): Werden und Wandel. Austellungskatalog und Handbuch* (Mainz, Ger.: Mainzer Verlagsanstalt, 1975), 277 and pl. 1; Muthesius, *Byzantine Silk Weaving*, 186 (item M68) and pl. 88A. On Willigis's connection to Theophanu, see Eickhoff, *Theophanu und der König*, 174–90.

87. David Ganz, "Divine Handcraft: The Power of Picture Textiles in the Middle Ages" ("Design of the In/Human," a three-day international symposium held from November 19 to 21, 2009, at Akademie Schloss Solitude, http://www.design-in-human.de/lectures/ganz.html).

88. Susan Boynton, *Shaping a Monastic Identity: Liturgy and History at the Imperial Abbey of Farfa, 1000–1125* (Ithaca: Cornell University Press, 2006), 166–74.

89. Muthesius, "Role of Byzantine Silks," esp. 308; Marcell Restle, "Das Gunthertuch im Domschatz von Bamberg," in *Byzantina Mediterranea: Festschrift für Johannes Koder zum 65. Geburtstag*, ed. Klaus Belke, Ewald Kislinger, Andreas Külzer, and Maria A. Stassinopoulou (Vienna: Böhlau, 2007), 547–68 (color images nos. 3–8).

90. Arthur Haseloff, *Pre-Romanesque Sculpture in Italy*, trans. Ronald Boothroyd (1930; repr., New York: Hacker, 1971), 44, 51, 61; Lafontaine-Dosogne, "The Art of Byzantium and Its Relation to Germany in the Time of the Empress Theophano," in Davids, *Empress Theophano*, esp. 228–30.

91. Belting, "Byzantine Art among Greeks and Latins," 18. For some examples, see Messerer, "Zur byzantinischen Frage," 51–55; J.J.M. Timmers, "Byzantine Influences on Architecture and Other Art Forms in the Low Countries with Particular Reference to the Region of the Meuse," in Aalst and Ciggaar, *Byzantium and the Low Countries*, 104–45, esp. 138.

FIGURE 40. Byzantine sacral imperial ideology, image of an emperor with halo and Greek cross found in a Latin *exultet* roll. Bari, Archivio Capitolare Exultet 1, sect. 7. © DeA Picture Library/Art Resource, NY.

repertoire in the Carolingian era and then often reemerged in the tenth and eleventh centuries when artists modeled their work on earlier manuscripts or ivories. Contemporary influence is suggested, howecver, by Ottonian evangeliaries which contain narrative illustrations of Gospel parables that evoke the iconographic tradition of Byzantine Gospels more than the traditional Carolingian Gospel books featuring only canon tables and author portraits.[92] Artistic images in illuminated manuscripts could

92. Palazzo, *History of Liturgical Books*, 104; Lafontaine-Dosogne, "Art of Byzantium," esp. 216–17; Martin Kaufman, "An Ottonian Sacramentary in Oxford," in Gameson and Leyser, *Belief and Culture*, 169–86, esp. 180–83.

bleed through frontiers, as, for example, a Greek-style haloed emperor holding a Greek cross in his right hand who appears in a Latin *exultet* roll from southern Italy.[93]

How did international artistic influence affect the Latin Church? Important Eastern iconographic motifs parallel, and seem to have helped foster, some Western developments in ecclesiastical material and spiritual culture. To illustrate this dynamic here, it will have to suffice to note some convergences related to sacral imperial art, to the veneration of Mary, and to devotion to the cross and the crucifix. These suggest Greek influence on Latin iconography and, through it, on Latin spirituality.

Byzantine art and ceremony focused on the sacred emperor.[94] Because Constantinople dominated court culture, its art had wide influence. Western artists would have been especially interested because after the coronation of Otto I they needed to develop their own parallel imperial imagery.[95] Unsurprisingly, therefore, some of the new images of sacral kingship in the millennial Church evoke Eastern prototypes. The divine hand reaching down from heaven to crown a ruler is an image appearing earliest at the Greek court and has counterparts not only in the Latin West but also in Georgian and Nubian circles.[96] Female personifications of nations or cities bringing tribute to the emperor, antique symbolism used in early tenth-century Constantinople, were employed to express Western conceptions of empire in the circles around Otto III.[97] Although images of the ruler completely prostrate before God (the *proskynesis*) are first seen in the West in the ninth century, tenth- and eleventh-century counterparts appear to be independently sustained and reinforced by Byzantine traditions.[98] Perhaps

---

93. Guglielmo Cavallo, *Rotoli di* Exultet *dell'Italia meridionale* (Bari: Adriatica, 1973), 31–35, sees these rolls as a Latinized Greek tradition; Thomas Forrest Kelly, *The Exultet in Southern Italy* (New York: Oxford University Press, 1996), esp. 20–22, 207, is less certain. On the Greek details, see Belting, "Byzantine Art among Greeks and Latins," 19–23; Palazzo, *History of Liturgical Books*, 80.

94. Neville, *Authority in Byzantine Provincial Society*, 14–31.

95. Hoffmann, *Buchkunst und Königtum*, 1:10–24.

96. Shepard, "Crowns from the *Basileus*," in Kaimakamova et al., *Byzantium, New Peoples*, 145–58. On the crown as the symbol of the emperor's God-given role, see Gilbert Dagron, "Couronnes impériales: Forme, usage et couleur des stemmata dans le cérémonial du Xᵉ siècle," in Belke et al., *Byzantina Mediterranea*, 157–74.

97. Wilhelm Weizsäcker, "Imperator und huldigende Frauen," in *Festschrift für Karl Gottfried Hugelmann zum 80. Geburtstag am 26. September 1959*, ed. Wilhelm Wegener, 2 vols. (Aalen: Scientia Verlag, 1959), 2: 815–832, esp. 819–20.

98. André Grabar, *L'empereur dans l'art byzantin* (1936; new pref. in London: Variorum, 1971), 85, 98–106; Cutler, "Proskynesis and Anastasis," in his *Transfigurations: Studies in the Dynamics of Byzantine Iconography* (University Park: Pennsylvania State University Press, 1975), 53–110. For post-Carolingian Western manifestations, see Anne S. Korteweg, "Thierry II, Count of Holland, and His Wife Hildegard and Their

most innovative in the West was the introduction of joint portraits of ruling couples that present lord and lady as figures of equivalent stature.[99] Note the ivory commemorating the marriage in 972 of Otto II and Theophanu in which, flanking Christ, they both appear in Byzantine dress.[100]

Devotion to Mary may also have been affected by Eastern images. In Ottonian circles, Marian piety had a "strong upsurge [*un vif essor*]."[101] Although Western Christians had always esteemed Christ's mother, early medieval devotion to her was less prominent than it would be in the High Middle Ages, when every Cistercian monastery and Gothic cathedral was dedicated to her, everyone learned the "Ave Maria," and popular piety delighted in the miracles of the Virgin. Constantinople, however, had always honored Mary as its all-important protector: its shrine churches had famous icons and relics of her.[102] Almost all the hymn and sermon writers of the Macedonian revival dedicated whole cycles to her.[103] Manifestations of this piety were exported to the West. The most common religious subject of the carved ivories, even more common than the Crucifixion, was Mary: 10 percent of the surviving ivory plaques are images of the Virgin holding the Christ Child with her right arm (an ancient image evoking the very popular *hodegetria* icon), an image that parallels the new West-

Donations to Egmond Abbey," in Aalst and Ciggaar, *Byzantium and the Low Countries*, 146–64, esp. 149; Edmond Voordeckers, "Imperial Art in Byzantium from Basil I to Basil II (867–1025)," in Davids, *Empress Theophano*, 231–43, esp. 241–42; Sarah Hamilton, "Most Illustrious King," esp. 265.

99. Lafontaine-Dosogne, "Art of Byzantium," 211–30, esp. 212; Karkov, *Art of Anglo-Saxon England*, 266–67. That women, especially imperial women, "exercised an unusual influence in Byzantium" is the central theme of Judith Herrin, *Unrivalled Influence: Women and Empire in Byzantium* (Princeton: Princeton University Press, 2013), esp. xvi, 8–10, 161–93.

100. Korteweg, "Thierry II," 146–64, esp. 148–49; on the colors of the plaque and its Byzantine connections, see Connor, *Color of Ivory*, 18.

101. Patrick Corbet, "Les impératrices ottoniennes et le modèle marial: Autour de l'ivoire du château Sforza de Milan," in Iogna-Prat et al., *Marie*, 109–35, esp. 113.

102. On Marian icons see Averil Cameron, "The Early Cult of the Virgin," in *Mother of God: Representations of the Virgin in Byzantine Art*, ed. Maria Vassilaki (Milan: Skira, 2000), 3–57; Bissera V. Pentcheva, *Icons and Power: The Mother of God in Byzantium* (University Park: Pennsylvania State University Press, 2006), esp. 189–92. On Marian relics see John Wortley, "The Marian Relics at Constantinople," *Greek, Roman, and Byzantine Studies* 45 (2005): 171–87; Stephen J. Shoemaker, "The Cult of Fashion: The Earliest 'Life of the Virgin' and Constantinople's Marian Relics," *Dumbarton Oaks Papers* 62 (2008): 53–74; Dirk Krausmüller, "Making the Most of Mary: The Cult of the Virgin in Chalkoprateia from Late Antiquity to the Tenth Century," in *The Cult of the Mother of God in Byzantium: Texts and Images*, ed. Leslie Brubaker and Mary B. Cunningham (Burlington, VT: Ashgate, 2011), 219–45.

103. Niki Tsironis, "From Poetry to Liturgy: The Cult of the Virgin in the Middle Byzantine Era," in *Images of the Mother of God: Perceptions of the Theotokos in Byzantium*, ed. Maria Vassilaki (Burlington, VT: Ashgate, 2005), 91–102; Alexander Kazhdan, *History of Byzantine Literature*, vol. 1, *850–1000*, ed. Christine Angelidi (Athens: National Hellenic Research Foundation, Institute for Byzantine Research, 2006), 3, 38, 60–61, 68, 89, 114–15, 262–64.

FIGURE 41. Emperor and empress portrayed with equal prominence in an ivory plaque representing the coronation of Otto II and Theophanu in 972, both presented in Greek imperial regalia. © RMN—Grand Palais/Art Resource, NY.

ern statues of Mary and Jesus.[104] Attempts at Greek inscriptions appear on some Western Marian images.[105] Byzantine ivories and coins showing Mary crowning the emperor are paralleled in the illustration of the War-

104. Cutler, *Hand of the Master*, 174–84, 250 (figs. 195–209) 250; Ciggaar, "Theophano," in Davids, *Empress Theophano*, 59–61; Henry Maguire, *The Icons of Their Bodies: Saints and Their Images in Byzantium* (Princeton: Princeton University Press, 1996), 8–9; Cutler, "The Mother of God in Ivory," in *Mother of God*, ed. Vassilaki (Milan: Skira, 2000), 167–75, esp. 167. On the increased prominence of the *hodegetria* icon in tenth- and eleventh-century Byzantium, see Pentcheva, *Icons and Power*, 109–41.

105. Von Euw, "Die ottonische Kölner Malerschule: Synthese der künstlerischen Strömungen aus West und Ost," in von Euw and Schreiner, *Kunst im Zeitalter der Kaiserin Theophanu*, 1:251–80, esp. 254; Pierre

mund sacramentary, in which she crowns Otto III.[106] The Chartres tunic of the Virgin, which emerges as an important Western relic at the end of the tenth century and which may actually be made of tenth-century Byzantine silk, echoes the plethora of garments of the Virgin already found at Constantinople.[107] Western devotion to Mary had its own ancient local roots, but in the millennial Church it appears to have received encouragement from the East.

Other parallels are furnished by the history of crosses and crucifixes. Their proliferation in the millennial Latin Church, their use in the liturgy, and their employment as paths to interior meditation have already been discussed, but here too Eastern practices may have influenced Western enthusiasms. After the fall of Jerusalem to the Muslims in the seventh century, the emperors in Constantinople had taken and exhibited much of the "True Cross," and—as a mark of imperial favor analogous to gifts of silks, treasures, and titles—they bestowed fragments encased in superbly crafted cross reliquaries.[108] These were highly valued in the millennial Church: St. Edward the Confessor, for example, would be buried wearing a Byzantine *enkolpion* around his neck.[109] Otto III died in the presence of a large relic of the True Cross.[110] From the tenth century onward, Latin fragments of the True Cross became increasingly common until they far outnumbered those noted in the East—one or more can be found in virtually every major ecclesiastical treasury.[111] Another way to measure this devotion is to count the churches dedicated to the Holy Cross, rare in Constantinople and its environs but increasingly numerous in the West.[112] The millennial Church also saw the triumph of the crucifix, and Greek

Alain Mariaux, *Warmond d'Ivrée et ses images: Politique et création iconographique autour de l'an Mil* (Bern, Switz.: Peter Lang, 2002), 213–14; Lasko, "Roger of Helmarshausen," 188.

106. Deshman, "Otto III and the Warmund Sacramentary," 1–20, esp. 1–2, repr. with additional bibliography in Deshman, *Eye and Mind*, 172–81, esp. 172–73; Mariaux, *Warmond d'Ivrée et ses images*, 224–25 (also pl. 1); Cutler, "Mother of God in Ivory," esp. 166, 169–70, 172.

107. Annemarie Weyl Carr, "Threads of Authority: The Virgin's Veil in the Middle Ages," in Gordon, *Robes and Honor*, 59–93, esp. 63 and 72–73; Margot E. Fassler, *The Virgin of Chartres: Making History through Liturgy and the Arts* (New Haven: Yale University Press, 2010), 21–23, 37–42.

108. Frolow, *La Relique de la Vraie Croix*, 125–34; Frolow, *Les reliquaires de la Vraie Croix*, 102–15; Klein, *Byzanz, der Westen und das "wahre" Kreuz*, 32–68.

109. Ciggaar, "England and Byzantium on the Eve of the Norman Conquest: The Reign of Edward the Confessor," *Anglo-Norman Studies* 5 (1983): 78–96; Lynn Jones, "From *Anglorum Basileus*," esp. 106–7; Lynn Jones "The *Enkolpion* of Edward the Confessor: Byzantine and Anglo-Saxon Concepts of Rulership," in Keefer et al., *Cross and Cruciform*, 369–85.

110. Bruno of Querfurt, *Vita Quinque Fratrum* vii, Miladinov, 230–31.

111. Frolow, *La Relique de la Vraie Croix*, 109–17, 133, 141–42, 228–300; Klein, *Byzanz, der Westen und das "wahre" Kreuz*, 69–141, 285–87. Both concur that in the West the number of relics of the True Cross increased in absolute and relative terms from the tenth century onward, but Frolow sees a relatively straight linear progression, while Klein sees a more rapid upturn in the later eleventh and twelfth centuries.

112. Frolow, *La Relique de la Vrai Croix*, esp. 117–18 and 134–35.

inspiration has been claimed for famous early Western examples such as the Lothar cross and the Gero crucifix.[113] In an odd parchment fragment filled with notes and sketches, it is possible to glimpse the Western monk Adémar of Chabannes (d. 1034), who as a young man had had an emotionally wrenching vision of a crucifix in the sky, apparently wrestling with a Greek Crucifixion image, perhaps one found on a Byzantine ivory, that he was trying desperately to record and remember.[114]

Asceticisms and Spirituality

A distinguishing feature of the tenth-century ascetical revival in the Greek world and the "new hermitism" in the West was the inspirational role played by new saints. Chapter 6 discussed the reappearance of new saints in the Latin West, a phenomenon already under way in the East. In the late ninth century, after the end of the disruptive fight over iconoclasm, contemporary ascetic saints began to reappear in the Byzantine Empire; in the tenth the ranks of its provincial saints came to include a host of charismatic, low-born hermit monks, many of whom lived in southern Italy, on Mount Olympus, and on Mount Athos. Greek authors collected lives of modern saints, and reformers such as Symeon the New Theologian proclaimed their importance.[115] Although *βίοι* of the new Byzantine ascetic saints may not have reached the Latin West, some of the holy men did.[116] Nilus was hailed as a "new morning star."[117] Latin lives of contemporary nonelite saints first reappear in Italy, the Western area most exposed to this eremitical glorification, and they proliferate a generation or two later in transalpine Europe.[118]

---

113. Lasko, *Ars Sacra*, 10; Haussherr, *Der tote Christus am Kreuz*, esp. 156–60. For images, see chapter 4 above.

114. Adémar, *Chronicon* III xlvi, Bourgain, *CCCM* 129:165–66; Caecilia Davis-Weyer, "Speaking of Art in the Early Middle Ages: Patrons and Artists among Themselves," in *Testo e imagine*, 2:955–991, esp. 973–82.

115. Kazhdan, *History of Byzantine Literature*, 1:381–95; Kazhdan, *A History of Byzantine Literature*, vol. 2, *850–1000*, ed. Christine Angelidi (Athens: National Hellenic Research Foundation, Institute for Byzantine Research, 1999), 185–225; Curta, *Edinburgh History of the Greeks*, 261–75; Efthymiadis, "Hagiography from the 'Dark Age' to the Age of Symeon Metaphrastes (Eighth–Tenth Centuries)," and André Binggeli, "Collections of Edifying Stories," in Efthymiadis, *Ashgate Research Companion to Byzantine Hagiography*, 1:95–142, esp. 100–25, and 2:143–59, esp. 150–51. On the hagiographical emphasis on new saints, see Kazhdan, *History of Byzantine Literature*, 2:25–29; Alfeyev, *St. Symeon*, 37, 136–42.

116. On the lack of contemporary Greek *βίοι* in the Latin West, see Sansterre, "Témoinages des textes latines," 22. On the presence of actual Greek holy men, see David Paul Hester, *Monasticism and Spirituality of the Italo-Greeks* (Thesssaloniki: Patriarchal Institute for Patristic Studies, 1991), 160–253; Howe, "Western Monks and the East."

117. *Vita Prior Adalberti* xv, ed. and trans. Cristian Gaşpar, in Klaniczay, *Vitae Sanctorum Aetatis Conversionis Europae Centralis*, 95–181, esp. 134–35.

118. Howe, "Greek Influence on the Eleventh-Century Western Revival of Hermitism," 2 vols. (PhD diss., UCLA, 1979), esp. 1:2 and 1:16–35.

Many of the new charismatic ascetics were hermits. In the West the eremitical tradition legitimized in the Benedictine Rule had been eclipsed to some extent in the late Carolingian and post-Carolingian era.[119] Greek monasticism, on the other hand, continued to embrace a whole spectrum of eremitic, cenobitic, and mixed communities, the latter often designated by the Greek term *laura* (λαύρα), which loosely describes a variety of compromises between anchoritism and community living.[120] The acclaimed father of this monastic tradition was St. Sabas (d. 532), who founded a laura in 483 on the route between Jerusalem and the Dead Sea, a community Western pilgrims would continue to visit over the centuries.[121] Laura communities predominated in Greek southern Italy, where Muslim raiders had caused problems for traditional cenobitic monasteries and their patrons, and where wandering hermit saints institutionalized their followers by establishing eremitical communities or small monasteries with dependent hermitages.[122] Latin Christians knew these communities, as evidenced by the visit of Otto III to Nilus at Serperi, whose laura there consisted of individual huts situated around a central oratory.[123] Also showcasing lauras was Mont Athos, whose original hermit colonizers were being upstaged by Athanasius the Athonite (d. ca. 1003), who in 963 at his "Great Laura" founded a cenobitic community with affiliated hermits living under the abbot's supervision.[124] Monastic customs on Mount Athos would have been directly known to the Italo-Latin Benedictine monks, many of them Amalfitani, who dwelled there and were favorably

119. Kathryn L. Jasper and Howe, "Hermitism in the Eleventh and Twelfth Centuries," forthcoming in Beach and Cochelin, *Cambridge History of Medieval Western Monasticism.*.

120. Enrico Morini, "Eremo e cenobio nel monachesimo greco dell'Italia meridionale nei secoli IX e X," *Rivista di storia della Chiesa in Italia* 31 (1977):1–39, 354–90; Anne-Marie Helvetius and Michel Kaplan, "Asceticism and Its Institutions," in Noble and Smith, *Early Medieval Christianities*, 275–98, esp. 277–78.

121. Joseph Patrich, *Sabas, Leader of Palestinian Monasticism: A Comparative Study in Eastern Monasticism, Fourth to Seventh Centuries* (Washington, DC: Dumbarton Oaks, 1995); Yizhar Hirschfeld, "The Founding of the New Laura," in Wimbush and Valantasis, *Asceticism*, 265–80. On the influence of Mar Saba, see *The Sabaite Heritage in the Orthodox Church from the Fifth Century to the Present*, ed. Patrich (Louvain: Peeters, 2001).

122. Agostino Pertusi, "Aspetti organizzativi e culturali del'ambiente monacale greco dell'Italia meridionale," in *L'Eremitismo*, 382–434, esp. 390–400; Hester, *Monasticism*, 60–101.

123. Βίος Νείλου ¶92, ed. Giovanelli, 128, trans. Giovanelli, 109. See Eickhoff, *Kaiser Otto III: Die erste Jahrtausendwende und die Entfaltung Europas* (Stutgart: Klett-Cotta, 1999), 141–43.

124. Peter Burridge, "Eleventh- and Twelfth-Century Monasteries on Mount Athos and Their Architectural Development," in *Work and Worship at the Theotokos Evergetis, 1050–1200*, ed. Margaret Mullett and Anthony Kirby (Belfast: Belfast Byzantine Enterprises, 1997), 78–89, esp. 79–82; Curta, *Edinburgh History of the Greeks*, 144–45; Kallistos Ware, "St. Athanasius the Athonite: Traditionalist or Innovator?," in *Mount Athos and Byzantine Monasticism, Papers from the 28th Spring Symposium of Byzantine Studies, Birmingham, March 1994*, ed. Anthony Bryer and Mary Cunningham (Aldershot, UK: Variorum, 1966), 3–16, esp. 12–14; Antonnopouolos and Dendrinos, "The Eastern Roman Empire at the Turn," in Urbańczyk, *Europe around the Year 1000*, 167–203.

described in a Georgian life from the 1040s.[125] It is probably no coincidence that communities resembling lauras spread throughout eleventh-century Latin Italy in the circles around Romuald and Peter Damian.[126] In the north there would soon be Carthusians, Grandmontaines, and a host of irregular eremitical communities that the new religious orders of the twelfth century would ultimately absorb.[127]

Another echo, albeit of short duration, involved imperially sponsored missionary monasticism. The Eastern Empire defined itself in missionary terms, with the emperor as chief evangelist.[128] The most spectacular Latin imperial missionary initiatives involved the half-Greek emperor Otto III and monks associated with him, whose enthusiasm for active "missionary monasticism" was somewhat atypical of the Western Benedictine tradition as a whole.[129]

Italo-Greek monks have been credited with fostering a revival of interest in manual labor among Western monks, including the use of lay brothers (conversi) working in the fields.[130] Hagiographical accounts suggest that Greek monks valued manual labor and accommodated peasants readily.[131] Westerners also had their own strong tradition of monastic labor enshrined in Benedict's rule, although in some houses it may have been eclipsed by the late Carolingian and Cluniac expansion of liturgical duties. New Latin and

125. George the Hagiorite, *Vitae of John and Euthymius*, xxvii–xvii, trans. Paul Peeters, "Histoires monastiques géorgiennes I," *Analecta Bollandiana* 36–37 (1917–19): 8–63, esp. 36–38; Pertusi, "Monasteri e monaci italiani all'Athos nell'alto medioevo," in *Le millénaire du Mont Athos*, 1:217–51. For traces of the Benedictine Rule on Athos, see Sansterre, "Témoinages des textes latins," 14.

126. Giovanni Tabacco, "Romuald di Ravenna e gli inizi dell'eremitismo Camaldolese," in *L'Eremitismo*, 73–119; Christian Lohmer, *Heremi Conversatio: Studien zu den Monastischen Vorschriften des Petrus Damiani* (Münster: Aschendorff, 1991), esp. 17–21, 36–55.

127. Jasper and Howe "Greek Influence on Western Monasticism," forthcoming. Italo-Greek and Italo-Latin eremitical influences on the formation of the Carthusians appear more likely with the adoption of the longer perspective on Carthusian institutional formation advocated in Adelino Giulani, *La formazione dell'identità certosina (1084–1155)* (Salzburg: Institut für Anglistik und Amerikanistik Universität Salzburg, 2002).

128. Shepard, "Spreading the Word: Byzantine Missions," updated in *Emergent Elites and Byzantium in the Balkans and East-Central Europe*, ed. Shepard (Burlington, VT: Ashgate Variorum, 2011), 1–17.

129. Leclercq, "Saint Romuald et le monachisme missionnaire," 307–23; Gregorio Penco, "L'eremitismo irregolare in Italia nei secoli XI–XII," *Benedictina* 32 (1985): 201–21, esp. 210–11; Eickhoff, "Otto III. in Pereum: Konzept und Verwirklichung seiner Missionspolitik," *Archiv für Kulturgeschichte* 83 (2001): 25–35.

130. Conrad Greenia, "The Laybrother Vocation in the Eleventh and Twelfth Centuries," *Cistercian Studies* 16 (1981): 38–45, esp. 40.

131. On manual labor and Greek monks, see Julien Leroy, "La vie quotidienne du moine studite," *Irénikon* 27 (1954): 21–50, esp. 36–46; Peter Charanis, "The Monk in Byzantine Society," *Dumbarton Oaks Papers* 25 (1971): 61–84, esp. 76–78; Roman Cholij, *Theodore the Stoudite: The Ordering of Holiness* (Oxford: Oxford University Press, 2002), 31–33. For Italo-Greek monks in particular, see Francesco Russo, "L'importanza delle opera ascetiche basiliane nella vita spirituale del monachesimo orientale del'Italia Meridionale," *Nicolaus* 7 (1979): 173–82; βίος Φαντίνου v–vi, ed. Follieri, *La Vita di San Fantino il Giovane: Introduzione, testo greco, traduzione commentario e indici* (Brussels: Bollandistes, 1993), 406–9.

Greek monasteries and hermitages on the frontiers naturally embraced manual labor as part of the challenge of entering the wilderness. Greater emphasis on solitude necessarily meant greater emphasis on manual labor.[132] Yet some Greek monks deliberately chose to live by the work of their hands for ascetical reasons—for example, Nilus meticulously copied a few manuscript pages every day.[133] They seem to have inspired some Westerners. Nilus's would-be-follower Adalbert of Prague, after he entered the Greek and Latin monastery of Boniface and Alexius, distinguished himself by working with his own hands.[134] John and Liutius, who in the late tenth century had left Monte Cassino for Mount Sinai and Jerusalem, shocked their brethren by their austerity, especially in regard to manual labor.[135] Stephen of Muret (d. 1124), according to his historically challenged twelfth-century vita, was inspired to embrace a simple self-sufficient eremitical life by a Calabrian hermit community that he encountered in the 1070s.[136]

Whereas Western Christians often saw asceticism as a penitential end in itself (see Chapter 6), Greeks, including the Greeks of southern Italy, assumed the connection between asceticism and mysticism postulated by Eastern theologians in Late Antiquity and saw ascetical practices as potential first steps toward a higher mystical spirituality.[137] When Greek ascetical practices reappeared in the millennial Latin Church, or at least became more prominent, there might have been some connection. Multiple repeated genuflections while praying the psalms had been a practice of the stylite saints. The practice was continued in the East, for example, by Patriarch Ignatios (d. 877) and in Greek Italy, for example, by Nilus; it reemerged in Latin Italy in the circles around Peter Damian.[138] Also

---

132. Bede K. Lackner, "Early Cîteaux and the East," in *One Yet Two: Monastic Tradition East and West*, ed. M. Basil Pennington (Kalamazoo, MI: Cistercian Publications, 1976), 373–400, esp. 387–90.

133. Βίος Νείλου ¶ 15, 74, ed. Giovanelli, 62–63, 113–14, trans. Giovanelli, 31 and 90–91.

134. *Vita Prior Adalberti* xi, Gaşpar, 140–43.

135. *Chron. Casin.* II xii, xxx, Hoffmann, 189–90, 221–23; McNulty and Hamilton, "Orientale Lumen," 1:212–13.

136. *Vita Stephani Muretensis* vi, ed. Jean Becquet, *Scriptores Ordinis Grandimontensis*, CCCM 8 (Turnhout, Belg.: Brepols, 1968), 105–37, esp. 108. Ahistorical elements in this vita are highlighted in Derek Baker, "'The Whole World a Hermitage': Ascetic Renewal and the Crisis of Western Monasticism," in *The Culture of Christendom: Essays in Medieval History in Commemoration of Denis L.T. Bethell*, ed. Marc Anthony Meyer (London: Hambledon, 1993), 207–23, esp. 216–20, but however dubious its literal historicity, it does demonstrate that a Western audience viewed Calabrian hermits as potentially inspirational ascetics.

137. Bernard McGinn, "Asceticism and Mysticism in Late Antiquity and the Early Middle Ages," and Gregory Collins, "Simeon the New Theologian: An Ascetical Theology for Middle Byzantine Monks," in Wimbush and Valantasis, *Asceticism*, 58–74 and 343–56, esp. 346–47; Annick Peters-Custot, *Les grecs de l'Italie méridionale post-Byzantine (IXe–XIVe siècle): Une acculturation en douceur* (Rome: ÉFR, 2009), 210–11.

138. Kazhdan, *History of Byzantine Literature*, 2:99; Βίος Νείλου ¶15–17, ed. Germanelli, 62–65, trans. Germanelli, 31–34; Patricia McNulty, *Saint Peter Damian: Selected Writings on the Spiritual Life* (New York:

apparently moving from east to west was radical hermit costume involving bare feet, bare legs, a staff, a sort of sackcloth garment, and perhaps a sheep or goatskin cape, worn by hermits who were bearded like Greek monks rather than clean-shaven like Western ones.[139] Greek reformers insisted that if possible monks and hermits should walk but that if riding was required, a holy man should ride an ass (following the example of Christ), a practice taken up by Italo-Latin hermits and ultimately so widely adopted in the West that Western hermit preachers became expected to have a donkey as part of their paraphernalia.[140]

Above and beyond the superficial ascetical details, however, was supposed to be a spiritual inner dimension, a withdrawal from the world to be closer to God. The gift of tears in prayer was continuously and frequently mentioned in Greek texts prior to the year 1000 and central to the spirituality of, for example, Symeon the New Theologian.[141] It was known but relatively rare in the West until mentions of it surge in the eleventh and twelfth century, particularly in Peter Damian's Italo-Latin milieu, the region in greatest contact with Italo-Greek spirituality.[142] Ecstasy, a concept always common in Greek hagiography and ascetical theology, especially in the period studied here when Symeon the New Theologian was developing his doctrine of the divine light, has resonance in Italo-Greek circles and reappears in the Latin West.[143]

THE MID-ELEVENTH-CENTURY LATIN CHURCH IN THE CHRISTIAN WORLD

In the nineteenth century, historians had a (Western) Eurocentric view of Christian history that understood the millennial Latin Church purely in

---

Harper, 1959), 39–40. On Irish parallels, presumably with independent paleomonastic roots, see Jungmann, *Pastoral Liturgy*, 172–80.

139. Howe, "Awesome Hermit," 106–19; Maguire, *Icons of Their Bodies*, 6–74; Howe, "Voluntary Ascetical Flagellation: From Local to Learned Traditions," *Haskins Society Journal* 24 (2012): 41–61, esp. 53–55; Howe, "Western Monks and the East."

140. Theodore the Studite, *Testament*, ed. Olivier Delouis, "Le *Testament* de Théodore Stoudite: Édition critique et traduction," *Revue des études byzantines* 67 (2009): 77–108, esp. 102–03; Becquet, "L'érémitisme clerical et laic dans l'ouest de la France," in *L'Eremitismo*, 182–211, esp. 194 and 203.

141. Irénée Hausherr, *Penthos: La doctrine de la compunction dans l'Orient Chrétien* (Rome: Pontificium Institutum Orientalium Studiorum, 1944), trans. Anselm Hufstader (Kalamazoo, MI: Cistercian Publications, 1982); Hannah Hunt, *Joy-Bearing Grief: Tears of Contrition in the Writings of Early Syrian and Byzantine Fathers* (Leiden, Neth.: Brill, 2004), esp. 25–37 and 169–223; Alfeyev, *St. Symeon*, 81, 90–91, 102–3, 208–15, 422–23, and 432–33.

142. Nagy, *Don des larmes au moyen âge*, 243–50; Nagy, "Individualité et larmes monastiques: Une expérience de soi ou de Dieu," in Melville and Schürer, *Das Eigne und das Ganze*, 107–29, esp. 112.

143. Alfeyev, *St. Symeon*, 241–49; Howe, "Greek Influence on the Eleventh-Century Western Revival," 1:142–49.

terms of its own dynamics. Any changes in its material, liturgical, spiritual, educational, or political culture could be explained as responses to local post-Carolingian crises and to the challenges of subsequent rapid demographic, economic, and institutional growth. Yet this model fails to explain why the competing churches of the Latin West and the Greek East often developed in surprisingly parallel ways. In opposition to a stand-alone model of the Latin Church, a few twentieth-century scholars made a case for cultural diffusion and attempted to see Western developments as reflections of broader Mediterranean patterns.[144] Emphasis on the light from the East is also insufficient, however, in that the churchmen trying to reform the Latin Church according to its own inherited authoritative models were probably less disposed to welcome exterior inspiration than they were to suspect that ideas that did not come from Simon Peter might have come from Simon Magus.

This present chapter's necessarily perfunctory survey suggests more complex connections. Christian churches shared related heritages. Moreover, the Latin and Greek churches were experiencing parallel external challenges: the Latin West in the ninth century confronted Vikings, Muslims, and Magyars; the Macedonian emperors were faced with Muslims, Bulgars, and Turks. Eastern and Western emperors attempted to use religion to bolster their positions. In both regions growing economies and governmental crises were impelling clerical elites to reorganize in increasingly sophisticated ways. Yet despite these commonalities the churches that resulted were not identical.

The Western Church, and the Western world it was creating, displayed a dynamism that was enhanced rather than diminished by its international contacts. A fitting symbol of the new Latin world might be Theophanu's wedding charter from 972, a five-foot-long roll of purple parchment with gold lettering, produced to be displayed, which looks ultra-Byzantine at first glance except that its language is Latin, its silk background is faux, and it somehow manages never to specifically identify the Byzantine Empire as "Roman." Close examination reveals it to be a recognizable local product that incorporates foreign resonances in order to proclaim the universality of the new German-Italian Roman Empire.[145]

---

144. The classic study in this regard was Walter Franke, *Romuald von Camaldoli und seine Reformtätigkeit zur Ottos III.* (Berlin: E. Ebering, 1913), which considered Romualdian hermitism Greek-inspired. For subsequent debates, see Howe, "Greek Influence on the Eleventh-Century Western Revival," 1:4–9, and "Western Monks and the East."

145. Anthony Cutler and William North, "Word over Image: On the Making, Uses, and Destiny of the Marriage Charter of Otto II and Theophanu," in Hourihane, *Interactions: Artistic Interchange*, 167–87; Nicolas Drocourt, "Ambassades latines et musselmanes à Byzance: Une situation contrastée (VIIIᵉ–XIᵉ siècles),"

Gerhart Ladner believed that in the West the idea of reform had developed as *reformatio ad melius*, an intellectual model that left some wiggle room for progressive improvement.[146] Historians rightfully hesitate to accept claims that abstruse theological differences could affect whole societies, most of whose citizens were not even literate, much less theologians. And yet in practice Latin Christianity, after violent disruptions in the post-Carolingian world—chaos that in retrospect may have been creative destruction—somehow messily managed to re-create itself in ways that proved to be productive. Reforming churchmen referenced biblical models, ancient books, and Roman and Carolingian ideals. They were aware of the best practices of neighboring churches. And somehow they helped to create a society that could and did advance.

Byzantion 74 (2004): 348–81, esp. 352–60; Hans K. Schulze, *Die Heiratsurkunde der Kaiserin Theophanu: Die griechische Kaiserin und das römisch-deutsche Reich 972–991* (Hannover: Hahn, 2007).

146. See introduction.

EPILOGUE

A POPE CAPTURED, A CHURCH TRIUMPHANT

Pope Leo IX was captured by the Normans of southern Italy after they had defeated his forces in the battle of Civitate (June 18, 1053).[1] He was a distinguished prisoner, a former prince bishop of Toul, descended from the late seventh-century Etichonids of Alsace, a scion of the counts of Egisheim, perhaps a nephew of the German emperor himself and certainly a blood relative of the greatest lords of northeastern France, the Lorraine, and Burgundy.[2] His situation was humiliating. In attempting to extricate himself, he had to beg for help from Henry III and Constantine IX, emperors whose dilatory military support had contributed to his troubles.[3] He had to absolve the Normans from their misdeeds.[4] He had to concede privileges to Benevento, now his prison, a city he had purchased from the German emperor in 1052 but which had been quick to hand him over to his enemies after the battle, enhancing its citizens' reputation as notorious rebels.[5] Now he found himself shielding Beneventan ecclesiastical

---

1. The sources on the battle of Civitate are described in Huguette Taviani-Carozzi, "Une bataille franco-allemande en Italie: Civitate (1053)," in *Peuples du Moyen Âge: Problèmes d'identification*, ed. Huguette Carozzi and Claude Taviani-Carozzi (Provence: Université de Provence, 1996), 181–211; and in Munier, *Pape Léon IX*, 212–15 and 249–51. For the Norman context of the battle, see Taviani-Carozzi, *La terreur du monde: Robert Guiscard et la conquête normande en Italie* (Paris: Fayard, 1996), 192–212; on its political consequences, see Loud, *Age of Robert Guiscard*, 110–23.

2. Leo's genealogy is investigated in Hans Hummer, "Reform and Lordship in Alsace at the Turn of the Millennium," in *Conflict in Medieval Europe: Changing Perspectives on Society and Culture*, ed. Warren G. Brown and Piotr Górecki (Aldershot, UK: Ashgate, 2001), 69–84, esp. 69–72; Munier, *Pape Léon IX*, 23–53 and 341; Frank Legl, "Die Herkunft von Papst Leo IX," and Jean-Noël Mathieu, "La lignée maternelle du pape Léon IX et ses relations avec les premiers Montbéliard," in Bischoff and Tock, *Léon IX et son temps*, 61–76 and 77–110.

3. Leo's communications with the emperors are discussed later in this chapter.

4. *Vita Leonis* II xxi, Krause, 228–31; "Anonymous of Benevento," *Vita Leonis* ix, ed. Albert Poncelet, "Vie et miracles du Pape S. Léon," *Analecta Bollandiana* 25 (1906): 258–97, esp. 288; William of Apulia, *Gesta Roberti Wiscardi*, II lines 261–66, ed. Marguerite Mathieu, *Guillaume de Pouille: La Geste de Robert Guiscard* (Palermo: Istituto siciliano di studi bizantini e neoellenici, 1961), 146–47, trans. Graham A. Loud, "The Deeds of Robert Guiscard by William of Apulia," Leeds Medieval History Texts in Translation website, http://www.leeds.ac.uk/arts/downloads/file/1049/the_deeds_of_robert_guiscard_by_william_of_apulia).

5. Hermann of Reichenau, *Chronicon* (1047 and 1050), ed. Georg Pertz, MGH SS 5 (Hannover: Hahn, 1844), 67–133, esp. 126–27 and 129, trans. Robinson, *Eleventh-Century Germany: The Swabian Chronicles*

properties with papal anathemas and awarding its archbishop the pallium, allowing him to wear it at major celebrations that included his own birthday parties.[6] Another potential indignity resulted from the traditional Greekophile orientation of southern Lombardy: the church associated with the ducal palace was Santa Sofia, a hexagonal building designed to evoke Hagia Sophia in Constantinople, not St. Peter's in Rome.[7]

In the aftermath of the disaster the pope was hit by a wave of criticism. Hermannus Contractus grumbled that the highest pontiff ought to have been fighting spiritual battles, and other German chronicles generally followed his lead.[8] Bruno of Segni, for whom Leo was otherwise a great hero, concedes that at Civitate he had been animated more by zeal for God than by military science.[9] Peter Damian, observing that St. Ambrose had led no armies against the Arians nor St. Gregory the Great against the Lombards, archly comments that Leo was holy but not because he had led troops, just as his predecessor the apostle Peter had been holy but not because he had denied Christ.[10]

Most upsetting, however, was the memory of the carnage. The Battle of Civitate was horrendously bloody. Although some chroniclers question the effectiveness, loyalty, and courage of Leo's petty Italian allies, all agree that his German troops had fought bravely until, as the chronicler William of Apulia puts it, "of all those men not one survived."[11] Afterwards the Normans allowed Leo, closely escorted, to wander through the battlefield and identify the bodies of his friends.[12] This affected him very deeply. He ordered a chapel to be constructed in honor of his fallen soldiers, whom

---

(Manchester, UK: Manchester University Press, 2008), 81 and 87. On Leo's earlier dealings with Benevento, see *Chronicon S. Sophiae (cod. Vat. Lat. 4939)*, ed. Jean-Marie Martin, 2 vols., Fonti per la storia dell'Italia medievale Rerum Italicarum Scriptores 3* (Rome: ISIME, 2000), 1:238–41.

6. Leo, *Epist. ad Uldaricum*, ed. Migne, *Pat. Lat.* 143:732–33, a document issued within several weeks of Leo's imprisonment, grants privileges to Benevento's churches. Perhaps he conceded these privileges somewhat willingly inasmuch as the archbishop was a Bavarian whom he himself had consecrated, a prelate who would later promote Leo's cult in Benevento: see Conradin von Planta, "Le dossier hagiographique de Léon IX," in Bischoff and Tock, *Léon IX*, 217–32, esp. 226.

7. On Santa Sofia in Benevento, see Thomas Forrest Kelly, ed., *La cathédrale de Bénévent* (Ghent: Ludion, 1999), 49–52, 78–81, 153–55; and McClendon, *Origins of Medieval Architecture*, 54–58. The eleventh-century *Translatio Sancti Mercurii*, ed. MGH *SS Rerum Langobardicarum et Italicarum* (Hannover: Hahn, 1878), 576–78, esp. 577, explicitly links Santa Sofia to Hagia Sophia, although the actual physical resemblance is slight, as it generally is with most early medieval architectural "copies."

8. Hermann of Reichenau, *Chronicon* (1053), Pertz, 132, Robinson, 96; Mireille Chazan, "Léon IX dans l'historiographie médiévale de l'Europe occidentale," in Bischoff and Tock, *Léon IX*, 589–621, esp. 590–602 and 620.

9. Bruno of Segni, *Libellus de Symoniacis* v, ed. Ernst Dümmler, MGH *Libelli de Lite*, 3 vols. (Hannover: Hahn, 1891–99) 2:543–62, esp. 550, trans. Robinson, *Papal Reform*, 377–90, esp. 383.

10. Peter Damian, *Epist.* lxxxvii, Reindel, 2:514–15, Blum, 3:299–308, esp. 307–8.

11. On the carnage of the battle, see William of Apulia, *Gesta Roberti Wiscardi*, II lines 142–265, esp. 256, Mathieu, 140–47, Loud, 21; "Anonymous of Benevento," *Vita Leonis* viii, Poncelet, 286–87; *Chron. Casin.* II lxxxiv, Hoffmann, 333.

12. "Anonymous of Benevento," *Vita Leonis* viii, Poncelet, 287–88.

FIGURE 42. Knights in southern Italy. Warfare illustrated in Rabanus Maurus, *De Rerum Naturis*. Archivio dell'Abbazia di Montecassino Cod. Casin. 132 (early eleventh century). Photo credit: Scala/Art Resource, NY.

he proclaimed martyrs for St. Peter. The holy war mentality that would blossom in later generations probably owed something to Leo's knights, who had earned their glory as martyrs by fighting the Normans.[13]

Leo had once been a dashing figure, described by an Italian chronicler as "very handsome, with red hair and a lordly stature."[14] In his last months, however, he became an ascetic in the severe Italian mode. Although the holy deeds reported in saints' vitae need to be evaluated cautiously, Leo's contemporary hagiographers may have some credibility here in that they

13. On the shrine of Leo's "martyrs" and multiple revelations about their blessed state, see *Vita Leonis* II xxi, Krause, 228–29, Robinson, 150–51; and the *Sermo Leonis* ii, ed. Poncelet, "Vie et miracles du Pape S. Léon IX," 289. Later hagiographers also emphasize Leo's vision: see, for example, Libuinus, *De Obitu S. Leonis* ii, ed. Johann Matthias Watterich, *Pontificum Romanorum Qui Fuerunt Inde ab Exeunte Saeculo IX usque ad Finem Saeculi XIII Vitae*, 2 vols. (1862; repr., Aalen: Scientia Verlag, 1966), 1:170–77, esp. 172; and, informed by Libuinus, Bruno of Segni, *Vita Leonis* vi, Dümmler, 2:543–62, esp. 550–51, Robinson, 377–90, esp. 384–87. Colin Morris, "Martyrs on the Field of Battle before and during the First Crusade," in *Martyrs and Martyrologies*, ed. Diana Wood, Studies in Church History 30 (Oxford: Blackwell, 19931), 93–104, esp. 97 and 103, situates these "martyrs" within a broader crusading tradition.

14. Amatus, *Ystoire* III xv, Guéret-Laferté, 318, Dunbar and Loud, 91.

had to produce portraits that his many surviving friends would recognize. According to these lives, Leo in his last days wore a hair shirt and slept on bare ground, attempted to learn enough Greek to read scripture, and recited the whole Psalter while genuflecting, a Greek ascetic practice now in vogue among Peter Damian's hermits. A long story describes him embracing a leper and ministering to his needs, anticipating a famous incident in the life of Francis of Assisi. His fasts and vigils, although at first voluntary, became so uncontrolled that he could hardly eat or sleep.[15] In March 1054, after nearly nine months of inconclusive negotiations, the Normans suddenly let their valuable captive go. They probably wanted to avoid having a dead pope on their hands. Carried back to Rome on a litter, he died on April 19, still in his early fifties.

᠍

How do a pope's last days relate to a history of ecclesiastical revival? Leo's captivity offers a vantage point from which we can look back and survey the progress that the Latin Church had made since the chaotic decades of the late ninth and early tenth centuries. According to the traditional narrative, Leo was a transitional figure, ruling at the end of imperial reform and at the beginning of the real Gregorian Reform that would free the Church from its feudal ties and lead to the canon-law-centered, Rome-centered Church of the High Middle Ages. Yet a closer examination of Leo's dark last days reveals that, long before the high drama of papal and imperial conflict over investitures, a renewed, powerful, and self-confident Latin Church was already occupying center stage.

One mark of the Church's progress is that Leo's captors behaved relatively well. The southern Italian Normans, or at least those leaders one can trace, were descended from Viking pirates.[16] Yet, like many other peripheral peoples whose depredations were described in the opening chapter of this book, these Northmen were now "Christianized." They treated Leo with all the respect that professional bandits and mercenaries could muster, begging for his blessing and forgiveness, holding him in relatively loose detention, and supplying his household with bread and wine (how they procured these is nowhere specified). They had allegedly become such devoted Christians that a contingent recently massacred near Monte Cassino was said to have been vulnerable because its soldiers had left their arms outside when they entered a church to pray.[17] Leo himself, for

---

15. *Vita Leonis* II xxii–xxiv, Krause, 230–37, Robinson, 151–54. On stories of saints' encounters with lepers, see Catherine Peyroux, "The Leper's Kiss," in *Monks and Nuns, Saints and Outcasts: Religion in Medieval Society: Essays in Honor of Lester K. Little*, ed. Sharon Framer and Barbara H. Rosenwein (Ithaca: Cornell University Press, 2000), 172–88.

16. Loud, *Age of Robert Guiscard*, 81–84.

17. Amatus, *Ystoire* II xxxi, Guéret-LaFerté, 304–5, Dunbar and Loud, 83 (where the division is II xxxii).

obvious reasons, was not willing to praise "this undisciplined and alien race with incredible and unheard of madness and more than pagan impiety . . . that refuses to distinguish between the sacred and the profane, that devastates the basilicas of the saints, burns them, razes them to the ground."[18] Norman apologists, however, saw a different reality and would describe how their heroes ultimately became defenders of the Church and "vassals of Saint Peter."[19] The truth is that, like other aspects of ecclesiastical reform, the conversion of the Normans was always a work in progress. Yet Leo was certainly treated more courteously than a bishop captured by Northmen would have been in the late Carolingian era.

Another milestone is that Bruno of Toul had become "Leo." As noted above, since the end of the tenth century newly elected popes had routinely changed their names, and in the mid-eleventh century they often chose names borne by the popes of Late Antiquity. But Bruno chose Leo explicitly because he wanted "to imitate the virtuous way of life and career of Leo the Great."[20] Leo I (440–61) was the pope who had not feared to confront Attila the Hun and Gaiseric the Vandal. He formally required clerical celibacy, a cause dear to the heart of Leo IX, whose eleven councils thundered against irregular marriages in general and clerical marriages in particular. Leo I had intervened at the Council of Chalcedon to check Greek errors and define orthodoxy. And, more explicitly than ever before, he had identified the papal office with Peter's headship over the apostles.[21] Bruno intended to bring his own age into better conformity with Leo's, and by choosing to become Leo he had committed himself to reform on a grand scale.

Also noteworthy is Leo's ability to direct the Church from captivity. Thanks to an improved and increasingly efficient Roman chancery, he was still able to issue bulls. Even in Rome's darkest days popes had produced volumes of legal documents, but in the late tenth and early eleventh century the German-dominated papal chancery improved its bureaucracy.[22] The Tuscolaner popes refined the system further, so well in fact that when Leo took office he chose to retain Peter of Tuscolo (d. 1050), the *bibliothecarius* who had been employed since 1037 by the last three popes.[23]

18. Leo, *Epist. ad Constantinum*, ed. Michel Parisse and Monique Goullet, in *Vie du Pape Léon IX (Brunon évêque de Toul)* (Paris: Les Belles lettres, 2009), 134–44, esp. 136 and 141.

19. Taviani-Carozzi, "Léon IX et les Normands d'Italie du Sud," in Bischoff and Tock, *Léon IX*, 29–39, esp. 312–17.

20. *Vita Leonis* II viii, Krause, 186–87, Robinson, 133–34.

21. Demacopoulos, *Invention of Peter*, 4, 39–72.

22. Elze, "Das *Sacrum Palatium Lateranense*, 27–54.

23. Karl-Augustin Frech, "Die Urkunden Leos IX.: Einige Beobachtungen," in Bischoff and Tock, *Léon IX*, 161–86, esp. 174–81. For the claim that major changes in chancery procedures occurred during the time of

Nevertheless, Leo, who had already acquired nearly twenty years of administrative and diplomatic experience as bishop of Toul, quickly made his own contributions. He literally left his mark on papal documents by replacing the traditional authenticating cross with a new mark, a "rota" monogram featuring a quartered doubled circle containing Leo's name, the cross, and a surrounding inscription (usually "The earth is filled with the mercy of the Lord"). This was a pious device that powerfully juxtaposed Leo, Christ, and the whole world inasmuch it visually evoked medieval "T maps," which present the Eastern Hemisphere as abstract continents within a circle (as in figure 43).[24]

During Leo's reign, papal charters became more numerous than imperial ones.[25] To help draft them, he brought to Rome fellow Lorrainers, men educated in northern schools distinguished for legal studies.[26] At the time when Leo was captured by the Normans, the papal chancery was headed by Frederick of Lorraine (the future Pope Stephen IX, 1057–58), a distant relative of Leo through the family of the counts of Lorraine. He was with Leo in Benevento at the end of 1053. Back in Rome other Lorrainers remained at work, including Humbert of Silva Candida (d. 1061), who, as titular archbishop of Muslim Sicily since about 1050, presumably had a special interest in Christians beyond the borders of the Latin West.[27]

During Leo's final months, he wrote three letters to Constantinople, at least two of them while he was confined in Benevento. The catalyst for this correspondence was a provocative sealed letter written by Archbishop

the Tuscolan popes, prior to the accession of the imperial popes associated with Henry III, see Munier, *Pape Léon IX*, 145–61.

24. Leo Santifaller, "Über die Neugestaltung der äusseren Form der Paptsprivilegien unter Leo XI.," in *Festschrift Hermann Wiesflecker zum sechzigsten Geburtstag*, ed. Alexander Novotny and Othmar Pickl (Graz: Historisches Institut der Universität, 1973), 29–38; Julius von Pflugk-Harttung, *Die Bullen der Päpste bis zum Ende des zwölften Jahrhunderts* (Hildesheim: Georg Olms, 1976), 161–70; Joachim Dahlhaus, "Aufkommen und Bedeutung der Rota in den Urkunden des Papstes Leo IX," in *Archivum Historiae Pontificiae* 27 (1989): 7–84; Iogna-Prat, *La Maison Dieu*, 392–94.

25. Hubertus Seibert, "Kommunication—Autorität—Recht—Lebensordnung: Das Papsttum und die monastisch-kanonikale Reformbewegung (1046–1124)," in Jarnut and Wemhoff, *Vom Umbruch zur Erneuerung?*, 11–29, esp. 14–15.

26. Michel Parisse, "L'entourage de Léon IX," in Bischoff and Tock, 435–56; Charles West, "Legal Culture in Tenth-Century Lotharingia," in Rollason et al., *England and the Continent*, 451–75.

27. John T. Gilchrist, "Cardinal Humbert of Silva Candida (d. 1061)," *Annuale mediaevale* 3 (1962): 29–42; Uta-Renate Blumenthal, "Humbert of Silva Candida," in *Medieval Italy: An Encyclopedia*, 2 vols. (New York: Routledge, 2004), 1:518–19; Parisse, "L'entourage de Léon IX," 437–39. Humbert's Sicilian office, apparently awarded even before he became a cardinal, is known from Lanfranc, *De Corpore et Sanguine Domini* ii, ed. Migne, *Pat. Lat.* 150:407–42, esp. 410, trans. Mark G. Vaillancourt, *Lanfranc of Canterbury* On the Body and Blood of the Lord *and Guitmund of Aversa* On the Truth of the Body and Blood of Christ in the Eucharist, Fathers of the Church Mediaeval Continuation 10 (Washington, DC: Catholic University of America Press, 2009), 27–87, esp. 32.

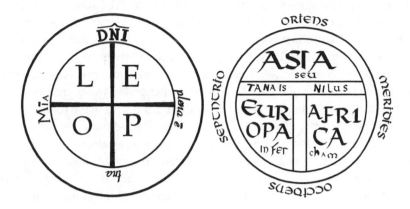

FIGURE 43. Rota of Leo IX compared with a T map of the world. Illustration by Holt Haley-Walker. Reproduced by permission.

Leo of Ohrid (d. post 1054), a former Constantinopolitan official who had become the autocephalous archbishop of the Bulgarians. The letter was sent directly to the senior Byzantine ecclesiastical official in Apulia but included instructions to forward it not only to local Christians but also to the Frankish bishops and to the pope. In it the archbishop exhorted all Christians to convert to the pure true faith and to renounce the Jewish and pagan practices of the Latin Church, especially the use of unleavened bread in the Mass.[28] Western churchmen assumed that this unexpected attack must have had the blessing of the patriarch of Constantinople, Michael Cerularios (1043–59).[29] Cardinal Humbert, who knew some Greek, brought a translated copy to Pope Leo.[30] Humbert and Leo probably both worked on a response.[31] Their first attempt was a long letter

28. The original Greek version of Leo of Ohrid's letter is in Cornelius Will, *Acta et Scripta Quae de Controversiis Ecclesiae Graecae et Latinae Saeculo Undecimo Composita Extant* (Leipzig: N. G. Elwert, 1861), 51–64; Humbert's Latin rendition is in Migne, *Pat. Lat.* 143:929–32. On the background, see Enzo Pettrucci, "Rapporti di Leone IX con Constantinopoli," *Studi medievali*, 3rd ser., 14 (1973): 733–831, esp. 751–69.

29. On Cerularios, see Franz Tinnefeld, "Michael I. Kerullarios, Patriarch von Konstantinopel (1043–58): Kritische Überlegungen zu einer Biographie," *Jahrbuch der Osterreichischen Byzantiniistik* 39 (1989): 95–127. On whether or not he really instigated Leo of Ohrid's letter, see Mahlon H. Smith III, *And Taking Bread . . . : Cerularius and the Azyme Controversy of 1054* (Paris: Éditions Beauchesne, 1978), esp. 77–83. On other things he may or may not have done in 1053–54, see Tia M. Kolbaba, "On the Closing of the Churches and the Rebaptism of Latins: Greek Perfidy or Latin Slander?," *Byzantine and Modern Greek Studies* 29 (2005): 39–51.

30. *Vita Leonis* xix, Krause, 218–25, Robinson, 146–48.

31. Stylistic comparison has been overused to assign works to Humbert, particularly by Anton Michel, whose Humbertine studies are listed in Pettrucci, "Rapporti di Leone IX con Constantinopoli," 740n–741n. Nevertheless, "Peace on Earth" likely reflects Humbert's influence both because it is related to his translation of Leo of Ohrid's letter and because it contains parallels to Humbert's later and clearly authentic *Three Books*

whose ostensible theme was "Peace on earth to men of good will."[32] It was probably never sent because a somewhat conciliatory letter soon arrived from Michael Cerularios and because the defeat at Civitate meant that the first priority had to be securing Greek military help. Yet the letters we choose not to send may still reveal our true sentiments, perhaps too well. Since some sections of "Peace on Earth" are echoed in the correspondence Leo actually sent from Benevento, this draft is a useful place to begin.

The opening line, "Peace on Earth to men of good will," begins a series of biblical exhortations to peace. Alas, this theme has already been undercut to some extent by the *intitulatio*, which addresses "Bishops Michael of Constantinople and Leo of Ohrid," failing to mention that his correspondents were the patriarch of Constantinople and the archbishop of the Bulgarians. Perhaps this slight resulted from an attempt to avoid Michael's formal Greek title, "Ecumenical Patriarch," which Latin churchmen, who translated it as *universalis patriarcha*, considered an illegitimate claim to universal authority.[33] Leo styles himself simply *Leo episcopus, servus servorum Dei*, a title that had been introduced into papal correspondence by Gregory I (590–604).[34] Although this formula is commonly translated as "servant of the servants of God," it is actually much more resonant. Because a *servus* was originally a slave, it might appear to be a humility topos, a form of self-presentation deliberately crafted to sound less arrogant than "ecumenical patriarch" (or than "universal pope," which Gregory VII would soon try out).[35] However, to be the slave of God is to be an agent of an omnipotent lord. And who are the other slaves of God the pope serves? In early Christian writings, all Christians are *servi Dei*; in Late Antiquity, just the clergy; later still, the saints alone, in the sense used in modern canonization documents such as the *Doctrina de Servorum Dei Beatificatione et Beatorum Canonizatione* of Pope Benedict XIV (1740–58). A servant of the saints of God ought to receive a respectful hearing.

against the Simoniacs: see Horst Führmann, ed., introduction to *Constitutum Constantini*, MGH *Fontes Iuris Germanici Antiqui* 10 (Hannover: Hahn, 1968), 15. The *Vita Leonis* II xix, Krause, 220–21, Robinson, 147, presents it as Leo's work without qualification, but ghostwriters rarely get due credit.

32. Leo, *Epist. ad Michaelem et Leonem*, ed. Migne, *Pat. Lat.* 143: 744–773. For context, see Annie Noblesse-Rocher, "Une source ecclésiologique de la letter *In terra pax hominibus* de Léon IX," in Bischoff and Tock, *Léon IX*, 205–16.

33. Petrucci, "Rapporti di Leone IX con Constantinopoli," 814–19; Aristeides Papadakis, "Ecumenical Patriarch," in *Oxford Dictionary of Byzantium*, ed. Alexander P. Kazhdan, 3 vols. (New York: Oxford University Press, 1991), 1:675–76.

34. Stephan Kuttner, "Universal Pope or Servant of God's Servants: The Canonists, Papal Titles, and Innocent III," *Revue de droit canonique* 31 (1981): 110–49.

35. On Western hesitation about "universal" titles, see Gilchrist, "Humbert of Silva Candida and the Political Concept of *Ecclesia* in the Eleventh-Century Reform Movement," *Journal of Religious History* 2 (1962): 13–28, esp. 22–24.

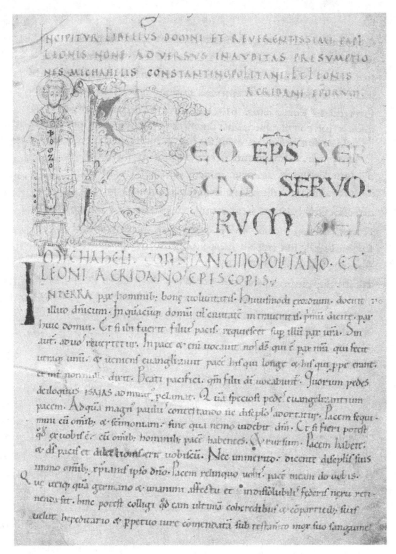

FIGURE 44. "Author portrait" of Leo IX, heading his treatise "Peace on Earth to Men of Good Will," written to respond to the "unheard of presumption" of Greek ecclesiastical leaders. Bern Burgerbibliothek/Berne Bibliothèque de la bourgeoisie cod. 292, fol. 2r. Image by permission of Burgerbibliothek Bern.

Although Humbert and Leo are responding to Leo of Ohrid's criticism of the Western use of unleavened bread in the Eucharist, they somehow fail to address this issue directly in their first forty chapters (i–xl). Instead, "Peace on Earth" segues from the peace of God to the heresiarchs who disturb it. Leo of Ohrid has displayed "unheard of presumption and incredible audacity. . . . Behold now, nearly 1020 years since the passion of Our Savior, you now begin to teach how the memory of His passion ought to be commemorated by the Roman Church! "[v]. Peter, Rome's patron, is the rock upon which the Church is built, whereas more than 90 heresies have appeared, most of them among the Greeks, some of which were opposed at the Council of Chalcedon by "Lord Pope Leo of blessed memory" (viii). Then chapters introduce and quote at length the "donation of Constantine," the odd and often discredited Roman legend in which Constantine, healed from leprosy by Pope Sylvester, gives the pope imperial power over Old Rome and shifts his capital to Constantinople (x–xiv). Specifically cited is Constantine's "law," conveyed in the *Actus Sylvestri*, which states that bishops ought to answer to the Roman pontiff just as justices ought to answer to the king (xiii).[36] The apparent intent here, although not expressed too clearly, is to claim that the authority of the Roman Church has been recognized by both councils and imperial laws and that therefore any murmuring against Rome ought to be deterred by "love of God and neighbor," by "reverence for divine canons," and by "the law of orthodox princes" (xi–xii). Leo sees the Latins as "truly Catholic [*Latinos vere catholicos*]!" (xx) and he states that, whatever his personal failings, "nobody should despise us because we are in the place of Peter . . . [and] by the action of God we preside from his throne [*cathedra*]" (xxxv). He who attacks us attacks the whole Church because there is one body of Christ" (xxxvi). "Why do you try to annul what has been divinely and humanly conceded to us?" (xxxix). At the very end of the draft Leo and Humbert finally get back to Leo of Ohrid's condemnation of the use of unleavened bread at Mass but only in an appended final chapter, which states that such details are hardly worth fighting about, especially with people who do not understand the bigger issues (xli). Although along the way this draft mentions Greek heresies and the irregular ecclesiastical career of Michael Cerularios, it is actually a very early systematic treatise on the primacy of the pope, affirming that the establishment of a well-ordered Christian community throughout the world requires an acceptance of unity under St. Peter, that is, under Rome.

The actual letters that the dying Leo sent to Constantinople were very different, shorter, more to the point, written to be carried and explicated by legates very much from his side: his occasional secretary Cardinal Humbert, his chancellor and relative Frederick of Lorraine, and Archbishop Peter of Amalfi, exiled from his see because of Greek machinations

---

36. See Amnon Lindner, "Constantine's 'Ten Laws' Series," in *Falschungen im Mittelalter: Internationaler Kongress der MGH, München, 16.–19. September, 1986*, 6 vols. (Hannover, Hahn, 1988–90), 2:491–507, esp. 494.

but knowledgeable about Constantinople. This embassy was probably doomed from the start by its incompatible goals: Leo wanted both to secure the emperor's help against the Normans and to rebuke the emperor's patriarch for his insolence. Even much more skillful diplomats would have found it difficult to be both friendly and harsh in a distrustful foreign land. The only glimmer of hope for the mission was that the emperor and his patriarch were somewhat estranged thanks to earlier personal and dynastic rivalries and to disagreements about the possible utility of Western alliances.

The first missive was a friendly letter from "Bishop Leo, servant of the servants of God, to his dear son, the glorious and religious emperor of New Rome, Constantine IX Monomachos [1042–54]."[37] Two initial chapters extol the emperor's virtues, praising especially his dedication to peace and his love of Holy Mother Church and characterizing the proper relationship between Rome and Constantinople as that of mother and daughter.[38] Leo emphasizes that "your conduct and the gifts which manifest your piety assure us that you will work faithfully to strengthen the holy catholic Church and to increase the imperial power in the world."[39] Playing with the emperor's name, Leo invokes "the first Constantine, a most noble and religious man."[40] Here the mentions of Constantine I's gift of the Western Empire to the pope found in the "Donation of Constantine" and in "Peace on Earth" are replaced by more subtle wording: "We exhort you then, great successor of great Constantine by blood, name, and power, to become also the imitator of his devotion toward the Apostolic See. And what he, the most admirable man next to Christ, gave to this See and confirmed and defended, we exhort you, according to the etymology of your name, to constantly help us recover, conserve, and defend."[41]

The heart of the letter concerns the problem posed by the incorrigible Normans, who "rise up against the churches of God and slaughter Christians." From day to day they go from bad to worse. Therefore, Leo proposes to organize a defense both "to liberate the lambs of Christ" and to punish "evildoers." Yet Leo knew all too well the limits of ad hoc military campaigns. More than once, both as an imperial prince bishop and

---

37. Leo, *Epist. ad Constantinum*, Parisse and Goullet, 134 and 139.

38. While the mother-daughter simile might have seemed likely to offend the Greeks, it had a long tradition, and within a few years Michael Psellus would also invoke it, albeit to deplore how mother Rome was revolting against her daughter New Rome: see Chrysos, "1054: Schism?," 1:547–71, esp. 556.

39. Leo, *Epist. ad Constantinum*, Parisse and Goullet, 134 and 139.

40. Ibid., 135 and 140, 137 and 142. Note H. E. J. Cowdrey, "Eleventh-Century Reformers' Views of Constantine," *Byzantinische Forschungen* 24 (1997): 63–91, esp. 74–79.

41. Leo, *Epist. ad Constantinum*, Parisse and Goullet, 137 and 142.

as the head of the Republic of St. Peter, he had failed in his own efforts to protect his people militarily. Now as a prisoner he was painfully aware of the threat that unchecked violence posed to the peace and order of the Church. He wanted more than just onetime military aid—he wanted a new world order.

The Latin West admired, but was very distant from, the ancient *pax romana*. It was ruled by military elites, bristling with fortifications, filled with jostling lordships fighting over territory. Now Leo proposes a remedy. He explains to the Greek emperor that from day to day he is awaiting the arrival of "our very dear and glorious son Emperor Henry," a descent of German forces into the contested Theme of Italy that would not necessarily have been welcome news to "dear son Constantine." But, Leo says, do not worry: "With God's grace, the interventions of the princes of the apostles, and me their vicar mediating and obtaining it, a very firm pact of peace and amity will be concluded between the two of you." Henry's forces and Constantine's, united under Leo's guidance, will crush the enemy "like two arms together." Implicit in this proposal is the hope that more general peace and order might be possible if the two Christian emperors would work together under the guidance of the pope.[42]

The closing paragraph, while stressing the need for peacemaking, deplores the "many and intolerable" things done by Patriarch Michael Cerularios, including burning Latin churches, anathematizing those who use unleavened bread in services, and depriving Antioch and Alexandria of their proper dignities. The emperor should discuss these problems with Leo's emissaries, and thus Leo's letter concludes with an introduction to Bishop Peter of Amalfi.[43]

In a separate letter sent directly to Patriarch Michael Cerularios, Leo itemizes his complaints at greater length. At least this time Michael is addressed as "archbishop" and the earlier conciliatory letter from him (today lost) is praised for offering an occasion in which the daughter may exult in reconciliation with her mother. Then, after other praises of peace, the hammer drops. Alas, "rumor has brought many intolerable things to our ears." All sorts of charges are cited as possible manifestations of pride and arrogance, but the major points at issue are four. First of all, Cerularios is a neophyte, irregularly raised to the patriarchate without respecting the proper canonical intervals of time, and perhaps his inexperience has contributed to his rash acts against Latin churches. Second, he has sought to reduce the ancient privileges and rights of the churches of Alexandria and Antioch.

---

42. Ibid., 136 and 141. On this proto-Crusade proposal, see Jean-Claude Cheynet, "La politique byzantine de Léon IX," in Bischoff and Tock, *Léon IX*, 259–72 esp. 268–69.

43. Leo, *Epist. ad Constantinum*, Parisse and Goullet, 138–39 and 143–44.

Third and most shocking, he calls himself "ecumenical," usurping the title of "universal patriarch," an "inane title [*inane nomen*]": "Even Peter did not claim to be a 'universal apostle' even though he had been established as prince of the apostles, and none of his successors would allow himself to be called by such a prodigious title even though the Council of Chalcedon had conceded it to blessed Leo and to his successors." The final charge is disparagement of Latin use of unleavened bread in the Eucharist. Michael should turn from heresies and accept the authority of the holy catholic Church, and then Leo will look forward to working with him as a "most dear brother."[44]

The mission failed spectacularly! The emperor tentatively discussed an alliance, but the patriarch, who had hoped for a better response from the West, not only refused to meet with Leo's legates but even refused to examine their credentials, which he claimed must have been falsified by his enemies. The legates finally excommunicated him July 16, 1054, but invalidly inasmuch as, unknown to them, their authority had expired more than two months earlier when Leo had died. The patriarch responded by summoning a local synod to excommunicate the legates and whoever had sent them (left unnamed). These events receive surprisingly little attention in contemporary Byzantine sources, suggesting that they were largely ignored back in 1054, although apparently they sparked enough outrage so that the emperor had to support Cerularios and refrain from allying with Rome in Italy. The resulting ecclesiastical posturing was nobody's finest hour. Humbert's bull of excommunication, among other wild claims of heresy, faulted Michael Cerularios for cutting from the creed the language specifying that the Holy Spirit proceeded from the Son, completely misunderstanding the history of the theological dispute about the presence of the *filioque* clause in the Nicene Creed.[45] Michael countered that the Latins had actually been heretics since the seventh century; that they rejected the authority of the Greek fathers such as Gregory Nazianzen, Basil the Great, and John Chrysostom; and that they intended to make Greek clergymen cut off their beards. His long list of the errors of the Latins inaugurated a polemical Greek literary genre that still flourishes today,[46] as Patriarch Bartholomew of Constantinople was recently reminded when he returned home after a meeting with Pope Francis in Jerusalem in May 2014. Although neither eleventh-century observers nor today's scholars see Leo's failed mission of 1054 as creating or finalizing a permanent

44. Leo, *Epist. ad Michaelem*, ed. Migne, *Pat. Lat.* 143:773–77.

45. Humbert, *Brevis et Succincta Commemoratio* iii, ed. Migne, *Pat. Lat.* 143:1001–4, esp. 1003–4.

46. Chrysos, "1054: Schism?," 561–64; Kolbaba, *Byzantine Lists*, 23–31; Bayer, *Spaltung der Christenheit*, 86–112.

break between the Latin and Greek churches, it obviously highlights a widening division between them.

∾

The primacy of the Roman Church was also an issue on December 17 of 1053 in two letters Leo dispatched from Benevento, one to "his dearest companion and fellow bishop, Thomas of Carthage"; the second to two other North African bishops, "Peter and John most beloved brothers in Christ."[47] Perhaps Humbert also collaborated on these letters.[48] The recipients were members of residual African Christian communities that had somehow survived centuries of Islamic regimes particularly hostile to "the land of Rome."[49] Now some African bishops were seeking Leo's help against the pretensions of the bishop of Gummi (modern Borj Cedria in Tunisia), who had called a local council and made other dispositions infringing upon the prerogatives of the archbishop of Carthage, the traditional metropolitan of Latin Africa.

Leo, again servus servorum Dei, cordially greets Thomas of Carthage as "most dear colleague and fellow bishop," emphasizing their common bonds. He commiserates with him about the African church's decline from its days of glory. Yet even though the precise point at issue is Thomas's ecclesiastical position, Leo never directly addresses him as "metropolitan" or "archbishop." Leo and his chancery intend to leave no doubt about Rome's superior status. The meat of the letter is that, although "beyond any possible doubt, after the Roman pontiff, the first archbishop and the metropolitan of all Africa is the bishop of Carthage," Thomas ought to be aware that "even if it is licit for you to examine some bishops, nevertheless it is not licit for you to give a judgment without consultation of the Roman pontiff . . . which, if you seek in the holy canons of statutes, you will be able to discover." Whatever statutes Leo might have had in mind, here he breaks off to bring in heavier artillery, invoking the proof texts regarding Peter's powers of binding and loosing (Matt. 18:18), the Petrine "Rock" (Matt. 16:18), and Christ's order to Peter to "strengthen his

47. Leo IX, *Epist. ad Thomam* and *Epist. ad Petrum et Joannem*, ed. Migne, *Pat. Lat.* 143:727–29 and 729–31.

48. The case for Humbert's authorship of the African letters is argued in Anton Michel, *Die Sentenzen des Kardinals Humbert, das erste Rechtsbuch der päpstlichen Reform*, MGH Schriften 7 (Stuttgart: Hiersemann, 1943), 185–90, but, on its skeptical reception, see Anette Hettinger, *Die Beziehungen des Papsttums zu Afrika von der Mitte des 11. bis zum Ende des 12. Jahrhunderts* (Cologne: Böhlau, 1993), 70–72.

49. The survival of the Latin Church in Africa is discussed in Hettinger, *Beziehungen des Papsttums zu Afrika*, 18–66: Mark A. Handley, "Disputing the End of African Christianity," in *Vandals, Romans, and Berbers: New Perspectives on Late Antique North Africa*, ed. A. H. Merrills (Aldershot, UK: Ashgate, 2004), 291–310, esp. 302–10; and Michael Lower, "The Papacy and Christian Mercenaries of Thirteenth-Century North Africa," *Speculum* 89 (2014): 601–31, esp. 613–14.

brothers" (Luke 22:32). Then Leo abruptly concludes the letter, explaining that he will reply more specifically to bishops Peter and John concerning the questions at issue. Perhaps the letter to Thomas was written simply for reasons of protocol so that Leo, who was in the process of communicating directly with Thomas's subordinate bishops who had appealed to him, would not be violating the prerogatives of an intermediate official. Indeed, repetitions in language and jumps in thought suggest that the letter to Thomas of Carthage could have been crafted by using as a starting point excerpts taken from the companion letter.[50]

Leo's reply to bishops Peter and John is twice as long. He presents in expanded form his lament on the present reduced state of the African church. He thanks Peter and John because they have prayed, as they have written him, "for the state of the Roman Church and for our health." If their prayers were simply generic, they were fortuitously apt; if their concern for Leo's health was more than coincidence, then even the isolated Christian communities of old Roman North Africa knew about Leo's travails. He thanks the two bishops for fostering the proper connection between head and members, and he agrees with them in affirming the primacy of Carthage, citing Carthage's role in the great councils of the African Church. Leo's observation that the archbishop of Carthage is the only bishop in Africa who is accustomed to receive the pallium from the Apostolic See suggests an ongoing connection between Rome and Carthage that little surviving evidence documents.[51]

Leo's letter has received some scholarly attention because of the argument he goes on to make regarding the rights of Rome. He contends that only Rome can levy a final definitive judgment against other bishops and supports this position not only with the Petrine Gospel texts but also with citations drawn from the Pseudo-Isidorian decretals. Leo quotes texts attributed in that collection to Clement, Anacletus, and others. The debate about the use of these forgeries by popes cannot be summarized here beyond noting that the most significant advance in recent decades was Horst Fuhrmann's attack on the scholarly consensus that the popes had largely ignored these dubious documents until the age of Leo IX (when the Lorrainers would allegedly have given them greater play). Fuhrmann's detailed studies identify scattered earlier traces of their influence during the tenth and early eleventh centuries. Yet he himself had to admit that the use of Pseudo-Isidorian material in these African letters is unparalleled in its extent, explicitness, and appropriateness. Leo and his Lorrainers,

---

50. Leo IX, *Epist. ad Thomam*, Migne, *Pat. Lat.* 143:727–29.
51. Leo IX, *Epist. ad Petrum et Joannem*, Migne, *Pat. Lat.* 143:729–31.

perhaps Humbert, were exhibiting greater legal expertise, albeit with problematic documents.[52] After those citations, Leo thanks his *charissimi fratres* once more for their prayers. He concludes with an invocation.

This African correspondence involves two parties in desperate circumstances: a pope dying in captivity and some African bishops whose own fractious communities had little life left. While they were corresponding, the physician Constantine the African was seeking asylum in Italy, the last indigenous medieval Christian Carthaginian for whom we have any detailed information. A few years later, Gregory VII, intervening in another fight between the bishop of Carthage and his subordinates, worried that the North African Christians might not have enough bishops left to consecrate new ones.[53] Unsurprisingly, Leo and his African correspondents found it easier to turn away from their present circumstances and look back on an idealized past: "We sorrow greatly," says Leo, "that the glory of the African churches has been so trodden underfoot by non-Christian tribes that now scarcely five bishops can be found where once two hundred and five could usually be counted at plenary councils; and that the few sheep who remain there are handed over to daily slaughter, where formerly the innumerable flock of the Lord enjoyed the highest peace under most numerous rams." That Africa and other areas had currently fallen to the *gentibus*, presumably "because of our sins," was a problem of theodicy Leo could not solve. Nevertheless, he believed he knew how things ought to be, and he and his fellows wanted to bring that world into being. They were proposing to reform the Church, and indeed the whole world, into a more just and righteous order.

In fact, the millennial Church had already developed structures that would make possible, perhaps even inevitable, the activist papacy, the investiture contest, and religious movements such as the Crusades. To adequately narrate the rest of this story would require, as Giles Constable suggested in *The Reformation of the Twelfth Century*, looking at the specific concerns and ideals of each subsequent reforming generation: the 1040–70 fight for the moral reform of the clergy; the 1070–1100 battle for the freedom of the Church and the power of Rome; the 1100–1130 transitional generation that sought to end the investiture controversy and develop new institutions; and finally the 1130–60 efforts to reform the life

---

52. Horst Fuhrmann, *Einfluss und Verbreitung der pseudoisidorischen Fälschungen: Von ihrem Auftauchen bis in die neuere Zeit*, 3 vols. (Stuttgart: Anton Hiersemann, 1972–74), 2:340–45.

53. Gregory VII, *Register* III. xix–xxi, Caspar, 285–88, Cowdrey, 202–4, on which see Hettinger, *Beziehungen des Papsttums zu Afrika*, 143–89. The last known of these African bishops appears in 1140 in the court of Roger II of Sicily: see Caspar, *Roger II. (1101–1154) und die Gründung der normannisch-Sicilischen Monarchie* (Innsbruck: Wagner'schen Universitaäts-Buchandlung, 1904), 422–23.

of every Christian, religious and lay.[54] Each generation stood upon the shoulders of its predecessors. But those reforming generations presupposed an earlier ecclesiastical recovery, a reconstruction of ecclesiastical structures after the shocks of Carolingian collapse, barbarian invasions, and societal reorganization. That reformation had been a great success. While the dying Leo was imagining the lost pastoral pastureland of Africa's ecclesiastical golden age, his own Church was already distinguished by many green pastures, numerous and spirited flocks, and increasingly indomitable "rams of the Lord."

54. Constable, *Reformation of the Twelfth Century*, 4–5 and 299–300.

SELECTED BIBLIOGRAPHY

This selected bibliography lists only those works cited more than once. Its purpose is to help readers expand the short-form footnotes, not to list all scholarship consulted or cited. Primary sources are listed first, separately, because, when possible, references to them privilege original language editions followed by English language translations. For primary sources, I cite 1) the original author (if one is known), short title, and any book or chapter references; 2) then the editor, edition title, and publishing information on the edition; and 3) bibliographic information on a translation in English if one is available. References to secondary scholarship in non-English languages cite English-language translations when these are at hand, the original languages otherwise. Reprints and reissues are not included unless they embody more advanced forms of the research. Series references have been omitted unless they provide unusual help in locating the works cited or in describing their nature.

Primary Sources

Abbo of Saint-Germain-des-Prés. *Sermones*. Edited by Ute Önnerfors, *Abbo von Saint-Germain-des-Prés: 22 Predigten: Kritische Ausgabe und Kommentar* (Frankfurt: Peter Lang, 1985).

Adam of Bremen. *Gesta Hammaburgensis*. Edited by Bernhard Schmeidler, *Adam von Bremen: Hamburgische Kirchengeschichte*, MGH SS Rer Germ 2 (Hannover: MGH, 1917). Translated by Francis J. Tschan, *History of the Archbishops of Hamburg-Bremen* (New York: Columbia University Press, 1959).

Adémar. *Chronicon*. Edited by Pascale Bourgain, *Ademari Cabannensis Chronicon*, CCCM 129 (Turnhout, Belg.: Brepols, 1999).

Adrevaldus. *Miracula Benedicti*. Edited by Eugène de Certain, *Les Miracles de Saint Benoît*, 1–83, Société de l'histoire de France publications in octavo 96 (Paris: Mme Ve Jules Renouard, 1858).

Aelfric of Eynsham. *Epistola* viii. Edited and translated by Christopher A. Jones, *Aelfric's Letter to the Monks of Eynsham* (Cambridge: Cambridge University Press, 1998).

——. *Epistola ad Uulstanum*. Edited by Whitelock et al., *Councils & Synods*, vol. 1, pt. 1, 242–55.

——. *Epistola de Canonibus*. Edited by Whitelock et al., *Councils & Synods*, vol. 1, pt. 1, 191–226.

——. *First Old English Letter to Wulfstan*. Edited by Whitelock et al., *Councils & Synods*, vol. 1, pt. 1, 255–302.

——. *Grammatica* (prefaces). Latin preface edited by Julius Zupitza, *Aelfrics Grammatik und Glossar* 1–2, 3rd ed. (Hildesheim: Weidmann, 2001). Old English preface edited by

Jonathan Wilcox, *Aeflric's Prefaces*, 36–37, 114–16, 151–53. Durham Medieval Texts 9 (Durham: Durham Medieval Texts, 1994, corrected reprint, 1996).

Aelfric Bata. *Colloquia*. Edited by Scott Gwara, translated by David W. Porter, *Anglo-Saxon Conversations: The Colloquies of Aelfric Bata* (Woodbridge, UK: Boydell, 1997).

Aimoinus of Fleury. *Miracula Benedicti*. Edited by Eugène de Certain, *Les Miracles de Saint Benoît*, 90–172 (Paris: Mme Ve Jules Renouard, 1858).

——. *Vita Abbonis*. Edited by Robert-Henri Bautier and Monique Labory, *L'abbaye de Fleury en l'an Mil*, 90–137, IRHT sources d'histoire médiévale 32 (Paris: CNRS, 2004).

Alcuin. *Epistolae*. Edited by Ernst Dümmler, MGH *Epistolae* IV: Karolini Aevi 2:1–481 (Berlin: Weidmann, 1895). Selected translations by Stephen Allott, *Alcuin of York, c. A.D. 732 to 804—His Life and Letters* (York, UK: William Sessions, 1974).

Amatus of Montecassino. *Ystoire de li Normant*. Edited by Michèle Guéret-LaFerté, *Aimé du Mont-Cassin: Ystoire de li Norman: Édition du manuscrit Bn F fr. 688*, Classiques français du moyen âge 166 (Paris: Honoré Champion, 2011). Translated by Prescott N. Dunbar and Graham A. Loud, *Amatus of Montecassino: The History of the Normans* (Woodbridge, UK: Boydell, 2004).

Andrew of Fleury. *Miracula Benedicti*. Edited by Eugène de Certain, *Les Miracles de Saint Benoît*, 173–276, Société de l'histoire de France publications in octavo 96 (Paris: Mme Ve Jules Renouard, 1858).

——. *Vita Gauzlini*. Edited by Robert-Henri Bautier and Monique Labory, *André de Fleury, Vie de Gauzlin, Abbé de Fleury*, Sources d'histoire medieval publiées par l'IRHT 2 (Paris: CNRS, 1969).

Annales Bertiniani. Edited by Félix Grat, *Annales de Saint-Bertin* (Paris: Klincksieck, 1964). Translated by Janet L. Nelson, *The Annals of St-Bertin* (Manchester, UK: Manchester University Press, 1991).

Annales Ultonienses. Edited and translated by Seán Mac Airt and Gearóid Mac Niocaill, *The Annals of Ulster* (Dublin: Dublin Institute for Advanced Studies, 1983).

Annales Vedastini. Edited by Georg Heinrich Pertz, MGH SS 2:196–209 (Hannover: Hahn, 1829).

"Anonymous of Benevento." *Vita Leonis*. Edited by Albert Poncelet, "Vie et miracles du Pape S. Léon IX," *Analecta Bollandiana* 25 (1906): 258–97.

Anselm of Liège. *Gesta Episcoporum Leodiensium*. Edited by Rudolf Koepke, MGH SS 7:189–234 (Hannover: Hahn, 1846).

"The Battle of Maldon." Edited and translated by Donald Scragg, "The Battle of Maldon," in Scragg, *Battle of Maldon*, 1–36.

Benedict, *Regula*. Edited and translated by Bruce L. Venarde, DOML 6 (Cambridge: Harvard University Press, 2011).

Bernard of Chartres. *Miracula Fidis*. Edited by Auguste Bouillet, *Liber Miraculorum Sancte Fidis* (Paris: Alphonse Picard et Fils, 1897). Translated by Pamela Scheingorn, *The Book of Sainte Foy* (Philadelphia: University of Pennsylvania Press, 1995).

βίος Νεῖλου. Edited by Germano Giovanelli, *Βίος και πολιτεία τοῦ ὁσίου πατρὸς ημων Νεῖλου νέου* (Grottaferrata: Badia di Grottaferrata, 1972). Translated into Italian with textual notes by Giovanelli, *S. Nilo di Rossano, fondatore di Grottaferrata* (Grottaferrata: Badia di Grottaferrata, 1966).

βίος Φαντίνου. Edited by Enrica Follieri, *La Vita di San Fantino il Giovane: Introduzione, testo greco, traduzione commentario e indici* (Brussels: Bollandistes, 1993).

Bruno of Querfurt, *Vita Quinque Fratrum*. Edited and translated by Marina Miladinov, in Klaniczay, *Vitae Sanctorum Aetatis Conversionis Europae Centralis (saec. X–XI)*, 183–313.

Bruno of Segni. *Libellus de Symoniacis*. Edited by Ernst Dümmler, MGH *Libelli de Lite* 2:543–62 (Hannover: Hahn, 1892). Partially translated by Robinson, *Papal Reform*, 377–90.

Charles the Bald. *Acta*. Edited by Arthur Giry, Maurice Prou, and Georges Tessier, *Recueil des actes de Charles II le Chauve, roi de France*, 3 vols., Chartes et diplômes relatifs à l'histoire de France 8 (Paris: Imprimerie nationale, 1943–55).

Chronica Monasterii Casinensis (*Chron. Casin.*). Edited by Hartmutt Hoffmann, *Die Chronik von Montecassino*, MGH SS 34 (Hannover: Hahn, 1980).

Chronicon S. Benigni. Edited by Louis Emile Bougaud and Joseph Garnier, *Chronique de l'Abbaye de Saint-Bénigne de Dijon suivie de la Chronique de Saint-Pierre de Bèze*, 1–195 (Dijon: Darantière, 1875). Partially edited by Andrew Martindale, "The Romanesque Church of Saint-Bénigne at Dijon and MS 591 in the Bibliothèque muniicpale" *Journal of the British Archaeological Association* 25 (1962): 21–54, esp. 47–51.

Chronicon Salernitanum. Edited by Ulla Westerbergh, *Chronicon Salernitanum: A Critical Edition with Studies on Literary and Historical Sources and on Language* (Stockholm: Almquist & Wiksell, 1956).

Concilium Meldense. Edited by Wilfried Hartmann, *Die Conzilien der karolingischen Teilreich 843–845*, MGH *Concilia*, 3:61–133 (Hannover: Hahn, 1984).

Corpus Consuetudinum Monasticarum (*Corp CM*). Edited by Kassius Hallinger, 12 vols. in 16 (Siegburg, Ger.: Franz Schmitt, 1963–87).

Desiderius. *Dialogi de Miraculis S. Benedicti*. Edited by Gerhard Schwartz and Adolf Hofmeister, MGH SS 30 (2): 1113–74 (Leipzig: Karl Hiersemann, 1929).

Diplomatarium Danicum, sec. 1, vol. 1, *Regester 789–1052*. Edited by C. A. Christensen and Herluf Nielsen (Copenhagen: C. A. Reitzels, 1975).

Einhard. *Vita Karoli Magni*. Edited by Georg Waitz and Oswald Holder-Egger, MGH SS Rerum Germ 25 (Hannover: Hahn, 1911). Translated by David Ganz, *Two Lives of Charlemagne: Einhard and Notker the Stammerer* (London: Penguin, 2008).

Flodoard of Rheims. *Annales*. Edited by Philippe Lauer, *Les Annales de Flodoard*, Collection de texts pour servir à l'étude et à l'enseignement de l'histoire 39 (Paris: Alphonse Picard et Fils, 1906). Translated by Steven Fanning and Bernard S. Bachrach, *Annals of Flodoard of Reims, 919–966* (Peterborough, ON: Broadview, 2004).

Fulbert of Chartres. *Epistolae*. Edited and translated by Frederick Behrends, *The Letters and Poems of Fulbert of Chartres* (Oxford: Clarendon, 1976).

Gerard I of Cambrai-Arras. *Acta Synodi Attrebatensis*. Edited by Steven Vanderputten and Diane J. Reilly, *Gerardi Cameracensis Acta Synodi Atrebutensis, Vita Autberti, Vita Tertia Gaugerici, Varia Scripta ex Officina Gerardi Exstantia*, CCCM 270:1–75 (Turnhout, Belg.: Brepols, 2014).

Gilo. *Vita Hugonis*. Edited by H. E. J. Cowdrey, *Two Studies in Cluniac History, 1049–1126*, 41–109 (Rome: Libreria Ateneo Salesiano, 1978).

Gozechinus. *Epistola ad Walcherum*. Edited by R. B. C. Huygens, *Apologiae Duae*, CCCM 62:1–43 (Turnhout, Belg.: Brepols, 1985).

Gregory I. *Dialogi*. Edited by Adalbert de Vogüé and Paul Antin, *Grégoire le Grand: Dialogues*, 3 vols., Source chrétiennes 251, 260, and 265 (Paris: Cerf 1979). Translated by Odo John Zimmerman, *Saint Gregory the Great: Dialogues*, Fathers of the Church 39 (Washington, DC: Catholic University of America Press, 1959).

Gregory VII. *Register*. Edited by Erich Caspar, *Das Register Gregors VII*, 2 vols., MGH *Epistolae Selectae* 2 (Berlin: Weidmann, 1920–23). Translated by H. E. J. Cowdrey, *The Register of Pope Gregory VII, 1073–1085: An English Translation* (Oxford: Oxford University Press, 2002).

Hariulf. *Chronicon Centulense*. Edited by Ferdinand Lot, *Hariulf: Chronique de l'Abbaye de Saint-Riquier (Vᵉ siècle–1104)* (Paris: Alphonse Picard et Fils, 1894).

Helgaudus of Fleury. *Vita Regis Roberti*. Edited by Robert-Henri Bautier and Gillette Labory. *Vie de Robert le Pieux, Epitoma Vitae Regis Rotberti Pii* [par] *Helgaud de Fleury*. Sources d'histoire médiévale publiées par l'IRHT 1 (Paris: CNRS, 1965).

Hermann of Reichenau. *Chronicon*. Edited by Georg Pertz, MGH SS 5:67–133 (Hannover: Hahn, 1844). Partially translated by I. S. Robinson, *Eleventh-Century Germany: The Swabian Chronicles* (Manchester, UK: Manchester University Press, 2008), 58–98.

Hugh of Farfa. *Destructio Farfensis*. Edited by Ugo Balzani, *Il Chronicon Farfense di Gregorio di Catino: Procedono la* Constructio farfensis *e gli scritti di Ugo di Farfa*, 2 vols., 1:25–51, Fonti per la storia d'Italia 33–34 (Rome: Istituto storico italiano, 1902).

John of Fécamp. *Confessio Theologica Recapitulatio*. Edited by Jean Leclercq and Jean-Paul Bonnes, *Un maître de la vie spirituelle au XIᵉ siècle: Jean de Fécamp*, 109–83 (Paris: Vrin, 1946).

John of Salerno. *Vita S. Odonis Abbatis*. Edited in *ASOSB* 7:150–86. Translated by Gerard Sitwell, *St. Odo of Cluny: Being the Life of St. Odo of Cluny by John of Salerno and the Life of St. Gerald of Aurillac by St. Odo*, 3–87 (London: Sheed & Ward, 1958).

Leo IX. *Epistola ad Constantinum*. Edited by Parisse and Goullet, *Vie du Pape Léon IX*, 134–44.

——. *Epistola ad Michaelem*. Edited by Migne, *Pat. Lat.* 143:773–77.

——. *Epistola ad Michaelem et Leonem*. Edited by Migne, *Pat. Lat.* 143:744–773.

——. *Epistola ad Petrum et Joannem*. Edited by Migne, *Pat. Lat.* 143:729–31.

——. *Epistola ad Thomam*. Edited by Migne, *Pat. Lat.* 143:727–29.

Liber Eliensis. Edited by E. O. Blake (London: Royal Historical Society, 1962). Translated by Janet Fairweather, *Liber Eliensis: A History of the Isle of Ely from the Seventh Century to the Twelfth Century* (Woodbridge, UK: Boydell, 2005).

Liber Tramitis. Edited by Peter Dinter, *Liber Tramitis Aevi Odilonis Abbatis, Corp CM* 10 (Siegburg, Ger.: Franz Schmid, 1980).

Liudprand, *Antapodosis*. Edited by Paolo Chiesa, *Liudprandi Cremonensis Opera Omnia*, CCCM 156:1–150 (Turnhout, Belg.: Brepols, 1998). Translated by Paolo Squatriti, *The Complete Works of Liudprand of Cremona*, 40–202 (Washington, DC: Catholic University of America Press, 2007).

——. *Legatio*. Edited by Paolo Chiesa, *Liudprandi Cremonensis Opera Omnia*, CCCM 156:185–218 (Turnhout, Belg.: Brepols, 1998). Translated by Paolo Squatriti, *The Complete Works of Liudprand of Cremona*, 238–82 (Washington, DC: Catholic University of America Press, 2007).

Martianus Capella. *De Nuptiis*. Edited by James Willis, *Martianus Capella* (Leipzig: Teubner, 1983). Explicated by James Willis, *De Martiano Capella Emendando* (Leiden, Neth.: Brill, 1971). Translated by William Harris Stahl and Richard Johnson, *Martianus Capella and the Seven Liberal Arts*, 2 vols. (New York: Columbia University Press, 1971).

The Northumbrian Priests' Law. Edited Whitelock et al., *Councils & Synods*, vol. 1, pt. 1, 449–68. Translated by Rabin, *Political Writings*, 197–206.

Notger. *Gesta Karoli*. Edited Hans F. Haefele, *Notker der Stammler: Taten Kaiser Karls des Grossen*, MGH SS Rer Germ, n.s., 12 (Berlin: Weidmann, 1962). Translated by David Ganz, *Two Lives of Charlemagne*, 45–116 (New York: Penguin Classics, 2008).

Odo of Cluny, *Vita S. Geraldi*. Edited in *AASS* Oct. VI: 300–331 (Paris: Palme, 1868). Translated by Sitwell, *St. Odo of Cluny*, 89–180.

Odorannus of Sens. *Liber Opusculorum*. Edited by Robert-Henri Bautier and Monique Gilles, *Odorannus de Sens: Opera Omnia*, Sources d'histoire médiévale publiées par l'IRHT 4 (Paris: CNRS, 1972).

Orderic Vitalis. *Historia Aecclesiastica*. Edited and translated by Marjorie Chibnall, *The Ecclesiastical History of Orderic Vitalis*, 6 vols., Oxford Medieval Texts (New York: Oxford University Press, 1969–80).

Peter Damian. *Epistolae*. Edited by Kurt Reindel, *Die Briefe des Petrus Damiani*, 4 vols., MGH *Briefe der deutschen Kaiserzeit* 4 (1–4) (Munich: MGH, 1983–93). Translated by Owen J. Blum, *The Letters of Peter Damian*, 6 vols. (the last two with Irven M. Resnick), The Fathers of the Church Mediaeval Continuation 1–3 and 5–7 (Washington, DC: Catholic University of America Press, 1989–2005).

——. *Sermones*. Edited by Giovanni Lucchesi, *Sancti Petri Damiani Sermones*, CCCM 57 (Turnhout, Belg.: Brepols, 1983).

——. *Vita beati Romualdi*. Edited by Giovanni Tabacco, *Peter Damian:* Vita Beati Romualdi, Fonti per la storia d'Italia 94 (Rome: ISME, 1957). Partially translated by Henrietta Leyser, *Medieval Hagiography: An Anthology*, edited by Thomas Head, 295–316 (New York: Garland, 2000).

Pontificale Romano-Germanicum. Edited by Cyrille Vogel and Reinhard Elze, *Le Pontifical romano-germanique du dixième siècle*, 3 vols. (Vatican City: BAV, 1963–72).

Popes (896–1046). *Epistolae*. Edited by Harald Zimmermann, *Papsturkunden, 896–1046*, 3 vols. (Vienna: Österreichischen Akademie der Wissenschaften, 1984–89).

Rather of Verona. *Epistolae*. Edited by Fritz Weigle, *Die Briefe des Bischofs Rather von Verona*, MGH *Briefe der deutschen Kaiserzeit* 1 (Weimar: Hermann Böhlau, 1949). Translated by Peter L.D. Reid., *The Complete Works of Rather of Verona*, 209–535, Medieval and Renaissance Texts and Studies 76 (Binghamton, NY: Center for Medieval and Early Renaissance Studies, 1991).

Regino of Prüm. *Chronicon*. Edited by Friedrich Kurze, MGH *SS Rer Germ* 50 (Hannover: Hahn, 1890). Translated by Simon MacLean, *History and Politics in Late Carolingian and Ottonian Europe: The "Chronicle" of Regino of Prüm and Adalbert of Magdeburg*, 61–283 (Manchester, UK: Manchester University Press, 2009).

Regularis Concordia Anglicae Nationis. Edited by Thomas Symons, Sigrid Spath, Maria Wegener, and Kassius Hallinger, *Consuetudininum Saeculi X/XI/XII Monumenta Non-cluniacensia*, 61–147, Corp CM 7 (3) (Siegburg, Ger.: Schmitt, 1984). Translated by Symons, *Regularis Concordia: The Monastic Agreement of the Monks and Nuns of the English Nation* (London: Thomas Nelson and Sons, 1953).

Richer of Rheims. *Historiae*. Edited and translated by Justin Lake, *Richer of Saint-Rémi: Histories*, 2 vols., DOML 10 (Cambridge: Harvard University Press, 2011).

Rodulfus Glaber. *Historiae*. Edited and translated by John France, *Rodulfus Glaber: The Five Books of the Histories* (Oxford: Clarendon, 1989).

——. *Vita Willelmi*. Edited by Neithard Bulst, and reprinted and translated by John France and Paul Reynolds, *Rodulfus Glaber: The Five Books*, 254–99.

Ruotger. *Vita Brunonis*. Edited by Irene Ott, MGH *SS Rer Germ*, n.s., 10 (Cologne: Böhlau, 1958).

Stephan, King of Hungary. *Monita ad Filium*. Edited by Migne, *Pat. Lat.* 151:1233–54.

Theophilus. *De Diversis Artibus*. Edited and translated by Charles Reginald Dodwell (London: Thomas Nelson & Sons, 1961).

Thierry of Amorbach. *Libellus de Consuetudinibus et Statutis Monasterii Floriacensis*. Edited by Anselme Davril and Lin Donnat, *Consuetudinum Saeculi X/XI/XII, Monumenta Non-cluniacensia*, 3–60, Corp CM 7 (3) (Siegburg, Ger.: Schmitt, 1984). Edited and translated by Davril and Donnat, *L'abbaye de Fleury en l'an Mil*, 167–251, IRHT sources d'histoire médiévale 32 (Paris: CNRS, 2004).

Thietmar of Merseburg. *Chronicon*. Edited by Robert Holtzmann, *Die Chronik des Bischofs Thietmar von Merseburg und ihre Korveier Überarbeitung*, MGH *SS Rer Germ* 9 (Berlin: Weidmann, 1955). Translated by David A. Warner, *Ottonian Germany: The Chronicon of Thietmar of Merseburg* (Manchester, UK: Manchester University Press, 2001).

"Vita A" (Old English) of Guthlac. Edited by Paul Gonser, *Das angelsächische Prosa-Leben des hl. Guthlac*, 97–200 (Heidelberg: Karl Winter, 1909). Translated by Michael Swanton, *Anglo-Saxon Prose*, 39–62 (London: Dent, 1975).

Vita et Miracula S. Bononii. Edited by Gerhard Schwartz and Adolf Hofmeister, MGH *SS* 30 (2):1023–33 (Leipzig: Hiersemann, 1934).

Vita Leonis. Edited by Hans-Georg Krause, *Die Touler Vita Leos IX*, MGH *SS Rer Germ* 70 (Hannover: Hahn, 2007). Translated by Robinson, *Papal Reform*, 97–157.

Walafrid Strabo. *Libellus de Exordiis*. Edited and translated by Alice L. Harting-Correa, *Walahfrid Strabo's Libellus de Exordiis et Incrementis Quarundam in Observationibus Ecclesiasticis Rerum: A Translation and Liturgical Commentary* (Leiden, Neth.: Brill, 1996).

William of Apulia. *Gesta Roberti Wiscardi*. Edited by Marguerite Mathieu, *Guillaume de Pouille: La Geste de Robert Guiscard* (Palermo: Istituto siciliano di studi bizantini e neoellenici, 1961). Translated by Graham A. Loud, "The Deeds of Robert Guiscard by William of Apulia," Leeds Medieval History Texts in Translation website, http://www.leeds.ac.uk/arts/downloads/file/1049/the_deeds_of_robert_guiscard_by_william_of_apulia.

Wulfstan of Winchester. *Vita Aethelwoldi*. Edited and translated by Michael Lapidge and Michael Winterbottom, *Wulfstan of Winchester: The Life of St Aethelwold* (Oxford: Clarendon, 1991).

Wulfstan of York. *Canons of Edgar*. Edited by Whitelock et al., *Councils & Synods*, vol. 1, pt. 1, 313–38. Translated by Rabin, *Political Writings*, 85–100.

——. "Edict When the Great Army Came to England" (Latin version). Edited by Whitelock et al., *Councils & Synods*, vol. 1, pt. 1, 373–78. Wulfstan, "Edict" (Old English version), edited by Whitelock et al., *Councils & Synods*, vol. 1, pt. 1, 379–82.

——. *Institutes of Polity*. Edited by Karl Jost, *Die Institutes of Polity, Civil and Ecclesiastical: Ein Werk Erzbischof Wulfstans von York* (Bern, Switz.: Francke, 1959). Translated by Rabin, *Political Writings*, 101–24.

——. "The Sermon of the Wolf to the English." Edited by Dorothy Whitelock, *Sermo Lupi ad Anglos*, 47–67 (New York: Appleton-Century Crofts, 1966). Translated by Whitelock, *English Historical Documents*, vol. 1, 854–59.

Secondary Sources

Aalst, V. D. van, and Krijna Nelly Ciggaar, eds. *Byzantium and the Low Countries in the Tenth Century: Aspects of Art and History in the Ottonian Era*. Hernen: A. A. Brediusstichting, 1985.

Abulafia, David, and Nora Berend, eds. *Medieval Frontiers: Concepts and Practices*. Aldershot, UK: Ashgate, 2002.

Adams, Jonathan, and Katherine Holman, eds. *Scandinavia and Europe, 800–1350: Contact, Conflict, and Coexistence*. Turnhout, Belg.: Brepols, 2004.

Al-Azmeh, Aziz, and Janos M. Bak, eds. *Monotheistic Kingship: The Medieval Variants*. Budapest: Central European University Press, 2004.

Alfeyev, Hilarion. *St. Symeon the New Theologian and Orthodox Tradition*. Oxford: Oxford University Press, 2000.

Antonnopouolos, Panagiotis, and Charalambos Dendrinos. "The Eastern Roman Empire at the Turn of the First Millennium." In *Europe around the Year 1000*, edited by Urbańczyk, 167–203.

Arbeiter, Achim. "Nordspanien zwischen Atlantik und Pyrenäen um das 10. Jahrhundert: Bau- und Kunstdenkmäler der erstarkenden christlichen Territorien." In *Europa im 10. Jahrhundert*, edited by Henning, 337–50.

Arnaldi, Girolamo, and Guglielmo Cavallo, eds. *Europa medievale e mondo bizantino: Contatti effettivi e possibilità di studi comparati (Tavola rotonda del XVIII Congresso del CISH—Montréal, 29 agosto 1995)*. Rome: ISIME, 1997.

Arnason, Johann P., and Björn Wittrock, eds. *Eurasian Transformations, Tenth to Thirteenth Centuries: Crystallizations, Divergences, Renaissances*. Leiden, Neth.: Brill, 2004.

Ashley, Kathleen, and Wim Hüsken, ed. *Moving Subjects: Processional Performance in the Middle Ages and Renaissance*. Amsterdam: Rodopi, 2001.

Austin, Greta. "Bishops and Religious Law, 900–1050." In *Bishop Reformed*, edited by Ott and Jones, 40–57.

——. *Shaping Church Law around the Year 1000: The Decretum of Burchard of Worms*. Burlington, VT: Ashgate, 2009.

Bachrach, Bernard S. *Early Carolingian Warfare: Prelude to Empire*. Philadelphia: University of Pennsylvania Press, 2001.

——. *Fulk Nerra, the Neo-Roman Consul 987–1040: A Political Biography of the Angevin Count.* Berkeley: University of California Press, 1993.

Bachrach, Bernard S., and David S. Bachrach. "Saxon Military Revolution, 912–973? Myth and Reality." *Early Medieval Europe* 15 (2007): 186–222.

Bachrach, David S. "Exercise of Royal Power in Early Medieval Europe: The Case of Otto the Great." *Early Medieval Europe* 17 (2009): 389–419.

——. *Religion and the Conduct of War, c. 300–1215.* Woodbridge, UK: Boydell, 2003.

——. *Warfare in Tenth-Century Germany.* Woodbridge, UK: Boydell, 2012.

Baldovin, John F. *The Urban Character of Christian Worship: The Origins, Development, and Meaning of Stational Liturgy.* Rome: Pontificium Institutum Studiorum Orientalium 1987.

Bandmann, Günter. *Early Medieval Architecture as Bearer of Meaning.* Translated by Kendall Wallis. New York: Columbia University Press, 2005.

Barral i Altet, Xavier, ed. *Artistes, artisans et production artistique au moyen âge: Colloque international, Centre national de la recherche scientifique Université de Rennes II—Haute-Bretagne, 2–6 mai 1983.* 3 vols. Paris: Picard, 1986, 1987, 1990.

——. *The Early Middle Ages: From Late Antiquity to A.D. 1000.* Cologne: Taschen, 2002.

——. "Les moines, les évêques et l'art." In *Religion et culture autour de l'an Mil,* edited by Iogna-Prat and Picard, 71–83.

Barré, Henri. *Prières anciennes de l'Occident à la Mère du Saveur: Des origins à saint Anselme.* Paris: Lethielleux, 1963.

Barrow, Julia. *The Clergy in the Medieval World: Secular Clerics, Their Families and Careers in North-Western Europe, c. 800–c. 1200.* Cambridge: Cambridge University Press, 2015.

——. "Recruitment of Cathedral Canons in England and Germany, 1100–1225." *Viator* 20 (1989): 117–38.

Bates, David. *Normandy before 1066.* London: Longman, 1982.

Bauduin, Pierre, ed. *Les fondations scandinaves en Occident et les débuts du duché de Normandie: Colloque de Cerisy-la-Salle (25–29 septembre 2002).* Caen: CRAHAM, 2005.

——. *Le monde franc et les Vikings VIIIᵉ–Xᵉ siècle.* Paris: Albin Michel, 2009.

Bauer, Franz Alto. "The Liturgical Arrangement of Early Medieval Roman Church Buildings: Architectural Changes at Santa Maria Maggiore and Santa Maria in Trastevere." *Mededeelingen van het Nederlandsch Historisch Instituut te Rome* 59 (2000): 101–28.

Bayer, Axel. *Spaltung der Christenheit: Das sogenannte Morgenländische Schisma von 1054.* Cologne: Böhlau, 2002.

Baylé, Maylis, ed. *L'architecture normande au moyen age.* Vol. 1, *Regards sur l'art de bâtir. Actes du colloque de Cerisy-la-Salle (28 septembre–2 octobre 1994).* Caen: Presses universitaires de Caen, 1997.

——. "L'architecture romane en Normandie." In *L'architecture normande au moyen age,* edited by Baylé, 13–35.

——. "La place des sculptures de Saint-German-des-Prés dans le cheminement des formes au XIᵉ siècle." In *De la création à la restauration,* 205–13.

Beach, Alison I., and Isabelle Cochelin, eds. *The Cambridge History of Western Monasticism.* 2 vols. New York: Cambridge University Press, forthcoming.

Bedingfield, M. Bradford. *The Dramatic Liturgy of Anglo-Saxon England.* Woodbridge, UK: Boydell, 2002.

Behrends, Frederick, ed. *The Letters and Poems of Fulbert of Chartres.* Oxford: Clarendon, 1976.

Belke, Klaus, Ewald Kislinger, Andreas Külzer, and Maria A. Stassinopoulou, eds. *Byzantina Mediterranea: Festschrift für Johannes Koder zum 65. Geburtstag.* Vienna: Böhlau, 2007.

Bellitto, Christopher M., and Louis I. Hamilton, eds. *Reforming the Church before Modernity: Patterns, Problems, and Approaches.* Burlington, VT: Ashgate, 2005.

Belting, Hans. "Byzantine Art among Greeks and Latins in Southern Italy." *Dumbarton Oaks Papers* 28 (1974): 1–29.

———. *Likeness and Presence: A History of the Image before the Era of Art*. Translated by Edmund Jephcott. Chicago: University of Chicago Press, 1994.

Benson, Robert L., and Giles Constable, eds. *Renaissance and Renewal in the Twelfth Century*. Cambridge: Harvard University Press, 1982.

Berend, Nora, ed. *Christianization and the Rise of Christian Monarchy: Scandinavia, Central Europe and Rus' c. 900–1200*. New York: Cambridge University Press, 2007.

Berg, Dieter, and Hans-Werner Goetz, eds. Ecclesia et Regnum: *Beiträge zur Geschichte von Kirche, Recht und Staat im Mittelalter: Festschrift für Franz-Josef Schmale zu seinem 65. Geburtstag*. Bochum: Winkler, 1989.

Bernhardt, John W. *Itinerant Kingship and Royal Monasteries in Early Medieval Germany, c. 936–1075*. Cambridge: Cambridge University Press, 1993.

Berschin, Walter. *Greek Letters and the Latin Middles Age: From Jerome to Nicholas of Cusa*. Rev. ed. Translated Jerold C. Frakes. Washington, DC: Catholic University of America Press, 1988.

Bischoff, Bernhard. *Mittelalterliche Studien: Ausgewählte Aufsätze zur Schriftkunde und Literaturgeschichte*. 3 vols. Stuttgart: Anton Hiersemann, 1966–81.

Bischoff, Georges, and Benoît-Michel Tock, eds. *Léon IX et son temps: Actes du colloque international organisé par l'Institut d'Histoire Médiévale de l'Université Marc-Bloch, Strassbourg-Eguisheim, 20–22 juin 2002*. Turnhout, Belg.: Brepols, 2006.

Blair, John. *The Church in Anglo-Saxon Society*. Oxford: Oxford University Press, 2005.

———, ed. *Minsters and Parish Churches: The Local Church in Transition, 950–1050*. Oxford: Oxford University Committee for Archaeology, 1988.

Blair, John, and Richard Sharpe, eds. *Pastoral Care before the Parish*. Leicester: Leicester University Press, 1992.

Bloch, Herbert. "Montecassino, Byzantium, and the West in the Earlier Middle Ages." *Dumbarton Oaks Papers* 3 (1946): 163–224.

———. *Monte Cassino in the Middle Ages*. 3 vols. Cambridge: Harvard University Press, 1986.

Bloch, Marc. *The Royal Touch: Sacred Monarchy and Scrofula in England and France*. Translated by J.R. Anderson. London: Routledge & Kegan Paul, 1973.

Blumenthal, Uta-Renate. *The Investiture Controversy: Church and Monarchy from the Ninth to the Twelfth Century*. Philadelphia: University of Pennsylvania Press, 1988.

———. "The Papacy, 1024–1122." In *NCMH* vol. 4, pt. 2, 8–37.

Blumenthal, Uta-Renate, Anders Winroth, and Peter Landau, eds. *Canon Law, Religion, and Politics:* Liber Amicorum *Robert Somerville*. Washington, DC: Catholic University of America Press, 2012.

Boehm, Barbara Drake. "Medieval Head Reliquaries of the Massif Central." 2 vols. in 1. PhD diss., Institute of Fine Arts, New York University, 1990.

Bolgia, Claudia, Rosamond McKitterick, and John Osborne, eds. *Rome across Time and Space: Cultural Transmission and the Exchange of Ideas c. 500–1400*. Cambridge: Cambridge University Press, 2011.

Bolton, Timothy. *The Empire of Cnut the Great: Conquest and Consolidation of Power in Northern Europe in the Early Eleventh Century*. Leiden, Neth.: Brill, 2009.

Borrelli, Arianna. *Aspects of the Astrolabe:* Architectonica Ratio *in Tenth- and Eleventh-Century Europe*. Stuttgart: Franz Steiner, 2008.

Bouchard, Constance Brittain. *"Strong of Body, Brave and Noble": Chivalry and Society in Medieval France*. Ithaca: Cornell University Press, 1998.

Bouet, Pierre, Giorgio Otranto, and André Vauchez, eds. *Culte et pèlerinages à saint Michel en Occident: Trois monts dédiés à l'Archange*. Rome: ÉFR, 2003.

Bougard, François, Régine le Jan, and Rosamond McKitterick, eds. *La culture du haut Moyen Âge: Une question d'élites*. Turnhout, Belg.: Brepols, 2009.

Bowlus, Charles R. *The Battle of Lechfeld and Its Aftermath, August 955: The End of the Age of Migrations in the Latin West.* Aldershot, UK: Ashgate, 2006.

Boynton, Susan. "Training for the Liturgy as a Form of Monastic Education." In *Medieval Monastic Education,* edited by Ferzoco and Muessig, 7–20.

Boynton, Susan, and Isabelle Cochelin. "The Sociomusical Role of Child Oblates at the Abbey of Cluny in the Eleventh Century. In *Musical Childhoods,* edited by Boynton and Kok, 3–24.

Boynton, Susan, and Roe-Min Kok, eds. *Musical Childhoods and the Cultures of Youth.* Middletown, CT: Wesleyan University Press, 2006.

Boynton, Susan, and Diane J. Reilly, eds. *The Practice of the Bible in the Middle Ages: Production, Reception, & Performance in Western Christianity.* New York: Columbia University Press, 2011.

Bozóky, Edina, and Anne-Marie Helvétius, eds. *Les reliques: Objets, cultes, symbols: Actes du colloque international de l'Université du Littoral-Côte d'Opale (Boulogne-sur-Mer) 4–6 septembre 1997.* Turnhout, Belg.: Brepols, 1999.

Brandt, Michael, and Arne Eggebrecht, eds. *Bernward von Hildesheim und das Zeitalter der Ottonen: Katalog der Ausstellung Hildesheim 1993.* 2 vols. Hildesheim: Bernward Verlag, 1993.

Brink, Stefan, and Neil Price, eds. *The Viking World.* London: Routledge, 2008.

Brooks, Nicholas, and Catherine Cubitt, eds. *St. Oswald of Worcester: Life and Influence.* London: Leicester University Press, 1996.

Browe, Peter. *Die Eucharistischen Wunder des Mittelalters.* Breslau: Müller & Seiffert, 1938.

Brown, Peter. *The Cult of the Saints: Its Rise and Function in Latin Christianity.* 2nd ed. Chicago: University of Chicago Press, 2015.

——. *The Rise of Western Christendom: Triumph and Diversity, A.D. 200–1000.* 2nd ed. Oxford: Blackwell, 2003.

Brown, Phyllis Rugg, Georgia Ronan Crampton, and Fred C. Robinson, eds. *Modes of Interpretation in Old English Literature: Essays in Honour of Stanley B. Greenfield.* Toronto: University of Toronto, 1986.

Bruce, Scott G. *Cluny and the Muslims of La Garde-Freinet: Hagiography and the Problem of Islam in Medieval Europe.* Ithaca: Cornell University Press, 2015.

Bruce, Travis. "The Politics of Violence and Trade: Denia and Pisa in the Eleventh Century." *Journal of Medieval History* 32 (2006): 127–42.

Bull, Marcus. *Knightly Piety and the Lay Response to the First Crusade: The Limousin and Gascony, c. 970–c. 1130.* Oxford: Clarendon, 1993.

Bulst, Neithard. *Untersuchungen zu den Klosterreformen Wilhelms von Dijon (962–1031).* Bonn: Ludwig Röhrscheid, 1973.

Butler, L. A. S., and R. K. Morris, eds. *The Anglo-Saxon Church: Papers on History, Architecture, and Archaeology in Honour of Dr. H. M. Taylor.* London: Council for British Archaeology, 1986.

Bynum, Caroline Walker. *Docere Verbo et Exemplo: An Aspect of Twelfth-Century Spirituality.* Missoula, MT: Scholar's Press, 1978.

Caillet, Jean-Pierre. "Reliques et architecture religieuse aux époques carolingienne et romane." In *Reliques,* edited by Bozóky and Helvétius, 169–97.

——, ed. *Les trésors de sanctuaires, de l'Antiquité à l'époque romane: Communications présentées au Centre de recherches sur l'Antiquité tardive et le haut Moyen Âge de l'Université de Paris X-Nanterre (1993–1995).* Paris: Picard, 1996.

Carr, Annemarie Weyl. "Threads of Authority: The Virgin's Veil in the Middle Ages." In *Robes and Honor,* edited by Gordon, 59–93.

Carver, Martin, ed. *The Cross Goes North: Processes of Conversion in Northern Europe, AD 300–1300.* York, UK: York Medieval Press, 2003.

Cavallo, Guglielmo. Exultet: *Rotuli liturgici del medioevo meridionale.* Roma: Libreria dello Stato, 1994.

Certain, Eugène de. *Les Miracles de Saint Benoît*. Paris: Mme Ve Jules Renouard, 1858.

Chazelle, Celia. *The Crucified God in the Carolingian Era: Theology and Art of Christ's Passion*. Cambridge: Cambridge University Press, 2001.

Chiarelli, Leonard C. *A History of Muslim Sicily*. Sta Venera, Malta: Midsea Books, 2011.

Christensen, C.A., and Herluf Nielsen, eds. *Diplomatarium Danicum*. Sec. 1, vol. 1, *Regester 789–1052*. Copenhagen: C.A. Reitzels, 1975.

Cristianità d'Occidente e Cristianità d'Oriente (secoli V–XI), 24–30 aprile 2003. 2 vols. Settimane di studio della fondazione CISAM 51. Spoleto: CISAM, 2004.

Chrysos, Evangelos. "1054: Schism?" In *Christianità d'Occidente e Christianità d'Oriente*, 1:547–71.

Ciggaar, Krijna Nelly. *Western Travellers to Constantinople: The West and Byzantium, 962–1204: Cultural and Political Relations*. Leiden, Neth.: Brill, 1996.

Claussen, Martin A. *The Reform of the Frankish Church: Chrodegang of Metz and the Regula Canonicorum in the Eighth Century*. New York: Cambridge University Press, 2004.

Cochelin, Isabelle. "When the Monks Were the Book: The Bible and Monasticism (6th to 11th Centuries)." In *Practice of the Bible*, edited by Boynton and Reilly, 61–83.

Colella, Renate L., Meredith J. Gill, Lawrence A. Jenkins, and Petra Lamers, eds. *Pratum Romanum: Richard Krautheimer zum 100. Geburtstag*. Wiesbaden: Dr. Ludwig Reichert, 1997.

Colombas, Garcia M. *Paradis et vie angélique: Le sens eschatologique de la vocation chrétienne*. Translated by Suitbert Caron. Paris: Cerf, 1961.

Conant, Kenneth John. *Cluny: Les Églises et la maison du chef d'ordre*. Cambridge: Mediaeval Academy of America, 1968.

Connor, Carolyn L. *The Color of Ivory: Polychromy on Byzantine Ivories*. Princeton: Princeton University Press, 1998.

Constable, Giles. *The Abbey of Cluny: A Collection of Essays to Mark the Eleven-Hundredth Anniversary of Its Foundation*. Berlin: LIT, 2010.

——. "Cluny in the Monastic World of the Tenth Century." In *Secolo di ferro*, 1:391–448.

——. "Commemoration and Confraternity at Cluny during the Abbacy of Peter the Venerable." In *Die Cluniazenser*, edited by Constable et al., 253–78.

——. *The Reformation of the Twelfth Century*. New York: Cambridge University Press, 1996.

——. *Three Studies in Medieval Religious and Social Thought*. Cambridge: Cambridge University Press, 1998.

Constable, Giles, Gert Melville, and Jörg Oberste, eds. *Die Cluniazenser in ihrem politisch-sozialen Umfeld*. Münster: LIT, 1998.

Contreni, John. "The Tenth Century: The Perspective from the Schools." In *Haut moyen-âge*, edited by LePelley et al., 379–87.

Contreni, John, and Santa Casciani, eds. *Word, Image, and Number: Communication in the Middle Ages*. Turnhout, Belg.: Brepols for SISMEL Edizioni del Galluzzo, 2002.

Cottier, Jean-François. *Anima Mea: Prières privées et textes de dévotion du Moyen Age latin: Autour des Prières ou Méditations attribuées à saint Anselme de Cantorbéry XIe–XIIe siècles*. Turnhout, Belg.: Brepols, 2001.

Coupland, Simon. "Holy Ground? The Plundering and Burning of Churches by Vikings and Franks in the Ninth Century." *Viator* 45 (2014): 73–98.

Cowdrey, H.E.J. *Lanfranc: Scholar, Monk, and Bishop*. Oxford: Oxford University Press, 2003.

——. "The Mahdia Campaign of 1087." *English Historical Review* 92 (1977): 1–29.

Cracco Ruggini, Lellia, and Mechthild Schulze-Dörrlamm. "Die Ungareinfälle des 10. Jahrhunderts im Spiegel archäologischer Funde." In *Europa im 10. Jahrhundert*, edited by Henning, 109–22.

Crook, John. *The Architectural Setting of the Cult of Saints in the Early Christian West, c. 300–1200*. Oxford: Clarendon, 2000.

Cuozzo, Errico, Vincent Déroche, Annick Peters-Custot, and Vivien Prigent, eds. *"Puer Apuliae": Mélanges offerts à Jean-Marie Martin*. 2 vols. Paris: Association des amis du centre d'histoire et civilisation de Byzance, 2008.

Curta, Florin. *The Edinburgh History of the Greeks, c. 500 to 1050: The Early Middle Ages*. Edinburgh: Edinburgh University Press, 2011.

Cutler, Anthony. *The Hand of the Master: Craftsmanship, Ivory, and Society in Byzantium (9th–11th Centuries)*. Princeton: Princeton University Press, 1994.

——. "The Mother of God in Ivory." In *Mother of God*, edited by Vassilaki, 167–75.

Dachowski, Elizabeth. *First among Abbots: The Career of Abbo of Fleury*. Washington, DC: Catholic University of America Press, 2008.

Davids, Adelbert, ed. *The Empress Theophano: Byzantium and the West at the Turn of the First Millennium*. Cambridge: Cambridge University Press, 1995.

Dédéyan, Gérard. "Les Arméniens en Occident, fin X^e–début XIe siècle." In *Occident et Orient au Xe siècle*, 123–39.

De Jong, Mayke. *In Samuel's Image: Child Oblation in the Early Medieval West*. Leiden, Neth.: Brill, 1996.

De Jong, Mayke, and Frans Theuws, eds. *Topographies of Power in the Early Middle Ages*. Leiden, Neth.: Brill, 2001.

De la création à la restauration: Travaux d'histoire de l'art offerts à Marcel Durliat pour son 75e anniversaire. Toulouse: Atelier d'histoire de l'art méridional, 1992.

Delaruelle, Étienne. "Le crucifix dans la piété populaire et dans l'art, du VIe au XIe siècle." In *Études ligériennes*, edited by Louise, 133–44.

——. "La vie commune des clercs et la spiritualité populaire au XIe siècle." In *Vita comune del clero*, 142–85.

Demacopoulos, George E. *The Invention of Peter: Apostolic Discourse and Papal Authority in Late Antiquity*. Philadelphia: University of Pennsylvania Press, 2013.

Deshman, Robert. *Eye and Mind: Collected Essays in Anglo-Saxon and Early Medieval Art*. Edited by Adam S. Cohen. Kalamazoo, MI: Western Michigan University Medieval Institute, 2010.

——. "Exalted Servant." *Viator* 11 (1980): 385–417. Reprinted with additional bibliography in Deshman, *Eye and Mind*, 192–219.

——. "Otto III and the Warmund Sacramentary." *Zeitschrift für Kunstgeschichte* 34 (1971): 1–20. Reprinted with additional bibliography in Deshman, *Eye and Mind*, 172–81.

Deswarte, Thomas. *De la destruction à la restauration: L'idéologie du royaume d'Oviedo-Léon (VIIIe–XIe siècles)*. Turnhout, Belg.: Brepols, 2003.

D'Haenens, Albert. "Les invasions normandes dans l'empire franc au IXe siècle: Pour une rénovation de la problématique." In *I Normanni e la loro espansione*, 233–98.

Díaz y Díaz, Manuel C. *Index Scriptorum Latinorum Medii Aevi Hispanorum*. 2 vols. Salamanca: Universidad de Salamanca, 1958–59.

Diebold, William J. *Word and Image: An Introduction to Early Medieval Art*. Boulder: Westview, 2000.

Dierkens, Alain. *Abbayes et chapitres entre Sambre et Meuse (VIIe–XIe siècles): Contribution à l'histoire religieuse des campagnes du haut Moyen Âge*. Sigmaringen, Ger.: Jan Thorbecke, 1985.

Doig, Allan. *Liturgy and Architecture from the Early Church to the Middle Ages*. Aldershot, UK: Ashgate, 2008.

Dumville, David N. *Liturgy and the Ecclesiastical History of Late Anglo-Saxon England: Four Studies*. Woodbridge, UK: Boydell, 1992.

——. "Vikings in the British Isles: A Question of Sources." In *Scandinavians*, edited by Jesch, 209–50.

Durliat, Marcel. "La Catalogne et le 'premier art roman.'" *Bulletin monumental* 147 (1989): 209–38.

——. "La sculpture du XIᵉ en Occident." *Bulletin monumental* 192 (1994): 129–213.

Efthymiadis, Stephanos, ed. *The Ashgate Research Companion to Byzantine Hagiography.* 2 vols. Burlington, VT: Ashgate, 2011 and 2014.

Ehlers, Joachim. "Dom- und Klosterschülen in Deutschland und Frankreich im 10. und 11. Jahrhundert." In *Schule und Schüler*, edited by Kintzinger et al., 29–52.

——. "Magdeburg—Rom—Aachen—Bamberg: Grablege des Königs und Herrschaftsverständnis in ottonischer Zeit." In *Otto III.–Heinrich II*, edited by Schneidmüller and Weinfurter, 47–76.

Eickhoff, Ekkehard. *Seekrieg und Seepolitik zwischen Islam und Abendland: Das Mittelmeer unter byzantinischer und arabischer Hegemonie (650–1040)*. Berlin: Walter de Gruyter, 1966.

——. *Theophanu und der König: Otto III. und seine Welt.* Stuttgart: Klett-Cotta, 1996.

Eldevik, John. *Episcopal Power and Ecclesiastical Reform in the Greater German Empire: Tithes, Leadership, and Community, 950–1150.* Cambridge: Cambridge University Press, 2012.

Elze, Reinhard. "Das "Sacrum Palatium Lateranense" im 10. und 11. Jahrhundert." *Studi Gregoriani* 4 (1952): 27–54.

Engels, Louk J. "The West European Alexius Legend: With an Appendix Presenting the Medieval Latin Text Corpus in Its Context (*Alexiana Latina Medii Aevi*, I)." In *The Invention of Saintliness*, edited by Anneke B. Mulder-Bakker, 93–144. London: Routledge, 2002.

L'Eremitismo in Occidente nei secoli XI e XII: Atti della seconda Settimana internazionale di studio, Mendola, 30 agosto–6 settembre 1962. Milan: Società vita e pensiero, 1963.

Erkens, Franz-Reiner, ed. *Die früh- und hochmittelalterliche Bischofserhebung im europäischen Vergleich.* Cologne: Böhlau, 1998.

Ettel, Peter, Anne-Marie Flambard Héricher, and Tom E. McNeill, eds. *Château et représentations: Actes du Colloque International de Stirling (Écosse), 30 août–5 septembre 2008.* Caen: Publications du CRAHM, 2010.

Euw, Anton von, and Peter Schreiner, eds. *Kaiserin Theophanu: Begegnung des Ostens und Westens um die Wende des ersten Jahrtausends.* 2 vols. Cologne: Schnütgen-Museum, 1991.

Facchini, Ugo. *San Pier Damiani: L'Eucologia e le preghiere. Contributo alla storia dell'eucologia medievale: Studio critico e liturgico-teologico.* Rome: Centro Liturgica Vincenziano—Edizioni Liturgiche, 2000.

Falk, Birgitta, ed. *Der Essener Domschatz.* Essen: Klartext, 2009.

Fassler, Margot E. *The Virgin of Chartres: Making History through Liturgy and the Arts.* New Haven: Yale University Press, 2010.

Fassler, Margot E., and Rebecca A. Baltzer, eds. *The Divine Office in the Latin Middle Ages: Methodology and Source Studies, Regional Developments, Hagiography: Written in Honor of Professor Ruth Steiner.* Oxford: Oxford University Press, 2000.

Fehring, Günter. *The Archaeology of Medieval Germany: An Introduction.* Translated by Ross Samson. London: Routledge, 1991.

Fernández-Armesto, Felipe. "The Survival of a Notion of *Reconquista* in Late Tenth- and Eleventh-Century León." In *Warriors and Churchmen*, edited by Reuter, 123–43.

Ferzoco, George, and Carolyn Muessig, eds. *Medieval Monastic Education.* London: Leicester University Press, 2000.

Fichtenau, Heinrich. *Living in the Tenth Century: Mentalities and Social Orders.* Translated and edited by Patrick J. Geary. Chicago: University of Chicago Press, 1991.

Fisher, Ernest Arthur. *An Introduction to Anglo-Saxon Architecture and Sculpture.* London: Faber and Faber, 1957.

Folz, Robert. *Les saints rois du moyen âge en Occident (VIᵉ–XIIIᵉ siècles).* Brussels: Bollandistes, 1984.

Foote, Sarah. *Aethelstan: The First King of England.* New Haven: Yale University Press, 2011.

——. *Veiled Women.* 2 vols. Aldershot, UK: Ashgate, 2000.

Forbes, Helen Foxhall. *Heaven and Earth in Anglo-Saxon England: Theology and Society in an Age of Faith.* Farnham, UK: Ashgate, 2013.

Forsyth, Ilene H. *The Throne of Wisdom: Wood Sculptures of the Madonna in Romanesque France.* Princeton: Princeton University Press, 1972.

France, John, ed. *Rodulfus Glaber: The Five Books of the Histories.* Oxford: Clarendon, 1989.

Frassetto, Michael, ed. *Medieval Purity and Piety: Essays on Medieval Clerical Celibacy and Religious Reform.* New York: Garland, 1998.

——, ed. *The Year 1000: Religious and Social Response to the Turning of the First Millennium.* New York: Palgrave Macmillan, 2002.

Freeman, Charles. *Holy Bones, Holy Dust: How Relics Shaped the History of Medieval Europe.* New Haven: Yale University Press, 2011.

Fried, Johannes, ed. *Dialektik und Rhetorik im früheren and hohe Mittelalter.* Munich: R. Oldenbourg, 1997.

Frolow, Anatole. *Les Reliquaires de la Vrai Croix.* Paris: Institut français d'études byzantines, 1965.

——. *La Relique de la Vrai Croix: Recherches sur le développement d'un culte.* Paris: Institut français d'études byzantines, 1961.

Fulton, Rachel. *From Judgment to Passion: Devotion to Christ and the Virgin Mary, 800–1200.* New York: Columbia University Press, 2002.

Gameson, Richard, and Henrietta Leyser, eds. *Belief and Culture in the Middle Ages: Studies Presented to Henry Mayr-Harting.* Oxford: Oxford University Press, 2001.

——. *The Role of Art in the Late Anglo-Saxon Church.* Oxford: Clarendon, 1995.

Garrison, Eliza. *Ottonian Imperial Art and Portraiture: The Artistic Patronage of Otto III and Henry II.* Burlingon, VT: Ashgate, 2012.

Gazeau, Véronique. *Normannia monastica: Princes normandes et abbés bénédictins (X^e–XIIe siècle).* 2 vols. Caen: CRAHM, 2007.

Gehl, Paul F. "Latin Orthopraxes." In *Latin Grammar and Rhetoric,* edited by Lanham, 1–21.

Gem, Richard. "Tenth-Century Architecture in England." In *Il secolo di ferro,* 2:803–36.

Genicot, Léopold. *Rural Communities in the Medieval West.* Baltimore: Johns Hopkins University Press, 1974.

Genin, Claude. *Fulbert de Chartres: Une grande figure de l'Occident chrétien au temps de l'an Mil.* Paris: Société archéologique d'Eure-et-Loir, 2003.

Giandrea, Mary Frances. *Episcopal Culture in Late Anglo-Saxon England.* Woodbridge, UK: Boydell, 2007.

Gibson, Margaret. *Lanfranc of Bec.* Oxford: Clarendon, 1978.

Gilchrist, John T. "Cardinal Humbert of Silva Candida (d. 1061)." *Annuale mediaevale* 3 (1962): 29–42.

Gilsdorf, Sean, ed. *The Bishop: Power and Piety at the First Millennium.* Münster: LIT, 2004.

Gittos, Helen. *Liturgy, Architecture, and Sacred Places in Anglo-Saxon England.* Oxford: Oxford University Press, 2013.

——. "Sacred Space in Anglo-Saxon England: Liturgy, Architecture, and Place." PhD diss., University of Oxford, 2001.

Glauche, Günter. *Schullektüre im Mittelalter: Entstehung und Wandlungen des Lektürekanons bis 1200 nach den Quellen dargestellt.* Munich: Arbeo-Gesellschaft, 1970.

Gneuss, Helmut. "King Alfred and the History of Anglo-Saxon Libraries." In *Modes of Interpretation,* edited by Phyllis Brown et al., 29–49.

Godding, Robert. *Prêtres en Gaule mérovingienne.* Brussels: Bollandistes, 2001.

Goffriller, Martin. "The Castral Territory of the Balearic Islands: The Evolution of Territorial Control in Mallorca during the Middle Ages." In *Château et représentations,* edited by Ettel et al., 109–13.

Gordon, Stewart, ed. *Robes and Honor: The Medieval World of Investiture.* New York: Palgrave Macmillan, 2001.

Goullet, Monique, ed. *Hagiographies*. vol. 6–. Turnhout, Belg.: Brepols, 2014–.

Graus, Frantisek. "La sanctification du souverain dans l'Europe centrale des Xe et XIe siècles." In *Hagiographie, cultures, et sociétés*, 559–72.

Griffiths, Fiona. "'Like the Sister of Aaron': Medieval Religious Women as Makers and Donors of Liturgical Textiles." In *Female* Vita Religiosa, edited by Melville and Müller, 343–74.

Haarländer, Stephanie. Vitae Episcoporum: *Eine Quellengattung zwischen Hagiographie und Historiographie, Untersucht an Lebensbeschreibungen von Bischöfen des Regnum Teutonicum im Zeitalter der Ottonen und Salier*. Stuttgart: Anton Hiersemann, 2000.

Hadley, Dawn M. *The Northern Danelaw: Its Social Structure ca. 800–1100*. London: Leicester University Press, 2000.

Hagiographie, cultures, et sociétés, IVe–XIIe siècles: Actes du Colloque organisé à Nanterre et à Paris (2–5 mai 1979). Paris: Études augustiniennes, 1981.

Hahn, Cynthia. *Portrayed on the Heart: Narrative Effect in Pictorial Lives of Saints from the Tenth through the Thirteenth Century*. Berkeley: University of California Press, 2001.

Hallinger, Kassius. *Gorze-Kluny. Studien zu den monastischen Lebensformen und Gegensätzen im Hochmittelalter*. 2 vols. Rome: "Orbis Catholicus" Herder, 1950–51.

Hamilton, Louis I. *A Sacred City: Consecrating Churches and Reforming Society in Eleventh-Century Italy*. Manchester, UK: Manchester University Press, 2010.

Hamilton, Sarah. "Most Illustrious King of Kings: Evidence for Ottonian Kingship in the Otto III Prayerbook (Munich, Bayerische Staatsbibliothek, Clm 30111)." *Journal of Medieval History* 27 (2001): 257–88.

Harper, John. *The Forms and Orders of Western Liturgy from the Tenth to the Eighteenth Century: A Historical Introduction and Guide for Students and Musicians*. Oxford: Clarendon, 1991.

Harris, Jennifer A. "Peter Damian and the Architecture of Self." In *Das Eigene und das Ganze*, edited by Melville and Schürer, 131–57.

Hartmann, Wilfried, ed. *Bischof Burchard von Worms, 1000–1025*. Mainz, Ger.: Gesellschaft für mittelrheinische Kirchengeschichte, 2000.

Hartog, Elizabeth den. *Romanesque Architecture and Sculpture in the Meuse Valley*. Leeuwarden, Neth.: Eisma, 1992.

Haussherr, Reiner. *Der Tote Christus am Kreuz zur Ikonographie des Gerokreuzes: Inaugural-Dissertation zur Erlangung der Doktorwürde der Philosophischen Fakultät der Rheinischen Friedrich-Wilhelms-Universität zu Bonn*. Bonn: Rheinische Friedrich-Wilhelms-Universität, 1962.

Häussling, Angelus Albert. *Mönchskonvent und Eucharistiefeier: Eine Studie über die Messe in der abendländischen Klosterliturgie des frühen Mittelalters und zur Geschichte der Messhäufigkeit*. Münster: Aschendorff, 1973.

——. "Ursprünge der Privatmesse." *Stimmen der Zeit* 176 (1965): 21–28.

Hawkes, Jane. "*Iuxta Morem Romanorum*: Stone and Sculpture in Anglo-Saxon England." In *Anglo-Saxon Styles*, edited by Karkov and Brown, 69–99.

Head, Thomas. *Hagiography and the Cult of the Saints: The Diocese of Orléans, 800–1200*. Cambridge: Cambridge University Press, 1990.

Head, Thomas, and Richard Landes, eds. *The Peace of God: Social Violence and Religious Response in France around the Year 1000*. Ithaca: Cornell University Press, 1992.

Heitz, Carol. "Influences carolingiennes et ottoniennes." In *L'architecture normande au moyen age*, edited by Baylé, 37–48.

Hen, Yitzhak. *The Royal Patronage of Liturgy in Frankish Gaul to the Death of Charles the Bald*. London: Boydell, 2001.

Henning, Joachim, ed. *Europa im 10. Jahrhundert: Archäologie einer Aufbruchszeit: Internationale Tagung in Vorbereitung der Ausstellung "Otto der Grosse, Magdeburg und Europa."* Mainz am Rhein, Ger.: Philipp von Zabern, 2002.

Henriet, Patrick. *La parole et la prière au Moyen Âge: Le Verbe efficace dans l'hagiographie monastique des XIᵉ et XIIᵉ siècles*. Brussels: De Boeck & Larcier, 2000.

Hermes, Nizar F. *The [European] Other in Medieval Arabic Literature and Culture: Ninth-Twelfth Century AD*. New York: Palgrave Macmillan, 2012.

Herren, Michael, W. C. J. McDonough, and Ross G. Arthur, eds. *Latin Culture in the Eleventh Century: Proceedings of the Third International Conference on Medieval Latin Studies, Cambridge, September 9–12 1998*. 2 vols. Turnhout, Belg.: Brepols, 2002.

Herrmann, Klaus Jürgen. *Das Tuskulanerpapsttum (1012–1046)*. Stuttgart: Anton Hiersemann, 1973.

Heslop, T. A. "The Production of *Deluxe* Manuscripts and the Patronage of King Cnut and Queen Emma." *Anglo-Saxon England* 19 (1990): 151–95.

Hester, David Paul. *Monasticism and Spirituality of the Italo-Greeks*. Thessaloniki: Patriarchal Institute for Patristic Studies, 1991.

Hettinger, Anette. *Die Beziehungen des Papsttums zu Afrika von der Mitte des 11. bis zum Ende des 12. Jahrhunderts*. Cologne: Böhlau, 1993.

Hicks, Carola, ed. *England in the Eleventh Century: Proceedings of the 1990 Harlaxton Symposium*. Stamford, UK: Paul Watkins, 1992.

Hinz, Paulus. "*Traditio* und *Novatio* in der Geschichte der Kreuzigungsbilder und Kruzifixe bis zum Ausgang des Mittelalters." In *Traditio—Krisis—Renovatio*, ed. Jaspert and Mohr, 599–608.

Hiscock, Nigel, ed. *The White Mantle of Churches: Architecture, Liturgy, and Art around the Millennium*. Turnhout, Belg.: Brepols, 2003.

Hodges, Richard. *Towns and Trade in the Age of Charlemagne*. London: Duckworth, 2000.

Hodges, Richard, and Brian Hobley, eds. *The Rebirth of Towns in the West, AD 700–1050*. London: Council for British Archaeology, 1988.

Hodges, Richard, Sarah Leppard, and John Mitchell. "The Sack of San Vincenzo al Volturno, 10 October 881, Reconsidered by Archaeology." *Acta Archaeologica* 82 (2011): 286–301.

Hoffmann, Hartmut. *Buchkunst und Königtum im ottonischen und frühsalischen Reich*. 2 vols. Stuttgart: Anton Hiersemann, 1986.

——. "Der König und seine Bischöfe in Frankreich und in Deutschen Reich 936–1060." In *Bischof Burchard von Worms*, edited by Hartmann, 79–127.

——. *Mönchskönig und Rex Idiota: Studien zur Kirchenpolitik Heinrichs II. und Konrads II.* Hannover: Hahn, 1993.

Hourihane, Colum, ed. *Interactions: Artistic Interchange between the Eastern and Western Worlds in the Medieval Period*. University Park: Princeton Index of Christian Art with Penn State University Press, 2007.

——, ed. *Objects, Images, and the Word: Art in the Service of the Liturgy*. Princeton: Index of Christian Art, 2003.

——, ed. *Romanesque Art and Thought in the Twelfth Century: Essays in Honor of Walter Cahn*. University Park: Princeton Index of Christian Art with Penn State University Press, 2008.

Howe, John. "The Awesome Hermit: The Symbolic Significance of the Hermit as a Possible Research Perspective." *Numen* 30 (1983): 106–19.

——. *Church Reform and Social Change in Eleventh-Century Central Italy: Dominic of Sora and His Patrons*. Philadelphia: University of Pennsylvania Press, 1997.

——. "*Gaudium et Spes*: Ecclesiastical Reformers at the Start of a 'New Age.'" In *Reforming the Church before Modernity*, edited by Bellitto and Hamilton, 21–35.

——. "Greek Influence on the Eleventh-Century Western Revival of Hermitism." 2 vols. PhD diss., UCLA, 1979.

——. "The Nobility's Reform of the Medieval Church." *AHR* 93 (1988): 317–39.

——. "Re-Forging the 'Age of Iron': Part 1: The Tenth Century as the End of the Ancient World?" *History Compass* 8/8 (2010): 866–87. doi:10.1111/J 1478–0542.2010.00707.x.

——. "Re-Forging the 'Age of Iron': Part 2: The Tenth Century in a New Age?" *History Compass* 8/9 (2010): 1000–1022. doi:10.1111/j. 1478–0542.2010.00708.x.

——. "St. Benedict the Hermit as a Model for Italian Sanctity: Some Hagiographical Witnesses." *American Benedictine Review* 55 (2004): 42–54.

——. "Western Monks and the East, 850–1050." In *Cambridge History of Medieval Western Monasticism*, edited by Beach and Cochelin.

Howe, John, and Michael Wolfe, eds. *Inventing Medieval Landscapes: Senses of Place in Western Europe*. Gainesville: University Press of Florida, 2002.

Howe, Nicholas. "Rome: Capital of Anglo-Saxon England." *Journal of Medieval and Early Modern Studies* 34 (2004): 147–72.

Hubert, Jean. *L'Art préroman*. Chartres: Jacques Laget, 1974.

Hughes, Andrew. *Medieval Manuscripts for Mass and Office: A Guide to Their Organization and Terminology*. Toronto: University of Toronto Press, 1982.

Iogna-Prat, Dominique. "Le croix, le moine et l'empereur: Dévotion à la Croix et théologie politique à Cluny autour de l'an mil." In *Études clunisiennes*, 74–92.

——. *Études clunisiennes*. Paris: Picard, 2002.

——. *La Maison Dieu: Une histoire monumentale de l'Église au Moyen Âge (v. 800–v. 1200)*. Paris: Éditions du Seuil, 2006.

——. "Les morts dans la compatibilité céleste des Clunisiens aux XIᵉ et XIIᵉ siècles." In *Études clunisiennes*, 125–50.

Iogna-Prat, Dominique, Éric Palazzo, and Daniel Russo, eds. *Marie: Le culte de la Vierge dans la société medievale*. Paris: Beauchesne, 1996.

Iogna-Prat, Dominique, and Jean-Charles Picard, eds. *Religion et culture autour de l'an Mil: Royaume capétien et Lotharingie: Actes du Colloque Hugues Capet 987–1987. La France de l'an Mil, Auxerre, 26 et 27 juin 1987—Metz, 11 et 12 septembre 1987*. Paris: Picard, 1990.

Irvine, Martin. *The Making of Textual Culture: Grammatica and Literary Theory, 350–1100*. Cambridge: Cambridge University Press, 1994.

Isla, Amancio. "Warfare and Other Plagues in the Iberian Peninsula around the Year 1000." In *Europe around the Year 1000*, edited by Urbańczyk, 233–246.

Le istituzioni ecclesiastiche della Societas Christiana dei secoli XI-XII: Diocesi, pievi e parrocchie: Atti della Settima internazionale di studio, Milano, 1–7 settembre 1974. Milan: Vita e Pensiero, 1977.

Iversen, Gunilla. *Laus Angelica: Poetry in the Medieval Mass*. Edited by Jane Flynn. Translated by William Flynn. Turnhout, Belg.: Brepols, 2010.

Jacobsen, Werner. "Saints' Tombs in Frankish Church Architecture." *Speculum* 72 (1997): 1107–43.

Jaeger, C. Stephen. *Ennobling Love: In Search of a Lost Sensibility*. Philadelphia: University of Pennsylvania Press, 1999.

——. *The Envy of Angels: Cathedral Schools and Social Ideals in Medieval Europe, 950–1200*. Philadelphia: University of Pennsylvania Press, 1994.

James, Liz, ed. *A Companion to Byzantium*. Oxford: Wiley-Blackwell, 2010.

Jannet, Monique, and Christian Sapin, eds. *Guillaume de Volpiano et l'architecture des rotondes: Actes du colloque de Dijon, Musée Archéologique, 23–25 septembre 1993*. Dijon: Éditions universitaires de Dijon, 1996.

Jarnut, Jörg, and Matthias Wemhoff, eds. *Vom Umbruch zur Erneuerung? Das 11. und beginnende 12. Jahrhundert: Positionen der Forschung*. Munich: Wilhelm Fink, 2006.

Jasper, Kathryn L., and John Howe. "Hermitism in the Eleventh and Twelfth Centuries." In *Cambridge History of Medieval Western Monasticism*, edited by Beach and Cochelin.

Jaspert, Bernd, and Rudolf Mohr, eds. *Traditio—Krisis—Renovatio aus theologischer Sicht: Festschrift Winfried Zeller zum 65. Geburtstag*. Marburg: N.G. Elwert, 1976.

Jaubert, Anne Niessen. "Some Aspects of Viking Research in France." *Acta Archaeologica* 71 (2001): 159–69.

Jeffery, Peter. "Eastern and Western Elements in the Irish Monastic Prayer of the Hours." In *Divine Office in the Latin Middle Ages,* edited by Fassler and Balzer, 99–143.

Jesch, Judith, ed. *The Scandinavians from the Vendel Period to the Tenth Century: An Ethnographic Perspective*. Woodbridge, UK: Boydell, 2002.

——. "Vikings on the European Continent in the Late Viking Age." In *Scandinavia and Europe*, edited by Adams and Holman, 255–68.

Jestice, Phyllis G. *Wayward Monks and the Religious Revolution of the Eleventh Century*. Leiden, Neth.: Brill, 1997.

Jones, Anna Trumbore. *"Noble Lord, Good Shepherd": Episcopal Power and Piety in Aquitaine, 877–1050*. Leiden, Neth.: Brill, 2009.

Jones, Lynn. "From *Anglorum Basileus* to Norman Saint: The Transformation of Edward the Confessor." *Haskins Society Journal* 12 (2002): 99–120.

Jung Wilhelm, ed. *1000 Jahre Mainzer Dom (975–1975): Werden und Wandel. Austellungskatalog und Handbuch*. Mainz, Ger.: Mainzer Verlagsanstalt, 1975.

Jungmann, Josef A. *The Mass of the Roman Rite: Its Origins and Development*. 2 vols. Translated by Francis A. Brunner. 1951–55. Reprint, Westminster, MD: Christian Classics, 1986.

——. *Pastoral Liturgy*. London: Challoner, 1962.

Jussen, Bernhard, ed. *Ordering Medieval Society: Perspectives on Intellectual and Practical Models of Shaping Social Relations*. Translated by Pamela Selwyn. Philadelphia: University of Pennsylvania Press, 2000.

Kaimakamova, Miliana, Maciej Salamon, and Małgorzata Smorąg-Różycka, eds. *Byzantium, New Peoples, New Powers: The Byzantino-Slav Contact Zone from the Ninth to the Fifiteenth Century*. Cracow: Towarzystwo Wydawnicze "Historia Iagellonica," 2001.

Karkov, Catherine E. *The Art of Anglo-Saxon England*. Woodbridge, UK: Boydell, 2011.

Karkov, Catherine E., and George Hardin Brown, eds. *Anglo-Saxon Styles*. Albany: SUNY Press, 2003.

Karkov, Catherine E., Sarah Larratt Keefer, and Karen Louise Jolly, eds. *The Place of the Cross in Anglo-Saxon England*. Woodbridge, UK: Boydell, 2006.

Kazhdan, Alexander P. *History of Byzantine Literature (850–1000)*. Edited by Christine Angelidi. Athens: National Hellenic Research Foundation Institute for Byzantine Research, 2006.

——, ed. *The Oxford Dictionary of Byzantium*, 3 vols. New York: Oxford University Press, 1991.

Keefer, Sarah Larratt, Karen Louise Jolly, and Catherine E. Karkov, eds. *Cross and Cruciform in the Anglo-Saxon World: Studies to Honor the Memory of Timothy Reuter*. Morgantown: West Virginia University Press, 2010.

Keller, Hagen, and Gerd Althoff. *Die Zeit der späten Karolinger und der Ottonen: Krisen und Konsolidierung, 888–1024*. Vol. 3 of *Gebhardt: Handbuch der deutschen Geschichte*. 10th ed. Stuttgart: Klett-Cotta, 2008.

Kelly, J. N. D., and Michael Walsh. *The Oxford Dictionary of Popes*, 2nd ed. Oxford: Oxford University Press, 2010.

Kelly, Thomas Forrest. *The* Exultet *in Southern Italy*. New York: Oxford University Press, 1996.

Kessler, Herbert L. *Old St. Peter's and Church Decoration in Medieval Italy*. Spoleto: CISAM, 2002.

Kenyon, John R. *Medieval Fortifications*. New York: St. Martin's, 1990.

Keynes, Simon. "Ely Abbey 672–1109." In *History of Ely Cathedral*, edited by Meadows and Ramsey, 2–58.

——. "The Vikings in England, *c.* 790–1016." In *Oxford Illustrated History of the Vikings*, edited by Sawyer, 48–82.

Kintzinger, Martin, Sönke Lorenz, and Michael Walter, eds. *Schule und Schüler im Mittelalter: Beiträge zur europäischen Bildungsgeschichte des 9. bis 15. Jahrhunderts*. Cologne: Böhlau, 1996.

Klaesø, Iben Skibsted, ed. *Viking Trade and Settlement in Continental Western Europe*. Copenhagen: Museum Tusculanum Press, University of Copenhagen, 2010.

Klaniczay, Gábor. *Holy Rulers and Blessed Princesses: Dynastic Cults in Medieval Central Europe*. Translated by Éva Pálmai. Cambridge: Cambridge University Press, 2002.

——, ed. *Vitae Sanctorum Aetatis Conversionis Europae Centralis (saec. X–XI)*. Budapest: Central European University Press, 2013.

Klauser, Theodor. *Der Ursprung der bischöflichen Insignien und Ehrenrechte*. 2nd ed. Krefeld: Richard Scherpe, 1953.

Klein, Holger A. *Byzanz, der Westen und das "wahre" Kreuz: Die Geschichte einer Reliquie und ihrer künstlerischen Fassung in Byzanz und im Abendland*. Wiesbaden: Reichert, 2004.

Knowles, David. *The Monastic Order in England: A History of Its Development from the Times of St. Dunstan to the Fourth Lateran Council, 943–1216*. Cambridge: Cambridge University Press, 1941.

Kobialka, Michal. *This Is My Body: Representational Practices in the Early Middle Ages*. Ann Arbor: University of Michigan Press, 1999.

Kolbaba, Tia M. *The Byzantine Lists: Errors of the Latins*. Urbana: University of Illinois Press, 2000.

Koep, Leo. *Das himmlische Buch in Antike und Christentum: Eine religionsgeschichtliche Untersuchung zur altchristlichen Bildersprache*. Bonn: Peter Hanstein, 1952.

Konstantinou, Evangelos, ed. *Byzanz und das Abendland im 10. und 11. Jahrhundert*. Vienna: Böhlau, 1997.

Körntgen, Ludger, and Dominik Wassenhoven, eds. *Patterns of Episcopal Power: Bishops in Tenth and Eleventh Century Western Europe*. Berlin: Walter de Gruyter, 2011.

Korteweg, Anne S. "Thierry II, Count of Holland, and His Wife Hildegard and Their Donations to Egmond Abbey." In Aalst and Ciggaar, *Byzantium and the Low Countries*, 146–64.

Kottje, Raymond, and Helmut Maurer, eds. *Monastische Reformen im 9. und 10. Jahrhundert*. Sigmaringen, Ger.: Jan Thorbecke, 1989.

Krautheimer, Richard. *Studies in Early Christian, Medieval, and Renaissance Art*. New York: New York University Press, 1969.

Kretzschmar, Hellmut, ed. *Vom Mittelalter zur Neuzeit: Zum 65. Geburtstag von Heinrich Sproemberg*. Berlin: Rütten & Loening, 1956.

Krüger, Kristina. "Architecture and Liturgical Practice: The Cluniac *Galilea*." In *White Mantle of Churches*, edited by Hiscock, 138–59.

Kselman, Thomas, ed. *Belief in History: Innovative Approaches to European and American Religion*. Notre Dame: University of Notre Dame Press, 1991.

Ladner, Gerhart B., *The Idea of Reform: Its Impact on Christian Thought and Action in the Age of the Fathers*. Cambridge: Harvard University Press, 1959.

——. "Terms and Ideas of Renewal." In *Renaissance and Renewal*, edited by Benson and Constable, 1–33.

Lafontaine-Dosogne, Jacqueline. "The Art of Byzantium and Its Relation to Germany in the Time of the Empress Theophano." In *Empress Theophano*, edited by Davids, 211–30.

Lahaye-Geusen, Maria. *Das Opfer der Kinder: Ein Beitrag zur Liturgie- und Sozialgeschichte des Mönchtums im hohen Mittelalter*. Altenberge: Oros, 1991.

Laiou, Angeliki E., ed. *The Economic History of Byzantium from the Seventh through the Fifteenth Century*. 3 vols. Washington, DC: Dumbarton Oaks, 2002.

Lanham, Carol Dana, ed. *Latin Grammar and Rhetoric: From Classical Theory to Medieval Practice*. London: Continuum, 2002.

La Rocca, Cristina, ed. *Italy in the Early Middle Ages, 476–1000*. Oxford: Oxford University Press, 2002.

Lapidge, Michael, and Rosalind C. Love. "The Latin Hagiography of England and Wales (600–1550)." In *Hagiographies*, edited by Philippart, 3:203–325.

Lasko, Peter. *Ars Sacra, 800–1200*. 2nd ed. New Haven: Yale University Press, 1994.

——. "Roger of Helmarshausen, Author and Craftsman: Life, Sources of Style, and Iconography." In *Objects, Images, and the Word*, edited by Hourihane, 180–201.

Lauwers, Michel, ed. *La Dîme, l'Église et la société féodale*. Turnhout, Belg.: Brepols, 2012.

Lavelle, Ryan. *Alfred's Wars: Sources and Interpretations of Anglo-Saxon Warfare in the Viking Age*. Woodbridge, UK: Boydell, 2010.

Leclercq, Jean. "From St. Gregory to St. Bernard: From the Sixth to the Twelfth Century." In *The Spirituality of the Middle Ages*. Edited by Leclercq, François Vandenbroucke, and Louis Boyer, 1–220. Translated by the Benedictines of Holme Eden Abbey. New York: Seabury, 1968.

——. *The Love of Learning and the Desire for God: A Study of Monastic Culture*. Translated by Catharine Misrahi. New York: Fordham University Press, 1961.

——. "Saint Romuald et le monachisme missionaire." *Revue bénédictine* 72 (1962): 307–23.

Lees, Clare A. *Tradition and Belief: Religious Writing in Late Anglo-Saxon England*. Minneapolis: University of Minnesota Press, 1999.

Le Jan, Régine, ed. *La royauté et les élites dans l'Europe carolingienne: Début IXᵉ siècle aux environs de 920*. Center d'histoire de l'Europe du Nord-Ouest 17. Lille: Université de Charles-de-Gaulle Lille 3, 1998.

Le Maho, Jacques. "La production éditoriale à Jumièges vers le milieu du Xᵉ siècle." *Tabularia "Études"* 1 (2001): 11–32.

Lendinara, Patrizia, Loredana Lazzari, and Maria Amalia D'Aronco, eds. *Form and Content of Instruction in Anglo-Saxon England in the Light of Contemporary Manuscript Evidence: Papers Presented at the International Conference, Udine, 6–8 April 2006*. Turnhout, Belg.: Brepols, 2007.

Lepelley, Claude, Michel Sot, and Pierre Riché, eds. *Haut moyen-âge: Culture, education et société. Études offertes à Pierre Riché*, Paris: Editions européennes Erasme, 1990.

Leyser, Karl. *Communications and Power in Medieval Europe: The Gregorian Revolution and Beyond*. Edited by Timothy Reuter. London: Hambledon, 1994.

——. "Die Ottonen und Wessex." *Frühmittelalterliche Studien* 17 (1983): 73–97.

——. "*Theophanu Divina Gratia Imperatrix Augusta*: Western and Eastern Emperorship in the Later Tenth Century." In *Empress Theophano*, edited by Davids, 1–27.

Lifshitz, Felice. *The Norman Conquest of Pious Neustria: Historiographic Discourse and Saintly Relics, 684–1090*. Toronto: PIMS, 1995.

Linehan, Peter, and Janet Nelson, eds. *The Medieval World*. London: Routledge, 2001.

Lobrichon, Guy. "The Chiaroscuro of Heresy: Early Eleventh-Century Aquitaine as Seen from Auxerre." In *Peace of God*, edited by Head and Landes, 80–103.

Logan, Ian. *Reading Anselm's Prosologion: The History of Anselm's Argument and Its Significance Today*. Burlington, VT: Ashgate, 2009.

Lorenz, Sönke, and Thomas Zotz, eds. *Frühformen von Stiftskirchen in Europa: Funktion und Wandel religiöser Gemeinschaften vom 6. bis zum Ende des 11. Jahrhunderts. Festgabe für Dieter Mertens zum 65. Geburstag*. Leinfelden-Echterdingen: DRW-Verlag, 2005.

Lowdon, John. "Illuminated Books: Some Observations," In *Objects, Images, and the Word*, edited by Hourihane, 17–53,

Loyn, H.R. "Church and State in England in the Tenth and Eleventh Centuries." In *Tenth-Century Studies*, edited by Parsons, 94–102 and 229–30.

Loud, Graham A. *The Age of Robert Guiscard: Southern Italy and the Norman Conquest*. Harlow, UK: Pearson Education Limited, 2000.

Louise, René, ed. *Études ligériennes d'histoire et d'archéologic médiévales: Mémoires et exposés présentés à la Semaine d'études médiévales de Saint-Benoit-sur-Loire du 3 au 10 juillet 1969*. Auxerre: Société des fouilles archéologiques et des monuments historiques de l'Yonne, 1975.

Luscombe, David, and Jonathan Riley-Smith, eds. *NCMH*. Vol. 4, *c. 1024–c. 1198*, pts. 1 and 2, Cambridge: Cambridge University Press, 2004.

Lutz, Cora E. *Schoolmasters of the Tenth Century*. Hamden CT: Archon Books, 1977.

Maccarrone, Michele, ed. *Il primato del vescovo di Roma nel primo millennio: Ricerche e testimonianze: Atti del symposium storico-teologico, Roma, 9–13 ottobre 1989*. Vatican City: Libreria Editrice Vaticana, 1991.

Magdalino, Paul, ed. *Byzantium in the Year 1000*. Turnhout, Belg.: Brepols, 2002.

Magennis, Hugh. *The Cambridge Introduction to Anglo-Saxon Literature.* Cambridge: Cambridge University Press, 2011.

Maguire, Henry. *The Icons of Their Bodies: Saints and Their Images in Byzantium.* Princeton: Princeton University Press, 1996.

Malone, Carolyn Marino. *Saint-Bénigne de Dijon en l'an Mil,* Totius Galliae Basilicis Mirabilior: *Interprétation politique, liturgique et théologique.* Turnhout, Belg.: Brepols, 2009.

Mariaux, Pierre Alain. *Warmond d'Ivrée et ses images: Politique et création iconographique autour de l'an mil.* Bern, Switz.: Peter Lang, 2002.

Martindale, Andrew. "The Romanesque Church of Saint-Bénigne at Dijon and MS 591 in the Bibliothèque muniicpale." *Journal of the British Archaeological Association* 25 (1962): 21–54.

Il matrimonio nella società altomedievale, 22–28 aprile 1976. 2 vols. Settimane di studio del CISAM 24 (1–2). Spoleto: CISAM, 1977.

McCarthy, T.H.J. *Music, Scholasticism, and Reform: Salian Germany, 1025–1125.* Manchester, UK: Manchester University Press, 2009.

McClendon, Charles B. "Church Building in Northern Italy around the Year 1000: A Reappraisal." In *White Mantle of Churches,* edited by Hiscock, 221–32.

———. *The Origins of Medieval Architecture: Building in Europe, A.D. 600–900.* New Haven: Yale University Press, 2005.

McCluskey, Stephen C. *Astronomies and Cultures in Early Medieval Europe.* Cambridge: Cambridge University Press, 1998.

McCormick, Michael. *Charlemagne's Survey of the Holy Land: Wealth, Personnel, and Buildings of a Mediterranean Church between Antiquity and the Middle Ages.* Washington, DC: Dumbarton Oaks, 2011.

———. *Eternal Victory: Triumphal Rulership in Late Antiquity, Byzantium, and the Early Medieval West.* New York: Cambridge University Press, 1986.

———. *Origins of the European Economy: Communications and Commerce, A.D. 300–900.* Cambridge: Cambridge University Press, 2001.

McCurrach, Catherine Carver. "*Renovatio* Reconsidered: Richard Krautheimer and the Iconography of Architecture." *Gesta* 50 (2011): 41–69.

McGinn, Bernard. *The Growth of Mysticism.* Vol. 2 of *The Presence of God: A History of Western Mysticism.* 5 vols. New York: Crossroad, 1994.

McGinn, Bernard, and John Meyendorff, eds. *Christian Spirituality: Origins to the Twelfth Century.* New York: Crossroad, 1985.

McGuire, Brian Patrick. *Friendship and Community: The Monastic Experience, 350–1250.* Ithaca: Cornell University Press, 1988.

McKitterick, Rosamond, ed. *Carolingian Culture: Emulation and Innovation.* Cambridge: Cambridge University Press, 1994.

———. *The Carolingians and the Written Word.* Cambridge: Cambridge University Press, 1989.

———, ed. *NCMH.* Vol. 2, *c. 700–c. 900.* Cambridge: Cambridge University Press, 1995.

———. "Ottonian Intellectual Culture in the Tenth Century and the Role of Theophano." In *Empress Theophano,* edited by Davids, 169–93.

———. *Perceptions of the Past in the Early Middle Ages.* Notre Dame: University of Notre Dame Press, 2006.

McNeill, John, and Richard Plant, eds. *Romanesque and the Past: Retrospection in the Art and Architecture of Romanesque Europe.* Leeds: British Archaeological Association, 2013.

McNulty, Patricia M., and Bernard Hamilton. "*Orientale Lumen* et *Magistra Latinitatis*: Greek Influences on Western Monasticism (900–1100)." In *Le Millénaire du Mont Athos,* 1:181–216.

Meadows, Peter, and Nigel Ramsey, eds. *A History of Ely Cathedral.* Woodbridge, UK: Boydell, 2003.

Meckseper, Cord. "Antike Spolien in der ottonischen Architektur." In *Antike Spolien in der Architektur*, edited by Poeschke, 179–204.

Meirion-Jones, Gwyn, Edward Impey, and Michael Jones, eds. *The Seigneurial Residence in Western Europe, AD c 800–1600*. Oxford: Archaeopress, 2002.

Melville, Gert, and Anne Müller, eds. *Female* Vita Religiosa *between Late Antiquity and the High Middle Ages: Structures, Developments, and Spatial Contexts*. Berlin: LIT, 2011.

Melville, Gert, and Markus Schürer, eds. *Das Eigene und das Ganze: Zum Individuellen im mittelalterlichen Religiosentum*. Münster: LIT, 2002.

Messerer, Wilhelm. "Zur byzantinischen Frage in der ottonischen Kunst." *Byzantinische Zeitschrift* 52 (1959): 32–60.

Meyers, Henry A., and Herwig Wolfram, eds. *Medieval Kingship*. Chicago: Nelson Hall, 1982.

Milis, Ludo, ed. *The Pagan Middle Ages*. Translated by Tanis Guest. Woodbridge, UK: Boydell, 1998.

Le Millénaire du Mont Athos, 963–1963: Études et mélanges. 2 vols. Vol. 1, Chevetogne: Éditions du Chevetogne, 1963. Vol. 2, Venice: Giorgio Cini, 1964.

Miller, Maureen C. *The Bishop's Palace: Architecture and Authority in Medieval Italy*. Ithaca: Cornell University Press, 2000.

——. *Clothing the Clergy: Virtue and Power in Medieval Europe, c. 800–1200*. Ithaca: Cornell University Press, 2014.

——. *The Formation of a Medieval Church: Ecclesiastical Change in Verona, 950–1150*. Ithaca: Cornell University Press, 1993.

Miquel, André. *La géographie humaine du monde musulman jusqu'au milieu du 11ᵉ siècle*. 4 vols. Paris: Mouton, 1967–88.

Moore, Michael Edward. "The King's New Clothes: Royal and Episcopal Regalia in the Frankish Empire." In *Robes and Honor*, edited by Gordon, 95–135.

——. *A Sacred Kingdom: Bishops and the Rise of Frankish Kingship, 300–850*. Washington, DC: Catholic University of America Press, 2010.

Moore, Robert I. *The First European Revolution, c. 970–1215*. Oxford: Blackwell, 2000.

——. *The Formation of a Persecuting Society: Power and Deviance in Western Europe 950–1250*. New York: Blackwell, 1987.

Morris, Colin. *The Sepulchre of Christ and the Medieval West: From the Beginning to 1600*. Oxford: Oxford University Press, 2005.

Mortensen, Lars Boje, ed. *The Making of Christian Myths in the Periphery of Latin Christendom (c. 1000–1300)*. Copenhagen: Museum Tusculanum Press, University of Copenhagen, 2006.

Mostert, Marco. *The Political Theology of Abbo of Fleury: A Study of the Ideas about Society and Law of the Tenth-Century Monastic Reform Movement*. Hilversum: Verloren, 1987.

Much, Franz J., ed. *Baukunst des Mittelalters in Europa: Hans Erich Kubach zum 75. Geburtstag*. Stuttgart: Stuttgarter Gesellschaft für Kunst und Denkmalpflege, 1988.

Mullins, Juliet, Jenifer Ní Ghrádaigh, and Richard Hawtree, eds. *Envisioning Christ on the Cross: Ireland and the Early Medieval West*. Dublin: Four Courts Press, 2013.

Munier, Charles. *Le Pape Léon IX et la réforme de l'Église, 1002–1054*. Strasbourg: Éditions du Signe, 2002.

Musset, Lucien. "Le mécénat des princes normands au XIᵉ siècle." In *Artistes, artisans et production*, edited by Barral i Altet, 2:121–34.

Muthesius, Anna. *Byzantine Silk Weaving, AD 400 to AD 1200*. Vienna: Fassbaender, 1997.

——. "The Role of Byzantine Silks in the Ottonian Empire." In *Byzanz und das Abendland*, edited by Konstantinou, 301–17.

Nagy, Piroska. *Le Don des larmes au moyen âge: Un instrument spirituel en quête d'institution (Vᵉ–XIIIᵉ siècle)*. Paris: Albin Michel, 2000.

Nees, Lawrence. *Early Medieval Art*. Oxford: Oxford University Press, 2002.

Nelson, Janet L. *Charles the Bald*. New York: Longman, 1992.

——. "The Frankish Empire." In *Oxford Illustrated History of the Vikings*, edited by Sawyer, 19–47.

——. "Royal Saints and Early Medieval Kingship." *Studies in Church History* 10 (1973): 39–44.

Nemerkényi, Előd. "The Religious Ruler in the *Admonitions* of King Saint Stephen of Hungary." In *Monotheistic Kingship*, edited by Al-Azmeh and Bak, 231–47.

Neuheuser, Hanns Peter, ed. *Bischofsbild und Bischofssitz: Geistige und geistliche Impulse aus regionalen Zentren des Hochmittalalters*. Münster: Aschendorff, 2013.

Neville, Leonora. *Authority in Byzantine Provincial Society, 950–1100*. New York: Cambridge University Press, 2004.

The New Cambridge Medieval History (NCMH). 7 vols. in 8. New York: Cambridge University Press, 1995–2005.

Newton, Francis. *The Scriptorium and Library at Monte Cassino, 1058–1105*. Cambridge: Cambridge University Press, 1999.

Nightingale, John. *Monasteries and Patrons in the Gorze Reform: Lotharingia ca. 850–1000*. Oxford: Clarendon, 2001.

——. "Oswald, Fleury, and Continental Reform." In *St. Oswald of Worcester*, edited by Brooks and Cubitt, 23–45.

Noble, Thomas F.X. *Images, Iconoclasm, and the Carolingians*. Philadelphia: University of Pennsylvania Press, 2009.

Noble, Thomas F.X., and Julia M.H. Smith, eds. *Early Medieval Christianities, c. 600–c. 1100*. The Cambridge History of Christianity 3. New York: Cambridge University Press, 2008.

Noble, Thomas F.X., and John Van Engen, eds. *European Transformations: The Long Twelfth Century*. Notre Dame: University of Notre Dame Press, 2012.

I Normanni e la loro espansione in Europa nell'alto medioevo, 18–24 aprile 1968. Settimane di studio del CISAM 16. Spoleto: CISAM, 1969.

Nussbaum, Otto. *Kloster, Priestermönch und Privatmesse: Ihr Verhältnis im Westen von den Anfänge bis zum hohen Mittelalter*. Bonn: Peter Hanstein, 1961.

Oakley, Francis. *Empty Bottles of Gentilism: Kingship and the Divine in Late Antiquity (to 1050)*. New Haven: Yale University Press, 2010.

Occident et Orient au Xᵉ siècle: Actes du XIᵉ Congrès de la Société des historiens médiévistes de l'enseignement superior public (Dijon, 2–4 juin 1978). Dijon: Société des belles lettres, 1979.

Ott, John, and Anna Trumbore Jones, eds. *The Bishop Reformed: Studies of Episcopal Power and Culture in the Central Middle Ages*. Aldershot, UK: Ashgate, 2007.

Palazzo, Éric. *L'espace rituel et le sacré: La liturgie de l'autel portative dans l'Antiquité et au Moyen Âge*. Turnhout, Belg.: Brepols, 2008.

——. *L'Évêque et son image: L'illustration du pontifical au moyen âge*. Turnhout, Belg.: Brepols, 1999.

——. *A History of Liturgical Books from the Beginning to the Thirteenth Century*. Collegeville, MN: Liturgical Press, 1998.

Parisse, Michel. "L'entourage de Léon IX." In *Léon IX*, edited by Bischoff and Tock, 435–56.

——. *Religieux et religieuses en Empire du Xᵉ au XIIᵉ siècle*. Paris: Picard, 2011.

Parisse, Michel, and Monique Goullet, eds. *Vie du Pape Léon IX (Brunon évêque de Toul)*. Paris: Les Belles lettres, 2009.

Parker, Philip. *The Northmen's Fury: A History of the Viking World*. London: Jonathan Cape, 2014.

Parsons, David, ed. *Tenth-Century Studies: Essays in Commemoration of the Millennium of the Council of Winchester and Regularis Concordia*. London: Phillimore, 1975.

Patzold, Steffen. Episcopus: *Wissen über Bischöfe im Frankenreich des späten 8. bis frühen 10. Jahrhunderts*. Ostfildern: Jan Thorbecke, 2008.

Pentcheva, Bissera V. *Icons and Power: The Mother of God in Byzantium.* University Park: Pennsylvania State University Press, 2006.

Pestell, Tim. *Landscapes of Monastic Foundations: The Establishment of Religious Houses in East Anglia, c. 650–1200.* Woodbridge, UK: Boydell, 2004.

Petersohn, Jürgen, ed. *Politik und Heiligenverehrung in Hochmittelalter.* Sigmaringen, Ger.: Jan Thorbecke, 1994.

Pettrucci, Enzo. "Rapporti di Leone IX con Constantinopoli." *Studi medievali,* 3rd ser., 14 (1973): 733–831.

Pfaff, Richard W. "The Anglo-Saxon Bishop and His Book." *Bulletin of the John Rylands University Library of Manchester* 81 (1999): 3–24.

——. *The Liturgy in Medieval England.* Cambridge: Cambridge University Press, 2009.

Philippart, Guy, ed. *Hagiographies.* Vols. 1–5. Turnhout, Belg.: Brepols, 1994–2010.

Philippart, Guy, and Michel Trigalet. "L'hagiographie latine du XIᵉ siècle dans la longue durée: Données statistiques sur la production littéraire et sur l'édition médiévale." In *Latin Culture in the Eleventh Century,* edited by Herren et al., 2:281–301,

Pierson, Leif Errol. "Evidence for Viking Disruption from Early Norman Histories and Commemorations of Saints." MA thesis, Texas Tech University, 1999.

Planavergne, Delphine. "Les Normands avant la Normandie: Les invasions scandinaves en Neustrie au IXᵉ siècle dans l'hagiographie franque." In *Les fondations scandinaves en Occident,* edited by Bauduin, 37–52.

Plant, Richard. "Architectural Developments in the Empire North of the Alps: The Patronage of the Imperial Court." In *White Mantle of Churches,* edited by Hiscock, 29–56.

Pleszczyński, Andrzej. *The Birth of a Stereotype: Polish Rulers and Their Country in German Writings c. 1000 A.D.* Leiden, Neth.: Brill, 2011.

Poeschke, Joachim, ed. *Antike Spolien in der Architektur des Mittelalters und der Renaissance.* Munich: Hirmer, 1996.

Poncelet, Albert. "Vie et miracles du Pape S. Léon." *Analecta Bollandiana* 25 (1906): 258–97.

Potts, Cassandra. *Monastic Revival and Regional Identity in Early Normandy.* Woodbridge, UK: Boydell, 1997.

Pounds, Norman J. G. *A History of the English Parish: The Culture of Religion from Augustine to Victoria.* Cambridge: Cambridge University Press, 2000.

Puhle, Matthias, ed. *Otto der Grosse, Magdeburg und Europa.* 2 vols. Mainz, Ger.: P. von Zabern, 2001.

Quinn, Patricia A. *Better Than the Sons of Kings: Boys and Monks in the Early Middle Ages.* New York: Peter Lang, 1989.

Rabin, Andrew, ed. *The Political Writings of Archbishop Wulfstan of York.* Manchester, UK: Manchester University Press, 2015.

Radding, Charles M., and William W. Clark. *Medieval Architecture, Medieval Learning: Builders and Masters in the Age of Romanesque and Gothic.* New Haven: Yale University Press, 1992.

Radding, Charles M., and Francis Newton, eds. *Theology, Rhetoric, and Politics in the Eucharistic Controversy: Alberic of Monte Cassino against Berengar of Tours.* New York: Columbia University Press, 2003.

Ramseyer, Valerie. *The Transformation of a Religious Landscape: Medieval Southern Italy, 850–1150.* Ithaca: Cornell University Press, 2006.

Redman, Charles L., ed. *Medieval Archaeology: Papers of the Seventeenth Annual Conference of the Center for Medieval and Early Renaissance Studies.* Binghamton: SUNY Press, 1989.

Reilly, Diane J. *The Art of Reform in Eleventh-Century Flanders: Gerard of Cambrai, Richard of Saint-Vanne and the Saint-Vaast Bible.* Leiden, Neth.: Brill, 2006.

Renoux, Annie. *Fécamp: Du Palais ducal au palais de Dieu: Bilan historique et archéologique des recherches menées sur le site du château des ducs de Normandie, IIᵉ siècle A.C.–XVIIIᵉ siècle P.C.* Paris: CNRS, 1991.

——. "*Palatium* et *castrum* en France du Nord (fin IXᵉ–début XIIIᵉ siècle)." In *Seigneurial Residence in Western Europe*, edited by Meirion-Jones et al., 15–26.

Reuter, Timothy. "Introduction: Reading the Tenth Century." In *NCMH*, 3:1–24.

——. "A Nation of Bishops: The Age of Wulfstan of York and Burchard of Worms." In *Strukturen bischöflicher*, edited by Körntgen and Wassenhoven, 17–38.

——, ed. *NCMH*. Vol. 3, *c. 900–c. 1024*. Cambridge: Cambridge University Press, 1999.

——, ed. *Warriors and Churchmen in the Middle Ages: Essays Presented to Karl Leyser*. London: Hambledon, 1992.

Reynolds, Leighton Durham, ed. *Texts and Transmission: A Survey of the Latin Classics*. Oxford: Clarendon, 1983.

Riché, Pierre. *Abbon de Fleury: Un moine savant et combatif (vers 950–1004)*. Turnhout, Belg.: Brepols, 2004.

——. *Education and Culture in the Barbarian West from the Sixth through the Eighth Century*. Translated by John Contreni. Columbia: University of South Carolina Press, 1976.

Rivard, Derek A. *Blessing the World: Ritual and Lay Piety in Medieval Religion*. Washington, DC: Catholic University of America Press, 2009.

Robinson, I. S. *The Papal Reform of the Eleventh Century: Lives of Pope Leo IX and Pope Gregory VII*. Manchester, UK: Manchester University Press, 2004.

Rollason, David. *Saints and Relics in Anglo-Saxon England*. Oxford: Basil Blackwell, 1989.

Rollason, David, Conrad Leyser, and Hannah Williams, eds. *England and the Continent in the Tenth Century: Studies in Honour of Wilhelm Levison (1876–1947)*. Turnhout, Belg.: Brepols, 2010.

Roma antica nel Medioevo: Mito, rappresentazioni, sopravvivenze nella 'Respublica Christiana' dei secoli IX–XIII: Atti della quattordicesima Settimana internazionale di studio Mendola, 24–28 agosto 1998. Milan: Vita e Pensiero, 2001.

Roma fra Oriente e Occidente, 19–24 aprile 2001. 2 vols. Settimane di studio del CISAM 49. Spoleto: CISAM, 2002.

Romano, John. *Liturgy and Society in Early Medieval Rome*. Burlington, VT: Ashgate, 2014.

Roper, Sally Elizabeth. *Medieval English Benedictine Liturgy: Studies in the Formation, Structure, and Content of the Monastic Votive Office, c. 950–1540*. New York: Garland, 1993.

Rosenwein, Barbara H. *Rhinoceros Bound: Cluny in the Tenth Century*. Philadelphia: University of Pennsylvania Press, 1982.

——. *To Be the Neighbor of Saint Peter: The Social Meaning of Cluny's Property, 909–1049*. Ithaca: Cornell University Press, 1989.

Rosser, Gervase. "The Cure of Souls in English Towns before 1000." In *Pastoral Care before the Parish*, edited by Blair and Sharpe, 267–84.

Rossetti, Gabriella. "Il matrimonio del clero nella società altomedievale." In *Il matrimonio nella società altomedievale*, 1:473–567.

Rouche, Michel, ed. *Fulbert de Chartres, précurseur de l'Europe médiévale?* Paris: Presses de l'Université Paris-Sorbonne, 2008.

——. "The Vikings versus the Towns of Northern Gaul: Challenge and Response." In *Medieval Archaeology*, edited by Redman, 41–56.

Rousseau, Philip, and Manolis Papoutsakis, eds. *Transformations of Late Antiquity: Essays for Peter Brown*. Burlington, VT: Ashgate, 2009.

Rudolph, Conrad. *The "Things of Greater Importance": Bernard of Clairvaux's Apologia and the Medieval Attitude toward Art*. Philadelphia: University of Pennsylvania Press, 1990.

——, ed. *A Companion to Medieval Art: Romanesque and Gothic in Northern Europe*. Oxford: Blackwell, 2006.

Saenger, Paul. *Space between Words: The Origins of Silent Reading*. Stanford: Stanford University Press, 1997.

Sansterre, Jean-Marie. "Les moines d'Occident et le monachisme d'Orient du VIᵉ au Xᵉ siècle: Entre textes anciens et réalités contemporaines." In *Christianità d'Occidente e Christianità d'Oriente*, 1:289–335.

——. *"Omnes qui coram hac imagine genua flexerint* … La veneration d'images de saints et de la Vierge d'après les texts écrits en Angleterre du milieu du XIᵉ aux premières décennies du XIIIᵉ siècle." *CCM* 49 (2006): 257–94.

——. "Témoignages des textes latins du Haut Moyen Âge sur le monachisme oriental et des textes byzantins sur le monachisme occidental." In *Revue Bénédictine* 103 (1993): 12–30.

Sapin, Christian, ed. *Avant-nefs & espaces d'accueil dans l'église entre le IVᵉ et le XIIᵉ siècle.* Paris: Comité des travaux historiques et scientifiques, 2002.

Sawyer, Peter H. *Kings and Vikings: Scandinavia and Europe, AD 700–1100.* London: Methuen, 1982.

——, ed. *The Oxford Illustrated History of the Vikings.* Oxford: Oxford University Press, 1997.

Sheingorn, Pamela, trans. *The Book of Sainte Foy.* Philadelphia: University of Pennsylvania Press, 1995.

Schmitt, Jean-Claude. *Le corps des images: Essais sur la culture visuelle au moyen âge.* Paris: Gallimard, 2002.

——. "Rituels de l'image et récits de vision," in *Testo e immagine nell'altomedioevo,* 1:419–62.

Schneidmüller, Brend, and Stefan Weinfurter, eds. *Otto III.–Heinrich II. Eine Wende?* Sigmaringen, Ger.: Jan Thorbecke, 1997.

Schulenburg, Jane Tibbetts. *Forgetful of Their Sex: Female Sanctity and Society ca. 500–1100.* Chicago: University of Chicago Press, 1998.

Scragg, Donald, ed. *The Battle of Maldon AD 991.* Oxford: Basil Blackwell in Association with the Manchester Center for Anglo-Saxon-Studies, 1991.

Il secolo di ferro: Mito e realtà del secolo X, 19–25 aprile 1990. 2 vols. Settimane di studio del CISAM 38. Spoleto: CISAM, 1991.

Shepard, Jonathan. "Crowns from the *Basileus,* Crowns from Heaven." In *Byzantium, New Peoples, New Powers,* edited by Kaimakamova et al., 127–48.

——. "Emperors and Expansionism: From Rome to Middle Byzantium." In *Medieval Frontiers,* edited by Abulafia and Berend, 55–82,

Sitwell, Gerard, ed. *St. Odo of Cluny: Being the Life of St. Odo of Cluny by John of Salerno and the Life of St. Gerald of Aurillac by St. Odo.* London: Sheed & Ward, 1958.

Skinner, Patricia. *Medieval Amalfi and Its Diaspora, 800–1250.* Oxford: Oxford University Press, 2013.

Smith, Brendan, ed. *Britain and Ireland 900–1300: Insular Responses to Medieval European Change.* Cambridge: Cambridge University Press, 1999.

Smith, Julia M.H., ed. *Early Medieval Rome and the Christian West: Essays in Honour of Donald A. Bullough.* Leiden, Neth.: Brill, 2000.

Smith, Katherine Allen. *War and the Making of Medieval Monastic Culture.* Woodbridge, UK: Boydell, 2011.

Smyth, Alfred P. "The Effect of Scandinavian Raiders on the English and Irish Churches: A Preliminary Reassessment." In *Britain and Ireland 900–1300,* edited by Brendan Smith, 1–38.

Snoeck, G.C.J. *Medieval Piety from Relics to the Eucharist: A Process of Mutual Interaction.* Leiden, Neth.: Brill, 1995.

Southern, Richard W. *The Making of the Middle Ages.* New Haven: Yale University Press, 1953.

Špidlík, Tomáš. *The Spirituality of the Christian East: A Systematic Handbook.* Translated by Anthony P. Gythiel. Kalamazoo, MI: Cistercian Publications, 1986.

Stahl, William Harris. *Martianus Capella and the Seven Liberal Arts.* 2 vols. New York: Columbia University Press, 1971.

Stalley, Roger. *Early Medieval Architecture.* Oxford: Oxford University Press, 1999.

Stephenson, Paul. *Byzantium's Balkan Frontier: A Political Study of the Northern Balkans, 900–1204.* Cambridge: Cambridge University Press, 2000.

Story, Joanna, ed. *Charlemagne: Empire and Society.* Manchester, UK: Manchester University Press, 2005.

Taft, Robert F. *The Liturgy of the Hours in East and West: The Origins of the Divine Office and Its Meaning for Today*. Collegeville, MN: Liturgical Press, 1986.

Taralon, Jean. "La majesté d'or de Saint Foi de Conques." *Bulletin monumental* 155 (1997): 11–77.

Taylor, H.M. "Tenth-Century Church Building in England and on the Continent." In *Tenth-Century Studies*, edited by Parsons, 141–68.

Tellenbach, Gerd. *The Church in Western Europe from the Tenth to the Early Twelfth Century*. Translated by Timothy Reuter. Cambridge: Cambridge University Press, 1993.

Testo e immagine nell'alto medioevo: 15–20 aprile 1993. 2 vols. Settimane di Studio del CISAM 41. Spoleto: CISAM, 1994.

Thoby, Paul. *Le crucifix des origines au Concile de Trente: Étude iconographique, Supplèment*. Nantes: Bellanger, 1963.

Tilliette, Jean-Yves. "La poésie métrique latine." in *Religion et culture*, edited by Iogna-Prat and Picard, 103–9.

Tinti, Francesca. *Sustaining Belief: The Church of Worcester from c. 870 to c. 1100*. Burlington, VT: Ashgate, 2010.

Töpfer, Bernhard. "Reliquienkult und Pilgerbewegung zur Zeit der Klosterreform im Burgundisch-Aquitanischen Gebiet." In *Vom Mittelalter zur Neuzeit*, edited by Kretzschmar, 420–39.

Toubert, Pierre. *Les Structures du Latium médiéval: Le Latium méridional et la Sabine du IXe siècle à la fin du XIIe siècle*. 2 vols. Rome: ÉFR, 1973.

Trilling, Renée R. "Sovereignty and Social Order: Archbishop Wulfstan and the *Institutes of Polity*." In *Bishop Reformed*, edited by Ott and Anna Jones, 58–91.

Ugé, Karine. *Creating the Monastic Past in Medieval Flanders*. York, UK: York Medieval Press, 2005.

Urbańczyk, Przemysław, ed. *Europe around the Year 1000*. Warsaw: Polish Academy of Sciences Institute of Archaeology and Ethnology, 2001.

Valante, Mary A. *The Vikings in Ireland: Settlement, Trade, and Urbanization*. Dublin: Four Courts, 2008.

Vanderputten, Steven. *Monastic Reform as Process: Realities and Representations in Medieval Flanders, 900–1100*. Ithaca: Cornell University Press, 2013.

Van Engen, John, ed. *Educating People of Faith: Exploring the History of Jewish and Christian Communities*. Grand Rapids: Eerdmans, 2004.

——. "Faith as a Concept of Order in Medieval Christendom." In *Belief in History*, edited by Kselman, 19–67.

van Winter Johanna Maria. "The Education of the Daughters of the Nobility in the Ottonian Empire." In *Empress Theophano*, edited by Davids, 86–98.

Vassilaki, Maria, ed. *Mother of God: Representations of the Virgin in Byzantine Art*. Milan: Skira, 2000.

Vauchez, André, ed. *Ermites de France et d'Italie (XIe–XVe siècle)*. Rome: ÉFR, 2003.

——. *The Spirituality of the Medieval West: From the Eighth to the Twelfth Century*. Translated by Collette Friedlander. Kalamazoo, MI: Cistercian Publications, 1993.

Vaughn, Sally N., and Jay Rubenstein, eds. *Teaching and Learning in Northern Europe*. Turnhout, Belg.: Brepols, 2006.

Vergnolle, Éliane. "Un carnet de modèles de l'an mil originaire de Saint-Benoît-sur-Loire (Paris, B.N. lat. 8318 + Rome, Vat. Reg. Lat. 596)." *Arte medievale* 2 (1985): 23–56.

——. "Les débuts de l'art roman dans le royaume franc (ca. 980–ca. 1020)." *CCM* 43 (2000): 77–104.

——. *Saint-Benoît-sur-Loire et la sculpture du XIe siècle*. Paris: Picard, 1985.

Verhulst, Adriaan. *The Rise of Cities in Northwest Europe*. Cambridge: Cambridge University Press, 1999.

Viladesau, Richard. *The Beauty of the Cross: The Passion of Christ in Theology and the Arts, from the Catacombs to the Eve of the Renaissance*. Oxford: Oxford University Press, 2006.

La vita comune del clero nei secoli XI e XII: Atti della Settimana di studio: Mendola, settembre 1959. 2 vols. Milan: Vita e Pensiero, 1962.

Webb, J.R. "Hagiography in the Diocese of Liège (950–1130)." In *Hagiographies*, edited by Goullet, 6:809–904.

Weinfurter, Stefan. *Heinrich II (1002–1024): Herrscher am Ende der Zeiten.* Regensburg: Friedrich Pustet, 1999.

Whitelock, Dorothy, ed. *English Historical Documents, c. 500–1042.* English Historical Documents 1, edited by David C. Douglas. 2nd ed. New York: Oxford University Press, 1979.

Whitelock, Dorothy, Martin Brett, and Christopher N. L. Brooke, eds. *Councils & Synods with Other Documents Relating to the English Church.* Vol. 1, pt. 1, *871–1066.* Oxford: Clarendon, 1981.

Wickham, Chris. *Framing the Middle Ages: Europe 400–800.* Oxford: Oxford University Press, 2005.

——. *The Inheritance of Rome: Illuminating the Dark Ages, 400–1000.* New York: Penguin, 2009.

Wimbush, Vincent L., and Richard Valantasis, eds. *Asceticism.* New York: Oxford University Press, 1995.

Wirth, Jean. *L'Image médiévale: Naissance et développements (VIᵉ–XVᵉ siècle).* Paris: Méridiens Klincksieck, 1989.

Wolf, Gunther, ed. *Kaiserin Theophanu: Prinzessin aus der Fremde—des Westreichs Grosse Kaiserin.* Cologne: Böhlau, 1991.

Wollasch, Joachim. "Monasticism: The First Wave of Reform." In *NCMH*, 3:163–85.

——. "Reformmönchtum und Schriftlichkeit." *Frühmittelalterliche Studien* 26 (1992): 274–86.

Wood, Ian. "Entrusting Western Europe to the Church, 400–750." *TRHS*, 6th ser., 23 (2013): 37–73.

Wood, Susan. *The Proprietary Church in the Medieval West.* New York: Oxford University Press, 2006.

Zettel, Horst. *Das Bild der Normannen und der Normanneneinfälle in westfränkishen, ostfränkishen und Angelsächsischen Quellen des 8. bis 11. Jahrhunderts.* Munich: Wilhelm Fink, 1977.

Zomer, Hiltje F.H. "The So-Called Women's Gallery in the Medieval Church: An Import from Byzantium?" In *Empress Theophano*, edited by Davids, 290–306.

INDEX